8

CLOTHING SELECTION | Fashions, Figures, Fabrics

SECOND EDITION

CLOTHING SELECTION

FASHIONS | FIGURES | FABRICS

HELEN G. CHAMBERS
Dean, School of Home Economics
Professor
Department of Clothing, Textiles, and Related Art
University of Connecticut

VERNA MOULTON
Associate Professor
Department of Clothing, Textiles, and Related Art
School of Home Economics
University of Connecticut

J. B. LIPPINCOTT COMPANY
Philadelphia · New York

Preface

This book was written to fill the need for an introductory text in clothing selection. More specifically, it was written for a course in clothing selection which is taken by both women and men. For some students the course is a basis for further, specialized work in clothing and textiles; for others, a terminal course. At the same time it is hoped that this book will prove helpful to women outside of the colleges who desire a reliable guidebook on problems of dress.

This book is not intended as a scholarly work; it is an attempt to answer simply some of the many questions that arise and to encourage interest in and the desire to learn more about dress and the numerous materials of which apparel is made. It does not pretend to make any profound contribution to the existing literature on the psychological, sociological, or economic aspects of the subject. This means neither that those aspects are unimportant nor that they are ignored; while an exhaustive study of those aspects is beyond the scope of this book, they do enter the discussion where this will be of help in solving individual or family consumer problems.

In approach and organization, this book attempts to present a different perspective in an ever-changing field. Parts I and II contain material that was felt to be important but had not been covered in a book of this nature. Part III discusses specific types and items of clothing and accessories.

Acknowledgments

Many of the ideas in this book are the result of years of assimilating knowledge from several sources and from associating with and learning from numerous people. We wish to express our appreciation for the suggestions and criticisms of all our friends and colleagues whose helpful advice contributed to this book. In particular, we wish to thank Mrs. Eleanor Boettke Hotte,

Associate Professor, Clothing, Textiles, and Related Art, School of Home Economics, University of Connecticut, for the drawings and for her many helpful suggestions.

Also we are grateful to: Miss Maude Bivins, High School, Franklin, N.C.; Mrs. Louise Johnson, Instructor, University of Connecticut; Mrs. Dorothy Lundblad Rainford, Educational Assistant, School of Business Administration, University of Connecticut; Miss Katherine Tingley, Retired Clothing Specialist, Extension, University of Connecticut; Dr. Albert Quade, Assistant Professor of Child Development, formally of the University of Connecticut; Dr. Sam Witryol, Associate Professor of Psychology, University of Connecticut; Miss Mary Whitlock, Retired Professor of Clothing and Textiles, University of Rhode Island; Mrs. Fred G. Boettke, Sr.; Miss Marian Chambers; Mrs. David Fisher; Mrs. Fred A. Moulton; Mrs. Carl R. Lloyd; and Miss Wilma B. Keyes, emeritus, Assistant Professor, Related Art, University of Connecticut; Mrs.

Allen Clapp, formerly, Instructor, textiles, University of Connecticut.

In addition, the following executives in the apparel trade were of great help: Mr. A. K. Bozadjian, of Joseph's Furs; Mr. Jess Chernak, Administrative Secretary, Fur Information and Fashion Council; Mr. Alfred Cohen, Retail Advisory Committee, Fur Information and Fashion Council; Mr. Leif C. Kronen, Secretary, Tanners' Council of America; Mr. William J. Leonard, Associate Buyer of Women's Shoes, G. Fox & Co., Inc.; and Mr. James H. Nolan, Director of the Technical Bureau, National Shoe Manufacturers' Association.

We appreciate the kindness of the many firms who granted us permission to use copyrighted photographs and illustrations, and we wish to give special thanks to the many people without whose loyal help in typing and editing the manuscript we could not have met the publishers' deadlines. Finally, we are grateful to our students for their helpful comments on chapters used as reading assignments in our courses.

STORRS, CONNECTICUT
FEBRUARY, 1961

HELEN G. CHAMBERS
VERNA MOULTON

Preface to First Revision

The reception of the first edition of this book was most gratifying. The revision is an attempt to update the material, to incorporate changes suggested by readers of the book, and to reorganize some of the chapters for more effective use. A few illustrations have been deleted and new ones added. Charts, glossaries, lists, and bibliographies have been revised to keep the information as current as possible. Chapter 1 has been rewritten.

Much of the philosophy of the book described in the original preface has been kept in the revision. Updating of some chapters are the major changes.

STORRS, CONNECTICUT
SEPTEMBER, 1968

HELEN G. CHAMBERS
VERNA MOULTON

Contents

Part One

TO
OR NOT
TO

Why clothes?

The questions "Do clothes make the man?" and "For whom do women dress?" have been favorite subjects of discussion for people of varied groups and ages for many years. These discussions generally ignore the many influences upon clothing selection.

The importance and "whys" of clothing have been theorized upon by many. Scholars have been interested in the historical, psychological, and economic aspects of dress. Recent thinking indicates that one can approach the study of dress by consideration of clothing as an *extension of the person,* as a means of *communication with others,* and as an assistance in *adjusting to a group.* Much stress has been placed upon the importance of dress in success; to certain groups, it has also been exaggerated in assessing the person.

The way you look and dress might be described by that frequently overused word, "image." It is the first communication you have with a stranger. The impression you give is largely determined by the attitudes the stranger has regarding expression in dress.

How important are clothes to the impression you are trying to create. Notice how frequently the author of your favorite novel uses appearance to describe a character, or think how the costuming of the actors in a play is used to create an impression of a person. It is not implied that costuming accomplishes all, but rather that clothing is used as a "tool." So it is with the individual; clothing should be no more than a tool, an aid in expressing what and who he is. It is a reflection of one's taste, one's life, and one's values. If one accepts this theory, it becomes necessary to think about what one's taste, life, and values are, not what one would like them to be. Too often our clothes reflect our friends' taste, the life we would like to lead, or timidity in expressing our own identity.

Clothing: a tool To communicate

GOOD TASTE *develops from knowledge of materials, design, color*

Good taste is a rather elusive but descriptive term. In clothing, it is the result of experience and knowledge of many factors. Most people feel deep in their hearts that they have excellent taste and that only lack of time, money, and opportunity hinder their expression of it. Although these factors enter the picture, neither time nor money will assure taste. In the clothing field as in other aspects of life, good taste implies knowledge. This knowledge includes proper use of materials, design, and color. For some people good taste is natural; others must struggle to attain it. The child who grows up in a home where good design, pleasing color, and proper use of materials are an integral part of life will develop taste more readily. It will become a part of him. Taste is influenced by common sense; it is a changing concept from area to area and from year to year, making it necessary to recognize the change that is

3

all about you and the changes that occur in yourself. What is considered in good taste one year may be the wrong thing another year. An article that is right for one purpose may be wrong in another situation. Science is constantly giving us new fibers and products that frequently suit a purpose better than did an old product. It is necessary to understand the new in order to use it correctly at the right time and place. Artists and color specialists are giving us new insights into the knowledge of color and line. Color combinations that were once taboo become popular and accepted when used with new understanding. The trend toward casual living created a need for informal clothing. What was once work clothing is now designed to be attractive and is used both in work and in play. Automatic household appliances have changed the problems of caring for clothing. Designers are eager to find new sources of inspiration. To exist, fashion must reflect what people are thinking and doing.

EXTENSION OF THE PERSON

If clothing is to be an extension of the person, it becomes necessary to think in terms of what we are really like and what we are attempting to express. There are many things in our responses to clothing that are not understood. Many are educated responses resulting from influences that have molded our lives, many of which we are unaware. We can, however, look objectively at those things which we do know about ourselves and try to relate them to what we want to express in clothing.

In creating an identity through clothing, you are designing and will be concerned with those things which concern designers. As such, your design choices will be *aesthetic, practical, social,* and *personal.*

Americans have always placed a high value on efficiency, which is reflected in an obsession for practical and functional clothing. Gradually, evidence of a greater interest in the art of apparel is being found. The individual might want to ask if beauty is important in his own appearance. If so, it becomes necessary for him to understand what will answer this need in clothing. There are many influences that impede the progress of a creative person. You should be aware of those factors that hinder the expression of individuality as well as those which assist in adding beauty to your own look.

In design, the second consideration will be practicality. Practicality suggests certain obvious things to the individual, such as comfort, health, and safety needs. However, it is important to become aware of the practical problems which you may not know exist, and to find where your awareness should be expanded. Often, it is the technical details which one does not understand that cause problems in dress and result in a lack of confidence in oneself. An example of such a problem would be fitting. If the garment is not properly fitted, the beauty of design may be lost or the garment may not be comfortable. Another example is the care of clothing. Sufficient knowledge of the care of fabrics is necessary in order to maintain their beauty, design, and durability.

In order to understand the social implications of design, one should look at the people and the cultures about him. Particularly important is awareness of the many changes which are occurring in our society. An individual's needs and wants will be strongly influenced by the ideas of those around him. Some of these ideas may be provincial and others may be cosmopolitan. Within any given area, there are many income levels and different standards of acceptance. It is essential, if one is to under-

4

stand the social influence upon clothing design, that he be aware of differences among cultural groups. MANY influences

Personal choices are frequently governed and influenced by many factors beyond our control. Lack of time and money may, for example, limit what we can achieve in clothing expression. However, choice often depends on the personal development of the individual and upon his past experiences. What he wishes to express in clothing will change as he matures. The young child is concerned primarily with the approval of parents and friends. As the child grows older, he obtains his values and goals from his group. The mature person is more aware of himself as an individual and wants clothes that are an extension of self. Education, occupation, religion, cultural interests, and social life will all be influences upon his choice of clothes.

Desire for conformity, desire for independence, or desire for recognition may affect the individual's choice of clothes. One person may use clothing to add what he assumes to be status in his life, others may want to relieve a dullness or drabness in their lives. There are also people who use clothing to attract the attention that they desire.

Americans are probably the most criticized and analyzed people in the world. Among other things, the American is accused of being unable to grow old gracefully. Age does play a part in clothing selection but is probably less important than we are inclined to believe.

As one grows older, he does not necessarily change his values, his preferences, or his activities. If, however, his physical characteristics change, he may need to make different choices from an aesthetic or practical standpoint. The person who has pride in self, regardless of age, will want to present a pleasing image. Problems of dress result when a person does not recognize the changes in physical characteristics that may occur with age. The favorite colors of youth may be less becoming or a style may no longer be attractive on the figure. These problems are just as crucial for the young person who insists on conforming to a group fashion that is unbecoming to him. must recognize age difference

Most older people do not want to be set apart in style of dress. Choice should be approached by consideration of what activities the person participates in, and what his energy and state of health demand. Some people are very active as they grow older. There are people who ski at fifty and need clothing which the sport requires. Their needs are still basically the same as when they skied in their youth.

COMMUNICATION WITH OTHERS

In dress, we visually communicate to others. The impact of what we convey depends upon the attitudes of the receiver, who interprets what he sees on the basis of his own experience and preference. A dean of an eastern school, when asked to talk to a group of men on the importance of dress, said he was not the person to choose since he was very skeptical of anyone who was too perfectly dressed—he always wondered what they were trying to hide. It is necessary, if we are to have an interchange of thought with people, that we know what we are attempting to say in dress. One may wish to compliment another by the way he dresses. He may honor him by dressing in a certain manner or he may show respect for the opinion of those with whom he associates. Experience and awareness are very important factors in understanding the reactions of others. We do not always anticipate a reaction such as that of the young Dane whose impression of Americans was that the "old ones" had purple hair and the "young ones" wore white socks. Ignorance of the customs of other people may hamper our attempt to communicate. For example, an American who likes Bermuda shorts and wears them in Europe may be creating a very negative impression. Many Europeans do not accept Bermuda shorts as suitable attire.

Another theory, the reverse of the idea that clothing is an extension of the person, suggests that people can change their personality by a change in their appearance. Advertisers use this idea to appeal to a person's ego. It is often suggested that by using the product advertised, one can become a "new person." There is little evidence to support the idea that personality may be changed by changing the appearance. However, there may be some basis for believing that certain kinds of clothing may affect the behavior of an individual. Some professors, for example, propose that the student who comes to class casually or carelessly dressed tends to be casual and careless in his work.

ADJUSTMENT TO THE GROUP

Dr. Ethel Alpenfels once said to a college group that we preach individuality but demand conformity. Nowhere is this more obvious than in clothing. The desire to conform to group patterns is strong from childhood on. Identity with a group generally appears more important than expression of self. The individual is made to feel secure if he dresses as his social group dictates.

Although we may want to encourage individuality, most of us are guilty of rejecting those who do not conform to the accepted standards of our group. Students have been dismissed from school for wearing apparel that is "different." Several banks in California supply employees with special suits or dresses on the theory that uniform dress inspires confidence both among customers and employees.

The individual who wishes to pursue an independent course will need a strong sense of identity. It is possible, too, that even within accepted standards the individual can find ways to express his uniqueness.

THE WELL-DRESSED PERSON

The well-dressed person is natural and never gives the impression of artificiality. He is usually someone who wants to be pleasing and interesting to others, but who has neither the time nor the desire to spend all his waking hours attaining this goal. There is no manner of nervousness or dullness about him. He wears clothes with graciousness unspoiled by awkward, jerky motions. There is no evidence that he is conscious of his clothes, and you would be unaware of his belonging to any particular age group, social group, school, or profession. In other words, you would not immediately "type" him, but rather you would think of him as an attractive or interesting person. Individuality, which is the key to being well dressed, is most easily attained by the mature person who would:

Recognize clothing problems and obstacles hindering the attainment of clothing goals.

Know that clothing is only a background and a reflection of self—not the personality.

Know better than to copy or imitate friends.

Know and recognize the importance of fashion and be aware of its individual values and limitations for him. He is able to recognize and resist fashions unbecoming to him or his way of life.

Know and accept himself. He recognizes his physical assets and liabilities and does not wish for what he cannot have, but makes the most of what is in the realm of possibility and uses the art of camouflage, color, and proportion to detract from irregularities over which he has no control.

Be realistic in recognizing that every age group has charm. He does not find it necessary to try to appear younger or older than he is.

Know that the reflection of individuality in dressing doesn't just happen; it is the result of knowing oneself, planning, and constantly developing good taste.

Know good quality and design.

Have planned and executed his wardrobe with enough thought that he can forget his clothes once he has put them on.

Be able to use self-discipline when tempted with clothing and accessories not suited to his needs.

Know that the smallest detail counts in clothing and in the way it is worn.

Know the facts about his clothes—size, fabric, quality, performance expected, etc.

Be satisfied with his purchases and his wardrobe and at the same time aim at improvement.

For a few, clothing may be a matter of covering the body, but most people find real pleasure and satisfaction in the buying, planning, and co-ordinating of a costume. If done in the spirit of meeting a challenge, buying a necessity can be a creative experience. Many a person has been given a lift by the purchase of a new hat, a necktie, a sport shirt, or an inexpensive string of beads. Further satisfaction is gained when the hat or shirt becomes a useful and becoming part of one's life. Only the individual can decide what he or she wants clothes to do for him or her. Aim at being a top designer for your own appearance.

REFERENCE READINGS

Anspach, Karlyne, "The American in Casual Dress," *Journal of Home Economics*, 55, 1963, pp. 255–257.

Compton, Norma H., "Personal Attributes of Color and Design Preferences in Clothing Fabrics," *Journal of Psychology*, 54, 1962, pp. 192–195.

Holtzclaw, Katherine, "Costume and Culture," *Journal of Home Economics*, 48, No. 6, 1956, pp. 401–404.

Rosencranz, M. L., "Sociological Aspects of Clothing Studied," *Journal of Home Economics*, 42, 1950, pp. 206.

———, "Social and Psychological Approaches to Clothing Research," *Journal of Home Economics*, 57, 1965, pp. 26–29.

Ryan, M. S., *Clothing: A Study in Human Behavior*, Holt, Rinehart and Winston, Inc., New York, 1966.

Chapter 2

What's new?

What is new in clothes each season is of primary interest to women of all ages and occupations. Each season, new fashions are created that are distinct enough from the fashions of the previous season to satisfy the almost insatiable appetite of most women for the new. New clothes seem to give a woman the sense of well-being and elegance she seeks.

The hordes of women who gather at "bargain" stores each season are an indication of the appeal of new fashions. Copies of models, from costly facsimiles to inexpensive items that are only token reminders of the real thing, provide thousands of choices for these eager women.

A woman is often in a quandary because she sees so many well-styled clothes from which to choose her own wardrobe. The woman with a limited clothes budget wonders how long the new styles will be fashionable; she cannot afford to buy clothing that will be dated in a short time. As Mark Twain said, "No woman can look as well out of the fashion as in it."[1] Although

[1] Clemens, S. L., Letter from New York to the *Alta Californian*, April 16, 1867.

women select and reject, since they make their selections from the fashions of the times, they all dress much alike at any given time.

FASHION TERMINOLOGY

Some understanding of how the fashion world works may help the consumer make wise decisions when she buys new fashions. Nearly every season the word *trend* is used in reference to fashion in newspapers, magazines, and radio and television broadcasts. Trend means the general course, direction, or tendency that fashions seem to follow in clothing, automobiles, housing, and other facets of life. Fashions tend to take on a pattern which is similar or characteristic throughout. For instance, there may be a trend toward seamless hosiery, cut-out shoes, knitted dresses, the color white, compact automobiles, split-level houses, or discothèques. In apparel, trends set the pace for the fashions shown in stores and accepted by many people.

Fashion, a strong influence in many phases of American life, is the prevailing or current mode or accepted manner of traveling, entertaining, living, and dressing. Like trends, fashions are not confined to apparel, interior decoration, and home appliances; they are also concerned with and influenced by many other developments, such as art, transportation, economics, society, government, and international affairs. Lightweight clothing and luggage evolved with the rapid growth of air travel. The fashion of outdoor cooking brought about new kinds of backyard clothes, cooking equipment, and entertainment. Depending upon the number of people who adopt a fashion, it may become so well established that it comes to be definitely characteristic of the period.

Some fashions are distorted or exaggerated designs accepted by only the few who can afford to indulge their desire to be different. The term *high fashion* describes the latest, and often the most extreme styles worn by fashion leaders and promoted by high-fashion publications. Some of these high fashions may last only a few weeks, while others may last several years. Fashions that have long acceptance are known as classics. Some examples are the shirtwaist dress, the box coat, and the pump.

Style is the characteristic mode of any art. It is distinctive enough to express the needs and tastes of the majority of people and to become associated with a particular period. The silhouette, fabric, color, and accessories used at a particular time and identified with a particular group of people are the style of clothes of the era. With increased demands on the time and energy of the individual in contemporary life, style emphasizes function and simplicity.

Indicative of the style that appeals to the greatest number of people during a significant period of time would be the size, color, trim, and lines of the automobile; the shape, materials, and decorative detail of architecture; and the speed, rhythm, and intricacy of the steps of a dance. The Tudor style of architecture, the surrealistic style of painting, and the "new look" in dress of the forties are typical uses of the word *style*.

A *fad* is a fashion adopted by a limited group of people for a short time. It is taken up with exaggerated zeal and quickly abandoned. In clothing, fads are common in small items and accessories such as the rope necklaces and men's striped blazers of the twenties, the beer jackets of the thirties, and the scarf hats of the sixties.

Occasionally, what appears to be a fad meets a real need and becomes a fashion or a style. When the bobby-socks fad began in the early forties, plain white athletic socks satisfied the younger set. Since that time, many styles and lengths in hosiery de-

Flapper of the 1920's with rope pearls.

signed for this age group have been adopted by others. There was some question whether the pallid look in make-up, a popular fad in the late fifties, served any purpose other than to attract attention to the wearer. Yet this pale-pale look, with added emphasis on eyes, appealed to an increasing number of women. Wigs that were popular among a limited group gained favor with many women as the convenience they offered became apparent.

FASHIONS OF THE TIMES

Within every new fashion lurks the spirit of the age. Periods of intense ferment have

The Gay Blade.

usually been periods of fantastic clothes. In early Renaissance Italy, men's clothing was extremely ornate. In Elizabethan England, the dress of both men and women was created in exaggerated silhouettes. In the revolutionary 1830's in Europe, women's dresses were full of whalebone, horsehair, and starch. Men of that period looked equally unnatural with their skirted frock-coats and flare-crowned top hats. In each of these periods, political and social struggles were going on. Thought, action, art, and politics affected contemporary apparel.

The eighteenth century, the Age of Enlightenment, was a classic age in costume. Formal elegance prescribed that men and women wear their hair, or their wigs, a uniformly powdered gray. Brocades, satins, knee breeches, and beauty spots were very much in evidence.

The violence of the French Revolution, which followed the Age of Enlightenment, altered costumes. Tousled hair, carelessly knotted cravats (or no cravats at all), and plain-fabric clothes succeeded the studied elegance of the previous era.

During the era of cold war and tension of the 1950's, clothes seemed to reflect the public's desire for escape. The novelty of new silhouettes like the chemise and the trapeze especially appealed to young women during this period of stress.

In the restless, affluent 1960's, hemlines rose above the knee; shifts, muu muus, and boots appeared, along with "op" and "pop" art designs and textures. The emphasis on youth influenced the fads and fashions of the decade.

In order to interpret fashion changes and recognize fashion trends, a knowledge of other factors which influence fashion may be helpful. Economic, political, psychological, and social influences on fashion have been significant throughout history. Government restrictions, taxes, strikes, and competition are some of the economic conditions affecting fashion. When money is abundant, opulence and elegance of fashion return as evidenced by the fabrics and styles of the sixties. Political influences include wars, international relations, and government. Fashion thrives in democracies and is less active under totalitarian regimes, where freedom of choice is limited.

A significant psychological factor in fashion is the effect of the word "import" upon consumers. Something imported seems to appeal to many people regardless of quality or design.

Several social influences have affected fashion change during the twentieth century: informal entertaining has promoted casual clothes; the growth of a large teen-age group of consumers who buy clothes in large numbers has developed teen-age

HOW FASHION WORKS

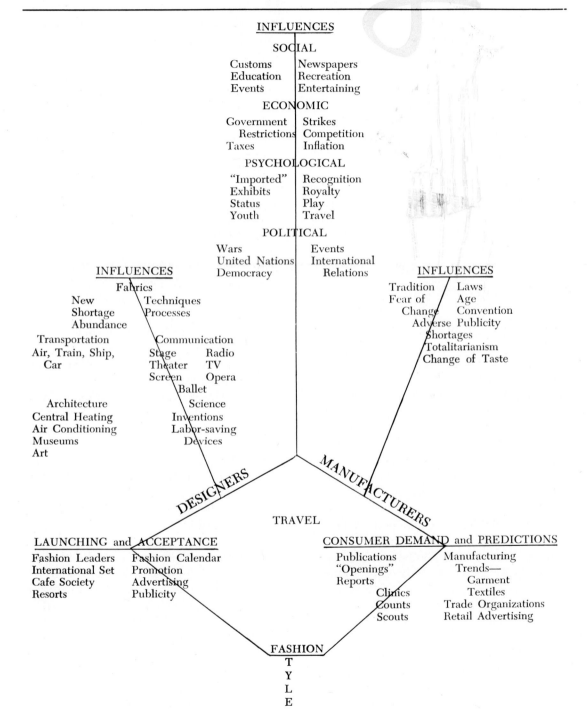

INFLUENCES

SOCIAL

Customs	Newspapers
Education	Recreation
Events	Entertaining

ECONOMIC

Government	Strikes
Restrictions	Competition
Taxes	Inflation

PSYCHOLOGICAL

"Imported"	Recognition
Exhibits	Royalty
Status	Play
Youth	Travel

POLITICAL

Wars	Events
United Nations	International
Democracy	Relations

INFLUENCES

Fabrics

New	Techniques
Shortage	Processes
Abundance	

Transportation	Communication
Air, Train, Ship,	Stage Radio
Car	Theater TV
	Screen Opera
	Ballet

Architecture	Science
Central Heating	Inventions
Air Conditioning	Labor-saving
Museums	Devices
Art	

INFLUENCES

Tradition	Laws
Fear of	Age
Change	Convention
Adverse	Publicity
	Shortages
	Totalitarianism
	Change of Taste

DESIGNERS   MANUFACTURERS

TRAVEL

LAUNCHING and ACCEPTANCE

Fashion Leaders	Fashion Calendar
International Set	Promotion
Cafe Society	Advertising
Resorts	Publicity

CONSUMER DEMAND and PREDICTIONS

Publications	Manufacturing
"Openings"	Trends—
Reports	Garment
Clinics	Textiles
Counts	Trade Organizations
Scouts	Retail Advertising

FASHION

STYLE

The Big Apple of the thirties.

fashions; high school and college student fashion consultants have boosted the sale of youthful fashions; and the increase in the number of women who work outside the home has promoted fashions for the working woman.

Social events, recreation, and customs have a bearing on what society in general will adopt. The Olympic games, a popular Broadway play, a presidential campaign, an inauguration, visits of international celebrities, world fairs—all inspire new color combinations, silhouette details, unusual accessories, and bizarre prints. Fashion leaders—the emulated men and women with social standing who launch fashions—creative designers, and the manufacturers who copy original designs are all influential in promoting new fashions.

REJECTION OF FASHIONS

Not all fashions that are promoted are adopted. The rejection of fashions by consumers is one of several retarding factors.

If people do not want to wear clothes that are not suitable to their tastes or their way of life, even the powerful forces of fashion cannot persuade them to do so. With a gradual improvement in public taste and an increasing consumer demand for personal choice, the sophisticated American consumer has become more discriminating and tends to reject conformity.

It has been said that some American women are afraid of change. The reluctance of a few women to try anything new slows down fashion change. In the commercial sense, a fashion is good only when it sells. If a fashion has good lines and is suited to the purpose for which it was created, it tends to be accepted by the majority. Many teen-agers and college students accept fads and frequent fashion changes, but some people are reluctant to do so because they are afraid of ridicule or of being stuck with something they cannot afford to discard.

The chemise of the 1950's was worn by many young people, but the extreme version of 1957–58 was never nationally accepted. The silhouette was not flattering to most women, there were too many ugly versions, men were very outspoken about their dislike of the "sack," and the fashion press was not complimentary. This style of chemise, originating in the mass market instead of high fashion and consequently ignored by fashion leaders, was rejected. However, the chemise never disappeared entirely. In modified versions and with different names it became fashionable later.

There have also been local ordinances, government restrictions, and legal regulations which retarded fashion. The L-85 rulings on garment manufacture during World War II slowed the progress of fashion for several years. Wartime shortages curtailed original designs and the amount of fabric that could be used for clothing.

People did not buy the new but repaired and renovated the old.

In the past, tradition and convention have indirectly delayed change in some fashions. The bride wore a red wedding dress in the Middle Ages. Later, a prominent queen who broke with tradition and wore white established a new custom.

Regulation clothing for the armed forces, the clergy, nurses, and officers of the law has undergone few—and only minor—changes, and only after much opposition and criticism. Although the change in these fashions is slow, more frequent changes are anticipated. Stretch nylon stockings, pleated skirts, tapered coifs, drip-dry habits, spongeable plastic collars, and other innovations have been accepted for some orders of nuns.

The textile and clothing industries have suffered as a result of the resistance to change and to improvements. Workers feared unemployment with the introduction of new methods or equipment; management fought the introduction of more costly equipment or improved methods, fearing that profits would not absorb the additional costs. Increased competition from foreign imports in the 1960's brought about some changes; profits were expended on research in products, methods, and distribution of apparel and textiles.

FASHION CYCLES

In the past the acceptance of new fashions was gradual, usually taking several years for a new fashion to achieve significant acceptance. For some items of clothing the length of the cycle was approximately seven years, while a general trend lasted from twenty to thirty years. A fashion passed through the stages of inception, publicity, presentation, mass acceptance, decline, and obsolescence. Since World War II new fashions have evolved faster.

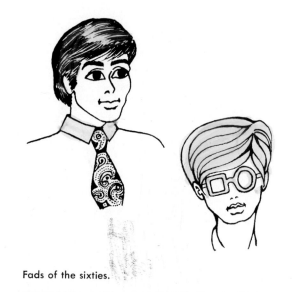

Fads of the sixties.

Reasons for this change include increased awareness of fashions, rapid pace of the spread of fashions, the increased buying of fashion. Other factors are the inclusion of couture designs by catalog houses, speedy communications, quick copying and adopting of high fashion which have shortened the period from origin to obscurity.

However, there is still a continuous and somewhat slow change of annual fashions accompanied by innumerable seasonal innovations and variations. Change must be sufficiently slow to prevent leaders of fashion from out-distancing their followers. Consumers can be fairly confident that there will not be major radical changes in a short time. Skirt lengths changed suddenly in 1929 and in 1947, yet whole wardrobes were not replaced immediately. There are always fashions in transition—the outgoing, the present, and the incoming—in which a woman can find what she desires. The student of fashion watches these stages of fashion for the change in patterns, periods of planned obsolescence, sociological developments that create a demand for the practical as well as the becoming, and

The chemise story.

styles that meet the needs of a changing society.

FASHION REPEATS ITSELF

Some well-established styles such as the Grecian classic drapery, the Napoleonic empire, and the silhouette of the Roaring Twenties have recurred several times.

In the 1930's, a famous actress turned the casual shape of the polo coat into a glamorous fashion. The coat itself never lost its appeal, and its wrapped look became evident in the 1960's in both daytime and evening wear. The slinky crepe-and-chiffon look of the thirties was also revived in evening gowns. The divided skirt designed for casual wear in the thirties was promoted for all occasions in the early sixties.

The chemise of the 1950's was not as new or as radical as consumers seemed to think. It first gained popularity in the Roaring Twenties. Loose lines and short skirts were prophesied by a leading French couturier in the early fifties when he showed bloused tops and low waistlines. The chemise silhouette evolved slowly through the years,

Bell or bouffant, back fullness variation, tubular.

with new features appearing each season —bodice drapes, the low-waisted two-piece look, the loose-at-the-middle silhouette, blousons and over blouses, the flat-back-and-front fit, and the semi-fitted look. In 1955, the new concepts of fit in the changing silhouette became apparent. Fit did not confine the body but provided room for it to move within the silhouette, especially at the unfitted waistline.

Although the extreme chemise was rejected, variations of the chemise appeared in the trapeze, the orbit sheath, the semi-fitted shift, and the easy look. These silhouettes continued along with a renewed emphasis on the normal waistline, a snug fit, and short length.

The silhouettes of women's clothing can be classified into two main categories—tubular and bouffant. From the straight tunic of the early Egyptians to the pencil-slim

sheath of the 1950's, the *tubular* silhouette has appeared several times. The full, round skirt of Marie Antoinette, the hoop of the 1860's, the flared ballet skirt of the 1950's, and the tent dress of the 1960's exemplify the *bouffant* silhouette.

A variation of these two silhouettes is the back fullness as evidenced by the French sacque of the 1770's, the waterfall bustle of the 1880's, and the bow-and-peplum back of the 1940's. In some periods, both of these silhouettes are popular at the same time. The existence of more than one type of silhouette in a period provides a wide selection for consumers, but requires more thought about wardrobe coordination.

HOW FASHIONS ORIGINATE

Helpful to further understanding of fashion is the fascinating story of a design from origin to obsolescence. In women's cloth-

1940's

1770's

1880's

Back interest.

ing, many of the original ideas occur abroad, primarily in Paris, and then are copied or adapted for American use. Paris has been the leading fashion center of the world for more than three hundred years. There are several reasons for this: Marie Antoinette and her court dressmaker, Rose Bertin, completely dictated fashion in their day. Much later, the creations of the first great couturier, Charles Worth, designed for the French Empress Eugenie, put women everywhere in crinolines and feathered hats.

After World War I Chanel, like all great designers, felt the flow of the new social tide with its greater freedom for women, and she expressed this freedom through clothing. Her designs led women to discard long skirts and throw away their inhibiting corsets. The knee-length chemise dress created by Chanel became the rage.

Paris, a cosmopolitan city, geographically located at the crossroads of Europe, is a center of culture and art. Couture, or dress designing, is an art, and the *haute*

couture, made up of several couturiers and couturières, is internationally famous. Chanel and Captain Molyneux returned after several years of retirement to triumphant leadership again—Chanel and her comfortable easy-to-wear elegance; Molyneux and his simple, timeless creations. In addition to their creative ability, these artists of apparel design have a choice of museums in which to study fine historic costumes as well as to acquire inspirations from invaluable art treasures. Hand-created fabrics and trimmings are made by skilled creators exclusively for the couture. The government encourages and fosters the couture, awards the highest distinction of the country, the *Legion d'Honneur*, to its members, and offers them protection from style piracy.

The genius of the Parisian couture is not exclusively French. Some of the famous Parisian designers came from Germany,

Tubular silhouette, in Egypt and in 1950.

Bouffants.

Greece, Denmark, Holland, Italy, and Spain. This combination of international talent and creative flair centralized in one city strengthens Parisian fashion leadership.

Several members of the couture have visited the United States to get ideas from the American way of life and the American woman. It has been questioned whether the Parisian couture is losing much of its originality in trying to please the American market. The lines of clothes are shown at one of the two major openings in February and July or at the mid-season openings in May and October. The various numbers in these lines are made by hand by the midinettes, or seamstresses, to fit the specific models who will show them at the openings.

Buyers representing retailers and manufacturers, well-known celebrities, and other private clients are admitted to these openings. The buyers have to produce proper identification and also purchase a *carte d'acheteur,* or buyer's card; others must show their engraved invitations. To protect the couture, the *Chambre Syndicale de la Couture,* the official organization of the industry, insists on rigid identification as well as conformation to the rule that the numbers shown in the line may not be sketched or copied. In many houses, the press is admitted after the buyers. Members of the press present very complete press identification and then receive special passes. After the showings, which are scheduled daily and in the evening and are interspersed with cocktail and champagne parties, a release date is announced. After that time, purchases are made, photographs and

The liberal fifties.

sketches taken, and the breathlessly awaited details of the haute couture opening are revealed to the world.

Usually there is a clear indication of a trend in these openings. While each house has its own individual expression, the basic silhouettes, colors, and fabrics of the Parisian couture are usually in accord. To the American buyer, this is an aid in determining the direction his own designing should take to eliminate some of the uncertainty and risk. To the consumer who follows these openings through news releases, it is a clue as to what is coming and what she should buy. Although many American consumers may never buy a Paris original or an exact copy, the Parisian ideas influence what American women wear through the great adaptation process at which American manufacturers are skilled. The Paris label seems to have a snob appeal for many manufacturers, retailers, and customers.

Some of the French originals are purchased to be sold as originals or to be copied or adapted. Those imported for promo-

tion and reproduction purposes only are purchased, brought over in bond, and admitted duty-free. The importer posts a bond with the United States Customs and within six months the bonded original is returned to customs and sent to some other country. Not having to pay the duty, which is more than half the original cost, makes importing in bond less expensive than buying and keeping indefinitely.

The growing ready-to-wear, *prêt à porter,* industry in Europe is an important source of imports for Americans. Imports with a great deal of style at prices much less than those of the couture models are popular in many stores in the United States.

More and more of the couture are concentrating on *boutiques* and *prêt à porter* in addition to or in place of custom designing. New young designers tend to tie in with large American stores and do exclusive lines. It is estimated that the shrinking couture will gradually be reduced as more buyers and manufacturers limit the number of houses they visit each season. For this great art, design, and creativity to dwindle seems unfortunate. Other gifted designers in the world include those from Austria, England, Holland, Germany, Ireland, Italy, and Spain who create clothes for a private clientele and for American buyers. Thailand, Israel, and Japan also furnish designs that serve as sources of ideas for American designers and manufacturers. Although these other areas do not have the history of leadership, the centralization, and all the other advantages of Paris, clothes from these countries are enjoying increasing popularity. With the emphasis on youth in the 1960's, the young designers of England met the fashion needs of the "under twenty" age group. The popularity of their venturesome fashions soared among several age groups all over the world.

Fashions in America

The story of fashions in the United States is different. Although there are many talented designers in the United States, the number of designers in the couture group is limited. Here, as in foreign countries, men and women are about equally represented as designers in women's wear. Some of them have produced well-known designs and gained name recognition. Unknown designers work for manufacturers who use corporate names or their own names, giving little or no recognition to their design staffs. However, the names of designers—especially of the young ones—are being more widely publicized. In the 1960's a change in the industry occurred in which the designer-owned firm emerged at the top of the dress market.

Mass production of ready-to-wear is the keynote of the huge, complex American clothing industry. Los Angeles, San Francisco, Dallas, Chicago, Kansas City, St. Louis, Cleveland, Miami, Philadelphia, and Boston are all apparel markets; but New York City takes the lead over all other centers in the production of women's apparel. While some of the top designers are established in other areas of that city, the bulk of the designing is confined to a few blocks in the Thirties on Seventh Avenue and Broadway. Fashion in the United States tends to be more a business and less an art, the major question being, "Will it sell?" However, fashionable ready-to-wear at a reasonable price and the American system of sizing have been important contributions to the world of fashion.

The history of American designing is brief compared to that of the French couture. Through the promotional efforts of the late Dorothy Shaver, president of Lord and Taylor's store, and many other people interested in fashion, American designers were recognized by the end of the thirties. During World War II, while the Parisian couture was struggling for existence, American designers gained needed experience and recognition. Fashion awards—including the American Fashion Critics Award, the Neiman-Marcus Award, the National Cotton Council Award, and others—have encouraged and promoted American designers.

Valentina, who retired in 1956, was one of the greatest international couturières to design in America. She was best known for elegant clothes with timeless lines. Her clothes were worn by many well-known socialites and stage celebrities.

The late Hattie Carnegie, a successful and influential designer, sold ready-made and custom-made clothes, and operated a wholesale business in hats, cosmetics, jewelry, and sportswear. The firm has continued under her name.

Claire McCardell, who died at the height of her career, was one of the best-known designers of casual wear and received numerous awards for her originality and for her "All-American designs for the All-American girl."

The late Philip Mangone, coat and suit designer, and Maurice Rentner, dress designer, were nationally famous for their fashion leadership.

Besides these famous leaders and current designers—Galanos, Mainbocher, Norell —who originate American clothes, there are skillful designers who adapt details so that fashionable garments are made available at prices nearly everyone can afford.

Major fashion trends are often started either by top designers or by manufacturers who interpret, develop, and reproduce European originals. American fashion trend-setters who have had a lasting influence on the look of American women are Pauline Trigere, Anne Fogarty, and Bonnie Cashin. Many casual clothes originate in the United States because Paris collections have seldom included casual clothing. Some children's clothes come from Europe, but many of them originate in America. The designers who create original designs have to anticipate trends and try to judge consumer taste and needs. Editors of fashion magazines, newspapers, and trade publications—through their keen observation, discrimination, and experience—are also able to forecast fashions and predict consumer demand.

Sources of inspiration

Designers of originals may get inspiration from travel, native costumes, historic costumes, museums, nature, occupational costumes, costumes of particular sports and professions, the theater, ballet, opera, military events and reviews, art exhibits, expositions, or new fabrics and materials. Films produced on foreign locations inspire new fashions, as is evidenced by the oriental and other Asiatic fashions adopted by the western world such as the Chinese sheath, slim and slit deep at the calf, and modified saris. When Alaska and Hawaii were granted statehood, designers had new sources of ideas for color, fabric, furs, and design.

The designer must have knowledge of his firm's market and price line, the previous season's successes, and the plant production requirements before beginning his work. He supplements his knowledge with information on fabrics, colors, and textures for the coming season. He resorts to national magazines, color-card associations, and fabric stylists. He must keep silhouette trends in mind by studying what the European couture is doing. He may not copy, but he notes changes and considers them in relation to the type of garment the American buyer will accept.

After careful study, research, and preliminary planning, the designer creates the numbers in the line of clothes to be presented in his showroom. The assistant to the designer helps in the creation, and a sample of each garment is made up in the workroom. At this stage, the designer works closely with the production manager, and plans are made and costs of manufacturing estimated in preparation for production. Then, provided the garments are popular with retail and other buyers at the showing, the clothes are put into production, orders are delivered, and soon the clothes are available in retail stores throughout the United States.

New high fashions are introduced and launched by fashion leaders, people who have the necessary leisure, wealth, social position, and interest in clothes. Their followers and fans tend to imitate their clothes, and these high fashions eventually spread in an adapted form throughout the country. This does not mean that all fashions in which these fashion leaders are photographed and publicized achieve mass acceptance. Even with the change of pace of fashion dissemination, acceptance does not move at the same rate throughout the nation. The rate of acceptance in different types of communities may be due to price or choice of fabric. What is worn in New York does not necessarily meet approval in Arkansas at the same time. Light cottons have a longer life in the South than in the Northern states.

Although there are many similarities in clothes for college students, college life would not be what it is without regional ways and local fads. Romantic ball gowns, long or short, may be worn in one region, while cocktail dresses or short formals reign elsewhere. Tennis shoes, often called sneakers or, at some colleges, "tennies," may be reserved for active sports in one locality but predominate as classroom footwear on other campuses. Knee socks and textured tights, fashionable in some regions, may never be worn at other colleges.

How do the manufacturer and the retailer predict fashion acceptance and know how many clothes to order and re-order? They follow various fashion publications, the couture openings, and fashion and merchandise reports; they make use of fashion services, fashion scouts, and fashion counts; and they note what competitors are advertising, promoting, and selling.

The remainder of this brief story of fashion lies with you, the consumer. What you approve, accept, and buy determines what will become a fashion and possibly the outstanding style of a particular period. You—as all other consumers—buy according to your creative, aesthetic, intellectual, and social needs, and the many other factors that influence personal choice of clothing.

"Do fashions control the consumer or does the consumer control fashions?" Actually, the consumer has the upper hand; that is, when the majority makes similar choices, a fashion is established. There may be some consumers who do not like the tastes of the majority, and they have less choice in their selection. In time, however, they can usually find what they want, because at any time both current and past fashions are worn, and new ones are on the way. Also, the so-called classics and basics are worn for a long time. Well-chosen apparel can be worn for five years or more and still fit into the current fashion picture.

An understanding of this story of fashion may be of value to you as a consumer. By careful observation of fashion publications, retail store merchandise, and well-dressed people, you should be able to recognize seasonal fashions, trends, styles, and fads and choose your clothing with ease and assurance. From the available choices try to choose what is appropriate for you, what you can wear a great deal, and what will not go out of date in one season. Choose styles that are not only in tune with the times but are in character with your personality.

FASHIONS IN MEN'S CLOTHES

The degree of interest in men's fashions has varied considerably throughout history. Henry VIII, Beau Brummell, and the gay Cavaliers were as much leaders of fashion as were Anne Boleyn, Catherine de Medici, and Josephine. Louis XIV, Lord Raglan, Napoleon, and other great political and military leaders were well known for the fashions they originated. European men have continued their interest in fashions, although with less color, elegance of fabrics, and radical style than in the past. The men's fashions of England, Italy, France, Austria, Germany, and Switzerland have been inspirations for the designers of men's clothes in the United States for many years.

The Egyptian   The French Court   The Victorian

Fashionable men of the past.

The early interest of American men in fashion waned during the twentieth century. An occasional recurrence of interest was sparked by aggressive manufacturers, retailers, and male fashion authorities. Men who are fashion-conscious like either new, distinctive, different, and flattering clothes or they like fashion in small amounts, to avoid being too different too soon.

Many American men have not been fashion conscious. They have seemed to consider it unfitting to think seriously about their appearance and so have pretended indifference. Men did not used to like to shop for clothes; they said they did not have time

to shop. They did not believe that clothes make the man. However, they have learned that a man seldom goes far in public without the help of suitable clothes. In the 1960's, with more time and money, men customers became more aware of fashions.

During the first fifty years of the twentieth century, fashions in men's clothing changed less frequently than women's fashions. A leading custom tailor once indicated that this infrequent change was due to men's reluctance to accept new ideas in dress, particularly those that would make them conspicuous in a crowd, and to men's determination not to sacrifice comfort for style. Men refused to be stampeded into accepting new styles. With the growing im-

22

Fifty years of change

portance of the Continental style of the middle fifties, many men did not buy this kind of suit merely because it was "what they were wearing."

After World War II, there was renewed interest in men's dress and an increase in buying by returning servicemen. The new casual living of the fifties increased the purchase of clothing over prewar days. Many young adults showed a keen interest in clothing and appearance. That women have taken over the dressing of the American male may account in part for the increase in sales of men's clothing. Another reason for the increased interest and for the speed of change in styles in the fifties and sixties is that men's fashions were trying to keep up with the speed of contemporary life. As the jet age took noted diplomats, politicians, scientists, and businessmen to all parts of the world, their dress received publicity. Some men's fashions became quite diverse and even difficult to pre-predict.

In the twentieth century, men's clothes have not been so fancy or colorful as they were in the past, when aristocrats dressed in resplendent finery to distinguish themselves from the commoners. In the age of democracy in America, a man does not dress to be different but to be accepted by the people with whom he associates. The security craved by teen-age boys leads them to adopt the fads of their group, which are often extreme but of short duration. The herd instinct of the college student causes him to adopt the fashions of his group even if it means wearing dirty white bucks, droopy socks, too-short chino slacks, open-collar shirts, and nondescript crewneck sweaters.

Fashion Terms

Adaptation. A copy of a garment, with features like those of an original.

Atelier. Workroom; studio of an artist or designer.

Bouffant. Puffed out; full, flaring.

Boutique. Shop where accessories, ready-to-wear, and apparel requiring one or two fittings are sold. In the United States, a shop where distinctive accessories and special ready-to-wear are sold.

Carte d'acheteur. Buyer's card for European couture.

Caution. Admission fee to European couture.

Chic. The expression of originality and style with correct taste.

Collection. Group of models shown by one designer.

Copy. A reproduction of a model, made outside the house that made the original.

Couture. Custom dressmaking industry.

Couturier. Male designer.

Couturière. Female designer.

Dummy. Wood or frame-and-fabric display unit built to resemble body contours. Used for designing purposes and to display apparel and accessories.

Exclusive designer. Designer who designs clothes featured in a salon in a retail establishment in the United States.

Fad. A short-lived fashion, quickly accepted and as quickly dropped.

Fashion. The accepted, prevailing style of any given time.

Fashion cycle. The periodic return of any fashion detail, in a form adapted to current trends.

Fashion obsolescence. The going out of use or fashion of an article outmoded by change in fashion or new trends.

Fashion trend. Tendency toward a future mode; the line or direction along which fashion moves.

Haute couture. High-class, prestige dressmaking.

High fashion. A new, costly, subtle fashion that has a limited but selective acceptance by fashion leaders.

House. Abbreviation for dressmaking house or firm.

In bond. Merchandise is "in bond" when imported duty-free for copying and then returned within a certain period.

La Chambre Syndicale de la Couture Parisienne. The trade association of Parisian couture.

Line-for-line copy. A copy of a garment whose outside appearance exactly duplicates the original.

Mannequin or **manikin.** Person who displays clothing; also dressmaker's dummy.

Market. Location of apparel manufacturers selling similar products.

Midinette. Seamstress.

Mode. Synonym for fashion.

Model. Person who poses for photographs, painters, designers; one who displays clothing; or a sample or original garment from which orders are taken.

Modiste. Milliner.

Openings. The first fashion showings of a new collection in the houses of the couture.

Original. Design created to be shown in a collection.

Prêt à porter. Ready to wear.

Resource. Supplier of fabrics; manufacturer of clothing for retailer's purchase.

Salon. Room in which collection is shown.

Silhouette. Outline; shadow profile (named after Etienne Silhouette, French author and politician).

Soignée. Well groomed; carefully done.

Style. The characteristic or distinctive expression of a mode; the distinguishing features, cut, design, or type of article.

Style piracy. Unauthorized copying of designs.

Toile. Linen or muslin models or sample dresses; also the cloth.

American fashions

The story of the development of men's fashions parallels that of women's dress in some instances. Many fabrics and styles are imported from Europe for reproduction or adaptation. Some custom-made originals are imported by individual clients.

The outstanding English fashions that originate in Savile Row and Bond Street in London are copied or adapted by many Americans. In England, dress is important to all classes of men. It is a badge of office, distinction, and occupation.

There are American leaders of fashion who launch new styles at resorts, sports events, and prominent social affairs. The clothing selection of stars of stage, screen, radio, television, and sports is imitated by many young adults. Even so, some men seem to be less fashion-conscious than women. Their wives still tell them when it is time to buy a new suit.

The three types

There are three types of men's clothing—ready-to-wear, made-to-measure, and cus-

The Natural Look   The Ivy Look   The Continental Look

tom-tailored. Many men have their own tailor or patronize a custom-made shop; others make use of the excellent alteration service provided by retailers of ready-to-wear or the made-to-measure service of some manufacturers.

Although New York is one of the leading men's-wear centers, there are several other manufacturing centers in the United States, including Rochester (N. Y.), Philadelphia, Chicago, and Boston.

There are fewer well-known creative designers of men's wear than of women's wear. The names of old and well-established custom-made shops and retail stores are more prominent. Of course all of the clothing is designed by someone, but the name of the designer of men's clothes is often obscured by a trade-name or the name of a firm.

The clothes available in stores are the result of the judgment and the efforts of several people, including the manufacturer, the designer, the fabric manufacturer, the clothing salesman, the clothing buyer, and the store owner. Although the majority of the people who work in men's fashions are men, there are a few women in the fields of designing, styling, buying, and selling men's clothes.

Various men fashion editors, authorities on men's wear, and prominent leaders in men's wear organizations predict trends, forecast consumer wants, and try to interpret manufacturers' showings to consumers as well as make consumer needs known to manufacturers. Some of these men are influential enough to introduce new ideas and launch new fashions.

Men's-wear fashion shows are held here and abroad to inform buyers. Forums sponsored by men's-wear publications and organizations are held for leaders of the apparel industry to present and promote fashions of the next seasons. The American Institute of Men's and Boys' Wear is one of several organizations responsible for promotion of men's fashions.

Women buy for men

Just as in women's fashions, it is the consumer who accepts or rejects a new idea and so determines fashion trends. Women are very influential in this phase of men's fashions. It is estimated that women suggest or decide on the purchase of 70 per cent of men's apparel. One retailer commented that either men do not care about clothes or they have renounced their shopping rights. The retail trade welcomes women shopping for men because they tend to buy more of the new.

The men's-wear industry has been promoting changes gradually since 1950. The natural line, unpadded suits and coats, neat shirt collars, slender ties, narrow hat brims, the suburban coat, the Ivy League look, the Continental look, tapered trousers and shirts, the fitted look, bright color in sportswear, and subtle color in evening wear are a few examples of fashion changes in men's wear. The promotion of flat-topped hats and boaters was not a national success.

Just as in women's fashions, different sections of the country have their effect on men's fashions, too. Colors, types of clothes, and furnishings worn in California, Florida, and Texas are different from those worn in the Central West or in the Northeast.

With men taking trips to the moon, they may set a fashion pace which women will be unable to surpass—until women are permitted to go, too.

DESIGNERS OF FASHION

In a short chapter on fashion, it is impossible to include a complete and descriptive list of designers in the fashion world. Some of the well-known creators and fashion firms are listed below with no attempt at classification. With this list as a guide, the student of fashion should be able to associate current fashions with these leaders and become familiar with their lines of clothes as pictured in fashion publications. It is recognized that designers' affiliations, lines of clothes, and prominence change occasionally. Students who are alert to fashion changes will want to make additions or deletions on this list.

Women's apparel—New York

Women designers: Helena *Barbieri—Miss Branell*, Ellen *Brooke*, Jeanne *Campbell—Sportwhirl*, Betty *Carol* of *Mam'selle*, Jeanne *Carr—Jonathan Logan*, Bonnie *Cashin*, Ceil *Chapman—Miss Winston*, Jo *Copeland* of *Patullo—Jo Copeland*, Eloise *Curtis*, Evelyn *Dawson—Suzy Perette*, Sylvia *de Gay—Robert Sloan*, Nellie *de Grab*, Mary *Douglas—L'Aiglon*, Anne *Fogarty*, Anne *Klein*, Tina *Leser*, *Lotte*, Rosalie *Macrini*, Vera *Maxwell*, Marie *McCarthy—Larry Aldrich*, *Molly—Jack Sarnoff*, Grace *Norman—Kay Windsor*, Alice *Oroven—Monte-Sano & Pruzan*, Toni *Owen*, Greta *Plattry*, Clare *Potter*, Sara *Ripault—Mollie Parnis*, Eva *Rosencrans—Ben Reig*, *Roxanne—Samuel Winston*, Gloria *Sachs*, Belle *Saunders—Abe Schrader*, Eleanor *Simmons—Malcolm Starr*, Adele *Simpson*, Stella *Sloat*, *Sophie—Saks Fifth Avenue*, Karen *Stark—Harvey Berin*, Pauline *Trigere*, Catalina *Villani—Mort Schrader*.

Men designers: Frank *Adams—Junior Accent*, Ronald *Amey* of *Burke-Amey*, Bill *Atkinson—Glenn*, Geoffrey *Beene*, Bill *Blass—Maurice Rentner*, Ole *Borden—Rembrandt*, Fernando *Bose—Paul Parnes*, Tom *Brigance—Sinclair*, Donald *Brooks*, Bob *Bugnand—Sam Friedlander*, Oleg *Cassini*, Maxzell *Cook—Cabana*, Victor *Costa—Suzy Perette*, *Dominic—Matty Polmach*, Seymour *Fox*, Harry *Frechtel*, Robert *Goldworm*, David *Gottlieb—Goethe*, George *Halley*, Charles *Howard—Townley*, Philip *Hulitar*, Victor *Joris—Cuddlecoat*, Herbert *Kaspar—Joan Leslie*, David *Kidd—Jablow*, Bud *Kilpatrick*, Charles *Kleibacker*, Robert *Knox—Laird Knox*, Oscar *de la Renta—Jane Derby*, Eric *Lund*, *Mainbocher*, Christian *Mann* at *Marquise*, Gerald *McCann* for *Modelia*, John *Moore*, Leo *Narducci*, Norman *Norell*, Patrick *Porter*, Sylvan *Rich* of *Martini*, Shannon *Rogers—Jerry Silverman*, Ferdinando *Sarmi*, Ted *Saulino—Anthony Blotta*, Arnold *Scaasi*, Harry *Schacter—Pembroke Squires*, George *Stavropoulos*, Jacques *Tiffeau—Tiffeau-Busch*, Philip *Tournaye—Modelia*, Illie *Wacs—Originala*, Chester *Weinburg—Teal Traina*, John *Weitz*, Sidney *Wragge—B. H. Wragge*.

Children's apparel—New York

Women designers: Joan *Bellew*, Betty *Brett*, Susan *Godart*, Helen *Lee*, Miriam *Norville*.

Men designers: Robert *Bart*, Bill *Beaton*, Tom *Brigance*.

Women's apparel—California

Women designers: Agnes *Barrett*, Georgia *Bullock*, Peggy *Hunt*, De De *Johnson*, Stephanie *Koret*, Addie *Masters*, Dorothy *O'Hara*, Pat *Premo*, Maggy *Reece—Catalina*, Irene *Saltern—Tabak*, Luella *Taylor—Montgomery*.

Men designers: Richard *Blackwell*, James *Galanos*, Rudi *Gernreich*, Don *Loper*, Jean *Louis*, William *Pearson*, Gustave *Tassell*, William *Travilla*.

Women's apparel—France

Women designers: Mlle. *Carven*, Gabrielle *Chanel*, Madeleine *de Rauch*, Jacqueline *Goddard*, Alix *Gres*, Emmanuelle *Khanh*, Nina *Ricci—Gerard Pipart*, designer, Maggy *Rouff—Michel Malard*, designer, *Simonetta*.

Men designers: Jean-Marie *Armand,* Pierre *Balmain,* Marc *Bohan—Dior,* Roberto *Capucci,* Pierre *Cardin,* Andre *Courreges,* Jules *Crahay—Lanvin,* Hubert *de Givenchy,* Antonio *del Castillo,* Jean *Desses,* Jacques *Esterel,* Louis *Feraud,* Miguel *Ferreras,* Jacques *Griffe,* Jacques *Heim—*Jean *Pomarede,* designer, *Hermes,* Ted *Lapidus,* Guy *La-Roche,* Jacques *Launay,* Serge *Matta,* Edward *Molyneux,* Jean *Patou—*Michel *Goma,* designer, *Sagardoy,* Yves *St. Laurent,* Jean-Louis *Scherrer,* Emmanuel *Ungaro,* Phillipe *Venet.*

Women's apparel—Italy
Women designers: Marella *Agnelli,* Maria *Antonelli—*Andre *Laug,* designer, Laura *Aponte, Carosa,* Gigliola *Curiel,* Sorelle *Fontana,* Irene *Galitzine,* Eleanora *Garnett,* Feranda *Gattfononi,* Lola *Giovanelli,* Germana *Marucelli,* Wanda *Roveda,* Mila *Schoen,* Jole *Veneziani.*

Men designers: Patrick *de Barentzen,* Renato *Belestra,* Piero *Bianco, Enzo,* Alberto *Fabiani,* Federico *Forquet,* Cesare *Guidi,* Pino *Lancetti,* Antonio *de Luca, Mingolini—Guggenheim,* Emilio *Pucci, Ognibene—Zendman,* Emilio *Schuberth, Tiziani, Valentino.*

Women's apparel—England
Women designers: Belinda *Belville,* Angela *Cash—Londontown,* Caroline *Charles,* Angele *Delanghe,* Jean *Muir,* Mary *Quant,* Sally *Tuffin—*Marion *Foale.*

Men designers: Hardy *Amies,* John *Cavanagh, Clive,* Norman *Hartnell,* Owen *Hyde-Clark, Mattli, Michael,* Roger *Nelson,* Charles *Owen—LaChasse,* Ronald *Paterson,* David *Sassoon—Belville,* Bob *Schulz,* Michael *Sherard,* Victor *Steibel.*

Men's apparel—United States
Women designers: Carroll *Draga* of *Arrow Shirts,* Countess *Mara,* and *Schiaparelli.*

Men designers: Bert *Bacharach,* Clyde *Bordner* of *Rogers Peet,* Brooks *Cadwallader,* Jimmy *Demaret,* Hugo *Gemignani* of *Hickey Freeman,* Howard *Greer,* Jay *Holliner* of *White Stag,* Paul *Mage* of *Robert Bruce,* and Pasquale *Trotta* of *Lebow Brothers.*

Men's apparel—France
Men designers: Pierre *Cardin, Dior, Lanvin, St. Laurent.*

Men's apparel—Italy
Men designers: Baratto, Brioni, Cavoda, Cucci, Datti, Duetti, Franzone, Giovanni, Litrico.

REFERENCE READINGS

Ballard, Bettina, *In My Fashion,* David McKay Co., Inc., New York, 1960.

Birmingham, Frederic A., *Esquire Fashion Guide for All Occasions,* Harper & Bros., New York, 1957.

Brockman, Helen L., *Theory of Fashion Design,* John Wiley & Sons, New York, 1965.

Dariaux, Genevieve Antoine, *Elegance,* Doubleday & Co., Inc., New York, 1964.

Daves Jessica, *Ready-Made Miracle,* Putnam Publishing Co., New York, 1967.

Garland, Madge, *Fashion,* Penquin Books, Ltd., Harmondsworth, Middlesex, 1962.

Jarnow, Jeannette A. and Judelle, Beatrice, *Inside the Fashion Business,* John Wiley & Sons, New York, 1965.

Langer, Lawrence, *The Importance of Wearing Clothes,* Hastings House, New York, 1959.

Levin, Phyllis Lee, *The Wheels of Fashion,* Doubleday & Co., New York, 1965.

Merriam, Eve, *Figleaf,* J. B. Lippincott Co., New York, 1960.

Morton, Grace Margaret, *The Arts of Costume and Personal Appearance,* 3rd. Edition, John Wiley & Sons, New York, 1964.

Nystrom, Paul H., *Economics of Fashion,* The Ronald Press, New York, 1928.

Picken, Mary Brooks, *The Fashion Dictionary,* Funk and Wagnalls, New York, 1957.

Picken, Mary Brooks and Miller, Dora Loues, *Dressmakers of France,* Harper & Bros., New York, 1951.

Roach, Mary Ellen and Eicher, Joanne Bubolz, *Dress, Adornment, and the Social Order,* John Wiley & Sons, New York, 1965.

Roshco, Bernard, *The Rag Race,* Funk & Wagnalls Co., Inc., New York, 1963.

Rudofsky, Bernard, *Are Clothes Modern?,* P. Theobold, Inc., Chicago, 1947.

Spanier, Ginette, *It Isn't All Mink,* Random House, New York, 1960.

Tate, Mildred Thurow and Glisson, Oris, *Family Clothing,* John Wiley & Sons, New York, 1961.

Chapter 3

Do your clothes express you?

Aperson's relationship to the clothes he buys or wears is often difficult for him and for others to understand. His usual explanation for his choice of the clothes he is wearing is that the shoes are comfortable, the shirt was the only clean one available, or the sweater was on top of the pile. Not only does he often see no personal reason for his daily choice of clothes, but he fails to realize that his original choice of the whole wardrobe was governed by his own personal preferences. This attitude is typical of many people who have never considered that they themselves or their tastes are being reflected in their clothes.

The suggestion of personal analysis seems to be considered an affront by many people. To others, especially to men, personal analysis will seem absurd, useless, and irrelevant. Perhaps these people are just pretending, but their reactions are sometimes indicative of personality traits. Nearly everyone has a philosophy about clothes, just as he does about life, people, recreation, and religion, although it may be

hidden or disguised. Each person thinks, acts, and makes choices as a distinct individual. The impression a person makes through the clothes he wears may or may not be indicative of his real personality. A person might also show by the way he dresses—and many do—that he really does not understand his own personality.

Adolescents tend to rely on conformity to the dress of their peers. However, in the late teens they begin to find themselves and develop self-confidence. When people know and accept themselves, their clothes often express how they feel about themselves and their environment.

PERSONALITY

Interests and clothes

The person who is uninterested in everything in life tends to reflect this lack of interest in his clothes. Studies reveal that young people who cannot afford appropriate clothing, who do not participate in social activities, and who are insecure in social situations often appear not to care about their appearance or their acceptance by others. Another type of person is one who becomes so involved in a multiplicity of interests that clothes seem unimportant, and, unfortunately, reflect this neglect. This person forgets that other people have to look at him and seldom find the sight pleasing.

Occasionally, a well-known public figure indicates by his personal appearance that he has not seen the connection between his public personality and dress. A man's clothes can be as eloquent a testimony of his talents and competence as any brilliant speech he might make. Yet there is many a well-known person who has never learned enough about himself to realize that his ego may be showing. He supposes his clothes to be appropriate for any place, occasion, or time because he feels his fame, personality, and self-assurance will see him through life.

A few women in the so-called intellectual group scorn clothing beyond the actual necessities. The statement that "a person not *interested in clothes* is usually not *interesting*" is not true. This person may have great potential for a charming appearance. It is just that she has never experimented and found that a pleasing appearance and intellectual attainments can be compatible.

Knowing oneself may help a person to make the most of himself and to choose clothes which are not only flattering but are expressive of the real person. A good appearance tends to boost one's morale, to promote self-respect, and to help in attaining success in the competitive economic and social world. With a feeling of security, a person gains inner strength, charm, and poise. In the rehabilitation of the mentally ill, becoming clothes and good grooming have helped in developing pride in self and renewed confidence. Tensions caused by concern about physical appearance disappear when a person feels at ease among people. A knowledge of what is becoming and what will express a person's individuality and role in life is an important part of his education. Interests, values, goals, personality traits, preferences, and physical characteristics should be considered by the person making a study of himself.

The person who is not aware of his own worth and potential will find that a study of self with or without the aid of others may be revealing and helpful. His hopes, aspirations, and desires may have been blighted by uncontrolled circumstances which have prevented him from developing self-respect, pride, and interest in people and activities. After finding out what he really likes and how he spends his leisure

time, a person begins to realize what he is like and how his personal interests may determine the kind of clothes he needs and chooses.

Values and goals

When considering individual values and goals, a person often discovers what he really values in life; his ultimate goals are a reflection of these values. To some, material things such as clothing, money, a new house, a new car, or a television set may seem to have more value than less tangible things such as the admiration of others, friendship, good health, happiness, and respect. This does not imply that these values are incompatible and that a person who owns a new car does not have friends and good health or that a happy, healthy person does not value money or a new house. If you examine carefully what you really value in life and why, you may learn why you make the choices you do in clothing, activities, college courses, and occupation.

It is wise to consider your goals to see what standards you hope to achieve in your own personal appearance. Do you wish to be well groomed and neat in every detail? Do you desire to be charming, cultured, poised? Do you want to be appropriately, becomingly, comfortably, fashionably, inconspicuously yet individually and strikingly dressed? The standards you maintain in everything you do may also be reflected in your clothing and grooming.

Many people consider other things in life more important than clothing. The family member who is satisfied with a few carefully chosen clothes may have money left to share with the rest of the family. Perhaps his real goal is to be well dressed on a minimum of the family income and to enjoy the pride of this achievement.

College students should be very conscious of their values and goals and should realize the importance of sharing the family income. They should, of course, be aware of the total income and should know whether they are demanding more than a fair amount. This amount will vary from family to family according to the number and the needs of the individual family members.

There may be certain times in one's life when it seems necessary to have a few more clothes. A high school girl, for instance, may need more clothes than her younger brother; a college freshman tends to buy more clothes than she actually needs; a homemaker who becomes very active in community affairs may increase her wardrobe noticeably; a man whose business requires a great deal of travel may need more than a basic wardrobe. Trying to meet individual needs without depriving others of their share of the family income can be a real challenge to each family member.

A real problem exists with some married college students. In some cases such couples may even have one or more children. Decisions on the clothing needs and expenditures, along with all of the other expenses, are major problems.

Some college students earn enough money for all their expenses, including clothing expenditures; it is their privilege to spend as they please. The student who earns only part of his expenses and then expects a large allowance from his family for clothes may be demanding more than he is entitled to. Brief reflection might reveal to him that he is being selfish.

It is the social stimulus value of one's basic personality or individuality that appeals to others, at home or in school, church, business, or the community. And more often than not, people base broad judgments about our basic personality on our appearance, especially our clothing.

Understanding one's own personality is a difficult and complex task. No one ever achieves complete self-understanding, but something in the way of self-knowledge can be gathered from our day-to-day behavior. To some extent we express our personality through actions, through facial expression, motions, posture, and voice, and particularly through the clothes we wear.

In doing a self-analysis, it may be helpful to seek the assistance of friends and relatives. If they are reluctant to talk to you directly, ask them to write a paragraph about you. Try to get a few different opinions. Ask relatives and friends, both male and female, and people both of your own age and of another generation.

A brief look at some common notions may prove helpful. Some people are referred to—redundantly enough—as retiring introverts and others as forthright extroverts. The extrovert-by-definition enjoys big parties and city life and likes to be fashionable, distinctive, and individual in dress. The introvert, who may prefer comfort and simplicity, usually enjoys casual and classic clothes more than high fashion. She may wear the same type of dress everywhere she goes and, if she can, avoid wearing any accessories other than shoes.

A consideration of remarks that have been made about American men and women in general may also prove interesting. American women have been described as women who either eat ice cream by the gallon or pursue crash diets, wear hair rollers in public, and try to look older if they are young and younger when they are older. They are good looking, with warm, friendly, sincere smiles. They are impatient and hurried, and seem to know just where they are going. American women are not types but individuals.

American men have been called just

nice, ordinary men who cover themselves with "just clothes"—clothes acceptable in their crowd and at their age. They wear conservative dark flannel suits and snap brims or blue worsteds and gray felt hats. Their socks are bought by their wives or knitted by their fiancées and their ties are Christmas presents. Their suits are neat and well pressed, their shirts are white, and their black oxfords well polished. They want to be thought of as "good dressers." Of course there are exceptions—the "fruit-salad man" dressed in, say, blue canvas shoes, red slacks, and a yellow sports shirt hanging free outside the trousers; the lawyer in tweeds; the doctor in pin-stripes; or the college student in chinos and button-down shirts.

When considering the remarks of others, one should realize that some people will never make flattering comments, and others will always be very complimentary. Careful evaluation is necessary. Self-analysis can be helpful, and many people find it so. Some, of course, may take it lightly and make no attempt to follow through where improvement would seem indicated. It is entirely up to the individual—personal analysis can be used constructively or can be considered nothing more than a waste of time.

DRESSING TO REFLECT CHANGE

The element of change should not be overlooked. Physical appearance, personality, and taste change. The contours of face and figure, the color and texture of complexion, posture, facial expression, temperament, and attitude—any of these may change gradually or suddenly, depending upon the individual and his pattern of life. This does not mean that a sweet, quiet, mousy girl will turn into a dazzling, sensational beauty overnight. Basically, she may always be a nice, quiet girl and never a

startling siren, yet it is possible for her to look prettier and more attractive through proper choice of make-up, hairdo, colors, and clothes. As she receives more compliments and more attention, she will gradually gain poise and confidence. It is better to look like the same person, with pleasing, subtle changes, than to look like "a new person" and then not be able to cope with the extreme change.

A person's attitudes, opinions, and outlooks may change as well as his appearance. College students have varying degrees of appreciation of many things, including clothing, but as their knowledge grows, they develop a better understanding of, and a clearer insight into, the reasons behind their choices of clothing. Their appreciation and their enjoyment of clothing increase as they develop objective attitudes, open-mindedness, and the willingness to observe, compare, and analyze dress. A person's opinion does not necessarily change radically, but his judgment and taste may improve. Some students learn to experiment and to discover a style of their own rather than to conform to the patterns of dress set by the leaders of their group.

Although a person's personality may not change greatly, his choice of clothing may vary according to time and place. A woman may look like an executive while on the job yet look quite different on an after-five dinner date. A student may look like a student at all times, but some students cannot be identified as such when dressed for special occasions. A businessman relaxing at his home in the country over the week end may not be recognized as an executive. Appropriate clothing for the situation defines one's role at that time.

Climate and seasonal patterns also affect changes in clothing and appearance. A person living where the weather is warm all year has a wardrobe quite different from that of someone who dresses for four seasons. People who move from one climate to another have to adjust to regional differences in clothing. Those who are realistic in the things they do change their habits of dress as their appreciations develop.

Age brings about changes in personality, attitude, and taste—and, consequently, in one's choice of clothes. The terms "pretty," "young," and "dainty" give way to "handsome," "mature," and "sophisticated." However, the kind of clothes a woman can wear often depends more on the kind of person she is—and on her proportions—than on her age. Clothes should be chosen for self-expression and identification of the wearer.

The differences in attitude and bearing that mark each generation make certain types of clothes seem the exclusive property of whatever age group happens to be wearing them.

DRESSING FOR MEN

The person who has pride in himself and wants to be accepted by others as an individual will dress accordingly. He values the opinions of others and lives by what he believes.

Many women in all age groups value the opinions of the men in their lives. Some women are willing to subordinate their own preferences for clothes and to wear what men like. A husband usually wants to be proud of his wife; he wants to show her off to his boss, to have his friends admire her, and to have their children approve of her. He seldom wants her to look like a show girl, a model, a sophisticate, a "beatnik," or a bizarre, arty type. He admires the happy, eager, winsome look that is a reflection of the way she feels.

A college student may have her hair long or wear short skirts or pale lipstick simply because her current boy friend likes her that way.

There are few people who are not appreciated by someone. Most people do not need the approval of the whole world—just the love and admiration of an intimate few.

IMPRESSIONS

In a fast-paced life with little time to get to know people well, people are often judged by first impressions. People sometimes remember a person for years, not only by his personality but also by his appearance and his clothes. A woman's chipped nails, uneven hemline, and scuffed shoes or a man's wrinkled trousers, frayed cuffs, and crooked tie leave a less flattering impression than do smartness, impeccability, and good grooming. People are often judged by personality, poise, charm, beauty of face and figure, individual style, and grooming.

If a person has a genuine desire to be well dressed, he will dress well without following the fashion leader in his group. He will develop enough confidence in himself to forget about his appearance once he has dressed. His clothes can be a means of "selling himself" as well as of expressing himself—his self-confidence, happiness, and leadership. Although clothes do not necessarily make the man, they do help. The person who is not aware of the importance of his total appearance fails to create the impression he really would like to make.

An example of the significance of clothes can be seen in the incident of the bank president who found it necessary to request one of his employees to return home for a change of clothing because the impression she made on the public in her sheer, transparent blouse was not favorable.

A similar instance involved the discharge of a young airline clerk whose extreme eye make-up, artificial hair color, and figure-hugging clothes were considered too distracting, provocative, and unbusinesslike.

The ability to recognize personal characteristics that distinguish one person from another, to see how these characteristics relate to clothes that are becoming to the wearer, to improve personal appearance, and to grow in aesthetic appreciation are all essential to one's knowledge of clothing.

PREFERENCES

Color

Personal preferences play an important part in determining a person's choice of clothes and may be affected by emotional experiences, loyalty to the past, childhood preferences, and parental choices. Take the subject of a "favorite color." Some people maintain that they do not have one favorite color. A check of their wardrobes may show all colors or a predominance of one particular color. Some people say that they like all colors but cannot afford to have them in their wardrobes. They may tend to choose brown, black, gray, or navy blue.

If a person has a favorite color, there usually is a reason. Perhaps he has received compliments or had a good time or felt poised and at ease while wearing that color. Or his liking for the color may go back to his childhood.

There is no obvious explanation for color preferences. Some individuals like certain colors and wear them almost constantly even though they may be unflattering; others may dislike intensely and refuse to wear some color that for them is very flattering.

Usually the colors an individual chooses and wears indicate something about him and his philosophy of clothing. A person may be known as "the woman who looks so smart in black" or as "the one who always wears" gray, light brown, or navy blue. She really loves red, but she never wears it. She admires blond hair, but will not change the color of her hair.

Texture

The choice of textures in clothing is another area where personal selection reveals individuality. Not all men wear rough-textured tweeds, pigskin gloves, and Scotch-grain shoes. One woman may prefer satin, velvet, polished cotton, doeskin, sequins, and patent leather while another likes crepe, seersucker, straw, suède, and jersey.

Some people like all textures and wear various ones at different times throughout the year. There are a few people who never wear wool, except, perhaps, in a winter coat for northern climates.

People are often identified by their tweeds, transparent sheers, or slinky satins. In other words, a texture may be associated with the individual and thought to indicate something about his personality.

Design

Many people have definite preferences in fabric designs—large floral prints, small geometric patterns, polka dots, bold stripes, pin checks, or plaids. Descriptions like "the woman who always wears plaid" and "the man who always wears a striped tie" are sometimes used to identify individuals.

A check of one's own wardrobe may reveal a definite trend toward, perhaps, plain fabrics, figured fabrics, or a combination of these. Similar preferences may also be evident in the decoration of a bedroom, in luggage, in umbrellas, or in the pattern of a golf bag.

Types of clothes

In types of clothing worn, there is a great deal of variation between different personalities. Some wardrobes are made up of all types, but may show a predominance of one type of clothing. There may be more suits and dresses, more casual clothes than dressy ones, more town clothes than sport clothes, or more after-five clothes than work clothes. In a man's closet, there may be more slacks and jackets than matched suits or more business than sport shirts.

The life a person leads and his personal preferences determine choices in clothes. A person who has no need for formal clothes will seldom have them in his wardrobe. However, some people do have definite likes for specific kinds of clothes but have no opportunity to wear them. The clothes a college student wears in the home community may not be needed at college, where campus customs control choice of clothing.

People for whom active sports are an important part of life will have many sport clothes in their wardrobes. There are a few women who do not own or ever wear shorts, slacks, or swimsuits while some women live in these clothes almost around the clock.

Silhouette

The kind of silhouette preferred in clothes also reflects an individual's tastes. The sheath, the shift, the princess style, the gathered skirt, and the bias cut may appeal to some women, while the bouffant, middy, or empire silhouette are chosen by others. Some men may choose padded shoulders, wide lapels, one-button jackets, long ties, and pleated trousers; others prefer narrow lapels, three-button coats, bow ties, and tapered trousers.

Accessories

Accessories, almost more than any other item, tell something about a person. In hats, for instance, there are the extremes of the college student who does not own a hat and the career woman who has an extensive hat wardrobe. Some women like small, flowery hats while others like plain, simple hats or big cartwheels or floppy brims. There are similar extremes among men, from the hatless to the hatted. One will wear only a cap, another a pork pie, snap brim, Homburg, or derby.

A few people make a habit of having a special "trademark" in their accessories—a fresh flower every day, a certain scarf, or a monogrammed handkerchief in a suit pocket.

A woman may wear doeskin gloves, expensive belts, beautiful shoes, one special perfume, or a strand of real pearls. She probably prefers one expensive dress to three of popular price, is always meticulously groomed, checks her nail polish every day, is fussy about her hair, and often wears white—pearls, a scarf, or a headband—near her face.

Shoes. Women's shoe preferences may include pumps, sling-backs, open-toes, or sandals. The high school or college girl who wears sneakers or loafers constantly and who has difficulty when walking on high heels usually chooses her footwear not only for comfort but also for conformity. The current college "culture" dictates many choices of students who need assurance and a feeling of security.

Some men would never be seen wearing formal pumps. They usually prefer wing tips, bluchers, loafers, bucks, or heavy-soled brogues. From time to time, fashion strongly influences their choice. "Dirty white bucks" and desert boots have been favorites with many college men, while others continued to wear conventional shoes. Comfort and cost are ordinarily given as reasons for the choice of shoes, but the pattern of the majority is usually the influencing factor. In their post-college careers, people tend to show personal tastes and preferences in clothes more obviously than during college days.

Jewelry. There are a few people who

never wear jewelry, while others feel undressed without it. Although jewelry should be a personal choice, it is often a gift chosen by friends or relatives. A person should not feel compelled to wear jewelry —and certainly not in excess—as pure adornment. A string of pearls is often enough.

One or two pieces of expensive jewelry in good taste are preferred by some; others like a great variety of costume jewelry—a set for every outfit, and not just earrings or a necklace but a whole array. Here again, color, design, texture, and appropriateness to outfit and occasion give the wearer the "added touch" that indicates individual taste and flair.

Men wear jewelry in varying degrees just as women do; in fact, some men show more individuality in their choice of jewelry than do women. While some men wear no jewelry at all, others wear collar pins, tie tacks, tie clamps, cuff links, key chains, and rings. A few men still prefer a pocket watch to a wrist watch and never wear rings or cuff links. Some men wear rings set with precious stones and diamond stick pins. Most high school and college men limit their jewelry to class rings.

TIME

The amount of time a person is willing to spend on the selection of clothes may affect the choices he makes. Of course some people do not mind spending the time, but they may actually not have as much time to spend in the selection of clothes as they would like. The greater their interest in clothes, the more time people will often spend on selection. A person with limited time may spend more time in preplanning before making the final selection, which can then be done in a relatively short time. There are people who spend very little time in selection. They buy as the need

arises, on the spur of the moment, or when they are in the mood for shopping.

The amount of time a person wants to or can afford to spend in the care of the wardrobe often has a bearing on the initial selection of clothes. A woman with a very busy schedule and limited time to spend on the care of clothing may choose fabrics, colors, and styles requiring a minimum of care. If, however, the care of clothing is done by others in the family, by domestic help, or commercially, a person may give little thought to the care required. This lack of thoughtfulness seems to reflect a trait of selfishness or carelessness. In planning, one might consider the many minimum-care fibers, fabrics, and finishes available.

IT'S YOUR CHOICE

Whether you select your clothing alone or with the help of a friend or a member of the family will also affect your selection. A mother may influence her daughter's choices to the extent that the daughter's clothes reflect not her own taste but her mother's. The girl may have difficulty in overcoming this influence when she leaves home. If easily swayed by others, including saleswomen, a person may lose individuality in her choice of clothes. In the final analysis, we are seldom satisfied with the choices someone else makes for us. Making one's own decisions is preferable to following the suggestions of others, even though the insecure person gets a greater feeling of assurance by conforming.

PHYSICAL SELF

In creating a style of your own, you are trying to present your individuality through your physical appearance. Physical characteristics, being inherited, are truly individual and, to a degree, are beyond your control. If you have a knowledge of the proportions of the human figure, and especially of your own, you will have an understanding of a part of yourself. Knowing your physical assets and limitations will enable you to use design not only to enhance your image but also to express the personality you wish to communicate. When you know what your figure is actually like, you will be able to choose becoming lines and find the size that really fits.

Recent data from the National Health Survey contains information about human figures which may assist us in understanding more about physical analysis. Ethnic, racial, and socio-economic background will be factors which make individuals differ in body build. Negroes, for example, are inclined to have longer extremities than do white people.

Age also affects body build. The individual generally reaches his maximum height between the ages of eighteen and twenty-four. After this period there is a slight but continuous decrease in height. Weight averages increase in middle age and decline again as one approaches old age. Fatty tissue deposits generally affect the figure through middle age.*

In America, the ideal woman's figure has come to be thought of as fairly broad-shouldered, with bust and hips of nearly the same measure and the waistline 8 to 10 inches smaller than the bustline and hips. This is quite different from the European ideal, according to which the hips should be larger than the bustline by 6 to 8 inches or even more.

The ideal masculine figure has been

compared to an inverted triangle: moderate shoulder width, full chest, tapered waist, and slim hips. It is fairly certain that the average man today is taller and has broader shoulders and a larger chest than he did a generation ago. Although in these respects he has increased in size, he generally has a somewhat smaller waist.

To wear clothes well, it is essential to have a well-proportioned figure. It should be understood before further discussion that a well-proportioned figure is not necessarily a "model" figure, nor is it always slim or tall. Within limits, a person of any height or weight can be well proportioned. A heavy person may have better proportions than a slim one. Posture, of course, will also have an effect on balance and appearance. Analysis over a period of years reveals that there are few "perfect" figures. It is not at all uncommon to find slight irregularities, such as one shoulder being higher than the other. One of the purposes of design is to camouflage slight imperfections.

In thinking through figure problems, we think in terms of *what can be controlled*, such as posture, and *what is beyond our control*, such as bone structure. You will learn to use will power to control what can be controlled and color, line, and fit to bring out good features and camouflage the less desirable. At some point, you may have to compromise a good feature in order to camouflage the bad. It is also possible occasionally to make an irregularity into an asset. A person with high, prominent cheek bones could appear thin and gaunt, whereas another person with the same kind of bone structure, through good choice of make-up, hair style, and dress, may be considered different, interesting, or stunning. Remember also that even a perfect figure can be spoiled by the wrong selection or fit of clothes. Above all, accept graciously that

* National Center for Health Statistics: Weight, Height, and Selected Body Dimensions of Adults. Vital and Health Statistics PHS 1000—Series 11—No. 8. U. S. Dept. of Health, Education and Welfare, Public Health Service. Washington, D. C. U. S. Govt. Printing Office, June, 1965.

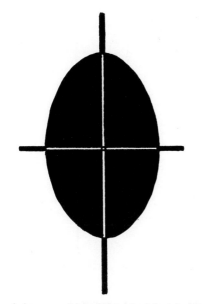

The oval, long considered the ideal facial shape, is symmetrical.

which you cannot control and concentrate on learning to handle it correctly.

In the analysis of your face and figure, various methods can be used. Silhouette photos are extremely helpful, but are not always easily obtained. Enlarged snapshots can reveal many things. Wear a simple swimsuit and take as many different poses as possible. Be sure that you have one with the body facing directly toward the camera and one profile shot. Candid shots of a person sitting or standing will also be enlightening. Old photographs can be equally helpful. A full-length mirror is necessary whether or not you use pictures. Those who can draw will find a natural alertness to detail. These are merely some of the aids you might enlist to help you. The point is to "dissect yourself" and, in what follows, put "you" back together.

The face

The face is the focal point of the person and therefore the most important area of the body. Since there is an abundance of material to help you understand the arts of make-up and grooming, our main concern is to deal with facial analysis as it will affect the selection of line and color in clothing. It would be an excellent idea to supplement this chapter with additional readings.

Although the oval face has long been considered the "ideal" of beauty, the factors affecting beauty are so numerous that this ideal should be used only as a basis for comparison in analyzing your own facial features. Many beautiful and interesting women have had faces far from the perfect oval shape. The oval itself requires just as careful treatment as do other shapes.

Before analyzing the various parts of the head, take a good over-all look at the size and general contours of your head. Many otherwise petite girls have large heads, and a tall person may well have a tiny head. The shape of the head will vary from long narrow to round, square, or rectangular. At this point, take a look at the ears. Are they large, small, pointed, narrow, or close to the head?

In judging facial features, you might first like to acquaint yourself with the oval. If you draw a vertical line and through its exact center another line at right angles, you will have the basis for drawing an oval. The oval will be longer in one direction than in the other, but it will be symmetrical. It will be exactly the same on one side of the vertical line as on the other and the two curves on either side of the horizontal line will likewise be symmetrical.

(Opposite) A comparison of some of the various head shapes with the oval: a. square jaw on a broad face; b. long square face; c. short square face; d. round face; e. pointed chin, broad forehead; f. long or high forehead; g. head narrow at forehead; h. long or high forehead on round face.

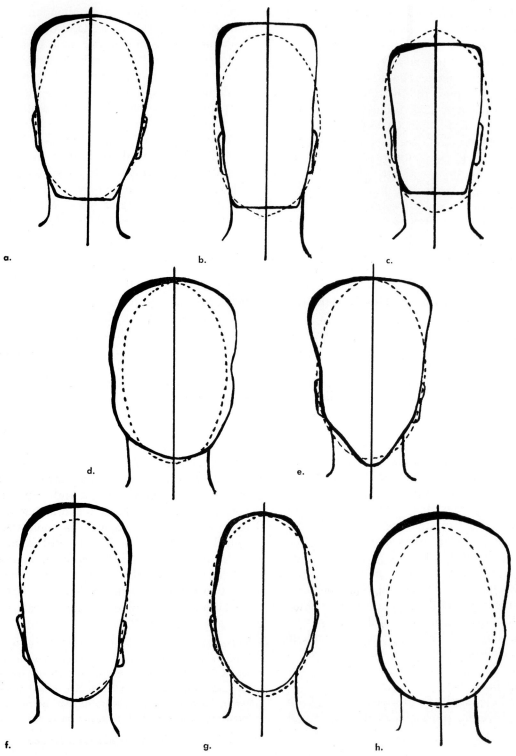

a.

b.

c.

d.

e.

f.

g.

h.

Having given consideration to the oval face, you may find it helpful to make a few generalizations before analyzing your own. A long face will generally get its length in a particular place. The forehead may be very long or high and the rest of the face in fine proportion, or the forehead may be low and the length could be from the eyes to the mouth or from the mouth to the chin. Each of these characteristics would call for different treatment in hair styles and hats. A long or a short face both may have a square jaw. An oval face may be in beautiful proportion but have extra fat or even puffiness on the cheek and give the illusion of being round. A good way to see the shape of your own face is to draw it, mentally or with pencil and ruler, as it is reflected in a mirror. Start with the widest part of the face—whether it is the forehead, the cheeks, the jawline, or the eyes. First, of course, you will need a center line. Then look at the distance from the widest parts to the remaining parts. How much distance is there between forehead and eyes, eyes and end of nose, cheeks and mouth, and mouth and chin? How do the distances compare with each other? Many faces will be long in one part and short in another part, or they may be round and full in one part and thin or even bony in another.

Next take a good look at the balance from one side of the face to the other. Are the two sides exactly the same? Is one side longer or irregular? Wider? If you have a full-view picture, you could actually measure your own face by drawing a line down the center and lines parallel to it at the fullest point. Lines at right angles would be drawn at the eyes, the nose, the mouth, and the chin. Is the shape symmetrical from top to bottom and from side to side, as in the oval?

Having obtained a clear picture of your

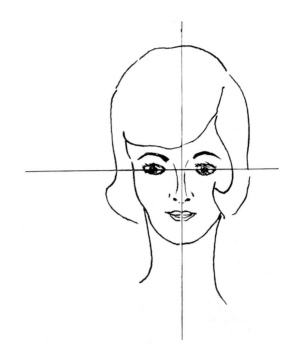

To analyze a face, sketch the outside contour of the front of the head. Then draw a vertical line through the long part of the face and a horizontal line through the widest part. Compare the parts with the parts of an oval. (See the illustration on page 38.)

facial silhouette, carefully evaluate those important factors that do not show up in a look at contour. The eyes should be judged for size, depth, and distance apart. Note the shape of the eyebrows and how the eyelashes show up. The relationship of any part to the rest of the face is always the important factor. The nose and mouth should be closely scrutinized as to length, shape, and size. You may observe slight deviations from side to side—one eyebrow lower than the other, a slightly lopsided jawline, or a crooked mouth. A profile analysis will be enlightening. The chin may be receding, jutting, uneven, pointed, or square. A last look should be concentrated on irregularities other than those of bone structure. Is there any puffiness under the eyes or the chin? What impression does the

mouth give—sulky, droopy, happy, smiling? The teeth will affect the contours of the whole face. Look at their size, straightness, and position in relation to the mouth and face. Noticeable delicacy or coarseness in the features of the face will also affect choice of colors, textures, and lines in clothing.

The neck

The neckline should be considered in the same terms as the face. As with the other parts of the body, it is difficult to "type" a neck. A long neck can be either thick or thin, as can a short one. The length of the neck should be judged in relation to the size of the face and the torso. Some experts would give the proportion of the neck as one third the length of the face. Again, many factors can affect appearance—a thin neck, for example, will look longer than a thicker one of equal length. Large veins or a prominent Adam's apple are other such features. The natural posture of the head and neck should be carefully studied and, where possible, improved.

The shoulders

Here, again, there is great diversity. Size and height are seldom an indication of what the shoulders will be. Prominent collar

The features of the face may vary in placement: a. oval face; b. oval face, eyes lower; c. oval face, nose lower; d. oval face, mouth lower.

bones may be found on anyone, tall or short, fat or thin. At various times in history, prominent collar bones were considered a mark of beauty. Most women have noticeable collar bones, and, unless extremely thin and bonelike, collar bones should not be of great concern. A rather fleshy woman may find her shoulders and neckline an asset to emphasize.

The shoulders may be square or sloping.

The two sides of the face may not be symmetrical: a. chin not centered; b. eyes not level.

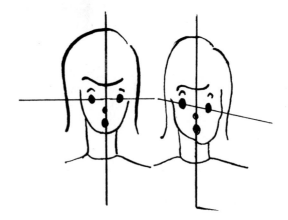

Women's shoulders vary in degree of slope.

The width of the shoulders in relation to the rest of the body should be closely inspected. Tall girls may be broad- or narrow-shouldered as well as short girls. Also to be noted are any hollows in the neck or shoulders and the straightness or roundness of the shoulders. Round shoulders with a forward head will show a lack of balance in the figure. The shoulder blades also have definite characteristics; some are prominent, others slightly seen.

Men will find the shape of the shoulders a most important factor in the selection of clothes, particularly of suits. Just as with women, the width and the slope of the shoulders are important factors in the balance and the proportions of the whole figure. Most men idealize the broad-shouldered look even when the "natural" silhouette is in fashion. A man should know whether his chest and shoulders are properly proportioned; a slight man may look top-heavy because of improperly selected clothing and so end up looking shorter than he is. Equally important are factors such as the roundness and straightness of the shoulders, mentioned above.

The torso

In analyzing her torso, a woman should remember that the measurements around

Depending upon the slope, men's shoulders may be round or angular.

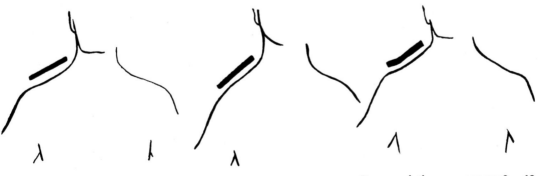

the bust and chest do not give a complete picture. A size 34 may have a full bust but a narrow back or a flat chest and a wide, full back. It is wise to measure the chest both above the bust and directly below. The fuller the bust, the larger will the difference in the two measurements be. The bust may be large, small, pendulous, high, low, round, pointed, fleshy, or firm or it may show a combination of several of these characteristics.

Fashion will attempt to dictate the bustline silhouette, but heredity has already determined shape and size. The degree to which it can be controlled is limited. This is one of the parts of the figure one must accept graciously. Maintaining proper weight and posture and careful selection of line will help. Women should never be so foolish as to let fashion interfere with the proper selection of foundation garments for health.

A very important measurement in sizing and fit is the length from the neck to the waist. A person may be tall and fairly short-waisted or short and long-waisted.

Analyze and measure the length of waist with those ideas in mind. A long-waisted person may be long from the shoulder to the bust while another person may be long from the bust to the waist. Some people lose or gain length from shoulder to chest; if you always feel that a garment is more comfortable if raised at the shoulder seams, you may be short in this area. Others may be long or short between chest and waist. If you are taller than average, your added height is in a certain place or places. The shorter-than-average figure is usually short in certain places. Either figure may be average in all other proportions. Generally the designers of women's clothes consider the average waist length (measured from the nape of the neck to the natural waist) to be from 15½ to 16½ inches. Anything over 16½ inches would be long- and under 15½ short-waisted. Some foundation garment manufacturers measure from directly

The length of the waist is measured from the base of the neck to the natural waistline, in front and in back.

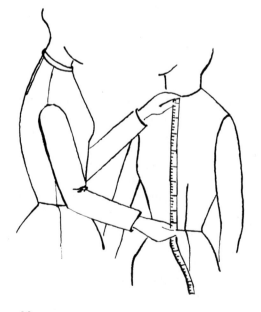

There is variation in the shape of the waistline, from the gently tapered to the straight. The waist may be fleshy or slim.

below the bust to the waist. A measure of 3 to 4 inches would be short-, 5 to 6 inches medium-, and 6½ to 7½ inches long-waisted. It might happen that a person's waist would be longer in the front than in the back.

The diaphragm may be fleshy or bony, broad or narrow. A prominent rib cage will create some problems of fit. A tapered waist is desirable for both male and female figures. Check for unneeded spots of fat around the diaphragm and the shoulders.

The arms and hands deserve the same consideration as do the other parts of the body. They play an important part in the design and in the selection of clothing. Check the length first—from shoulder to elbow and from elbow to wrist. You may find either part longer or shorter than good proportions allow. You may have long fingers and a stubby hand. There is no set pattern for shape and size. All hands are

interesting, so do not worry about what the ideal is. Know the breadth and length of the hand and fingers and the way the parts taper. Later, you may decide that a certain line in a glove is just right for you. The girth of the upper arm should always be watched, since people tend to add weight there easily. The ideal arm would be neither thin nor fat and would taper gently to the wrist. Note where the hand ends in relation to other parts of the body.

The waist

For the ladies, there is no greater figure asset than a small, trim waistline. Without it, you will find many styles and silhouettes —the princess line and the gathered skirt, for example—eliminated from your selections in outerwear. Carefully observe thickness and width at the waistline. Most authorities agree that for a good figure the waist should be about eight inches smaller than the bust or hips. Some figures are almost straight from the waist to the hips. Although some styles will necessarily have to be eliminated, there are many interest-

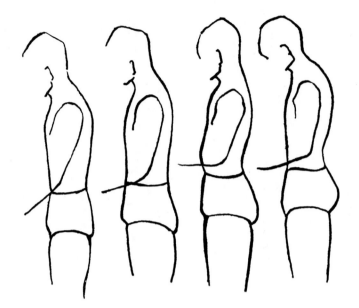

ing treatments that can be used to an advantage. Other factors such as the curve of the hips and the width of the shoulders affect the proportions to such an extent that it is difficult to give a definite rule. There are people with perfect measurements who do not seem to have good proportions.

Men, of course, are straighter through the waistline. The waist should taper gently without rolls or "stomachs." The man with a bulging middle will need expert tailoring to hide and proportion this fault. And what will he do in a pair of swimming trunks? This comes under the heading of "that which we can control."

The hips

There is no more deceiving way to analyze hips than by a tape measure. A tape measure's main purpose should be to warn from time to time that "things are not as they used to be" or that "things are looking up." Hips are not just "big" or "small." They are big or small in a certain place. To begin, take a good look at the width of

The contours of the male hips also vary in slimness.

your hips. Where is the broadest part? Most sizing takes the hip measure 7 inches below the waist, but individual figures can have the greatest width at any spot from 3 to 9 or 10 inches down from the waist. See whether the width is the result of your bone structure or of a pad of fat that has

Hip and thigh contours range from the very flat to the very rounded.

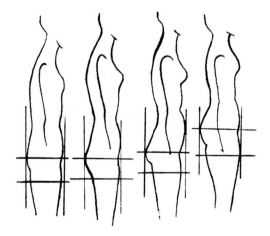

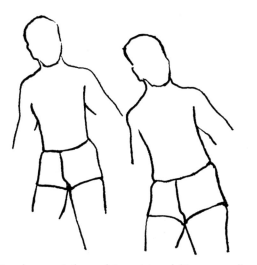

The shapes of the male's waist and hips generally are straighter than the female's.

Variation in women's leg and thigh shapes, front view.

widened you in a certain area. Not uncommon is a pad at the beginning of the thigh that results from much sitting and lack of exercise. Do the hips gently taper from the waist to the widest part or are they fairly straight? The back view may indicate flat, straight hips, a sway back, a definite hip curve, or a little shelf a few inches down from the waist. Hips with a bustle effect may still have a thin front line. Hip bones are frequently protruding and thin even though the remainder of the hips is well padded. Fat has a nasty habit of settling unevenly over the body. Another frequent irregularity is that one hip is slightly larger or higher than the other, which can occur in the front or in the back.

The thighs

Of the things listed under "what you can control," the thighs are perhaps the most difficult actually to control. It is here that the years show very fast—for even the thin thigh is likely to become flabby. Age is not

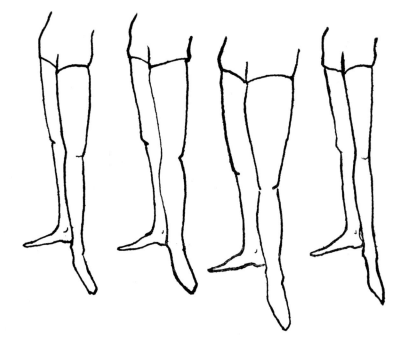

the only factor. Many young people have thighs that are large for their other proportions. A critical eye should be kept on this part of the body for changes. With proper selection of skirts, a fault here can readily be hidden, but, unfortunately, it will become a problem in the selection of bathing suits, shorts, or slacks and other trousers.

The legs

The length of the upper leg and the lower leg should be analyzed as carefully as the other parts of the body. A short woman or man may have longer legs than another person who is four or five inches taller. This would indicate that height had been lost in the length of waist, neck, or torso.

Many people gain or lose height in the upper or lower leg or in both. Men with short legs will find the proportions of their coats to their trousers quite different from those of men with longer legs. Similarly, the woman with short legs will have less skirt than her long-legged sister.

After a good look at length in the various parts of the leg and the foot, check the girth measures of the thigh, the calf, and the ankle. Check the straightness of the legs and the trimness of the ankle. Proper fitting and corrections in children's shoes

have greatly improved the legs of our young people, and it is seldom that "piano legs" and extreme bow legs are seen. Mothers should realize that corrections in shoes can be made to help the development of nice straight legs. Only a doctor should prescribe these corrections. You wouldn't consider dental corrections without a dentist, would you?

Correct body alignment.

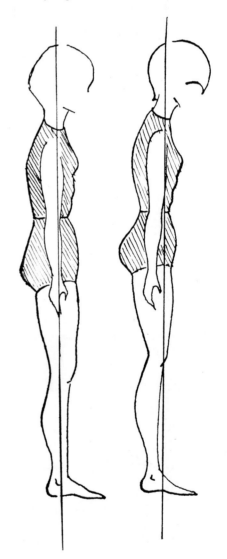

Variation in the shape of the legs, side view.

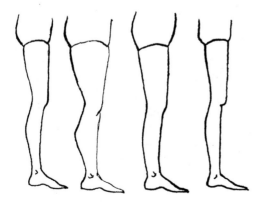

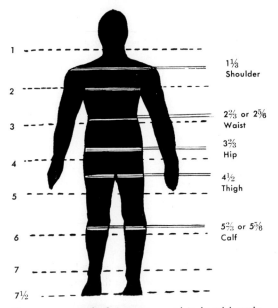

1	1⅓ Shoulder
2	
3	2⅔ or 2⅝ Waist
	3⅔ Hip
4	4½ Thigh
5	
6	5⅔ or 5⅝ Calf
7	
7½	

The average male figure measured in head lengths.

Average body proportions of women, using the head as the unit of measure.

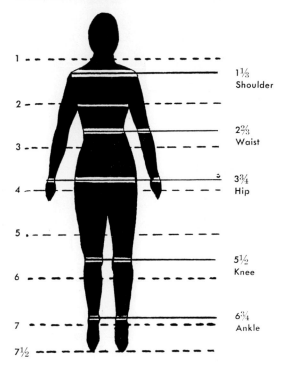

1	1⅓ Shoulder
2	
3	2⅔ Waist
4	3¾ Hip
5	
6	5½ Knee
7	6¾ Ankle
7½	

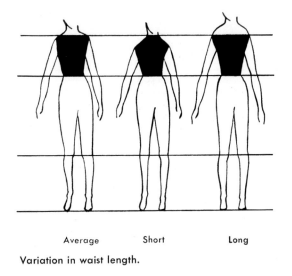

Average   Short   Long

Variation in waist length.

Knees are usually the least attractive feature of the leg, and apparel lengths that emphasize this area will not be becoming. Feet should be studied and related to the over-all size of the body. A small body with large feet may give a feeling of awkwardness and a heavy, large body with small feet the impression of being top-heavy unless shoe selections are carefully made.

Note also any irregularities in the legs and the feet that might affect your selections. Examples would include bow legs, prominent veins, knotty or muscular calves, sharp, protruding bones, and calluses on the feet. Determine the best features of your legs and feet.

Head lengths

Having taken into close scrutiny all of the various parts of the body—and it's the small details that make up the whole—make an over-all analysis of the figure. Using the head as the unit of measure—and we have found no better way—you will quickly be able to review and to discover differences. Use both a front and a side view where possible. The average

PROPORTIONS

| MEASUREMENTS | AVERAGE (HEADS) | | MY PROPORTIONS |
	WOMEN	MEN	
1. Top of skull to chin	1	1	
2. Top of skull to shoulderline	$1\frac{1}{3}$	$1\frac{1}{3}$	
3. Top of skull to bustline or chest	2	2	
4. Top of skull to waist and elbows	$2\frac{2}{3}$	$2\frac{5}{6}$	
5. Top of skull to hipline and wrists	$3\frac{2}{3}$–$3\frac{3}{4}$	$3\frac{5}{6}$	
6. Top of skull to knee	$5\frac{1}{3}$–$5\frac{1}{2}$	$5\frac{1}{2}$	
7. Top of skull to ankle	$6\frac{3}{4}$–7	7	
8. Top of skull to sole of feet	$7\frac{1}{2}$	$7\frac{1}{2}$	
9. Width of shoulder	$1\frac{1}{2}$	2	
10. Width of bust or chest	$1\frac{1}{4}$	$1\frac{1}{2}$	
11. Width of waist	$\frac{7}{8}$–1	$1\frac{1}{16}$	
12. Width of hip	$1\frac{3}{4}$–$1\frac{1}{2}$	$1\frac{1}{2}$	

All four figures have the same waist length; they vary in length from the waist to the hips.

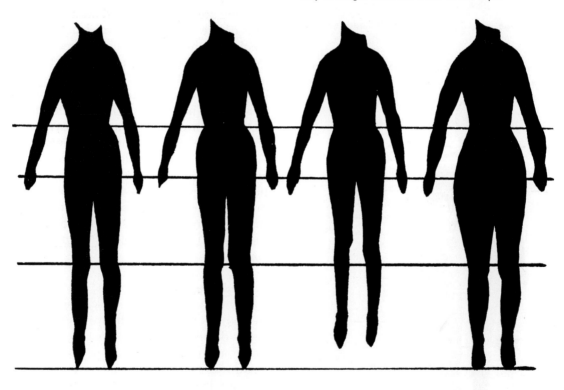

Average

Short waist
to hip
Long upper
leg

Short waist
to hip
Short upper
leg

Long from
waist
to hip
Short legs

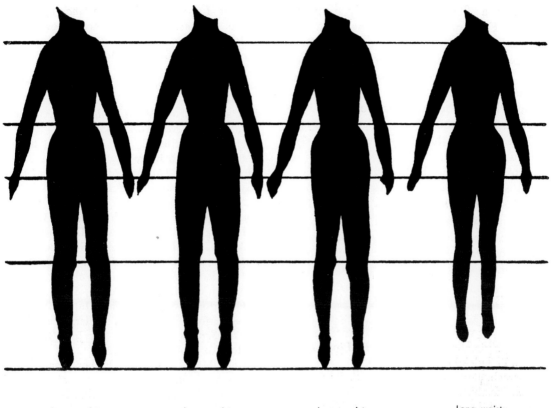

Long waist
Average
leg length

Long waist
Short
upper leg

Long waist
Short
lower leg

Long waist
Short upper
and lower leg

All four figures have the same long waist length but vary in leg proportions.

figure is 7½ or 8 heads high. Recent developments indicate that most figures are now about 8 heads tall, but more research is needed to determine what more exact proportions will be as the average person becomes taller. Although fashion drawings may be 8 to 10 heads tall, few will have what are sometimes considered such ideal proportions. Since the small details play such an important part, analysis by head lengths will not be entire story, but rather a helpful aid. Measure the head length, and using that measure, mark off the body as in

the illustration on this page. Using a colored pencil or a firmer line, indicate the natural breaks of the body, the bust, waist, hips, etc. To see how your proportions compare with the average, enter your measurements in head lengths in the space at the right in the chart on page 50.

It is to be remembered when using the head length as a unit of measure that some people, regardless of height, have very large or very small heads. If the head is large, the body proportions could be measured by using a unit of measure $1/7\frac{1}{2}$ the total height in inches of the figure. There are other factors that help to determine whether a figure is pleasingly proportioned. For example, extra length in the legs is generally considered an asset unless the proportions of the other parts of the body are not attractive. A long waist is an asset except where the rest of the body is extremely short or long. Posture is very important to a good figure. All proportions will seem better than they are if the body alignment is good.

After completing the breakdown by head lengths, go back and see how the detailed analysis and the head lengths compare. Do not assume you have the final answers; you will now be more alert to detail and you will continually find out new things about yourself.

REFERENCE READINGS

Books

Archer, Elsie, *Let's Face It*, J. B. Lippincott Co., Philadelphia, 1959.

Bacharach, Bert, *Right Dress*, A. S. Barnes & Co., Inc., New York, 1955.

Bell, Quentin, *On Human Finery*, The Hogarth Press, Ltd., London, 1948.

Daché, Lilly, *Glamour Book*, J. B. Lippincott Co., Philadelphia, 1956.

Flugel, John, *Psychology of Clothes*, Hogarth Press, Ltd., London, 1950.

Hawes, Elizabeth, *It's Still Spinach*, Little, Brown & Co., Boston, 1954.

Head, Edith, *The Dress Doctor*, Little, Brown & Co., Boston, 1958.

Hurlock, Elizabeth B., *The Psychology of Dress*, The Ronald Press, New York, 1929.

Langer, Lawrence, *The Importance of Wearing Clothes*, Hastings House, New York, 1959.

Laver, James, *Clothes*, Horizon Press, New York, 1953.

Lynes, Russell, *Snobs*, Harper & Bros., New York, 1950.

McCardell, Claire, *What Shall I Wear?*, Simon & Schuster, New York, 1956.

McJimsey, Harriet T., *Art in Clothing Selection*, Harper & Row, New York, 1963.

Morton, Grace, *The Arts of Costume and Personal Appearance*, 3rd Ed., John Wiley & Sons, New York, 1964.

National Center for Health Statistics: Weight, Height, and Selected Body Dimensions of Adults, Vital and Health Statistics PHS 1000—Series II—No. 8, U. S. Dept. of Health, Education and Welfare, Public Health Service, Washington, D. C., U. S. Government Printing Office, June, 1965.

Powers, John Robert and Miller, Mary Sue, *The Secrets of Charm*, The John C. Winston Co., Philadelphia, 1954.

Roach, Mary Ellen and Eicher, Joanne B., *Dress, Adornment, and the Social Order*, John Wiley & Sons, New York, 1965.

Ryan, Mary Shaw, *Clothing: A Study in Human Behavior*, Holt, Rinehart & Winston, New York, 1965.

Tate, Mildred Thurow and Glisson, Oris, *Family Clothing*, John Wiley & Sons, New York, 1961.

Veblen, Thorstein, *The Theory of the Leisure Class*, Reprint by the New American Library of World Literature, Inc., New York, 1953.

Chapter 4

What are your tools?

There is more to being well dressed than having a well-designed suit or dress. Being well dressed is the combination of many small details and the manner in which they are combined. One must not only understand what quality and good design are but must develop creativity and a feeling for the use of the various items that are aesthetically pleasing to oneself and to others.

Good design in dress is more than the proper use of line and color. It is the combination and integration of many factors—color, line, texture, workmanship, fit, form, shape, materials, proportion, balance, and scale. There is also an elusive and a somewhat difficult to define feeling that might best be called the "idea"; a pleasing and imaginative integration of the structural and decorative parts of the whole design. It is this "idea" that may be the most important factor in the expression of individuality in clothing. As the one who puts the articles of clothing together into the "whole picture," you will express or create a mood or an idea. You will want each part to be interesting and pleasing but subordinate to the whole idea. In dress design, you are concerned with elements which are less important than the person who is part of the finished design.

The person and his personality, then, are at the focal point of design in dress. It is from the person that the factors which make up the design radiate and move. A good designer will develop all the possibilities that material, color, texture, and other ingredients of design offer to transmit his ideas. As the designer of the way you look, you will use the tools of the designer. They are knowledge, observation, inspiration, and experimentation.

The good designer has creative ability and is not just a technician who imitates. He has learned to criticize his work and discards many ideas. He knows he must allow time to develop his ability. In the clothing field, there must be cooperation among designers, technicians, and consumers for free development of new concepts in design. The problems of the designer and the consumer are those of personality attitudes, technical problems, and functional problems.

The designer must keep in mind that apparel is designed for man, should serve man, and make him a better person. In order to do this the designer must ask, "Is the garment I am designing right? Does it fill a need? Is it beautiful? Is it honest?" Ornamentation should not be confused with design. The apparel designer works under a greater handicap than other designers in that the final success depends upon how the person who wears the garment uses it. The designers must then have an understanding of the functional and emotional needs of people. The consumer

Design features may express an idea. Youthful lines on the mature are inconsistent.

has the responsibility of selecting the right design for his needs *and* of trying to communicate his needs.

COLOR

Color is the design factor to which many people react first and most strongly. In clothing, color is the "spice" of the outfit. It is essential to sense our own response as well as the response of others to the color we are using. Color can enhance the beauty of the outfit or it can be the factor that does the most to impair good looks. It is the connecting link between the individual parts of the outfit. Color can lift your spirits.

It might be interesting to observe how colors are used to call attention to the actors in a play. Loud, brilliant colors that attract the eye immediately are often used to draw attention to one particular actor. An actor can also be brought into the spotlight by the use of strong contrasts. The main character might be dressed in a light color and the other actors and the background might be kept in a darker color, in which case the other actors would also serve as background and by comparison emphasize the main character.

Color is a challenge, it is fun, and it is a strong determining factor in your ultimate satisfaction with how you look. In order to use this tool most effectively, one must have a keen awareness for seeing actual color and to all of the elements that affect the use of color, such as lighting and texture. *Observation* and *experimentation* with the use of color in the materials used for dress are essential; along with the insights that color specialists have given us, they will help build the knowledge necessary in creating a color composition that expresses the ideas you want to convey. It is fun because there are no cut and dried rules for using color; the individual will develop his own.

Color observations

Individuals react differently to color. A hue that may give one person a lift may depress another. Some people find certain colors very tiring to wear in large amounts or for long periods of time; yet the same tiring color might add variety to an otherwise monotonous color scheme. Most individuals have definite color likes or preferences that might be dependent upon old experiences.

Association of age with a color is not uncommon. We think in terms of "baby blue," and we consider lavender a color typical of old age. It is possible to convey a "too sweet" or "too loud" or even vulgar feeling with color. A color can appear loud because of its intensity, the place it is used, the texture of the article, or the way it is combined with another intense color. Changing the amount of the color or the texture of the material might change the whole reaction to the color. Bright red in some fabrics might be garish, but in a fine velvet it could be subtle and elegant.

Factors

Fashion, too, plays a part in the use of color. What is considered in excellent taste at one time is not always acceptable at another. Tastes in color harmonies change. Green and blue, at one time considered unacceptable, later became a very popular combination of colors. What one generation finds to be garish, the next generation may consider expressive. In due time, however, a new generation swings the pendulum in a new direction. The youth of the 30's tired of the multicolored prints worn by their mothers. The youth of the 50's and 60's in turn rejected the conservative "well bred" navy of the former generation, and demanded the gay outlandish color prints of the mod look.

The apparent color will depend on more than color alone. The size and shape, the texture of the surface, the uniformity and transparency will affect the visual appearance of the object.

Most colors can be combined under certain conditions. A pleasing relation of such factors as the amount of color, the value of the color, and the texture of the fabric to each other and to the person is important; the misuse of any one of these factors could spoil the effect.

A few of the factors that affect the use of color harmony have been mentioned above, but special attention should be given to lighting, background, distance involved, the amount and strength of the colors used, and the skin tone and the size of the person. In the choice of colors, consideration should be given to where they will be used and worn. The amount and the kind of light will affect color. In bright sunshine, intense colors may seem less bright; incandescent light will cast a yellow tone and add a tinge of yellow and green to most colors. Many people have seen purple-blue lips—the effect of ultraviolet light on lipstick—or have purchased an article in the store and found that in daylight its color was completely different. Consider where you will be wearing an outfit most and buy it to go with the lighting and the background of the surroundings. You will know the lighting and the colors used in your place of business or your home, and many of your clothes will be worn in these places. In choosing colors to be worn in many places, select colors which will not clash with the colors most frequently used in interiors. Certain colors such as greens, blues, yellows, and neutrals do not "fight" with background colors to the same degree that reds and oranges will. A multicolored print background may not enhance a dress of a different vivid print. The background color of a room may emphasize the color of clothing; a green room, for example, will intensify red in a dress. Or background colors may absorb color, making clothing appear less bright against the background. In a dark-paneled room, bright colors seem less intense than they really are. Evening clothes should be chosen to be worn under artificial light, and clothes that are to be worn in daylight should be examined in the daylight rather than under store lighting.

Intensity, the brightness or dullness of a color, is especially important in co-ordinating the costume. Few clothing materials are made in full intensity. A small amount of bright color with a neutral outfit may be very effective, whereas a whole dress of an intense orange could be too strong and tiring for many situations. For festive and gay occasions, a brilliant color would be very effective. The light reflection of fluorescent fabrics makes color very intense. Excellent for use in clothing as a safety precaution, these fabrics tend to become garish if used at other times.

Colors also give a feeling of weight. Value—the lightness or darkness of the color—will affect this illusion. Dark colors seem to have a heavier feel than light colors. Dark red will seem heavier than pale pink, and black, of course, heavier than white. The more intense colors heighten the feeling of weight. This will be important to remember in choosing color in relation to the parts of the figure. White shoes worn with dark clothes would not appear to give the body a solid foundation. The feeling of weight will also be affected by texture. A black woolen will appear heavier than a black chiffon, since the sheerness and filminess will seem less heavy.

Distance may change the effect of two colors next to each other. A color change results when two colors which are put close to one another merge and appear as a third color. A small printed fabric or stripe is very likely to change color if seen at a distance; thus a red and white stripe seen at a distance will blend to a pink. Where colored fibers are twisted together into yarns, as in tweeds, the colors may blend and produce another color. In co-ordinating an outfit where two colors are woven or spun together in the fabric, it is usually wise not to pick out one of the colors in matching accessories. Look at the fabric at a distance to see the appearance the colors give together. A small fleck of color in a tweed may be seen when very close, but at a short distance may disappear. Where there is blending of different colors in fabric, choice of color for accessories should harmonize with the blended color rather than with any one color in the fabric.

Color criteria

In the study of color in dress, one should think in terms of the materials used in clothing and establish a criterion for judging color combinations. A good color accord not only (1) pleases the wearer but (2) is suitable and becoming to the wearer and (3) creates a pleasant over-all effect with the figure and skin. It (4) is appropriate to the occasion and the place and has (5) variety and interest and (6) a pleasing harmony.

The selection of color in clothing and in co-ordinating the various articles is aided by a knowledge of how color is obtained. Fabric, leather, and fur are the most commonly used materials in clothing; metals and stones are used for decorative additions. A color in one material will differ from the same color in another. Color effects will vary from paper samples to fabric samples. Most fabric color is obtained from dyes, although some pigments are used. The manner by which color effect is achieved will depend upon the weave, the yarn, and the finish. The same combination of colors will create different effects and appearances according to the way color is obtained. The methods used include printing and yarn, piece, skein, and cross-dyeing. The combination of the fiber, the way the yarn is spun, the dyeing process, the weave or knit, and the finish create the final color. A change in one may change the apparent color.

In looking at your over-all wardrobe, it is important to ask yourself what you want color to do. Obviously, it must be flattering; you yourself should be happy in your color combinations and others should find them pleasing to see. Ask yourself: Is it becoming to your skin, hair, eyes, and size?

Warm colors tend to advance and to have intensity. Cool colors are more subdued and tranquil than warm colors.

Cool   Warm

Different fabric textures will appear as different colors even though the same dye is used.

Color appeals. Color changes. Color entertains.
Color is rampant! (Courtesy United Air Lines)

When different colored yarns are mixed in weaving, the apparent color may change with the amounts of the colored yarn used.

Does it emphasize your best features and flatter less attractive points? What colors should you combine and how many colors should you use? When and where will you wear the outfit you are co-ordinating? What idea or mood do you wish to create? How simple or elaborate are the other items—such as jewelry and trim—that you will use?

A clear, smooth skin is, of course, a valuable aid in wearing clothes well. Your choices of color must, above all, emphasize good skin or flatter skin that is not perfect. Since the condition of the skin does not remain the same always—weather and health can change skin coloring very quickly— it is necessary constantly to experiment with colors. No two individuals have the same skin color. For this reason you cannot depend upon a set of rules—you must use color principles only as guides in experimentation. Normal skin coloring is determined principally by the relative amounts of melanin, carotene, and haemoglobin— the brown, yellow, and red pigments— present in the skin. Skin containing an excess of yellow pigment will look pale and sallow; too much red in skin will cause it to look ruddy or florid. Ideally, the skin has orange-pink tones. The texture of the skin —smooth, clear, or fine—will affect choice of color in clothing.

The relationship of the colors of hair and eyes to skin coloring will be important in the choice of colors. It is not always possible to flatter all three—skin, eyes, and hair. When there is conflict, the skin must be considered first. Care of skin and make-up will play an important part in maintaining the clear, smooth skin so important to wearing colors well. Make-up is important to all skin coloring, but it is essential to the woman who has little definiteness in coloring or who is very pale. A person with dark blond or light brown hair, pale coloring,

and pale gray eyes will need to add color by using make-up or by selecting colors to bring out the color in her skin. Paleness will be especially dull and drab where hair and eyes lack contrast. Other problems will result from freckles, shadows, or blemishes. Because men do not have the aid of make-up, choice of color in clothing is their tool for improving or playing up their coloring.

In experimenting with colors for your skin, you will find that a color may not be becoming in one texture, but tried in another texture or value it might be very suitable. A bright blue, shiny taffeta may be very trying to the skin. but the same blue in a soft woolen could be very becoming. The difference is the result of light reflection. Pure color is less likely to be becoming than a shade or a tint of the same hue. Many people believe they can wear all colors or hues. Rarely, however, do we find a person on whom certain colors are not more attractive than others. Few people can wear all colors in all textures. In experimenting, start to work with colors that are—or that you think are—complementary. Complementary colors are those opposite one another on the color wheel. Green will intensify the red in the skin; yellow will be emphasized by purple. Purples containing red will often give a greenish cast to yellow skin. Shadows under the eyes are usually a bluish purple and will be emphasized by yellow-greens. Blue-green is flattering to many people, since it complements the desired skin tones of orange-pink.

Remember that within the range of yellow and red tones there are skins which are very fair and skins which are dark in tone. Within this same group of tones, you will also find skins which are very clear and flawless and those which have blemishes or flaws. A skin tone can be subdued by using the same hue in a less pure and less intense color in clothing. A pure hue will emphasize the color by repeating it. In other words, yellow in the skin can usually be subdued by a yellow with an orange hue such as a warm beige or a warm brown. Yellow-greens would subdue yellow where no dark shadows are present. It is important in selecting color to compliment the hair to consider the degree of contrast between the hair and skin. People with dark hair and fair skin have the advantage of contrast in their personal coloring. Those with light hair and dark eyes will obtain the same kind of contrast. The person who has neutral hair, light skin, and light blue or green eyes or both dark hair and dark skin will have to achieve a contrast of color through clothing and make-up. This person can use color to emphasize the color of hair and eyes.

Soft blues will complement and accent the color of red hair and will probably be kindest to the florid skin which so frequently accompanies red hair. Soft blues will also emphasize freckles; if this is objectionable, one cannot emphasize the hair and will tone down both it and the freckles. The girl with lovely, clear, petal-like skin and red hair will have fewer problems; she will avoid only those colors which do not bring out and accentuate her skin and hair. She may deliberately emphasize her hair by wearing one of the pinker tones.

Color is chosen to bring out lights and to make hair seem bright and shiny rather than dull and lifeless. The redhead will try to subdue only hair that is too brassy. Blondes will avoid colors which emphasize a straw effect rather than the golden lights. People with medium brown or medium blonde hair will try to bring out the golden or red lights.

Combining colors

Matching hues is very difficult. Colors which are just a little different in hue will not be harmonious. It is usually better to have two contrasting hues than two colors which are almost the same hue. The person who attempts to match must be perceptive to slight differences in hue.

In working out color proportions, you will find that a small amount of intense or warm color will offset a large amount of dull, dark, or cool color. Most combinations of colors should aim at creating variety through the use of interesting proportions of light and dark, bright and subdued, and warm and cool colors. For most occasions, it is best to keep large areas of color a reasonably subdued shade with gay or lighter accents. Generally, bright colors should be used in small areas of importance which emphasize a good feature. A great deal of experimenting for effect should precede using several bright or strong colors together. Two brilliant colors may appear garish or striking. A very bright dress can be startling and most effective—at the right time. Texture and the proportions of the colors used will affect what will be pleasing together.

Most dark shades look well with tints or pastels; navy, for example, with pink, pale green, or apricot, forest green or purple with pink, pale blue, or lavender. Texture will again be a factor. Two satins might not blend in any color as well as would a satin and a mat finish. Red and black may appear too heavy without the aid of a light contrast. The contrast need not necessarily be in fabric; it may be a piece of jewelry or even a physical characteristic such as hair. Sports clothes, evening clothes, or clothes for special occasions are effective in bright colors. Festive occasions suggest a gay mood with warmer colors.

It is not unusual to find that one's favorite color is not becoming to one's skin. That does not necessarily mean it must be eliminated from one's wardrobe. An unbecoming color can often be worn in small quan-

Figures of the same height but different waistlines. Observe the effect of contrasts and pattern.

tities and relieved near the face by another color.

Bright colors can seldom be used effectively together, but with certain textures, the person with color knowledge can do so with dramatic effect. Bright colors in chiffons, silks, or in sheer fabrics are often very dramatic. Muted, neutral colors, such as beige and gray, are usually not effective together. White can be used with all colors, dull or bright. It is best to treat black and white as you treat all other colors, giving careful consideration to proportions. Remember that few whites are pure white; they may tend toward creamy or gray. Blacks vary in depth of color. Many people use a great deal of white contrast in a color scheme where small touches would be more effective.

Not only do different fabrics and materials take dyes differently, but colors change with texture. Turn back the face of a fabric over the reverse and you will see the effect of texture on color in one fabric. A common mistake is putting together two colors only a little different in hue; trying to match color is almost always disastrous. Work for a blending of shades and tints rather than matching colors. Overmatching —in color or in fabric—will often appear too studied. Red leather shoes with a red coat or a complete red outfit are common examples of color matching that misses completely. In working with one-color outfits, contrast is a most important factor; there should be enough use of texture and value contrast to avoid monotony. The color chosen must, above all, be becoming to the individual. In a one-color outfit, coloring too near that of the individual may be very dull.

When you have experimented with these ideas and tried every color and combination of colors, you will begin to find color effects that suit you and "become yours."

The effect of different trouser lengths on the proportions of the same figure.

Lines created by yokes, pockets, and seams divide space and emphasize the hip area.

LINE

To understand line in dress, you should have a knowledge of your body and its movements. You should know the proportions of the figure and the progression of size in the parts of the body, regardless of the shape or height of the figure. The body is seldom inert, and lines change with the movements of the body—walking, standing, or sitting. Lines break up and shape surfaces, affecting apparent body proportions. In discussing line, we must stress the importance of correct fit. If a garment does not fit properly, the lines will be changed and new lines, such as wrinkles, will be created.

Kinds of lines

There are those lines which are structural and those that are decorative. Structural lines result from seams and construction points that are essential for holding the garment together. Seams, darts, and fullness are the means by which the materials are controlled to allow for body movement. Structural lines may also be decorative, as when a seam or a collar edge is top

The effect of the contrast of light and dark.

stitched in a contrasting color. Decorative lines result from purely decorative trim without functional purpose. Cording, appliqué, braid, and embroidery are examples. Decorative lines are usually incorporated mainly for emphasis of a particular feature.

Effect of line

When a garment is put on the human body it acquires line and shape from the body curves. Lines also result from the fullness and drape of the design. You might trace the lines of any picture to actually become aware of the number and the kinds of lines found in a dress or suit. As you trace, you will notice that all lines have direction and are not found alone but will at some point meet other lines. When two lines meet it is important that they give a feeling of continuity of movement in the direction you want the eye to travel on the figure. The direction in which lines carry the eye is often deceiving. For example, most people will tell you that a vertical stripe carries the eye up and down and

The flared skirt on the short-waisted figure. Note the effect of the different necklines on the apparent length of the bodice.

creates an illusion of height. Whether or not this is true depends on the width, the spacing, and the color of the stripes. A broad, balanced black-and-white stripe, because of the repetition of strong color and of spacing, may carry the eye across the fabric rather than up and down. Train yourself to be alert to the direction in which your eye travels when you look at a line. Notice the effect of color on line and the dominance of one line over another. Dominance becomes important in camouflage or emphasis. It is a result of the relationship of the line to color, texture, decorative trim, and placement. A line may be emphasized by decorative trim such as

cording or by a change of color at the structural points. Movement of the body will also emphasize certain lines.

When a designer creates a dress, suit, or hat, he must be aware of the lines that are essential in holding an article together and the numerous lines that are created by the pattern or by the weave of the material. If he uses a fabric such as a plaid, the designer must not change the idea of the fabric; with such fabrics, he will generally use as few structural lines as possible. For the same reason it is necessary that textile designers be aware of what will be done to make a straight piece of fabric conform to the curves of the human body. The designer knows that the dominant line, which must be placed attractively on the human figure, may be in the pattern of the fabric. He would not place a dominant stripe off-center unless it were balanced in some way. Every line is cut to make the most effective use of the pattern without disturbing the original idea of the fabric.

In addition to meeting the functional requirements in clothing, we are attempting to break up spaces in the most interesting manner possible and to create balance. In speaking of balance, we are referring to interesting proportions that relate to the human form and are pleasing in relation to each other rather than to equal spacing. The human body itself is not divided into equal parts. It is a progression of sizes. For example the arm is relatively large at the shoulder and decreases in size down to the fingers. In structure, the body might be compared to a tree, with the limbs growing out of the trunk.

(Opposite) Top: The width of the lapel should be in proportion to shoulder width and silhouette. Center: The gathered skirt adds bulk to the waist area and emphasizes the shape of the waist. Bottom: The width of the set-in waistline should be proportional to the waist length.

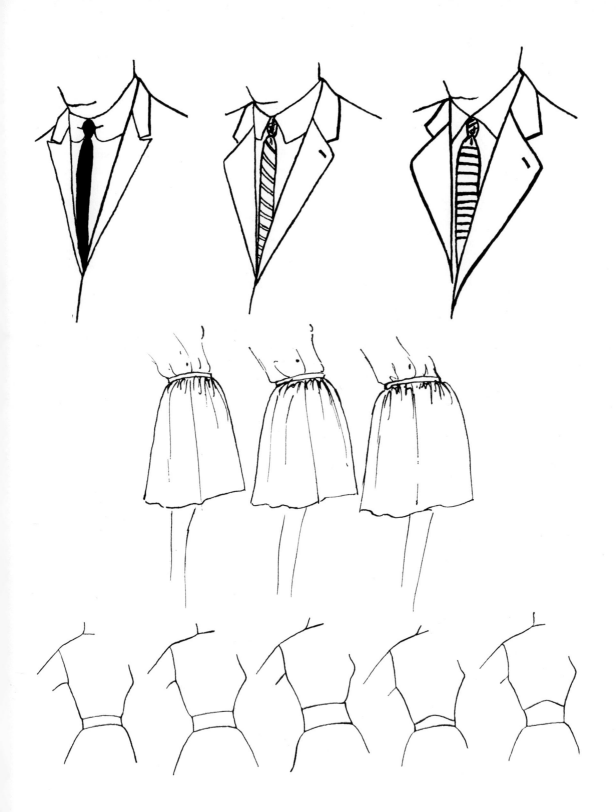

Exaggeration of detail in the bodice area may create a top-heavy appearance, particularly on a short-waisted figure or a long-waisted figure with short legs.

Most good design conforms to the human figure at least at some point. One reason for the need for some conformity to the body is the relationship of design to body movement; too great a deviation from the lines of the human form would cause bulk which would interfere with movement. Excess bulk resulting from too much fabric becomes apparent in a garment which is full and bulky throughout—full blousy bodice, full gathered skirt, and full sleeves. In this respect, the kind of fabric used will make a difference; a soft chiffon, for example, will mold to the figure and so lend itself to greater bulk than will a heavy fabric that does not cling.

Lines for the individual

Lines for a particular figure should be chosen so as to break up the areas of that figure in an interesting manner. If, for example, you have a wide, broad figure, you will want to divide it so as to stop the eye from traveling across the figure. The person who has a short waist would want to keep the eye moving in a lengthwise direction and would not break the figure with opposing lines that would stop the eye.

Individuals will also remember that some figures are small in bone structure; others have large frames. Scale and proportion in clothes should be related to the frame of the body as well as to areas that are longer or shorter than average. Petite women will dress in a petite scale. Tall women can also be small-boned, and petite bone structure does not always correspond to height.

The face and the neckline should always be considered first. Becoming necklines and correct collar and hat sizes are of prime importance. The person with a head that is small in relation to the other parts of the body will keep collars, hats, and necklines in proportion; the strong contrast of a bulky collar would make the head seem even smaller. Similarly, a relatively large head surrounded by dainty collars and jewelry would seem even more out of proportion.

After considering the size and shape of the head, you will think in terms of the areas of the body. After analyzing the various areas of the figure, make allowances for the relationship between the various parts of the anatomy. A woman who is long from the shoulders to the bust could break the space between those points; she would

(Opposite) Top row: The peak cut on a set-in waistband helps direct the eye up the center of the figure regardless of width. Center: The illusion of a small waist can be achieved by the placement and direction of seams. Bottom: Direction and placement of darts can change the apparent waist size in addition to affecting the bust and hip area.

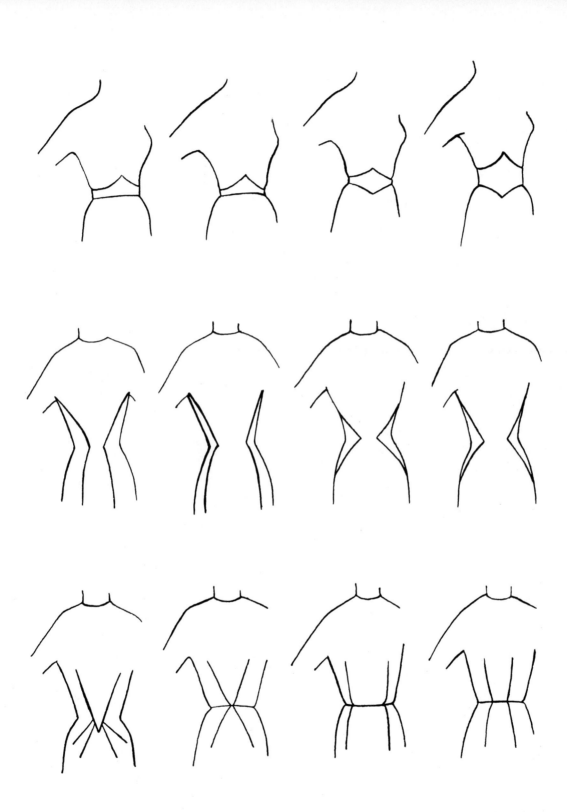

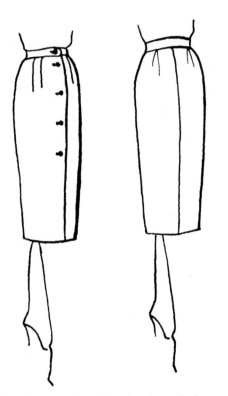

Tubular skirts vary in width. The width of pleats or the division of space by seams will affect body proportions.

The long torso line may be an effective way to add length to the waist. The proportion of torso to skirt will be important.

avoid things, such as high turtle-neck sweaters, that give a long line to that area. The length of a skirt is another example of spacing. Too often the length of a woman's skirt is determined by the shape of her legs. Although that enters into the picture, it is more important that the skirt be in pleasant proportion to the bodice. A short-waisted woman may have height from her waist to her knees; she would not want a great deal of skirt and very little blouse. A woman of the same height with a longer waist would have less skirt. She would want to lengthen her skirt to create a better proportion, whereas the woman with the shorter waist would shorten her skirt within the limits of fashion. The kind of lines within the skirt would play an important part in the overall effect. Straight lines, in themselves, shorten and in a skirt will need careful fitting to the particular figure.

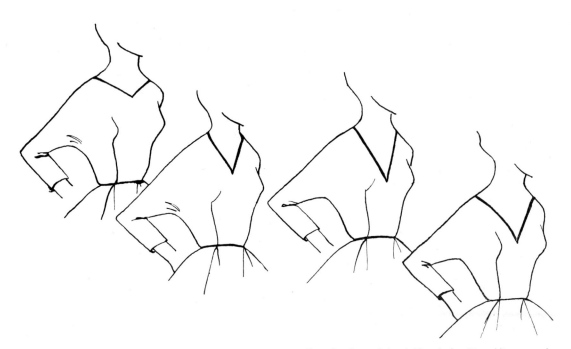

The depth and breadth of the V-neckline can be adapted to the individual's neck and facial structure.

The deeper the cut of a U-neckline, the more length is added to the face and neck of the individual; the broader the U, the more emphasis will be on a square face.

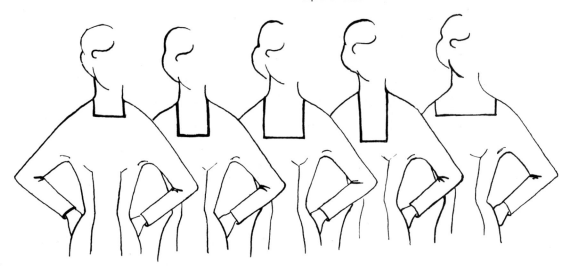

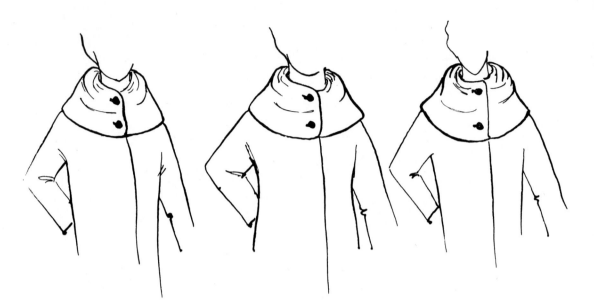

Large, high, rolling collars affect neckline proportions.

Regardless of height, it is the figure that determines
the shape and form of the dress.

Bertha   Convertible   Peter Pan

Mandarin   Notched

Shawl   Stand-away   Sailor

Experiment with different collar styles.

Bateau

Cowl

Halter

Scoop

Decolleté

Sweetheart

Jewel

Tie

The length of a man's jacket would depend not only on his over-all height, but on where his height is obtained. A man with short legs will avoid a full drape in trousers and jacket. Lapels will be scaled to chest and shoulder width; a wide lapel will look broader on a slight figure than on a very broad-shouldered one. Jackets may be shortened slightly within the limits of style of the suit.

A well-proportioned figure, rather than height, should be the first concern of the design. A tall woman will probably have obtained her height in certain parts of the body. It is better to design for the long area than to try to counteract over-all height. In handling over-all height, one could cut an area that is not long and so distort the relationships between the various parts of the body. If a very tall person who has a

(Opposite) Neckline styles create eye movement.

The effect of two different designs on each of three figures of different waist lengths. Compare the amount of bodice on each figure in the top row with that on the figure below.

long neck, a short waist, and long legs were to cut lines of length in the bodice she would appear all skirt. If she disguised the length of the neck with collars and lines to help give the illusion of a shorter neck and wore her skirts proportioned to her bodice, she would appear less tall—and in good proportion. If she tried to cut height at all parts of her outfit, she might end up with a very poorly proportioned figure.

The short person will try to create an illusion of length in the areas where she has found herself to be shorter than average. If a short person of average proportions except for the legs tried to create a feeling of length in all parts, she would still

The length of the skirt affects the proportions of the average figure.

give the impression of being poorly proportioned. Her solution would be to adjust her skirt length to the over-all proportions. Regardless of height, the individual will break up areas that are too long or too broad in relation to other parts of her figure with lines that lengthen or broaden

the areas that are too short or too narrow.

Lines should not carry the eye across a broad figure or up and down a figure that is taller than average. The eye is directed not only by line, but by scale, color, texture, and shape. Repetition of line, color, or texture is one way of guiding the eye in the direction in which you want it to move. Contrast of line, color, or texture will stop the eye where you want it to. Slight varia-

The effect of skirt length on the figure with a short waist and long legs.

tions in length and width should not be taken too seriously, since pleasing appearance is possible with many figure variations; concern is justified only when there is a wide deviation from what is considered a pleasing figure.

Line and accessories

The structural and decorative lines of accessories are as important as those of dresses and suits. In considering the choice of line for an accessory, it is wise to think in terms of the part of the anatomy where this accessory will be. It should always compliment that part and relate to it in scale and proportion.

The line of an accessory will have a direction just as any other line. If you will observe gloves, for example, you will find that the structural lines vary a great deal. Seam construction can add bulk or can flatter a heavy hand. Lines added for decoration may run across the hand or in a lengthwise direction. In your choice of gloves, you will consider the size of the hand, the kind of outfit you will be wear-

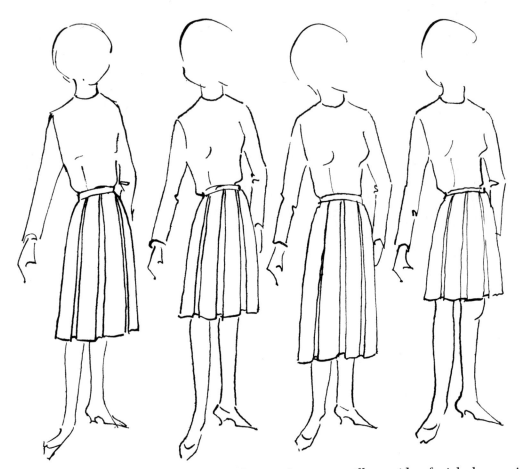

The effect of the skirt length on the proportions of the figure with a long waistline and short legs.

ing, the sleeve, and the hips. Decoration may take the form of hand stitching, hand embroidery, or applied bands and cuffs.

In selecting a hat, one will choose lines that are becoming to facial shape and features and will give better proportions to the figure. A person whose face is widest at the cheek and narrow at the forehead may wish to have trim that ends at the forehead to help make the shape more nearly oval. Bulk in material, construction, and trim may overwhelm a small head.

With jewelry, an item of pure decora-

tion, you will consider facial shape, size, and color. Choker necklaces vary in size and should be scaled to the thickness and the length of the neck. The choker would cut length at the base of the neck and make a short neck seem shorter. The reverse would be true of a long string of pearls. A pendant may end in a point and repeat the

(Opposite) Top row: In this illustration and in those below the effect of the princess line on figures of varying waist lengths can be seen. Second row: As the space between the princess line widens, width is created and length decreased. Third and Bottom rows: When value contrast is introduced, the emphasis is greater.

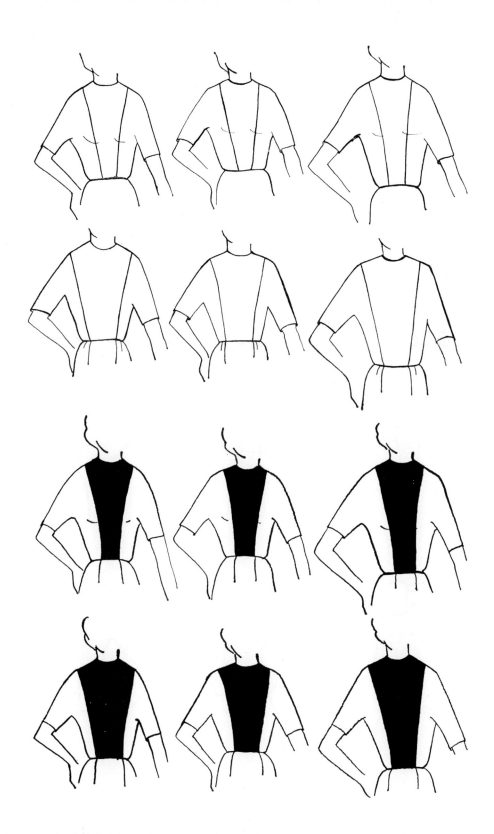

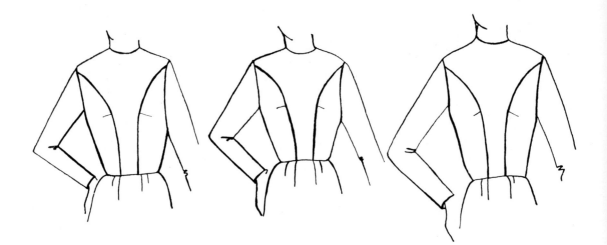

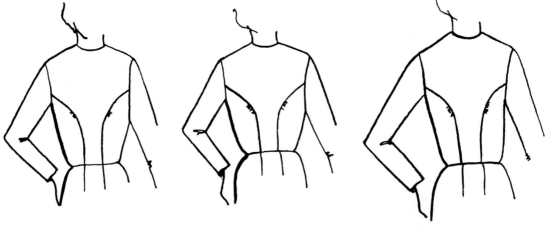

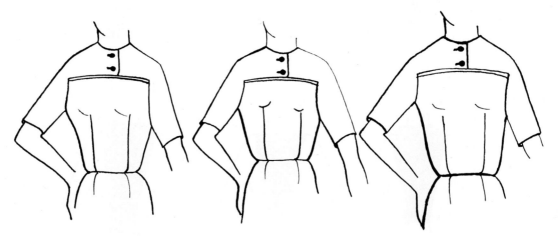

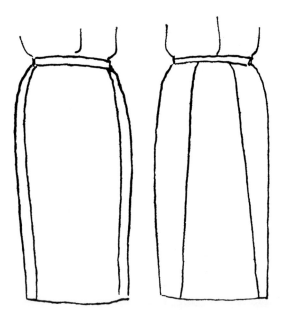

The varying width of the skirt panels changes the apparent size of the hips of an average figure. The broad, unbroken panel broadens the hips.

Optical illusions created through the use of gores of different widths on the large figure.

(Opposite) Top and center: Curved seams are a subtle way of breaking the bodice above and below the chest. The shoulder width is affected as well as the waist length. Bottom: The straight line of the yoke is a line of opposition to the upward movement of the eye and decreases waist length.

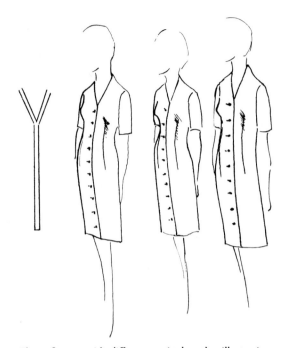

Three figures with different waist lengths, illustrating the effects on different body proportions of center openings ending at the base of the neck or in a V-neck. The short-waisted figure may gain in length, while for the long-waisted figure there may be too much bodice for the skirt proportions.

The neckline stops the upward movement of the eye. Compare the lines with those on the equivalent figures in the illustration on the left.

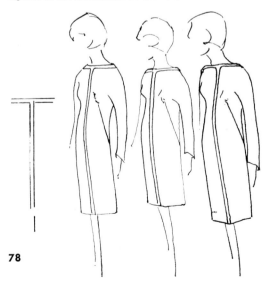

line of a pointed chin. It is possible to use a necklace to soften an otherwise unattracttive neckline. If a woman with a short waist wanted to wear a high neck to gain length in her bodice but needed to add length to the face, she might wear a long necklace over the high neckline. This compromise could be used where the bodice needs one treatment and the shape of the face another.

Long, dangling earrings would tend to add length in the cheek area; button earrings would concentrate the eye at one point and would seem to widen that particular area. The scale and shape of the earring should fit the facial shape at that point. Jewelry is chosen for the part of the body where it will be worn. The kind of jewelry is determined by the place where emphasis is desired. Rings should be scaled to the hand; the length, width, and shape of the ring should be chosen to either lengthen or shorten the fingers. The effect of large rings, if the shape is becoming, depends on the size of the wearer. Rings and other jewelry should be chosen so as not to create lines that distort other accessories such as gloves. The petite person who wants to direct the eye up the figure will not choose jewelry, belts, or other decorative items that stop the movement of the eye upward.

The scale of masculine jewelry will be governed by the size of the individual. Cuff links should be in keeping with the style and the size of the cuff. Necktie width should complement the lapels of the jacket, the shape of the face, and shoulder width. The man with a smaller physique will not choose a tie that is heavy because of width, fabric, or texture; he should also avoid bulk

(Opposite) Top: The width of the pleats in a full skirt will affect the apparent width of the hips. Bottom: Skirt styles create silhouettes that affect body proportions.

Box   Unpressed   Inverted   Knife

Side drape   Peg top   Eight-gore   Circular

Breaking up space with gores of different widths to create optical illusions on the average figure.

in the knot. Bow ties have crosswise direction and stop the eye at the neckline. Although they cut length from the face, the association of joviality with the style often makes them seem right even on people with full faces.

Texture and fabric

As with color, our first impression of texture comes from sight, and there will be some reaction to what we see. Satin is shiny; other fabrics are dull or smooth. The result of seeing something may be the de- sire to touch it. This desire to feel the fabric is related to the term "hand" used in the textile industry. Few people will buy fabric without feeling it. Sound—like the rustle of taffeta—also plays a part. A person without sight could derive pleasure from handling the fabric and from the sounds it creates.

Most people are aware of the psychological effect of color and the relation of color to their own coloring; few people realize how much texture affects them. A certain fabric may make a woman feel lovelier or more feminine. Most men have definite

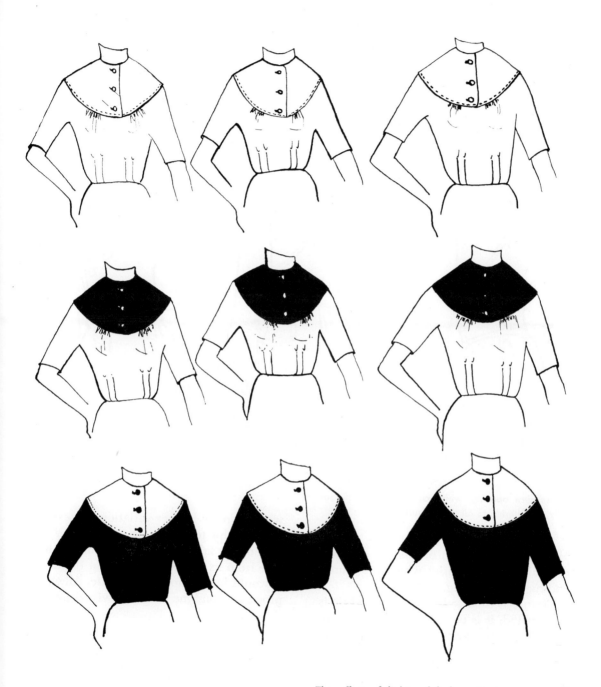

The effect of light-and-dark contrast on a curved yoke and its relationship to three different waist lengths. The dark yoke creates a feeling of heaviness on all three figures, while the light yoke over the dark bodice is flattering to all three.

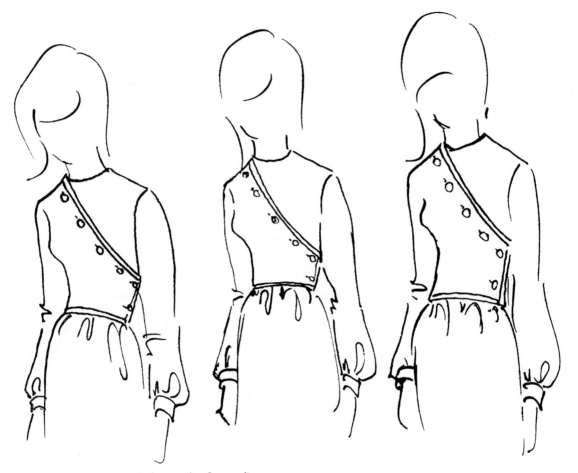

The surplice opening, which cuts the figure diagonally, is flattering to all three figures.

preferences for rough or smooth and will generally choose fabrics which are sturdy and rugged in feeling.

Texture is the result of the way fabric is constructed; it is created by the treatment of yarns, weave, knit, embroidery, and the finish given to the final product. Variety in texture can be obtained through the use of different yarns and through the closeness or looseness of the weave. Fiber will also give textural interest; wool is warm and linen cool to the touch. The numerous patterns resulting from the combination of

weaves create further variations in texture. Finish helps to determine the feel and the look of the fabric. Organdy obtains its texture from its crisp finish; without the finish it would be a limp cotton fabric. All these processes combine to give a visual impact

(Opposite) Top row: Compare the effect of the width of the stripes on emphasis and on how the shoulders and chest are divided. Center: Wide stripes and strong colors call attention to the part of the figure they are placed on. Bottom: The sweater at the left does not emphasize any particular part of the body so much as do the sweaters at the right.

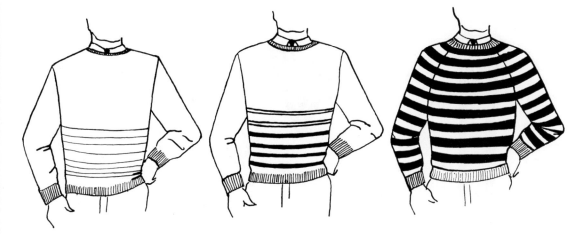

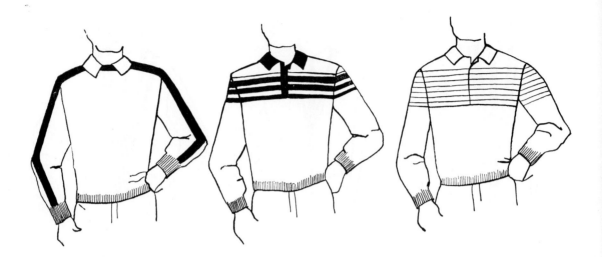

The relation of the skirt length to the apparent size of the leg.

of richness, elegance, crispness, lightness, or refinement.

The designer knows how fabrics will drape on the figure. He must consider the weight of the fabric and what the fabric will do for the person for whom the article is being made. He must also remember the occasion for which the garment is intended. He must not forget the importance of permanence of texture; a crisp-looking dress loses all charm if it becomes limp

(Opposite) Top row: Emphasizing the shoulder area through color contrast. Broad lines call more attention to the chest area than thin lines. Center: Emphasis on the center of the body through contrasts of light and dark direct the eye upward. Bottom: Lines and their direction are strengthened by color contrast.

after washing. He will experiment with varying degrees of fullness in various fabrics; garments cut from the same pattern will look different in different fabrics and textures. Jersey, for example, will cling and mold to the body; taffeta stands away from the figure. Denim suggests a certain crude durability; he would not put a fabric of lush, elegant, soft texture with denim. He would, nevertheless, try various combinations of fabric and texture in order to find new effects.

The consumer will find the textures of different fabrics helpful in conveying a desired impression. Chiffon has a soft, flowing appearance; sheers suggest softness, femininity, and sometimes—as in the case of

What are your tools? 85

Width and placement are more important than the direction of the separate stripes. Fine chalk stripes are less dominant than broad or colorful stripes. The two sweaters on the right emphasize different parts of the anatomy.

The strong contrast of color in the sweater on the left draws attention to the bodice and does not direct the eye up the figure. The placement of the stripes in the bodice on the right carries the eye up the center of the figure.

The effect of the waistline yoke on three different waist lengths.

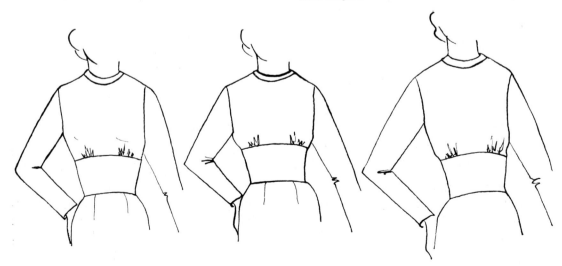

tulle—youth. Piqué is crisp and fresh. Satin reflects light and glistens. If it is a quality fabric, it will have an elegance that suggests dressy clothing such as ball gowns. The weave and the fiber used in satin are not the most durable; it has been associated with extravagance in evening clothes. Velvet suggests richness, elegance, and refinement. Until recently, it was seldom seen in essentially functional clothes; new finishes, however, have given it greater versatility. As opposed to the rich pile of velvet, we find the clarity of a worsted fabric such as gabardine. Tweeds suggest heaviness and durability.

The texture of any fabric depends on the quality of the yarn and on construction and finish. Variations in methods of construction create textural effects in fabrics. Bonded fabrics such as felt create interest through fiber and finish. Knits—lacy, loose, close, ribbed, or cable—offer a great variety of textural effects.

The effect of different toe shapes in men's shoes on the apparent length of the same foot.

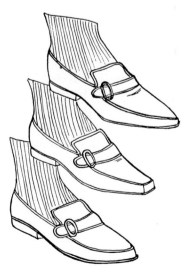

The same foot in shoes with rounded, pointed, and square toes.

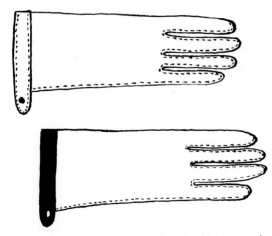
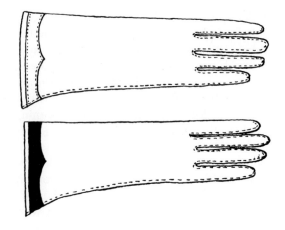

Gloves have decorative lines that should be considered in the total effect.

Texture effects

All textures have certain characteristic effects. Shiny fabrics that reflect light and heavy, bulky fabrics will increase the apparent size of the individual. A heavy fabric increases bulk and therefore creates more surface. Crisp fabrics that stand away from the body may make the body seem larger. Mat surfaces, thin fabrics, or crepes in fine wool will not increase size and may help to detract from or camouflage largeness. This is determined by the color and line that is used with the texture. Textures that have dominance or eye-catching appeal will also call attention to a feature.

Texture also influences the appearance of the skin. A shiny fabric may reflect color on the skin. Crisp, hard fabrics may not be as flattering as those which are napped in finish. Velvet and other napped fabrics are generally becoming to skins. Fabrics similar in texture to the skin will repeat and therefore accentuate the characteristics of the skin.

It is important to experiment not only with textures of all kinds but with combinations of different textures. Observe the effect of large areas of two different textures together and then try a large area of one texture with a small area of another. New fabrics are created every year and more textures with more uses are available than ever before.

Reading about design will not bring understanding of it. Reading will open new avenues of thought; but, to understand design, one must see and be aware of what he sees and then experiment with the elements such as color, line, texture, shape, and proportion. Observation and experimentation cannot be over-emphasized in the process of understanding design.

In the aesthetics of dress, all articles worn are seen together—not in isolation. The person is seen with a background, which must be considered because the way a person appears is affected by his surroundings. Thus the beginning of understanding effective appearance is to see all the components of a total design and the inter-relation of all these components.

Before one attempts to understand his own total design, it is helpful to study design which does not necessarily involve him personally. The individual can create exercises in awareness. Wherever one goes there is color, texture, and line to observe. Nature is a wonderful source of inspiration

Deep crowns create a feeling of height.

Shallow crowns and wide brims create a feeling of width.

and knowledge. A walk where one really *looks* can be a study in design. Concentrate on color first, then line and texture. You will note many things. Color is never uniform or matched in nature. There are always shades and variations. Vibrant color is present in small amounts. As you look you will see that color is never alone. It is mingled with texture, shapes, and light. If you study and re-study one spot as the light changes at different times of day, you will become aware of the complexity of the picture. A close look discloses the coarse texture of bark, the lines of a leaf, the velvety texture of a flower petal. It will be apparent that despite the endless variety there is little confusion.

Nature is an obvious source, but there are numerous other experiences which increase your knowledge. Analyze the texture and color of costumes for a play—one piece of fabric, a piece of wood, or a piece of costume jewelry. Use lighting to change effects. Experiment with colors and textures on your skin. Try matching colors of fabric and leather. Combine different textures and observe effects. Train yourself to constantly be aware and really *see*.

Another important exercise will be to analyze the reaction of people. Observe a child at play; notice his movement, the way he plays. Find out the color and texture he likes, the preference he shows for shapes. Dress a child. Ask his opinion about a shirt. The individual can make each experience an exercise in learning about design and people.

Most important in these exercises will be to keep an *open mind* and to really *see*. One should approach all observation as if it were a new experience.

REFERENCE READINGS

Books

Birren, Faber, *Color, Form and Space*, Wittenborn, New York, 1961.

Birren, Faber, *Creative Color*, Wittenborn, New York, 1960.

Birren, Faber, *The World of Color*, Wittenborn, New York, 1960.

Bond, Fred, *Color, How to See It and Use It*, Wittenborn, New York, 1956.

Brockman, Helen L., *The Theory of Fashion Design*, John Wiley & Sons, Inc., New York, 1965.

Emerson, Sybil, *Design: A Creative Approach*, International Textbook Co., Scranton, 1953.

Fogarty, Anne, *Wife Dressing*, Julian Messner, Inc., New York, 1959.

Graves, Maitland, *The Art of Color and Design*, McGraw-Hill Book Co., New York, 1952.

Hardy, Kay, *Costume Design*, McGraw-Hill Book Co., New York, 1948.

Renner, Paul (Translation Nesbiet Alexander), *Color: Order and Harmony*, Reinhold Publishing Corporation, New York, 1964.

Spears, Charlezine Wood, *How to Wear Colors*, Burgess Publishing Co., Minneapolis, Minn., 1965.

Magazines

American Fabrics, Numbers 6, 9, 12, and 32, Doric Publishing Co., Inc., 152 East 40th Street, New York 16.

Chapter 5

Does it fit you?

For man, woman, or child, nothing is more important in being attractively and comfortably dressed than having properly fitted clothes. A garment may be perfect in line and beautifully cut, but it must fit correctly to do justice to the design. A well-designed and well-fitted garment will look right and be comfortable to wear.

A properly fitted garment conforms to the figure and has adequate ease for movement; its lines are not strained or changed by the body. It is the sum of many details of cutting and manipulating fabric that makes the garment seem a part of the wearer. A wrinkle is an indication that either the garment is too long, too wide, too short, or too narrow or the grain is not controlled where and as it should be. Wrinkles should not be confused with folds that are an integral part of the design, like the folds at the shoulder of a kimono or dolman sleeve.

Fashion also plays a part in the way the article is fitted. You have already been introduced to silhouettes. The amount of ease or the control of fullness will change with current styles, but changes are limited to what can be done with fabric on the human body. The designer will plan for the looseness or snugness of the garment in relation to the silhouette being designed.

The processes of fitting and designing cannot be separated. At the time designing is begun, provisions are made for cutting, darting, and draping a straight piece of fabric to mold around the curves of the body. Fitting is the adjusting of the design to the human figure. Alteration is the changing of certain parts of a completed article to fit a particular person. Custom fitting refers to adjusting the design of an article on the individual for whom it has been especially made. In custom houses a dummy form padded to the exact proportions of the individual is used for first fittings.

In fitting, the following factors must be considered:

1 The hang and drape of the garment.
2 Grain and grain control.
3 The cutting and assembling of the parts of the garment.
4 The control of fullness for the type of fabric, body proportions, and silhouette.
5 The balance of the parts of the garment on the figure.
6 Figure irregularities and special problems.

It will be noted that the first four points are concerned with the design of the garment and the last two are related to the individual. In determining the properly fitted garment, one must be aware of the effect the designer wanted to create in the construction of the design. The process of fitting and alteration will usually be done on structural lines and will not affect the decorative lines except where decoration

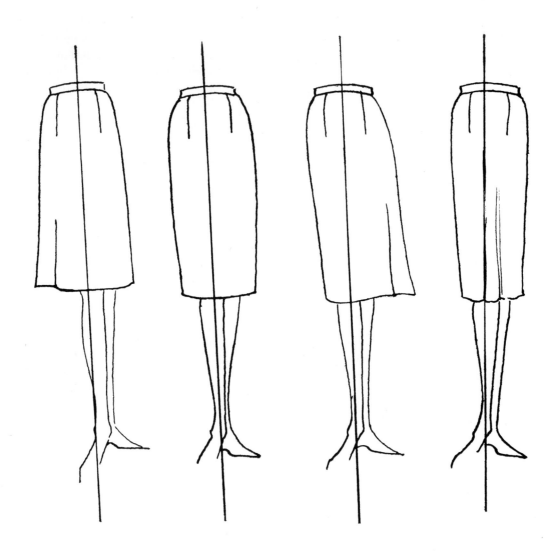

A straight skirt should hang evenly, as in the figure second from the left. Other views show uneven hang to the sides or the center.

has been applied to or incorporated in a structural line. An example of the latter is cording in a seam.

HANG AND DRAPE

Few garments conform completely to the body; the amount of fullness and the way the fullness falls is called the "hang" of the garment. There should be good balance in the hang of skirt or trousers, from side to side, in front and in back, and in the fullness from the side view. A slim or tubular skirt is generally flat on the sides, the fullness falling below the knees on both sides. Fullness in a slim skirt back will fall behind the knees.

"Drape" refers to the manner in which the fullness is handled and controlled. A

The hang of a full skirt should be evenly distributed. The figure at the left illustrates correct hang. In the figure at the right, the fullness falls to the center instead of being balanced on both sides of the center. In the figure in the center, the skirt swings to the side.

man's suit jacket that allows more than usual fullness from the shoulder—a double-breasted jacket, for example—is re- the fabric lies to the natural contours of the body, the less the drape. This is called a "natural" drape. Drape should not be con- ferred to as having a full drape. The closer fused with the draping done by the designer when he designs on a dress form.

Every garment must have ease for movement, and the ease must be controlled at the point of the movement; when adequate ease is not properly controlled, wrinkles may appear or the garment may bind.

Fabrics with different textures will drape differently. The weight and body of the material will also affect the hang of an outfit; a stiff fabric such as taffeta will drape differently than will a soft jersey.

Bonded fabrics have greatly increased the possibilities in the draping of fabrics. They also eliminate labor costs of separate backings.

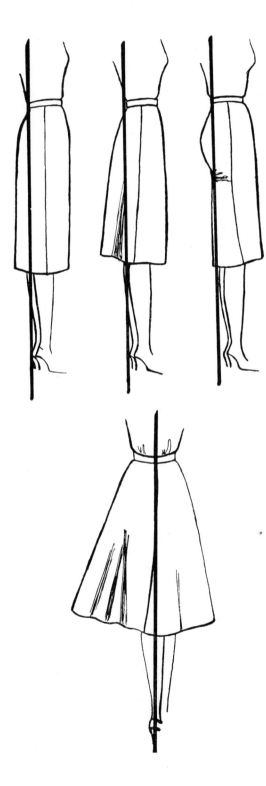

(This page) Top left: From the side view, the skirt should be proportioned as in the figure on the left. In the figure in the center, the skirt hangs to the back. The skirt on the right does not hang evenly and cups under the hips. Bottom left: Back view of full skirt, showing uneven hang to one side. Top right: The fullness in a man's suit should hang evenly in jacket and trousers, as in the figure on the left.

(Opposite) Top left: A woman's dress which does not hang evenly may pull up in front. Bottom left: Left, the natural drape; right, the full drape. Right: The seams in a man's trousers should fall at right angles to the floor.

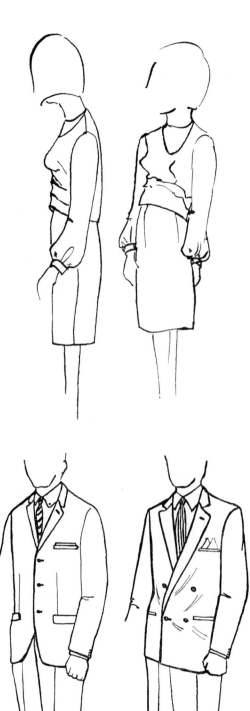
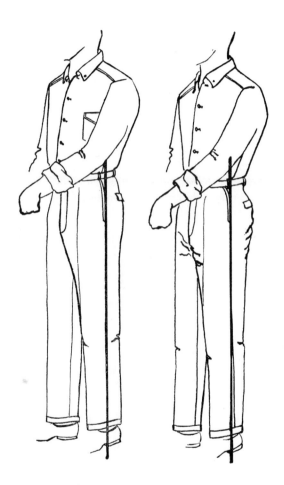

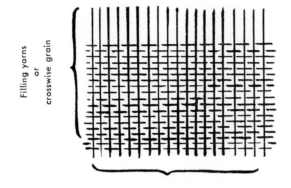

Filling yarns or crosswise grain

Warp yarns or lengthwise grain

GRAIN CONTROL

Grain refers to the direction of the yarn in woven cloth. True bias is the diagonal from one corner of the fabric to the opposite; it cuts a 45° angle between the warp, the lengthwise yarn, and the weft, or filling, the crosswise yarn. Garment bias may have an angle of less than 45°.

Garments cut on the straight of the fabric are cut with the warp yarns at right angles to the floor in center front and center back. "Biascut" means that the bias is at right angles to the floor in center front. The bias of the fabric stretches and can therefore be molded, whereas straight lengthwise yarns cannot; the closer the design is cut to the true bias, the more the fabric will stretch. The designer uses this knowledge of fabric in draping. How well an operator reproduces a design depends on his knowledge of grain and fabric construction and his ability to cut accurately.

Accuracy in cutting fabric maintains the grain as the designer intended it to be on the figure. Accuracy of cut is illustrated in the matching of plaids at seams or in the placement on the figure of a dominant stripe in the design of the fabric. The process of

Grain as it relates to the tubular silhouette on the figure. The heavy horizontal lines are parallel to the filling yarns; the vertical line in center front is on the warp grain of the fabric.

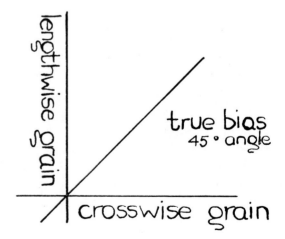

lengthwise grain

true bias
45° angle

crosswise grain

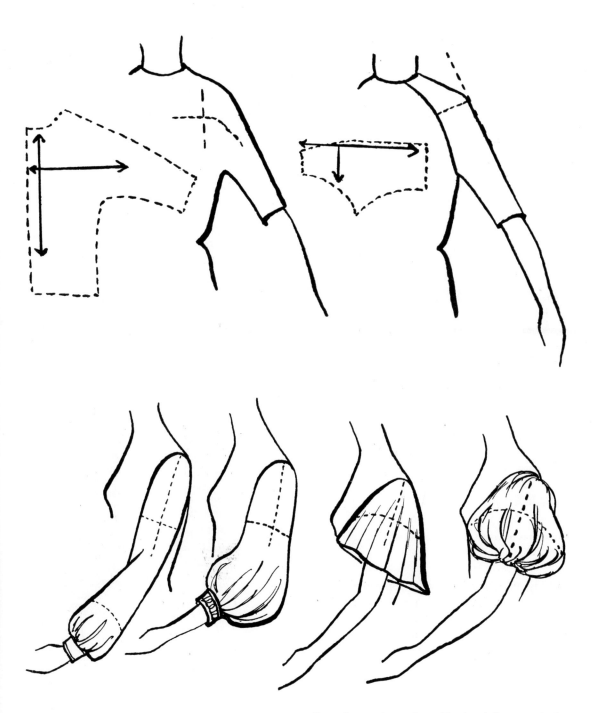

Crosswise grain varies with the fullness and the shape of the sleeve, as shown in the kimono and raglan sleeves.

A gusset is an extra inset of fabric which allows ease of movement.

cutting an article cannot be separated from grain control, hang, or drape. Good cutting reproduces a design with exactness, so that darts, seams, and fullness are placed on the form as the designer intended.

CONTROL OF FULLNESS

Darts are a means of controlling fullness. The direction and placement of darts will be determined by the fullest part of the body curve. For example, the shoulder

Plaids in a well-cut garment will match as in the figure on the left. The skirt at the right is poorly cut.

blade is usually the fullest part of the back; a dart will, therefore, take out fullness below this point and its direction will be toward the fullest part of the shoulder. On a woman's figure, the basic dart of a bodice front should be directed to the point of the bust. The depth of the dart is determined by the difference between the fullest and the smallest parts of the figure. A person with a full bust will have deeper darts than a person with a flatter bust. The straighter the figure, the less the depth of the dart.

Pleats, tucks, and gathers are other methods of controlling fullness, but do not give the same effect in fit. Control can also be obtained by easing or by shrinking the fullness into a seam—an example is the shrinking or easing of the sleeve into the armscye.

The construction of the garment is an important factor in maintaining fit. The treatment of seams, proper staying for fullness, and reinforcement at points of strain will help a dress or a suit retain the correctly fitted line. The direction of the seams, darts, or gathers is determined by their purpose and the design. Center

Tucks or pleats control fullness for the shoulder blade.

Skirt and trouser darts control fullness to the hip.

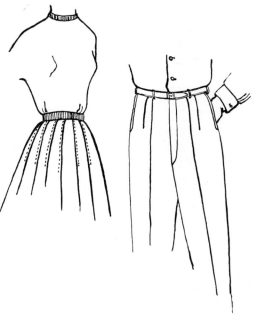

Control of fullness for the elbow through darts. The dart at the shoulder controls fullness for shoulder movement. Gathers replace darts for bustline control.

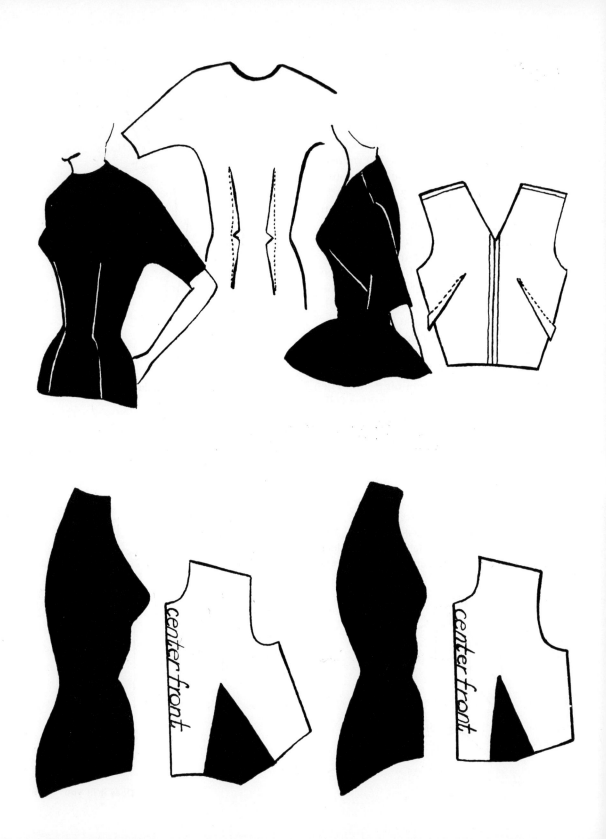

center front

center front

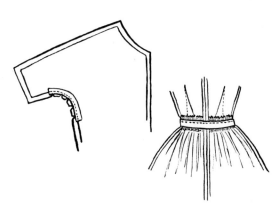

Reinforcements such as tape are needed where there will be strain from the movement of the body.

Back fullness can be controlled by a lining stay inside the bodice.

Fullness can be held by a stay on the inside of the skirt.

seams, front or back, should lie in the center of the body, and, like side seams, should fall straight from the hips toward the floor.

Even though silhouette and fashion will govern, to some extent, the snugness of a garment, the individual will also find that his needs and activities will call for an easy or close fit. This is one detail which will contribute to a person's expression of self.

THE RELATIONSHIP OF FITTING TO THE INDIVIDUAL

If your proportions are different from those of the model used by the manufacturer, your clothes will not fit as well as you may desire. Ready-made clothes are

(Opposite) Top: The control of fullness through bustline darts in different locations. Bottom: The size of the bustline dart is related to the size of the bust. The fuller the bust, the larger the basic dart.

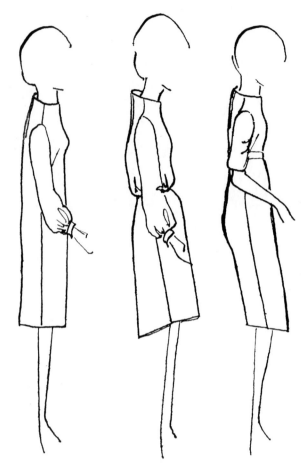

In a well-made garment, seams meet seams and fall straight to the floor. Left: The seams on the figure on the left are straight. In center figure, shoulder and neck swing back and skirt seams swing forward. Right: Seams fall forward and skirt cups under the hips.

The seams on the figure on the right fall straight and meet center seam of bodice. Left, the seams do not fall straight and center seams do not meet at waistline seam.

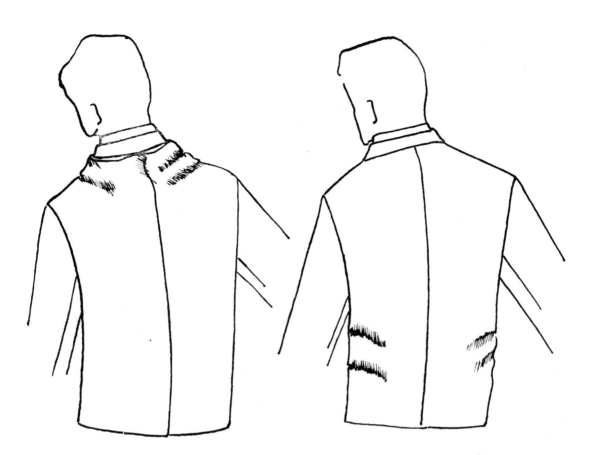

An article that is too long will create wrinkles. The coat at the left is too long in the shoulder area. That at the right is too long in the waist.

designed for the "average" figure, but manufacturers do not always agree on what the average figure is.

Observe the lengths from the neck to the waist, the waistline to the hip, and the waistline to the hem of the skirt or trousers in relation to your proportions. If the garment is too long in the waist, a crosswise wrinkle will appear between the shoulder blades and the waistline; if the bodice is too long between the neck and the shoulders, you will find a wrinkle across the shoulders. A short waist will be quite evident, since the deepest part of the waistline dart will be above the natural waistline and will appear skimpy in this area. It is not unusual to find individuals whose

lengthwise proportions are longer in the front than in the back, or vice versa. The proper length of waist is most important in articles with no waist seam, since alteration will be more difficult and often impossible.

The lengthwise proportions that determine the fit of a skirt are those from the waist to the large part of the hips and from the hips to the hem. The length of the skirt from the waist to the hem should be checked for appearance after a careful check of lengthwise proportions. Skirts that have inadequate ease will tend to push up

Excess length in the bodice will cause wrinkles in the rib area or may cause the front to poke out.

ment of the arm at the elbow. If when the arms are bent the darts or gathered fullness fall below the elbow, the sleeve is too long from the shoulder to the elbow. This places the controlled fullness at the wrong point on the arm. If the controlled fullness falls above the elbow, the sleeve is too short from the shoulder to the elbow. In a regular set-in sleeve, the girth of the sleeve is always several inches larger than the arm to allow for ease of movement.

A check of crosswise proportions will aid your knowledge of fitting. The width of the shoulders is extremely important. There must be adequate controlled ease for movement of the shoulders and arms so that no strain appears with movement, but too much ease or fullness will allow the armscye to move down to a point on the arm where it will hamper rather than aid movement. The chest and the bust must have adequate ease and should not strain at any point. There must be fullness in any article of clothing or there will be lack of movement. The amount of ease in the crosswise proportion will depend upon the style, the silhouette, and the method the designer used to control the fullness. Depending upon the style, of course, from 2 to 4 inches ease is allowed in the average bodice. There is generally adequate ease in what appears to be a form-fitting garment.

Individual irregularities—such as one shoulder being lower than the other—will require alteration of ready-made clothing, since manufacturers cut clothes symmetrically. Those alterations will be similar for most garments; if you had one shoulder lower than the other, you would probably find it necessary either to raise the seam of the low shoulder or to use padding to raise the lower shoulder to balance the higher. Padding the shoulders may, however, create too bulky an effect, especially for someone with a short neck.

to a smaller part of the body. If the girth through the hips is not sufficient, the skirt will move to the smaller part of the body and cause a wrinkle under the waist or across the thigh. This is not to be confused with the skirt's being too large. A skirt may cup for different reasons. It may be too narrow across the hips and thighs or the back may be too long, allowing the grain to fall too low on the figure.

In trousers, the depth of the crotch is of utmost importance for appearance and comfort. If the crotch is too long, there will be downward wrinkles under the inseam, if too short, the fabric will draw too close to the body and cause upward wrinkles.

In the sleeve of a dress or suit, there usually is controlled fullness for the move-

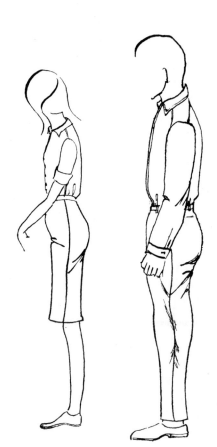

Top left: A dress that is too long from the waist to the hip will push up on the figure, causing wrinkles, and will not hang correctly. Top right: When the crotch of the trousers or a skirt from waist to hips is too long, wrinkles will appear under the hips. Right: When a sleeve is too long in the upper arm, the darts will fall below the elbow, and wrinkles will appear in the sleeve.

Many factors such as the construction of the fabric will also affect fit. Knitwear, because of the nature of its construction, will allow more movement than will woven fabrics. The closeness of the weave and the

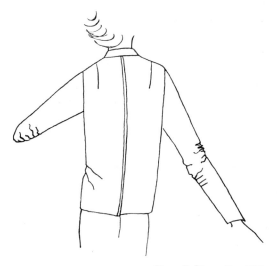

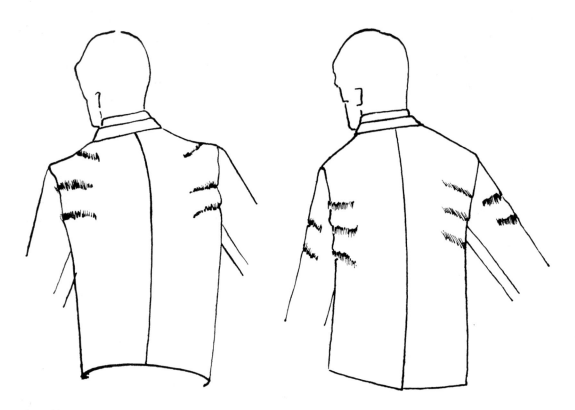

When the wearer's shoulders are too large for the shoulders of the jacket, there will be wrinkles of strain, as in the figure on the left. If the shoulders of the jacket are too large, the armscye may move down on the arm and interfere with movement, as in the drawing on the right.

treatment of the finish will affect the amount of give in a fabric; crepe fabrics, for example, usually have more give than firmly woven ones.

The use of the article will make a difference both in choice of fabric and in the amount of ease needed. Sports clothes must provide more ease for movement than is necessary in clothing to be worn for occasions not requiring great freedom of action. A dancing dress must have adequate fullness for movement of the legs, a golf shirt ample room for arm movement. A coat must allow for the bulk of the garments to be worn under it. Designs for children's clothes must allow enough ease for the activities of play, whereas most clothing for adults need provide only adequate ease for walking, sitting, and arm movement. Care must be taken that garments have adequate ease without hampering movement through too much fullness.

Accessories and underwear also play an important part here. If the undergarments are smooth and close to the body, the outer garments will be smooth. Undergarments that are fuller than the outside clothing will create bulk under otherwise nicely fitted clothes. Fabric construction will affect the closeness of fit and ease of movement in underclothing. Children's underwear should allow for plenty of ease and should not bind; at the same time it should not be so full as to catch on toys. Knitted

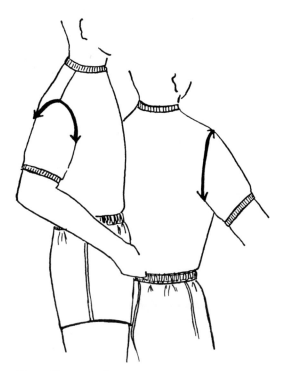

fabrics mold to the figure, but allow movement. Girdles and brassieres should mold to but not confine the body. An undergarment that distorts or changes the body contours will more often than not make the body less attractive. A heavy woman who binds the fat will usually create a bulge or a roll that will show when she is dressed. Comfort and appearance in underwear or accessories involve the same factors that are considered in outer wear.

When one shoulder is lower than the other, the excess fabric will create wrinkles on the low side.

Above: The natural armscye seam.

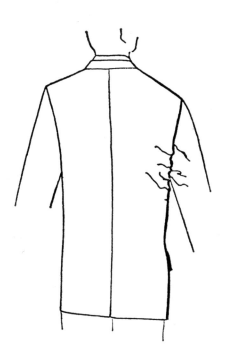

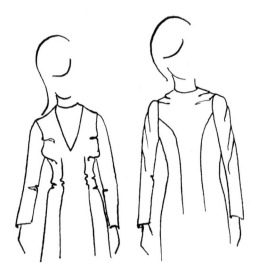

When a dress has inadequate ease, wrinkles of strain appear in the tight area.

With all the factors that influence fit, you may feel that understanding the fitting process requires an expert. However, there is much the individual who wants to look well and be comfortable in his clothes can do to understand his or her own fitting problems. If you understand how you like your own garments to fit, you can tell your fitter what alterations you want made. People who sew are often dissatisfied with the things they make simply because they have not learned to fit them properly. If you do not sew, it will probably be wise to allow some alteration cost when purchasing a new outfit.

SIZING

In order to have fashion at a price, there must be some compromise between custom fitting and mass production. Often the consumer is unable to find the correct size when purchasing ready-made clothing. Many alterations could be avoided if there were uniformity and consistency in sizing among manufacturers. However, each year

brings improvement in the sizing of clothing.

The National Health Survey studies in body measurements have many implications for use in the sizing of clothing which should supplement the size standardization proposed by the Department of Commerce.

In turn, the retailer could aid his customers by making available information about

A poorly fitted garment, as indicated by seam placement and wrinkles.

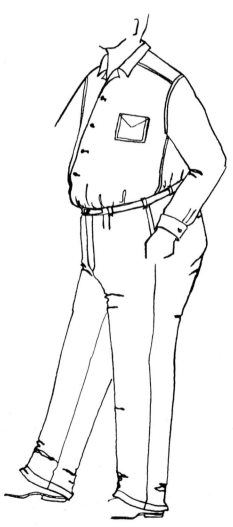

A petticoat fuller than the skirt interferes with the hang and drape of the skirt, as in figure at right.

the sizing of the products sold in his store. Larger stores should consider having fitting co-ordinators just as they have fashion co-ordinators or bridal consultants. Until manufacturers adopt size standardization, the consumer will be dependent upon the sales person for information concerning sizes.

REFERENCE READINGS

Lonie, Mansfield, "Size Coordination in Women's Apparel Lines," *Stores,* January 1954.
National Health Survey, "Weight, Height, and Selected Body Dimensions of Adults, United States 1960–1962." *Vital and Health Statistics.* PHS Washington, D.C.: U.S. Government Printing Office, June 1965.

Chapter 6

Do
you
co-ordinate?

Co-ordinating is the combining and relating of many different items and elements in such a way that the result gives the individual a new and special identity that is greater than the accumulation of the parts. When coordination is well planned a "total look" results, which makes order of chaos rather than a hodgepodge of ideas. Whenever things are put together, they become something other than what they are alone. All things seen together change each part. Thus a look can be changed from restraint to boldness or from subtle to obvious by changing the relationships of separate articles.

TERMINOLOGY

Basic is used here to mean an essential or fundamental part or the foundation of an outfit. What is basic to one person is not necessarily basic to another. A suit might be basic in one woman's wardrobe but nonessential in another's. The much-talked-about basic black dress would hardly be basic for someone who cannot wear black well. What is basic depends also on the individual's life and his social and professional needs. An article that for city life would be considered fundamental could easily be nonessential in country life. A suit may be basic to a banker, but a civil engineer who uses a suit only for contacts in the business world and so will need fewer suits may not find the suit basic.

Overdressing may refer specifically to dressing too elaborately for the occasion. More generally, it is used to mean the wearing of too many items not suited to the purpose the wearer intended or the presence of too many ideas within one picture. *Underdressing* would be the selection of an outfit not worthy of the occasion or one so plain as to make the wearer appear unimportant as a person. *Understating*, however, would be co-ordinating important items in an outfit in a subtle manner that would make the articles seem less important than they really are. A beautiful fabric made in a simple design would be one example of understatement.

Simplicity of dress refers to apparel that is plain and unadorned or which is not elaborate. It is surprising how often one may hear women say that they like simple things yet see them the very next day in an elaborate blouse or dress. It is possible to have a simple style in a luxurious fabric or an elaborate design in a simple fabric. Simplicity in dress is gained in the total picture rather than in the separate items. When trying for simplicity, it is important not to lose personality or individuality and not to create a plainness that is dull or too severe. Let the purpose of the outfit govern your choice. In a place of business, for example, one would want to be a pleasant addition but not so different as to be a distracting force.

Just as one can overdress, one can overdo simplicity in clothing. A great deal will depend upon the individual. Some people are in themselves decorative, while others are very plain in appearance. Some people need the help of clothing to bring out a definite personality. Simplicity used in extremes or in the wrong way can become dullness. Such misuse generally is the result of a misunderstanding of what simplicity really means and a lack of understanding of oneself. If you feel that you are always in the shadow of someone else, you might re-evaluate what aids you have that might help you bring out your personality. To say that simplicity is a distinctive style for some who understand how to dress and is a studied style with others does not fully explain simplicity to those who do not understand or have not accomplished simplicity.

PERSONAL ATTRIBUTES

Beautiful coloring, lovely skin, a good figure, and pretty hair have identity to begin with. There are some people with very dynamic and charming personalities who yet need more decorative and color assistance than those who are blessed with beauty. This does not imply that they are not attractive; if their clothing is carefully co-ordinated, they may present a far more attractive appearance than others who start with a little more. Some people can wear more jewelry than others without seeming loaded down. To be able to "carry off" an unusual idea requires a certain degree of poise or daring. This is a matter of personality rather than of physical characteristics.

You may appear as two different personalities to your business associates and to your friends. Keeping your contacts, the background, and activities foremost in mind when co-ordinating will help you create the mood that you want. Knowing yourself is, as we have said, an essential factor. You may wish to create a mood of restraint or a gay, abandoned mood. Whatever the idea, keeping all the various factors in mind will help you develop it.

VARIETY

Variety, it has often—and unnecessarily—been said, is the spice of life. Used in the right way it will help you express yourself and reflect your personality. Too much variety may result in confusion and make you appear mixed up. If you tend from habit to be comfortable in one kind of clothes, one color, and one kind of fabric, people may become so accustomed to seeing the same look that they will really not look at you. A surprise treatment—perhaps a new silhouette, color, or texture—once in a while will help to relieve the monotony and create interest.

At the other extreme is the person who overdoes the variety treatment and so loses identity and effectiveness in dress. Variety that is often lacking within the wardrobe can easily be overdone within an outfit. Too many textures, too many patterns, and too much variety in color can create an overdressed effect as easily as too much jewelry or trim. What in one place is restraint can against another background be exotic. The variety we are seeking can be controlled if in our co-ordinating we keep foremost in mind communication with the people we are to be with, the activities in which we will participate, and the background.

The outfit should always be co-ordinated as it will be worn. If it is to be worn without a hat, it should be co-ordinated as a whole without the hat. If the coat will be removed, the outfit should look complete without the coat. When you begin combining all of the items that make up the outfit, remember that the idea of all the various articles should be interesting in themselves but the sum of all should create *one* defi-

CORRECT MALE FORMAL ATTIRE

	FORMAL DAYTIME	SEMI-FORMAL DAYTIME	FORMAL EVENING	SEMI-FORMAL EVENING	FOR FUN (RESORTWEAR)
Coat	Cutaway coat with plain or bound edges, peaked or notched lapels.	Single-breasted jacket with 1-, 2- or 3-buttons, peak or notch lapels, bound or plain edges.	Evening tailcoat with satin or gross-grain lapels.	Dinner jacket (tuxedo) with peak, notch or shawl lapel.	You name it: Anything from white to batik, brocade to Madras.
Fabric	Oxford gray or black regular weight or tropical worsted or worsted cheviot.	Oxford gray or black regular weight or tropical worsted or worsted cheviot.	Black tropical worsted or mohair/worsted blend.	Same as formal plus white for summer and tropics.	Worsted, silks, brocades, blends, cotton, man-made fibers.
Trousers	Black and light gray or black and silver tone stripes of regular or tropic weight worsted.	Black and light gray or black and silver tone stripes of regular or tropic weight worsted.	Same material and color as coat with side stripes to match lapels.	Same material and color as coat with side stripes to match lapels.	Usually side-striped black. But white, red or Madras, too. May match colored coat.
Waistcoat	Single- or double-breasted to match coat or of light gray or faun flannel or white or gray washable fabrics.	Single- or double-breasted to match coat or of light gray or faun flannel or white or gray washable fabrics.	White pique to match shirt bosom in low cut backless evening model. Can be single- or double-breasted.	Cummerbund to match lapels or vest same as formal in black or white. To match lapels if black.	Wear one, or don't. It can be classic or exotic.
Shirt	Plain white with stiff or pleated bosom.	Plain white with stiff or pleated bosom.	Stiff white pique bosom and cuffs.	Soft or semi-stiff pleated bosom.	Pleated or plain, white or a color, maybe striped.
Collar	Starched bold wing or fold model.	Starched fold or wing. Latter is correct but not often worn.	Starched bold wing only.	Soft fold collar attached; semi-stiff fold on same type bosom.	Take your pick.
Necktie	Ascot or four-in-hand in moire stripes of black and silver or neat silver checks.	Ascot or four-in-hand in moire stripes of black and silver or neat checks.	White pique bow to match shirt bosom and vest.	Black bow to match fabric of lapels and vest or cummerbund.	Be sure it's a bow.
Shoes	Black polished straight tip calfskin.	Black polished straight tip calfskin.	Black polished calfskin or patent leather pumps or plain toe oxfords.	Black polished calfskin or patent leather pumps or plain toe oxfords.	Pumps, oxfords or updated "casual formals."
Socks	Black calf-length; silk, nylon or lisle.	Black calf-length; silk, nylon or lisle.	Black calf-length; silk, nylon or lisle.	Black calf-length; silk, nylon or lisle.	Black calf-length.
Hat	High silk.	Black homburg.	High silk.	Black homburg or black snap brim.	In town, yes. At resorts if it is raining.
Jewelry and accessories	Pearl or jeweled tie pin. Cuff links of gold, silver or semi-precious stone. Gray silk scarf.	Pearl or jeweled tie pin. Cuff links of gold, silver or semi-precious stones. Gray silk scarf.	Studs and cuff links: White pearl or precious stones. White silk muffler.	Studs and cuff links: Smoked pearl or semi-precious stones. Black & white silk muffler.	Studs and cuff links with some shirts.
Gloves	Gray, white or faun (to match waistcoat).	Gray, white or faun (to match waistcoat).	White kid, cape or doeskin or white fabric.	Gray mocha or gray fabric.	None.
Overcoat	Black, oxford gray or navy Chesterfield. May have velvet collar.	Black, oxford gray or navy Chesterfield. May have velvet collar.	Black, oxford gray or navy Chesterfield. May have velvet collar.	Same as formal plus raglan balmacaan in same colors.	Raincoat if needed.

Reprinted by permission of *Men's Wear* Magazine, A Fairchild Publication.

Top left: Semi-formal daytime. Top middle: Formal daytime. Top right: Formal evening dinner jacket. Bottom left: Semi-formal evening white dinner jacket. Bottom right: Semi-formal evening. Grooms fashions by permission of After Six Formals.

nite idea. Each article will create a textural quality and add color tones. Study each separately with the intent of creating an overall oneness which adds variety.

OCCASION

Knowing that you are attractively and well dressed at the right time is one of the main concerns of dressing. Whether you are really well dressed depends in large measure on the people you are with; you are only as well dressed as they think you are. Always wearing the right thing at the right time is not easy to accomplish. Most people prefer the feeling of "belonging" to that of being a stranger in the group. This natural, characteristic desire to be accepted and recognized as an individual is behind most people's desire to be appropriately dressed for the occasion.

The "air of belonging" some people have, which makes them seem at home in almost any situation, may be the result of experience. By experience, we mean familiarity with the place, the people, and the activities involved. When you dress for an occasion, you call on past experience. When you are approaching a new situation, there are certain things that will help you decide what to wear. One is alertness to, and another, observation of, life as it is lived *now*.

Certain indications people give with invitations can help you decide what to wear. First of all, there is a considerable difference between a public affair, where you will be associating with people who do not know you, and one held in a private club or home. If you are known in the private home and at the club, you are being invited for yourself; you already belong, and there will be less rigidity in dress. In a public place, you are judged by your appearance, not according to personality or achievement.

In going to a place where you are un-

A brocade dinner jacket (courtesy American Institute of Men's and Boy's Wear, Inc)

known and will meet new people, conformity is in order. You will be on display and you will want to be dressed in a manner acceptable to all. A public occasion that calls for white tie or black tie demands a conservative approach and strict conformity. At a club or fraternity party where people know you, a plaid cummerbund or tie may be acceptable, or if you are entertaining in your home, it might be a charming relief to wear a plaid dinner jacket. A formal invitation that specifies black tie or white tie is an indication to both men and women. "White tie" means full dress for the men and formal ball gowns and shoulder length gloves for the ladies. "Black tie" suggests a little less formality but enough to require dinner jackets. The ladies may assume that their dress may be a little less formal in fabric or design.

However, even when custom dictates conformity of dress, try to have some individual touches which will identify and express you.

If you are invited to an occasion, think back to what you know about the people and their activities. In the process of getting to know them, you have probably found out a number of things about them. Your real problems arise when you know neither the place where you are going nor the people you will be with. If, in this situation, you know someone else who is invited and whose judgment you respect, ask what you should wear.

What is called intuition is usually a knowledgeable feeling for what is right, based on experience and observation of place and people. People with "intuition" are people who are aware of places and people and have made note of things people say or do that might help them in making decisions on what to wear when.

In almost any invitation you will be able to find some clues as to planned activities and appropriate dress. Several kinds of clothes might be suitable for a picnic. A simple cotton shirtwaist or a cotton skirt and blouse would be safe. If you know the people, you may know pant suits would be acceptable. If some particular sport is specified, you will know what kind of clothes to wear. If you are the hostess and you are inviting strangers to your home, you should give them a tactful clue to the kind of clothing you expect them to wear.

When you will be in a strange location for any length of time, it may be wise to leave your planning until you have had a chance to observe local customs. Many a college freshman buys her clothes before going to college, only to find that she has bought the fashion magazines' concept of what the college student is wearing and that she has many things that do not fit into the life at her school.

When you are not sure, it is wise to wait. Most local stores have a readily available stock of merchandise suited to the life of that particular locality. When you are adjusting to a new situation, there is more need than ever to express yourself through clothing. Within conformity and good taste, it is a challenge to communicate your individuality.

CONTRAST

Contrast is the key to emphasizing good points or to creating moods. Too much contrast can detract from a total look and create confusion.

Contrast creates opposition by *contrast of color hue, contrast of light and dark, contrast of pure and clouded color*. There is also textural contrast such as *rough and smooth, shiny and mat*, and *crisp and soft* which will affect the color appearance. The different means of obtaining contrast can be combined in numerous ways. Thus one outfit may have contrast of colors and textures. It will be important to attempt to keep some similarity and avoid having contrast in all of the elements of purity, value, hue, and texture.

COLOR IN CO-ORDINATION

It is obvious to the student of color in dress that color is not independent of other elements. Color is also a result of an individual's senses and is therefore hard to measure. It then becomes difficult, if not impossible to evolve systems and rules to guide the untrained eye. Thus when an attempt is made to give guidelines to follow in combining color in dress, the individual must still evaluate and discard that which does not please.

In co-ordinating colors in dress, consideration is always given to the many elements such as light and background which affect the use of color. Each co-ordination has three dimensions which must be considered in combining colors—*degree of purity, the value*, and *hue*, including the warmth or coolness. In most pleasing combinations one of the dimensions remains similar. For example, where there is a contrast of hue, the colors may be similar in purity and/or value. The individual should experiment with combinations of contrast of hue, contrast of value or contrast of purity. The most pleasing co-ordinations will generally have similarity in one of these dimensions.

For example, experiment with contrast of two colors such as blue and green, which fall into the same value and purity range. Emerald green and royal blue in the same degree of purity and lightness will create a pleasing combination. Then proceed to experiment with these same colors with a difference in purity *but* in the same value range. Lastly, try emerald green and royal blue in different values but with the same degree of purity. After experimenting with two colors, use only one color and see the effect of contrast of value or contrast of purity. This process will give a feeling of how colors combine harmoniously. There should usually be one factor which is similar.

As you work with different colors, you will find that the degree of warmth and coolness will also create stronger contrast. Red and blue will cause more opposition than blue and green.

In using pure colors with gray, it will be important to keep value and color similar. The gray must have some of the pure color —a warm gray with red or a cool gray with green or blue.

Most pleasing combinations are built on a few main colors. This does not eliminate graduation of the colors. In dress, the pleasing effect is usually obtained by giving dominance to one of the colors. The student of color should analyze the colors in fabrics to observe the dominance that is usually present. It will also be wise to experiment with fabrics in different lights, on varied backgrounds, and on the human form. Learning about color combination will be never ending. As the awareness develops, the individual will develop sensitivity to pleasing co-ordination.

The way the individual combines colors frequently is more expressive of individuality than the use of a single preferred color. The important thing is to have the contrast at the point you wish to emphasize and subordinate other factors to this point of emphasis. This will help to create a dominant idea. Repetition can also be used as a means of emphasis. Your aim is to combine your tools so that the eye moves in the direction in which you wish it to travel. Obviously, you will eliminate decorative trim or bright color from points at which you do not want the eye to stop. Repetition of textures and colors will help to guide the eye from one item to the next.

If a heavy-set person finds it desirable to carry the eye to the face, there will be no breaks in contrasts of color, line, or texture. Bright or light colors will be used to attract the eye to good points through contrast.

In co-ordination, remember the effect that results when two colors are placed in juxtaposition. A black-and-white tweed will frequently appear gray and should be co-ordinated as gray rather than as black. Too often people pick out a color that is very obvious at close range but disappears with a little change in light or distance.

It is seldom wise to choose hat, gloves, bag, and shoes in a color and texture that is in contrast to the dress or suit with which they will be worn. When using contrast, it is important to tie the accessories and the rest of the outfit together in some way. This might be done with a scarf that picks up the color of the hat or a handbag containing both the color of the accessories and the color of the dress. It may be more interesting to pick up the color of the dress in one accessory.

THE INDIVIDUAL

Where do you start co-ordinating? With yourself. The individual is the basis of the design. Purpose also is an essential part of co-ordinating; you will not want to use all of the ideas or moods that express you at one time. You need not feel that different kinds of clothing must express the same mood. You may have one philosophy for sports clothes and a completely different approach to evening or business clothes. Most people will also find that there is a definite pattern to their needs, and, unless they are making a complete change of position or locality, they should know what these needs are.

You have thought about the kind of outfit and when it will be worn and the mood you wish to create. You already know the colors you wear best and your physical characteristics such as the texture and coloring of your skin and hair. These factors are already a part of the picture you are creating. You yourself will have certain decorative features. A woman's hair style might in itself be a dominant, elaborate idea and suggest simplicity in dress. A person with tight curly hair might consider that as a decorative part, and one that she might be reluctant to change. You may have decided that certain parts of your body would look best in subdued colors and textures. Your good features, perhaps a small waist or lovely hands, are points that can stand emphasis. Make-up must also be considered in co-ordinating; nail color, for example, will be a part of your color co-ordination.

A man may have good coloring, broad shoulders, or handsome features. A child often has lovely skin and attractive hair and eyes. The foundation (assuming you have done your best through perfect grooming) is already determined and beyond your control; you must work around and build upon this foundation. You want each part of the picture to have interest, particularly where the part in question is a good point, but the interest must not be so important as to overshadow the main idea. The main idea should be dominant.

Since co-ordinating is where you express individuality in designing "your look," you might start with something you like very much—a piece of jewelry, a dress, a coat, or a favorite color for a woman; a jacket, a shirt, or slacks for a man.

CO-ORDINATING WOMEN'S CLOTHING

Review in your own mind the relationship of the parts to yourself. What colors and textures are best for your skin and hair? What color values—light or dark—should you use at certain parts of the body? Your choice of color will be governed by your own coloring and by the points you wish to emphasize. If, for example, your feet and legs are nicely shaped, you can, occasion permitting, wear shoes that are gaily colored or, if in a neutral or dark color, decorative in line. However, if your feet are too large or poorly shaped, you might wish to keep to simple shoes in a plain, neutral hue or a dark shade. The weight of the color and the weight of the material in shoes should be consistent with the size of the feet. A woman with a large body and small feet would not want to wear delicate-looking shoes. Delicacy might result from too light a shape, too fine a texture, or from shoes that are too open. If a small person wore heavy shoes or heels, she might appear to be all feet. Although the hands might be a very good feature, it is rarely advisable to put intense color on the hands. The color will call at-

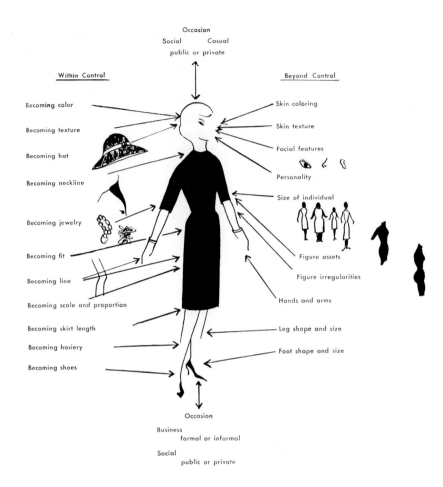

Occasion
Social   Casual
public or private

Within Control

Becoming color
Becoming texture
Becoming hat
Becoming neckline
Becoming jewelry
Becoming fit
Becoming line
Becoming scale and proportion
Becoming skirt length
Becoming hosiery
Becoming shoes

Beyond Control

Skin coloring
Skin texture
Facial features
Personality
Size of individual
Figure assets
Figure irregularities
Hands and arms
Leg shape and size
Foot shape and size

Occasion
Business
formal or informal
Social
public or private

tention not only to the hands but to any part of the body the hands may be near, creating a great deal of movement and emphasis where you might not want it.

You will use contrast to play up your best points, and less dominant and inconspicuous colors and textures to tone down less attractive points. For the person who feels she cannot wear large-pattern designs or bright colors, there is always the opportunity to use a pattern in an accessory. Jewelry can be used not only for emphasis but as a tool to dramatize and give distinction to the person who needs a little more color and texture identity. Identity could be attained through a trademark of your own such as a color, a certain plaid, or a

particular kind of jewelry. The accessories should complete the design rather than look like separate items.

Knowing yourself and your limitations and assets, you can decide whether you will start your co-ordinating with apparel or physical characteristics or accessory items. If it is to be a decorative item such as an exquisite hat or piece of jewelry, do not add any other decoration until you have completed the structural co-ordination. The item with which you start will determine other items. Diamonds will not suggest heavy tweeds. A heavy silver piece, on the other hand, would be more in keeping with the texture of tweed. Think of the textures you have in one outfit. There are the texture of the decorative item you start with, the textures of your skin and hair, and the textures of the dress or suit, shoes, handbag, gloves, hat, and stockings. If each of these items has a different texture, you will have a great many contrasts at different points of the body. Do your size or your features allow the eye to stop at all these points of contrast? Too much textural contrast in these items might result in your appearing overdressed. Imagine the further impact of having all these articles in different colors. If all the items were in one color, there would, of course, be less contrast, but since different materials take dyes differently, you would probably find differences in color effect creating further contrast. Add to this confusion various dominant lines of the various items, and you would have a complete lack of unity.

If the decorative item you start with is a piece of jewelry, your suit, shoes, belt, and stockings should be simple in texture, color, and line, though not necessarily the same. Shoes would not have eye-catching decorative stitching or bows. Gloves would not have elaborate design. The dress or suit should be simple in line and cut, without decorative trim or fancy buttons. These articles can and should be of good materials and have good structural lines that fit properly and pleasant textures that do not overshadow the basic decorative piece or the individual. Texture and line will be chosen to flatter the skin and the figure. Color will be chosen to highlight the decorative addition and to complement the hair and the skin.

If, on the other hand, you decide to start your co-ordination with a dress or suit that is becoming in color and flattering in line, you should first check necessary details such as fit and then add the necessary accessories. Color, texture, and line in accessories should be interesting in themselves but should not detract from the suit or dress. They should reinforce or accent the theme of the costume.

There are different approaches to planning an outfit. In the costume approach, the separate items are planned to complete one picture and are not meant to be worn with other items in the wardrobe. In the basic approach, the individual expects all of the items to be interchangeable between outfits. Most people use both approaches.

Since the costume look is not dependent upon the rest of the wardrobe, the costume is more likely to look complete and unified. With this method, there is more opportunity for unusual color, design, or silhouette. The woman who prefers a few well-chosen clothes may prefer the costume approach.

Choosing basic items to be worn with many outfits requires more time in planning the whole wardrobe. An item chosen this way too often looks like an item meant to go with everything but nothing in particular. With the basic approach, it is necessary that one become an expert in small accessories such as jewelry and scarves, in combining color and texture, and in ways of wearing clothes. It is most effectively done with simple background clothes that lend themselves to added decoration. As basic items must co-ordinate with other items in the wardrobe, it is easiest to have variety in design and color in accessories. When using the basic approach, you should start your co-ordinating with the larger items, keeping in mind the dual purpose of each article. In this way you can avoid overdressing or underdressing. Colors should be chosen to fit into various color backgrounds. Those who have a limited clothes budget may prefer neutral colors.

It is also possible to look too basic. One might, for example, use the basic approach for professional needs and the costume ap-

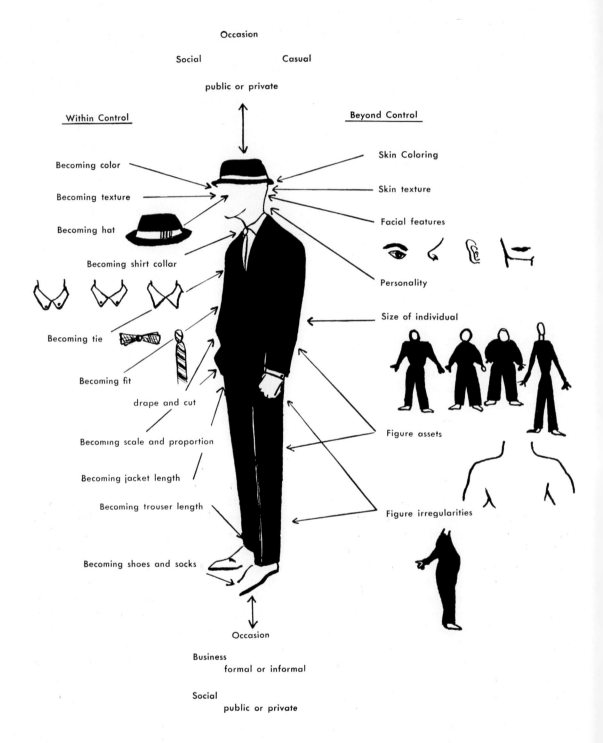

Occasion

Social   Casual

public or private

Within Control   Beyond Control

Becoming color →   ← Skin Coloring

Becoming texture →   ← Skin texture

Becoming hat   ← Facial features

Becoming shirt collar

Personality

Becoming tie

Size of individual

Becoming fit

drape and cut

Becoming scale and proportion

Figure assets

Becoming jacket length

Becoming trouser length

Figure irregularities

Becoming shoes and socks

Occasion

Business
      formal or informal

Social
      public or private

proach for evening dress. Many women co-ordinate business clothes as complete, individual outfits and use the basic approach in sports clothes.

CO-ORDINATING MEN'S CLOTHING

For purposes of co-ordination, men's clothing falls into the general categories of business, sport, leisure, and formal attire. The use of these terms, as has been noted, may vary from locality to locality. Business wear is not necessarily a suit; in many localities where dress has in general become more casual, sport coats and slacks may be worn to work. Men who have to commute often wear car coats. The kind of clothing will be determined by the occasion and the place.

As we have already noted, the person is the foundation of any outfit. A man, too, should consider his skin coloring as related to colors in clothing, the texture of his skin, his features, his over-all size, any figure irregularities or assets, and his personality. Unless he has an extensive wardrobe, he should generally start co-ordinating with a large item such as a suit or a jacket and slacks. In selecting this basic item, he will consider good fit, fabrics that are suitable to his stature, and colors and textures that are becoming to his skin first.

A man who is slight will probably choose fabrics that are a little thicker and heavier than most of the smooth-finished fabrics; he would not, however, go to the extreme of buying a very heavy, bulky fabric but would pick a fabric like a flannel or a light, rough-textured tweed that suited his build. In patterns he would avoid large plaids and checks. The fashion of the day will to some extent govern the drape of the suit, but soft padding may be added to correct figure irregularities such as a low shoulder. A fuller roll in the lapel will add girth to the chest. Whether the man is thin or heavy, he should always consider lines that are chosen for a natural, easy fit. The short or stocky man will avoid the double-breasted suit, the full drape, and too close a fit. A well-fitted suit, whether the wearer is tall, short, thin, or heavy, does more than anything else to create suitable lines.

A heavy man will choose dark-toned materials and fabrics without bulk. The straighter lines of the single-breasted suit, correctly fitted, will be more becoming than the full drape of the double-breasted. Any padding, like that to lift a low shoulder, must be very skillfully done. Lapels will be as narrow as the shoulder width will allow. Lapels that are too narrow may through contrast exaggerate heaviness. The fitting of the sleeves should allow adequate fullness to conceal heaviness in the arms. A smooth-hanging coat will help to decrease the apparent size of a large abdomen. Fabrics that have definite or dominant patterns such as plaids should be avoided. The man must then choose a necktie, shirt, and hose that complement the design of the suit and do not clash with each other.

A suit will generally give a dominance of color to the outfit. The necktie will be chosen as an accent to skin coloring and to direct the eye to the face. It must from necessity be a good choice to go with the shirt and the material of the suit. With a solid color suit, stripes, checks, prints, plaids, and textured ties can be worn. In most co-ordinating, it is wise to keep in mind that there should be only one dominant pattern in any outfit. However, a plaid suit, a striped shirt, and a printed tie is acceptable on some men if done without confusion of pattern. With a patterned fabric in suiting or in shirting, a good selection is a tie in a solid color. The color of the shirt may pick up the color of the suit or may be a contrast. When a striped shirt is worn, a small print in the tie is acceptable. However, it is important to remember that when two patterns are worn one pattern should have dominance over the other. With a solid-color suit and shirt, a wide variety in tie patterns can be worn. A plain tie with a solid-color suit or shirt may be monotonous unless there is a contrast in color or texture. Colored shirts, which are a fashion item from time to time, give a little more variety to the outfit and are very smart for those people who need a little color to flatter the skin. Shirts are also available in checks, stripes, and small dobby designs. In co-ordinating the total wardrobe, one may gain variety by having one suit in a plain fabric and another in a pattern. If the figure does not warrant even a muted tweed, variety in color is refreshing. Variety can also be obtained through different styles in shirt collars, patterned shirts, and different neckties.

As a general rule, black shoes are best with blues and dark grays. Brown shoes look well with brown and tan clothes. The hat will blend with the suit and may be in a neutral tone. A light gray hat might look very nice with blue, and so might a light tan. Much will depend on whether a man plans to have a hat for each suit. If a hat has to go with several colors, it is wise to experiment with colors that would look well with both the suits and the topcoats in the wardrobe.

A short or slight person should consider carefully before buying a hat that is darker than his suit or topcoat. The feeling of weight should be scaled to the proportions of the person. In general, light over dark has a greater tendency to carry the eye upward than dark over light. The overcoat or topcoat will generally be of a neutral shade, look well with several suits, and be becoming to the wearer. Some men like the dashing black chesterfield for dressy city wear. The coat with raglan sleeves, a more casual style, is quite popular.

Belts, if worn, are generally chosen to match the shoes or to blend with the other colors in the outfit. Most tailors feel that trousers hang better when worn with suspenders.

There should be some consistency in the kinds of textures used. One would not wear a delicate tie with a heavy tweed or a bulky tie with a thin, lightweight suit. If contrast is used, careful consideration must be given to the degree of interest found in the color and the pattern. Wool, knitted, and plaid ties in rough textures will generally go with the heavier suit fabrics. The texture of all ties should be suitable and flattering to the texture of the skin. Heavy knit hose go best with the heavier suit fabrics. Socks are generally chosen to be as inconspicuous as possible. Knee length stockings give a neat and trim appearance.

Chapter 7

Do you wear clothes well?

Just as the selection of clothes requires thought and deliberation, the proper way of wearing them needs more attention than some people give it. One of the secrets of smartness in dress is the way a man or woman wears clothes. Often the well-put-together look can do more than money for one's appearance. We all wear clothes, but it is what we wear and how we wear it that makes the difference. You may be one of those people who think that everyone knows how to put on his clothes and that it is only the selection that presents any great difficulty. You may not have observed that the stunning appearance of a person can be lost just by the poor way he wears an outfit. Fashion affects ways of wearing, and a new way is often more flattering than the old; the single lapel pin is replaced by several scatter pins, long necklaces follow chokers, or several bracelets on one arm become more fashionable than one on each arm. All of the following topics are discussed in detail elsewhere; the main emphasis here is on the way apparel is worn.

POSTURE

Since posture has already been analyzed, the consideration here is the realization that posture has a great deal to do with the way your clothes look on you. If your body slumps, sags, or protrudes where nature did not intend, the best-selected garment in your wardrobe cannot do you justice.

From a careful study of your physical self with the aid of a silhouette and a full-length mirror, become familiar with your own posture. Good body alignment is most important to your appearance and to the way your clothes look on your figure. As you already know, the features of good standing posture are head erect, neck straight, shoulders back and down, rib-cage lifted, back flat and straight, derrière tucked under, knees relaxed. If you maintain good posture, you will feel better, look better, and wear your clothes with confidence.

WOMEN'S WEAR

Underwear

With your posture aligned and your figure in good shape, a little undercover help in the way of proper, well-fitted foundation garments will act both as a reminder and as a restraining influence. For some young women, bra and panties or will-o'-the-wisp shapers may be sufficient. However, these privileged few might take a good look in a full-length mirror before putting on a pencil-slim skirt or tight stretch pants. No matter how slim or how perfect your figure, appropriate undergarments are important to a trim appearance and an attractive carriage. For some women, a garter belt or a brief, feather-weight girdle that smooths and molds gently without confining may be adequate. A firmer girdle may be necessary to give others those extra-smooth body lines. An all-in-one foundation garment

Do you look like this?

that is lightweight and flexible will help control pouches, spare tires, and wagging derrières until the good habits of posture, exercise, and diet are formed. Seek professional aid for proper fit.

It is always important to wear a length of underwear which is compatable with the outerwear. A panty girdle that shows below the length of a thigh length skirt or a jump suit is unattractive.

Correctly chosen undergarments should be put on properly and worn as they were designed to be in order to do justice to the outer clothing. The appropriate choice of bra for the kind of outfit to be worn is also important, like the long-line bra for the bodice that fits snugly from bustline to waistline. A bra should be worn with the lower edge parallel to the waistline instead of dropping in front and riding up on the shoulders in back. If a body stocking does not give adaquate support, a nude bra under it should create a moulded appearance at the bustline. A girdle should be pulled on far enough to lie flat at the waistline; it should be pulled down on the thighs and worn straight rather than at an angle.

These undergarments should be put on so they stay in place, to eliminate constant adjusting—a common habit with many American women.

The way slips and petticoats are worn should be carefully considered. You might check to see that the slip or petticoat is the correct length for the dress or skirt under which it is worn. Not only should a slip not be so long that it shows below a skirt, it should not be so short that it ends above the double thickness of the hem. Such space between a short slip and the top of a skirt hem allows light to show through the outside fabric. A slip with a very wide lace band deeper than the hem of a dress gives the same effect as a too-short slip.

Wearing the appropriate color slip with each outfit is important. For instance, a black or dark blue slip worn under black or other dark-colored clothes provides more opaqueness than a white or a light-colored one. Also a dark slip that is too long is not

Ways of wearing foundation garments.

quite so conspicuous as a white one showing below a skirt.

Care should be taken when choosing a slip or petticoat to wear under sheer outerwear. A petticoat with several layers of fabric or a slip with an effective shadowproof panel should be worn under thin dresses. A slip should cover the bra enough so that only the lines of the slip are visible through a sheer dress or blouse. Some lace and eyelet dresses are made with natural-color net lining and straps so that there is no contrasting lingerie visible. A close-up view in a mirror plus a see-through test in bright sunlight or artificial light will help you to decide what lingerie to wear with each outfit. Petticulottes, pant-liners, and

Reflections.

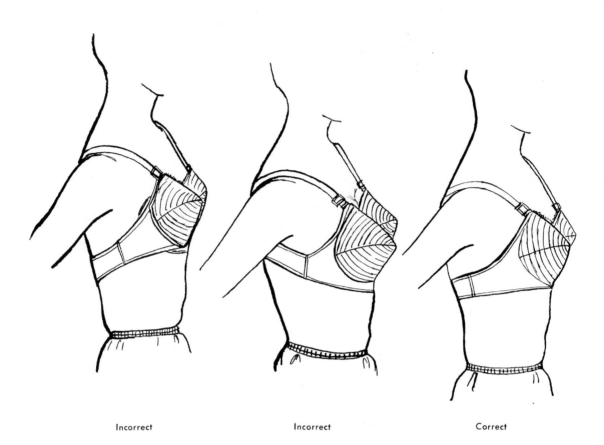

| Incorrect | Incorrect | Correct |

Ways of wearing brassières.

panti-slips provide other choices. Keep in mind the effect of static electricity on slips and outerwear. Some people find it impossible to wear a nylon or Dacron slip with a silk or wool dress because of the clinging and creeping of the fabrics. It is wise to discover this before appearing in public.

Hosiery

Even though correct size and length were selected originally, careful fastening of stockings is still very important to help prevent crooked seams of full-fashioned hosiery and wrinkles at the ankles or bags at the calf of seamless hosiery. To insure proper fit and appearance, circular knit hosiery should be pulled on straight and snug. Textured hose with definite patterns should be put on with care so that the designs are straight with the leg.

Fitted body hose may be a flattering choice if a person does not wear a gartered girdle under a tight, straight skirt or culottes. Heavy patterned or colored knee socks or tights are appropriate with short casual outfits.

If you want to maintain a well-groomed look throughout the day, you should check your stockings every now and then—but do it privately, not in front of a store window. Activities like driving or riding in a car, crossing and uncrossing your legs, or wearing a straight skirt tend to cause stockings to shift in spite of care in selecting and putting on hosiery. If you drive or travel a great deal, seamless hose without patterns may be a wise choice.

Outerwear

After you have checked the way you wear your underthings, turn your attention to your outer garments. Try to wear your dress, suit, coat, or whatever in the most flattering and comfortable way. Shoulder pads are a fashion detail; they come and go. If there are pads in your clothes, make sure they are in the proper place, flat, and balanced on the shoulders. A folded or bunched pad or one that has moved down

A poor way of wearing—awkward in public.

the sleeve length detracts from the smooth appearance of the shoulder line. Additional fastening is occasionally necessary.

A small detail, ignored by some people, is shoulder straps of underwear showing at the neckline or on the arm. Conspicuous straps plus the awkward probe for them detract from even the most flattering outfit. Lingerie tapes or guards on the shoulder seams not only hold straps in place but control necklines that do not stay in position.

The use of stays adds to the wear-rightness of some pieces of clothing. For instance, stay-tapes on a wrap-around skirt hold the overlap in place when the wearer is walking or sitting. Tapes on the seams of a jersey blouse that pulls over the shoulders prevent stretching and straining of the neck-

Good and poor fit in a full-length foundation.

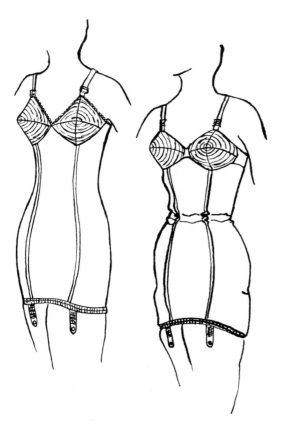

Your slip can show without being too long.

really informative, it has no further value to the wearer. Stuffed pockets are unsightly and detract from the beauty and fit of coat, suit, dress, or separates.

All facings at necklines, armholes, and sleeves should be tucked in, smooth and flat. If your collar does not roll as it should or fit snugly to the neck, put your hand under and roll the collar, and at the same time pull the whole garment up from the back so that it rests squarely and does not pull away from the neck and shoulders.

Both cuffs should be turned up on the sleeves and the belt should be the proper length, so that no extra length flaps around or requires pinning. All fastenings such as buttons, snaps, and hooks and eyes should be securely anchored.

Fit and wearing

If you have chosen correctly fitted apparel, you should be able to put a garment

line. If stays or "anchors" on a blouse can be fastened to a skirt, they will hold the blouse inside the skirt. Another way to keep a tuck-in blouse in place is to use a strip of nylon cockleburr hooks on the blouse and a matching strip of loops on the skirt band.

Minor alterations and improvements on a new dress can often add chic to an inexpensive garment. The hem should be level. Removing or changing buttons or ornamental detail may improve the appearance. The dress should be checked for split seams, loose buttons, and gaping.

If the label shows through the back of a garment or always flips over the edge of the collar, it should be removed. Unless it is

Check your hose!

The view *you* never see.

on with ease, place it in correct position, fasten it, and then relax and be comfortable.

Since hemlines do not always remain even, it is wise to check them regularly, especially on a bias-cut skirt. While checking hemlines, note whether dresses, skirts, or suits show below the hem of your coat. Hems of other clothes seldom should show below a full-length coat.

Make sure that the lining of your suit jacket or coat has not stretched enough to show below the hemline. Jackets or coats designed without buttons or other fastenings should be put on with care so that the two front edges fall evenly at the hemline.

All clothes designed to fit close to the neckline should be pulled up and forward at the neckline and shoulders. Whenever stand-away collars and necklines are fash-

ionable, care should be taken to adjust the garment on the shoulders.

Blouses and shirts

The way blouses are worn with suits, skirts, shorts, or slacks is not considered carefully by some people. For instance, if a suit has a collar and lapels, a collarless blouse may look better than one with a collar that refuses to stay flat and in place.

The tuck-in type of blouse should be long enough to stay inside the skirt and provide a flat, smooth fit at the waistline instead of a blousing roll or a half-inside, half-outside effect. This problem is eliminated if an overblouse or blouse slip is worn or if stays or other controls are used.

Nearly all suits are designed to be worn

Do you wear clothes well?   129

Lumpy shoulder
padding

Poorly placed
shoulder padding

Well-balanced
shoulder padding

with the jacket on. A suit skirt and blouse without the jacket seldom present a co-ordinated appearance, especially if the blouse tails are showing and one or more buttons down the back have been not buttoned. Of course, there are skirts and blouses which look well together, but these are usually designed as separates to be worn either with or without a jacket. The person who insists on removing her suit jacket should wear a belt to tie the skirt and blouse together or an overblouse. If the problem of co-ordinating a blouse and suit cannot be solved, wear the suit without a blouse.

In addition to the design, the fabric of the blouse can add to or detract from your appearance. Very sheer fabrics reveal lingerie as well as bony necks, moles, freckles, or rolls of avoirdupois. Whenever sheerness is fashionable, check yourself and your lingerie before wearing transparent garments.

Details
The grace with which you wear your

Shoulder straps should not be seen.

These labels serve no purpose.

Details are important.

accessories adds so much to your attractiveness. For instance, if you wear a scarf to add that essential spot of color or texture, try not to destroy the desired effect by the way you wear it. Drape, tie, knot, or pin a scarf; or try one of the scarves shaped to the neck so that it stays where you put it and you will forget you have one on. Other people find it annoying when you fidget with your accessories all the time. Try new and different ways to wear scarves; avoid always looking as though you were nursing a sore throat. Here again, fashion provides ideas with which to experiment. The way you drape a stole, whether it is fabric or mink, can also lend an individual flair to your appearance. The way varies with the individual; notice what models do in fashion shows and magazines, then develop a method of your own.

Jewelry can be worn very effectively if various ways of wearing it are considered. A pin may be worn on the collar, shoulder, sleeve, pocket, or purse. Beautiful, well-chosen jewelry can also lose its effectiveness through the way it is worn. Too much matching jewelry on one outfit becomes monotonous and loses its appeal. When,

Check your hemline!

where, and how much jewelry is worn depends upon the outfit, the effect desired, the occasion, and personal preference. Experimentation with lengths of necklaces, sizes of earrings, and numbers of bracelets is helpful.

Shoes

Shoes that fit correctly and are in good repair must be worn properly to look well and feel comfortable. Once on, your shoes should be left on until it is time to remove them. Avoid dangling or swinging your shoes while sitting or standing. It is not

good for your shoes or your appearance to take a one-foot-on-the-other stance, to roll on the sides of your feet, or to stand with one foot out.

It is embarrassing to try to find shoes you have removed under a table, chair, or desk. If your shoes hurt your feet and you feel you must remove them, your original selection may have been poor. Shoes are to be worn once they are put on and should not be removed except in privacy.

Hats

A hat, often as much a part of an outfit as shoes, should be worn properly to do justice

Do you wear these?

to the hat and the wearer. If you have made a good selection (see the chapter on millinery), you should not have to clutch your hat at the slightest puff of wind. There are combs and pins for anchoring hats. A hat that stays on and is correctly anchored, worn at the appropriate angle, and flattering can be your crown and worn with the aplomb of royalty. Few people can carry a hat effectively in the hand; hats should either be worn or left at home.

Handbags

A handbag is an accessory to be carried comfortably, gracefully, and conveniently. Your bag should be organized so that you can carry the necessities without stretching the bag to its, limit and so that you can easily find what you want without a frantic search. Purse organizers with various compartments are useful aids. An occasional cleaning of the bag and discarding unnecessary items reduces bulk and bulging.

A shoulder bag is a good selection when both hands are needed in shopping, traveling, carrying extras, and holding children's hands. Avoid swinging and twirling a bag. It is a mark of grace and poise to carry a handbag inconspicuously.

Gloves

Gloves are either to be worn or to be put in your handbag, not to be carried. Wear

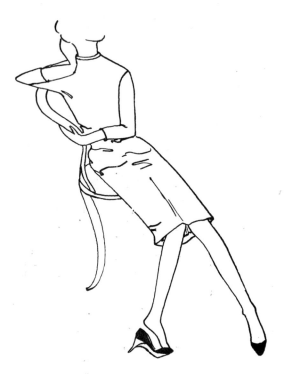

Sit up!

them until it becomes awkward or inconvenient, and then remove them and place them in your bag.

If you carry gloves, you tend to handle them too much, crush and twist them, or drop one or both and make yourself conspicuous in retrieving them. Gloves complete an outfit when worn but look like an afterthought when carried.

Miscellaneous

Little things like handkerchiefs, corsages, and artificial flowers are important. The use of many of these small items varies with changes in fashion. A handkerchief, besides being useful, is sometimes decorative, and never should be crushed, twisted, or mussed into a sodden rag. It should be carried in your purse or pocket or protruding perkily from a handkerchief pocket, as

fashion decrees. Avoid tucking a handkerchief up your sleeve, inside your neckline, or under your belt.

Flowers, artificial or real, are a lovely accent when worn correctly and appropriately. They should be fastened securely so that they do not flop, slide, or droop. Try wearing flowers in different places and check the effect before a mirror. Wear them high on the shoulder, at the waistline, on the wrist, or on your purse. Some hair styles lend themselves well to flowers. The occasion and your costume should determine the way you wear flowers. At a luncheon, for instance, you might wear your corsage at the shoulder so that it would be visible at

Watch your stance.

the table. At a ball, you could wear flowers on your left wrist or at the back waistline to avoid crushing them.

Occasionally, artificial flowers are worn at the base of the neck on high necklines. Flowers are seldom attractive at the point of a V-shape or other deep neckline; flowers there tend to give the impression that you are trying to cover up too much exposure. Flowers should be worn with the stem down and the blossom up, as they originally grew.

Motions

A person's movements and activities, gracefulness, speed of movement, and body positions may make clothes look quite different on the person than they looked on the store dummy. It is advisable to check your appearance when sitting, standing, walking, or driving a car to see that the original effect has not been changed. If you stand with one foot slightly ahead of the other, your stance is not only graceful and comfortable but your clothes look well, too.

A sheath skirt or dress may look well when you stand but may pull, bind, and creep to mid-thigh or higher when you sit. When you sit down, try to avoid the awkward motion of smoothing your skirt to eliminate wrinkles while sitting. It is better to sit down easily, with a minimum of motion, and then gradually and inconspicuously ease your skirt out at the sides. You might check your sitting position from a front view and note your leg position and the way straight skirts and full skirts look on you. When a woman crosses her knees, she usually displays inches of hose or bare thigh, touches of lingerie, and the calf of one leg flattened against the other leg. Awkward sitting positions—knees spread far apart, feet twisted around chair rungs, sitting on one foot, or swinging one leg—

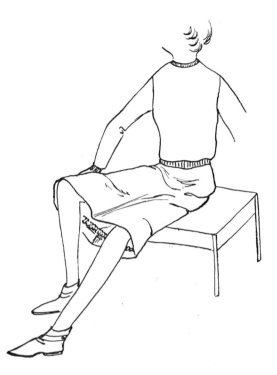

Position counts.

do nothing for a woman's appearance. Rising from or sitting down in a chair should be a graceful motion. The average woman's entrance into or exit from a car of any kind is an extremely clumsy and often embarrassing maneuver. Instead of climbing in, it is better to sit on the end of the seat and slowly pivot the body as you swing both legs in and toward the front. In reverse, this procedure is a graceful way out.

The way you walk is important. It has been said that a person's walk is indicative of age—children toe in; youth points its feet straight ahead; old age toes out. The height of the heels on a woman's shoes influences her walking movements. Mincing steps, a long stride, deliberate and heavy steps, and swinging arms are char-

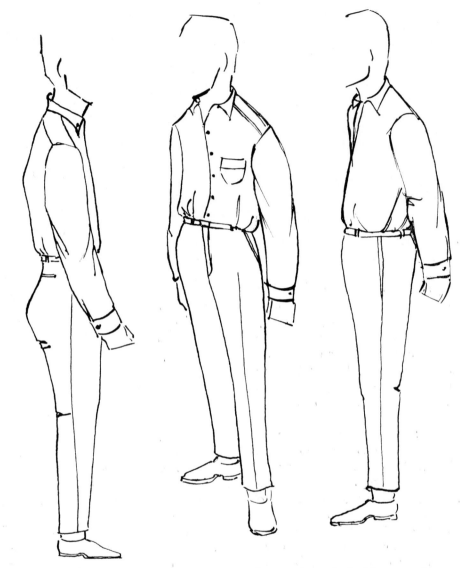

Posture counts for men, too.

acteristic motions affecting appearance. A graceful swing from the hips is usually more flattering than a jack-knife knee walk, especially in a straight skirt.

Grooming

Good health; graceful posture; cleanliness of body, hair, and clothes; neatness of hair style and clothing; good manners; and a friendly smile are essential to an attractive appearance.

Flawless make-up, neatly groomed nails, a dainty and fresh body, a subtle perfume —all should be part of your grooming for the public.

Public manners

A woman who wears her clothes well will

not want to detract from her appearance by forgetting the social graces that are so much a part of the over-all impression she makes on others.

Distracting gestures and other habits can destroy the harmony of her whole appearance. Among these are biting her nails, combing her hair with her hands, removing lipstick smeared at the corners of the mouth, running her tongue over her teeth, wiping rather than blotting perspiration from her face, twisting a strand of hair, chewing gum or the end of a pencil or her eyeglasses, "talking" excessively with her hands, raising her voice when angry, yawning in the presence of others; interrupting someone who is speaking; displaying unsightly smoking mannerisms.

She should take time to find the discordant notes that may be spoiling her appearance, and correct them. However, a person should retain the charming gestures that distinguish and add attractiveness.

To maintain a good public appearance, a woman should avoid performing personal grooming chores in public. It is also in poor taste to wear hair in rollers, open sandals with dirty feet, or slacks or shorts when in museums, government buildings, and other cultural areas.

MEN'S WEAR

Many of the suggestions on ways of wearing clothes apply to men as well as to women. The man who looks better will generally do better in his public life. Many men have gained satisfaction and confidence through dress.

Although college men need not be fashion plates, they should realize that one measure of a college man is his appearance, and that what he wears and how he wears it is as important on campus as anywhere else.

Posture

A forward head, stooped shoulders, a flat chest, and a prominent abdomen are a poor foundation for good-looking, well-chosen clothes. Men who are interested in making a good appearance might check their posture before a full-length mirror to see whether exercise, diet, and determination should not perhaps be considered.

Following this physical inspection, a man should turn his attention to the ways of wearing the clothes he has chosen—or the woman in his life has chosen for him. Correct dress is often a matter of exacting detail in ways of wearing.

Underwear

The undershirt or T-shirt should be tucked into the shorts, and both it and the shorts should stay in place. The elastic waistband on shorts helps in this respect. Should a man need control for a prominent pouch, he might be wise to wear shorts that provide a wide elastic support at the front waistline.

Socks

It is generally agreed that hose that stay up instead of rolling down sloppily over

the tops of the shoes are an indication of good grooming. This is achieved by methods varying from the wearing of very short socks, socks with elasticized tops, and knee-length socks to the use of garters. Whatever the method used, socks should be smooth and neat, since they are usually exposed when a man is sitting. It is also important to wear socks properly with walking shorts or other casual or sports clothing.

Shirts

Men's shirts, if correctly fitted, should be no problem. They should be kept smooth and securely tucked inside the trousers unless designed to be worn outside. A tapered shirt of adequate length usually stays inside the trousers.

The points of the shirt collar should stay down; buttons, stays, and collar pins help keep collar points in place. Very sheer shirts, whether they are worn with or without an undershirt or T-shirt, do little for a man's appearance.

Suits

When a man puts on a suit, he should make sure that the slide fastener on the trousers is completely closed and locked and that the trousers are held in place at the waistline. The waistline of the trousers should come above rather than below a protruding abdomen. Trousers that look too short or too long are often merely carelessly adjusted. If they are worn too low on the hips—intentionally or because of loose adjustment of belt or suspenders—they will appear much too long. If hitched up too high, they will seem too short.

The suit coat should be put on so that it is square on the shoulders and snug at the neckline, with the collar a half inch below the shirt collar at the back. Sleeve lengths should be checked to be sure that the sleeves of the coat are half an inch shorter than the shirt sleeves.

The way the suit coat or jacket is buttoned varies with the individual. Whenever the double-breasted suit is fashionable, the common practice is to wear the coat completely buttoned except when sitting; then

A good shirt looks well only if properly worn.

138

The Battle of the Bulge.

Sleeve length deserves attention, too.

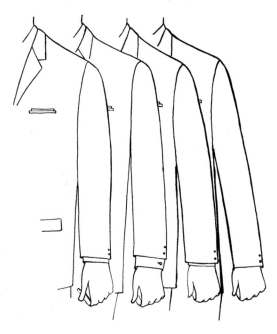

the lower button may be unbuttoned. With the single-breasted suit, the coat may be worn unbuttoned if a vest or a weskit is worn underneath. With a coat that has a two-button front, the top button is usually buttoned; with a three-button jacket, either the second button or both the first and second buttons are buttoned. This difference in buttoning depends upon the type and style of the coat and on regional fashions. Since topcoats or overcoats are usually worn for extra warmth, they are worn buttoned all the way. When the wearer is sitting, however, the lower button may be unbuttoned.

Ties

A man's tie is often the most noticeable item in his whole outfit. It should be tied securely and fastened with a tie clip, tie chain, tie tack, or button so that it will stay in place. A tie clip is usually worn below the V-zone of the suit coat.

A bow tie should be carefully tied and worn straight and even so that it does not twist or slide out of position. A crooked bow tie, a twisted long tie pulled off center, or a sloppy ascot can spoil an otherwise impeccable appearance. Men should avoid pulling at their ties and collars as though they were choking. With a properly fitting shirt and a carefully knotted tie, there should be no binding at the neckline.

To look right, neckwear must fit.

Shoes

Many men might pay more attention to the proper way of wearing shoes. Each campus "culture" includes apparel—and shoes are included in that category. Campus fashions in footwear are often objectionable elsewhere. Leather shoes that are kept clean, shined, and in good repair are more indicative of good grooming than dirty bucks or threadbare sneakers. Metal clips may protect the lifts on heels, but the noise they make when men drag or clank their heels may be very annoying to others. Loafers, moccasins, and sandals should be properly fitted and worn correctly so that the toes do not slip over the sides or the heels work over the edges, beating down the shoes at the heel. Improperly worn footwear is not only unsightly but uncomfortable.

Hats

The attitude of many men toward hats is like that of many young women. Many young men do not like hats and will not wear—and usually do not even own—a hat. Knowing that hats are as much a part of the well-dressed man's wardrobe as other fur-

A hat should be worn at the proper angle.

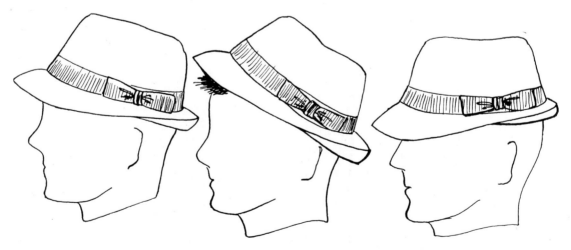

The importance of minor details.

nishings and that hats are becoming when carefully chosen, many of them might learn how to choose and wear hats.

A man should wear his hat with a flair that indicates his pride in his appearance. To be effectively worn, a hat must always be clean, brushed, and in its original shape. It should be put on and then forgotten until the time comes to remove it. The man who lifts and adjusts his hat constantly gives the impression that either the hat makes his head ache or he is nervous and ill at ease. Details on selecting and putting on hats are discussed in the chapter on millinery.

Jewelry

Details—jewelry, handkerchiefs, scarves, mufflers, and gloves, for instance, and the way he wears them—are important to a man's appearance. Jewelry can be worn with distinction when worn with the right outfit and not in excess. Tie clasp, cuff links, studs, ring—all help to complete an outfit, but the wearer should forget about them once they are in place. A man who constantly adjusts his tie clasp, twists his ring, or fidgets with his cuff links can be distracting.

Handkerchiefs

While some men do not use decorative handkerchiefs, others have individual and distinctive ways of wearing them. A handkerchief may be folded square and placed in the breast pocket or it may be folded so that two or more points protrude above the edge of the pocket. Fashion influences the placement and the folding of the decorative handkerchief. When one handkerchief is worn as decorative detail, another should be easily accessible for practical use. If a man insists on carrying this second handkerchief in his back hip pocket, he ought to tuck it out of sight and not let it cascade over the edge.

Gloves

Gloves are worn for warmth, for comfort, and because certain formal occasions demand them. When not being worn, gloves should be placed in a pocket large enough to hold them or inside the hat if it is removed.

Scarves

A scarf or muffler worn with a topcoat or overcoat should be carefully placed around the neck so that it does not protrude in front but lies flat and smooth and extends about one half inch above the collar line in back.

Pockets

Some men stuff their pockets until they bulge; pens, pencils, and cigars in the breast pocket of a jacket make the front view look a little crowded. Might not some of these items be put in an inside pocket?

A thick billfold—plus the miscellaneous items usually carried in trouser pockets—can also add unsightly bulges. A flat money case and a cigarette case carried in an inside coat pocket can relieve the strain on the back hip pockets of many a pair of trousers. Other objects men consider necessary should be distributed as evenly as possible between the various pockets in the trousers and the coat or jacket. Some men stretch and tear their trouser pockets by keeping their hands inside them.

Motions

Men might check the effect of the movements, activities, and body positions on their appearance. The constant raising of trousers that slip below the normal waistline is an unsightly but very common gesture. A man's suit coat or jacket may look just fine when he is standing but push up at the neckline, bulge at the waistline, or wrinkle at the armscye when he sits down. A man will improve both his com-

These are common mistakes.

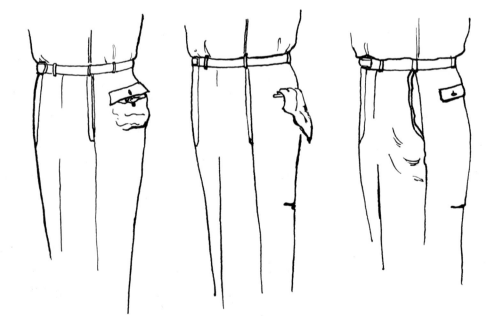

142

fort and his appearance if he unbuttons his coat when he sits. When he sits down, he should just sit down and then gradually pull up his trouser legs so that they will not stretch at the knees. This way, sitting down is easy and natural rather than a demonstration.

Most men tend to cross their legs at the knees, and the amount of sock or bare leg exposed varies with the distance the trousers creep up on the leg. Careful selection improves this particular view of the sitting man.

Grooming

People see the back of a man's neck every time he turns around—frequent haircuts are a necessity for the man who wears short hair. A moustache, beard, and long hair require careful shaping and trimming. Cologne, after-shave lotions, and deodorants with a "manly" fragrance are a part of men's good grooming.

"WEAR WITH ALL"

What boys say about a girl's appearance and the converse might be worth noting by both sexes. Do they like the current fad on you?—the pierced ears; the beard, the moustache, the long hair?

The well-put-together look does a great deal for the appearance of both men and women. In present-day society everyone wears clothes—the difference lies in what clothes and how. The expression of good taste does not require a huge clothing budget. You can look smart even on a small budget if your clothes have been carefully chosen, if they are well co-ordinated, and if you wear them in the most comfortable and flattering way.

Anything worthwhile takes time, and time you devote to making the most of what you have is well spent. A good appearance pays off—in self-assurance and in the priceless elation of knowing that you look your best.

REFERENCE READINGS

Archer, Elsie, *Let's Face It*, Rev. J. B. Lippincott Co., Philadelphia, 1968.

Bacharach, Bert, *Book for Men*, A. S. Barnes & Co., New York, 1953.

Bacharach, Bert, *Right Dress*, A. S. Barnes & Co., New York, 1955.

Broadbent, Adah, *Teen-Age Glamour*, Doubleday & Co., Inc., New York, 1955.

Colby, Anita, *Anita Colby's Beauty Book*, Prentice-Hall, Inc., New York, 1952.

Daché, Lilly, *Glamour Book*, J. B. Lippincott Co., Philadelphia, 1956.

Dariaux, Genevieve Antoine, *Elegance*, Doubleday & Co., Inc., New York, 1964.

Erwin, Mabel D., Kinchen, Lila A., *Clothing for Moderns*, 3rd ed. The Macmillan Co., New York, 1966.

Fogarty, Anne, *Wife Dressing*, Julian Messner, Inc., New York, 1959.

Harper's Bazaar, *Beauty Book*, Appleton-Century-Crofts, Inc., New York, 1959.

Hillhouse, Marion S., *Dress Selection and Design*, The Macmillan Co., New York, 1963.

Jones, Candy, *Finishing Touches*, Harper & Brothers, New York, 1961.

Jones, Candy, *Look Your Best*, Harper & Brothers, New York, 1964.

McCardell, Claire, *What Shall I Wear?*, Simon and Schuster, Inc., New York, 1956.

McJimsey, Harriet T., *Art in Clothing Selection*, Harper & Row, New York, 1963.

McLeod, Edyth Thornton, *Lady Be Lovely*, Wilcox & Follett Co., New York, 1955.

Powers, John Robert, *How to Have Model Beauty, Poise, Personality*, Prentice-Hall, Englewood Cliffs, 1960.

Ryan, Mildred Graves, *Dress Smartly*, Charles Scribner's Sons, New York, 1956.

Stote, Dorothy, *Men Too Wear Clothes*, J. B. Lippincott Co., Philadelphia, 1950.

Stratton, Dorothy C. and Schleman, Helen B., *Your Best Foot Forward*, McGraw-Hill Book Co., Inc., New York, 1955.

Part Two

SO YOU HAVEN'T
A THING
TO WEAR

Chapter 8

What do you have?

Few people ever buy a complete new wardrobe; they can neither afford to nor do they wish to. The best-dressed people are collectors at heart—collectors of good clothing. It takes time to build a good wardrobe; one does not just go out and start over but attempts to look well groomed and dressed at all times. Frequently, after analyzing the figure and thinking in terms of color, line, and fabrics, we may think everything we have is wrong. It would be a great mistake and a waste of time and money to remedy this by buying all new clothes at one time.

WHAT ARE YOUR RESOURCES?

It is doubtful that many people discard clothes because they are worn out. Frequently, clothes are discarded because they no longer fit, appeal, or appear out-dated. As you have been developing a philosophy of clothing, you have, hopefully, been expanding your knowledge of what being well dressed means to you. *Knowledge* is one of your greatest resources. The more

you know about yourself, your values and needs, the sooner you will have control over the way you dress. As you develop, you will learn more about design and quality in clothing. Your knowledge of fabric, care, and fitting of clothing will allow for more effective buying. *Physical assets* such as a good figure and clear skin are resources not to be overlooked. The *skills* you have developed also increase your effectiveness. The individual who can perform some of his own services has increased his ability to meet a need. *Services* available are also important resources. A knowledgeable dry cleaner can keep a garment in good condition; a poor dry cleaner can ruin a new garment. For those who have little time to spend, good services are a valuable resource. *Time* is also an asset. The individual who can do some services for himself is not dependent on others. The kind and amount of equipment in the home may eliminate hours spent in care of clothing.

Before you proceed with planning for future needs, it would be well to take an honest look at what you have to start with in clothing. Everything you have should be wearable or should probably be discarded. Clothes take a great deal of handling—and it may be extravagant to keep items which you do not wear since they demand much of that valuable resource, *time*. Last but not least, of course, is the money you have to spend.

TAKING STOCK

Good wardrobes are built slowly and thoughtfully. Most people would be surprised at the large stock of clothing they have on hand. Make a game of checking what you now have in your wardrobe. A good time might be when you are going to clean your closet or drawers or when you are thinking of mending or repairing clothing. The beginning of a new season is one

147

time we are likely to be thinking about what we would like in clothing. Or perhaps a better time would be when you feel that you have nothing to wear. Whenever you decide to do it, look critically at all you have—from foundation garments and hosiery to coats, dresses, and suits. If you do not have the time to take everything out and look at it at one time, as many people feel is the only way, you might do it as you dress each day for various occasions.

Before you start, look through fashion magazines and newspapers or, perhaps, at store windows. This will give you not only new ideas but some indication of what will be available when you later wish to buy. Note hem lengths, sleeves, the kinds of fabrics being used, color combinations, the way clothes are fitted, priced, and the way it is being worn. All of these points will have fashion timeliness, and many ideas can be gleaned from a glance through a magazine. You may be surprised to see styles you already have in your wardrobe now being worn in a different way. You may find a new color combination or a different way of wearing jewelry.

As you look at your clothes, you will be looking for improvements and, maybe even more important, you will be noting for future buying certain factors that you like or dislike about articles you already have. You are looking to see what place these clothes have in your life, how long you can expect service from these same articles, what care and how much storage space they require, when replacements will be needed, and what alterations or repairs must be made for the coming season. As you put on an outfit, think in terms of where and for what occasions you will wear it. In other words, what place does it have in your total wardrobe? Put on the various articles, try them with different scarves or jewelry, and you may find that you have just the right outfit. Keep in mind the fashion trends and adopt those which you think suit your life and personality. If you are dissatisfied with an article, take a good look at the various factors which make up a satisfactory outfit. Is the color at the neck becoming? Does the dress need a little fitting? Is the hem straight? What condition is the fabric in? How long do you think you will be able to wear it? And what alterations or repairs are needed?

Make a mental note of—or, if you are a list maker, jot down—the replacements needed to complete the outfit. If you do not like or wear an article, try to determine the reason. Perhaps it requires more time in care than you can allow. Any article of clothing that is not being worn frequently is not only taking up storage space, which is usually scarce, but may be out of date before it has served its purpose.

The way you check and evaluate your present wardrobe is an individual procedure. The family might make a habit of discussing what is going to be needed and checking over the various things in individual wardrobes. Parents should listen to children and consider their ideas, for they may have been thinking of a child's needs in an adult manner. People who are extremely well organized might even have a master list of things that are bought every year, listing particularly satisfactory brands and where they are available. It is important, however, if you do keep a master list, to re-evaluate it carefully each season, before doing any buying. Remember that your needs may change in a year's time.

EXPERIMENTATION

Since appearance is foremost in the minds of most people, a good look at the factors that contribute to a pleasing appearance might be your first step. If the garment you are checking is in a color you like very much, does it express you as a person? What mood has the color created?

Is it really one of your most becoming colors? If you are fashion-conscious about color—you might feel that color is not a fashion item you are going to follow—are you wearing this color in fashionable combinations and good proportions? If not, what changes might you make? Maybe the color at the neck is not becoming, and a change of shirt or scarf might make it just right. This is where experimenting is most important. Try a combination you have not considered before. Take out all your accessories and experiment with just color in mind. Also think in terms of the relationships of colors in the total wardrobe.

Next, note the textures you have found particularly pleasing and becoming. Think as you did with color. Were they suitable when you wore them? Was the fabric too warm? Did it scratch or otherwise interfere with comfort? If one of your favorite dresses is in a texture which scratches, it might be worth the expense of having it lined. Or perhaps you have a knit which needs the staying qualities of a firmer fabric than is usually found in a regular slip. For future use, you might jot down the textures that looked well on you, were comfortable, and that you found particularly pleasing.

Note the lines in the dress or suit and the way they direct your eye. It might be that a change of buttons would be an improvement in guiding the eye in a certain direction. Check the outline of the body. Does the outfit make your figure appear as you would like it to look? Pay special attention to the areas which, in your analysis, you decided needed improvement. Have you perhaps put an eye-catching color at some point you do not wish to emphasize or does some line direct the eye toward rather than away from some less attractive feature? Note hem lengths, the sleeve length, the way trousers break over the ankle, and the size of collars or lapels. Are these as you

would like them to be? Some of these points will have fashion timeliness, others may be all right and need just a little correction in construction, such as straightening a hem.

In order to understand your fitting needs, you might try experimenting first with clothes you already have in your wardrobe. Observe the success or lack of success of these garments in relation to the factors we discussed in the chapter on fitting. First, look for the fabric grain and its direction. Try to capture the designer's idea for the design and the silhouette. Note how the garment is cut. Are the seams falling at the right places on the body? Look at both the front and the side views. Is the hang right? Is the garment balanced on the figure? Hold the waistline seams slightly on one side and see what happens to the hang of the skirt or the trousers. See whether you can raise your arms and move them back and forth. Check all your movements and think of the purpose of the item you are trying on. Are the darts directed towards the full part of the body? Bend the arms in every direction. Is there action where needed? If the material is a plaid, are the plaids matching?

Move again and note what happens when the body moves. Sit in front of a mirror. Move naturally, observing any wrinkles or binding. Hold some of the fabric snug against the body and see how much ease there is. Check for fashion rightness in the fit of the article. Is this the amount of ease currently being shown? Is this the way designers are currently handling fabric?

This kind of observation and thinking will help you when you go to buy new outfits. Note what you liked in other outfits and avoid the errors in clothing you found unsatisfactory. If you have figure irregularities, allow for the cost of alterations when planning your clothes budget.

CLOTHES FOR WHAT

After checking appearance, think specifically about where you wear these articles of clothing. What need, in other words, does this outfit fill? Where have you worn it? Where will you wear it? What kind of occasion does it suit? What part does it really play in your total wardrobe? Do not forget to consider the frequency with which you wear a garment; it may be an indication of what you need in your wardrobe. When something is not worn, there is probably a good reason. It may, of course, be a special-occasion outfit which you really need—but not often. It may be that there is something about the outfit—the fabric, perhaps—that you do not like, or it may be that on an impulse you bought something which, while you like it very much, does not fit into your life.

There are times when we are just plain tired of an old article and feel the need for a change. You may find that putting clothes out of sight for a period of time relieves this boredom. People who live in sections of the country where there are definite seasons will get the natural relief of putting things away for a season. Those living in climates where the same kind of clothing is worn the year round, lucky as they are in having to buy clothes for only one season, may want to put a suit or a pair of slacks away just to relieve the monotony. Another solution might be to find a new way of wearing the clothes or a new occasion for which they might be worn. Perhaps the outfit needs some little fashion change to make it look different.

REPLACEMENTS

As you think in terms of outfits, make a note of the items that will have to be replaced. Remember that hosiery and underwear are part of the outfit. Thinking in terms of the length of service you can ex-

pect from various articles will be a help in planning later on. Replacement costs will, of course, be something to consider in coordinating your wardrobe; they will help you determine just how much you will do to put an old outfit into use. The length of service expected from a suit may not warrant the addition of a new blouse or shirt. With items such as underwear and hosiery, you will find that a pattern evolves as you constantly evaluate your wardrobe. This pattern can be a time-saver: as you plan ahead, you will know when to buy and will be able to ask your store to send out these items.

UPKEEP

The care required for the upkeep of any item deserves more than a little thought. Could it be that the upkeep of some special item will require more time than you have to give? This could also be a key to future buying. You may like a blouse, but if you simply do not like to iron and the blouse consequently is out of service a good part of the month, is the blouse practical in your wardrobe? Or consider how frequently any piece of clothing will need dry cleaning. The money involved here might perhaps be spent more satisfactorily otherwise. At times you might prefer things which can go to the cleaners or the laundry to things demanding a great deal of home care. One problem in clothes care is pressing. Ironing may be necessary because the fabric wrinkles easily, or the garment may need a touch-up after hanging in an over-crowded closet. In future selections, you might avoid that particular fabric. The amount of available closet space and storage space may well be a factor in deciding the size of your wardrobe. Consider whether a particular item is giving enough service to warrant the closet space it takes up. Unless an item is worn often, it may also not be worth the time and effort required for seasonal care, handling, and mothproofing.

Alterations and repairs also take time and money. Is the item worth repairs or a fitting alteration? Simple alterations may give more wear than you expected. On the other hand, unless one has the time to do the altering oneself, or the money to pay for having it done, the style may not warrant the expenditure of time and money. Remember that things which are out of service are still taking up space. Some of the busiest, most efficient people make a practice of repairing all clothing as they go, so that each article is ready when needed. The well-dressed person does not have slits in seams or hems that are coming out.

NOW AND LATER

In checking your entire wardrobe, you have been doing two things—trying to put all of your articles of clothing into better use and forecasting a little for the future, which will help you in planning a continuing wardrobe.

Try to think back to the shopping trip on which you bought some item you do not wear or like. Was it a spur-of-the-moment purchase? Did you buy it for an occasion which has not been repeated? Did you buy a certain hat to raise your spirits or because you admired a similar one on your girl friend?

Parents can apply a great many of the same questions in planning children's wardrobes. It is wise, as soon as a child is old enough, to discuss with him why things are worn and to let him help determine why something was satisfactory. Note what it was he especially liked about various articles.

You have noted many small but important details for future planning. Remember that it is wise to think in terms of original cost plus upkeep. Know which items will have to be replaced; then you will be able to shop for these items when the prices are most reasonable. Remember to consider the part an article of clothing will play in your wardrobe and, most important, begin now to make everything in your wardrobe work for you. It will work for you if it is ready when you need it—with all repairs done and with co-ordination well thought out.

Chapter 9

Planning for what?

Being well dressed takes time, money, and thought. The less money, the more time and thought—or, the less time, the more money and thought—are needed; all are necessary in some degree. If you have to turn down an invitation because you "have nothing to wear," it is time to reorganize your wardrobe planning. You will miss a lot of fun if you haven't suitable clothes to wear. A little thought before you go shopping or before you plan your wardrobe for the next season will probably save you time and money and give you much more satisfaction. Your greatest pleasure will come when you find that you have a workable wardrobe which lets you look and feel as you want to—a wardrobe that meets your needs yet requires minimum time.

PLANS

Planning is concerned with using the knowledge of self, design, values, and needs to organize your wardrobe to serve you and *not control you.* It is part of the process of making *order* out of chaos so necessary for good design. It is making decisions that allow you to spend your money as you *want* to spend it. It requires an answer to "what do you want your clothes to do for you?" With so many influences on your life and so much knowledge available, you must organize your activity to make the best use of your resources. Planning allows you to satisfy your immediate and *ultimate* goals and also to constantly evaluate your values to see if they require change. Certain factors in your life are already established and dictate certain solutions. You will have just so much money to spend on clothing for the family or yourself. You have a certain amount of time in which to accomplish all that is to be done, including shopping and care of clothing. Your place of residence is established, as are your place of work and the climatic conditions under which you live. Your community may have an accepted mode of behavior, and your selection may be based on conformity to the patterns of your group. Your professional needs are established by the nature of your work.

What is within your control? First, although there is just so much money available, its division can be decided by the family members. You decide the amount and the kind of clothing you buy. How effectively you use your time in taking care of it or in clothing selection is up to you. You will use your originality in co-ordinating various articles. The will power and control you develop in the way you spend your money will be strong contributing factors to your success in solving your clothing problems.

WILL POWER

You have been developing your own philosophy concerning clothes and have probably made a great many decisions about clothing. Honesty about your desires and sincerity in expressing yourself will help you to control impulse buying and to develop the will power to control your money. Expressing yourself as an individual does not require money so much as the development of good taste in selection and wearing.

TIME

Time is an element to be considered in purchasing and using clothes. If you have more time than money, you may want to reduce the cost of services such as laundry. You might develop the ability to make some of your clothing or to do the alterations on clothing you purchase. Time may, however, be at a premium for you. Most people live busy, active lives. It is important that you think in terms of what your time is actually worth. You will buy services when you feel your time would be better spent in other ways. In the previous chapter, you noted how the time element is involved in the storage, mending, and other care that is necessary for clothing. Also involved is the time you spend in doing the actual shopping. The person who has limited time will want to keep at a minimum those items which require such extra care as hand washing. The amount of time you can spend in the care of clothing will in turn be an influence on the amount of equipment you should acquire for the purpose.

The amount of clothing you have will be determined by the kind of storage space you have, the length of time that articles are away for cleaning, and the kind of services available to you where you live. Many areas do not have pick-up and delivery service, which means that you may have to spend time doing this for yourself. It is possible to have too few clothes just as it is possible to have too many. It takes more time to put some outfits on correctly; those that have to be fussed with to look right may have to be eliminated from the clothes you wear often.

You can also reduce the amount of time spent shopping if you know what you want and where and how it can be obtained. Some stores have services for doing your shopping for you; you have only to use the telephone. In these cases, remember that correct terminology and a knowledge of the product and of your size are essential when you write or telephone for merchandise. If you do not express adequately what you want, you may spend more time returning articles or making adjustments than it would have taken to do the shopping in the first place.

STORAGE

In your planning, you should consider whether you are making the best possible use of the available storage space. Clothes that will be worn together should be stored relatively close to each other. Shoes, for example, should be stored close to hosiery and underwear. Clothing that is worn often should be easily accessible.

FAMILY

Young people frequently ask what part of their income should be spent for clothing and personal care. Many studies have been done which give estimated clothing expenditures, but it is difficult to give a definite amount. The amount spent will be influenced by the needs of the family, the income bracket, where the family lives, and the climate. Whether the wife is employed outside of the home and the kind of work she and her husband do may affect the percentage of the income spent on clothing. A U.S.D.A. study estimates that if the wife is employed outside the home, extra expenses such as clothing, taxes, and traveling are between $900–$1,000.

Individual families differ; how much money is to be spent on clothing should be decided on after consideration of the needs of the family.

BE REALISTIC

The cost of clothing varies from person to person; what one person finds expensive another may not. A woman may be shocked at the price of another woman's dress but think nothing of the dress in her own wardrobe which she never wears. Any article is expensive if it does not pay its way. The spur-of-the-moment purchase which does not go with anything, the blouse which does not fit, the pair of shoes you don't like, the dress you don't wear— all are high-priced items, regardless of their actual cost in dollars and cents. An article which is seldom or never worn may be more expensive than the dress which you think another woman paid too much for.

If you stretch your budget by making some of your own clothing, remember that fabric which is not used is also expensive. A sewing machine is a large investment and, when not used sufficiently, may cost more than it saves. The woman who sews should use the same kind of will power in her planning as the woman who buys.

Most people, regardless of the amount they spend, would like their clothing to look better than it is. It is human to want to feel you have a bargain.

In considering the needs of the individual or the family, it is important to be realistic in analyzing demands. One member of the family may have professional needs that must be met and considered first. Most professions demand certain standards in dress regarding appearance or safety. Certainly comfort will be of prime importance in determining needs; social and leisure time activities are next in importance in the minds of most people.

After you have gone over your present wardrobe, you will want to compare what you need and want with what you already have. In planning for your shopping, list the minimum essentials first.

FUN CLOTHES

After you get your plan working, you may have enough money left over to get some articles for pleasure and fun. When you are thinking about your needs, plan for a two- or three-year period in order to be sure that you will eventually have what you want. After you have thought of your needs, you should consider the amount you really have to spend on clothing and compare this with the essential needs. Jotting down approximate prices you expect to pay will help you when you shop and keep you from spending too much on one item.

RECORDS

Until you have reached the point where you feel that you understand your needs and have accomplished your goal of being well dressed, it might be wise to keep records to see where your money is going as a means of evaluating your progress. You should know not only how much you spend, but whether your money is being spent on the things which give you the most satisfaction and happiness. Keeping records is the secret of future improvement. You do not have to itemize everything in a book. Receipts for clothing can be kept and evaluated all at one time, thus eliminating your always having to make entries. The way you evaluate your records will depend on what you are most anxious to find out. You might have separate categories for outerwear, shoes, hosiery, and lingerie; or you may evaluate by costume.

Planning enables you to have what you

want when you want it. Planning is using the thought necessary to being well dressed. There are many things time and money cannot do; money won't make a dress fit at the last minute and you can't buy a dress when the store is closed. There are many services which cannot be bought. Planning allows you to use your money and your time to best advantage.

Remember that good wardrobes are not purchased in one shopping trip but are built over the years with much thought. People build their wardrobes differently. Some plan to buy one complete outfit a year, including hat, shoes, and accessories. Others make one large purchase such as a coat or a suit and the next year perhaps a good wool dress. When buying a new outfit, consider what is already in your wardrobe. You might concentrate on your greatest weakness in the first year.

STRENGTHS AND WEAKNESSES

It is possible to make your weakness your strength. If, for instance, your hips are big, you might start building a collection of beautiful skirts in becoming designs. If your bust is large and you feel that you cannot wear sweaters or clinging fabrics, you might concentrate on shirts and blouses. If you sunburn easily, you could use smart beach coats and jackets in a variety of colors and fabrics. It is not unusual to find a fashion which was started because someone of necessity chose a certain kind of garment.

Everyone has a weakness—in what he buys as well as in what he doesn't buy. Many people will put off purchasing items in which they are not interested even though they need them. Some women do not like to change handbags; they might make a specialty of unusual and versatile handbags. Women who dislike buying lingerie might plan for a few lovely pieces. It is a challenge to be an expert in the thing you don't care for.

Your weakness may be that you are too absorbed with how you look. Although you can use clothing as an art, dressing is not a ritual. Your problem will be to plan your co-ordination to the best of your ability and then, once dressed, forget how you look.

You have probably kept in mind what you think fashion can do for you. Fashion is a tool you will use to bring interest and variety to old articles in your wardrobe. It can help you keep your wardrobe current and aid you in buying for a greater length of time. If you understand fashion, it is simple to skip a year when the current fashion is not becoming to you. If you always skip fashion, however, it is an indication of poor buying or observation and you will always feel a little behind the times.

Some people feel comfortable in old clothes. They would not part with a "mellowed" tweed jacket, an old pair of shoes, a familiar hat, or a classic flannel robe. Some things acquire distinction with age. Know what your "old faithfuls" are and make sure they are kept in good condition.

In developing a feeling for your individual look, you may find it helpful to keep an envelope of clippings of things which appeal to you. When planning a shopping trip, you can check to see how these would fit in with the items you need.

Women do a great deal of buying for men; they should be able to communicate a man's needs to the salespeople.

Plan and buy each purchase as though you were investing in a priceless treasure. There is no item too small for beauty.

REFERENCE READINGS

Winakor, Geitel, "Consumer Expenditures For Clothing," *Journal of Home Economics*, Vol. 54, No. 2, pp. 115–118, February, 1962.

Chapter 10

How
do you
buy?

Do you read labels? Before you answer, you should perhaps ask yourself, "What is a label?"

You will find different labels on apparel, labels showing price, size, brand name, trademark, fiber content, care instructions, and other information. Which of these do you read, or do you read them all? Of what value is the information to you in making your selection? With the increasing number of textiles, processes, and finishes, you need all the information available. Such information is found on printed hang tags, inserts, button-ons, packaging, and permanent sewn-in fabric labels.

LABELING

All labels give some information. However, few are ideal and give all of the following:

1. What is the article made of? The label should give the fiber content of the fabric, listing the various fibers and the percentage by weight of each in the fabric, as required by the 1960 Textile Identification

Act. For leather, it should tell what kind and how processed. The kinds of thread used and how they were processed should be listed, e.g., "mercerized, two-ply cotton." A permanent sewn-in label is of value to the dry cleaner as well as the customer.

2. How is it made? Construction features such as double-stitched seams, reinforced elbows, or shadow-proof panels may give some indication of the service one may expect from the garment.

3. What will it do? Is the garment washable? Colorfast? Wrinkle- or stain-resistant?

4. How should you care for it? May it be laundered? Dry cleaned? If washable, what kind of detergents should you use? What is the proper water temperature? How should you dry the garment?

5. For what purpose is it recommended? While this information can be helpful it is not essential. It sometimes gives the manufacturer's recommendations as to use.

6. Who made it? Who sold it? If, for any reason, you have to return a purchase, it is good to know the manufacturer's name and address or the retailer's name and address or both.

A label giving all the above information is ideal but not available on all merchandise since labeling and the technicalities involved add to its expense.

Basic materials

If you have preferences in materials, a label which gives the fiber content is helpful. You may prefer cotton to other fibers or you may prefer different fibers for different seasons. Perhaps you do not wear nylon in the summer or wool in the winter; knowing whether either fiber is contained in a fabric will help you decide upon your purchase. Some people have allergies which prevent their wearing any fabric containing certain fibers. If you prefer patent leather to plastic in certain accessories such as belts or

Style : #473
Size : 10
Price : $7.95
Color : white

Price tag—front side.

Price tag—reverse side.

100%
orlon
acrylic

bags, a label indicating the material will be valuable to you.

Durability

When buying apparel in which you desire special durability, a label pointing out

Trademark.

Madame
Bovary

Care label.

THIS GARMENT IS GUARANTEED WASHABLE

To HAND WASH use moderate water temperature (120°) with mild soap. DO NOT twist or spin dry. Rinse thoroughly. DRIP DRY on plastic hanger. Use cool iron for touch-up. Dry Cleaning may also be used.

construction features—especially hidden ones—such as single-needle-stitched seams on shirts for better fit, reinforced toes and heels in socks, hand-picked seams in a suit, or extra-durable interfacing or interlining in a coat is desirable.

Performance

Some indication of what you can expect from your purchase in the way of performance is useful. The specific explanation of colorfastness, for instance, indicates whether the clothing is colorfast to sunlight, to washing, to perspiration, to pressing, to fume fading, or to all of these. A limited number of fabrics are colorfast under all these conditions, but, depending upon the use to which you will put the article, you may not need all of these colorfast characteristics. Will plastic stick together in warm weather or crack in cold? Will suède *crock,* or rub off color, on other fabrics?

Care

With the large variety of materials being used, care can be a problem. Should you dry clean or wash the garment? If it is washable, by what method? Must you avoid bleach? Do you press or iron, and at what temperature? A well-written label will answer at least some of these questions for you. Though a set of sure-care symbols to guide the consumer was developed for labels, it did not gain wide acceptance.

Uses

In general, you will probably know how to use ready-to-wear items. Advertisements and catalog descriptions may suggest occasions and possible combinations. In the case of textile fabrics, suggestions may be given which you would find helpful in making clothing for yourself or for others in the family.

BRAND NAMES

Knowing the manufacturer's or retailer's name and address may be of value if, for any reason, you must return merchandise or need further information. Your retailer can usually help you, but if he cannot, it may be necessary to contact the manufacturer. Noting whether the label indicates a national brand or a store brand will help if you find it necessary to check on your purchases or if you wish to reorder.

For those who buy by brand name or registered trademark, more informative labels may be of little value. You should remember, however, that a brand name or registered trademark does not necessarily indicate that a particular piece of merchandise will meet all your qualifications.

Many shoppers find labels and tags aids in judging quality. Yet, a label alone is not enough; it must be backed up by adequate quality control and identification programs. Quality does not mean the same to all consumers. The relative importance of the features of goods we buy varies with our purposes and our ability to pay for desirable characteristics. To the individual, quality merchandise usually means merchandise of the most importance to him, merchandise from which he will get the greatest degree of satisfaction for the amount spent.

Some specific points which indicate value in apparel are: basic materials—fibers, yarns, trimmings, linings, buttons, and other details—of good quality; good design with regard to color, pattern, fit, comfort, and fashion; full-cut and accurate sizing; good construction features, such as seams, edges, and reinforcements; standard initial cost; upkeep costs at a minimum in relation to price; and a reliable store.

IMPORTS

There are shoppers who think that the word "imported" indicates quality. That is not so; imported goods, especially fabrics, are not necessarily better than, or even as good as, those made in the United States. There has, however, been a steady improvement in the quality of many imported textiles.

Many imported fabrics do have aesthetic value and good appearance; these imports may be worth their high cost. However, if you are going to pay the price, make sure that you are actually getting an import. "Imported" on a label may mean only the material; "French silk," for example, refers to the fabric and not the garment. Labels should have full information on whether one or all manufacturing processes took place in a foreign country, e.g., "Imported —woven in France; Finished in U. S." Names of foreign countries should not be used unless the merchandise originated there. A trade-name or brand name for a product made in the United States embodying the name of a foreign country should be accompanied by a legend in equally large type showing that the product was made in the United States. Merchandise coming from United States possessions should not be described as imported.

HELPFUL SOURCES

There are organizations and groups which attempt to furnish the consumer with information, satisfaction, and protection. Included are non-commercial organizations like Consumer's Research and Consumer's Union as well as educational groups like the American Home Economics Association and the American Association of University Women.

The National Retail Merchants' Association; the National Better Business Bureau, which has locals in many cities; the American Standards Association; and the Federal Trade Commission also provide help and protection for the consumer. At least one state has a Department of Consumer Pro-

tection in the executive branch of government, where many different consumer-protective services are concentrated. Other states have consumer counsels, divisions, leagues, and associations. On the national level, an assistant to the President on consumer affairs has been appointed, a Consumer Advisory Council formed, and a department of the consumer considered.

There are store, independent, and manufacturers' testing laboratories whose test results provide information for your use. The laboratories which certify merchandise provide seals which guarantee the claims of manufacturers on labels or in advertisements. Certification seals are always reliable; frequent checking ensures that the standards warranting the original certification are maintained. The American Institute of Laundering and the National Institute of Dry Cleaning provide reliable information.

INDUSTRY REGULATIONS

Another means of consumer protection is provided by government acts, Federal Trade Commission rules, and production standards of company and trade associations, technical societies, local, state, and national—both voluntary and mandatory.

The *Wool Products Labeling Act* of 1941 requires labeling of apparel and wool fabrics that are made of 5 per cent or more wool or the specialty hair fibers. *Wool* refers to fibers from sheep, lamb, or specialty hair fibers. *New wool* and *virgin wool* mean that the fibers have been through the manufacturing process only once. *Reprocessed wool* is obtained from scraps of new woven or felted fabrics made of previously unused wool. *Re-used wool* is obtained from used rags and clothing.

The *Fur Products Labeling Act* of 1951 requires that all furs be labeled with the following information: the name of the true animal of origin; if imported, the country of origin; if dyed, bleached, or otherwise changed from its natural state; if the fur contains pieces of less valuable parts of the animal.

The *Flammable Fabrics Act* of 1954 provides that clothing or fabric, manufactured or imported, that is dangerously flammable when worn, is unlawful. The Federal Trade Commission established the standards of flammability which must be met by manufacturers and importers.

The *Textile Fiber Products Identification Act* of 1960 covers all textile fibers except those included in the Wool Products Labeling Act. The generic name of each fiber present in an amount sufficient to change the characteristics of the fabric is to be mentioned and the percentage indicated. In some instances the term "other fibers" is used to denote fibers making up less than 5 per cent of the total weight.

The American Standards Association *L-22 Performance Requirements* for textiles provide voluntary standards for use by manufacturers of textile fabrics, women's, girls', men's, and boys' apparel. When these minimum performance standards are met, and even surpassed, by some manufacturers, the consumer benefits from the improvements in textiles and apparel.

Federal Trade Commission rules, effective in 1963, for labeling and advertising footwear provide for the accurate use of the terms leather, split leather, and imitation leather, as well as the designations of the parts of the shoe or slipper where used.

The 1961 *National Fair Claims Adjustment Guide for Consumers of Textile Products* dealing with fair adjustment for consumer complaints on damaged or inferior quality textiles is of value to consumers, retailers, and manufacturers.

COMPARATIVE SHOPPING

Most people have preferences as to where they buy. Some of the factors influencing their choice are the time available for shopping; the price and value of merchandise; the kind of salespeople, store services: credit, installment, approval plans, parking facilities, and evening shopping hours; and the store's reputation and reliability.

Kinds of stores

In *department stores,* all apparel can be purchased in the various departments within the store. *Specialty shops* appeal to the shopper who likes variety within a special kind of merchandise. *Mail order* houses provide convenience through catalogs with easy selection by mail or through retail outlets. This "armchair" buying eliminates the possibility of racial slights. *Sample stores* and *manufacturer's outlets* have a certain amount of exclusiveness along with lower costs. Often, sample houses take for resale merchandise which did not sell in high fashion stores within a specified period of time. *Popular-price* or *volume merchandise stores* offer quality goods at low prices; they buy in large quantities and offer only limited customer services. Special purchases of off-season merchandise often provide bargains which appeal to customers who do not mind crowds and a minimum of service. The low price of unbranded and private brand merchandise appeals to many consumers. The *discount store* usually sells some nationally advertised brand goods below the suggested list price. *Super-discount stores,* named after the super-market grocery store which they resemble, provide carts, self-service, and a check-out cashier; some are clusters of individual stores under one roof with cashiers in each section. The *closed-door discount house* is a co-operative store operated for special groups who pay membership fees and are the only ones allowed to shop in the store. *Neighborhood stores* and *suburban shopping centers* provide easy access, free parking, and leisurely shopping. In the *drive-in* store, the distance from car to counter is 75 feet or less. *Super-markets* and *drug stores* provide quick pick-ups of miscellaneous items such as packaged yard goods, hosiery, underwear, blouses, plastic raincoats, and many other staples. Canned soft goods in super-markets appeal to many consumers, perhaps partly because of the novelty of the packaging. *Variety* stores usually feature large assortments of general merchandise in the low-price range. *Boutiques* provide exclusiveness and high style in accessories and specialty items; a boutique often is a separate shop within a larger store. *Yard goods stores* and *mill stores* often provide both variety and quality at prices which appeal to the home sewer. Fabrics found in these stores are often seconds, irregulars, and surplus goods, which may account for the low cost; they should be carefully checked for flaws. *Clothing-exchange* centers, often operated by civic groups on a small commission and *clothing house* parties are less common than retail stores.

Consumer services

The organization of the store and the services provided are important; credit, installment buying, C.O.D., merchandise on approval, and return privileges, for example, are definite conveniences. Lacking time and energy, a consumer often takes advantage of telephone and mail order, personal shopping, delivery, self-service, car parking, and alteration services. For effective and satisfactory shopping, stores have well-informed salespeople, well-labeled merchandise, apparel easily located and well displayed, discounts to cash customers, and clothes displayed by live models.

Fascinating to the "thrifty" customer are bargain basements, sales, "special offerings," contests, trading stamps, free gifts with purchases, and one-cent deals; many of them fail to realize that they actually pay for these added "features." The consumer who enjoys shopping because it is a pleasant experience shops in a store providing courteous salespeople, fashion shows, exhibits and displays, air conditioning, and other facilities like snack bars, nurseries, rest rooms, and waiting rooms. Store organization and policy are important to the person who puts faith in the store with a good reputation for standing behind its merchandise, fair customer relationships, fair prices, legitimate sales, honest advertising, good labor policy, responsible personnel, lack of confusion, and clean, fresh, well-presented apparel.

Knowing what is available and where is also important. Stores provide the information through advertising in newspapers and magazines, on radio and television, and through direct mail promotion as well as through fashion shows and telephone inquiry services.

It is up to the consumer to decide which services are important to him. If he does not use many of the services, he will be wise to shop at stores with limited services. Services are a part of the retailer's expenses and are added onto the retail cost of goods.

GOOD SHOPPERS

Co-operation in returning goods is a responsibility of the customer. Some abuse the privilege of returning goods, while others do not return unsatisfactory merchandise. A change of mind, damage due to your failing to follow the prescribed care procedure, or your having damaged the goods in some other way are not legitimate reasons for returning goods. The unscrupulous practice of buying a garment on approval, wearing it for a special occasion, and then returning it is certainly an abuse of the return privilege. Some retailers make adjustments when neither they nor the goods are at fault, not because of any obligation, but as a matter of store policy.

Returns add to the retailer's expenses by causing waste, through soiling and taking goods out of stock and by creating costly delivery service. You can help cut these costs by knowing what you want, by following directions for care and use, and by making all necessary returns promptly and in person.

Of course it is your duty to return goods that are unsatisfactory through no fault of yours. Nearly all retailers accept the responsibility for faulty merchandise. They try to offer satisfactory goods and to meet your needs as nearly as possible. Unless you return faulty merchandise, the retailer has no way of knowing that it is not satisfactory, and therefore he does not contact the wholesaler or manufacturer, who might make adjustments. Each item sold encourages the manufacturer to continue to produce it. To ensure the availability of good merchandise for your money you must return unsatisfactory items and avoid buying poor values.

Many consumers do not follow through on this kind of return because of the unpleasantness involved. If the right approach and the proper channels are followed, there is seldom any dissatisfaction. The clerk from whom you purchased the item is not responsible, and an irate customer who places the responsibility on the salesperson will gain nothing but high blood pressure. Depending upon the organization of the store, you should approach the buyer, the merchandise manager, or the adjustment department. If your complaint is legitimate, you should have no trouble in making the return. Remember that you are doing the retailer a favor as well as receiving satisfaction yourself. It is true that returning faulty merchandise takes time and tact; many customers do not follow through for

that reason. That merchandise is not returned is no indication it was satisfactory.

Efficient management of shopping time is your responsibility to the retailer as well as to yourself. Factors affecting the best time to buy include the conditions in your shopping area, your needs, your pocketbook, and your own time limitations. Since many people are free to shop only at certain times like lunch hours, after work, or on Saturdays, it may be to your advantage and the retailer's to shop at other times if possible. Shopping during the less crowded hours is easier on both you and the salesperson. You can feel free to take adequate time to make your selections and to make use of the information and service provided when the salesperson is not hurried and harried, and you avoid being jostled by crowds of customers.

Some consumers with limited shopping time use mail orders and the telephone, but they often miss good buys, which they might not if they visited the stores and did some comparative shopping. Sometimes substitutions on your original plan prove satisfactory when you actually go to the store in person and discover special merchandise on sale. Here again, it is up to the customer to decide on the importance of the time element in the shopping plan.

Lack of adequate shopping time is a common complaint. Although not all stores offer time-saving services, a growing number do, and the busy shopper is wise to seek them out. If you establish a good personal relationship with one saleswoman in every department of a large store and always deal with her, she will learn what kind of clothes you prefer. As soon as she understands your preferences, she may be able to preselect what you will like, and alert you, by telephone, to new stock you might like to see before it is sold out. The personal shopping services set up by many stores also save time for busy people. After the personal shopper knows you, she will be able to shop for many items which you can order by telephone. If you want her to, she will also call you about items she thinks you would like.

Some stores cater to the working woman who has only her lunch hour in which to shop. She can make an advance reservation for a fitting room and a saleswoman who knows her will have a selection of merchandise ready. The store may also arrange to round up from other departments a selection of accessories suitable for the garment the customer is buying. Other special services may include the sending out to customers of cards announcing new stock, personally signed by the saleswomen; identification cards for customers so that salespeople may know speedy service is needed; fashion shows scheduled at lunch time or after five; and emergency delivery service within a local area.

THRIFTY SHOPPING

Sales, bargains, and discounts are fascinating to many consumers. For some, they offer real advantages, while for others they ruin budgets and sometimes even dispositions. A sale does not always mean good buys and thrifty shopping. There are all kinds of merchandise available, good values and poor; you really have to be more discriminating at a sale than at other times. "End-of-the-month," "inventory," and "out-of-season" clearance sales may be profitable for you if you know what you need. Other sale offerings include "special purchase," "irregulars" or "seconds," soiled merchandise, and samples or discontinued lines. These may be good buys, but require careful inspection and weighing of values. If the cost of cleaning a piece of soiled merchandise plus the sale price adds up to the pre-sale cost, you save nothing. If the flaws

in irregulars or seconds are inconspicuous and will not affect durability, this kind of merchandise is a good purchase. Be sure that "sample purchase" and "novelty" goods are not in such high style as to limit length of service.

Do not be taken in by sales designed purely to attract interest during slack seasons. Learn to distinguish between real reductions and sales designed merely to attract you to the store. Sometimes fictitious prices are put on the tag by the manufacturer in agreement with the retailer, and the store marks down the item from its "original" cost for the consumer who likes sales and bargain prices; at times these "sale prices" may be higher than the real prices. The following are common times for bargain sales:

January: Store-wide clearance sales with substantial markdowns on winter clothing.
February: Fur sales; resort wear.
April: Clearances on Easter clothing.
May–June: Anniversary sales.
July: Clearances on spring and summer clothing.
August: Furs; summer clothing sales.
September: Back-to-school clothing clearances.
November–December: Pre-Christmas "specials."

There are Founders' Day sales, inventory sales, going-out-of-business sales, end-of-season sales, special-purchase sales, promotional sales, and Saturday morning sales. Such sales often attract customers to non-sale merchandise.

When taking advantage of sales, you should go early, when both the selection and the service are better; make sure you have the money, decide whether the purchase fits in with your original plan of buying, and compare sale merchandise with regular stock for price and quality. Do not buy bargains just because they are bargains; remember that a bargain is not a bargain unless you really need the merchandise. If the item is necessary, suitable for your purposes, available when you need it, and if it costs less than you had planned to spend, it is a bargain. If you cannot resist bargain counters or sales, you probably have a closet full of clothes which have no real purpose because you really did not need them in the first place. They are markdowns—but not bargains.

A bargain has been described as something you cannot use at a price you cannot resist. A true bargain is an item that is less expensive today than it was yesterday; it is something you have given thought to, will use, really have a desire for, can afford, and would buy anyway.

Many consumers are completely sold on discount houses. Here again, a careful inspection of merchandise is necessary and a knowledge of brands and of quality helps. If unsatisfactory merchandise cannot be returned, you have saved little by purchasing it at a discount. Ask yourself whether the low price represents a discount or the actual value of the merchandise. Buy from a discount house if you have shopped around enough to know that it offers the best price and you get the manufacturer's guarantee and a receipt with a description of what you bought.

SHOPPING ETHICS

As a consumer you have other responsibilities, sometimes called shopping ethics. Know what you are going to buy; if not, be able to describe or indicate its intended use, so that the salesperson will have some idea of what to show you. Wait for your turn. State your request well; be courteous and you can in turn expect courtesy.

Do not expect the whole stock to be on the counter. Buy enough of yard goods or findings so that you will not have to keep returning only to find the supply exhausted. If you have a charge account, using it for items costing a dollar or more will usually save time for you and the salesperson. Do not abuse the approval system; try to make a satisfactory selection the first time. If you are buying a blouse for a suit, wear the suit and the other accessories the day you buy the blouse instead of taking several blouses home on approval. Carry small purchases rather than having them sent, especially during rush seasons like the Christmas shopping period. Be considerate of others' feelings. Be a lady or a gentleman. Do not make scenes; make any complaints in a low, quiet voice, stating the case briefly, and wait for a reply. Be fair to others and to yourself; most important of all, be honest. Have you ever asked yourself what kind of shopper you are? A price-tag hunter? A drifter? A dawdler? A spontaneous shopper? An erratic, spontaneous spender? It might be interesting to analyze your shopping practices to see whether there is room for improvement. Being conscious of your mood when shopping is helpful. Shopping during a period of stress, after a crisis, during periods of loneliness, or after a period of long restraint often results in impulse buying which you may later regret.

You become a good shopper by developing desirable attitudes, techniques, and skills, which in the end will save you time, money, and effort. In addition, you have the responsibility of showing interest in buying beyond your own individual needs and desires. Be aware of marketing conditions and problems, consumer legislation, labor conditions, government regulations, and other developments; be willing to express your interest, share your knowledge, and encourage others to become more aware of consumer issues.

A few basic observations on buying: When goods are plentiful, easy and normal consumer buying keeps the economy running; buy according to your normal needs. When goods are scarce, heavy consumer buying brings inflation; buy only what is necessary. Watch markets and consider your needs; learn to judge markets both for prices and for types of merchandise; learn to judge by inspection all the various characteristics of merchandise; and study goods you have bought for hints on evaluating future purchases.

PLANNING

You already know that planning is the key to effective, efficient, and satisfactory buying. It is estimated that only three out of every ten purchases are firmly decided upon before the shopper gets to the store, that almost half of all purchases are made on impulse, and that two out of three shoppers never bother to prepare even a partial shopping list. A well-thought-out plan helps you to reach your goals—first consider your goals, then plan accordingly. With good planning it may even be possible to buy some of the items you only dreamed of. You will recall that in planning you should consider actual needs, activities and occasions for which you need clothing, the number of clothes you need, when they will be needed—now or in the future, what you have now, and what of the old will fit in with the new.

To be of real value, this preplanning should be done on paper. First you will probably write down ideas as they occur to you. Make a master list of all the items you buy often and regularly, like cosmetics or hosiery. This prevents the hit-or-miss shopping that results in your being out of these items at awkward moments. A list of the items you buy occasionally plus a long-range listing will also help you in planning before buying.

This does not mean that strict adherence to a plan is the answer. In fact, well-planned shopping provides for flexibility. You may not find what you want at the price you planned to pay, or you may happen to find what you want for less and therefore have more to spend on other items in your plan. A plan need not be rigid to help keep your leakproof budget from becoming a sieve.

If you share the clothing money with other members of a family, a family council will help in deciding who needs the most, at what time, and how much money is available for all. Are you willing to adjust your personal plan to permit other members of the group to benefit? The college student who demands a new dress for every formal dance may be depriving her high school sister of needed skirts and sweaters or her father of the new suit his position demands.

Although it may not be possible to determine the care and upkeep requirements of apparel before actual purchase, they should be considered in your planning. Knowing that some apparel can only be dry-cleaned and that it would require cleaning after limited wearing may enable you to do a better job of preplanning. If some garments require special care for which you do not have the space or facilities or if expensive alterations are needed, you may find it necessary to make adjustments in your original plan.

Buying habits in the United States have changed with the way of living. Increased leisure time has heightened interest in hobbies, do-it-yourself projects, sports, and vacation travel. These activities have promoted the buying of appropriate clothing.

Nearly all of the information on buying applies to men as well as to women. All men should become informed on buying clothing: the sole providers of the family income; those who take a dim view of women's buying habits; those contemplating marriage; those who let a mother, wife, or fiancée buy their clothes; and those who buy their own clothes.

Children need to learn not only about the value of money but also about quality of merchandise in preparation for shopping on an allowance. Nowadays it is not unusual for teen-age boys and girls and college men and women to shop together for clothes. Pooling their knowledge of buying often helps them make more satisfactory purchases.

A WORD ABOUT GIFTS

Gifts are very special items. They are tokens of the giver's love, esteem, and appreciation. Most people get as much pleasure from giving a present as from receiving one. Since "it isn't the gift, it's the thought," you will want to be careful in the selection of gifts, especially with items of apparel. It is a great compliment to have someone say that you have the knack of choosing "just the right thing." That requires thinking about what would most please the person for whom the gift is intended. Impulse buying may prove expensive to the giver, and the gift might not be suitable for the receiver. A little thought before purchasing and some investigation of the person's interests and preferences will help.

Gifts play an important part in many wardrobes, especially in children's. Some gifts are chosen to replace clothing that might have been purchased by the recipient; others may be items the individual would not buy for himself. In choosing an article of clothing as a gift, remember that it should suit the receiver's needs and his personal preferences in color, texture, and design. It should be in keeping with his interests and it should co-ordinate with his present wardrobe.

Some people do not like useful presents such as hosiery; others much prefer practical gifts. Some people will use whatever is given to them, but there are a few who have very definite preferences and will never use a gift they do not like.

Many a gift item is given away or stored in a drawer simply because it is unsuitable or not wanted. If you are not with a person enough to know the colors in her wardrobe or what fabrics she wears, it would be a mistake to try to buy items of apparel which must be co-ordinated with others. A blouse which does not go with any of the receiver's skirts means she will have to purchase a skirt to use your gift. Gifts should not require additional expense on the part of the wearer and should seldom have to be exchanged.

Some people do not like solid colors. Others do not like plaids or prints. You would not want to give a wool sweater to someone who is allergic to wool. There are women who have collections of gift jewelry they do not wear because it is not appropriate for them or their wardrobes.

Large gift items should be carefully considered; one should be sure the receiver really wants the present. This applies especially to expensive articles of clothing. Most people would rather be consulted than receive a gift which does not suit them. It might be a good idea to take the person along to help select a large gift such as a coat or an expensive piece of jewelry.

Unless you have a truly wonderful memory for detail, it might be a smart idea to keep a notebook of sizes and other pertinent information about those for whom you frequently buy gifts.

For women

Items frequently chosen as gifts for women might be considered in more detail. In general, you should remember that the gift must fit and that most women have preferences as to color and style.

Lingerie. Slips, nightgowns, and robes are favorite gifts in this category. Most women enjoy receiving them, provided, of course, that they are the correct size and becoming in style and color. A young girl might appreciate something—pettipants or stretch tights, perhaps—in keeping with the current fad.

Sweaters. Sweaters are another favorite gift item, but it is especially important with sweaters to consider individual preferences in color, yarns, and style. The correct size in sweaters is usually a larger size than the person would wear in other clothes. A luxury item such as a cashmere sweater will, of course, appeal to any girl.

Hats. As a rule, you should never try to buy a hat for anyone but yourself. It may be quite all right, however, to buy some item of casual headgear that happens to be in fashion, like a hood, headscarf, or headband for a young person.

Hosiery. No woman ever has too many stockings. To be really sucessful in buying stockings for someone else, you must know the correct size, including the proper length proportions. You should also know the woman's preferences as to sheerness, texture, pattern, and color and whether she prefers seamless, full-fashioned, or tubular.

Handbags. Before you give a woman a handbag, observe what kind she uses and try to find out whether she would prefer leather, patent leather, fabric, or straw. You should know something about her wardrobe and about the other accessories she uses, you should consider the relation between the size and shape of the handbag and the woman's proportions, and you should pay special attention to color. A handbag can be a very appropriate gift if the receiver does not have to buy a new outfit to go with the bag.

Cosmetics. Perfume, cologne, or other toiletries are acceptable and suitable gifts if you know the woman's preferences.

Gloves. Gloves of the correct size and a suitable color are generally appreciated. If you do not know the colors in the lady's wardrobe, white or light beige would be a good choice. You should, of course, know something of her preferences in style and design.

Jewelry. Since jewelry is a very personal expression of individuality, it is necessary to know the person's preferences for metals, designs, and kinds of jewelry.

For men

The necktie is the single most popular gift for men. It is also one of the least appreciated by men; six out of every ten ties bought by women for men are never worn. If you feel you must give a man a necktie, you must know his preferences in color, fabric, and style. Age is not a good guide; some young men are conservative and some older men may enjoy bright colors. Above all, give him a tie only if you know he would want one.

Fine white linen handkerchiefs are usually acceptable. Wool, silk, or cashmere scarves are good gifts for the man who wears a topcoat. Wallets, brief clips, and money clips are old stand-bys; if you are giving one of these, however, check to see what kind he is using before replacing it.

Jewelry. A man may receive a pair of cuff links and then have to go out and buy a shirt with French cuffs. If you are buying cuff links for a man who does wear French cuffs, you should know what size, color, and design he prefers. Other suggestions include identification bracelets; tie chains, tacks, and clips; collar pins; pocket knives; key chains.

Slippers. Slippers are available in a wide range of styles and textures, ranging from inexpensive slipper-socks to fine alligator slippers. The man probably will have some preferences, and it would be helpful to know what they are.

Hosiery. Socks are another ever-popular gift for men. All too often, however, too little thought is given to color, pattern, fiber, and length. If a woman knows the size, she may buy or knit socks. The thoughtfulness that has gone into a pair of hand-knit socks will make the gift especially appreciated. Personal preferences, especially in fibers, are again an important consideration.

Toiletries. With such variety available, you should be able to choose a man's favorites among cologne, soap, talc, and skin conditioners.

Sweaters. If you know the proper size and the gentleman's preferences in style, color, and fiber, he will probably be pleased with a sweater. Sweaters can also be chosen keeping in mind the activities in which the man participates. Design should be considered in relation to his physique.

Closet accessories. Extra-large coat and trouser hangers are often welcome gifts. They are available in various materials—such as wood, plastic, metal, or tortoise shell—and in shapes and sizes to fit men's coats, trousers, and slacks. If you know that a man is in need of closet accessories, you can give him a gift which is not only appropriate but will simplify the care and storage of his clothes.

For children
In buying for children, size is extremely important; you should frequently check on the child's size. You should buy children's clothing according to weight rather than age. Ask the store for a chart to assist you in finding the correct size. Most stores do an excellent job with children's mittens and gloves. When you buy a gift for a child, consider the parents' wishes as well as the child's. No matter how wonderful you may think a dress or suit would look on the child, if the mother has other preferences, she may not use the gift. Relatives should remember that mothers are busy and do not always want clothing that requires time-consuming care.

General tips
There are certain articles for which you do not need so much information; they may often be your best way out of a quandary. For women there are compacts, toilet soaps, bath powders, handkerchiefs, and "travel-mates" for friends on-the-go. For umbrellas you need only know the recipient's color preferences.

Scarves are welcome gifts for both men and women. Some articles are made of stretch fabrics and fit several sizes. Neutral or black velvet slippers will go with many things.

Stationery and books are a better choice than apparel if you really do not have the necessary information. Of course, if you have no idea at all, money or a gift certificate is always welcome.

REFERENCE READINGS

Books
Danville, Bea, *Dress Well on $1 a Day*, Wilfred Funk, Inc., New York, 1956.
Dooley, William H., *Economics of Clothing*

and Textiles, D. C. Heath & Co., New York, 1934.

Evans, Mary, *Better Clothes for Your Money*, J. B. Lippincott Co., Philadelphia, 1952.

Katona, George, *The Mass Consumption Society*, McGraw-Hill, New York, 1964.

Morgan, James N., *Consumer Economics*, Prentice-Hall, Inc., New York, 1955.

Packard, Vance, *The Hidden Persuaders*, D. McKay, New York, 1957.

Tate, Mildred Thurow and Glisson, Oris, *Family Clothing*, John Wiley & Sons, New York, 1961.

Trollstrup, Arch W., *Consumer Problems and Personal Finance*, McGraw-Hill, New York, 1957.

Wharton School of Finance and Commerce, *Men's Clothing*, Merchandising Division, National Retail Dry Goods Association, New York, 1952.

Wingo, Caroline E., *The Clothes You Buy and Make*, McGraw-Hill, New York, 1953.

Wolff, Janet, *What Makes Women Buy?*, McGraw-Hill, New York, 1958.

Bulletins

Bilkey, Warren J., *Stretching Your Family Income*, University of Connecticut, 1957.

"Do Shoppers Need Help from the Government?" *Changing Times,* August 1964, pp. 7–12.

Gault, Jr., M. B., "A Matter of Price," *Journal of Home Economics,* Vol. 54, No. 7 (1962), pp. 560–563.

LaBarthe, Jules, "Your Money's Worth In Clothing and Textiles," *Journal of Home Economics,* 46: 64–644, November, 1954.

Lampman, Robert J., "An Appraisal of Consumer Protection," *Journal of Home Economics,* Vol. 54, No. 7 (1962), pp. 555–559.

Nelson, Don, *Stretching Your Family Income* (TV Series), University of Connecticut, 1959.

"Shop By Mail?" *Changing Times,* April 1964, pp. 37–40.

The Mail Order Shopping Guide, M. Barrows and Co., New York, 1964.

Warne, Colston E., *Consumer Protective Movements on the State and Local Levels*, Amherst, Massachusetts, 1964.

White, Rose U., "Standards Protect the Consumer," *Forecast for Home Economics,* November 1961, pp. 48–54.

Whitlock, Mary C., "Adjustment Guide for Consumers of Textile Products," *Journal of Home Economics,* Vol. 54, No. 2 (1962), pp. 109–111.

Winakor, Gertel, "Consumer Expenditures for Clothing in the United States, 1925–1958," *Journal of Home Economics,* Vol. 54, No. 2 (1962), pp. 115–118.

Chapter 11

Who's the caretaker?

Good clothes deserve good care. The best-designed and most stunning clothes lose their appeal when not properly cleaned, pressed, and stored. Without habitual care, one may not have a thing to wear. Care of clothing is easy if done regularly and systematically on a daily, weekly, and seasonal schedule. With organization and management of time, setting aside twenty minutes a night and working out a regular weekly plan, a person should have no trouble keeping clothes in top-notch condition. Faced with an accumulation of care problems, people tend to become discouraged and neglect their wardrobes. Although today the care and cleaning of clothing requires less manual labor than in the days of the scrub board, it requires knowledge of the innumerable fibers and finishes used in clothing today.

The care of all wardrobes is too often left to one person in the family, usually the mother. Care of clothing should be a shared responsibility; with a little help, encouragement, and direction, the men and boys can care for some of their own clothing as well as the women and girls. The hang tags on ready-to-wear apparel tell enough about fiber, finish, and care that family members should find the care of clothing quite simple. College students should not send or take their clothes home for care and repairs by other members of the family; if they do not have the time or the facilities away from home to care for their clothes, they should use commercial laundries and cleaners. When going home for week ends or vacations, they should plan to take care of their clothes instead of greeting their mothers with collections of soiled and neglected clothes.

STORAGE

Only a small part of an individual's wardrobe is worn at any one time; most of it is stored in closets and other storage space and should be clean, pressed, repaired, and ready to wear whenever needed. With careful storage, care, and choice of care equipment, the serviceability of and the satisfaction derived from one's wardrobe are greatly increased. Good storage means accessibility; protection from dust, unusual atmospheric conditions, moths, and mildew; and that garments and accessories will retain their original shape. A well-kept closet suggests well-groomed clothes. Whether the closet is in a house, an apartment, or a dormitory room, whether shared with others or used by one individual, it should be cleaned during seasonal cleaning and the floor kept vacuumed or similarly cleaned at all times. Deodorizers or air sprays keep closets and clothes fresh.

Since proper storage, in a closet or elsewhere, is so important a part of the care of clothing, it includes daily as well as seasonal storage. As soon as clothes are removed at night, they should be properly stored. A brushing, a quick pressing, or maybe a spot removal precedes hanging of outer garments. Proper hanging—on a hanger of the correct size and shape, in the right place, and protected from dust and moisture—helps keep a coat, suit, or dress in proper shape and condition. Men should realize that keeping a suit clean and in repair will extend its useful life. The suit jacket should be neatly centered on a shaped or slightly curved wooden hanger; the trousers should be hung evenly, with the creases and the grain straight, on a hanger of the proper width. Frequent brushing helps to prevent moth damage. Dust and lint should be brushed from trouser cuffs; dirt and grit tend to reduce wearing qualities, especially if lodged in creases and folds.

It is a good idea for both men and women not to wear the same suit, or any outer garment, for more than two successive days. Give it a rest the third day; this gives the weave or knit a chance to reset itself and reduces the need for frequent pressing. Owning several good suits pays dividends in lasting good looks and lowers the cost of upkeep per suit.

Pockets should be emptied before the suit is hung in the closet. Necklines should be kept clean and any shine should be removed from the sleeves and from the seat of the trousers.

EQUIPMENT

There is a large selection of special items for use in the storage and care of apparel. While some of them are both attractive and functional, others are ineffective; a knowledge of the function, construction, and cost of these accessories is important. A few examples are tie, belt, purse, and shoe racks; glove, sweater, sock, and trouser frames for shaping garments while drying; and drawer dividers, hat-boxes, garment bags, and hanging shelves. Peg boards with hooks placed at convenient intervals provides hanging space for many small items.

Hangers. There is a hanger for nearly every kind of garment. The sharp-crease trouser hangers that clip under the cuffs and occupy less room than the cuffs themselves hold trousers securely, as do the clamp hangers for cuffless trousers. There are wooden or heavy plastic hangers for coats and jackets, padded ones for soft or crisp fabrics, notched hangers that fit inside the skirt band and are held taut by spring action, skirt hangers with clips that adjust to the size of the skirt band and are padded so as not to leave marks, and clamp hangers that hold slacks and shorts. For suits, there are the padded, shaped shoulder bars for jackets and padded spring clips for skirts or trousers; for furs, strong wooden hangers with flattened-out ends to hold sleeves and shoulders in shape. Thin metal wire hangers allow garments to become creased and lop-sided.

The scoop gripper keeps scoop-neck blouses and dresses on their hangers. Made of elastic with a ring that slips over the hanger and clamps at both ends that fasten to the garment to keep it in place, it fits any hanger. Quilted padded fabric hangers keep garments from slipping.

A very popular belt hanger is the ring type that hooks over the closet rod like a regular hanger. It is easy to open; simply pull it apart, insert the belt, and snap it closed. To remove an individual belt, just slide the ring opening around to that belt.

Protective coverings. Shoulder coverettes protect clothing from the dust that seems to penetrate all closets. In addition to these individual coverettes, there are large closet coverettes that drop over the closet rod and cover several garments. These give protection similar to that given by garment bags.

Zippered garment bags are available for single garments or groups. Made of transparent plastic, these bags protect clothing from dust and still allow easy selection and

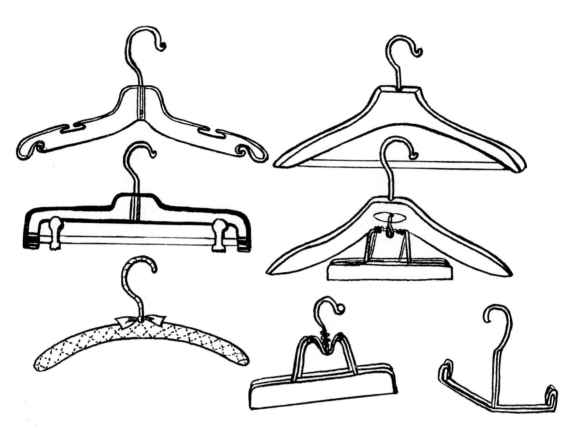

Variety in hangers.

removal of clothes. A disadvantage of garment bags is that clothes are often crushed and require ironing upon removal from the bag.

The shirt and blouse booklet will hold four individual shirts, blouses, or sweaters. Made of heavy, scuff-resistant plastic with zipper closings across the cover, it provides airtight storage and keeps clothes neat and clean. If hanging space for blouses and shirts is limited, this storage is a good substitute.

Sweater cases of transparent plastic with heavy binding and full-length, side-opening zippers for easy access provide airtight moth- and dust-free storage. Each holds at least two sweaters.

Shoe storage. Shoe racks with metal forms to hold shoes in shape and off the floor store from four to twelve pairs of shoes. A cover prevents the accumulation of dust. Shoes stored in a shoe bag that can be hung on the closet door are protected from dust but do not get the support provided by the metal shoe rack. Stuffing shoes stored in a shoe bag with paper helps to preserve their shape.

A shoe box that holds four pairs of shoes in separate compartments and has a front cover, with a transparent window for easy viewing, that lifts up for quick shoe selection fits handily on a closet shelf. It provides good storage for shoes that are not worn daily.

Hat storage. Similar storage is available for hats. A set of hat-boxes with front windows that open outward for easy removal or replacement of hats without taking the

Belt hanger.

Closet hang-a-chain.

box off the shelf keeps hats free from dust and eliminates crushing.

Trays and drawers. Sectioned sliding trays in drawers are convenient for orderly storage of jewelry and the odds and ends so difficult to store and to find. Flock-lined metal trays slide from the front to the back of the drawer on adjustable metal drawer dividers. The space under the tray in a deep drawer can be utilized for the storage of other items, which can be reached by sliding the tray backward.

Adjustable drawer dividers, which are easy to install, are a solution to the problem of the untidy drawer. They provide separate sections in a large drawer for gloves, socks, handkerchiefs, lingerie, and cosmetics and cut down on searching time.

The stow-a-way bed drawer is convenient when storage space is limited; it turns waste space under the bed into clean, dust-free storage room. It can be used for extra blankets, bed linens, slippers, sweaters, shirts, or any number of items for

which there is no other space. The runners clamp onto any wooden or metal bed frame. The sturdy metal drawer with dust cover conveniently slides out from either side of the bed and hangs clear of the floor.

Lingerie storage. Storage for petticoats and crinolines is provided by a tubular plastic case with quilted top, binding, and a hook by which to hang it. Just roll up the skirt, place it in the tapered bag, and hang the bag in the closet. A handy substitute for this case, especially for traveling, is an old full-length stocking.

Novelty. The closet hang-a-chain is a novel accessory consisting of eight three-inch hooks attached to a continuous chain that can be hung from the closet rod. It holds odd items like purses, umbrellas, and belts.

Storage sacks. The car sack, when not being used in travel, can be used to store clothes. For travel, it provides convenient temporary storage and eliminates the wrinkling that results from folding garments in a traveling bag.

Store seldom-worn evening dresses in

dust-free garment bags, and along with each dress store the dyed-to-match shoes, sandal-foot stockings, slips, and other special appurtenances. Then, when that special occasion comes, the whole outfit is dust-free, spot-free, and assembled ready to wear.

Efficient storage

In order to accommodate clothes and closet accessories, it is often necessary to expand the closet space. If the closet is narrow and deep, two parallel hanger bars will help, with the one at the back holding garment bags for off-season clothes. If the closet is high and small, try two bars, one above the other; this works especially well if you have a pole with a hook on the end to reach the hangers on the upper bars.

If special hangers are too bulky for the closet-space available, it means getting rid of those clothes which are never worn yet are still cluttering the closet. Hanger bulk guarantees that clothes will have room to breathe and wrinkles will hang out. Clothes should be moved and shaken from time to time to remove hanging wrinkles.

If your storage space is limited, the dry cleaner will store a winter wardrobe for a small fee including full insurance coverage.

Care before storage

A garment should be ready to wear when it is taken out of the closet. This means not only that it must be properly stored but that it must be clean and in good repair.

Cleaning. Clothes should be aired thoroughly after each wearing before they are put away. A thorough airing reduces unpleasant odors. Knitted garments should be aired on a flat surface to prevent stretching.

Brushing garments extends the time between cleanings. Use a medium soft brush for sturdy fabrics and a piece of velvet for delicate ones; always brush with the grain of the fabric. Clothes brushes are available for all types of fabrics. To remove balling, pilling, and matting from sweaters and all napped fabrics, use a nonabrasive nylon-loop comb designed for this purpose. Lint removers pick up lint, dog hairs, and surface dirt ordinary brushing does not remove. A clothes brush, fabric comb, and a lint remover kept in the clothes closet will be convenient for frequent use.

In hanging clothing, close all fastenings so the clothes will keep their original shape. Belts should be hung separately. Clothing to be stored in drawers or chests should be folded carefully to avoid excess wrinkles and folds. Knits should be carefully folded to avoid a crease down the center and should be stored in a plastic bag or other tight container in a drawer or on a shelf. However, some double knits and lined knits may be hung on padded hangers.

Hats, particularly felt hats, should be kept free from dust. If a hat is dusty, a drop of water will make a muddy spot that will soak into the felt and be difficult to remove. A soft bristle brush is better than a whisk broom or an ordinary clothes brush for cleaning hats. Always brush with the nap. If the leather hat band inside a man's hat is damp from perspiration, the band should be turned out and allowed to dry naturally without artificial heat to prevent staining of the ribbon, felt, or straw. The hat should be stored separately on a block or frame and not piled up with other hats.

Men's ties should be dry-cleaned or washed frequently. Spot removal between cleanings is necessary for ties that are not washable.

Before storing clothes, remove wrinkles by pressing or by bathroom steaming. Hang the clothes in a closed bathroom and run a hot shower or tub until the room is steamy. After a short time, remove the garments from the bathroom and allow time for wrinkles to hang out and for the fabric to dry thoroughly.

Repairs. Clothing should be checked after each wearing for necessary repairs, missing or loose buttons, tears, rips, "popped" seams, and loose hems. Everyone should be able to sew on buttons and make minor repairs. Some dry cleaners will do this for you, however. New clothes should be checked for these same details. In deciding whether to repair clothing and what kind of repairs to use, one should consider the value of the garment and the fabric, what kind of wear it will receive, how repairs can be done inconspicuously, and whether the time required is available or worth it. For a favorite wool skirt, sweater, or coat, or a new cocktail dress, it may be wise to seek professional repair services for burn, moth, or tear damage. If a slip seam is pulling apart, open the seam and mend the pulled place by putting tape on the underside; when resewing, let the seams out a little to prevent further strain and pulling. Lace may be inconspicuously repaired by machine stitching back and forth or using a zigzag attachment over a net reinforcement on the underside. When clothes return from being dry-cleaned, the cleaner's tag should be removed carefully.

Seasonal storage

For off-season storage at home, woolens should be protected from moths and carpet beetles. They should be washed or dry-cleaned before storing, because soiled areas are quickly attacked by moths and carpet beetles. Clothing should be thoroughly aired, sunned, and brushed, pockets turned inside out, cuffs down, and collars up to expose all parts of the garment. Although man-made fibers do not attract moths, certain types of soil do; all fabrics

should therefore be cleaned before storing. Blends containing even a small amount of wool need protection because moth larvae can badly damage the fabric in getting to the wool content. Orlon or nylon fleece coats should be laundered and fluffed up in a dryer before storing. Imitation furs made of thermoplastic fibers should be dry-cleaned by a cleaner familiar with the special procedure necessary or by a fur cleaner.

Insecticides give various degrees of protection and there are some liquids to be used in wash or rinse water as a precautionary measure. Sprays, crystals, or flakes are effective if the vapors are held in by airtight containers—boxes, chests, clothes-bags, and closets which can be sealed with masking tape. When winter clothes are removed from storage, they should be thoroughly aired for at least a day.

Summer clothes should be clean when stored. If they are hung, they can be ironed; if stored in a box, ironing is not necessary. Cottons and linens should be left unstarched, since starch may deteriorate the fabrics and attract silver fish. The clothes should be stored in a dry place to prevent mildew. No special treatment is needed for silks and the synthetic fibers. In humid climates where dampness causes mildew, a well-aired closet is important. Small dehumidifiers or an electric light burning in the closet and calcium chloride in an open container help to reduce moisture. Adequate space for each garment to have good air circulation is important, as are frequent airing and sunning. An electric fan run occasionally in the closet freshens the air. The selection of clothing made of mildew-resistant fibers is advisable.

LAUNDERING

Some articles in almost every wardrobe will need special care. If a knitted dress or suit, for example, is labeled washable, the care can be done at home. Otherwise, it should be sent to a dry cleaner who specializes in blocking knitted clothes.

The Importance of labels

Many ready-to-wear clothes have either hang tags or sewn-in cloth labels giving directions for care. If the label gives no information other than the trade name, the consumer should proceed with caution where care is concerned. One should try to get factual, informative instructions from tags, advertisements, or from the salesperson; any oral information should be noted on the sales slip. It is impossible to tell whether a fabric is washable by looking at it. Washable is interpreted in many ways by as many people. The following classifications are generally used:

Completely Washable—Wash any way; bleaches may be used; dry as desired.

Fully Washable, Do Not Bleach—Wash in a machine but dry away from the direct sun. If an automatic dryer is used, follow the manufacturer's directions.

Wash in Warm Water, Do Not Bleach—Wash in a machine at 120° temperature; dry away from heat or sun. If a dryer is used, follow the manufacturer's directions.

Wash By Hand In Lukewarm Water, Do Not Bleach—Wash separately with a mild detergent, at 100 temperature; dry away from heat or sun; do not wring.

Informative labels should be kept on file with a notation of the garments to which they belong for future reference. Envelopes to hold the tags, extra buttons, and matching yarn for each garment are convenient. Additional information to be kept on file includes washing machine instructions and current newspaper and magazine articles and tips on laundering. Clothes should be handled properly or the benefits

of new fibers and processes will be lost. Since proper home laundering is important to the appearance, fit, and length of life of clothing, it is essential to read and follow the laundering directions given on labels.

If you use a self-service laundry, the coin-operated automatic washers and dryers are usually different from home appliances. There is a choice of hot or warm water on washers, and a time selector but no control of heat on dryers. The hot setting and full cycle is used for white clothes; the warm setting for colors. The premeasured detergent tablets, bleach, and fabric softener are accurate and convenient to use in these washers.

Pre-laundering procedure

As before dry cleaning, pockets should be emptied; facial tissues in pockets leave clinging white flecks on the clothes after laundering. Small rips should be mended and loose buttons tightened. Clothes should be separated carefully; deep colors often bleed during the first washings even if the dyes are colorfast. Nylon picks up color readily; it is less likely to become gray if washed by itself. To prevent shirt sleeves from tangling during washing, button the cuffs to the front of the shirt.

Heavily soiled areas should be rubbed with a soft brush dipped in a heavy-duty detergent or a paste of detergent granules and water. Rubbing lipstick stains with vaseline to soften them and following with the application of carbon tetrachloride before washing is a very effective pretreatment. Mild bleaches can be used only on washable colorfast fabrics and those without resin finishes.

Detergents and bleaches

The right combination of detergents and water is important in all good laundering, especially in view of the great number of detergents, water softeners, bleaches, starches, rinses, and other laundering aids available. *Detergents* are cleansing agents which in water solution remove soil by wetting out and emulsification. Although only syndets are usually referred to as detergents, soaps are also included in the category. *Soaps* are the result of the chemical reaction of fats and oils with alkalies. *Syndets* are by-products of petroleum refining or may be derived from fats and oils. Some syndets are mixed with water softeners.

These are mild detergents, both soaps and syndets, for light laundry and all-purpose ones for general use. The all-purpose varieties contain alkali builders to assist in soil removal. Fluorescent dye is added to some detergents to increase the whiteness of fabrics or the brightness of colors. All soaps and most syndets make suds; a few syndets with low sudsing action are manufactured for use in automatic washers in which excessive suds may hamper the washing action.

In order to determine the type of soap or syndet to use for best laundering results, it is helpful to know whether the water is soft or hard. In soft or softened water, soaps clean well; in hard water they form a curd that is difficult to rinse away unless a water softener is used. Syndets clean in either hard or soft water, but clean better in soft water. Mild soaps or syndets are recommended for fine fabrics and all-purpose ones for general family laundry. Mild soap should be used on some fabrics with special finishes such as anti-static, because syndets may remove the finish.

There are two types of dry oxygen bleaches for fine fabrics: sodium perborate and potassium monopersulphate—light-duty bleaches. They are made for all kinds of washable fabrics on which chlorine bleaches cannot be used—whites and colors in silk, wool, spandex, wash-and-wear

cottons and rayons, and wrinkle-resistant or resin-treated fabrics labeled unbleachable. Sodium perborate performs best in the hottest water the fabric will stand, while potassium monopersulphate bleaches well in lukewarm water. Chlorine bleaches are more effective but directions must be followed very carefully because of the effects of bleach on some of the synthetic fibers, finishes, and elastic. Fabric conditioners added to the laundry makes fabrics feel softer and fluffier and wrinkle less and they reduce the tendency of synthetics to cling to wool. An assortment of starches is available. Fabrics with permanent finishes, however, do not require starch; heavy starches interfere with the finish. Untreated cottons take a light starch. The semi-permanent plastic starches eliminate weekly starching. Cold water starches are quick and easy to use. The aerosol spray-as-you-go starch eliminates prestarching and predampening and makes ironing easy.

Special washing

Many washable items require special handling and laundering supplies. Directions for care should be followed very carefully, especially for sweaters and other knitted apparel, fine lingerie, and leather gloves. The wash-in-net nylon knit laundry bag can save time and work by safely machine washing blouses, hosiery, and fine lingerie.

Knitted garments should be washed or dry-cleaned as soon as they begin to soil. Manufacturers' instructions for cleaning should be followed carefully. For hand-washable knits, cold water and a cold-water wool-washing compound minimizes shrinking and stretching. Always handle garments gently. Many knits are machine washable, depending upon the fiber and the construction. They should be removed from the dryer just as soon as the are dry;

do not use too hot a dryer. A rack on which the garment can be laid flat inside the dryer can be used used in place of the usual tumble drying. Some knits are only dry-cleanable and should never be washed.

Washing girdles, bras, and other lingerie with elastic in cold water soaps especially designed for elastics extends the life of these garments.

Wash-and-wear

Wash-and-wear clothes are easy to launder if one follows directions accurately. Many of the natural fibers are treated with special finishes for wash-and-wear purposes or are blended with synthetic thermoplastic fibers. These fibers are heat-set in shape and retain the original appearance until creases are forced into them through wear or in washing. The total load of wash-and-wear should equal about half the washer's normal capacity, because overcrowding causes wrinkles. Too much heat can destroy the advantages of the wash-and-wear finishes. Wrinkling, especially in synthetics, is minimized with warm or cold water and a short wash. Washing and ironing temperatures should be kept low for best results. Machine washing is a satisfactory method if cotton wash-and-wear fabrics have labels of reputable brand names, wash-and-wear assurances and laundering instructions; and if the clothes are of the following blends: polyesters alone or in blends—50 to 60 per cent polyester with 35 to 50 per cent cotton, rayon, or linen; acrylics alone or in blends—80 percent acrylic with cotton, 60 per cent acrylic with rayon or wool, 50 per cent acrylic with polyesters; nylon tricots, other knits, crepes, nylon alone or blends with special types and texturized nylon; triacetate tricot knits—100 per cent.

Since the temperature of the water is so important to successful laundering, several factors should be kept in mind to determine the temperature to be used: the kind of fiber in the fabric, the sensitivity of the dye to water temperature, the construction features of the garment, and the amount and the kind of soil in the garment.

For home laundering, standard water temperature ranges for washing and rinsing are:

Cold—cold water tap temperature, usually 75° F. or less.
Cool—approximately 80° F.
Warm—approximately 100° F.
Medium hot—approximately 120° F.
Hot—temperature as delivered by hot water tap, approximately 140° F. or more.

Use *hot water* for white and colorfast cottons, linens, white nylon, and sturdy wash-and-wear; for heavily soiled or greasy clothes to release embedded dirt and remove perspiration odors. Use *warm water* for non-colorfast cottons and linens, acetates, rayons, silks, woolens, resin-treated and stretch fabrics. Use *cold water* for not-so-soiled clothes and to protect non-colorfast dyes, to lessen wrinkling of wash-and-wears, to prevent shrinkage of troublesome fabrics, and to prolong the life of elasticized garments.

Findings such as thread, slide fasteners, facings, and trim must meet the same requirements as the fabric. Clothes that have a great deal of exposed stitching, French or flat-fell seams, pipings, bindings, and excess trimming do not always meet the wash-and-wear standards of appearance and often require pressing or ironing after washing and drying. The rows of stitching in double stitched seams should be stitched in the same direction to prevent puckers and ripples between the rows. If the fabric has already been pulled off grain by improper stitching, the seams will never be flat. Good workmanship adds a great deal to the final appearance of wash-and-wear clothes. This is especially true of durable-press clothes because the finish is set after the garment is made and puckers and other unsightly features will never come out.

Durable-press garments are the easiest clothes to care for of all wash-and-wear. A blend of 50 per cent polyester fiber with cotton, rayon, acrylic, or with a combination of these fibers stands up in all washing and drying methods. Cotton with 15 per cent nylon provides strength for good wear. Efforts to get satisfactory results on 100 per cent cotton durable-press are continuing.

Added improvements are being made constantly on laundry appliances. Large washers can easily handle a load from 12 to 15 pounds, twice the capacity of earlier machines, and use the same time as the smaller washer. The amount of water can be adjusted to the size of load and speeds adjusted for sturdy or for delicate wash; models with a cold-water rinse do a load of compatible fabrics safely.

Several laundering tips help prolong the wearable life of garments and reduce the amount of ironing: (1) sort clothes properly before washing according to the type of fabric and its construction; (2) close zippers, fasten hooks, remove pins, ornaments, decorations not suited for machine agitation; (3) avoid lint—do not include "lint producers" in same load with other items; shake each article before it goes into the washer; for white cotton loads, add a little more detergent than usual; use a fabric softener in the final rinse; (4) wash stretch garments frequently; use warm water, a short agitation cycle, cool rinse with fabric softener added; use fine fabric bleaches, short spin, wash-and-wear setting for best results.

There are dryers to match the washers'

proportions and automatic devices for control of heat and length of drying. Automatic dryers with special setting tumble the clothes in warm air, remove wrinkles forced in by washing, and then run an additional period of time without heat to restore the shape of the garment. If a wash-and-wear garment is clean but needs pressing, it can be put in the last cycle of the automatic dryer. Clothes should be removed the minute the tumbling stops, otherwise wrinkles will be forced in by the weight of the fabric. Suggestions for dryer-drying clothes: for best results, do not stuff dryer; do not combine whites and dark colors if lint is to be avoided; dry wash-and-wear clothes in small loads to lessen wrinkling; dry starched items separately to avoid spread of starch to whole load; use de-wrinkle, air, fluff, or no-heat setting for airing clothing, fluffing stored items, removing musty or mothball odors; for stretch fabrics, use low to medium heat setting and remove clothes while still slightly damp.

Steel trouser creasers save the time and work of ironing wash trousers, shorts, or pedal pushers which are not durable-press garments. Drying on these frames gives trousers the sharp creases of a well-ironed garment.

A touch-up with a warm iron is sometimes necessary on some wash-and-wear clothes around collars, facings, and interfacings and along puckered seams, especially on clothes to be worn in public. Some work clothes and children's play clothes may not need ironing.

Commercial laundry

If a commercial laundry is used, pockets should be cleaned out and jewelry, nonwashable buttons, and other ornaments should be removed. Tears should be mended unless the laundry provides this service. Here, as for dry cleaning, a note should indicate fiber content, nature of spots and stains, any first aid already given, and whether clothes should be folded or returned on hangers. The commercial laundry prefers receiving the soiled clothes unfolded and in a laundry bag—not a pillow case or a sheet. Be sure the laundry list is made out in duplicate; this will help in case of loss. If your laundry also does dry cleaning, be sure to put clothes for dry cleaning in separate bags. Some clothes can be either laundered or dry-cleaned; but others, such as washable leathers, lose their washability after cleaning. Washing of clothes that should be dry-cleaned decreases freshness, body, and depth of color.

SPOT AND STAIN REMOVAL

Since cleaning is often harder on clothes than wearing, one of the first steps in the home care of clothes is to prevent spots and soil by changing clothes or by wearing a protective covering when working around the house, garden, garage, or similar places. Before hanging clothes back in the closet, check for spots and stains. The proper use of deodorants and antiperspirants as well as underarm and back shields prevents perspiration stains and damage. If it is not overdone, pressing clothes between cleanings improves their appearance; but remember that pressing may set stains permanently.

Although on-the-spot stain removal is seldom recommended because amateur treatment often makes stains permanent, many people insist on doing their own spot cleaning. Before a spot or stain is removed, one should know the fiber content of the fabric, the kind of stain, the type of remover suitable for the stain and the fabric, the proper procedure for applying the remover, and whether the weave, dye, or finish will be affected by the process. Since it is difficult to identify the fiber content of

fabrics by appearance or feel, it is advisable to consult the hang tags or labels that were on the garment when it was purchased. As stated earlier, a file of these labels, with the identity of the garment written on each tag, will be useful in all clothing care.

Some small spots may be removed at home with proper cleaning agents and techniques. It is essential to have a reliable guide to clothing care and to follow it closely. Speed is important; some stains from chemical bonds with the fibers and on drying form insoluble compounds. Spots should be removed before both laundering and dry cleaning because heat may set some stains, and alkali, others.

Some solvents commonly used in stain removal are water, acetone, alcohol, and turpentine for non-greasy stains and carbon tetrachloride, methyl chloroform, and petroleum naphthas for greasy stains. Because of the hazards of toxicity and flammability of all solvents except water, they should be carefully used in small amounts. Absorbents include fuller's earth, talc, powdered chalk, corn meal, and cornstarch. Detergents, both soaps and syndets, will remove many non-greasy and some greasy stains. Stubborn stains on wash-and-wear can be removed by rubbing liquid detergent into the dry fabric before washing.

Chemical stain removers include acetic acid, ammonia, bleaches, iodine, oxalic acid, and sodium thiosulphate. Since some chlorine bleaches cannot be used on all fibers, directions should be followed exactly. Other bleaches used in the home include sodium perborate, potassium monopersulphate, hydrogen peroxide, and color removers. The removal of some stubborn stains like lipstick or road oil requires the use of a lubricant as well as a solvent and can become quite a task—with no guarantee of satisfactory results. To make sure that a reagent will not harm a fabric, you should test it on a seam, a hem, or some other hidden area. Grease can often be removed by rubbing nonwashables with cleaning fluids and washables with liquid syndets. Fresh paint can usually be removed with turpentine. Hot water poured through fresh fruit stains is effective on washables. Cold water is usually recommended for other stains.

DRY CLEANING

When in doubt about stain removal, go to the cleaner as soon as possible with the necessary information before the stain or soil sets. Mark the spot by pinning a piece of paper on it or by basting around it with contrasting thread. Stains from spilled liquids may not show until heat, moisture, and the chemicals in the cleaning solution bring them out and perhaps make them permanent. Inform the dry cleaner of the fiber content of the fabric; many fibers require special handling. Dry cleaners have not only knowledge and experience but cleaning materials and equipment not available to the average consumer. Most reputable dry cleaners are members of dry cleaning institutes whose services they use in keeping up-to-date on new methods.

Home dry cleaning, beyond removal of minor spots and stains, can be hazardous and is not recommended. A reputable dry cleaner will get much more satisfactory results than will an amateur. After finding a reliable dry cleaner, make him your friend and he may provide extra services such as mending, tightening buttons, small tailoring jobs, reweaving, and dyeing. The cleaner who suits you and your budget may do all of your ordinary cleaning, but you may have to contact a custom cleaner to do elaborate evening clothes, leather goods, and imitation fur coats. Many cleaners offer seasonal bargain rates, but it is not wise to save stained clothes for these sales. Speed may make the difference between a temporary and a permanent spot.

The self-service coin-operated dry cleaning machine appeals to the economy-minded person. However, it has some limitations: not all spots are removed; if the machine is overloaded, garments tend to tangle and crease; pressing or ironing may have to be done at home; the cleaning compound has some undesirable effects on items which are made of leather, fur, rubber, or imitation suede.

PRESSING AND IRONING

Ironing or pressing is becoming less a burden with wash-and-wear and durable-press clothes and with the excellent equipment available. Proper equipment is essential to speed, ease, and satisfactory results in ironing and pressing.

Equipment

Useful but not absolutely necessary equipment might include: an adjustable ironing board with a thick, spongy pad and a flameproof cover; a sleeve board; a "tailor's ham" or thick pads of various shapes and sizes for pressing difficult seams, trimmings and other design features; a spray steam and dry iron; a needle board; and suitable press-cloths.

A steam iron is excellent for both pressing and ironing; it eliminates redampening when clothes dry on the board. Some types have a water window that tells when to add water, a soleplate designed for rate, pattern and distribution of steam without spurting, and a non-spotting sprinkler. A steam iron, either regular or travel size, is a good investment for college men and women.

Clothes should be dampened evenly before ironing for best results. The damp-dry cycle on some washing machines leaves clothes ready to iron; dryers can be stopped and the clothes removed at the proper ironing dampness. The plastic laundry bag provides another means of dampening clothes. The dry clothes are put in the bag, two cups of water are poured in, the bag is sealed, and in one hour the clothes are evenly dampened. Some bags have two sections, one for white clothes and one for colored items. If clothes are dampened by sprinkling, lukewarm water instead of cold should be used because it penetrates more evenly. The clothes should be folded lightly, and as little as possible, to avoid putting in wrinkles which have to be removed later. If it is impossible to iron sprinkled clothes on schedule, it is suggested that the clothes be placed in the refrigerator or deep freezer to prevent mildew and mustiness.

Special ironing

Irons which are both steam and dry irons have temperature control dials marked for fabric types in order of increasing temperatures. For blended fabrics, it is wise to follow the directions on the hang tag or to start at the lowest temperature. If this is too cool, work gradually up until the iron glides easily; beyond this point high temperatures will cause some of the synthetic fabrics to glaze or melt. A press-cloth is required for some fabrics even with a steam iron. Fabrics which shine should be pressed on the wrong side or with a press-cloth. Leave woolens slightly damp to avoid scorching and shrinking; use a press-cloth. Silks need little dampness and should be pressed on the wrong side with a press-cloth. Press dark-colored fabrics and all rayons on the wrong side. Acetates should be pressed on the wrong side at low temperature to avoid shine and fusing.

Pile fabrics like velvet, velveteen, and corduroy should be steamed to bring up the flattened pile. Bathroom steaming is effective for the whole garment. Extremely flattened areas may be raised by placing a damp press-cloth over the fabric and holding an iron slightly above the surface. A needle board is helpful in pressing pile fabrics. Place the right side of the fabric on the protruding needles and press lightly on the wrong side with a steam iron, or use a damp press-cloth and a regular iron.

Some synthetics and specially treated cottons may not need ironing if they are allowed to drip dry. Seams, double edges, and wrinkles may be smoothed out with the fingers. If pressing is necessary, a cool iron is used. Permanent-press garments require no ironing.

When pressing one-way stretch fabrics, use a warm iron or a steam iron and press in the direction opposite the stretch.

For garments requiring ironing the general procedure is to iron sleeves, collar, trimmings, facings, and pockets first, then the seams, front and back, and then to touch up the collar, trimming, and sleeves if necessary. Fabrics should be ironed with the lengthwise grain to maintain the shape and to avoid wrinkles at the hem. Easy-care and wash-and-wear clothes may require a light touch-up on the collar, the trim and, occasionally, the seams.

An automatic ironer is valuable at the price the consumer pays only if he learns to use it properly, a procedure which takes time. It is used for flatwork, shirts, some children's clothes, and simple dresses and blouses which should be ironed with the grain of the fabric, a difficult feat for the amateur operator.

When using aerosol starch try the following: hold the can at the distance from the fabric specified by the spray manufacturer; spray evenly in a back-and-forth motion; work on a small area at a time; iron with a slightly lower heat than normal for the fabric; give collars and cuffs the heaviest treatment; apply spray a second time to areas that need more body.

Hand ironing means pushing an iron back and forth with the grain of the fabric to remove wrinkles.

The ironing instructions on wash-and-wear labels include the classifications:

Needs No Ironing—The garment requires no ironing throughout its wearable life.

Needs Little or No Ironing—The garment may sometimes be worn without ironing but for an immaculate appearance, it must be touched up with a warm iron.

Needs Only Touch-Up Ironing—The garment usually requires touching up at seams, lapels, collar, and cuffs.

Pressing is a molding and shaping process accomplished by lifting the iron and putting it down, with little or no back-and-forth movement.

Pressing with steam is effective in removing shine from woolens or worsteds. As the steam rises from the fabric, gentle brushing with a fine clothes brush revives surfaces which have become flattened and smooth. It is also possible to reduce bagginess at the seat of trousers and skirts and at the elbows of jackets and knees of trousers and slacks. Concentrated moisture and heat tend to shrink the stretched areas back to their original shape.

When pressing pleats, slip a piece of heavy wrapping paper up into each pleat to prevent marks on the right side of the garment. When pressing seams, especially on wool garments, place a two-inch strip of wrapping paper under each side of the seam to avoid leaving an imprint of the edges.

WARDROBE INSURANCE

There are innumerable property floaters adapted to the needs of private individuals, covering, for example, loss of clothes sent to the cleaners, theft of a hat at a ball game, clothes stolen from unattended automobiles, and students' clothes, in dormitories or on school premises. A tourist baggage floater covers wearing apparel, trunks and suitcases, and certain personal property. There are also fur floaters and jewelry floaters. In a number of states the personal effects floater can be endorsed to cover property on the premises of the insured.

The personal property floater is probably the most comprehensive form available. It provides in one contract all the property insurance protection an individual ordinarily requires for himself and his family. This is not low-cost insurance, but it is considered preferable to a group of individual policies for comparatively simple insurance needs.

REFERENCE READINGS

Books

Delavan, Betty C., Adams, Aurelia K., and Richards, Louise J., *Clothing Selection—Application of Theory*, Burgess Publishing Co., Minneapolis, Minnesota, 1964.

Gilbreth, Lillian M., Thomas, Orpha M., and Clymer, Eleanor, *Management in the Home*, Dodd, Mead, Co., N. Y., 1955.

LaBarthe, Jules, *Textiles: Origins to Usage*, The Macmillan Co., New York, 1964.

Stout, Evelyn E., *Introduction to Textiles*, 2nd Ed., John Wiley & Sons, New York, 1965.

Bulletins

McLendon, Verda I., *Removing Stains from Fabrics—Home Methods*, Home and Garden Bulletin No. 62, U. S. Dept. of Agriculture, Washington, D. C. Revised 1964.

U. S. Dept. of Agriculture, *Clothes Moths and Carpet Beetles and How to Combat Them*, Home and Garden Bulletin No. 24, 1953.

U. S. Dept. of Agriculture, *Home Washing Machines—Operating Characteristics and Factors Affecting Performance*, Technical Bulletin No. 1088, 1954.

Chapter 12

Do you pass inspection?

Whether you are tastefully and well dressed will be judged by you, by the people with whom you associate, and by strangers, who may be appraising your community or your country. You have many audiences. In your profession and in your social life you are seen as an individual. You appear in your community as a representative of your family. A college is often judged on the basis of its students. If you travel abroad, people may form opinions about your country from the impression you create. Unless the individual is entirely selfish, he will give some consideration to the aesthetic and moral sensitivities of his public.

Although nearly everyone has a theory on the question of for whom we dress, we really dress to please many different people and to suit many different situations. A little girl may "dress up" for her daddy, a grandmother for her children, a college girl for her fiancé, a woman for her husband, or a young businessman for his boss; but at other times, these same persons will dress for others in their audiences.

STANDARDS

As in all behavior patterns, there are pressures to meet certain standards even in dress. The student of dress may feel a conflict between the expression of his personality and the demands of our society for conformity to predetermined standards. We urge individuality but demand conformity. Much has been said about the widespread practice of companies' prescribing to employees and their wives how to entertain and dress. Many of these people resent being just cogs and losing identity. The individual must in some cases yield to local, social, or business demands but can maintain some identity just in the way he uses clothes. Analysis of the demands of a profession frequently indicates that the main things expected of the individual are that he present a neat, clean appearance and be suitably dressed. Most businesses are not concerned with color, line, fit, or many of the other factors that help create individuality. Even where a uniform is worn, many persons find ways of expressing themselves. We have seen that the same dress looks different on any two people. It is a challenge to be an individual on a small income or in a demanding job while conforming to a given set of patterns. It can be accomplished by knowing oneself and by expressing oneself through color, line, or just through the way one wears one's clothes. Since few people are really alike physically, we start with some individual characteristics. The person who has a fairly true picture of himself and wants to be an individual will seldom lose identity through clothing. It is far more likely that the individual who wants the security of identity with a certain group will end up losing his individuality. The person who really wants personal uniqueness or self-identity will usually find that he can attain it with a little thought about what is actually demanded of him and what is his own choice. One should not use freedom of expression in dress as an excuse for a slovenly appearance.

TASTE

Having good taste in dress means knowing what not to do as well as knowing what to do. Overdressing may be the result of having too much of a good thing at the wrong time or place—too much make-up; too much jewelry; too elaborate, simple, or casual a dress; too-tight clothes; too-short shorts; or too much fashion adherence. Naturalness and an unself-conscious manner are always in good taste.

EXPERIMENTATION

There are many intangibles in learning to dress well, and it is for this reason you are urged to observe, experiment, and learn all you can. Those in the fashion field would be the first to tell you that there are no easy rules to follow.

Often the individual, after studying the various phases of clothing, will react with the feeling, "There isn't anything I have that is right." After you have analyzed yourself and your appearance, you are ready gradually to put into effect the decisions you have made about your clothing. If you remember that the feeling is not uncommon and that experimentation is necessary because there is no one way to use clothing, you will begin to realize how very much you have to start with. For every rule and every example we might give there is always an exception.

Some people have a natural flair for dressing, which may be the result of keen observation. Those who are just beginning should begin slowly by experimenting with what they have in their wardrobes.

Observation, experimentation, and acquiring knowledge about clothing is a continuous process for the person who wishes to express himself in dress.

GROOMING

Although the subject of grooming has not been included in a separate chapter in this book, the importance of impeccable grooming to the person who wishes to be well dressed cannot be overemphasized. If in our dress we want to please others, cleanliness of body and of clothing is essential.

TEST YOURSELF

The questions below are designed to help you check yourself as the designer of your look. A question you cannot answer might give you a clue to something that requires more thought, experimentation, and observation on your part.

For the ladies

Do you understand the way fashion operates?

Do you find that observation and awareness in all things keep you current in fashion outlook?

Do you use fashion to complement your image?

Do you use fashion to add variety to your old wardrobe—perhaps a new length or a different way of wearing accessories?

Do you skip a fashion that is not becoming?

Do you know when you should ignore a fashion?

Do you sense when a particular fashion will enhance your individual look?

Do you extend the length of the useful life of garments by understanding when a fashion is coming in—and when it is on the way out?

Do you understand what the lines of decorative items such as jewelry do for your "whole picture"?

Have you discovered the most flattering shoe styles, lines, and textures for you?

Do you know the styles and lines that flatter your figure?

Do you know which necklines are most becoming to your face?

Do you know which skirt length—within the limits of fashion—is most becoming to your legs and figure?

Do you know which patterns in fabrics look best on you?

Do you choose color remembering the background and lighting in the place where it will be worn most frequently?

Do you know which is the most becoming color for your skin and figure?

Have you found certain colors that look well in small quantities?

Have you discovered new combinations of colors that are not "run of the mill"?

Do you use color to express your personality?

Have you become expert at co-ordinating color in pleasing proportions for you?

Have you found ways to incorporate in your wardrobe colors that you like but are not becoming to your skin?

Are your shoes "well heeled" and polished rather than scuffed and run over?

Have you taken time during the current season to observe new trends in hair styles, make-up, and beauty aids?

Have you read additional references on grooming and make-up?

Do you have a regular time scheduled for grooming?

Do you feel that your hair style is as becoming as you can make it?

Have you kept your hair shaped regularly—either professionally or by learning to do it yourself?

Is your hair clean and well groomed at all times?

Do you know the color and texture of your skin?

Is your skin clear and smooth?

Do you feel your make-up is the most flattering you can find?

Have you conquered the problem of superfluous hair on the face?

Do you make up your neck and shoulders, when they will be exposed, as well as your face?

Have you learned that cleanliness really is next to godliness?

Do you remove nail polish before chips appear?

Do you manage to keep nails free of hangnails and dead cuticle?

Are your nails clean and well groomed at all times?

Do you give your toenails the same care you give your fingernails?

Do you know what your physical characteristics are?

Have you been able to control annoying mannerisms?

Do you work for good posture at all times?

Is your voice as pleasant as training can make it?

Do you know that a little time spent organizing and planning clothing helps to release the individual from worry when dressed?

Can you forget your clothes completely once you have put them on?

Do salespeople find you a pleasant person to wait on?

Have you been able to dress smartly without getting that too-studied look?

Do you honestly feel that you do not use being well dressed as a substitute for other accomplishments?

Do you have a personal trademark such as a piece of jewelry?

Do you consider all articles of clothing—including hosiery, belts, etc., when co-ordinating your wardrobe?

Have you experimented enough with the fitting of the articles to know when they look well on you?

Do you always move in a dress or suit before purchasing it in order to observe the effect of movement on line?

Are most of the clothes in your closet ready to wear?

Are most of the clothes in your closet worn fairly frequently?

Have the clothes you have purchased been such that you have adequate time to care for them?

Do you really enjoy all of the clothes you have in your wardrobe?

In the past month, have you felt that you have had something ready to wear on all occasions?

Do you feel your selection of clothes includes something suitable for all of the occasions in which you participate?

Have you been able to avoid being conspicuous and showy and still retain identity in a group?

Does your wardrobe suit the places you go?

Do your clothes reflect indifference or boredom?

Do you feel people appreciate your appearance?

Are the members of your family proud of the way you look?

Have you avoided offending your town by keeping within accepted standards of dress of the locality?

Do you avoid imposing your clothing standards on other people?

Do you try clothes on at home before wearing them for a big occasion or a trip?

Did someone recently say, "That's just like you!"? Was it a compliment?

Do you have a philosophy of your own about the place of clothing in your life, the way you want to appear, and the factors that affect your dressing?

If you buy for others

Do you consider what clothes express the individual's personality—not your own?

Do you in buying for others consider carefully what is suitable to their activities?

Do you avoid choosing clothing that is a background for you rather than for the individual for whom you are buying it?

Do you know as much about men's and children's fashions as you do about women's?

Do you keep a record of the sizes, color preferences, and style preferences of those for whom you buy?

Do you resist the temptation to buy a tie for the man who likes to select his own?

For the gentlemen

Do you know how fashion changes occur in men's suits—in the width of the lapel, the closeness of the fit, the length of the jacket, etc.?

Do you use fashion to express you?

Do you know when a fashion detracts from your distinctiveness?

Are you willing to try a new style or color?

Do you know the weights and patterns of fabric that suit your skin and figure?

Do your clothes give you the confidence that allows you to move with comfort and ease?

Do you study the length of the jacket in relation to your proportions?

Do you know the correct sleeve and coat length for you?

Are you impeccably groomed at all times?

Are your shoes polished and in good repair at all times?

Are you able to stay clean shaven throughout the day?

Do you know the color and texture of your skin?

Have you discovered the colors and textures that are most becoming to you?

Do you know the collar and necktie widths that flatter your face?

Do you know what hair style is most flattering to you?

Do you look best in trousers with or without cuffs? With or without pleats?

Do you know which pattern scale in suits and ties is good for you?

What clothing standards are you expected to maintain in your profession?

What standards of dress are you expected to maintain socially?

Do you know what kind of jacket—with two, three, or no buttons—looks best on you?

For everybody

Do you ever relax your high standards of grooming and dress?

Are you tolerant of "all right" or "good enough?"

Are you adaptable and able to communicate in a variety of cultures?

Part Three

LET'S
BE
SPECIFIC

Chapter 13

Textiles

Since a high percentage of all apparel is made of textiles, it might be helpful to consider what these textiles do for the wearer and why consumers prefer one fabric to another for some of their clothing. Appearance means a great deal to many people; they want fabrics that are pretty, fashionable, and interesting in design or pattern. Comfort is another important consideration. The hand of a fabric is significant to the person who is texture-conscious and prefers a soft, pliable hand in some fabrics and stiffness, body, and bulkiness in others. Nearly everyone wants textiles that do not wrinkle easily, are durable, and will be easy to care for.

You may have wondered why some textiles possess certain characteristics while others do not; the explanation is that differences in fiber content and quality, yarns, weave and other construction, dyeing, and finishing are responsible for the variety of characteristics found in textiles.

When you buy apparel, do you ask such questions as "Is it wool?" "Will it shrink?" "Will it fade?" Some consumers are confused by terms like blend, thermoplastic, solution-dyed, and lofted yarn. Rayon and cotton blends are made to look like silk;

Dacron and linen, like pure linen; some Dynel-and-Orlon pile fabrics resemble fur; and nylon can be spun to look like silk. The facts about fabrics are numerous and may seem confusing to the uninformed consumer. Some basic knowledge is essential. Informative labels and salespeople will help to answer some of the consumer's questions.

What questions arise when you are selecting textile fabrics or ready-made clothing? Let us presume you saw an advertisement that ran something like this:

Fine 2x2 pima cotton broadcloth; mercerized; sanforized.

What does this mean? Is it a good buy? Will it wear well? The advertisement tells a great deal when analyzed. The "two by two" refers to the yarns, which are made of two strands, or plies, instead of a single strand, in both the lengthwise and the crosswise yarns. "Pima" is one of the better grades of cotton grown in the United States; broadcloth is a durable, plain-weave fabric easy to care for. "Mercerized" means that the fabric has been chemically treated to increase strength, sheen, and dye affinity. "Sanforized" goods have a residual shrinkage of not more than one per cent.

Once you become familiar with some of the basic terminology, you will have little difficulty in understanding textile information. There is a list of terms for reference at the end of this chapter to which you may want to add.

For many people, beauty in a fabric has the greatest appeal. Beauty is achieved through design, color, finish, construction, and fiber. Surface designs may be printed color patterns, embossed patterns on plain colors, or embroidered patterns. The design of a fabric may also be obtained in construction, through weaving, knitting, or felting. Color can be applied at various stages, from the fiber—or the solution, for some of the man-mades—to the finished fabric. Finishes add to the texture of fabrics by making them shiny or dull, crisp or soft. The method of construction and the fiber used can add beauty by texture and color.

The same factors also add durability and wearability to fabrics and give quality as well as beauty. With the increasing number of fibers and combinations, mixtures, or blends of fibers, plus all the finishes available, the consumer has a wide selection.

A fabric is any cloth or textile material produced from fibers, filaments, or yarns in woven, knitted, lace and net, or non-woven form. As indicated earlier, differences in fabrics are due to variations in fibers, yarns, and methods of construction, dyeing, printing, and finishing. These variations affect the characteristics—appearance, hand, and durability—and the use and care of the fabrics.

Fibers, in staple or filament form, used alone or in blends, mixtures, or combinations, give fabrics their characteristic sheen or dullness, softness or roughness, and crispness or drapability. Differences in yarns are due to the number of filaments or strands, the amount of twist and direction, and the size and weight of yarns. Crepes are made of highly twisted yarns, while the yarns used in sharkskin fabrics have a minimum of twist.

CONSTRUCTION

Woven fabrics

Three basic weaves, in many variations and combinations, are used in the construction of all woven fabrics. The *plain* weave has at least two sets of threads, the lengthwise, called the warp, and the crosswise, called the filling, interlaced at right angles to each other. Examples are taffeta, organdy, seersucker, muslin, and poplin. Var-

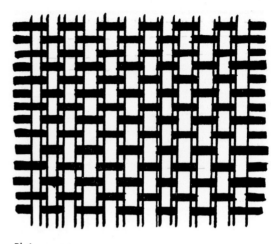

Plain weave.

iations of the plain weave include the basket weave, where two or more yarns are handled as one in the interlacing, such as oxford cloth in men's shirts or monk's cloth. The cord weave or rib is another variation.

Another basic weave is the *twill* weave, in which the filling yarns are interlaced with the warp yarns in such a way as to form diagonal lines across the fabric. Serge, covert, foulard, flannel, gabardine, jean, and chino are typical examples of fabrics made in the twill weave. The most common variation of the twill is the herringbone or chevron form found in many tweeds.

Twill weave.

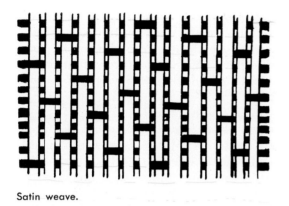

Satin weave.

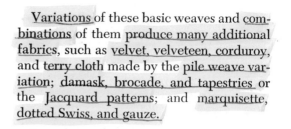

Variations of these basic weaves and combinations of them produce many additional fabrics, such as velvet, velveteen, corduroy, and terry cloth made by the pile weave variation; damask, brocade, and tapestries or the Jacquard patterns; and marquisette, dotted Swiss, and gauze.

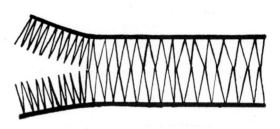

Side view of double-woven velvet. Two pile surfaces are formed as a sharp blade cuts through the center.

A third basic weave is the *satin* weave, which gives a beautiful sheen to fabrics because the interlacing of the two sets of yarns is such that more warp yarns than filling yarns are exposed on the right side of the fabric. If more filling than warp shows on the right side of the weave, it is usually called sateen. The points at which threads cross are not, as with twill, in a diagonal line; the exposed yarns, called floats, reflect light and give luster to the surface. Dress satin, slipper satin, and sateen are made with the satin weave.

As stated earlier, weaving, which is the most common method of making cloth, uses two or more sets of yarns that interlace at right angles. The outer edges of woven fabric, which are parallel to the lengthwise or warp yarns, are finished so that they do not ravel. These finished edges are called selvages. Fabrics made on shuttleless looms do not have regular selvages, but require other types of side finishing.

Top and side views of pile weave.

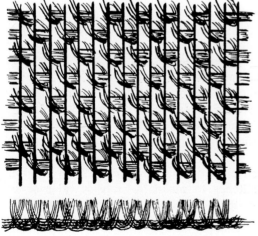

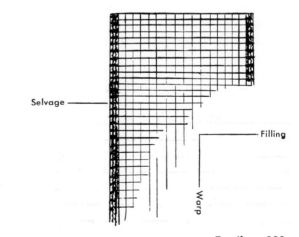

Selvage

Filling

Warp

Grain refers to the direction of the yarns in materials, the filling yarns forming the crosswise grain and the warp yarns, the lengthwise grain. To say a garment is cut on the grain means that the lengthwise direction of the garment follows the warp grain of the fabric and the crosswise direction of the garment, the crosswise grain of the fabric. When a garment or a part of a garment is cut on a forty-five degree angle between warp and filling, it is said to be cut on the bias. If the garment is cut slightly off grain but not on the true bias, the results in hang, drape, and fit are usually poor.

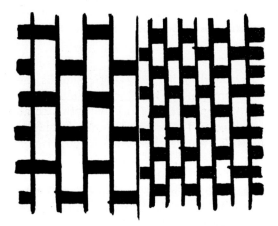

Loose weave: low count.   Close weave: high count.

The term *thread count* refers to the closeness or looseness of the weave. It is determined by the number of warp and filling yarns per square inch of fabric. A count of eighty warp yarns and eighty filling yarns to the inch is expressed as 80×80 or 80 square. A count of 80×80 is typical for percale. Surgical gauze, which has fewer warp and filling yarns per square inch, has a thread count of 28×24. There are high-count and low-count fabrics for different purposes.

Stretch fabrics provide both fit and comfort. Depending upon the type of stretch and the method of construction, fabrics stretch lengthwise, crosswise, or in both directions. One method involves the use of curled, coiled, or crimp yarns; a second uses spandex core yarns which are wrapped with conventional yarns of almost any fiber content; a third type is produced by subjecting yarns or fabrics to chemical and heat treatments. *Power* stretch fabrics have snap, extensibility, and quick recovery for foundation garments; *action* stretch is designed for sports wear; *comfort* stretch is used for everyday wear.

Knitted fabrics

In knitting, a continuous yarn or set of yarns is interlooped to form rows of loops, each row caught into the previous row and depending for its support on both the row below and the row above. This makes an elastic, porous fabric that shapes itself to the body. There are two methods of constructing knitted cloth: *weft* or filling knitting, with crosswise loops, and *warp* knitting, in which two or more yarns form loops in both directions. In weft knitting, which is the way hand knitting is done, there are three basic stitches—purl, plain, and rib—with a number of variations such as openwork, tuck, and Jacquard patterns. In warp knitting, the basic stitches are single-bar, double-bar, and multi-bar, such as raschel.

Knitted fabrics can be made *flat* or in *circular* form. For a tubular knit, the needles on the machine are arranged in a circle and loops are made around the fabric; in flat knitting, the loops are formed across the fabric.

In flat weft knitting, the fabric can be shaped during the process by adding stitches to make the fabric wider or by knitting two or more stitches together as one to narrow the fabric. This shaping process, called fashioning, is used in full-fashioned hosiery and sweaters. These flat-knitted fabrics hold their shapes and fit better than tubular knits, which are shaped by changing the tension of the yarns, increased tension making the fabric narrower. Tubular goods can be shaped after they are knitted by being put on forms and steamed to the shape and size desired. With nylon and other thermoplastic fabrics, because of the heat-setting qualities of the fibers, this method makes the shape permanent.

Double knits, made with two sets of needles, have a fine ribbed appearance with the reverse side in a tiny diamond pattern. These fabrics have more body than single knits, are durable, and require no lining.

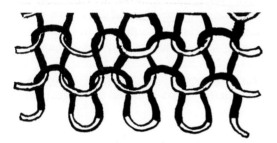

The construction of knit fabric.

Felted fabrics

Felting, another process by which fabrics are constructed, is the interlocking of fibers by heat, moisture, and pressure to form a compact fabric. The fibers are interlocked and interlaced in every direction to form a dense material of great strength. The natural characteristics of wool make it one of the best fibers for this purpose. Felt is used for hats, skirts, jumpers, dresses, jackets, slippers, and other accessories.

Bonded plastic and laminated fabrics

With the advent of synthetic fibers with thermoplastic qualities came *bonded* fabrics made of synthetics or blends of synthetics and natural fibers fused together. These fabrics are used for interfacings in tailored garments, hats, shoes, interlinings, padding, and as washable stiffening material to give shape to apparel. To produce bonded fabrics, fibers are made into a web, which is bonded into a firm mat or sheet by use of solvent bonding, heating, printing, padding, or needle punching. The resulting fabric can be dyed, printed, embossed, or used as it is, depending on its intended function.

Plastic fabrics made of vinyl compounds or polyethylene are either unsupported film or supported film with woven, bonded, or knit fabric backing. The resulting materials have good wrinkle recovery, high durability, waterproofness, and low cost for their use in jackets, rainwear, and footwear.

Laminated fabrics are made by joining fabrics to polyurethane foam, or by forming a "sandwich" with foam center, or by bonding fabric to fabric such as lace to tricot backing.

Lace and net fabrics

Another method of construction provides the lace and net fabrics with openwork patterns and designs. Lace is made up of a pattern or design that forms the solid portion and the ground, or filling, which serves to hold the pattern together. The two main types of lace are "real," or hand-made, and machine-made. They are either needlepoint, bobbin, darned, crocheted, or knotted. Net is a fabric in varied meshes made on a lace machine in round, regular, or irregular sizes like bobbinet or large novelty meshes often called fishnet.

Lace and nets are made in nearly all fibers; they have many uses, from evening dresses to lingerie and from collars and cuffs to lace-covered shoes and purses. Durability depends upon fiber, construc-

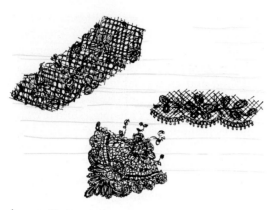

Lace patterns.

tion, finish, and use. For instance, nylon net is strong and has a lasting crispness; a compact, all-over-design lace is more durable than an open-mesh, widely scattered pattern. A wilt-resistant finish adds to the permanent crispness of net.

YARNS

Differences in the yarns affect the appearance, durability, and texture of fabrics. Yarns are made by twisting fibers or filaments together by a process called *spinning*. Yarns made from the long, continuous strands called *filaments* are different from those made of staple fibers of varying lengths. *Carded* yarns, made from fibers that have been laid parallel before spinning, differ from *combed* yarns, which, besides being carded, have been combed to remove short fibers and leave only the long ones. Cotton fabrics made from combed yarns have a fine, smooth texture and are less likely to develop a fuzzy surface. Carded and combed wool yarns are usually made into worsted fabrics like gabardine, while carded wool yarns are used in napped fabrics like flannel.

The amount of twist, the direction of the twist, and the size of the yarn are other factors that affect the characteristics of yarn. A single yarn is made of many fibers twisted together to form a single strand. A ply yarn is made up of two or more single yarns twisted together. The strands within one yarn may vary in fiber, color, size, and twist. Yarns may be tightly or loosely twisted, small or large, hard and tight or soft and bulky, knobby, corkscrew, looped, or knotted.

Specialized yarns

Some of the yarns made of synthetic fibers, the bulky yarns used in sweaters and the crepe yarns used in hosiery, for example, undergo special processing. *Textured yarns* provide many desirable features. These continuous-filament yarns have been modified so that fabrics made from them have more loft and are more absorbent, soft, opaque, warm, and fluffy. Most of the processes can be applied to nearly all fibers, natural as well as manufactured, and to blends of different fibers. There are many processes and resulting yarns, with an equally great number of trade names.

Types of yarn: a. single; b. ply; c. filament; d. staple.

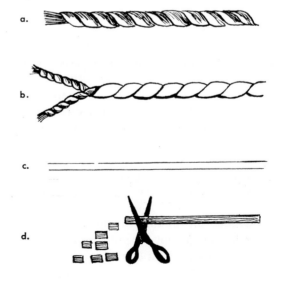

Textured yarns are coiled, curled, crimped, or looped, depending upon the particular end product desired. Some of these textured yarns add stretch to fabric.

The advantages of textured yarns offset the additional cost of the processing. There are no slubs or knots, which means better evenness of yarns. The finished product does not pill, fuzz, or shed.

Another kind of yarn is *high-bulk* yarn, a spun yarn made by blending high-shrinkage and low-shrinkage staple fibers. It differs from textured yarn in that it is made from staple fibers rather than continuous filaments. Many manufacturers prefer the textured filaments to the bulky spun yarns.

Although metallic yarns are not new, processing and finishing have been improved so that the yarns are washable, non-irritating, and nontarnishing. Metalized polyester film and laminated sheets of aluminum foil between sheets of plastic, colorless or colored, produce attractive and durable yarns.

FIBERS

Fibers are the raw materials from which fabrics are made. They are the fundamental units in the fabrication of textile yarns or fabrics. Many consumers know the natural fibers—cotton, linen, silk, and wool—and their characteristics; however, the new manufacturing processes being used on the familiar fibers change the end product a great deal. Some of the man-made fibers like Antron, Arnel, Acrilan, Avril, Zefran, Vyrene, Kodel, Vectra, Dynel, Verel, Fortisan, and Cantrece are less familiar.

Natural fibers—with the exception of asbestos, the only mineral fiber—are derived from either plants or animals. Many of the man-made fibers start as chemical solutions. In that stage, some of the characteristics of the fiber are controlled; color, for example, with dye being added in the

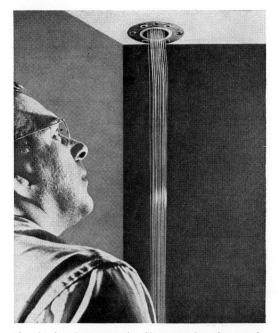

The birth of man-made filaments for the textile industry. (Courtesy E. I. du Pont de Nemours & Co.)

solution, or "dope," stage to assure color fastness. The finished fibers and filaments go through the yarn and fabric stages like other fibers. A process used with both natural and man-made fibers is *blending*, in the fiber stage. Another process is *combining* unlike fiber strands in the construction of yarns. In a woven fabric, when the warp yarns are of one fiber and the filling of another, the process is a *mixture*.

Any of the fibers, natural or synthetic, may be woven into a variety of fabrics, and any fabric may be made up of different fibers. Nylon may be made into chiffon, crepe, lace, jersey, taffeta, or velvet. Flannel is no longer made only of wool or cotton; it may be made of Orlon and wool, acetate and rayon, or cotton and rayon, which closely resemble each other in appearance and feel but may differ in use, care, and durability. End use is one of the

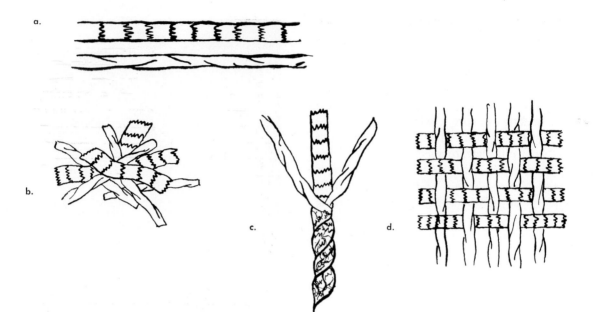

Blends, mixtures, and combinations: a. two different fibers; b. a blend of these fibers; c. the combining of fibers in ply yarn; d. mixing yarns of different fibers in weaving.

determining factors in making choices; if you want an outfit that will hold its pleats and yet be washable, you will choose one made of a fabric that provides these qualities. You may not need these characteristics in a silk organza cocktail dress.

No one fiber is perfect, yet all have desirable characteristics in varying degrees. In blending, mixing, or combining two or more fibers the good qualities of each fiber tend to minimize less desirable features. The resulting fabric often gives more satisfactory performance than a fabric made of single fiber content. To obtain the characteristics of pleat-retention and wrinkle-resistance of some of the synthetics, percentages of 65–35 or 55–45 have proven satisfactory. When buying, check on this information.

As to quality in performance, there is wide variation due to differences in the standards used by manufacturers. The fiber manufacturer makes only fibers, and the fiber name usually applies to fibers only; spinners, weavers, dyers, and finishers may also influence fabric quality. Variations in the size and the twist of the yarn, the closeness and uniformity of the weave, and the permanence of dye and finish cause differences in fabrics made from the same fibers. By knowing the names of reliable textile and clothing manufacturers and by shopping in dependable stores, you can avoid some disappointments.

If you make your clothes, you would apply the same knowledge in selecting yard goods; in addition, you should find out the suggested procedures and techniques of handling the fabric. These would include length of stitch, tension, type of sewing thread and needle, and pressing temperatures.

Further information is furnished by the

Fiber sources.

provisions of the Textile Fiber Products Identification Act discussed in Chapter 10. The Act protects consumers against misbranding and false advertising of the fiber content of textile fiber products. The generic name of each fiber present in an amount sufficient to change the characteristics of the fabric is to be mentioned and the percentage indicated. In some instances, the terms "other fibers" are used to denote fibers making up less than 5 per cent of the total weight. Labels and tags bearing this information must be firmly affixed to garments, so that they shall be on the merchandise when it reaches the consumer.

In this chapter, the classification of the fibers includes the generic names estab-

lished by the Federal Trade Commission rules and regulations under the Textile Fiber Act. Many of the trade names are also included in the chart on page 208–209.

Cellulose fibers

Cotton, one of the oldest and most widely used of the natural fibers, is a vegetable fiber which comes from the boll of the cotton plant and is chiefly composed of cellulose. There are several different varieties of cotton, with a wide range in quality. For example, a cross of five varieties,

Fiber sources.

known as supima cotton, with a staple length of two inches, has been developed. Fibers vary in length, the longest and finest being used for sheer fabrics like organdy and the shorter fibers for coarser materials like Indian Head. Fabrics made of cotton fibers are economical, versatile, easy to care for, durable, and comfortable. Cotton has innumerable uses in clothing and is fabricated in a variety of weaves and textures: silky cotton satin, straw and tweed effects, slub novelties, meshes, knits, and laces. Cotton wrinkles easily, and is weakened by sunlight unless finished. Contemporary finishes make cotton fabrics resistant to shrinkage and creasing, fire-resistant, and water-repellent. The wash-and-wear and minimum-care cottons are examples of fabrics to which special finishes have been applied. Through special finishes, cotton fabrics can be polished for high sheen, embossed, and permanently pleated. Although these finishes are desirable, there are some that complicate care; for example, some bleaches cannot be used on cottons with certain of the resin finishes. For years, cotton was used alone, but it can now be blended with almost any other fiber in proper amounts.

Linen, another old natural fiber, is a vegetable fiber, chiefly cellulosic, obtained from the inside of the stalk of the flax plant. Linen fibers are larger and coarser than cotton fibers and in general make heavier, hard-surface fabrics. The long, smooth, lustrous fibers, called "line," are used for handkerchief linen and sheer linen. Shorter lengths, called "tow," are used in fabrics with irregular appearance. Like cotton, linen is versatile, easy to care for, and durable; it wears even longer than cotton. It is not so plentiful and because of the expense of production cannot compete in price with good quality cottons. People like it for warm weather wear because it is cool, comfortable, and very absorbent. In spite of its crisp, smooth finish, linen tends to wrinkle easily unless it has a crease-resistant finish. Like other natural fibers, linen is blended with polyesters, rayon, cotton, silk, and worsteds.

Rayon, the oldest man-made fiber, is also cellulosic in substance. It is produced by the viscose or the cuprammonium process. Wood pulp or cotton linters are treated with chemicals to form a viscous solution which is formed into strands or filaments and hardened. Rayon fabrics range from the dull to the lustrous in texture; they have good color and are absorbent, easy to care for, and durable. White rayon does not turn yellow. Since the length, size, and luster of rayon fibers can be controlled, the fibers can be made into all fabrics. They can be made to resemble closely fabrics made of natural fibers—in many instances at a lower price. As rayon is absorbent, fabrics may shrink unless stabilized by special resin finishes. Rayon is cool and drapes well, but tends to wrinkle unless treated with a wrinkle-resistant finish.

Improved and higher-strength rayon fibers give greater wet strength to fabrics made of rayon and rayon blends. Thus one of rayon's original weaknesses, low tensile strength, has been overcome.

Solution-dyed rayons, with the color "built in" while the rayon is still in liquid form, are highly resistant to fading. A one-third rayon, two-thirds cotton blend has become a very satisfactory fabric. Rayon-and-polyester or rayon-and-acrylic blends make very successful wash-and-wear fabrics.

The slubbed yarns resembling duppioni silks and other novelty yarns such as the yarn with color applied at irregular intervals make interesting fabrics for dresses and blouses. Thick-and-thin filaments, flaked yarns, and flat monofilaments are other variations in rayon yarns used in fabrics for apparel and accessories.

Rayon fabrics can be washed or dry-cleaned, depending upon the fabric construction. They should be ironed when nearly dry, on the wrong side, at a wool or low cotton setting. If rayon is blended with fibers that are more sensitive to heat, a lower setting is used.

Further developments in rayon have produced fibers described as high-wet strength and cross-linked rayons. They give softness and richness of texture and dimensional stability alone or in blends with regular rayon, cotton, and wool. These include the fibers known as Avril, Corval, Fortisan, Lirelle, and Zantrel-Polynosic.

Saponified rayon is a fiber of high tenacity which provides good shape retention, dimensional stability, and fine textures to light weight fabrics. Saponified rayon is sold under the trademark "Fortisan."

Protein fibers

Wool, an animal fiber, is composed chiefly of protein. The many varieties of wool depend upon the breeds of sheep, where the sheep are raised, and their health and care. The fact that a garment is labeled "all wool" is not always a guarantee of top quality because of the many sources of wool and the kinds of wool used.

The Wool Products Labeling Act includes the definitions of wool, reprocessed wool, and re-used wool. The term *virgin wool,* not defined in the act, was defined by the Federal Trade Commission. Virgin wool is wool that has never been processed in any way before its complete manufacture into the finished fabric. The term *wool* refers to fibers from the fleece of the sheep or the lamb or the hair of the mohair or cashmere goat, and may include the so-called specialty fibers from the hair of the camel, alpaca, llama, guanaco, and vicuña.

Fibers reclaimed from new knitted scraps and from waste and broken threads in textile mills are called wool, never new wool or virgin wool. *Reprocessed* wool is obtained from scraps and clips of new woven or felted fabrics made of previously unused wool; the scraps discarded by tailors and garment manufacturers are one source of this wool. *Re-used* wool is obtained from used rags and clothing. The rags are cleaned, sorted, and shredded into fibers. A label or tag stating the fiber content of the fabric by percentages of total weight must be firmly attached to any product containing wool, except upholstery and floor coverings.

Wool fibers are made into two types of fabrics. *Worsted* fabrics, made from long, smooth, carded, and combed, highly twisted wool yarns, are hard finished and durable, hold a press, and tailor well. Serge, gabardine, and covert are examples of worsted fabrics. Although they are very durable, some of the worsteds, especially the semi-finished worsteds in men's wear, develop shine where abrasion is concentrated.

Woolen fabrics are made of shorter fibers spun into fuzzy, loosely twisted, carded but not combed yarns; they are usually bulkier and have a softer finish. Examples of woolen fabrics are wool flannels, fleeces, and some tweeds. The nap, or brushed surface, on many of these woolen fabrics tends to wear off and show the weave beneath.

Wool fabrics are resilient, absorbent, warm, wrinkle-resistant, and fire-retardent. The characteristics of water resistance, moisture absorption, and resiliency are due to the natural curl of the wool fiber. Special finishes are applied during manufacturing to lend the fabrics shrinkage resistance during home laundering and pressing. Mothproof finishes are necessary to protect wool fabrics from moths. The felting characteris-

Woolen yarn & fabric

Worsted yarn & fabric

tic of wool, which is a disadvantage in washing and pressing, permits the making of a strong, durable fabric by felting.

Wool fibers blend well with cotton, silk, linen, and all of the synthetics; wool fabrics range from tweeds, crepes, and flannels to sheers and lace.

Wool is only one of the several hair fibers used in clothing; but because it is more plentiful and less expensive than the other hair fibers, it is more commonly known and used. Other hair fibers, often referred to as specialty wools, are obtained from the goat family and the camel family. These fibers are cashmere and mohair from goats and alpaca, camel's hair, guanaco, llama, and vicuña from the camel and its relatives. The hair of the Angora rabbit and other fur fibers are also used.

Cashmere, from the cashmere goat, is extremely fine, soft, smooth, and beautiful. Since there are many qualities of this fiber, the consumer should consider cost, brand name, and the reliability of the retailer when purchasing apparel made of cashmere.

Mohair, from the Angora goat, is lustrous, smooth, soft, strong, and resilient. It is often blended with other fibers to lend durability and lustre to the fabric.

Camel's hair from the Asian camel provides warmth without weight; it is used primarily for coat fabrics. The hair is lus-trous and soft, and is used either by itself or combined with wool and other fibers. Inasmuch as there are many different qualities of camel's hair, consumers should be guided in their selection by the hand of the fabric as well as by the reputation of the manufacturer or the retailer.

There are four species in the South American branch of the camel family—the llama, alpaca, vicuña, and guanaco. The fiber obtained from the *alpaca* is fine, long, lustrous, and soft. It is used alone or blended with wool for pile fabrics for use in linings, collars, trimmings, and coats. The *llama* is closely related to the alpaca, but its hair is coarser and the fibers are seldom used for clothing in the United States.

The hair of the *vicuña* is very fine, lustrous, short, and soft. Because of its rarity, the fiber is expensive. It is used mainly in coats. The *guanaco* has shaggy red-brown outer guard hairs and soft fine under hair. The pelts of the young are sometimes used for fur trim.

The *Angora rabbit* has fine, fluffy, long, smooth, soft, and slippery hair, which is used alone or blended with wool to lend novelty effects in knitted and woven fabrics. The limited supply makes the fiber expensive. Other hair fibers are included in the discussion of furs.

202

Silk, another animal fiber and the longest natural fiber, is produced by the silkworm, which feeds on mulberry leaves, converting them into protein. The fibers are fine, glossy, continuous filaments that make soft, smooth, lustrous, and pliable fabrics. *Reeled* silk is made from filaments unwound from several cocoons and joined to form a long, continuous strand. The rough or irregular yarn made of silk reeled from double or triple cocoons is called duppioni silk. *Spun* silk is made of short, broken silk fibers and waste from cocoons, carded and spun into a yarn less lustrous than reeled silk. *Wild* or *tussah* silk is strong, irregular in diameter, and brown in color; it is used in novelty fabrics. Silk fabrics are attractive, warm for their weight, durable, strong, and absorbent; they dye well and resist wrinkling. Some can be washed by hand and a few, by machine; others must be dry-cleaned. This difference in care is determined by the finish and the manufacturing process. Good quality silk is ordinarily more expensive than the other natural fibers and is less commonly used now than it was in the early days of its use. It has become an important blend fiber to be combined with other natural fibers or with synthetics in both men's and women's wear. Screen-printed silk and silk tweeds are favorite luxury fabrics.

Thermoplastic fibers

Because thermoplastic fibers soften at high temperatures, a relatively cool iron must be used for ironing fabrics made of these fibers. They absorb little moisture and are therefore easy to wash and dry fast, depending upon the construction of the fabric and the garment. The disadvantage of nonabsorption is that with no moisture to conduct it away, static electricity builds up. Thermoplastic fibers are difficult to dye, but improvements in dyeing have alleviated many of the problems.

The thermoplastics are sturdy and lightweight; they resist wrinkling and are dimensionally stable, mothproof, allergy-free, and easy to care for. Some fabrics made of thermoplastic fibers tend to pill; textured yarns are used to reduce pilling to a minimum.

Acetates. Acetate is a man-made fiber with a cellulosic base made from wood pulp or cotton linters, which are treated with acetic acid to produce cellulose acetate. Its smooth, sleek appearance makes it desirable for taffetas, satins, and failles. Being thermoplastic, it is used for permanently embossed fabrics, like moire. Acetate fabrics, having a low melting point, require cautious care. The low melting point, however, is advantageous in providing the heat setting qualities which make possible permanent embossing and pleating. Acetate washes easily and dry-cleans well. It must be ironed damp and with a cool iron. Nail polish remover containing acetone will dissolve acetate if it comes in contact with the fabric. Lofted-filament acetate is used in knitted dresses which require no steam pressing or blocking. Acetate absorbs little water in laundering and so dries quickly. It requires special dyes and finishes to prevent color change. Solution-dyed fibers produce fabrics that are colorfast to sunlight, washing, salt and chlorine water, perspiration, and fading.

Arnel, a triacetate fiber, makes fabrics that resist wrinkles, hold pleats permanently, dye readily, will not stretch or shrink, and have a crisper hand than does acetate. It is not as sensitive to heat as acetate and can be pressed or ironed at the wool setting. Arnel fabrics are hand and machine washable; some can be tumble-dried, depending upon the construction of the fabric and the garment. A permanently pleated skirt is dried more satisfactorily by hanging after the final rinse.

Acrylics. Acrylic fibers are lightweight, warm, resilient, crease resistant, and of medium strength. Pilling and static electricity are characteristic of some of the acrylics. *Acrilan,* an acrylic fiber, is lightweight but warm, soft, and bulky. It can be heat set, it has good recovery from wrinkling, and it dries faster than Orlon and has less static. Its tendency to pill is being overcome. Acrilan is used as a blend with other fibers in suitings, interlinings, and dress fabrics. It can be used in almost any fabric construction, and lends stability when blended with other fibers because it neither stretches nor shrinks. Acrilan jersey has become increasingly popular because of its dimensional stability. A type of Acrilan fiber with a different dye reaction combined with regular Acrilan creates interesting multicolored effects. Its easy washability makes Acrilan desirable for children's clothing.

Orlon is a man-made fiber classified as an acrylic. The staple form of this fiber has a variety of uses, including sweaters and woven fabrics in both men's and women's wear; it can be blended with other fibers, including wool, cotton, and synthetics. A blend of Orlon and Dynel in pile fabrics for coats closely resembles fur in appearance. The desirable features of Orlon are lightweight; resistance to moths, mildew, and sun rot; washability; little or no shrinking; durability; and soft, luxurious hand. It is almost as strong as nylon. Bulk Orlon yarns are used for sweaters. Orlon keeps size and shape and holds heat-set permanent creases or pleats. One of its disadvantages is its tendency to create static electricity. Blended with wool, Orlon is used in fabrics for men's and boys' suits, slacks, and sport coats.

Creslan is resilient, has soft hand, is lightweight, and resists sunlight damage, abrasion, and wrinkles. Creslan fibers, of which there are several types, make fabrics dimensionally stable and fast drying. Permanent pleats and good shape retention are other characteristics of Creslan fabrics.

Zefran is an acrylic fiber that can be blended successfully with wool, mohair, cotton, rayon, and silk. It is resistant to abrasion, common types of soil, odors, pilling, sunlight damage, and wrinkles. Zefran fabrics are soft, smooth, warm without being heavy, and comfortable to wear. They hold their shape, they can be permanently pleated, and they are machine washable. *Zefchrome* is the solution-dyed form of Zefran.

Modacrylics. Modacrylic fibers are closely related to acrylics; they can be made flame resistant and are heat sensitive. *Dynel* is classed as a modacrylic. It blends satisfactorily with Orlon to make pile fabrics for coats. It is wholly resistant to moths, mildew, and chemicals; it is nonflammable, resilient, and quick drying; and it has good dimensional stability. It has a pleasing wool-like hand and makes fabrics warm, comfortable, and durable. When blended with wool, it produces a wash-and-wear fabric with a true woolen hand. Its disadvantages are the low melting point and the electrostatic property. Finishes counteract this disadvantage. Dynel-and-rayon blends are used in popularly priced slacks, shirts, and jackets.

Verel, another modacrylic fiber, is used in men's socks, pile linings, and knitted sport shirts. It is also blended with Dynel in pile fabrics. It has controlled shrinkage and a soft hand, and it is easy to dye. Originally used for men's wear, it has become important in all apparel.

Nylon. Nylon is a synthetic fiber, a polyamide made from chemical elements. It is made in both filament and staple forms. The outstanding characteristics of nylon are strength, elasticity, and resistance to abrasion. Nylon is also wrinkle-resistant, mothproof, lightweight, and easy to care for. It will not shrink, and it dries quickly. Nylon blends well with all fibers. Wear-resistance is one of its chief advantages in blends containing twenty per cent or more. It takes deep, rich colors, and it never loses its shape. Spun nylon was originally used in sweaters, but pilling was so common that the filament yarns which have been lofted or bulked have gained favor. Nylon can be made into a variety of fabrics, from the sheerest hose and chiffon to textured, wool-like tweeds and velvets. Nylon yarns with a special high twist make stretch yarns for hosiery and lingerie. Nylon is excellent for hosiery because of its elasticity, resistance to abrasion, and ability to hold its shape. A unique use of nylon is in cockleburr closures for apparel. A strip of nylon bristles of filaments tipped with microscopic hooks is pressed against a matching strip covered with soft loops of nylon yarns and is clamped to form the closure.

Being thermoplastic, nylon must be ironed with the iron set for synthetics or rayon to prevent fusing. This same characteristic, however, makes permanent pleating possible.

Modified forms of nylon giving different hand and performance characteristics include Antron, Cadon, Cantrece, Caprolan, and Qiana.

Olefin fibers produced from either polyethylene or polypropylene are resilient, flexible, odorless, and resistant to mildew and insects. The shrinkage of fibers at high temperatures makes interesting texture effects when these fibers are combined with fibers which remain stable. Some of the trade names are D.L.P., Voplex, Herculon, Polycrest, Reevon, and Vectra.

Polyesters. Polyester fibers, resilient and crease-resistant, are widely used in blends for wash-and-wear fabrics. *Dacron* is a trade name for a man-made polyester fiber.

Its crispness, springiness, beauty, durability, wrinkle-resistance, and its rapid-drying, easy-care, and little-or-no-ironing qualities make it a popular filament or staple fiber, used alone or in blends or combinations. Although blend levels vary greatly, one of the most successful fabric blends for easy care, beauty, and comfort consists of sixty-five per cent Dacron and thirty-five per cent cotton. A mixture of sixty per cent Dacron and forty per cent cotton is a satisfactory blend in men's suiting. One of its disadvantages, pilling, is being overcome.

Kodel fibers are resilient and resistant to heat, acids, alkalies, common solvents, cleaining agents, weather, and pilling; Kodel fabrics retain creases when properly processed and at the same time resist wrinkles. These fabrics are wash-and-wear and dry rapidly. Many of these characteristics are contributed to other fabrics through the use of Kodel as a blend.

Kodel IV with built-in and lasting whiteness and brightness is the result of a unique chemical compound with brightner properties being added to the Kodel polyester polymer producing fluorescent whiteness.

Fortrel is similar to Dacron. *Vycron* is resistant to pilling, has good drying properties, and may be ironed up to 300° F. temperature.

Metallics

The term *metallic* applies to manufactured fibers composed of metal, usually aluminum foil, plastic-coated metal, metal-coated plastic, or a core completely covered by metal. Fabrics made from these metallic fibers or yarns are hand or machine washable and non-irritating; they can be dry cleaned, do not tarnish, and can be embossed. The yarns are very strong, durable, and flexible; they have great abrasion resistance and add beautiful luster to fabrics. They are made in a variety of colors in addition to the usual gold and silver. If plastic-coated yarns are combined with fibers which may be ironed at high temperatures, precautions must be taken to avoid melting the coating of the metallic yarns.

Rubber

The term *rubber* refers to a manufactured fiber composed of either natural or synthetic rubber. The yarns are usually covered with other fibers and used in knitted and woven fabrics under a variety of trade names.

Spandex

The manufactured fibers in this group are known as synthetic elastomers. They are extremely fine, yet tough, with the physical characteristics of rubber. Fabric made from this material has greater strength and resistance to abrasion, body oils, heat, and solvents than rubber. *Spandex* fiber can be made into filament yarns and used uncovered or covered with other textile fibers. It is used in stretch fabrics, foundation garments, swimwear, and hosiery. Trade names include Blue C, Glospan, Lycra, Numa, Spandelle, and Vyrene.

Urethane foams

Plastic materials derived from thermoplastic resins, these foams have found ready use in apparel as interlinings because they offer warmth without weight. Foam interlining withstands repeated washing or dry cleaning and will not mat or shrink. It is used in cold-weather leisure wear, in rainwear, and in utility underwear for outdoor workers.

Expanded vinyls

Plastic resins can be produced to contain millions of microscopic pores resulting in a fabric that breathes. The expanded vinyls have been used to imitate leather in outerwear.

Corfam, a poromeric material provides breathability, comfort, and easy care in its use for shoes and other accessory items.

FINISHES

The process that gives a fiber, yarn, or fabric its characteristic appearance is called finishing. The crispness of organdy, the smooth softness of batiste, the watered effect of moire, and the water repellency of rainwear—all are the results of finishing treatments. Finishing is as important as, and in some instances more important than, the fiber used. The properties of fibers can be changed by finishes, and swatches of the same fabric can be so differently finished as to bear little or no resemblance to each other.

Finishes make fabrics attractive and serviceable; they improve the hand and provide specific characteristics to meet the special needs and desires of consumers. There are finishes to make fabrics crease-, soil-, mildew-, perspiration-, odor-, and fire-resistant; to make them crisp, absorbent, warm, fast drying, water and waterspot repellent, and mothproof; and to give them antiseptic and insulating qualities, resistance to atmospheric and fume fading, and shrinkage control.

Bleaching makes fabrics white; brushing raises a nap on the surface, singeing removes fuzz and makes fabrics smooth; mercerization increases strength, luster, and absorbency and makes fabrics easier to dye; and embossing adds surface design.

Some of the fabrics made of synthetic fibers, because of the built-in characteristics of the fibers, require less finishing than others. Some finishing, however, is necessary on all textiles. Fabrics made of natural fibers have been greatly improved by the greater variety in weights and textures and by special finishes which give them qualities similar to those of some of the synthetics.

Steady improvements are being made in finishes and dyes. One finish can make fabrics resistant to oil as well as to water-borne stains. Another type of finish increases the wearing comfort of nylon and other synthetics by making the fiber more absorbent and eliminating clamminess. Another finish makes fabrics softer to the touch and more comfortable to wear. Another finish makes permanent pleating of woolen fabrics possible.

Specialized finishes

There is an increased use of finishes which inhibit the creation of body odors and resist mold and mildew. Resin finishes ensure the permanence of embossed designs, luster or glaze, durable pleats, weighting, body, or stiffness. It is possible to finish a fabric so that it is crease resistant and will at the same time take permanent pleats.

Finishes which give cotton and rayon wash-and-wear characteristics are resins which coat or impregnate the fabrics. The resulting fabrics become versatile in washing and ironing, have a pleasant feel, and are less expensive than synthetics. Some strength, however, is lost with the resin treatment.

Waterproof finishes coat fabrics to make them waterproof and airproof. Water-repellent finishes on fabrics resist water but allow the passage of air. Durable water-repellent finishes survive at least three dry cleanings and are affected little by laundering. Renewable finishes, which are removed by laundering and dry cleaning, must be renewed after each cleaning.

Fire-retardant finishes are classed as durable and nondurable. They are applied to fabrics that do not meet the flammability test, a requirement of the Flammable Fabrics Act. Any fabric that meets the requirements of the act will not flame for more than two seconds after the ignition flame is withdrawn. The terms "flammable" and "inflammable" mean "capable of being set on fire easily." "Nonflammable" means "will not burn." "Fire retardent" means that the material ignites slowly and will burn for only a short time.

There is still room for improvement in the permanency of some finishes; ideally, the finish should last as long as the fabric. Some of the finishes having some particular advantage will at the same time have one or more disadvantages. Fabrics that have a soil-resistant finish, for instance, are often difficult to clean once grease and oil have adhered to the fabric. In home sewing, it is often difficult to press flat seams or sharp edges on wrinkle-resistant fabrics. One finish to serve all purposes is an eventuality in textiles.

A revolutionary development is the durable or permanent press garment in which pleats and sharp edges are permanently stabilized. The fabric is treated with a resin-forming chemical in a dormant state. After the garment is made, it is placed in a large oven and baked for a designated time at a controlled temperature. The chemicals react with the fibers in the fabric and permanently set a pressed smooth shape, pleats, and sharp edges—a no-iron garment. Maufacturers differ in their method of production, but the processes are usually described as either a deferred cure or a pre-cured approach.

DYEING AND PRINTING

Have you ever considered how drab your wardrobe would be if you had only white clothes? The color we have come to expect in our clothing is the result of numerous

	CELLULOSE			THERMOPLASTIC		
FIBER TYPE						
COMMON PROPERTIES	Fabrics: *Advantages* —Comfort—high absorbency; free from static electricity —Durability—withstand high heat; no pilling —Launderability—strong detergents, syndets —Resistant to moths		*Limitations* —Wrinkle a great deal —Absorb stains —Attacked by mildew —Weakened by sunlight —Ignite easily; burn quickly	Fabrics: *Advantages* —Highly resistant to moths, mildew —Strong; resistant to pulling; rubbing —As strong wet as dry (except acetate) —Wrinkle resistant —Washable; quick drying —Stable heat-set pleats, embossed designs, edges		

	NATURAL		MANUFACTURED	ACETATES	ACRYLICS	MODACRYLICS
	COTTON	LINEN	RAYON			
SPECIFIC PROPERTIES	Very absorbent Easy care Inexpensive	Natural luster and body Strong Dries quickly Does not lint	Inexpensive Good resistance to sunlight Dyes easily Absorbent	Inexpensive Mildew resistant Soft hand, natural body; drape well Dry quickly	Lightweight bulk Resilient Dimensional stability Good pleat retention Soft, luxurious hand	Bulk without weight Low flammability Resilient Good pleat retention
	Untreated—wrinkle easily; degraded by mildew, sunlight, strong acids	Wrinkles readily Heavy linen difficult to dye	Wrinkles easily Susceptible to mildew Weakened by long exposure to light	Heat sensitive Dissolve in acetone Weaker when wet (except triacetates)	Heat sensitive Pill easily Accumulate static electricity	Very heat sensitive Pill Accumulate static electricity
TRADE NAMES			*Viscose* Avicron—Crimp F * Avlin—Crimp F Avron—strong F DuPont—thick & thin—F Englo—dull F Fortisan—strong F Narco—F Ondelette—slub F Perlglo—Semi-dull F Rayflex—F Avisco—S * Enka—S Fibro—S *Solution-dyed* Avicolor Coloray Dry-Lok Jetspun Kolorbon *Cross-Linked* Avril Corval Lirelle Moynel Suprenka Zantrel *Cuprammonium* Bemberg—F Cupioni—thick & thin Matesa—dull Nub-lite—thick & thin Sunspun—S Cupracolor—solution dyed	Acele—F * Avisco—F & S * Celanese—F & S Celaspun—S Estron—F & S *Solution-dyed* Celaperm Chromspun Arnel—triacetate	Acrilan—F * & S * Creslan—F & S Orlon—S Orlon Sayelle-crimp Zefran—F & S *Solution-dyed* Acrilan Spectran Zefchrome	Aeress—F * Dynel—S * Teklan—S Verel—S
CARE	Hand or machine wash Line or dryer drying Dampen well; iron with hot iron For resin finish—little or no ironing; use perborate bleach	Hand or machine wash Iron while damp with hot iron	Lukewarm water for hand washables Hot water for machine washables Iron spun fabrics when almost dry Iron filament fabrics when fairly damp with hot iron Dry clean some garments	Hand or machine wash; dry clean Avoid wringing to prevent permanent wrinkles Press while still damp with warm iron	Generally washable Use warm iron for hand or machine wash Dryer dry at low heat	Wash or dry clean—low temperature Use lowest heat plus press cloth when ironing

*F—Filament
S—Staple

THERMOPLASTIC—continued			PROTEIN		METALLIC	RUBBER	SPANDEX
Limitations —Glaze or melt under hot iron —"Heatset" creases difficult to remove in pressing —Difficult to dye —Build up static electricity —Feel cold and clammy or hot and clinging			**Fabrics:** *Advantages* —Comfortable in cool, damp weather —Tend to hold shape —Wrinkles hang out between wearings —Do not burn readily; self extinguishing *Limitations* —Weaker when wet —Build up static electricity —Damaged by chlorine bleach —Weakened by alkalies —Become brittle, yellow with dry heat		**Fabrics:** *Advantages* —Washable —Non-irritating —Do not tarnish —Can be embossed *Limitations* —Sensitive to abrasion and flexing	**Fabrics:** *Advantages* —Resistant to acids —Strong, durable elasticity *Limitations* —Sensitive to extremes of temperature	**Fabrics:** *Advantages* —Fine yarns —Very strong —Resistance to abrasion —Lightweight *Limitations* —Yellow with heat, light exposure

NYLONS	OLEFINS	POLYESTERS	SILK	WOOL	METALLIC	RUBBER	SPANDEX
Abrasion resistance Elasticity Resiliency Great strength Lightweight Good pleat retention	Resilient Flexible Impervious to mildew, moths Lightweight	Wrinkle resistance Good dimensional stability Good strength Excellent wash-and-wear characteristics	Lustrous Resilient Strong Dyes well	Resilient Warm Resists mildew Easily dyed Holds shape	Strong Durable	Yarn covered with other fibers Natural rubber affected by sunlight Synthetic rubber resistant to natural aging	Physical characteristics similar to rubber Monofilament core covered with other fibers
Heat sensitive Low moisture absorption Accumulate static electricity Pill Absorb and hold body oils and perspiration	Shrink at high temperature Difficult to dye Low strength and abrasion resistance	Pill Poor affinity for dyes Filament yarn-slippage	Expensive Water spots Weakened by sunlight, perspiration Generates static electricity	Damaged by moths, alkali Special care needed to prevent felting and shrinkage in laundering, dry cleaning			
Antron—Trilobal Cadon—Multilobal Cantrece—Texturized Caprolan—F * Chemstrand—F & S * (Blue C) DuPont—F & S Enka—F & S Qiana—F	D.L.P.—F * & S * Herculon—S Reevon—F Vectra—F	Dacron Fortrel Kodel Kodel IV Vycron	*TYPES* Doupioni Tussah	*HAIR FIBERS* Alpaca Angora Rabbit Camel Cashmere Guanaco llama Mohair Musk Ox Vicuna	Fairtex—acetate or polyester cover Lame—alone or with polyester cover Lurex Malora—with polyester cover Metlon—with acetate cover Raymet—covered metal	Lactron—pure rubber fiber Lastex—covered rubber strand Laton—covered with cotton	Blue C Duraspan Glospan Interspan Lycra Orofil Rheeflex Spandelle Uralon Vyrene
Hand or machine wash Separate white garments Hand squeeze for line drying Low heat for dryer and ironing	Washable at low temperature; dry rapidly; no ironing	Hand or machine washable Need little or no ironing	Dry clean unless labeled washable Hand wash, warm water, mild detergent; press on wrong side at medium heat when damp-dry	Dry clean unless labeled washable; Hand wash in cold water detergents Protect from perspiration; moths	Hand or machine wash; dry clean Iron at low temperatures	Wash with cold water detergents Do not iron Avoid exposure to excessive heat	Hand or machine washable, depending on construction of garment at warm temperatures

dyeing and printing processes, applied at various stages in the manufacturing.

Methods of dyeing

If the fibers are dyed before they are spun or felted, the process is known as *fiber* or *raw stock* dyeing. Fibers of different colors can be blended to produce interesting effects; for instance, mixing white and black fibers in the correct proportion produces gray; a mixture of white and red, pink.

Dyeing yarns after they have been spun from fibers or filaments is called *yarn-dyeing*. Yarn-dyed plaids and checks are made of yarns that were dyed in the yarn before the fabric was woven.

Piece dyeing means dyeing the fabric after it is woven. Fabrics dyed in this way are usually in a solid color. However, not all dyestuffs have equal affinity for all fibers, and interesting two-toned and frosted effects can be obtained by *cross* dyeing. With cloth containing cotton and wool or rayon and acetate, a dye may be used that will color the cotton and not the wool or the rayon and not the acetate; a stripe, check, or heather effect can also be achieved.

Still another method of dyeing, used by some manufacturers of synthetic fibers, is known as *solution* or *dope* dyeing. During an early stage in the manufacturing process, the synthetic fibers are in a viscous solution; dye may be added at this point. When the solution is solidified and changed into filaments which become yarns, the color is locked in, and the fiber is colorfast to all conditions to which the finished fabric may be subjected.

Printing

Color is also applied to fabrics through printing. The design is not woven into the cloth but printed on it. Of the many differ-

ent ways of printing fabrics, *direct printing* is the simplest and most often used. The cloth is passed over a series of etched rollers which revolve in the dye. There is a separate roller for every color in the design, and each roller retains its particular color in the etched design and prints it on the fabric.

Discharge printing or dyeing is often used when the design is to contain not more than two colors. The whole cloth is first dyed a solid color; then the design on the roller is covered with a chemical which removes or discharges the color from those portions of the cloth which correspond to the design on the roller, leaving the design white. Another color can be applied to the discharged parts if desired.

The opposite of this method is *resist printing* or dyeing, in which the design is printed first with a chemical which resists dye. The parts of the cloth covered by the chemical will not take the dye, and retain their original color.

In *screen printing*, often used on silks, color is pressed through a silk or nylon screen. The background around the design is made impenetrable, and color passes through onto the fabric only in the design areas. Just as in direct printing a different roller is required for each color, in screen printing a separate screen is required for each color in the design.

Other methods of printing include *duplex, warp,* and *photographic printing* and several hand methods, such as *stenciling, block printing,* and *painting*.

A fabric made from good raw materials, beautifully and strongly fabricated, can be enhanced by the application of proper coloring—or ruined by the use of poor dyes and improper methods of application.

Dyes are constantly being improved. The promotion of existing dyes and the dissemination of information on improvements are of great value to the consumer. For instance, promotion points out that vat dyes, although costing a little more, are generally regarded as the colors most durable and fade-resistant to sunlight and washing.

USES AND CARE

Knowing the effect of excess heat on various fibers may help you in pressing and ironing. Cotton, rayon, and linen scorch; wool and silk burn; and thermoplastics shrink and become hard. Heat, moisture, and friction in washing and pressing cause wool to shrink and felt. The use of cold-water soap and the elimination of rubbing while washing wools reduces this shrinkage. Using a press cloth over wool tends to eliminate shrinkage and felting while pressing.

Comfort

Silk, linen, rayon, and cotton are considered the most comfortable for hot weather because they absorb a great deal of moisture rapidly. However, the way the yarn and the fabric are made is equally important. A closely woven, heavy cotton seersucker is not as cool as a loose or open construction like dimity. The first provides insulation; the second allows air to pass through.

The thermoplastic fibers—acetates, nylons, acrylics, and polyesters—sometimes feel clammy because they do not absorb perspiration. Special finishes and blending with other fibers make them more comfortable to wear.

Colorfastness

Colorfastness depends not only on the kind of fiber but also on the treatment of the fabric, on the type of dye used, and on the method of application. There are so many factors that may harm colored fabrics that it is impossible for one fabric to be colorfast to all of them—sunlight, washing, dry cleaning, ironing, pressing, atmospheric fumes, perspiration, salt water, and chlorinated water. If you know that the garment must be subjected to one or more of these conditions, you should look for a specific guarantee on the label when purchasing.

Wrinkle resistance

When buying clothing for traveling, you may look for wrinkle resistance. Wool and Dacron recover from wrinkles very readily; silk, Orlon, Acrilan, Dynel, acetate, and Arnel are good. Cottons, rayons, and linens are poor in wrinkle recovery unless treated with special finishes. Here again it is impossible to judge wrinkle-resistance by fiber or finish alone. For instance, crepes, knits, and fuzzy, textured, and printed surfaces help to shed wrinkles or to make them less apparent.

Shrinkage

Fabrics made from nylons, acrylics, modacrylics, acetates, and polyesters usually hold their shape well during washing and dry cleaning. Since these fibers are sensitive to heat, however, if the temperatures you use during washing, drying, and pressing are higher than those used to "heat set" the fabric or garment when it was manufactured, a sweater may stretch during laundering or a blouse may shrink when pressed. Fabrics made from absorbent fibers—wool, silk, linen, rayon, and cotton—are sensitive to moisture as well as to heat, and need special finishes to control shrinkage. Washing, steam pressing, vigorous agitation, long washing periods, or over-drying in an automatic dryer may increase shrinkage. Therefore, it is very important to read and follow the directions on the labels of yard goods or ready-to-wear.

Textile Terms

General

Abrasion. The wearing away of the surface of a material by friction.

Absorbency. The ability of a fiber to take up moisture.

Atmospheric fading. The tendency of certain colors in acetate fabrics to change or fade due to smoke, soot, or acidic fumes in the air.

Bias. Diagonal or oblique direction across the lengthwise and crosswise grain of a fabric.

Bleaching. A process to remove natural and artificial impurities in fabrics in order to obtain clear whites for even dyeing and printing.

Bleeding. Excess dye tends to "bleed" or run when fabrics are washed.

Blending. The combining of two or more fibers in the spinning process.

Bonded fabrics. Webs of fibers adhesively bonded to one another with a bonding material or by the action of thermoplastic fibers.

Bulk yarns. Increased in mass, bulk, or size without increase in weight or length.

Carding. Process of separating fibers from each other, laying them parallel in a thin web.

Combing. Process that produces even, compact, fine, and smooth yarns by eliminating short fibers.

Combination. Plied yarn composed of two or more strands, each made of a different fiber.

Cotton boll. Seed pod of the cotton plant, from which the cotton fiber is taken.

Cotton linters. Very short cotton fibers clinging to the cotton seed after the regular staple fibers have been removed.

Count (of cloth). The number of yarns or threads per square inch of fabric.

Crocking. Tendency of dye in a fabric to rub off.

Cut pile. Fabric woven with an extra set of either warp or filling threads that form a pile, which is later cut, on the surface of the fabric. If the pile is not cut, it is known as looped or uncut pile.

Detergent. A cleansing agent or solvent, including soap; a synthetic detergent is called a syndet.

Dimensional stability. The ability of a fabric or garment to maintain its original width or length in laundering and dry cleaning.

Drip dried. Removed from rinse water without wringing and allowed to hang until moisture has evaporated.

Dry wrinkles. Wrinkles resulting from wringing in laundering; tend to remain when the fabric is dry.

Dyeing. A process of coloring fibers, yarns, or fabrics with either natural or synthetic dyes.

—**Cross-dyeing.** Process of dyeing yarn or fabric containing fibers with different dye reaction with one dye, so that different colors are obtained from the same dye.

—**"Dope" dyeing.** See *Solution dyeing.*

—**Piece dyeing.** Dyeing fabrics after weaving.

—**Solution dyeing.** Adding color in the solution or "dope" stage in the production of synthetics.

—**Stock dyeing.** Dyeing fibers, or "stock," before spinning.

—**Yarn dyeing.** Dyeing the yarn before the fabric is woven.

Elasticity. The characteristic that enables fibers, yarns, and fabrics to return to shape after being stretched.

Embossing. The process of pressing a raised design into a fabric by passing the fabric between hot engraved rollers.

End use. The ultimate use for which a manufacturer makes a material for consumer consumption.

Fabric. Any cloth or textile material produced from fibers, filaments, or yarns in woven, knitted, or non-woven form.

Felting. Natural characteristics of wool fibers which cause wool to mat or felt when subjected to abrasion, heat, moisture, pressure; the felting property of fibers.

Fiber. Smallest textile unit, from which yarns and fabrics are made.

Filament. A single strand of silk or synthetic fiber, as extruded by the silkworm or from a spinnerette.

Filling yarn. The crosswise yarn in a woven fabric, at right angles to the warp yarn.

Grain. The warp (or lengthwise) and filling (or crosswise) yarns make up the grain of a woven fabric.

Hand. The feel of the fabric—soft, smooth, hard, rough, light, or heavy.

Jacquard. A type of weave with intricate patterns or designs woven into the fabric on the Jacquard loom.

Knitting. A method of making fabric by interlocking a series of loops of one or more yarns.

—Circular knit. Knitted fabric made in tubular form without seams.

—Courses. Horizontal ridges in knitted fabrics.

—Double knit. Knitted fabric with more body and durability than single knit.

—Flat knit. Knitted fabric made in flat, not tubular, form, which permits shaping or fashioning.

—Full-fashioned. A flat-knitted fabric shaped on the machine by adding or dropping stitches.

—Wales. Lengthwise line of loops in knitted fabrics.

—Warp knit. A knitted fabric like tricot and melanese; it is a flat and close knit, less elastic than weft knit.

—Weft knit. A knitted fabric in which the yarn runs back and forth crosswise in the fabric, as opposed to warp knit; it is made in plain, purl, and rib stitches.

Laminated. Made up of several layers bonded into one sheet with resins or glues.

Linen, line. The long linen fibers.

Linen, tow. The short linen fibers.

Lofted yarns. Yarns with increased bulk or thickness but without an increase in weight; when pressure is applied to and then removed from a lofted-yarn fabric, the fabric will spring back to its original thickness and bulk.

Mat. Lusterless and dull in surface. To finish with a mat surface. Mat jersey.

Mercerization. A process that increases the strength, luster, absorbency, and dyeability of cotton.

Mixture. The warp yarns are of one type of fiber; the filling yarns are of another type.

Monofilament. A one-filament strand used as a yarn.

Multifilament. A yarn made of a number of single filaments.

Noils. The short fibers that are separated from the long fibers in the combing process in preparing worsted yarns.

Pellon. Trade name for any of several non-woven interfacings and/or interlinings.

Pile fabrics. Fabrics with cut or uncut loops on the right side; velvet is an example of cut pile, Turkish toweling of uncut pile.

Pilling. The tendency of yarns and fabrics to show little balls or tufts of fibers on the surface after wear.

Pima. A fine, strong, American-grown cotton.

Ply. Strand. Ply yarns are formed by twisting together two or more single strands.

Printing. Method of applying dye to a fabric in a design or a pattern.

—**Block printing.** Method of stamping a pattern on the fabric in which wood or linoleum blocks carry the dye.

—**Direct printing.** Method in which the design is applied by means of engraved rollers; a separate roller is required for each color.

—**Discharge printing.** Process in which color is discharged from or bleached out of piece-dyed goods, leaving a white pattern to which color may be added or which may be left white.

—**Duplex printing.** Printing a pattern on both the face and the back of the fabric; imitates woven design.

—**Photographic printing.** Application of a photographic image to cloth.

—**Resist printing.** Method in which substances that resist dye are applied to the fabric in designs and are removed after the cloth has been dyed.

—**Screen printing.** Method in which the background of the design is painted on the screen with paste and the dye printed through the exposed screen; separate screens are used for each color.

—**Stencil printing.** Similar to resist printing: portions of the fabric are covered with paper or metal; the dye is applied to the exposed fabric through openings in the stencil.

—**Warp printing.** Process of printing a design on the warp yarns before weaving. Filling yarns may be white or a neutral color. The process produces a muted or shadowy pattern.

Resiliency. Property of fibers which causes them to return to or resume the original position in shape after crushing.

Silk

—**Cocoon.** The case spun by the silkworm serving as a covering; the source of the silk filament.

—**Doupione** or **duppioni.** Silk from two silkworms who spin their cocoons together; the resulting yarn is irregular, uneven, and large in diameter.

—**Reeled.** Long, continuous filament.

—**Spun.** Waste silk and silk from pierced cocoons.

—**Wild** or **tussah.** Silk from the wild, uncultivated silkworm; fibers shorter than reeled silk.

Spun yarns. Yarns made of staple fibers.

Staple. Term used to denote lengths of any fiber which requires spinning and twisting to form a yarn.

Static electricity. Electricity generated by friction of a fabric against itself or against other objects.

Supima. Long-staple cotton fiber developed and grown in the United States.

Syndet. Synthetic detergent as distinguished from a soap.

Tensile strength. Breaking strength of yarns or fabrics. High tensile strength means strong yarns or fabrics.

Thermoplastic. Having the property of becoming soft under application of heat; rigid at normal temperature.

Vat dye. One of the best kinds of dye, resistant to both washing and sunlight.

Warp. The lengthwise yarns in woven fabrics.

Wicking. The characteristic that allows water to travel rapidly along fibers and through the fabric, as opposed to absorbency, which means that the moisture is retained within the fibers of the fabric.

Wool

—**Reprocessed wool.** Wool obtained from

scraps and clips of new woven or felted fabrics made of previously unused wool.

—**Re-used wool.** Wool obtained from used rags and old clothing that has been worn.

—**Virgin wool.** Wool that has never been made into cloth or used for any other purpose.

—**Wool.** New scraps and fibers reclaimed from knitted scraps, broken threads, and other waste from the manufacturing process.

—**Woolen fabrics.** Carded, short wool fibers spun with medium twist into soft, bulky yarns for soft, fuzzy-surface fabrics.

—**Worsted fabrics.** Carded and combed long fibers spun with high twist into smooth, light yarns for smooth-surface fabrics.

Yarn. Product of fibers twisted into a continuous strand or strands to be used for weaving and knitting fabrics.

Textured yarn—trade names

Agilon. Stretch yarn; nylon or nylon in combination with cotton; Dacron; applicable to all thermoplastic and blended fiber yarns.

Antron 24. Bulked trilobal nylon filament.

Avicron. Rayon yarn with a latent crimp, developed by wet processing.

Ban-Lon. Gives moderate stretch and bulk to nylon and Dacron yarns; name applied to yarns, fabrics, garments.

Cantrece. "Engineered" stretch nylon for hosiery.

Duclé. Texturized acetate, polyester, nylon yarns.

Fluflon. Coiled, false-twist continuous process for plied yarns of Dacron or nylon.

Helanca. Coiled process for high-stretch yarns of Dacron or nylon.

Lofted Chromspun; Estron. Acetate yarns looped by air jet process.

Loft-Set. False twist nylon filaments.

Mylast. Crimped Dacron or nylon yarns.

Saaba. Modified stretch Dacron or nylon yarns.

Spunize. Crimped nylon, polyester, polypropylene yarns.

Superloft. Stretch yarn produced by false twist; any thermoplastic fiber.

Synfoam. Crimped thermoplastic filament yarn.

Taslan. Process that fluffs any kind of yarn and combinations of yarns by air jet.

Tycora. Continuous-filament yarns processed by several texturing methods.

Textile finishes—trade names

Absorbent. Increase the ability of fabrics to absorb moisture and permit more rapid evaporation: Fabulized, Nylonized, Sorbinol, Sorbtex, Telezorbent, Zelcon.

Antiseptic. Reduce tendency for growth of bacteria and retard absorption of odors by fabrics: Dowicide, Eversan, Permachem, Perma-cide, Permaseptic, Puritized, Sanitized.

Anti-static. Prevents accumulation of static electricity.

Crease-resistant. Fabrics are impregnated with synthetic resins to resist creases and wrinkles: Aerotex, Bradperma, Bradura, Casual Care, Dela Shed, Disciplined, Dri-smooth, Fresh-Tex, Norfix, Martinized, Resloom, Sanforized plus, Stazenu, Staze-Rite, Superset, Tebelized, Unidure, Vitalized, Wrinkle-Shed, Zeset.

Crease-retention. Finishes applied to fabrics to maintain pleats and creased edges: Si-Ro-Set, applied to woolens; Koratron.

Crispness. Finish is a permanent sizing that will not wash out: Apponized, Bellmanized, Ceglin, Everglaze, Heberlein, Ice,

Resi-Perm, Sabel, Saylerized, Stabilized, Stazenu, Trubenized, Vitolast, Vitalized, Wat-a-Set, Unisec.

Durable Press. Pre-cure or post-cure treatment of fabrics. Burmi. Coneprest, Dan Press, Koratron, Never Press, Primatized, Reeve Set, Super-Crease.

Flameproof; fire-repellent. According to the finishing treatment, fabrics can be made flameproof or fire-repellent, resistant, or retardent: Aerotex, Anti-pyros, Banflame, Ellicote, Erifon, Fire Chief, Flamefoil, Flame Retardent, Permaproof, Pyroset, Saniflammed, X-12.

Mildew-resistant. Antiseptic finish retards or prevents the growth of mildew: Aerotex, Ban-Dew, Dowicide, Fresh-tex, Permaseptic, Puritized.

Mothproofing. Finish tends to make fabrics moth repellent rather than permanently mothproof: Amuno, Berlou, Boconized, Eulan, Larvonil, Mitin, Moth Snub, Woolgard.

Shrinkage-resistance. Finishing treatment for yarns or fabrics to reduce shrinkage of finished fabric, the degree varying from one to two per cent: Aerotex, Ap-ponized S, Avcoset, Avcosol, Bradura, Cyana, Delta-Set, Definized, Dylanize, Evershrunk, Facility, Fiberset, Harriset, Kroy, Lanaset, Perry-ized, Permathol, Protonized, Redmanized, Resloom, Rigmel, Sabel, Sanco 400, Sanforized, Sanforlan, Sanforset, Saylaset, Schollarized, Shrink-Master, Stazenu, Tebelized, Tub-Allied, Unifast, Wat-a-Set, Zeset.

Stain-resistance. Resin finish to resist soil and stains: G.E. Silicones, Repel-A-Tized, Scotchgard, Sylmer, Zepel.

Thermal or **insulation.** Metallic finishes applied to fabrics tending to keep body heat in and reflecting sun rays away from body: Milium, Temp-Resisto.

Waterproof. Finish coats the fabric to prevent the passage of moisture or air through: Beautanol, Koroseal, Reevoir.

Water-repellent. Finish resists water yet permits passage of air through the fabric.
Durable: Cravenette, Durasec, Four Star, Hydro-Pruf, Lovely-on, Norane, Norfix, Nortex, Permel Plus, Silicone, Unisec, Zelan.
Renewable: Aqua-sec, Aridex, Cravenette, Dry-dux, Impregnole.

Easy care

The "wash-and-wear" feature of fabrics and apparel intrigues many consumers. Garments that can be washed and worn with little or no ironing have become quite popular. They are made of the non-cellulosic fibers that possess the properties of moisture resistance and shrinkage resistance, making them quick to dry and ideal for wash-and-wear apparel. Cellulose fibers with special finishes or proper blends of cellulose and synthetic fiber are also used for wash-and-wear fabrics. A wash-and-wear fabric is "one that can be made into a garment that will satisfactorily retain its original neat appearance after repeated wear and laundering, with occasional or no ironing." This means that garments retain their creases or pleats after washing and require only an occasional light ironing. In addition, they meet consumer demands for durability, color fastness, and shrinkage, and remain neat in appearance during normal periods of wear.

The earlier "wash and drip dry" requirement became a decided limitation when wash-and-wear garments increased from underwear and blouses to bigger and heavier apparel like men's summer suits. In fact, the next development in this area was "automatic wash-and-wear." In addition to the qualities of wash-and-wear, automatic wash-and-wear has the ability to go through the full cycle of the automatic washer and be dried in a home tumble dryer to a condition described as smooth and wearable with little or no subsequent ironing needed. Any wrinkles put in the garment by the spin cycle or by wearing are actually removed by the tumble dryer.

Cotton obtains wash-and-wear characteristics through resin finishes. Blending of natural with synthetic fibers also increases wash-and-wear features. Cotton is blended with a new nylon staple fiber developed especially for blending with cotton and rayon. A Dynel-and-wool blend and an Orlon-and-wool blend have put woolens into the wash-and-wear class.

Garments with the durable-press finish have the shape locked in and wrinkles, stretch, and shrinkage are eliminated. Continued washing and machine drying of cotton or blends with cotton have no appreciable effect upon the appearance of the garments.

An aluminum-based finish has been developed to give water-repellency, stain-resistance, and quick-drying properties to cotton, wool, rayon, and blends.

Blends, combinations, mixtures

Do blends, combinations, or mixtures of fibers puzzle you? Fabric will behave somewhat like each fiber it contains, according to the proportion of each. It is advisable to treat a fabric as you would the most sensitive fiber included. Orlon or Dacron added to cotton or rayon will increase the speed of drying; if the proportion used is high enough, very little moisture will be needed in pressing. To help retain the washability, quick drying, wrinkle resist-

ance, and easy care features of acrylics and polyesters, there should be at least 55 per cent of these fibers in mixtures with wool and 65 per cent or more in mixtures with cotton or rayon.

Polyesters add wrinkle resistance to cotton and rayon blends. Nylon and silk give added strength and luster. Polyesters, acrylics, and tri-acetates blended with rayon or cotton in the proper amounts produce fabrics in which the consumer can readily press pleats that are durable to laundering. Cotton and rayon in turn lend absorbency that improves the comfort of these blends.

It used to be difficult for the consumer to identify fibers without labels indicating fiber content. With the Textile Fiber Products Identification Act requiring that the percentage of fibers be indicated on labels, the information is there if the consumer wants to use it. See explanation of blends, mixtures, combinations page 197.

Fiber content, however, is only one of the items that determine how a fabric will react to care. As stated earlier, all steps of manufacturing influence the final fabric. Although each of the synthetic fibers is washable, any one of them could be used in a type of fabric that is not washable but used for another of its qualities. Consequently, the statement of fiber content does not necessarily indicate the proper care methods. Directions for care on the labels should be followed because the end-use performance of the fabric determines the care methods.

Care labels

When buying, note whether the label refers to the garment or to the fabric alone. If trim, paddings, and interfacings are not washable but the fabric is, the garment is not washable.

For best results it is very important to follow directions for minimum care of garments given on informative hang tags. The direction "Don't soak or rub" means that soil is removed easily because the resin finish forms a coating which resists soil. "Don't wring or twist" means that creases will set and be hard to remove even with pressing. Drip dry or tumble dry is usually the suggested care. Another example of the importance of care directions is the "Don't starch or bleach" warning, which means that the resin finish gives the fabric enough body without starch. Plastic starch cuts down on the efficiency of the resin finish. It is wise to check the label concerning the use of bleach since some resin finishes are chlorine-retentive and will become discolored.

Care tips

Separate white garments from colored ones. Garments with well-made seams can stand the automatic wash, but some clothes may require hand washing no matter what the fiber content. Washing sweaters inside out prevents fuzzing and pilling.

When ironing fabrics containing two or more different fibers, use some moisture; either use a steam iron or dampen the fabrics lightly. Blends containing Dynel always require a damp press cloth between fabric and iron, even with a steam iron, because Dynel is unusually sensitive to heat.

Test your iron to make sure it heats evenly. If not, use a lower setting. Move quickly; temperatures build up when you hold the iron in one spot. Be careful not to press in unwanted creases, since they are sometimes hard to remove.

When pressing wools on the right side, use a press cloth between the iron and the garment. To avoid shine, use a dry wool cloth topped by a damp cotton one. If you use a steam iron, only the dry wool cloth is necessary. Stop pressing while the steam is still rising, before the cloth is completely dry.

You must remember that although there are hundreds of different fabrics, there is no single one that can possibly fill all needs. The characteristics that make a fabric desirable for one purpose often make it undesirable for another. It is helpful to think of fabrics in terms of what you want them to do for you. Buy the right fabric for the right purpose. It is better to buy a garment with clear instructions for care on the label than a similar garment without directions.

Remember also that the manufacturer's recommendations regarding dry cleaning or washing are to help you. Each fabric reacts just a little differently, depending on how it is constructed, dyed, and finished.

REFERENCE READINGS

American Fabrics, Nos. 63, 64, 65, Doric Publishing Co., New York, 1964.
American Fabrics, Nos. 66, 67, 68, Doric Publishing Co., New York, 1965.
American Home Economics Association, *Textile Handbook*, 3rd ed. (Revised), Washington, D. C., 1966.
Campbell, Jerome, "Profit Opportunities in Man-Made Fibers," *Modern Textile Magazine*, Rayon Publishing Corp., N. Y., March, 1959.
Cowan, Mary L., *Introduction to Textiles*, Appleton-Century Crofts, Inc., New York, 1962.
Denny, Grace G., *Fabrics*, J. B. Lippincott Co., Philadelphia, 1953.
Federal Trade Commission, *Trade Practice Rules for the Silk Industry*, 1938.
——, *Trade Practice Rules for the Linen Industry*, 1941.
——, *Trade Practice Rules for the Rayon and Silk Dyeing, Printing, Finishing Industry*, 1941.
——, *Trade Practice Rules for the Rayon and Acetate Textiles Industry*, 1951.

————, *Rules and Regulations Under the Wool Products Labeling Act,* 1953.

————, *Rules and Regulations Under the Flammable Fabrics Act,* 1954.

Federal Trade Commission, *Rules and Regulations Under the Textile Fiber Products Identification Act,* June, 1959.

Henry, M. Frances, "Why Textured Filament Yarns?," *What's New in Home Economics,* September, 1958.

Hess, Katharine P., *Textile Fibers and Their Use,* J. B. Lippincott Co., Chicago, 1954.

Hollen, Norma and Saddler, Jane, *Textiles,* 2nd Ed., The Macmillan Company, New York, 1964.

Joseph, Marjory L., *Introductory Textile Science,* Holt, Rinehart and Winston, Inc., New York, 1966.

LaBarth, Jules, *Textiles-Origins to Usage,* The Macmillan Co., New York, 1964.

Lee, Julia Southard, *Elementary Textiles,* Prentice-Hall, Inc., New York, 1953.

Linton, George E., *Applied Basic Textiles,* Duell, Sloan, and Pearce, New York, 1966.

Linton, George E., *The Modern Textile Dictionary,* Little, Brown & Co., Boston, 1954.

Stevens, Hazel Thorp and Richey, Helen L., *Introduction to General Textiles,* Burgess Publishing Co., Minneapolis, Minn., 1950.

Stout, Evelyn E., *Introduction to Textiles,* 2nd Ed., John Wiley & Sons, Inc., New York, 1965.

Tingley, Katherine A. and Bivins, Maude, *Today's Textiles,* University of Connecticut, September, 1959.

United States Department of Agriculture, *Clothing Fabrics,* Home Economics Research No. 1, Washington, D. C., 1957.

Wingate, Isabel B., *Textile Fabrics,* Prentice-Hall, Inc., New York, 1963.

Women's Wear Daily, June 24, 1959, "FTC Generic Names Paired with Trade Names of Manufactured Fibers."

Chapter 14

Suits
and
coats

Suits and coats generally represent the largest investments in a wardrobe. Because people expect more wear from a suit or a coat, they are willing to spend more in its purchase. Fashions in suits, as in other articles of clothing, change with living patterns; contemporary living has particularly affected fabrics. Air conditioning in buildings and heaters in cars have eliminated much of the need for very light and cool or very heavy, warm clothing. Travel has encouraged the development of items of lighter weight, and the demand for easy care has increased the use of man-made fibers and crease-resistant finishes.

Although individual criteria for judging suits and coats will vary, the following points should be considered in all suit or coat purchases:

1 Fabric
2 Workmanship
3 Design
4 Fitting

A good suit has quality fabric suitable to the design, to the person, and to the occasion. Fine tailoring is essential in any suit, whether custom made, made to order, or ready made. The fitting of the suit is a fine point; it will in large measure determine becomingness and comfort.

FIBERS

Just about every fiber has been or will be used in suits. The fibers most frequently used are wool and other hair fibers, silk, cotton, synthetics, and blends of two or more of these fibers.

Woolens, worsteds, and hair fibers

Because of its superb tailoring qualities, wool has always been a favorite for suits and coats. Wool has an elasticity that resists wrinkling; it takes dyes well; and it gives warmth without clamminess.

The choice between a woolen or worsted fabric will depend on the end use of the garment. (See Chapter 13.) Woolens, because they are softer, may wrinkle more readily than worsteds. A woolen with a long nap tends to show wear more readily than one with a shorter nap. A worsted fabric generally holds a press well, but may become shiny with wear and pressing. Unfinished or semi-finished worsteds are given a slight nap to help prevent shine.

Among the luxury fibers used in suits and coats, we find vicuña, cashmere, and camel's hair. These luxury fibers should be judged as are the other hair fibers. They are generally considered less durable than wool of equal fiber quality and are expensive. Vicuña, the most costly hair fiber, is to casual wear what mink is to dressy fur coats.

Cotton and linen

Cotton has always been a popular fabric for summer suits, but unless it has a wrin-

Duffle coats.

kle-resistant finish or is woven to resist wrinkling, it will wrinkle and soil readily. Seams in a fabric with a wrinkle-resistant finish will not press as crisply as seams in woolen suits. Cotton is easily laundered, durable, and comfortable to wear. Linen suits also require a finish resistant to wrinkling but launder well when unlined.

Silk

There is nothing to surpass the beauty of a fine silk suit. Beautiful textures result from the use of the natural uneven yarns of raw silk. Pongee, shantung, and duppioni have long been prized for coats and suits. Tie silks and foulards are light in weight and make excellent spring suits. Perspira-

tion is harmful to the silk fiber, and in summer, when most people perspire more readily, a silk suit will have to be cleaned frequently. Silk is blended with synthetics, worsteds, and linen for interesting textures.

Blends

Among the blends most commonly found in suits are those of silk and worsted, polyester and acetate or rayon or both, polyester and mohair, and polyester and cotton. A popular blend for cord suits is nylon with acetate and rayon. Acrylic is blended with wool and synthetic fibers. Modacrylics have been used in fabrics of napped finish, like fleece. Because modacrylic can be laundered, a white coat is no longer strictly a luxury item. Blends of triacetate and nylon create velours which are elegant yet practical for evening suits and smoking jackets.

The advent of stretch fabrics makes possible styling for ease of body movement without bulk. The first men's suits made of stretch fabrics were not successful because the trousers did not retain a crease, but improved finishes have solved the creasing problems. Stretch fabrics will have advantages in designing for greater comfort and fit, as the use in slacks and trousers has already indicated. Important in the development will be better shape retention. Stretch slacks, when not properly finished and constructed, tend to sag at the knees.

Continuous studies to determine the amount of stretch needed for specific uses will be a necessity as improvements in stretch fabrics are made.

Choice of stretch fabrics should be made with the end use of the garment in mind. It is essential to choose the correct size when buying articles of stretch fabric. The stretch of the fabric should not be used as a means of fitting into a smaller size—or the purpose for which the stretch fabric is designed may be lost. Certain suits do not require extra ease.

Bonded and laminated fabrics

Bonded and laminated fabrics have limitless potential in the design of coats and suits. Fabrics, such as open lacey weaves, which in the past were not suitable for coats and jackets, may be bonded for this use. Numerous combinations of fabrics suggest new design concepts that were never before possible. Bonding may also help solve some of the problems of the suit industry which have been created by the scarcity of fine tailors.

INTERFACINGS

Interfacings are a means of reinforcing a garment and giving it shape and body; they are used particularly in collars, lapels, and the revers of suits and coats. Interfacings are always covered with facing cloth or lining, and do not show. An interfacing in the back and shoulder area protects and reinforces the outer fabric; occasionally a suit or coat is completely interfaced. Interfacings and linings increase resistance to stretching and wrinkling. Interfacings must be compatible with the outside fabric being used, and are chosen for the amount of body needed and the purpose they are to serve. In men's suits, a good grade of hair cloth is generally used. Tailor's canvas, an excellent coarse linen interfacing, was used for many years, and is found occasionally in good quality suits today, but the cost of linen makes it expensive. There are numerous other interfacings on the market. Nonwoven, bonded interfacing fabrics include Pellon, Interlon, and Keybak. Muslin of a good quality which has the sizing removed is an inexpensive but durable interfacing. Other fabrics such as Veri-form, Siri, and Acro have been created especially for wash-and-wear articles.

The interfacing will affect the drape of the collar and lapels and is chosen for the amount of body and shape needed. It is an additional stay to the front of the jacket. Although the interfacing does not show in a ready-made suit, it is wise to feel the amount of spring and body at the collar and lapels.

INTERLININGS

Interlinings are used in coats between the outer fabric and the lining for added warmth. Loosely woven, napped woolen is an excellent interlining. The air spaces created by the open weave and nap have excellent insulation powers. Highly napped cotton has been used. Cotton is less expensive, but it is not as warm and does not hold up in cleaning as well as the woolen fabric. A cotton napped surface may mat and lose the quality for adding warmth.

Napped cotton is soft and is excellent as an interlining for children's ski pants. Later developments for interlinings are made of various synthetic fibers and those of urethane which are similar to a foam rubber fabric. Glass fiber is also made into a fabric to be used as an interlining. Many fabrics made of glass fiber will not be comfortable worn close to the body.

LININGS

A lining covers the inside construction of a coat or suit. Linings are also used in skirts; they take the strain of sitting and help to prevent stretching and wrinkling. Linings should be made with a firm weave and should slip readily over other fabrics and over the body. The lining protects the outer part of a coat or suit from perspiration, wear, and movement of the body and the body from irritation by wool or scratchy fabrics. Women's suit jackets are generally fully lined. A man's suit may have a full lining only in the front and in the sleeves and a partial lining over the shoulders in the back. Linings are now frequently treated to resist soil and perspiration. Coat linings of alpaca or pile fabrics of Orlon or Dynel are very warm and decorative.

COMBINATION LINING AND INTERLINING

Combination lining and interlining is constructed as double fabric. The napped backing fabric is made of synthetics such as Acrilan or Arnel or of wool. If carefully tailored, these fabrics make excellent linings; their only disadvantage is that they may be bulky around the armscye and shoulder seams. Metallic coatings on lining fabrics give less warmth than interlinings of a napped fabric but are lighter in weight; since the advent of heaters in cars, they are adequate a good part of the year.

A fabric made by laminating a lining fabric with urethane is light in weight, gives added warmth, and can be dry-cleaned. Synthetics like urethane and glass fiber which are bonded to lining fabrics with adhesive may not withstand dry cleaning.

Linings bonded to fabrics change the textural effect of the fabric and add new possibilities in draping the fabric.

TRIM AND NOTIONS

Trim such as buttons, braid, and thread is also an indication of quality. Plastic buttons should be cleanable and colorfast. Fabric-covered buttons are attractive but may wear on the edges. Bone, pearl, and leather of good quality give excellent service. Most good suit manufacturers now furnish extra buttons, in case one should be lost or damaged. Other notions, such as tapes and zippers of good quality, are essential for a good suit. The quality of all materials used in the suit, inside and out, should be considered.

PERFORMANCE

Fabrics—whether interfacings, linings, or woolen outerwear—that shrink will be expensive investments. A good tailoring house will have preshrunk woolens, tapes, and interfacings. If an interfacing shrinks and the outside fabric doesn't, the jacket will pucker and will be very unattractive. Ideally, a label on the garment should give performance facts about all materials and trim used in making a suit or coat.

CONSTRUCTION

Tailoring builds shape and molds fabric through proper interfacing, padding stitches, stay taping, and pressing. The finest tailoring is done by hand. Construction often makes the difference between a good suit and a poor one.

The custom tailor is skilled in hand-tailoring into the suit qualities which hold fabrics where they should be held. He shapes and molds the right places and builds permanent shaping in the suit. There is much more to tailoring than appears in the finished garment. The quality of the work which goes into a suit has a definite relationship to how long the garment will retain a good appearance.

The best suits begin with the treatment of the fabric for cutting. Custom-made suits are cut individually. The fabric is sponged prior to cutting. Materials are straightened so that the warp and filling yarns run at right angles to each other. Fabrics which are not straightened before cutting will not hang properly on the figure. Patterns are cut accurately on the grain of the cloth; materials with plaids, checks, and designs are cut so that patterns can be matched where they meet at the seams. Armscye seams are an excellent place to look for the matching of patterns, and, of course, center front and center back should match. Pockets and decorative details should match the area where they are placed. The center back of the collar should match the center back of the jacket.

Tapes used to stay the fabric on the center front prevent stretching and swinging. The bridle is a diagonal tape placed on the fold of the lapel. It is taut in order to hold the fullness for the chest and prevents the jacket from standing away from the body. Stay tapes are frequently used on the armscye to prevent stretching and to ease fullness. Some tailors use a drawing-in stitch which holds the fabric of the armscye. The collar is usually taped on the outside edge to give it a thin, crisp edge. In women's fitted suits, waistlines are generally taped to prevent stretching of the waistline where no seam is present.

Seams may be an indication of workmanship. A good seam is straight, flat, and carefully pressed open. Thinness at the junctions of the seams is attained by proper trimming and clipping. The armscye seam of the jacket does not have puckering or fullness showing where the sleeve was attached to the body of the jacket. Exposed seams, as in a partially lined man's jacket, are generally bound with seam tape of good quality. Seams which are not bound are overcast or turned under and stitched to prevent raveling. There are no bumps or thick areas along the edges of a good coat or suit. In a fine hand-tailored suit, the edges of lapels, collars, and pockets are slightly turned or curled inward to keep the seam from showing. The front of the coat does not swing, but hangs perfectly straight and at right angles to the floor. There is no rolling or waving of the edges of the front.

In well-made trousers or slacks, there is no skimping in size of seams or in fabric. The crotch is not pieced and will be reinforced for greater durability. Seams are generous and the inseam is particularly wide to allow for alterations in the trousers. Many of the facings are hand hemmed over seams to avoid an overhandled and bulky appearance.

Much hand sewing is not observable at a glance. A great deal of hand basting is necessary to hold pieces while shaping, molding, shrinking, and pressing. Collars are generally hand sewn to the body of the jacket in order to prevent tight stitches from pulling and drawing the collar. Linings are attached to the body of many jackets with hand hemming. In suits of poorer quality, machine stitching replaces much of the hand sewing.

In addition to the processes of cutting,

staying, darting, and easing, pressing is an important operation in molding and shrinking parts to allow fullness at strategic places. Underpressing is the operation of smoothing and shaping the body contours of the jacket as work progresses. Darts and seams are pressed open, and armholes are shrunk to proper shape. Off-pressing refers to the final shaping and smoothing out of the finished jacket.

While many of these details are hidden, many can be seen in the finished product. The straightness of the stitching, the roll of the edge seams, top stitching, the symmetry of the pockets, and the sewing of buttons, with adequate shanks to prevent puckering between buttons, are obvious. Men's suits have hand-worked buttonholes and fine women's suits have bound buttonholes. Many of the details of shaping and pressing will be evident when a suit is tried on.

Not all good suits are custom made. Custom-made suits have the advantage of fitting the figure which does not conform to a standard size or which has slight irregularities. Ready-made manufacturers have done an excellent job of adapting the tailoring methods of the custom houses to machine methods. Many ready-made suits have several details of fine hand construction. Inexpensive suits may lack the shaping and pressing which mold and build permanent shape into suits.

MEN'S SUITS AND COATS

Since the suit is the most important item in a man's wardrobe, it is important that he concern himself with line and silhouette, proper fitting, and color. He may receive assistance from his wife or from a salesman in the selection of fabric and workmanship, but no other person can know his needs as well as he himself.

The design of men's suits has a definite fashion element. Although the male likes to

Car coats.

consider himself conservative and unchanging, his clothes reflect style changes just as do women's clothes. The changes may be more gradual and less drastic, but there are changes.

The pattern of buying coats has changed considerably for men in recent years. Few men own a really heavy overcoat. On the other hand, whereas most men used to have one heavy woolen jacket for outdoor sports, they now have a wide range of jackets and car coats of different weights.

Design changes in men's suits and coats can be analyzed by the details. Silhouette changes occur as a result of changes in the width of the shoulders, the amount of fullness or drape, and the length of the jacket. When wide shoulders are in fashion, the suit will generally have considerable padding. The broad shoulder is usually accompanied by a full drape. With a natural

Fur-lined and fur-trimmed coats.

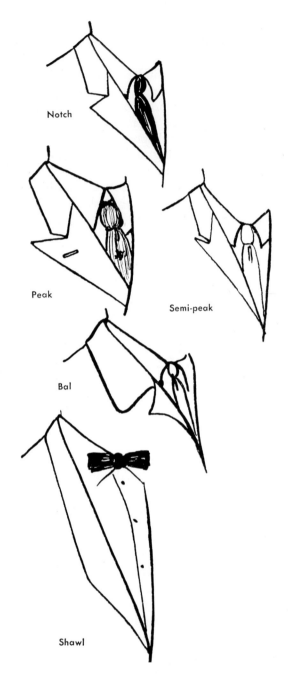

Notch

Peak

Semi-peak

Bal

Shawl

shoulder, there is usually little or no padding and an easy but closer fit.

Details within the silhouette make up the style. The suit may be either double-breasted or single-breasted. The double-breasted suit jacket has four or six buttons. The single-breasted may have four, three, two, or no buttons. The placing of the buttons varies with the fashion of the day; it will usually correspond to the length of the roll of the lapel.

The lapel and collar vary in width and the fullness of the roll. Collars are notched, peaked, semi-peaked, convertible or bal, or shawl. With a full silhouette and broad shoulders, the lapel will generally be wide. The narrower lapel is usually in better proportion with the natural shoulder line.

Pockets and the way they are placed will vary with the fashion and the model. Patch pockets are most often seen on sports jack-ets. Bound, flap, or welt pockets may be placed straight or diagonally; they are popular on business suits. The placement of

the vents, if any, also varies. Some jackets have a center back vent; others have side vents. Center vents which are "locked in" or hooked are stitched across the vent top for extra strength.

The set-in sleeve is used almost exclusively for business suits. The raglan, half-raglan, and kimono sleeves are found in coats and sportswear.

Trouser details include the amount of fullness, location and style of pockets, and the taper of the leg. Fashion may at times include cuffs of varying widths on the trousers; at other times, the cuff may be completely removed.

The wearing of a vest is a fashion item. The vest may be single or double breasted, or of matching or contrasting fabric. The fabric and trim will also vary with fashion and occasion.

A quarter-century panorama from the pages of Esquire. From left to right: 1933, double-breasted, waist-hugging jacket and wide-kneed trousers; 1937, the British drape influence showing in a looser jacket and tapered trousers; 1947, the bigger, broader, bolder look of the full drape; and 1961, the stream-lined appearance of the natural drape. (Courtesy American Institute of Men's and Boys' Wear, Inc.)

The design and the cut of the trousers should receive the same fine workmanship as the suit jacket. The amount of fullness in trousers depends on the current fashion. Trousers should never be cut so full as to appear sloppy; they are generally most flattering when tapered to give a tall, slim look. The amount of taper will depend upon the individual's build and his preferences. Too much fullness may interfere with easy movement. The trouser leg should barely

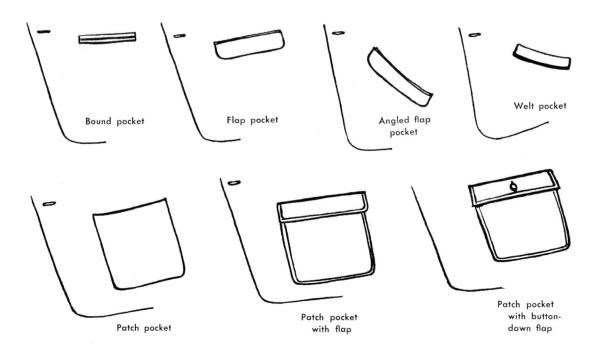

Bound pocket   Flap pocket   Angled flap pocket   Welt pocket

Patch pocket   Patch pocket with flap   Patch pocket with button-down flap

break on the instep or be even shorter. The shorter trouser is generally most becoming to the slim, young person.

Slacks come in numerous fabrics and in

Traditional side pocket and welt or flap back pocket.

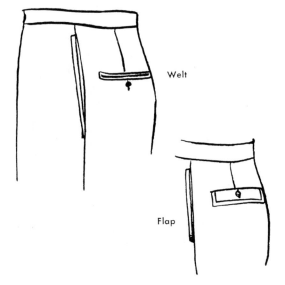

Welt

Flap

assorted style variations. Variation will be found in the rise of the trousers, the kind of pockets and their placement, adjustments in waistbands, and in decorative detail, such as hand picking or corded belts. Slacks, like other garments, are chosen for their purpose and for the kind of care they will need. Slacks worn with sports jackets may be a fine flannel; if worn for active sports, they will probably be of "no iron" durable-press that they may be machine washed and dried. There are slacks with stretch waistbands for very active sports such as bowling.

Proper fitting is the key to maintaining a well-cut suit. The clean, uncluttered, easy look is the result of men's insistence on comfort. A well-fitted suit maintains line and drape. A poorly fitted suit creates wrinkles and discomfort. A suit which fits

(Opposite) Styles in men's coats. From left to right: top: chesterfield and ulster; bottom: balmacaan, fly-front raglan, and split raglan.

The look of 1967. Left: Double breasted suit. Far right: Single breasted suit with vest. (Courtesy of Institute of Men's and Boy's Wear, Inc.)

figure or it has not been properly held by a bridle stay. Width of the lapel is determined by the fashion of the day.

There should not be wrinkles across the chest or the back or under the collar. The front should hang straight and never toward the center. The jacket should be just long enough to cover the seat. Certain styles, such as the Edwardian jacket, may be designed to be worn longer and may be fuller in cut at the bottom. The sleeves should permit about one-half inch of the shirt cuff to show. The waist is gently tapered but not so close as to pull on the buttons.

Trousers are trim and hang straight but are full enough in the crotch and seat for comfort in sitting. Good fit depends upon accurate sizing at the waist and in the

The more fitted look of 1967. (Courtesy of Institute of Men's and Boy's Wear, Inc.)

too closely to the body hampers movement and binds or confines. A suit which is too easy in fit may also constrict movement by allowing the garment to shift on the figure.

In a properly fitted suit, where a turtleneck sweater, a scarf, or a Nehru shirt is worn, the height of the neckline should flatter the individual. (1) the collar should set low enough to show about one-half an inch of the shirt collar. It should be a comfortable but snug fit; (2) the shoulders of the suit should ride easily on the individual's shoulders, but remain in place. Both shoulders of the suit should be the same height and width. (3) Lapels, if properly constructed, remain close and smooth against the chest. If they gap in front, either the suit is not right on the

proper length of the inseam and the out-seam. There should be no puckering, the result of excess fullness, in the cuff. Cuffless trousers are a little shorter than those with cuffs. Pleats in trousers should lie flat.

Posture will play an important part in the way a man's trousers fit. It will be important for the person to move, sit, and bend to determine if the fit is comfortable. Well-fitted trousers will move with the person and not pull at any point. When an individual is being fitted, he should put the same items he normally carries in his pockets so that the fitter may make allowances for these items.

The man should experiment by trying on the various designs. He should observe lines, pocket detail, and lengths which look good on him and should adopt those features in current fashion. He will ignore the overly exaggerated features which are seldom in good taste.

Suits for every occasion

Men's suits fall into the following general categories: (1) Business wear; (2) Daytime wear—formal, semi-formal, and informal; (3) Evening wear—formal, semi-formal, and informal; and (4) Sportswear. There are variations within each category. The fashion of the day in one category will generally carry through in the other categories.

Change in the width and style of the hat accompanies a change in the style of the suit. (Courtesy American Institute of Men's and Boys' Wear, Inc.)

The break in trousers. From left to right: correct; too long; and too short.

The business suit generally has trousers and jacket of a fabric such as flannel (the famous gray flannel suit), gabardine, or serge. Sportswear is more casual than the business suit; jackets and trousers usually are of contrasting fabric and color. In some areas, where life is more casual, sports jackets may be worn for work. The fabric of a sports jacket is usually a fine woolen, a tweed, or, in summer, madras.

Evening wear includes the tailcoat for formal wear, the tuxedo or dinner jacket for less formal occasions, and a dark suit for informal evenings. The tailcoat is worn after six P.M. with a white tie, a white waistcoat, a stiff dress shirt, a top hat and white gloves of capeskin or fabric. In college, men often wear business suits to formal occasions. Even though at college this may be accepted as proper dress, they should never consider this as acceptable practice elsewhere. Semi-formal wear includes a black or midnight-blue dinner

The business suit, the American look of 1966. (Courtesy American Institute of Men's and Boys' Wear, Inc.)

Variations in the treatment of the front pocket.

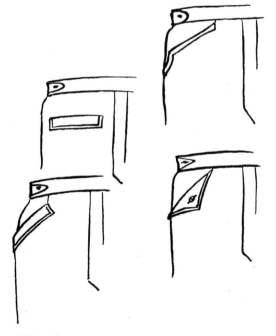

jacket, black bow tie, pleated-front shirt, and black Homburg. It is worn for those "less than state" occasions when something more than informal wear is desired. In certain situations, where the individual knows his group, a white or plaid dinner jacket may be permissible. Informal evening wear calls for a dark gray or navy business suit. Informal wear should never be worn when a woman wears a formal gown.

Daytime formal calls for a cutaway coat, striped trousers, gray waistcoat, white pleated-front shirt with wing collar, and silk topper. The ascot or four-in-hand tie is proper. In America, formal occasions are limited to weddings and very important

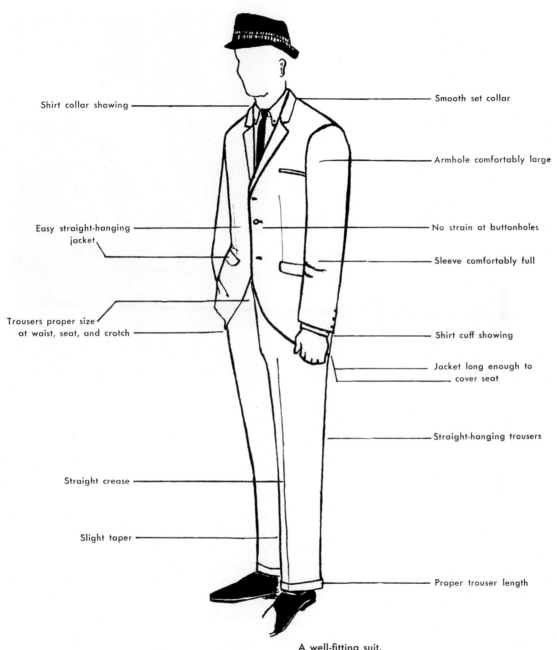

Shirt collar showing

Smooth set collar

Armhole comfortably large

Easy straight-hanging jacket

No strain at buttonholes

Sleeve comfortably full

Trousers proper size at waist, seat, and crotch

Shirt cuff showing

Jacket long enough to cover seat

Straight-hanging trousers

Straight crease

Slight taper

Proper trouser length

A well-fitting suit.

occasions such as inaugurations. Daytime semi-formal calls for an oxford jacket or stroller, striped trousers, pleated-front shirt, gray waistcoat with turn-down collar, and gray four-in-hand tie. This would be worn where a woman wears a gown that is dressy but not formal. Daytime informal indicates a business suit in a suitable color and fabric.

Sportswear refers to a wide range of

The tuxedo in the American Continental style has a shawl collar. (Courtesy American Institute of Men's and Boys' Wear, Inc.)

A 1967 sports jacket. Notice the texture of the striped double-breasted jacket with side vents. (Courtesy American Institute of Men's and Boys' Wear, Inc.)

sports jackets and slacks. Suburban life has made the sports jacket a very popular item in men's wardrobes. The tweed jacket in winter and the cotton jacket in summer are worn most of the time, except for formal or city occasions.

Sizing

Men's suits are sized according to chest size measure, but for a number of body types. For the short man there are short regular, short stout, short portly, and extra short sizes. The tall man can obtain long,

long stout, long portly, medium long, and extra long. The man of average height can buy regular, stout, and portly. There is strong indication that, since men appear to be more weight conscious, the number of men needing the portly size is decreasing. Several large stores have discontinued stout sizes.

One enterprising retailer sells suit jackets and trousers separately in order to fit most people with a minimum of alteration. Other custom shops specialize in outsize clothing.

Care

Wherever possible, suits should be alternated and rested between wearings. This allows the suit to return to its natural shape without excess pressing. Brushing after each wearing will extend the length of time between trips to the cleaners. A good suit or coat deserves a special hanger that helps maintain the shape that has been so carefully built in. To minimize overpressing, trouser creases are finger pressed before the pants are hung on a trouser hanger. Many people do not realize that the sleeves of a jacket and the lapel roll should not have a crease.

NECKTIES

The necktie is a most important accessory; it must complement not only the wearer's skin and coloring but his suit, his personality, and his good taste. Profession and personality will play an important part in the selection of colors and patterns. A doctor, for example, would probably choose a more conservative tie than would an entertainer.

Design

Ties may have pointed or square ends and range in width from one to three inches. The average length is about 52 inches, but there will be some variation. Ties up to four inches longer, made to be worn mainly with a sport shirt, are available for the very tall, long-waisted man.

The design of a tie involves more than width and the pattern of the fabric; allowance must be made for the way the tie will be tied and its relationship to the kind of collar worn. The four-in-hand knot, straight and thin, is generally worn by those who prefer a regular shirt collar and who are slight in build. The triangular Windsor knot is popular with the spread shirt collar. Bow ties, which enjoy fashion popularity from time to time, are neat and youthful in appearance.

Color and pattern

Color is chosen to enhance the wearer's coloring and the colors of his shirt and suit.

How to tie a four-in-hand: (1) Cross the wide end over the narrow end. (2) Bring it around behind the narrow end and (3) cross over once more. (4) Bring it up through the center and (5) pull it down through the loop; with your index finger form the dimple under the loop. (6) Tighten the knot.

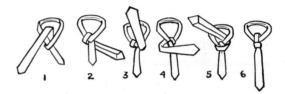

How to tie a Windsor: (1) Starting with the wide end about twelve inches longer than the narrow end, loop it over the narrow end as shown. (2) Bring it around behind the narrow end (3) up and over on the other side. (4) Cross over in front, (5) bring it up through the center, and (6) pull it down through the loop. Form the dimple with your index finger and tighten the knot.

How to tie a bow tie: (1) Start with the end in your left hand an inch and a half longer than the other and in front and (2) bring it up through the loop. (3) Fold the short end to form the front part of the bow and (4) bring the long end down over the bow. (5) Form the back part of the bow by pushing the long end through the knot. (6) Even the ends and tighten the knot.

How to tie a Half Windsor: (1) Start with wide end on right about 11″ to 12″ below narrow end. (2) Cross wide end over and under the narrow end. (3) Bring wide end up and through the loop. (4) Place wide end over front. (5) Pull wide end through the loop. (6) Slip wide end through the knot and adjust.

The man who seeks individuality will experiment with various colors and with combinations of those colors that are becoming to him. One way to co-ordinate an outfit is to have the tie include the color of the shirt and/or the suit.

Fashion governs the width of the tie, the kind of designs shown, and colors.

Materials

All men want a tie which is resilient and will give a nicely shaped knot and stay in place. A tie should not stretch or wrinkle easily.

Fabrics in ties include almost every known fiber in a weave or knit heavy enough to hold shape well. The resiliency of the fiber, the cut of the tie, and the interlining used will help determine shape. Silk and wool ties have always been favorites because of their natural resiliency and their ability to return to their natural shape. Man-made fibers, especially Dacron, which has good resiliency, are popular because they are washable and require little if any ironing. They do not require pressing and extra care between cleanings. Fabrics such as acetate and rayon will generally have an interlining which helps keep the shape. Interlinings are made of numerous fibers and fabrics. The wool interlining is popular because of its natural resiliency. It would, however, not be suitable in a Dacron tie since it would interfere with laundering. An interlining that has properties similar to those of Dacron would be excellent. New bonded interfacings and interlinings such as those made of urethane are frequently used in ties made of synthetic fibers.

Construction

Ties should be cut on the bias. The stitching should not be too tight or too small, since otherwise it may hold when resiliency is desired. The finest ties are hand tailored and hand sewn to eliminate the possibility of too-tight stitching. Knit ties have elasticity and do not wrinkle as much as a woven tie. They are usually not lined. Some men consider that a knit tie does not stay tied as well as a woven tie.

Care

Men differ as to what they want in a tie; some would not consider a tie which has to be dry-cleaned. Generally, ties which are lined will need to be dry-cleaned, although those which have interfacings that can be shaped are washable. When a tie is washed, it should be smoothed out before drying. Knit ties are rolled for storage to prevent stretching. Some people store all ties by rolling the tie, from the narrow end to the wide. Light pressing will eliminate wrinkles, but great care should be taken that the temperature of the iron will not fuse or melt a tie of synthetic fiber. Silk and wool ties may be pressed lightly, but overpressing will ruin the edges.

WOMEN'S SUITS AND COATS

The importance of the suit in the wardrobe varies with the individual and with the fashion of the day. At times, as it was during World War II, the suit may be the most important article in almost every woman's wardrobe. Suits, at that time, were worn to just about every occasion. After the war, the popularity of the suit as an all-purpose garment declined. People had more leisure time, and the amount of casual clothing purchased increased. Fabrics and labor were no longer at a premium, and dressier clothing was welcomed back. Despite the return of different "occasion" clothes, the suit had become an American institution. The average woman still feels that her wardrobe is not complete without at least one suit.

There are women who will have only suits—or equivalent garments—in their wardrobes. They may include not only classic and dressmaker models, but suits in fine brocades and damasks for dress occasions. Other women include suits in their wardrobes only to fill some certain need.

Women have a much greater variety of suits or coats to choose from than men. Although this variety gives them more opportunity to select a becoming garment, it also can mean greater confusion in making a choice. Men must choose between certain design features within limited silhouettes. Women must choose between endless variations in silhouettes, design details, fabrics, and colors. A woman's figure is harder to fit than a man's.

It will lessen confusion if, before she begins her shopping, a woman will review in her mind the purpose for which she wants the suit or coat, considering the warmth needed and where and to which occasions it will be worn; silhouettes and design features that have looked well on her in the past; and her preferences in colors and textures. This does not mean that she would avoid anything new, but rather that she looks at the article on the basis of her past experience.

Women's suits and coats are not easily classified. Each silhouette has many variations in fabric and line. The most likely classification would be the classic suit, the dressmaker suit, and the ensemble.

The classic suit is simple in line and generally conservative in color and fabric. The term tailored is misleading, since the tailoring process of construction is used in all suits. Sometimes the classic suit is described as man-tailored, suggesting that the style features of a man's suit are the classic line. The blazer styled in this manner has remained a classic, but many other styles— the cardigan, for example—have been classics.

The dressmaker suit is softer in line and fabric and may have decorative details and trim such as braid, appliqué, or fur. Design and cut of the dressmaker suit may be elaborate or simple.

The ensemble may be a dress with a jacket or coat or a suit with matching blouse and lining. The ensemble is planned for the costume look. Design and cut may be simple, with the emphasis on a lovely fabric, or it may be a more complicated design in a plain fabric. The ensemble is not necessarily—although it may be—classic in line; it may be an elaborate and detailed design. The difficulty of this classification is obvious; there is of necessity much overlapping of categories.

Silhouette

In almost every season, coats and suits are found in the basic tubular or bell silhouettes or in combinations of these two. The silhouette changes with the design details. It is usually given a seasonal fashion name such as A silhouette, H silhouette, tent etc. Most suits are best described by the well-known style names box, bolero, peplum, tunic, bloused, cardigan, or belted. Familiar coat styles include the princess, box, Chesterfield, reefer, polo, fitted, and greatcoats.

The skirt of a suit is designed to complement the jacket. Frequently, the skirt has little decorative design and is simple in cut. Full skirts, whether pleated or flared, generally accompany a short cropped jacket. Most women's figures look best when some part of the silhouette follows the human form.

Box
suit

Bloused
suit

Demi-
fitted
suit

Belted
suit

Bolero
suit

Details of fashion and design can be studied best by observing the various areas of the suit and coat. A woman should note especially those details which are becoming to her.

Collars will vary in shape and size with the fashion of the day. The currently fashionable collar may be round, pointed, or square. It may be extremely large or small; it may roll or lie flat. Collar accessories and the way the collar is worn will change with fashion. One year the collar may be

Cardigan

Classic

Double-
breasted

Blazer

Tunic

Styles in suits.

Box
or
Chesterfield
or
Boy

Polo

Capecoat

Clutch

Reefer

Princess

Styles in coats.

Bloused coat

Duster

Redingote

Cut-away coat

Some coat styles from fashion history.

Wrap-around

Tuxedo

Swagger

Greatcoat

Styles in coats.

turned up or it may be worn with a scarf or with a certain kind of jewelry. The individual should look for features which will complement her face and neck. For example, the woman with a short neck may choose a collarless suit or a collar which is flat and away from the neck. The woman with a long neck might choose a collar which stands or rolls high on the neck.

Lapels, of different styles and widths, may be peaked, notched, shawl, or rounded. In a double-breasted jacket, there is occasionally an asymmetric lapel treatment. The individual will observe the becomingness of the size, width, and depth of opening of the lapel in relationship to the length of her waist and her neck and the shape of her face. For example, a deep V cut may give added length to the person who has a short waist or a round face.

The style, shape, size, and length of the sleeve will be chosen to complement the arm, chest, and shoulders. The person with wide shoulders would avoid sleeves which add width in this area. For women's suits, there are various styles in sleeves; the kimono, raglan, split raglan, puffed, or regular set-in provide for differences in individual preference. Sleeve length will be governed by the length of the arm and the style of the jacket.

The style and the placement of pockets and other trim should be chosen to attract the eye to good features of the figure. The petite woman would avoid large patch pockets, and instead choose bound or welt pockets which would be in better proportion to her size.

The style of the front of the jacket should be observed with consideration for the effect it creates on the figure. The double-breasted suit may have a broadening effect on some figures.

Fabric choices are unlimited; in every season one finds an excellent selection of different weights and textures. The woman will have to limit herself only to choosing colors and textures which suit her figure and skin. Materials for coats will, of course, include fur, furlike fabrics, and leather as well as the numerous varieties of woven and knitted fabrics. Fur and leather are treated in separate chapters.

There will be many variations in the way the designer controls the fullness. The individual should check the placement of darts and seams on her figure. She should carefully check for the proper amount of fullness for her figure; fashion may in one year decree closely fitted jackets and in the next, an easy, semi-fitted look.

Fitting

Probably the greatest problem in buying a woman's suit or coat is finding one which is well fitted. No matter how lovely a suit or coat is, it will not look right on a person unless it fits properly. An inexpensive suit which really fits will look better than the most expensive suit on the market which does not. The amount of alteration that can be done on a suit is limited. Because of the shaping and underpressing that has been done in a ready-made suit, alteration may ruin the permanent shape of the suit.

In your selection you should consider the following: (1) Collar and lapels should fit snugly but smoothly. If the neck edge is wide, it should move with the body but remain near the body without slipping. (2) The shoulders must allow movement of the body but should remain in place. (3) There should be no wrinkles across the shoulders or chest or under the collar. (4) If tapered, the waist should fit without creating wrinkles across the back, and it should be neither too long nor too short. (5) When a sleeve is too long, the whole

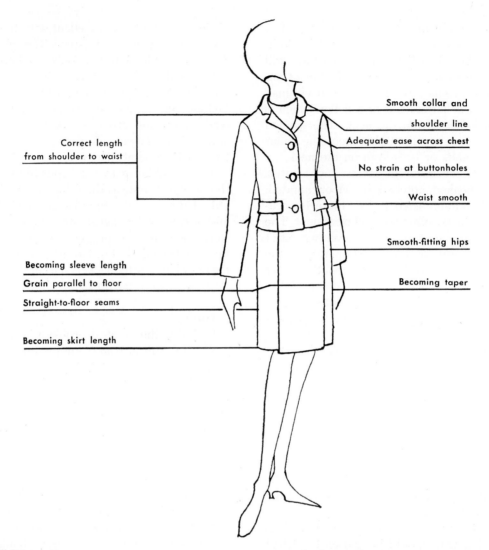

Correct length
from shoulder to waist

Becoming sleeve length

Grain parallel to floor

Straight-to-floor seams

Becoming skirt length

Smooth collar and
shoulder line

Adequate ease across chest

No strain at buttonholes

Waist smooth

Smooth-fitting hips

Becoming taper

A well-fitting suit.

jacket or coat will appear too large. The
sleeve should be just long enough so that
the wrist bone is not exposed. (6) The
jacket or coat should be of the correct
length for the wearer and in proportion to
the length of the waist and skirt length.
Before buying a coat that must be shortened, make sure that the shortening will
not destroy the effect of the design.

It is seldom wise to purchase a suit or
coat which needs alterations in the shoulders and collar. It is also difficult—and
often impossible—to change the length of
the waist in a fitted suit. Alterations are
usually limited to taking in side seams and
basic darts. Seams are seldom adequate
enough at the waist to increase the girth in
this area.

In a well-fitted suit, the skirt will fall
straight, with a balanced hang. Seams
should fall straight to the floor. There will
be adequate ease across the hips, with no

straining of fabric at the seams. Darts will be related to the curves of the figure. There will be no wrinkles under the waistband and no cupping under the seat. The lining will fit smoothly into the skirt. The skirt will be properly tapered and the hemlines will be straight.

When you attempt alterations in a skirt, make sure that the seams are adequate. The control of the hang and drape of the skirt is in the waistband. If alterations are attempted, the waistband and zipper must be removed to maintain the hang and drape of the skirt.

Before making a final decision, try the garment on; move your arms, sit down, and walk around in order to observe the effect of movement on the line and the comfort of the garment.

Sizing

Women's sizes are not standardized and often vary from one manufacturer to another. The woman who wears a size 10 in one brand may need an 11 or 12 in another brand. However, there is improvement in the size ranges available each year. Many women who could not be fitted ten or twenty years ago are now finding clothes that are proportioned to the different figures and need little alteration. Many stores have departments that specialize in clothes for, say, the tall girl or the petite girl. Separate skirts are made in proportioned sizes— short, regular, and tall—in both misses' and junior sizes.

Women's sizes are generally stated in misses', junior petite, junior, petite, half sizes, and women's sizes. Misses' sizes are 8 to 18 or 20 and are for the average figure. Junior petites are scaled for the figure 5'1" and under, and range from 3 to 13. Junior sizes, 3 to 17, are for the youthful figure with a high bust, a slightly shorter waistline than misses' size, and slightly larger hips.

Petite sizes, 10 to 18, are scaled for the figure shorter than 5'4" but otherwise proportioned as the misses' figure. Half sizes, 12½ to 20½, are for the woman who is stockier in build and shorter in the waistline and large sizes, 36 to 42 or 44, are for the heavier mature figure.

If you cannot find a ready-made suit jacket that fits you without having the alterations that are not recommended, you might have to eliminate this kind of clothing or you may choose the coat-and-dress ensemble. Your only other choice is to have your suits custom made, which is usually more expensive. The disadvantage of custom-made suits is that you must choose the design without seeing it on yourself. The success of a custom suit will depend upon the skill of the tailor who makes it. It is important to have it made by someone who understands the fitting of the female figure —and who has an understanding of fashion in women's clothes.

CARE

The care of men's and women's suits is essentially the same. Suits that are rested between wearings look better for a longer time. Brushing, airing, and removing spots or make-up after each wearing will keep the suit fresh and presentable between dry cleanings. A scarf cannot only enhance many co-ordinations but will protect the collar of a woman's coat from make-up. Coats with napped surfaces like fleece should be brushed frequently to maintain the beauty of the fabric. Most lined suits and coats should be dry-cleaned. There is no practice which can do more harm to the appearance of a coat than stuffing the pockets. Shaped suit hangers with fasteners for skirts help retain the shape of the garment. As an added protection, suits and coats should be given a mothproofing finish when dry-cleaned.

Chapter 15

Dresses

What appeals to you first when you see a dress in a store? The design, the color, the fabric, the construction, that it is the latest thing in fashion, or that it will be easy to care for? Maybe you consider all of these factors before making your selection. On the other hand, you may buy simply because the dress fits you, because you like the color, or because the dress seems to meet your immediate needs.

VARIETY

There are dresses of all kinds and qualities in various price ranges and many choices of values within each price range. For your convenience, dresses are usually classified as house, casual, street, afternoon, after-five, and formal evening dresses. In each of these types, a variety of styles and silhouettes includes the sheath, the shift, princess, dirndl, shirtwaist; tubular, bouffant, ballet, and strapless.

From this variety, the customer chooses what is becoming to her in color, fit, and silhouette; something that fits her needs, goes with her present wardrobe, will give the desired service, can be cleaned easily and satisfactorily without undue expense, and is reasonably priced in relation to the desired

features. Many value-conscious women will pay more for a dress that will receive hard wear than for one that is to be used only occasionally.

Your preferences in design often determine your choice of dresses as well as of other apparel. Good design may appeal to you through line within the silhouette, through the straight lines of pleats, the full, round curves of scalloped flounces, or the restrained curves of a scooped neckline. If you like straight lines in dresses, do you prefer vertical, horizontal, or diagonal lines or some combination?

You may also have a preference for some particular silhouette, outline, or contour. Form-fitting silhouettes, extended silhouettes, and silhouettes reflecting current fashions afford some variety from which to choose. Designers try to provide variety and at the same time produce unified designs. If you recognize and appreciate this kind of design, you will usually demonstrate this in your choice of dresses.

If you know what constitutes good design and learn to distinguish real beauty and elegance from the gaudy and merely eye-catching, you will have little difficulty. You should also know from previous discussion what design is most appropriate for your personality, your figure, and the occasion for which you want the dress. It may be a distinguished, sleek, sophisticated line and silhouette or a soft, clinging crepe, skillfully shaped in restrained curves.

DESIGN

The point is that several aspects of the design of the dress must be considered: the design itself as a whole; whether it is in

(Opposite) From left to right: top row: sheath style, strapless style, tunic style; bottom row: princess style, empire style, dirndl style.

Shirtwaist style.

cocktail length; semi-fitted dresses become snugly fitted. Fashion may move the waistline from directly under the bustline to the natural waistline, on down to the hipline, and up again.

FABRICS

Having made up your mind about the design of the dress, you should consider what it is made of. The rapid increase in the number of different fabrics available, with new and unusual names appearing from season to season, can make selection difficult. New fibers, weaves, knits, and finishes are constantly changing the appear-

Tiered style.

good taste; its fitness to the purpose of the dress—bias cut, action sleeves, kimono sleeves; and its relation to you, your actual needs, and your wardrobe. Design includes line, form and shape, color, and texture.

Some prefer the shirtwaist dress to other designs for nearly all occasions, while others might choose a sheath for both daytime and evening wear. Still others may do housework in a two-piece dirndl, shop in a sheath, dine in a softly draped gown, and dance in a flounced bouffant. Some wardrobes contain a variety of styles, while others exhibit uniformity and consistency.

Fashion, of course, affects dresses as it does all apparel. Changes in length, silhouette, design, fabric, and trim provide a wide choice for the fashion-conscious consumer. Wide padded shoulders change to sloping ones; floor-length gowns are shortened to

ance and the feel of fabrics. What appears to be wool may be one or more other fibers. Informative tags and labels are the safest guides to fiber content, since the names of the fibers as well as the percentages are given. However, important as fiber content may be as a guide to use and care, it is not necessarily a complete guide to quality. There are varying qualities of fabrics, according to the fiber, construction, dyeing, and finishing. Price is not always a dependable guide to the quality of a dress because costs of materials and production vary, making it difficult for manufacturers to maintain uniform quality in the same price lines.

Knitted dresses are available in all sizes and fibers, for nearly all purposes, from

Flared with a flounce

Draped style.

Flared with a godet

Flared styles.

mass produced to couture. In selecting, one should note whether they are single or double knit, lined or unlined, and what method of care is recommended.

Cotton

Cotton fabrics, ranging from delicate laces, organdies, and voiles to stronger fabrics such as gabardine, piqué, and velveteen, enjoy continuing popularity as dress fabrics. While a dainty voile is serviceable for summer wear, a strong, firm percale is more suitable for classes or house dresses. Cotton and Dacron polyester blends in seersucker, fine broadcloths, batistes, and voiles are favorite "packables" for summer vacations. Some cottons are given resin finishes to make them wrinkle-resistant and wash-and-wear. It should be noted, however, that it is very difficult to remove stains from these treated cottons.

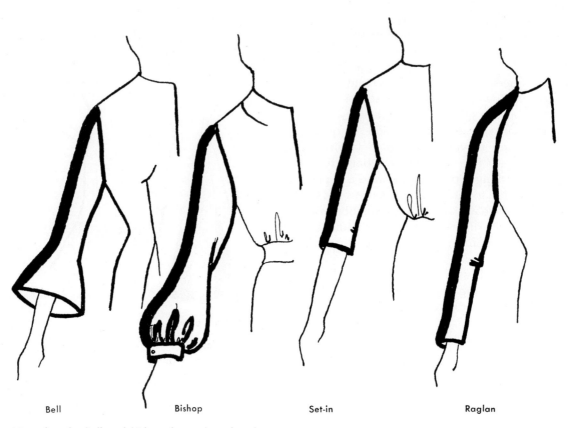

Bell   Bishop   Set-in   Raglan

Note that the bell and bishop sleeves broaden the figure at the sleeve ending.

Linen

Good dress linens are generally more expensive than cottons but for certain dresses the special qualities of linen may be worth the extra cost. A dress made of crease-resistant dress-weight linen in a classic style is appropriate for many occasions and will always look crisp and fresh. However, many linens wrinkle easily. Some dyed linens do not always maintain a clear color throughout. Linen fanciers often do not care for less expensive fibers woven to look like linen, or even a mixture of linen with some other fiber. However, for some purposes, part-linen dresses that combine the characteristics of two fibers are desirable.

With finishes to counteract excessive wrinkling and with the development of new yarns, weaves, designs, and blends, linen is used in all types of dresses, for sport, street, afternoon, and evening wear.

Silk

Silk is a desirable dress fabric. Good dress silks must be firmly woven so that the yarns will not snag, shift, or slip, causing pulled seams and unsightly bulges across the shoulders, under the arms, and through the hips. Firm, regular weaves that give little in either direction make good dress fabrics in that they tend to keep their shape through wear and cleaning. Silk dress fabrics vary from smooth, shiny satins and soft *peau de soie* to slub-yarn shantungs and

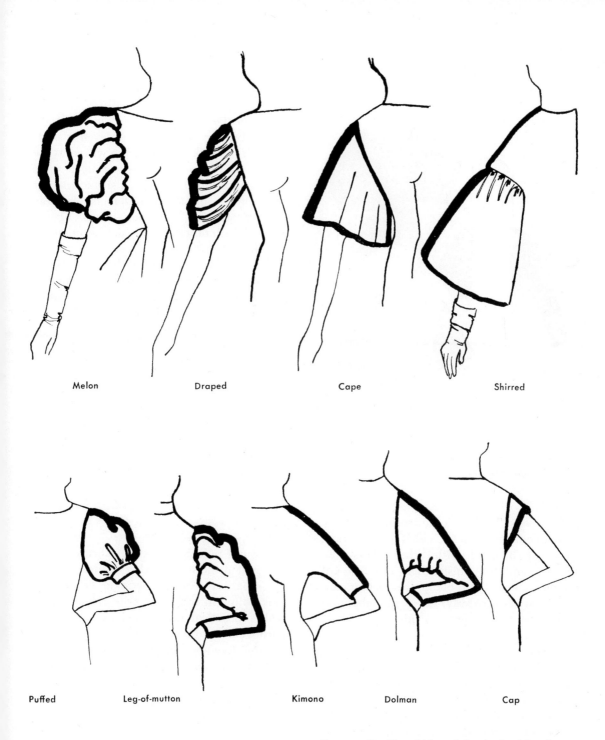

Melon   Draped   Cape   Shirred

Puffed   Leg-of-mutton   Kimono   Dolman   Cap

Sleeve styles. The width and the depth of the sleeve affect the apparent body proportions.

Exaggerated sleeve design may add weight to the shoulder and bust area.

silk tweeds. The fabric depends on the silk —filament, spun, wild, cultivated, or raw, pure or blended with other fibers—the weave, and the finish. Silks that do not water spot are desirable in dresses that cannot be washed. Always check the label of a silk dress for suggestions on care.

Wool

Wool fabrics today are different from those of the past, but the marks of quality remain the same. Good quality wool fabrics are evenly woven from firmly twisted yarns made of long, high-grade undamaged fibers. Worsteds, made of long, fine-quality combed wool fibers, have clear weaves and firm finishes; materials made of worsted yarns—such as challis, gabardine, and crepe —tend to hold shape and resist wrinkles.

Woolens, made of shorter fibers, are generally heavier and warmer than worsteds. When buying an all-wool or even a part-wool dress, look closely at the weave to see that it is of even weight, not thin in some places and thick in others. A surface nap or other finish can hide such defects. Note the surface of sheer, gossamer wools. Blends of wool with other fibers which supplement its characteristics make very satisfactory dress fabrics. Wool-and-Orlon and wool-and-Dacron blends in proper percentages are washable and dimensionably stable More detailed information on blends is included in the chapter on textiles.

Man-made fibers

Rayon may be used in filament form or the long filaments may be cut into staple length and spun into yarns. Consequently, rayon can be used in practically all kinds of fabrics, from coarse crash to fine chiffon. Washable rayons include chiffons, sheers, and a spun rayon resembling linen. They are inexpensive yet generally serviceable and practical. Rayon sheers with fine yarns and close weaves are better buys than those with open weaves and coarse yarns that catch and pull. Some rayon fabrics stretch and pull at the seams; others, unless treated for crease resistance, wrinkle easily and look wilted in warm weather. Rayon jersey makes practical dresses which will stand hard wear and do not wrinkle readily. Some of the rayons resembling wool, called challis and alpaca, wear well, but will wrinkle unless given a crease-resistant finish. Stiff rayons such as taffeta and moire, popular for evening dresses, wear well.

When buying dresses made of rayon fabrics, look for strong yarns and examine the weave carefully. To guard against fraying and seam pulling, look for generous seam allowances and secure seam finishes.

Other man-made fibers—including the acetates, nylons, acrylics, polyesters, modacrylics, Verel, and Darvan—are made into a variety of dress fabrics. The specific qualities of the fabric depend on the method of fabrication, and on whether the fiber is used alone or in a blend. Textured nylon prints and Antron nylon tricots and soft crepes of Dacron polyester are easy-care fabrics for summer wear. Orlon and wool blends make good washable dress fabrics. Moiré taffeta made of acetate has a permanent surface design because of the thermoplastic quality of acetate. Dacron, alone or with cotton, is popular for summer wear because of the crispness and crease resistance of the fabric. Acrilan and Arnel lend dimensional stability to jerseys. Creslan and Zefran are wrinkle-resistant. A blend of Dynel and wool makes a good wash-and-wear dress fabric.

Novelties in dress materials are leather and fur for evening wear. When these are chosen, consider the suggestions for selection of these non-textile materials as indicated in Chapters 20–21.

THE LITTLE THINGS

Materials used in dresses—other than the fabric—include trim, thread, tapes, backings, interfacings, linings, and fastenings. Do not be deceived by items used by the manufacturer to catch your eye. Attractive buttons, decorative stitching, or intricate braid designs may "sell" a dress to people who fail to notice the quality in material and workmanship of the rest of the garment. Some fastenings, such as buttons, slide fasteners, buckles, clips, pins, and lacings, are also decorative. Others, such as snaps and hooks and eyes, are hidden. All fastenings, whether they are hidden or used as trim, either add to or detract from the appearance of the garment, as well as affect its wearability. Buttonholes should be on the straight grain of the fabric with the stitching sufficiently deep, close together, and securely fastened.

If a dress is washable, the fastenings, backings, linings, and trimming materials should also be washable. Pearl, glass, and rustproof metal buttons are classified as washable; painted glass, wood, and some plastic buttons often do not hold up in laundering. Buttons that have been glued or cemented together will generally soon fall apart, those covered with loosely-woven fabric frequently pull out, and glass breaks easily. Buttons with rough, decorated edges quickly wear out buttonholes or loops. Pearl buttons of uniform thickness, well-made covered buttons, and many plastic buttons stand up well under wear and care.

Thread used for stitching and for buttonholes should match the fabric in color and last the life of the garment. Some colors of thread fade quickly; for example, the thread used in the outside stitching on some red dresses often fades to pink. This characteristic is difficult to discover just by examining a dress. Labels do not indicate this information.

Slide fasteners vary in color, size, and material. Lightweight metal fasteners that have been properly set in make a smooth, neat closing and usually are quick and easy to operate. A synthetic filament fastener made of polyamide or polyester requires the same precautions as some plastic buttons—avoid extreme heat in laundering and dry cleaning; a hot iron may melt a synthetic-monofilament fastener.

Metal snaps and hooks and eyes, in the right size and properly placed and sewed on, are desirable fastenings. A snap so large that it makes a bulge in the fabric, or a hook-and-eye fastener set too near the edge of an opening, will be unsightly. Fastenings placed so that they pull an opening out of line should be moved or replaced. If they are insecurely sewed on, they are likely to come off the first time the garment is worn.

TRIM

Trim that is simple, conservative, and in good taste can add a great deal to a dress. The trim may be of varied material, including contrasting fabric, embroidery, appliqué, braid, lace, ribbon, flowers, sequins, jewels, fur, or leather. Some ready-made dresses are so overtrimmed that the trim detracts from the dress as well as the wearer. A dress trimmed with, for example, a sequin collar, a lace insert in the bodice, and a gold leather belt would be a rather "busy" outfit.

Besides the attractiveness of trim, serviceability should also be considered. All trim should be comparable to the dress in quality and durability. Trim which requires different cleaning and white or light trim which cannot be removed for washing are examples of poor choices. Washable collars, cuffs, and other trim made to snap on or to be easily slip-stitched in place actually cut down cleaning costs on dresses which can only be dry-cleaned. All trimming on washable dresses should also be washable and easy to iron. Avoid trims that tarnish, rust, become dull, cut the fabric, are easily marred, or pull out in ordinary usage. Attached trim such as braid, stitching, lace, and ribbon should be as easy to clean as the dress and should not hinder pressing and ironing.

Belts made of the same material as the dress should be made so that they can be as easily cleaned as the dress; a belt backed with material which cannot be either dry-cleaned or washed is of little value on the dress. Colorfastness is also important. Colored leather, contrasting fabrics, metals, and other materials may rub off on dresses and leave stains and smudges which cannot be removed. Buckles and eyelets should be well made, because they are subject to a great deal of abrasion and strain. Fabric-covered buckles tend to fray unless edges and corners are securely fastened; thread eyelets fray and some metal ones pull out.

SIZE

Correct size and proper fit are of course essential considerations. A dress which does not give both smart appearance and comfort is a poor choice at any price. With little or no standardization of sizes, there is no assurance that any two dresses marked the same size will fit equally well or that a dress marked the desired bust measurement will have corresponding measurements in the waist, the hip, and at other points important to comfort and fit. Consequently, you should try on every dress you purchase. This means putting the dress on over the foundation garments with which it will be worn and checking it from all sides before a full-length mirror. Holding a dress up to the shoulders or trying it on over another dress is not a good way to judge fit. The woman who has a size 12 figure and size 14 shoulders or some other figure irregularity should carefully check the fit of a dress and note necessary alterations.

American women have more clothes in more size ranges to choose from than any other women. Partly, the difficulty that women have in finding the right size may be due to their really not knowing their own sizes. Consequently, they look for—and find—the wrong size. Junior sizes, 3 to 17, generally have a high bustline and are shaped for a youthful figure. Misses' clothes are cut in sizes from 8 to 18 or 20. Half sizes,

12½ to 24½, are short-waisted and cut for a more fully-developed figure than the junior size. Clothes for the large figure are cut in women's sizes 36 to 44, and occasionally larger. Another size range, sometimes called Petite, Diminutive, Short Cut, or Brief, in sizes 8 to 18, is designed for women who are 5'3" to 5'5" in height but do not have a junior figure. Junior petites, scaled for the figure 5'1" and under, range from 3 to 13. The average American woman is 5'4" or under, without shoes, and is short-waisted. Tall sizes are designed for the very tall figure.

Progress has been made in sizing so that many designs are available in several sizes. Many attractive styles are cut to carefully studied proportions so that the woman who has passed beyond her junior years and proportions can still find a smart dress.

There is some variation in manufacturers' sizes. Some women shop until they find a manufacturer's size and design which fits. The designer's label is usually inside the dress, so that once you find out which designs fit you best, you can look for the same brand again. Catalog companies have garments made to size standards developed by the U. S. Dept. of Commerce to assure more accurate fit than the traditional sizes.

FIT

We have already discussed fit in a previous chapter, but a review of the factors to be considered may be helpful. Fit varies according to fashion, individual preferences, and the design and the use of the dress. Some details, however, should always be observed. A dress should stay in place and not ride back or up on the neck. Shoulder seams and armholes should neither slide down on the arms nor push up too high. With long sleeves, elbow darts or gathers should come at the bend of the elbow. If there is a definite waistline on the dress, designed to fit the wearer's normal waistline, it should be a straight line around the figure and should not sag below or rise above.

Skirts—whether straight or full—should be comfortably wide at the lower edge to permit easy and natural walking. Skirts designed to fit smoothly about the hips should not be so tight as to be unflattering to the figure and pull into folds just below the waistline. For sitting, enough extra ease is needed to keep the back of the skirt from stretching out of shape and the seams from straining or pulling out. Skirts that are lined with a firm fabric stretch less than unlined ones, but the lining must be properly fitted or it can ruin the fit and the appearance of the dress. Unless the skirt is differently designed, the side seams should hang straight from the waist. If they swing to the front, the back of the skirt will cup under the figure. If they swing to the back, the skirt will hang unevenly.

Room for action is important in dresses for housework, golfing, driving a car, and many other activities. Walk, reach, and sit to test the dress for shifting, "give," pulling, or binding at the neck, shoulders, and sleeves and in the skirt. Check items such as neckline and sleeve length for general coolness and comfort. For a dress to be worn when a great deal of sitting is involved—for office work, travel, or classes—choose one in which you can sit comfortably all day and still appear neat at the end of the day.

Dresses for social occasions should fit to assure comfort as well as appearance. The bodice—especially of a strapless gown—should fit smoothly and snugly. The wearer will take more pleasure in dancing if her dress fits so that it stays in place and at the same time allows for easy movement.

Fit and size are important in all dresses, but whether a dress fits snugly or loosely depends on fashion, the end use of the dress, and the wearer's desire for comfort and appearance. The emphasis of a snug fit may be at the bustline, at the waistline, or at the hipline, depending upon the design and silhouette currently in fashion.

CUT

An important factor, which affects both fit and appearance, is the cut of the dress. Cut refers to the way in which each pattern piece has been laid so that the thread runs accurately, whether crosswise, lengthwise, or on the bias. The crosswise threads should not run up- or downhill but straight across the back and front; a true bias-cut skirt falls into even flares—not into uneven, one-sided ones. In a plain sleeve, properly cut, crosswise threads run straight across the upper arm and lengthwise threads drop straight from the highest point of the shoulder. If the threads slant, unsightly fullness shows and the fit is strained. When hundreds of dresses are cut simultaneously from many layers of fabric, the material tends to shift, with the result that some of the pieces will be cut off grain. With fabrics in which the designs or figures have been printed "off grain," the cut of the garment is quite obvious.

In a dress which is well cut, plaids, checks, and stripes will match at the seams of the skirt. In a plaid, the crosswise lines in the top of the sleeve will match those of the bodice across the width of the back and the chest. Additional information is included in the chapter on fitting.

CONSTRUCTION

Besides the cut of the dress, you should note several other construction features if you want good value for your money. Start with the seams of the dress. Note whether there are more seams than are necessary to the design, such as a seam up the back of a straight skirt or a plain bodice or the center front of a closed bodice, or a seam concealed under applied trimming. They are often added in adaptations and reproduc-

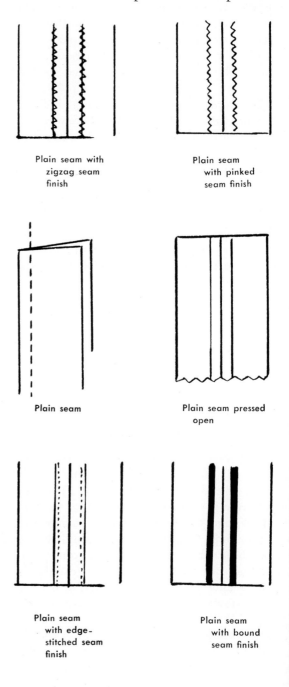

Plain seam with zigzag seam finish

Plain seam with pinked seam finish

Plain seam

Plain seam pressed open

Plain seam with edge-stitched seam finish

Plain seam with bound seam finish

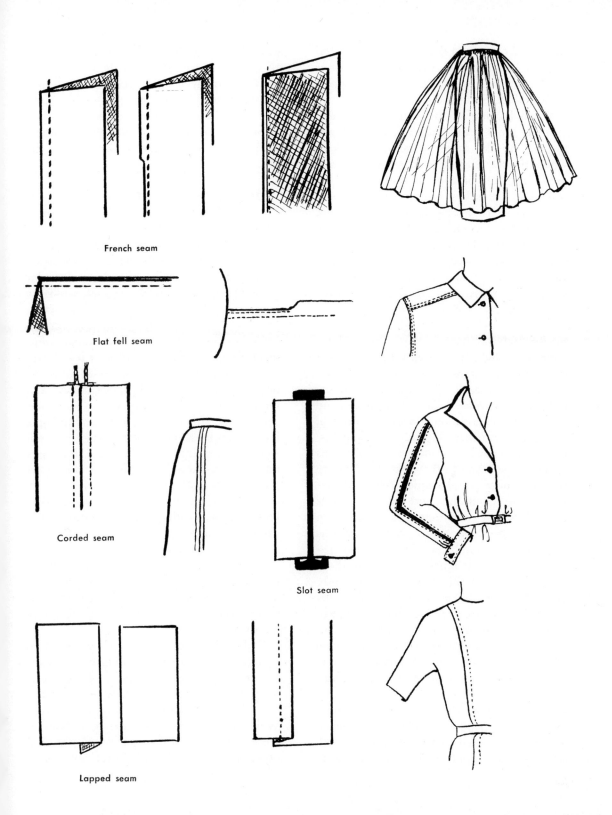

French seam

Flat fell seam

Corded seam

Slot seam

Lapped seam

tions, and often ruin the design of the original which was copied. Although extra seams may not affect wear, they affect appearance and ease of care.

When looking at the seams of a dress, examine them in full length rather than just turning up the lower edge of the skirt, where the seams often look better than they do in the rest of the dress. Look at the waistline, armscye, hipline, and at any seams where there is a slant or curve; these require great care in stitching and finishing and are often irregular and quick to pull out. Of course, seam allowance and finish vary with the material and its thickness, weight, firmness, and tendency to fray. Plain seams, half an inch wide and pinked or machine overcast, are usually adequate for firm fabrics like percale or broadcloth; plain seams which are wider than one half inch stay flat. More loosely woven fabrics, however, like crash, spun rayon, and linen, require generous seam allowances and some kind of additional finish to prevent fraying. Loose threads catch on slide fasteners. The rows in double-stitched seams should be stitched in the same direction to prevent puckers and ripples. Sheer fabrics like voile, chiffon, and some blends through which construction is readily seen require narrow yet secure seams—such as French, net-bound, or double-sticthed—which give a neat finish. Plain, unfinished, fraying seams in thin fabrics are not only unsightly; they are not durable. All seams should be smooth, even, adequate in width, and of suitable finish for the fabric.

The thread, length of stitch, and tension on seams should suit the weight of the dress fabric. Fourteen stitches per inch is average, but in many dresses it is only seven. Correct tension, which prevents frequent breaking or "popped" seams, is evidenced by stitching which looks the same on both sides. Thread which matches the fabric in color improves the appearance. In general, thread of the same fiber as the fabric is desirable. However, silk thread is often used on wool and some synthetics; mercerized cotton is used on some blends, depending upon the percentages of the different fibers in the blend and on the construction of the fabric.

INSIDE INFORMATION

Hems are important; a generous hem which can be adapted to various heights, which has invisible stitching, a firm binding, or edge stitching, and is flat and inconspicuous adds to the value of a dress. Circular hems are usually narrow, because a narrow hem is easier to turn in the construction process. Facings, bindings, interfacings, reinforcements, and stays are additional items to notice. Facings and bindings which are not properly fitted cause ripples, bunches, or pulling. Interfacings, tapes, stays, and linings should stand the same wear and care as the dress fabric, so that shrinkage, loss of crispness, and color change will not ruin the appearance of the dress. Backings and linings should be cut and sewed to provide a smooth fit and flat seams.

Tapes, particularly on jersey and other knitted fabrics, add to the durability of the dress; the tapes are usually placed at the shoulder seams, the waistline, and at other areas where stretching might occur. Reinforcements and stays at pocket corners, underneath buttons, at ends of slits, and at other areas where needed are desirable features.

If shoulder pads are used, they should be attached to the shoulder and armscye seams with enough stitches to hold them securely. Snap-in pads, which are easily removed, are desirable, especially in washable dresses. Well-fitted linings—for parts of dresses or whole dresses made of jersey, crepes, and other fabrics needing shape retention or of

Width of hem on
straight skirt

Width of hem
on circular skirt

fabrics which scratch—add to the cost, but improve appearance, comfort, and serviceability.

PERFORMANCE

Performance—such as colorfastness, dimensional stability, or crease resistance—is another important characteristic. If a label indicates colorfastness, note to what conditions; the garment may be colorfast to light, water, heat, atmospheric fumes, dry cleaning, or perspiration, but you may not need all of these in any one garment. Vat dyes are among the best, especially on cotton and rayons. Solution-dyed fabrics are excellent for many of the above-mentioned conditions of colorfastness.

A dress that will not shrink more than one per cent or will not stretch is desirable as a wash dress. Resin finishes and blends of fibers give fabrics wash-and-wear characteristics. Crease-resistant or wrinkle-resistant finishes also improve the quality of a dress. Mercerization of cotton fabrics

adds luster and strength. Polished cottons have a special finish for a durable, polished, lustrous appearance. Permanently crisp organdy, net, taffeta, and moire are popular for formal wear. Nets, tulles, and other evening-wear fabrics which have been treated for fire resistance are also available. Fire-retardent finishes are important in dresses which may come in contact with a candle flame or a lighted cigarette. Moth-repellent finishes on wools help in care and storage.

CLEANING AND CARE

With the wash-and-wear, minimum-care, and durable-press characteristics of dresses, care is no longer the problem it once was. There are, however, a few general instructions to keep in mind in addition to the specific ones for individual garments. Dresses should not be permitted to become too soiled before they are washed, as the rubbing necessary to remove the soil may damage the fabric. Even though labeled colorfast, dresses of colored materials should be washed separately in water that is not too hot and hung in the shade to dry or machine dried. If directions for washing are available, they should be followed carefully with regard to water temperature, method of washing, and use of bleach. Follow instructions on pressing and ironing temperatures and the use of press-cloths to avoid scorching, glazing, or melting certain fabrics.

Remember to help the dry cleaner by informing him of the location and the nature of any stains. Remember also that the cleaner may not be able to do a good job if the garment is excessively soiled and the soil has been in the fabric too long.

Dresses should be placed on suitable hangers. Those of perishable materials and those worn less frequently should be covered with shoulder covers or placed in garment bags. The covers dry cleaners use are excellent for protecting dresses hanging in the closet, but be sure that all clinging, transparent plastic is kept out of the reach of small children; playing with the film over their heads endangers their lives.

Frequent brushing and airing of wool dresses safeguards against moths. Dresses should be protected from perspiration and from contact with deodorants. There are many sizes and shapes in dress shields: shields to be worn as separate garments, and those to be attached to lingerie, thus eliminating shoulder straps. Except for dry-cleanable shields which often are permanently attached and cleaned with the garment, all dress shields need regular washing. Unless a fabric is white and washable, it is advisable to let the dry cleaner take care of spot and stain removal. An amateur not sure of fiber content, color-

fastness, or finish can ruin a dress in attempting to clean it. Keeping your dresses in good repair is another way of giving them the care the deserve and prolonging their usability. Additional points on care are included in Chapter 11.

IT'S YOUR CHOICE

It is not always possible to find all desirable features at the price you are willing to pay; you may have to make choices. If you consider color and design more important than workmanship, if you are not disturbed by plaids that do not match, if you can refinish carelessly stitched seams and other points of poor workmanship, then you may well choose a less expensive dress.

It will be to your advantage to make use of all the information available at the point of sale, from tags, labels, display cards, and sales personnel. Comparative shopping, among brands, in various departments, and in a variety of stores, is one means of helping yourself make wise decisions. You may find items of similar quality and characteristics at different prices, or items that are priced alike but differ in quality.

In the final analysis, your decisions and your selections are entirely up to you. It is your responsibility to yourself to shop carefully.

REFERENCE READINGS

Evans, Mary, *Better Clothes for Your Money,* J. B. Lippincott Co., Philadelphia, 1952.
Hillhouse, Marion S., *Dress Selection and Design,* Macmillan Co., New York, 1963.
Tate, Mildred Thurow and Glisson, Oris, *Family Clothing,* John Wiley & Sons, New York, 1961.
Wingo, Caroline E., *The Clothes You Buy and Make,* Mc-Graw-Hill, New York, 1953.

Chapter 16

Separates and sports clothes

Separates and sports clothes are among the best examples of the strong influence of a way of life on dress. Separates and sports clothes are truly American; they are a result of the increased leisure time the majority of people have now. This leisure has meant more time for the garden, for sports, and for do-it-yourself projects. The weekend is longer and the workday shorter. Improved appliances have lightened the work of the women of the house. Almost everyone has time to relax in the sun and to participate in more activities, and both men and women have developed new hobbies and interests that require new and comfortable clothing.

DEVELOPMENT

No longer is there the big difference between city and rural living. Suburbia requires clothes for outdoor interests and casual living. Even the city dweller has acquired casual clothes, and comfortable and relaxing separates are found in every home. Swimming pools, which once were for only the very wealthy, can now be found in many back yards. The automobile has brought lakes, forests, and other recreation areas close to all. All these social and economic changes in our way of life have brought with them the development of suitable clothing for new activities and situations.

The concept of what is ladylike has changed since the Victorian age. The proper lady of today is an alert, energetic person, not a prima donna. It is impossible to climb around in a boat in a full, bulky skirt, and women have consequently taken to slacks and shorts. You can't be ladylike in a dress while weeding the garden. What was once strictly work clothing is now more generally used. Jeans, denims, and sturdy fabrics have become popular. Television has brought entertainment into the home, and with it has come a more casual way of living, which is reflected also in clothing. Separates and sports clothes were comfortable enough, but the desire to be a little more decoratively dressed prompted the development of a new kind of "at home" clothes. Because of the wide variety of activities, there has been a demand for separates which meet more than one need and are easy to care for. Clothes for skiing, swimming, golf, riding, and tennis are still specifically designed for the activity; even some of these articles, however, can be used for other activities.

SELECTION

Separates should be chosen with a view to the intended use of the article. All separates must be comfortable, becoming, and durable. If you find that you never have quite the right thing to wear, you probably do not give casual clothes the same concern and consideration you give your dress clothes. Because casual clothes have developed gradually, many women have not given them much thought. If you will consider how and where the outfit is to be used, you will find yourself more attractively and more comfortably dressed in situations that call for casual clothes. There is no feeling more uncomfortable than that of knowing one is interfering with the fun of others.

In selecting casual clothing—whether for sports, active or spectator, or just for wear around the house—the most important thing is good sense. When going on a picnic, you would choose your clothes with consideration for the weather, the activities in which you expect to participate, and, of course, for appearance.

Do-it-yourselfers have found that clothing for work around the home must be practical; it must provide freedom of movement and protection for the body. When one paints a house one must be able to move freely and safely, without having to fuss with or adjust clothing; it is difficult to concentrate on painting when you are worried about your skirt blowing up. For painting and other dirty jobs, many women wear "cover-up" smocks or old shirts to protect clothing.

There was a time when some women wore an old dress which they felt could no longer be worn in public for working around the house. Since they were seldom selected for that purpose in the first place, these dresses generally were inappropriate for work. Some women still wear "house dresses," but most prefer dual-purpose work and play clothes. Those who do not feel comfortable in slacks generally wear sports dresses or skirts and blouses or sweaters, which can be worn equally well for shopping.

SPORTS CLOTHES

Sports clothes are good-sense clothes. Although there is some fashion element, most sports clothes are classic enough to be used until worn out. Clothes for most active sports and many spectator clothes obtain design interest from the fabric itself rather than from added trim. Jewelry is superfluous in active sports. Although clothes for boating, bowling, and walking do not have to meet requirements as specific as those for skiing, skating, and swimming, all sports clothes should protect the body from the weather and from scratching or burning, they should provide adequate ease for active movement, and they should be designed for safety, comfort, and appearance.

For swimming

The requirements for swimwear seem so obvious that when visiting a beach one is often surprised to see how many people are inappropriately dressed. First and foremost, swimming clothes must provide room for action; the whole body moves in the sport of swimming. The fit of the bathing suit must be perfect. Proper stays and construction are essential. There should be no bulk or additional weight. Things such as sleeves that fill up with water only hamper movement. Knit fabrics and those with elastic qualities are excellent for the serious swimmer. Most of the form-fitting bathing suits are woven with spandex or power stretch fabrics of synthetics and cotton. Cotton in combination with Lastex and other stretch fabrics has always been a favorite. Since the form-fitting suit is not very attractive except on a perfect figure, dressmaker suits are produced in great numbers.

Fashion influences swimming suits as it does all clothing. A "covered-up look" may be popular one year and a "bare look" the next. But all swimwear must be designed for movement. One should not have to worry about ripping of seams or insecure fastenings. Knits should be such that they do not become heavy with the absorption of water. Nonknits should not cling or become limp in the water. Many of the wash-and-wear fabrics that have sufficient body are used in dressmaker suits. The fabric must be able to take the strain of movement in both swimming and beach activity. Construction must be durable, with strong, reinforced seams at points of strain. Swimming suits that dry quickly are desirable. If you practically live on the beach during the summer months, you may want to—or find it necessary to—have more than one

There is a style of bathing suit for every figure.

bathing suit. Important in the choice of a swimming suit is colorfastness—to the sun, to salt water, and to chlorine. Many colorfast fabrics are colorfast only for a certain number of hours and will fade with long exposure to the bright sun. Halter necks may cause strain on the neck and be uncomfortable when worn for any length of time.

A woman chooses her suit for her figure. The woman who is large will want a slightly flared but not gathered skirt to make her hips and legs appear less large. Prints have excellent camouflage value, unless, of course, they are very bright and large. For the woman with slender hips, the clinging suit is wonderful. Shirred suits are excellent for the very thin. Also good for the slender are the suits with broad panel effects. For the bustline, there are built-in brassières and padded inner structures. Pellon and other bonded fabrics are being used to give bathing suits extra body and shape. Suits that are cut low have boning to hold them securely in place. Two-piece suits are becoming to the woman with a nicely tapered midriff, but will also expose and accentuate any prominent ribs or rolls of fat. Camisole-type suits, because of the high cut and the close fit above the bust, are usually more becoming to the girl who has a small bustline. Generally speaking, the close-fitting suit displays the figure; for the less-than-perfect figure, the dressmaker suit, with fuller cut, pleated skirt, and carefully tailored top with well-built inner structures, is best.

Lines in swimming suits are similar to lines in dress. The woman with some particular figure problem or irregularity may find a custom-made suit well worth the cost. Bathing suits emphasize form and shape more than most clothes, and, since so much of the body is exposed, too much care cannot be taken in the selection of a swimming suit.

Color in bathing suits is chosen as are other colors, with the exception that the person who tans beautifully will select a color that plays up the tan. One may at this time be able to wear colors one normally would not. Whites and strong contrasts of black and white or brown and white will accent a beautiful tan. Selecting a swimsuit and a foundation garment is similar. Brassière, as well as dress or slip size, will be on labels. A snug suit will not flatter a heavy figure. There are some places where the bikini would be considered in poor taste.

Accessories. At the beach, most people will need some protection, either from the cold or from too much sun. Terry cloth is absorbent and easily cared for, and is often used in beach coats. In mountain areas where the air is cool, warmth may be important. A smart shirt can serve as a beach coat where just a little protection is needed. Many beach coats have water-repellent finishes. A beach bag that is not too large but large enough to allow for the needed equipment will be useful. Beach bags are made of many materials, but those made of fabrics which can be wiped off or washed are best, since beach bags will receive hard wear. Beach bags lined with plastic or some other waterproof material are very satisfactory. Beach shoes come in many styles and materials. A favorite is the sandal, which eliminates the problem of sand in the shoes. The style should be such that the shoes are easy to care for, do not interfere with play activity, and are easy to put on. Most people use shoes only to walk to the beach or pool; a few want shoes that can also be worn in the water as a protection from sand or pebbles. Zoris are favorites of younger people and have been adopted by many groups. A good rubber bathing cap has an added rim inside as a protection for the hair. Ear plugs are available for those who do not wear caps. Elaborately decorated caps have at times been in fashion. In choosing a decorated cap, one should keep weight in mind; many elaborate bathing caps are too heavy for comfort. Beach hats are worn by people who sunburn quickly and, occasionally, as a fashion item. Generally, beach hats are made of a coarse straw or a water-repellent cotton fabric such as denim. The visor cap, a favorite with men, is occasionally used by women as a protection for the hair.

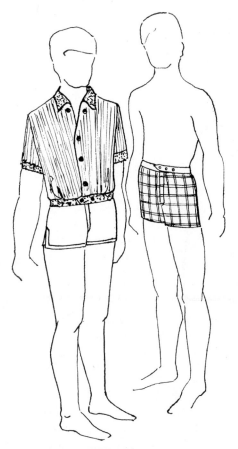
Bathing trunks and shirt co-ordinates.

Men's swimwear. Men's swimwear comes mainly in two styles, boxer shorts and knitted or Lastex swim trunks. Fashion variations include the amount of taper, the length of the shorts, the styling of the belt or waistband, the kind of fabric, design, and color. Comfort is, as always, the prime consideration; the longer swim trunks designed to give some protection for water-skiing or surfboarding are an example of design for comfort. Adequate weight of fabric is important in appearance. The wide range of fabrics and variations in styles and designs available today give some opportunity for individual expression.

For golf

Since golf requires much arm movement, the golf shirt is designed with an "action back." The action back has added ease in a deep pleat in center back or in two large pleats controlled over the shoulder blades. For any active sport, this kind of shirt, which allows movement without creating bulk, is excellent. Bermudas and other shorts have in large measure replaced the golf skirt. For skirts, there should be pleats or other controlled fullness to permit free and graceful movement of the body. Golfing equipment also includes sport sweaters, and, for the serious golfer, special golfing shoes with spikes. Some golf courses require that golf shoes be worn. In all sports, the hair—unless it is very short and looks well when wind-blown—could be controlled by either a scarf, a band, or a hair spray.

Men's golfing clothes naturally have the same basic requirements as women's. Slacks and bermudas are made of durable and easily laundered fabrics. Durable-press fabrics have made these clothes easy to care for. The knit sports shirt, which allows for free movement of the arms and shoulders, is a favorite with golfers. The golf course is one place where men can indulge a love of color and bold, unusual patterns.

The feet should be protected with cotton socks, which absorb moisture readily. Socks and stockings should be washable and should not need special hand laundering.

For riding

Riding clothes differ in various sections of the country. In the East, riding with clubs and on hunts, one still sees the conventional riding habit of fitted trousers, riding coat, and derby hat. In the West, on the plains or in the mountains, you would wear Levis or frontier pants. There are certain common requirements, whether for blue

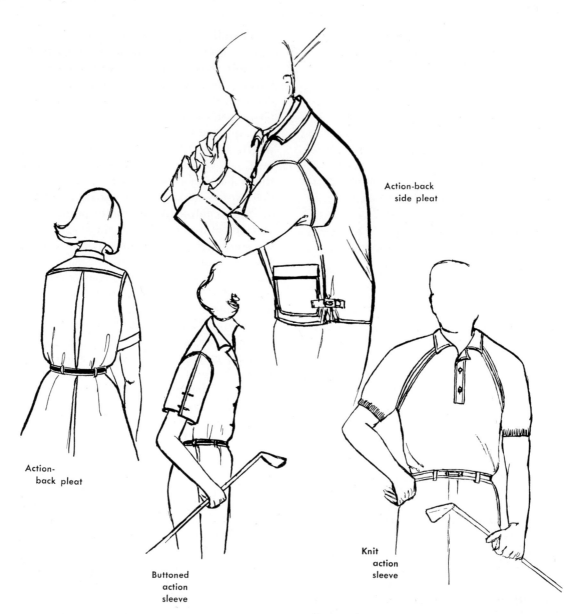

Action-back
side pleat

Action-
back pleat

Buttoned
action
sleeve

Knit
action
sleeve

Action clothes for golf.

jeans or for the beautiful twill trousers of the conventional habit. The trousers will be subject to a great deal of abrasion at the knees and must be of a durable, strong fabric, such as found in a covert cloth. Most riding clothes have reinforced areas at the

inside of the legs and the seat. The legs of the trousers are always closely fitted or tapered to avoid any bulk that would interfere with riding.

Most horseback riders respect the weather and carry a sweater or a waterproof jacket; some carry a slicker on the saddle. As in other sports, a T-shirt worn under another shirt or a knit shirt will help to maintain the body temperature if the weather should change suddenly. Most riders require socks for the protection of feet and ankles. Boots—whether the conventional high boots, jodhpurs, or cowboy boots—are mandatory. Many a dude has come home with sore and blistered ankles from riding without proper footwear.

Some kind of head covering is generally desirable. This, of course, depends a great deal upon where your ride takes you. In dense woods, protection is needed from brush and branches. For those who sunburn easily, a hat is a necessary precaution.

For tennis

Tennis clothing requires ease for movement without excess bulk. Short shorts are

Tennis clothes.

popular with young women, but the professionals often wear tennis dresses. A tennis dress is best designed with pleats that allow movement and are well controlled. Because there is so much arm movement, the one-piece dress is a favorite; it moves with the body and the shirt or blouse does not pull out. The tennis dress may be more flattering to the player who is large in the hips and thighs than shorts would be. As with golf shirts, you will find the action-back pleat. The blouse will generally be sleeveless, but this in itself does not allow for more action. In selecting an action back for tennis or any other sport, select a style that you are sure has the controlled action where you need it. The action back is usually controlled in a yoke; if the yoke falls too far down on the shoulders it may fall below the point where action is needed. For men, there are T-shirts and shorts especially designed for tennis.

For ice skating

Clothes for ice skating and skiing must give more warmth than those for any other active sports. Professional women skaters wear skirts that are very short, full, and either flared or pleated. These skirts are very becoming on a good skater—and look foolish on one who has not developed grace. Trousers worn for skating should be trim and tapered in order to avoid interfering with movement. Stretch fabrics that cling to the body are excellent, since they give the necessary warmth without adding bulk. Many skating outfits are worn over knit tights; above all, the skating outfit must afford free leg movement.

For skiing

Skiing is not an inexpensive sport. Ski clothes are of necessity not versatile; they are designed to meet special requirements.

In no other active sport has high fashion

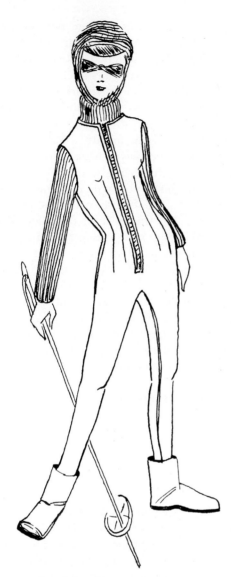

The one piece jumpsuit.

struction allow movement without excess bulk. One piece jumpsuits may, on occasion, replace trousers.

Ski trousers are slim and tapered. When properly fitted, they are held taut by an extension of the trouser leg or an added band which fits under the foot. Trousers that blouse over the boots add unnecessary bulk and do not give movement where needed; ski trousers are tapered at the ankles and vented. Motion in skiing is a smooth turning of the shoulders and bending of the knees rather than violent movement. Important to the fit, as in all trousers, are the length of the crotch and adequate ease over the hips.

Boots are especially designed to fit the clamps of ski bindings and are made in all kinds of shoe leathers. Ski boots should fit; control of the skis is lost if the boots are too large. Sometimes ski boots are bought a half size smaller than other shoes. The boots should be large enough to allow for a pair of woolen socks or stockings for warmth. Cotton socks, which are absorbent, should be worn under the woolen socks.

Ski jackets are frequently purchased as prestige items but do have specific requirements which good skiers will check. Easy movement of the shoulders and arms is imperative. Action pleats give controlled fullness to classic jackets. Fur parkas usually are made in accordian type construction to give stretch qualities. The head should be protected by a hood, knit cap, stocking cap, or water-repellent helmet.

Where you will be skiing will make a difference in the kind of ski clothing you will need. In the United States, eastern slopes are more humid, and cold is felt more. Western slopes, although cold, are often very dry, and when one is exercising as hard as one does in skiing, one needs less warm, bulky clothing. The time of year will

so completely taken over. Expensive fur parkas and hats, costly ski boots, and hand knit sweaters are common.

Despite the emphasis on fashion, serious skiers want clothes that do not interfere with activity. Stretch fabrics are favored in ski pants, although knitted fabrics are sometimes used. Both types of fabric con-

Ski clothes without bulk. The trousers should be taut
and the jackets cut for action.

Jerkins, bulky knits, and lounge boots for after skiing, and ski headgear.

also be a factor; in the spring, many places are pleasantly warm for skiing. In the Alps and on our western slopes, one can ski in shirt sleeves during the spring months. Helanca stretch tights or thermal underwear may be needed in very cold areas.

In most clothes for active sports, decoration is provided by the fabric and the weave or by prints on the fabric. Seldom do we find decorative additions. Quite naturally, we have adopted many of the customs of those who brought the sport of skiing to America. Bulky sweaters of Scandinavian and Tyrolean design are appropriate both on the slopes and after skiing. Generally speaking, some type of boots will be needed to replace the ski boots after skiing, since the ski boots, extremely heavy and tiring, are not made for walking. A change of socks may also be necessary; the heavy woolen socks may be too warm off the slopes.

For boating

Boating clothes must protect the body from the elements. When the sun is shining, be especially careful to avoid sunburn; you are getting sun not only directly, but reflected from the water. There is always a good chance of getting wet; even if it does not rain, there will usually be spray from breaking waves or from the wake of the boat. Shoes must not mar wooden decks; high heels or black rubber heels can make a boatman hate you. Skidproof soles are best for boating; sneakers and espadrilles are excellent. Clothes should be both washable and durable; they will be exposed to frequent laundering, because you will find engine grease and soil on even the best-kept boats.

For bowling

Bowling clothes, like clothes for boating and for all other sports, must afford freedom of action without excess bulk. Both arms and legs need adequate freedom for movement. Bowling shoes, with flat, soft, nonskid soles, are required; they can be rented at most bowling alleys.

For the spectator

The clothing needs of the spectator are, of course, different from those of the active player. The general requirements are much the same, however; the body must be protected and the clothes should afford adequate freedom of movement. There are sport occasions—like certain horse shows and some college football games—for which people dress quite elaborately. However, comfortable and casual clothing are more suited to the atmosphere of indoor and outdoor sports events.

Football games. Experienced spectators have learned that stacked heels and handsome, durable knits are in the end more attractive than more elaborate dress; high-heeled shoes are awkward for climbing around in the bleachers, and delicate fabrics and fine furs may be ruined by exposure to wind and rain or to the enthusiasm of the crowd. Clothes that protect the wearer from the elements and allow for comfort and easy, graceful movement permit the wearer to forget the clothes and enjoy the game. Tweeds, blazer jackets, sturdy fabrics, and comfortable shoes can be just as effective in a simple way as the most elaborate of furs and decorative additions.

In selecting and co-ordinating spectator clothes, we often have to take into consideration after-the-game activities. A woman might come from some distance to see a game and then go directly from the bleachers to a party for which she would prefer to be more dressed up. She can plan for this. There are suits which can be slightly dressed up by a change of shoes or hats and the addition of jewelry. Small tote bags and large handbags are practical for carrying the extra accessories. It would be wise to choose as additional accessories things which can be folded and packed into a small space without crushing.

SLACKS AND SHORTS

Slacks and shorts, practical and comfortable, have become an important part of many wardrobes. Fashion change is slow and gradual, and slacks or shorts can be chosen which will remain in fashion for a long time. Some one style—perhaps bermudas, jamaicas, or short shorts—will probably be the most popular in any one year, but that does not mean that the other styles will be out of fashion. Fashion changes affect the degree of taper, the kind of fastenings used, belts and belt lines, length, pocket design, and the style of the cuffs—if cuffs are in fashion.

Slacks or shorts do not look equally well on all women. In fact, some men think women should never wear slacks. There are some women who will sacrifice appearance for the sake of comfort and practicality. It should be remembered that women borrowed the fashion from men; trousers were designed for men's figures and have therefore always looked best on the trim-hipped person. Slacks are not particularly flattering to legs or thighs, and expert tailoring is just as important as a good figure and good posture. Some women are willing to wear light foundation garments to improve the appearance or for the additional support for the figure during active participation in sports. Slacks take their form and shape from the figure; the woman who likes slacks should do everything she can to improve her figure.

The fabrics used in slacks and shorts will vary according to fashion, but there is some consistency in the general characteristics of those fabrics. Closely woven, firm weaves lend themselves better to use in shorts than do loose weaves. With loose weaves, interlinings should be used. Interlinings are also used in madras shorts which are meant to bleed and mellow. As in all other kinds of clothing, luxury fabrics are used also in slacks and shorts. Examples are certain beautiful silks and linens in interesting weaves. Stretch or knit fabrics, being easy to move in, are, of course, among the most popular. All slacks and shorts must fit well, have good workmanship and strong seams, and be easy to care for.

From left to right: calf-length tapers, clam diggers or pedal pushers, and frontier or Western pants.

(Opposite) Three popular styles of shorts: short shorts, jamaicas, and bermudas.

KNITS

Knitwear, which at one time was limited to sweaters and underwear, now also includes coats, suits, dresses, shirts, and even trousers. Because of the nature of their construction, knits do not wrinkle readily and are therefore excellent for travelers and for others who must look fresh for longer periods of time. Knits have added appeal in that they do not restrict or hamper movement. They are comparatively easy to care for; new finishes and methods of construction have produced excellent knit fabrics not only from wool but from cotton and synthetics.

Fashion in sweaters can be observed in changes of yarn construction and in neckline styles. Bulky yarns, looped mohair, or smooth, fine yarns are examples. A sweater that is loosely knit will result in an "airy" look.

Line and fit

Few people seem to realize that in the selection of knitwear, line should receive the same consideration it receives in the selection of other clothing. If a woman needs a line which "breaks" or stops the eye at a certain point in other clothes, she will need the same kind of line in knits. There are structural lines in knits just as there are in other kinds of clothing. In knits, these lines are often the result of the kind of stitch used.

Knits get their form and shape from the figure. This is an important fact to remember; close-fitting knitted outfits should be bought large enough to provide adequate ease over curves. Fit is more important in knits than it is in woven fabrics. Many people hand knit as a hobby; for them it is essential to know where in a knitted garment ease for movement will be required, where to control fullness, and how to construct a knitted article.

Sizing, especially in sweaters, is not uniform. A few companies mark sweaters in sizes corresponding to dress sizes. It is usually wise to buy sweaters slightly larger than the dress size, since sweaters generally run smaller than the corresponding dress size. Men's sweaters are sized according to chest measurement. When buying a sweater, you should always try it on; that is the only way to be sure of a good fit. This is especially true with imported goods; English or Italian sweaters, for example, may be sized according to a system different from that used in the United States.

Construction

There is a great variety of knitted fabrics; knits include jerseys, suede-finished knits, ribbon knits, fleeces, poodle cloth, and imitation furs, to name only a few. In knitted as in woven fabrics, texture is the result of yarn, finish, and construction, and knits are available in many interesting textural effects.

The inner construction of a knit garment will to a great extent determine fit, especially the degree in which the garment clings to the figure and the way in which ease and fullness are controlled. Most knits stretch and will need stays in construction points such as the shoulder and waistline seams and on underarm and center seams. In addition to being stayed, many jerseys and other knits are lined to give body to the garment and to help to control stretching. It is recommended that skirts, and even bodices, be lined if possible. If a knit is not lined, a slip of a firm material such as taffeta will take much of the strain and help to retain the shape of the garment. Knitted coats and jackets are often interfaced in the same manner as coats and jackets of woven fabrics.

The three types. There are three basic types of knits—circular, full-fashioned, and

Fashion marks. The sweater at the left is full fashioned; the one at the right shows mock fashion marks.

Stitches. In the plain stitch, lengthwise rows of loose stitches form ribs. The backstitch or inverted plain stitch is referred to as purl. The shaker knit is a plain knit in a heavy yarn and has a coarse feeling. The cable stitch, a combination of plain and purl stitches twisted to give a cable effect, is popular for bulky sports sweaters. The Swiss rib is a knit-two-and-purl-two stitch. The knit is more in evidence than the recessed purl, and the resulting rib effect makes the Swiss rib popular for bands and waistlines. Jacquard knits, such as those seen in Swiss or Tyrolean sweaters, are generally done in a double knit and involve yarns of different colors. The Jacquard is usually confined to one area, such as across the shoulders. Purl stitching looks alike on both sides; it appears rather coarse and seems to have a crosswise direction rather than the rib effect of the plain knit. Much design and textural interest are obtained by combining various stitches.

Yarns and fabrics. In knits, as in all other fabrics, quality begins in the fiber. The construction of the yarn is of great importance; it will govern many performance qualities. A four-ply yarn will, of course, be stronger than a two-ply yarn. The more twist the yarn is given, the more durable will it be—but too tight a twist may result in loss of softness. Worsted yarns, which are tightly twisted and given a soft finish, are less likely to pill than are woolen yarns with less twist. Fabrics made from the woolen yarns will be more loosely knitted and therefore softer. Cotton yarns are frequently finished to resist snagging and to help to hold the shape of the fabric. Some inexpensive cotton knits are loose and tend to snag. The washable and quick-drying man-made fibers are popular for sweaters. Some of the man-made fibers, however, tend to pill. Pilling, caused by abrasion, is the formation of little balls of fibers on the surface of the fabric. The

interlock. Circular knits are made in tubular form. They can be shaped during construction by changing the tension of the yarns or they can be steamed to size and shape on forms after being removed from the machine.

Full-fashioned knits are shaped by the adding or dropping of stitches on the knitting machine. Marks known as fashion marks are left where stitches are added or dropped. Full-fashioned garments can be identified by parallel stitches along the edge of the fabric where it joins another piece, as at the armscye seam. False fashion marks are stitches added to imitate full-fashioned garments in appearance.

Interlock knits differ in appearance from knits made by the circular or full-fashioned methods in that both sides of the fabric look the same. Interlock knits are made on circular-knit machines, and stitches are varied for design purposes or to give the fabric added elasticity.

stronger the fiber, or the looser the twist, the more likely is the yarn to pill. Pilling can be controlled in some measure through the use of textured yarns.

Blouses, sweaters, and skirts

In any knit garment, the finish of the seams, the edges of the ribbing, and the way stays—such as the grosgrain ribbon facing on the sweater—are applied to maintain the shape of the front edge are good indications of quality. Seams should be trim and smooth, without raveling or loose threads.

Knitted blouses and sweaters are either full-fashioned or cut and sewn like those of other fabrics. Skirts are either tubular knit or cut and sewn. The full-fashioned sweater or bodice is shaped and bound off as the machine knits. Cut and sewn sweaters will vary in style and appearance. The cutting of a flat piece of fabric is less expen-

sive than full fashioning, but not all cut and sewn sweaters or dresses are inexpensive. Many of the best-fitting knits are cut just as woven garments would be, with the direction of the pattern straight with the lengthwise stitches or the crosswise rows.

Ribbing, which is more elastic than plain knit, is generally used in the necks of sweaters. The ribbing on many men's and boys' sweaters is double and forms the facing for the entire front of the sweater. Important in neck facings is a smooth, flat neckline which is shaped by the knit. Ribbing of poor quality may be too full and the excess yarn may make the edge roll. In many of the better grades of sweaters, an elastic thread may be included to help to hold the shape. On occasion, wool or cotton fibers may be reinforced with nylon 420

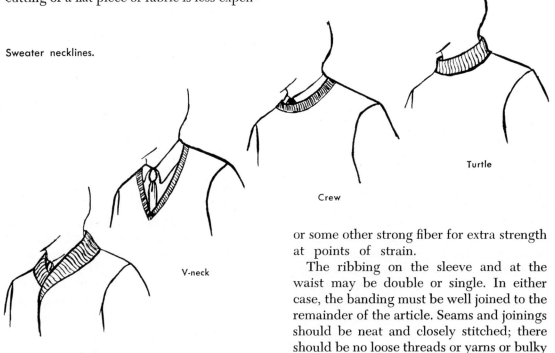

Sweater necklines.

Turtle

Crew

V-neck

Shawl

or some other strong fiber for extra strength at points of strain.

The ribbing on the sleeve and at the waist may be double or single. In either case, the banding must be well joined to the remainder of the article. Seams and joinings should be neat and closely stitched; there should be no loose threads or yarns or bulky seams.

Variation in shirts can be obtained through pattern and color. From left to right: dobby, pin stripe, wide stripe, and checks or tattersall.

A good knit product, then, is the result of many factors, from the quality of the fiber to the size and twist of the yarn, the tension of the knit, its compactness and the way it is constructed, the kind of stays used and their quality, and the finish of edges and seams.

SHIRTS

Shirts and blouses are almost universally worn. Women have adopted and adapted the man's shirt for their own use. Men's shirts are classified as either dress or sports shirts. Blouses are made in dressmaker styles and in the lines of the simple, classic shirt. Fashion change in shirts is slow and gradual. While there is little obvious change, the fashion element is noticeable in collars, cuffs, and sleeves and in the color and kind of fabric.

Collars

The fit of a shirt depends upon the control of the fullness for arm and shoulder movement in the fullness of the armhole, in the length of the body as related to the person, and in the tapering of the waist. Men's dress or business shirts differ from sport shirts in the collar style and in the fabric. The dress shirt is usually more conservative in color than the sport shirt.

There are many different styles of collars,

Wide spread
Long points

Wide spread
Short points

Medium
spread

Pointed

Button-down
collars—

Rounded

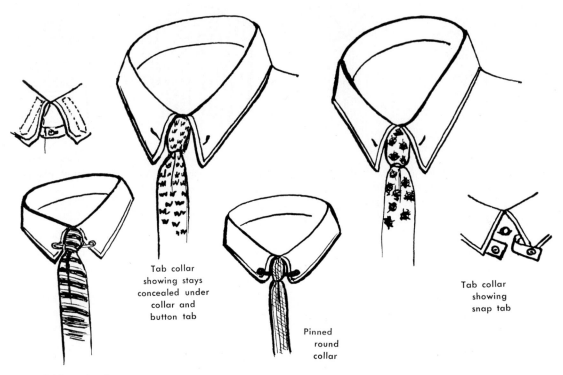

Tabless tab collar

Tab collar
showing stays
concealed under
collar and
button tab

Pinned
round
collar

Tab collar
showing
snap tab

varying in shape, spread, and slope. There is variation also in the length of the points. A man can choose a slope becoming to the length of his neck—high neckband, regular neckband, or low-slope collar. The dress shirt may have wide stitching around the edge. In addition to variation in the kind of collar, there are differences of style in the points, which may be rounded or pointed. The spread and the line of the collar can flatter the features of the face. The long, pointed collar flatters the full, round face; the short, wide-spaced points would be more attractive on a longer or oval face. The individual with a very short neck will choose the low slope, which does not cut the neck length. The person with a very long neck might choose the high-neckband collar. Button-down collars give a more youthful, and a more casual, appearance than does the widespread type. Round collars are also a little more youthful in feeling. Those that have a fastening to hold the collar stay neat and do not rumple so readily.

Cuffs

Cuffs are made in mainly three styles—the barrel cuff, the convertible cuff, and the French cuff. The combination barrel cuff can be buttoned as a straight cuff or turned back as a French cuff. There are variations in fashion and design from time to time. A cuff may button with two buttons or one. The French cuff has varied in the amount of turnback given to the cuffs. At various times in fashion history, we have seen contrasting cuffs, or white collars and cuffs on colored shirts.

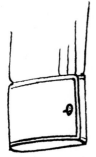

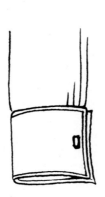

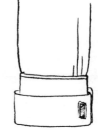

Top left: Regular one-button barrel cuff. Bottom left: Two-button barrel cuff. Center: Convertible cuff. Button or cuff links. No turnback. Top right: French cuff. Bottom right: Narrow-turnback French cuff.

Sleeves

Top-quality shirt sleeves are cut in one piece, with the straight of the material at the top fold of the sleeve. Sleeves are occasionally pieced at the back of the arm. A good sleeve is set in at a precise angle to allow freedom of movement. The sleeve should have an armhole wide enough for freedom without being too deep for comfort when worn under the suit coat. The sleeve tapers gradually toward the cuff, and the best shirts have a control by pleats into the cuff rather than uneven gathers. Cuff plackets are long to allow the arm to enter easily through the opening and to make ironing easier. The sleeve facing for the opening above the cuff is best done with a two-piece placket that comes together when the cuff is bottoned.

Shirt body

The body of the shirt is cut with a natural shoulder line and a high sleeve head to fit smoothly over the arm. The shirt front should lie flat, whether it is a regular box front with a pleat or a French coat front without pleats. In a well-designed shirt, the body is tapered at the waist and is related to the neck and sleeve size. A good shirt is long enough when tucked in and has a gusset at the lower edge where the side seams are joined. The interfacing used in a good shirt is generally made of the same material as the body of the shirt. Other materials used as interfacings should be of comparable quality. Buttonholes are done with a close, firm stitch, securely fastened at the end of each buttonhole. Seams in men's shirts are generally made with flat felled seams. Most seams are double stitched to add strength. Single-needle construction indicates the direction which the seam is sewn and has only one row of stitching showing. Single-needle construction does not pucker the seam as when two rows are sewn at one time, and is usually found in higher priced shirts. Some shirts have single-needle construction on the armscye seam only. Pleating of back fullness and fullness into the cuff is more time consuming than the gathered fullness but is more easily cared for and looks much more attractive. Of course all parts of the shirt are symmetrical.

Fabrics

The numerous fabrics used in shirts include many old favorites in addition to a wide variety of new wash-and-wear fabrics. The fabric plays an important part in durability and comfort. The kind of fiber and yarn used, the way the yarn is woven, the evenness and firmness of the weave, and the finish will make a great deal of difference to the durability of the shirt. The basic shirtings include broadcloth, madras, oxford, and chambray in dress shirts, with percales, ginghams, and twill weaves popular in sportswear. Although the white shirt is the favorite for business, a colored or striped shirt reflecting the fashion of the day is acceptable. Broadcloth comes in various weights and different qualities; the finest are made of a mercerized, combed cotton, generally in a single-ply yarn, although it may be found in two-ply. Characteristic of broadcloth is a crosswise yarn effect resulting from the warp's having twice as many threads per inch as does the filling. Madras generally has a balanced number of threads in the filling with precise weaving. Madras frequently has a striped effect in the lengthwise yarns or a small pattern. Oxford cloth is a heavier fabric than madras or broadcloth and is made in a basket weave. It is soft, has a dull finish, and has a round, full yarn. Oxford makes a sturdy fabric in a close weave. Chambray has colored warp threads and white crosswise threads. Generally speaking, chambray is a fairly balanced weave and a durable fabric. The finer grades of these fabrics are found in better shirts. The smoother the fabric and the better the balance between warp and filling threads, the less uneven wear will be found. Cotton may have a resin finish that gives wash-and-wear characteristics. Most wash-and-wear cottons are of heavier fabric than is found in the fine pima cotton shirt.

Care and comfort

The claims of the manufacturer should be stated in definite terms such as "Wash-and-wear, no ironing" or "Wash-and-wear, little or no ironing." Blends of polyester and cotton are made in oxford and batiste. Taslan-textured Dacron is a yarn that is opaque, static free, quick to dry, and long wearing. To date, the wash-and-wear shirts have been a little more expensive than the cotton. Value can be judged by the cost of washing at home as opposed to additional laundry costs. Some shirt collars are permanently stiffened by using a fused material between the collar and its facing. Dress shirts for formal wear have wing collars, pleated fronts, and French cuffs. Now a softer, lightweight but stylish wing collar has been developed to give more comfort in the dress shirt.

Sport shirts

Sport and leisure shirts add variety to the wardrobe. The sport shirt has much gaiety in fabric, ranging from very loud prints, stripes, and plaids to smaller prints and textured materials. Variety in styling is found in the collar and neck openings. Knits are popular in shirts for leisure wear. In the woven fabrics, the action back allows for easy movement. The fly front is a trim and neat opening on the sport shirt. The cardigan shirt styles, which are collarless, give variety and are particularly becoming to the man with a shorter, thicker neck.

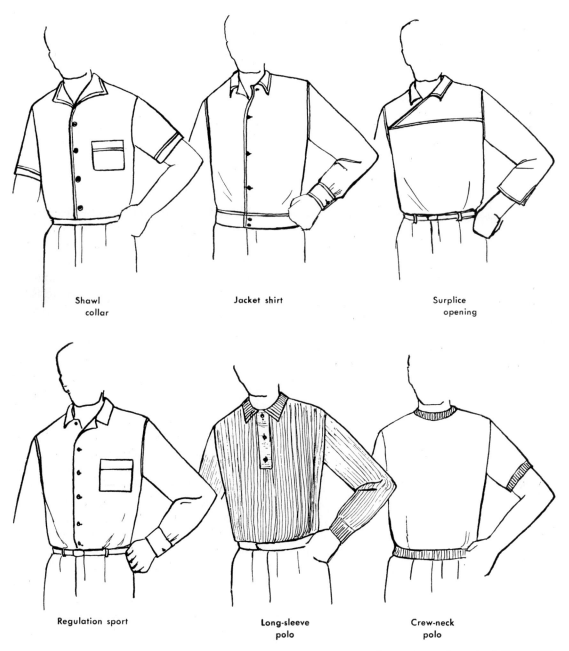

Shawl
collar

Jacket shirt

Surplice
opening

Regulation sport

Long-sleeve
polo

Crew-neck
polo

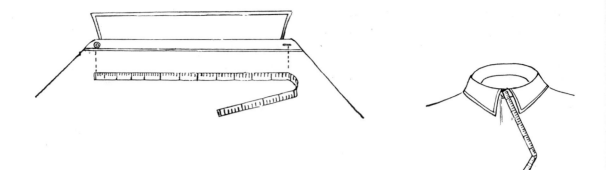

Measuring a shirt collar to determine correct sizing: Measure the collar band from the center of the button to the center of the buttonhole for the correct size; to determine the length, measure the length of the tab along the collar edge.

Sizing

Men's shirt sizes are given by sleeve length and the circumference of the neck. The sleeve length is taken from the center back of the collar, over the shoulder, and to the wrist. The length of the collar is measured from the center button to the buttonhole. Size is printed on the inside rim of the collar. If the collar length is 15½ inches and

To measure a shirt sleeve, measure from the center of the back of the collar over the shoulder and down the sleeve to the edge of the cuff.

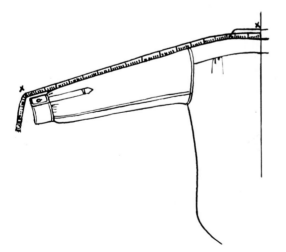

the sleeve length 33 inches, it will read 15½–33. Depth of collar point is measured along the edge of the collar at the fullest point.

WOMEN'S BLOUSES

Blouses and shirts fall into two categories —classic sport and dressmaker styles. The difference between the dressmaker and the sport is found in the structural and decorative lines. The sport shirt, or classic blouse, is cut with many of the same characteristics as a man's shirt. A dressmaker blouse results when a rich, luxurious fabric is styled in a decorative manner. A woman's shirt may be made in a luxurious and elaborate fabric or the simply cut shirt might be made into a decorative blouse by the addition of jewelry. Design, decorative trim, or fabric may change the idea the blouse creates.

A suit blouse generally has a collarless neckline and fits closely at the base of the neck. Many people feel that this simple, round neck, often referred to as a jewel neckline, lends itself to change of jewelry. This blouse is generally designed to be worn with the jacket on and may look incomplete if the jacket is removed. It is a supplement to the suit and should be chosen with great care. Collars, bows, or trim should not interfere with the design of the suit. The color and neckline of a shirt or blouse must be becoming to the face and to the clothes it

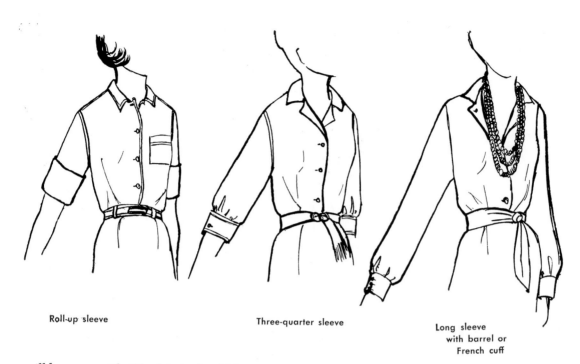

Roll-up sleeve   Three-quarter sleeve   Long sleeve with barrel or French cuff

Styles in women's shirts.

will be worn with. The fabric should be suitable to the design of the suit or skirt.

When worn as separates, blouses should be chosen to look complete with the skirt even if worn without a jacket. Three-quarter or full-length sleeves usually look more complete than short sleeves. The lines of the blouse should harmonize with the lines of the separate skirt. The separates idea often requires a belt to make the two pieces look as though they belong together.

Selection

In choosing for durability, the fiber and the construction will be strong determining factors. The fit of a blouse is one of the first concerns a person should have in selecting a blouse. The blouse should have adequate anchoring for the tail. Those who are long-waisted may find blouses and shirts are cut too short for them. Those who are short-waisted may find that the darts which control the fullness to the waist will fall too low on the figure.

Sizing

Women's shirts and blouses are sold by dress size—10, 12, 14, etc.—or by bust measure—30, 32, 34, etc. There is wide variation in sizing in different makes of shirts. It is essential to know your brand or to try on the blouse or shirt in order to get a proper fit.

AND SKIRTS

Separate skirts differ from suit skirts mainly in design. Suit skirts are cut to complete the design of the jacket. Separate skirts are designed to be worn with blouses or sweaters. They have more decorative detail and variation in silhouette than is usually found in suit skirts. Top stitching, decorative pockets, and decorative trim are examples of the kind of design found in separate skirts. The skirt and accompanying

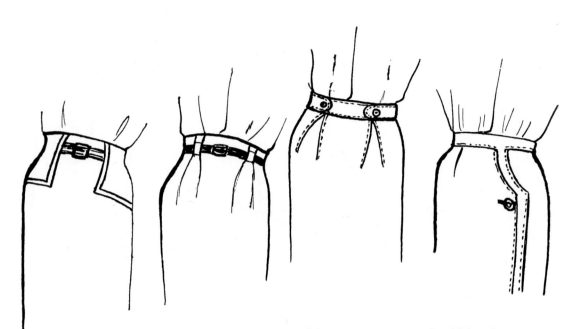

Design variations in separate skirts.

blouses or sweaters should be chosen to go together, as complete units. One will seldom want elaborateness in both the blouse and the skirt. A wide variety of fabrics is used in separate skirts.

Variation in vest styles.

Lounging pajamas and culottes.

AT-HOME CLOTHES

"At home" clothes have come to indicate a dressy but casual kind of separates worn in the home. They are very decorative in treatment. What is actually worn in the home varies a great deal but the comfort and ease of care of the casual clothes has had a strong influence on the clothes used for work and play in the home. The increase in home entertaining has inspired a number of styles in which women can look attractive and yet be comfortable. In the home you are not on public display and meeting the demands for conformity of public life.

Your home is your castle, and you are the fashion dictator. The kind of clothes you wear will be governed only by your family, your activities, and your interests. Designers of work clothes have taken their clue from sports clothes that give the necessary ease and comfort for your leisure time and activities at home.

For clothes at home there is a wide variety of patterns. Women who may have to cook a meal, do dishes, or make a snack want clothes that will go into the kitchen and still be attractive in the living room. The desire to be a little more decorative has always been a feminine characteristic, and gay, quilted full skirts, culottes, comfort-able, smart jerseys, and velvet trousers can be found in many wardrobes. In colder climates, we find that the long wool skirts or the quilted skirts add greatly to comfort and decorativeness and still allow freedom of movement.

The exotic in clothes for the home is not new. Men have enjoyed smoking jackets and decorative coats for many years, and women have always liked the long hostess robe. Whatever your choice of clothing for the leisure at-home hours, the clothes should be attractive, comfortable, and easy to care for and should provide adequate freedom of movement.

Chapter 17

For rain and storm

What kind of raincoat should you buy? Do you want an all-purpose coat or just a raincoat? Do you want an all-season coat or a summer raincoat? Do you want a stormcoat that you can wear for cold as well as for rainy weather? A survey on preferences in rainwear revealed that certain characteristics are preferred. They are, in order of preference: light weight, ability to stay neat, year-round wearability, and durability. Wash-and-wear is an added advantage, and some raincoat buyers are willing to pay more for them.

Rainwear is made in a variety of styles, materials, and colors. There are jackets, cape coats, ponchos, and full-length coats —with attached hoods or detachable hoods, with mandarin collars or convertible collars. Materials include film plastic, plastic-coated fabric, laminates; expanded vinyles; oilskin, wool covert and gabardine, cotton, rayon, silk, cotton-and-Dacron blends, nylon poplin, gabardine, puckered nylon, and quilted ciré, velvet, corduroy, and wool jersey. The coats may be lined or unlined. They are available in solid colors, prints, plaids, checks, and stripes. Children's raincoats made of plastic over plaid have had great popularity. Fluorescent colors are also used. Fastenings used include buttons, zippers, snap fasteners, and hooks.

FINISHES

Materials may be waterproofed so that they are impervious not only to water but to air as well. Tiny eyelets, or "breather holes," are usually provided under the arms in waterproof coats. Film plastic coats, plastic-coated raincoats, and oilskin slickers are examples of this type of rainwear. These coats are usually warm when worn on hot days and cold in cooler weather. Expanded vinyls have more breathability.

Water-repellent finishes applied to fabrics vary in their degree of effectiveness and permanency. When choosing rainwear, it is advisable to read labels carefully for information concerning water repellency. Note whether the finish is permanent to dry cleaning or whether it is a renewable type that must be restored after each cleaning or after a certain number of cleanings. Silicone finishes and durable-press fabrics provide water, stain, and wrinkle resistance.

LININGS

Linings in raincoats are similar to those in other coats; rayon or silk twills or satins and fabrics coated with a metallic finish on the inside, which add warmth by reflecting body heat. Laminates often have foam backing for light-weight body and warmth. Heavy storm coats and jackets are often lined with pile linings such as alpaca and furlike fabrics. Some expensive raincoats are lined with genuine fur.

CONSTRUCTION

Construction features that add to the serviceability of rain and storm wear include sufficient overlapping of the fronts to keep out rain and wind. The number and

Printed-fabric raincoat.

Rain-or-shine coat.

coat is to be worn over a suit or other coat or jacket, it should be sufficiently large—especially in the sleeves and armholes—to be comfortable; raglan sleeves provide this kind of comfort. Flat, leak-proof seams provide both comfort and protection.

TYPES

Many people find it convenient to have a film plastic raincoat that can be folded into a compact case and easily carried or stored for use during warm weather when weight and warmth are not needed. In addition, they purchase an all-purpose coat in a style, color, and fabric appropriate for sev-

the kind of fastenings used in rainwear are also important. If the fastenings extend only to the waistline or slightly below, a tab-and-button closing near the knees may be used to hold the garment together at the bottom. The front edges of the coat, which support the fastenings, should be well reinforced—especially in the film plastic coats. If the

Children's raincoat styles.

eral occasions in various kinds of weather.

Rainwear, if chosen with care, can offer smartness, attractive appearance, comfort, and serviceability—all in the same coat. The wrinkle-resistance and shape-retention of the blended and synthetic fabrics provide a fresh, neat appearance in any weather, so that the wearer will not look crumpled upon arrival at his destination. Some rainwear is easy to pack, resists wrinkling, and looks ready to wear when you arrive. Rainwear that is lightweight and comfortable yet durable enough for many seasons of wear is desired by many people.

Some people prefer rainwear that is washable by hand or by machine, dries quickly, and is ready to wear with little or no ironing. The blends of Dacron and

cotton or cotton and nylon will take several washings before requiring reprocessing.

Oilskins in various colors appeal to various age groups. The heavy plastic fabric and the plastic-coated fabric provide a choice, the coated fabric being preferable in cold weather, since stiffness and cracking occur in some plastic fabrics at low temperatures. Raglan sleeves, a high, close neckline, and reinforced fastenings are important features of this type of raincoat, which generally receives hard wear. The cotton poplin raincoat, lined with bright-colored prints, plaids, and stripes, is often worn as an all-weather campus coat.

Trench coats.

Balmacaans.

MEN'S WEAR

Men seem to like versatile raincoats that can double as topcoats and look well rain or shine. The classic raglan-sleeve coat made of fine Egyptian-cotton poplin, plaid lined and with a fly front, appeals to many men, especially college students. Golf jackets, college windbreakers, and car coats of Dacron-and-cotton blends serve as raingear for some students.

The heavier all-wool gabardine coat for protection from rain, snow, and cold weather gains favor among men who live where seasons are long and cold. The trench coat and the balmacaan are other popular styles of all-weather men's coats.

LABELS

In addition to checking closely all of the characteristics desired in rainwear, it is wise to read all tags and labels carefully. Try to find out about:

The fabric—cotton, nylon, wool, a blend, or others.

Construction—seams, stitching, fastenings, overlap, collar, and lining.

Performance—type of finish, degree of water-repellent protection provided, durability, and guarantee of claims on label, such as: is color permanent to care and various exposures? Will treated silk coats waterspot?

Care—washing or dry cleaning; whether —and if so, how often—refinishing is required.

Uses—will it meet your needs for rain only

or have many uses; color is a significant item here.

Name and address of retailer or manufacturer.

It is up to you to make the final decisions when choosing, after careful consideration of the items suggested above.

CARE

If a raincoat is marked "washable," it can be washed quite safely in a washing machine. Usually the original water-repellent finish will last as long as the finish in a coat that must be dry-cleaned. When the original finish is gone—usually after several washings—it may be renewed with a water-repellent spray.

To wash a raincoat, pretreat the collar and any badly soiled spots by brushing on a liquid syndet; put the garment in the washer, using hot suds; rinse thoroughly; and let it drip dry or put it in a dryer set at medium heat.

To apply a water-repellent spray, make sure the coat is clean and dry, work in a well-ventilated room or outdoors, and follow the directions on the container. Water-repellent sprays are not permanent and must be applied after each washing. A touch-up with a steam iron improves the appearance of the coat and helps "set" the water-repellent fluids. A steam or wash-and-wear setting should be used for this job.

Professional cleaners clean washable raincoats as well as dry-clean nonwashable ones and renew water-repellent finishes. You should furnish the cleaner with the information on the label attached to your raincoat when you purchased it.

Whether you clean your own coat or send it to a dry cleaner, you can keep down the upkeep cost by taking good care of your coat. After it has been out in the rain, it should be pressed to keep it from looking rumpled the next time you wear it. A steam iron achieves a smooth finish and avoids damaging the water-repellent surface.

Remove all soil spots as soon as you see them, using a damp cloth, a damp cloth with soap, or cleaning fluids—as required by the fabric and the nature of the stain. Work quickly; if you use soap, rinse it out at once, as soap left on the fabric for any length of time tends to counteract the original water-repellent finish.

If it is impossible to press a raincoat soon after it was worn in the rain, be sure to hang it up instead of dropping it on a chair. Whether your destination is a classroom, a public gathering, a private home, or a church, try to find a place to hang your coat. There is a loop at the neckline on some coats for this purpose. If space permits, place each shoulder over a hook, so that the weight of the coat is distributed.

UMBRELLAS

Ever since umbrellas have been used for protection from the elements, they also have been a fashionable item in women's wear. Fashion seems to influence size, color, shape, material, and length of handle.

Types and sizes

Umbrellas are available in various sizes, which are determined by the length and the number of ribs in the frame; this number being eight, ten, or sixteen. Weight as well as size is controlled by the number of ribs, an eight-rib being much lighter than a sixteen-rib. Some umbrellas have very long handles and when tightly closed resemble a walking stick, a smart accent to a woman's outfit. Others are designed with short ribs and handles and can be carried inside a weekend case or attached to a large handbag or tote bag. Matched bag-and-umbrella combinations are often sold as units. The folding umbrella is a convenient design: when open, it is regulation size; when it is closed, hinges at the center of each rib allow it to be folded in half, the fabric swirled into a tight roll, and the umbrella inserted into a carrying case one half the length of the open umbrella. Umbrella handles may be plain or intricate in design, ranging from knobs and curved handles to animal heads. A loop of cord, leather, or metal is attached to most handles for carrying the umbrella on the arm.

Materials

The handles of umbrellas are made of bone, plastic, and wood, or wood covered with alligator, calfskin, lizard, or morocco leather or decorated with gold, mother-of-pearl, or silver. The frame is usually made of steel or aluminum with bone or plastic tips on the ends of the ribs and the end of the spine opposite the handle.

The materials used for covers are cotton, rayon, and acetate, nylon and silk taffeta, and plastic, all with water-repellent finish. There is a wide range of colors and patterns—light or dark, bright or dull, solid colors, iridescent colors, stripes, plaids, dots, and other patterns. Umbrellas of plastic film may be transparent or opaque, colorless, colored, or printed. With a transparent one, you can see where you are walking.

Points of selection

In choosing an umbrella, there are several points to keep in mind. Consider color and design in relation to the color and design of the clothing with which the umbrella will be carried, especially if it is to be the only one in the wardrobe. Decide which size and type of umbrella will fit specific needs. Colorfast fabric should mean that the umbrella will maintain its original color in all types of weather and atmospheric conditions. The weave of the fabric should be very close to keep out the rain and to withstand the strain of being tightly stretched when the frame is open. The way to check the fabric is to open the umbrella and note whether light shows through readily. The stitches on the seams should be close together and the cover fastened securely to the frame. Raw edges of seams should be finished to prevent fraying. The cover should be anchored to each rib of the frame in at least two places. Plastic film covers should be of heavy gauge to prevent easy tearing. The loop for carrying and the tape for fastening the closed umbrella should also be securely fastened. Aluminum steel frames that are rustproof are the most durable. Note whether there is a case in which to carry or store the umbrella when it is not in use. A windproof frame to snap back into shape if strong winds turn the umbrella inside out; a small cup at the base of the shank to collect water when you carry a folded umbrella on a bus, train, or car; a self-opening device; reflective tape and trim that glows at night are features of some umbrellas.

Men's umbrellas are usually black cotton, nylon, or silk with the traditional crooked handle of wood—ash, malacca or whangee—and with either eight or ten ribs. The variety in selection is quite limited. Umbrellas are less popular with men than with women, and the men who have umbrellas use them for protection only, with little regard for fashion.

Care

Proper care of an umbrella will prolong its usefulness. A wet umbrella should be opened and allowed to dry thoroughly away from direct heat. It should be brushed free of dust, rolled neatly, and stored in a cool, dry closet.

Chapter 18

Millinery

Of all the items of clothing in the wardrobe, hats are probably the least functional. Throughout the centuries, headdresses have been used for adornment first and for comfort and warmth secondarily. Actually, for study one might divide millinery into two categories—those hats that are for adornment and those that are made for protection. Although men like to laugh about women's hats, a look at a man's hat might also raise a question about function and comfort. True, there is protection for the top of the head from the sun and the elements, but the ears and the neck are certainly not protected.

"HATTITUDE"

Some women and men are loath to wear hats, and it would appear that they feel strange and uncomfortable wearing hats. We rarely like that which is not familiar. The rigidity of custom in the thirties which demanded that hats must be worn by all well dressed women is in conflict with the casualness of present day living. Men and women who seldom wear hats generally buy their hats to go with everything. Since few hats are made as basic items, hats chosen in this way are usually not well co-ordinated. Instead of being an adornment, the hat chosen to go with everything often looks it, and ends up going well with nothing.

Since a hat can add a great deal to the appearance of a man or woman, take a look at your hat needs. You may discover that if you do not care for hats, you will wear a hat with very few articles and only for special occasions. Why not, then, buy the hat for the outfit and the occasion it will be worn? Hats, first, should make a person more attractive. If a hat is only adornment, buy it "to adorn." When one sees how well a hat can complete and enhance the whole picture, one may even come to enjoy wearing a hat—or, if not to enjoy it, at least to feel at ease.

WHY HATS

The hat is a part of the whole picture and should always be considered in relation to the over-all effect. The hat will either dramatize or complement other articles in the outfit. A look at a person's hat wardrobe would reveal much about him—his life, activities, and personality—and would probably suggest what other clothing might be found. A becoming hat may not only give the wearer a lift but improve his appearance. The hat is the background for the center of interest, the face.

Just as other articles of clothing can be traced through historical periods, hat styles have been repeated throughout the ages, and inspiration for millinery design is frequently found in history. A knowledge of styles will help the consumer communicate his needs to the salesperson.

MATERIALS

Every conceivable raw material has been used in the designing of millinery, from straw to velvet, feathers, fur, and trim of

The fantasy of fashion.

fine jewels. Most hat materials fall into the categories of fabrics—synthetic or natural —plastics, straw, and fur. Those most peculiar to millinery are felt—both fur and wool —and straw. Fur felt is usually made of rabbit, beaver, seal, or nutria. It is soft to the touch and usually quite smooth in feeling. It can be molded and blocked with ease and beauty. Wool felt is made from hair fabric, mainly wool, and can be made from reclaimed products. Wool felt is generally a little less soft to the feel than fur felt, but in most cases the quality of the felt will depend upon the quality of the original material. In other words, a wool felt may be finer and more luxurious than a fur felt of poor quality.

Straw is obtained both from natural fibers and from synthetic materials, and frequently it is very difficult to distinguish between the natural and the synthetic. Natural straw is obtained from grasses, barks, grains, palms, wheat, and rye. The kind of straw, particularly in men's hats, will be a fashion factor. Sennits and coconuts may be in favor one year and Milan or Panama the next. Different fibers will adapt to certain construction such as braiding and each will vary in coarseness, in the amount of body, and in durability.

Every fabric or material imaginable has been and is used in the making of hats. Women's winter favorites vary from those used in dressier hats—such as faille, grosgrain, taffeta, velvet, and brocade—to fabrics such as jersey and wool flannel for less dressy occasions. Summer fabrics include linen with interesting textures, piqués, nets, and laces, to name but a few. The quality of the hat may be greatly increased by the quality of the trimming used on the hat. Fine feathers such as bird-of-paradise or aigrette would add a great deal to the cost of a hat. Flowers of all types, leather, fruits,

Tricorn Fedora Slouch brim

Watteau Tam or Beret Breton

Cartwheel Picture

sequins, and fur are just a few other materials used for trim. Nets, gauzes and chiffons are used for veiling. The quality of these trims and their availability will greatly affect the cost of a hat. In selecting a hat, an individual should look at the trim, the basic material, and the body of the hat for indications of quality.

CONSTRUCTION

Methods of construction are as varied as the kinds of materials and the numerous designs and styles available. Generally speaking, felt hats, whether fur or wool, are blocked on a wooden head block, steamed, and molded to shape. Most straw hats require some blocking on a head form. Depending upon the material used, construction may be a process of tedious hand shaping, or it may go very quickly because of the properties of the fiber. Fabric hats are frequently draped and cover a stiff hat body that has previously been shaped. The hat body is generally made of highly sized material like crinoline. Some hats need wiring to hold brims or to shape the hat in the desired place. Others need particular fabric finishes such as napping or special care in pressing and steaming. Water-repellent finish for weather and sports caps is probably the most common special finish. The steps needed in creating a hat always relate to the kind of fiber or material used.

Many of the features that make a good hat will not be obvious in the finished product, but details such as stitching, handling of the trim, and pressing will give some indication of quality.

WEARING

Comfort is a strong factor in the wearing of a hat. A hat that slips, binds, or is too heavy will make one feel self-conscious and uncomfortable. A hat should stay in place without effort on the part of the wearer. Women's hats range in size from 20 to 25. Most hats for women have adjustable headbands, and adjustments can be made easily in a hat department. The lady with an exceptionally large or exceptionally small head, however, will find she will have to devote more time than usual to the selection of a comfortable and well-proportioned hat. Aids that help hold a woman's hat in place include hat pins and combs sewn in the front of the hat. Most of these satisfactorily anchor a small hat if properly placed when the hat is put on. The elastic bands that go under the hair are generally unsatisfactory since they tend to separate and disrupt the well-combed hairdo.

SIZES

Men's sizes are not stated by circumference of head as are women's sizes. The chart below gives American hat sizes and corresponding measurements of circumference.

SIZE	INCHES	SIZE	INCHES
6⅞	21½	7¼	22⅝
7	21⅞	7⅜	23
7⅛	22¼	7½	23½

FIT

In judging the fit of a hat, it is well to try it on and adjust it to the head to find the proper placing and the intended arrangement for that hat. People from the industry recommend starting at the front of the head and working toward the back. When you are trying on a hat without the aid of a salesperson, it is wise to spend a little more time on this. A hat should fit the head closely but without binding. If it is too large, it may slip and move on the head

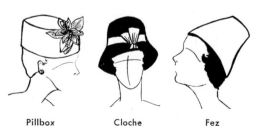

Pillbox   Cloche   Fez   Toque   Halo   Coolie

to a place where it might be uncomfortable or unbecoming. We are all familiar with the clown effect of the hat that fits too far down on the head or the lack of poise suggested by the hat perched at the wrong angle.

COST

With few exceptions, brand names have not assumed the importance in women's millinery that they have in other clothing. Much more important has been the name of the designer of the hats. Outstanding in America are the names of Lily Daché, Sally Victor, Mr. John, Walter Florel, Irene Anello of Emme, and Susie. A number of dress and suit manufacturers, like the House of Hattie Carnegie, have designed hats to complement their clothes. There are many others, like Vincent Borg and Harmik Gasparian, who are very important in this field.

The cost of the hat is influenced by many different factors—the designer and his reputation, the basic materials used, and the time needed to make the hat. If a very rare feather or fabric is used, the cost of the material alone will naturally raise the price of the hat. Many construction details, including the time involved in blocking by hand or machine, may be an item in the end price of millinery. The markup on hats is high also because of the timeliness of hats, the sales risk, and packing costs. Small details such as the trim and the lining are good clues to value in millinery.

Some women have found hats most valuable aesthetically and will pay fabulous sums to obtain one that flatters their appearance.

CARE

In the care of all clothing, prevention is the best treatment. This is particularly true of millinery, which in many cases requires professional repairs and is often impossible to restore after hard treatment. Careful storage will do much to prevent an accumulation of dust and the hat's being squashed or pushed out of shape. Most good hats come in hat boxes; a little tissue inside the hat and around the hat will help to retain the shape. Prevention also includes proper protection from rain, snow, and wind whenever possible. Plastic covers that can be carried in pocket or purse and can be slipped on easily in the event of sudden storms are useful and, of course, the use of an umbrella is obvious. Some hat fabrics like taffeta and felt will rain spot readily.

The ways of cleaning hats are as numerous as the kinds of materials used. For felt hats there are many chemically treated sponges and brushes. In addition, there are powdered cleansers that are helpful particularly in removing oil or grease spots. Brushing a napped fabric will do a great deal to keep the hat and the nap in good condition. Very few hats are washable. If a hat, particularly a felt hat, is in good condition but slightly soiled, reblocking by a good cleaner is very satisfactory. Many good hat manufacturers offer restoring services. There are tricks—like pressing veils with wax paper—that help to prolong the life of a woman's hat. A dusty, spotted hat or one with wilted-looking trim such as a mussed veil or frayed ribbon quickly loses the power to enhance the wearer's looks.

Men should protect the brims of their

Turban   Derby   Sailor

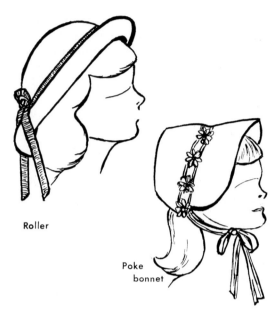

Roller

Poke
bonnet

hats when putting them on. Holding the
brim firmly and close to the crown in front
and in back will protect it and make it easier to put the hat on correctly. One should
be particularly careful when setting a hat
down. It should not be placed so that the
brim will support the weight of the hat.

SELECTION

In selecting the style of hat most becoming and suitable to you, you should give
consideration to the following factors:

The shape of the face.
The size of the head.
The length of the neck.
The size and height of the body.
The features of the face.
The silhouette, shape, and lines of the out-
    fit to be worn.
The hair style.
The idea, or mood, of the outfit.
Fashion rightness.
The co-ordinated outfit.
The occasion for which it will be worn.
The personality of the individual.

298

Selection would be simple if a person
could choose the hat for just one factor, but
the relationship of all the factors to the hat
is the important consideration. Attention
to all of the above factors is what makes a
hat most becoming. It is also the reason selection is sometimes difficult. Consideration
of all these factors helps to create that individual look.

HATS AND THE INDIVIDUAL

In selecting a hat, an individual must give
first consideration to complementing the
face. Then the relationship between the hat
and the various parts of the body will need
thought. The wide variation here demands
experimentation, and suggestions are given
merely to help the individual determine
which factors he should observe in trying
to find the most becoming lines for him.
The camouflage of poor features is a very
suble thing, and a person who aims at extreme camouflage may call more attention to the feature he is trying to hide than
he would by wearing something less extreme. For example, extremely tall people
frequently feel they must wear large hats.
A big hat will attract attention because of
its size and may tend to emphasize the
largeness of the wearer.

HATS AND THE FACE

It is difficult to discuss facial shape without considering all the various features of
irregularity or symmetry within the face.
The shape of the outside contours might
suggest one treatment and the contours
within the face—nose, eyes, and forehead
—another. Generally, the lines of the hat
are chosen to help create the illusion of an
oval and symmetrical shape. One person
may have a long face and very regular,
smooth features while another person with
a face of the same length and outside contours may have irregular and angular fea-

tures. This applies to the oval, round, square, or any other facial shape. The oval, which is considered the ideal shape, may have irregular, broken features within the outside contours. If you have come to know the shape of your face, you will know what features you wish to emphasize and where added length or width is desirable. You will also have noted any features you might wish to camouflage. The size and shape of the face should be the first and most important consideration even if it is in conflict with the over-all proportions of the body.

Repetition of line will emphasize a good or bad feature. A too-round hat will make the face appear more round. The person whose facial shape is decidedly round may be interested in creating lines that add length rather than width to the contour. Circular and extremely curved hats and brims or visors will tend to emphasize or repeat the line of roundness. A high hat like a pill box or a derby with a deep crown will add height to the face. Hats with width in the brim will add to the width of the face. Hats that frame the hair and are in a line of length will lengthen the face. Small, narrow brims that tend to go upward in line may be very becoming to the round face, particularly when combined with deep crowns.

The person with a long face would want to create a different impression than would the person with a round face. It is important to decide first where the face gets its length. Length in the face may be in the forehead or from the mouth to the chin. Both of these characteristics would need a treatment different from the one for length throughout the face. For example, a person with a high forehead might cut the length by wearing a hat forward on the head, but if the length were elsewhere in the face and the forehead narrow, this would create a poorly proportioned appearance. For a short person with a long face the wearing of

vertical necklines and deep crowns which might add height to the figure would also add height and length to the face. Remember that full, plump cheeks give any face, regardless of shape, a rounder look.

A person with an oval face and regular features can wear symmetrical hats; but where irregularity is found in features like the nose, symmetry will only emphasize the poor feature. If the nose is too large, too long, or irregular in bone structure, the lines should not be repeated in the hat, nor should symmetrical hats with center trim and emphasis be used. An irregular brim or a hat that projects a little over the forehead may be more becoming to irregularities in bone structure. Abrupt, harsh, and angular lines will be severe on any face that has irregular contours. The relationship of the eyes, nose, mouth, and eye glasses to the outside contour may change the effect of the facial shape. The person who wears glasses may choose her hat according to shape and size—with one exception: she will try to keep the area around the glasses free and unencumbered by brims or veils that might interfere with vision.

HATS AND THE HEAD

The size of the head will be almost as important in choosing a hat as the facial shape. A very small hat will tend to exaggerate any largeness of the face and head; a small, petite head would be overwhelmed by a large brim or a deep-crowned hat that is bulky in effect. The head also has a shape —oval, round, or flat—and may have irregularities in shape.

HATS AND PROPORTION

It is recommended that in trying on a hat, you use a full mirror in order to be able to judge the relationship of the hat to the proportions of the figure. It should be stressed that becomingness to the face is most im-

Millinery Terms *

Aigrette. (Egret). A tuft of long, plume-like feathers or jewels to be worn on the head. It is unlawful to import the plumes of egrets to the United States, so most aigrettes are of imitation feathers.

Baku. Expensive, dull-finished, fine, lightweight straw made from buri palm.

Ballibuntl or **balibuntal.** Lightweight, fine, glossy, smooth straw made of buntal, a white Philippine fiber obtained from palm leaf.

Bird-of-paradise. The colorful, brilliant plumes of the male bird of paradise. It is unlawful to import these plumes into the United States.

Braiding. To weave, interlace, or entwine fabric, ribbon, or straw cords to form braid.

Chip. Inexpensive straw, coarsely woven of woody material.

Coconut. Coarse straw from the leaves of the coconut tree.

Emu. The largest bird in existence, closely related to the ostrich.

Exotic. Any smooth, fine, closely woven straw, natural or synthetic.

Horsehair. Stiff, loosely woven, transparent fabric of horsehair, used for stiffening.

Leghorn. Finely plaited straw made from wheat, made for the export trade in Italy.

Lisere. Bright-finished, split-straw braid, used in making blocked hats.

Milan. Fine, closely woven straw used in finest quality women's hats, manufactured in Milan, Italy.

Osprey. A kind of long feather used on hats.

Panama. Fine, hand-plaited straw from the choicest leaves of the jipijapa, a palm-like plant.

Peanit. An inexpensive straw of the exotic type.

Plaiting. Braiding, as of hair or straw.

Plush. Rich fabric of various fibers, in pile weave, with a longer pile than velvet.

Ramie. The strong, glossy fiber of an Asiatic plant, used in making woven fabrics and hat bodies.

Sennit. Braided cord or fabric made of straw, grass, or fiber; used for making men's hats.

Sisal. Finely woven, smooth, expensive straw with a linen finish, made from sisal, a kind of hemp.

Toyo. Shiny, smooth, expensive straw woven from cellophane-coated rice paper. Similar to Panama.

Velour. Velvet-like felt used for hats.

* Adapted or taken by permission from Mary Brooks Picken, *The Fashion Dictionary*, Funk & Wagnalls Co., New York, 1957.

portant, but for the person with a small head and ample figure, a reasonable compromise would be a hat selected according to facial shape and head size but not too extreme in either width or height. With the numerous style of hats available, this should not be too difficult. The very short woman who wears a hat with too wide a brim might be hiding her face from a taller companion. The very tall person should remember that people will often be looking up at his face. The relationship of the size of the hat to the size of the body is well exemplified by the expectant mother, who will want to use her hat to give balance to the figure. A woman who would ordinarily wear a small hat may at this time choose a larger brim or bulkier hat to offset the lack of balance in the figure.

The person who has a conflict of size between head and body will avoid extremes—both the large and the very small hat and trim that juts out, such as large, high feathers. This person would be wise to avoid textures that are too heavy or too delicate in feeling, and should also avoid the extremes of height and width. The hat should usually be at least as wide as the widest part of the face in order to avoid the effect of the face bulging out under the hat.

The size of a man's hat is very important. The depth, taper, and height of the crown and the width, roll, and snap of the brim should be scaled to suit his face and his build.

The relationship of the length and contours of the neck will also affect the hat shape. The person with a short, thick, or stubby neck will avoid hats that cover the neck or have downward lines.

HATS AND COLOR

Since the hat is near the hair and the skin, it is essential that the color chosen compliment the skin color. With some hats, there is direct reflection of color onto the face; if the hat is in an unbecoming color, it may cast an unpleasant glow on the face.

HATS AND TEXTURE

The texture of the skin should to some extent govern the choice of texture in hats. Soft, napped finishes like velvet will generally be much kinder to rough-textured or coarse skin. Some straws and other hat materials are very severe in texture; these are harsh and unkind to a blotchy skin. Shining and bright hats may also be hard on a coarse skin; rich, soft materials like velours will be a much better choice. Soft fabrics will also be kinder to hard and sharp features. Texture will also influence the feeling of weight and bulk, and should be considered in selecting the size of the hat. A hat in a filmy, lightweight fabric will look more delicate than one of the same size in a heavy felt or straw. A large cartwheel or wide-brimmed hat might seem to overpower a small face and figure. In a delicate net or lace, however, the cartwheel would probably be more becoming to a smaller woman than to one with a large head or a very large frame.

Veiling and tulles are very flattering, but they should be part of the design; they should not look "just stuck on." Many hats can be improved by removing a veil that is not an integral part of the original design of the hat. This does not refer to veiling and nets that have definitely been planned as a part of the design. The texture of fabric and trim will affect the proportions of the hat in relation to the face and the figure as well as the apparent size and shape of the hat.

HATS AND HAIR STYLES

The hairdo should be chosen much as a hat is, keeping the same factors in mind— the contours, the features, and the proportions of the head. It is usually well determined before a hat is chosen. The hairdo can change the facial shape and so allow for more freedom of choice in hat styles. For example, bangs would cut the length of the forehead and make the face seem less long in that area. Young women often allow most of the hair to be exposed. A hat may be more effective if some of the hair at the temple is tucked under the hat. The hat is not necessarily background to the hairdo, and experimentation in this particular area is important. Because fashions and styles in hats change, it is always an excellent idea to try a hat at different angles on the head. Too many women tend to put all hats on the back of the head, which is not always best for the style of the hat or the facial shape.

HATS AND FASHION

Fashion rightness in hats is usually more evident than it is in other articles of clothing. Fashion can be observed by following the kind and style of hat, the fabrics used,

Bowler   Homburg   Top hat

Tyrolean   Sports-car hat   Cap

the kinds of trim used, and the shape of the hat. In women's hats you may in one year see a sailor, a bonnet, and a tricorn. They may disappear the next year and then reappear at a later time. Velour may be used in many, many hats one season and then disappear from the scene for a number of years. Trim may be flowers one year and feathers, ribbons, or veils the next. Color, of course, in the millinery trade is the most important factor. Wigs in elaborate hairstyles frequently replace hats now, and have been popular at various periods of history.

Although men's hats do not change as quickly in fashion as do women's, there is a definite fashion element. The derby or bowler enjoyed popularity in the 1920's and was forgotten until the late 1950's, when it again became fashionable. Hatbands vary in width and pattern. The edge of the brim may be bound, top-stitched, or plain. Hat brims vary in width and in the way they

(Opposite) Top: Changing crease styles. Bottom: Styles in men's summer hats.

302

Center dent

Center dent
and
side dents

Telescope
crown

Boater

Snap-brim,
center-crease
Panama

Snap-brim sennit

The diplomat's badge. (Reprinted from *Life* by courtesy of Time, Inc. Copyright 1959, Time, Inc.)

shortened, height is added to the hat. Full, bulky silhouettes will often be accompanied by hats small in shape and size. When collars are high, hats are small so as not to interfere with the drape of the collar. When the natural drape in men's suits is fashionable, hat brims have become narrower. Whenever the full drape and the padded shoulder are popular in suits, the brim of the hat is considerably wider.

YOUR HAT AND YOU

The hat is a personal expression of the wearer. It not only expresses the person; it can give an impression of dignity, poise, and self-assurance. Association of a hat with people, professions, or an age may create a mood or an idea. This idea may result from a combination of factors. An example of the association of a hat with a certain age would be that of the poke bonnet, which suggests a little girl. Hats that tie under the chin may have a baby or little-girl look. A flat-top or porkpie brings to mind a college man. *Life* magazine referred to the Homburg as the diplomat's badge. The idea created here is that of "the man of distinction." The style may be associated with a person, as the derby with Al Smith. When he threw his hat in the ring, it was a derby. The love of hats is associated with Hollywood columnist Hedda Hopper. Just as some women collect antiques, Bonnie Cashin, the noted designer, collects fabulous hats from all over the world.

are dipped, snapped, or rolled. The amount of taper, the depth and the kind of dent, and the stiffness and fullness of the crown will also be changing factors in fashion.

Certain dress silhouettes are generally accompanied by certain hat silhouettes. When the waistline is high, as in the empire silhouette, hats are higher in the crown; to add length where the waistline has been

The changing brim width of the snap-brim hat.

A suit is sometimes just a suit. A hat is never just a hat. It is a success or it is a flop. The hat frames the face, which is the most important part of the person, and must complement the face. If it does not do this, it is not a success and should be discarded.

Women ask how many hats there should be in a wardrobe. The industry—interested, of course, in each woman's having more hats —says six. The number of hats in the wardrobe will depend upon how often, where, and for what purpose a hat is worn. It may be one or ten.

The best way of discovering a good hat for yourself is to experiment with different hat styles and bodies, trying on as many styles and types as possible, and analyzing why you like a certain one and why you do not like another. When you have purchased a new hat, wear it enough before an important occasion to be completely at ease in it.

REFERENCE READINGS

Books

Chambers, Bernice G., *Color and Design,* Prentice-Hall, Inc., New York, 1951.

Hardy, Kay, *Costume Design,* McGraw-Hill Book Co., Inc., New York, 1948.

Morton, Grace Margaret, *The Arts of Costume and Personal Appearance,* John Wiley & Sons, Inc., New York, and Chapman & Hall Ltd., London, 1955.

Pickens, Mary Brooks, *The Language of Fashion,* Funk & Wagnalls, 1939.

Wilcox, R. Turner, *The Mode in Hats and Hairdress,* Scribner's Sons, Inc., 1945.

Pamphlets and booklets

Klepp, Amelia L., *Selling the Right Hat,* New York University School of Retailing, New York.

Merchandise Facts to Help You Sell Millinery, Research Bureau for Retail Training, University of Pittsburgh, Pittsburgh.

Chapter 19

Leather and shoes

History seems to indicate that one of the first things man learned to do was to make leather. Leather is the skin of an animal, preserved and transformed into a useful, durable substance by a process known as tanning. The process probably was a gradual development, and may have come about accidentally. One may presume that man learned to wrap himself in the skins of the animals he killed for food to protect himself from the elements. Hanging the skins over a fire to dry, he eventually noticed that smoke preserved them. Later, he found that the sap of certain woods and tree barks preserved skins even better, and that pounding and chewing made the skins soft and pliable; and so evolved primitive methods of tanning. The uses of leather in ancient times were as numerous and as varied as they are today. Leather has been used for jackets, headgear, shoes, bottles and water bags, rugs, shields, and sails, to name a few. Today, leather is a fashionable item used extensively in shoes, apparel, ac-

cessories, home furnishings, automobiles, and luggage.

LEATHER

The principal sources of raw materials for making leather are the hides and skins of cattle, goats, and sheep, which are by-products of the meat industry, and the hides and skins of deer, horses, kangaroos, ostriches, pigs, and reptiles. The skins of each of these various animals are especially suitable for a number of different purposes.

Cattle hides and calfskins, from which most leather is made, are supplied primarily from cattle slaughter in the United States, although some hides are imported. The lighter, softer, more pliable leather made from sheepskins and lambskins is also widely used, although in smaller quantity than cattle leather. New Zealand and the United States are the chief suppliers of these skins. Kidskins are imported from Africa, India, Pakistan, South America, and from other areas where goats are raised as a source of milk and meat.

Terminology

A brief explanation of terms may be helpful. A *skin* means the covering of a smaller animal—alligator, calf, deer, goat, or sheep—and generally has a raw weight of less than fifteen pounds. A *hide* is the pelt of a larger animal, such as a full-grown buffalo, cow, horse, ox, or walrus, and has a raw weight of twenty-five pounds or more. *Kip* is the intermediate size; generally used to mean the hide of young or small cattle, a kip usually weighs from fifteen to twenty-five pounds.

After being removed from the animal, the skin is cured to prevent decay before the tanning process. Various curing methods are used, including green salting, pickling, flint drying, and dry salting.

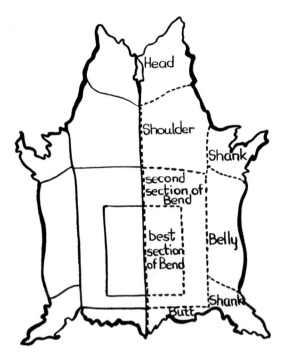

The division of a hide.

Tanning transforms hides and skins into leather and makes them soft and pliable. The Latin term *tannum*, meaning oak bark, is the origin of the word "tan," which means the preserving of skins of animals. The methods used are (1) formaldehyde, (2) mineral (alum and chrome), and (3) oil and vegetable tanning. Only a small percentage of hides is tanned by the alum process, used mainly for pure white leather and furs, and the oil process, used mainly for chamois leather; the chrome and vegetable methods are the two principal ones used. Chrome tanning, a rapid process producing long-wearing leather with good heat resistance, is used for garments, gloves, handbags, and shoe uppers. Vegetable tanning, a longer process producing firm leather with good water-resistance, is used for harness, industrial belting, luggage and small leather goods, shoe soles, and upholstery. Formaldehyde tanning is used a great deal for washable glove leathers. Any hide or skin may be tanned by either the chrome or the vegetable process or by a combination of the two methods.

Tanning

The initial steps in all tanning processes are similar: washing, soaking, liming, unhairing, fleshing, deliming, and pickling. Only the dermis, or true skin, is tanned; the epidermis, or outer layer of dead skin, and all the natural liquids and oils in the skin are removed. Only the tiny, interlaced fibers of the dermis are converted into leather. On arrival at the tannery the cured skins are washed and then soaked to dissolve all curing materials and to replace the moisture lost during curing. After being subjected to the liming process to loosen the hair, the skins are fed into an unhairing machine with blades similar to those of a lawn mower, and all of the hair is removed. There is a distinctive pattern where the hair protruded; this side of the skin is referred to as the grain side. Bristles removed from pigskin leave very noticeable, distinctive holes, which are identifying marks of pigskin. The tiny holes left on calfskin are so indistinct that it is difficult to see them; in contrast, the spiral markings with a hole in the center of ostrich skin are very pronounced and are responsible for the characteristic beauty of the skin. Reptile skins have scales instead of hair markings on the right side.

The inner side, or flesh side, of the skins must be freed of all flesh and muscle tissue. In a manner similar to that of the unhairing process, sharp knives remove the major part of the residue, and hand fleshing completes the job. The skins are then delimed by being soaked in a weak acid solu-

Leather Terms

Alligator-grained leather. One of various types of leather such as calfskin, cowhide, and sheepskin embossed to resemble alligator; not genuine alligator leather.

Alum leather. Leather produced by alum tanning, one of the mineral tannages; it is used mainly for gloves and is not washable.

Aniline-dyed leather. Leather dyed with any of the organic dyes produced from a coal-tar base, as distinguished from leather colored with pigments or other opaque materials.

Antelope leather. Fine, soft leather made from antelope skin, sueded on the flesh side. It is so rare as to be almost nonexistent. The term antelope-finish suede is applied to calfskin, kidskin, and lambskin finished to resemble antelope.

Boarded leathers. Leathers finished on the grain side in a distinct pattern such as box, pebble, or willow. The leather is folded with the grain side in and rolled and creased by pressure applied on the flesh side with a cork board which is fastened to the arm of the worker. Boarding is sometimes done by machine and can be imitated by embossing.

Buckskin. Genuine buckskin comes from the skins of deer and elk. The term applies only to the outer cut of the skin from which the surface grain has been removed; leather from the split, or undercut, of deerskin is called *split buckskin. Buck sides* are cattle hides with the grain surface buffed to simulate genuine buckskin.

Buffalo leather. Imported leather made from the hides of domesticated land and water buffalo.

Buffing. A finishing process in which a fine nap is produced on leather by the action of an emery wheel.

Cabretta leather. Leather made from the skins of hair sheep.

Calfskin. Leather made from the skins of calves.

Capeskin. Sheepskin with the natural grain preserved; that of South African hair sheep is superior to that of wool sheep.

Carpincho. The hide of a large water rodent also known as the *capybara*. The leather is classed as pigskin; it is chrome-tanned and washable and is mostly used in gloves.

Cattle-hide leathers. Leather made from the hides of cows, bulls, and steers.

Chamois leather. Originally, leather made from the skin of the chamois, a goatlike alpine antelope; now an oil-tanned, suede-finished leather made from the undersplits of sheepskin; used for gloves, apparel, and cleaning and polishing cloths.

Chrome leather. Leather produced by a mineral tannage using chromium salts. It is frequently used for shoe uppers.

Clothing leathers. Leathers used in the manufacture of clothing such as leather breeches, coats, hats, and jackets; chiefly cabretta, cowhide, horsehide, sheepskin, and goatskin.

Combination tanning. A process combining two or more tannages, as, for example, chrome and vegetable.

Cordovan. Term originally applied to leather from Córdoba, Spain, a city noted for fine leather; now applied to horsehide split so as to leave the grain intact. *Shell cordovan* is a nonporous, very durable, scuff-resistant leather frequently used in uppers for men's shoes.

Corrected grain. Term applied to leather from which slight scratches or imperfections in the grain have been removed by light buffing with an emery wheel.

Cowhide. Leather made from the hides of cows, steers, or bulls. The term is synonymous with cattle hide or steerhide.

Crocking. The rubbing off of coloring or finishing materials from leather on other materials.

Crushed leather. Leather whose natural grain is accentuated during tanning; also, leather that has been grained artificially.

Deerskin. Deerskin finished with the grain surface intact rather than removed as in buckskin.

Doeskin. Genuine doeskin is rarely used; the term generally applies to lambskin and sheepskin splits tanned to resemble doeskin. It is called American, English, or French doeskin, according to the country of origin and the tannage.

Ecrasé. Crushed.

Elk. Genuine elk leather is designated by the term buckskin. *Elk, smoked elk,* and *elk side* refer to specially tanned and finished cowhide shoe leather and are labeled as *elk-finished cowhide.*

Embossed leather. Leather finished with designs stamped on by etched, engraved, or electrotyped plates or rollers; the design may imitate some natural grain or may be artificial.

Fancy leather. Leather of commercial value primarily because of its distinctive appearance, whether due to grain or finish. It may be natural grain or the result of processing such as embossing, graining, ornamentation (gold, silver, and aluminum finishes, for example), printing, or any other finishing operation to improve the appearance.

Flesher. The flesh side or undercut of a sheepskin split before tanning.

Formaldehyde leather. A white washable leather obtained by a tannage using a formalin solution.

French antelope. In France, a lustrous suede finish applied to lambskin from Algeria, the Balkans, France, and Spain. In the U. S., French antelope finish is applied to suede leather made from pickled lambskins from New Zealand and South America.

French kid. Formerly, a fine quality kidskin from France, used for gloves and shoes. Now, alum- or vegetable-tanned kidskin from any country. *French Kid Finish* and *Real Kid* are terms used in the glove trade.

Full grain or **full top grain.** The outer surface, or grain portion, of a hide from which only the hair has been removed.

Glazed finish. A finish obtained by polishing the grain surface under heavy pressure with a roller of agate, glass, or steel; a varnish or shellac coating can also be used, but seldom is.

Glazed (glacé) kid. Chrome-tanned goatskin and kidskin leather, black or some other color, which has been given a glazed finish.

Goatskin. From a mature goat, but also referred to as kidskin.

Gold kid. Kidskin on whose grain side thin gold leaf has been applied so that the gold adheres and shows the pattern of the grain on the surface.

Grain. The outer, or hair, side of a hide or skin split into two or more layers; also, unsplit skins finished on the grain side. In *grained leather*, the natural grain is highlighted by a finishing process.

Hair calf. The skin of an unborn or prematurely born calf; slunk.

Hide. The pelt of one of the larger animals, having a raw weight of twenty-five pounds or more. See *Kip* and *Skin.*

Horsehide leather. Leather made from the hides of either horses or colts.

Imitation leather. Material—coated fabric, rubber, rubber composition, or plastic—made and finished to resemble leather.

Kangaroo leather. From the hide of the kangaroo or the wallaby; the leather resembles glazed kid.

Kid leather. For shoe upper leather, kidskins or goatskins are used; goatskins or lambskins are tanned for glove leather.

Kip or **kipskin.** Refers to the skins of young or small cattle, between the size of a calf and a full-grown animal; a skin of a raw weight of between fifteen and twenty-five pounds.

Lambskin leather. Leather made from either lambskin or sheepskin, since the skins are almost identical in appearance after tanning.

Leather. The hide or skin of an animal, or any portion of such, tanned or otherwise treated for use.

Lining leather. Leather, usually split, used for shoe linings; calf, cattle, goat, kid, kip, lamb, and sheep are used.

Mat finish. A smooth, dull finish applied to chrome-tanned leather for belts, handbags, and shoe uppers.

Mineral tanning. A tanning process in which some mineral, such as chromium salts or alum, is the tanning agent.

Mocha leather. Obtained from Somali blackhead or whitehead sheep and from Egyptian and Sudanese sheep. The grain is removed by a liming process called frizzing, and the fine fibers below the grain are sueded. It is a popular glove leather.

Mocha suede. Chrome-tanned leather from Arabian blackhead hair sheep. The grain is mechanically removed, and the leather is suede finished on the flesh side.

Morocco leather. Originally, fancy goatskin leather from Morocco, vegetable tanned and with a distinctive grain produced by boarding or graining. Genuine Morocco is now so labeled. *Morocco grain* is a term applied to imitations of this grain embossed on other leathers.

Nap finish. A finish in which the natural grain is removed and the outer surface then given a soft, buffed finish.

Oil tannage. A tanning process used with soft leathers like chamois and certain kinds of buckskin in which fish oils are used as the tanning agent.

Parchment. Extremely thin alum-tanned sheepskin used for diplomas, documents, scrolls, drumheads, and lampshades. Paper is used to imitate real parchment.

Patent leather. Leather for handbags and shoe uppers—calfskin, cowhide, kidskin, and horsehide—surface finished with successive coats of lacquer or varnish.

Peccary leather. Obtained from the peccary, a wild mammal of Central America, Mexico, and South America resembling the pig, it is classed as pigskin. It is a chrome-tanned, washable leather used for gloves.

Pigment finish. A finish in which the surface of the leather is coated with material containing pigments or other opaque substances.

Pigskin leather. Leather obtained from the skins of domestic pigs and hogs or from the skins of the carpincho and the peccary.

Pin seal or **pin grain.** The natural grain of high-grade sealskin, tanned for fancy leather. It is also imitated on calfskin, cowhide, goatskin, and sheepskin, in which case it should be described as, for example, pin-grain sheepskin.

Plastic patent. A material made from vinyl resins or other materials to resemble genuine patent leather.

Pyroxylin finish. A plastic finish sometimes used on leather.

Rawhide. Cattle hide subjected to the pre-tanning processes—dehairing, liming, and stuffing with oil or grease—but not tanned. It is creamy white and pliable; it is used in luggage and for some accessories.

Saddle leather. Vegetable-tanned cowhide, tan in color, used for saddles, harness, and some women's accessories; it is produced in various thicknesses.

Satin finish. A dull or mat finish on leather as distinguished from glazed finish.

Scotch grain. A coarse, pebble-grained cowhide or calfskin used for men's shoes, embossed to resemble a heavy, coarse-grained leather originating in Scotland.

Sharkskin. Leather made from the top grain of the hides of certain species of sharks, used in belts, fine leather goods, luggage, shoes, etc. It has varying natural grain markings or a fine, smooth, mesh-like grain similar to pin seal; other leathers are embossed to resemble true sharkskin.

Shearlings. Sheepskins or lambskins tanned with a short length of wool left on the skin. See the chapter on furs.

Shoe leather. *Sole leather*—for outer soles, insoles, heels, toe caps, and counters—usually is cowhide; *upper leather*, calfskin, cattle hide, goatskin, horsehide, and others; *miscellaneous shoe leathers* are used for weltings, linings, facings, and tongues.

Skin. The pelt of a young or small animal, having a raw weight of less than fifteen pounds.

Skiver. A thin top-grain split of sheepskin, used for handbag linings, fancy leather goods, and sweatbands for hats.

Slunk. The skin of an unborn or prematurely born calf.

Snuffed finish. Corrected grain.

Split. The under part of a hide or skin split into two or more thicknesses. Must be marked as such.

Suede finish. The surface of the leather is run over an emery wheel to separate the fibers and give a nap to the leather. Although the grain side may be suede finished, the process is usually applied to the flesh side of chrome- or alum-tanned leather. The term *suede* always refers to the finish, not to a type of leather.

Top grain. The grain (hair) side of cattle hide, reduced to a specific thickness according to a standard leather gauge.

Vegetable tanning. A process using tannins from barks, woods, or other parts of plants and trees, as distinguished from mineral, oil, and other tannages.

Vellum. Calfskin prepared as is parchment.

Washable leather. Leather tanned, dyed, and finished to be colorfast, soft, and pliable under normal washing conditions.

Water-repellent leather. Leather treated in tanning with chemical compounds to reduce the absorption of external water without interfering with the porosity.

tion; next they go into a bacterial fermentation to dissolve horny fibers; after that they go into a pickling solution; and finally they are rinsed in clean water.

In the vegetable tanning process, the skins are soaked for a period of weeks in tannin liquors obtained from certain barks, woods, or other parts of plants or trees.

The next series of steps for the bend leathers and heavy cattle hides includes increasing the tannin content, extracting the uncombined tannin, rinsing, bleaching, and stuffing to improve wearing qualities; next is a lubrication to compensate for natural oils removed in tanning. After this the leather is rolled, coated with a finishing compound, and brushed under a revolving cylinder.

Vegetable tanning makes an attractive, durable, firm leather; the color produced by this process varies from a light cream to a deep, reddish brown. The leather is porous but resistant to moisture and is often washable. Sole leather for shoes is usually vegetable tanned. Skins that are vegetable tanned include alligator, calfskin, cowhide, ostrich skin, pigskin and sharkskin.

In chrome tanning, used on light cattle hides, calfskins, and kidskins, the tanning agent is a chromic salt. It transforms the raw hides or skins into leather quite rapidly—in days rather than weeks. The skins are tumbled in revolving drums of tanning liquor, washed, and "set out," a squeezing process to remove water and wrinkles.

In order to produce leather of a desired uniform thickness, the skins are split into two or more layers. The layer with the grain surface produces the finest leather, called "top grain." The flesh layer, or split, is used for medium quality leather. All hides and skins are then shaved, on the flesh side, to a uniform thickness on a machine similar to the fleshing machine.

To restore the natural oils and greases to chrome-tanned leather, the fat-liquor process, which lubricates the leather and makes it soft and pliable, is used. The desired color is given the leather by a dye liquor, either aniline or pigment dye. Leathers may be colored on both sides by dip dyeing or on one side by brush dyeing or spraying. After "setting-out" comes the drying process, which requires extreme care to prevent shrinkage. Usually the grain side of the skin is pasted onto frames of glass or porcelain, which are then moved into a drying tunnel where temperature and humidity are rigidly controlled. Later the skins are dampened and then staked, or pulled, until soft. Chrome-tanned leather is extremely durable. The process is adaptable to calfskins, kidskins, and cowhides for use in shoe uppers, gloves, bags, and other accessories.

Some leather is tanned by a combination of the chrome process and the vegetable process, so that the advantages of both types of tanning are combined. Chrome tanning requires less time; vegetable tanning produces a higher yield of leather from the same hide; chrome-tanned leather has greater resistance to heat and abrasion; and vegetable-tanned leather has greater resistance to the effects of perspiration and humidity.

Shearling leather, sheepskins and lambskins tanned with a uniformly clipped short length of wool still on the skin, is used in the manufacture of many types of cold-weather clothing. Shearlings may be tanned by either the vegetable or the chrome process, with certain deviations necessary because the skins are tanned with the wool on. The wool must be clipped to the desired length and combed to fluff it up by separating the fibers.

Another mineral tannage is alum tanning, used for soft glove-like leathers. The skins are tumbled in an alum solution that changes them to leather in a very short time, but the seasoning period requires several weeks or even months. The resulting leather is soft, pliable, and white in color, but unfortunately cannot be washed and must always be dry-cleaned.

Leather tanned with formaldehyde is similar to alum-tanned leather, with the exception that it is washable. Consequently this tannage is superior to the alum process for glove leathers.

In oil tanning, cod oil is kneaded into the skin until the skin changes to leather. The excess oil is then removed, leaving a soft, yellow skin. Chamois skin is oil tanned and buckskin and doeskin may be also.

Finishing

After all this, the leather is still dull, stiff, and unattractive until properly finished. Finishing varies according to the use to which the leather will be put. If the grain surface is marred by imperfections, which may result from several causes, the appearance is improved by a light buffing or sandpapering of the grain surface, producing "corrected-grain leather." Buffing may also be used to give hides or skins a nap known as a suede finish, although this process is more often applied to the flesh side than to the grain side. Bucko and mocha leathers, however, are usually napped or buffed on the grain side.

In giving smoothness and a lustrous color to leathers, several steps are involved. *Seasoning* means treating the leather with a mixture of pigments, shellac, synthetic resins, and wax. After a thorough drying, the leather is then *glazed,* giving it a highly polished surface. If an extra-smooth surface is desired, the leather is plated by being placed under pressure and heat in a hydraulic press. *Patent leather* is made by putting a number of lacquer coatings on the grain side of any smooth-surfaced leather. This should not be confused with plastic that resembles it; in true patent leather, the distinct grain of the leather is visible through the lacquer.

Some leathers are given a distinctive surface pattern by a process called *boarding,* which produces a series of tiny parallel creases in the grain. *Box grain* results when the skin is completely boarded in one di-

rection and then boarded again in a direction at right angles to the first. *Pebble grain* is the result of boarding in a direction diagonal to the other two. Boarded calf, pin seal, and morocco are examples of leathers that have been boarded. After boarding, the grain side is ironed to make the surface smooth without destroying the pattern.

Embossing is a finishing process by which designs are imprinted in relief on the surface of leather. The desired grain is etched on a large steel plate, which is then placed on the leather, and under great pressure and heat the grain is permanently stamped on the leather. By means of embossing, calfskin or cattle hide may be made to simulate the skins of reptiles or other skins with distinctive markings. Two-tone effects, a mottled appearance, and printed patterns and designs are also applied to leathers by embossing. Split leathers can be made to resemble top-grain leathers, and marks and scars can be covered by this process.

Sorting, grading, and testing

The finished leather is sorted and graded on the basis of evenness of color, fineness of grain, and general appearance and feel; then it is measured on a machine that marks the size on the flesh side. The leather then is ready to be sold in lots with other leathers of similar kind, weight, and grade.

There are many characteristics of leather that make it desirable for use in apparel and allied accessories: its beauty; its comfort, due to leather's breathing quality, called porosity; its durability; its elasticity, which helps leather articles to keep their shape; its softness; and its strength.

Leathers are subjected to a variety of tests in research laboratories; these include tests for tensile strength, stitch-tear-resistance, resistance to cracking, puncture-resistance, scuff-resistance, and crockproofness.

CATEGORY	COUNTRY OF ORIGIN	CHARACTERISTICS	USES
AQUATIC			
Alligator	Africa Central America Philippines South America United States	Beautiful markings; tiny oval and round marks to large squares and rectangles. Expensive; skill needed in matching adds to cost.	Fancy leather goods, handbugs, luggage, shoe uppers, belts.
Seal	North America Arctic Zone	Smooth, soft leather. Boarded for beautiful pebbly grain.	Fancy leather goods, handbags.
Shark	Australia United States (Pacific Coast)	Diamond-shaped grain. Scuff resistant.	Handbags, belts, tips of children's shoes.
Walrus	North America	Several inches thick. Hides are split and embossed.	Luggage, polishing wheels for buffing gold and silver jewelry.
BIRD			
Ostrich	Arabia Africa	Markings are spiral-shaped rosettes with a hole in the center. Rare and expensive.	Fancy leather goods—billfolds, book covers, key cases, men's shaving kits—handbags, luggage, shoes.
BUFFALO			
(domesticated, land and water)	Asia Eastern Europe	Coarser than cowhide. Usually badly scarred; embossed with artificial grain.	Heavy work gloves, handbags, luggage, shoe soles and uppers.
CATTLE			
Calf	North America South America Europe	Smooth surface, fine grain, firm, durable. Does not scuff easily. Patent, suede, or boarded finish. Vegetable-tanned calfskin is known as saddle leather. Embossed to resemble alligator. Stretches moderately, cleans well, takes polish well.	Handbags and other personal leather goods, luggage, shoe and slipper uppers and linings, sweatbands for men's hats, belts, tooling leather.
Cow, steer, bull	North America South America Europe	Hide thicker, heavier, and larger than in calfskin; grain more distinct. Durable and pliable.	Bags, belts, brief cases, gloves, luggage, shoes, upholstery.
DEER			
Antelope Deer Elk	Canada United States Europe	Porous, fine texture. Stretches. Rare; often imitated in calfskin and cowhide. Suede-finished antelope is very rare; lambskin is often buffed and finished to imitate antelope.	Gloves, handbags, shoe uppers, trimmings.

Care

Since proper handling and care of articles can both preserve their beauty and prolong their useful life, it is wise to find out how to care for them at the time of purchase provided such information is available.

It is advisable to note whether leather articles are labeled washable. If directions for washing are given, they should be followed accurately, with special attention to temperature of water, type of detergent, shaping, and drying. Usually, mild suds, lukewarm water for both washing and rinsing, gentle pressing out of excess water, and drying slowly away from sunlight, with occasional "finger pressing," which is a pulling gently between the fingers to re-

CATEGORY	COUNTRY OF ORIGIN	CHARACTERISTICS	USES
EQUINE Colt Horse Mule Zebra	America Europe	Firm, less porous than most leathers. Resistant to scuffing. Colt has a fine texture.	Belts, gloves, handbags, luggage, shoe uppers (men's shoes), tips for boys' and girls' shoes.
GOAT and KID	Africa Asia Europe South America	Fine, thin, smooth skin with tiny markings on the grain side; the finer the grain, the better the quality. Strong and porous. Takes glacé and suede finishes. Morocco, goatskin boarded to give a fine, pebbly surface, is often imitated in other leathers.	Gloves, handbags, shoe uppers and linings, belts, wallets, garments.
KANGAROO (and wallaby)	Australia	Comfortable and durable, resembles kidskin but is stronger. Takes a glazed finish. Scuff-resistant.	Men's street and athletic shoes.
PIG Carpincho Peccary Pig Hog	Mexico South America United States	Vegetable tanned and left in natural color (tan). Carpincho (actually a rodent) provides a heavy leather with smaller hair holes than peccary. Durable, but tends to stretch.	Fancy leather goods, gloves, handbags, luggage, shoes—uppers, innersoles, and counters.
REPTILE Lizard	Africa South America	Markings resembling grains of uncooked rice; side and tail sections have tiny rectangular scales resembling alligator markings. Durable.	Decorative trim on gloves, belts, handbags, and shoes. Handbags, shoe uppers.
Snake (cobra, diamondback)	Africa South America	Thin skins, loose scales; attractive markings. Durable.	As lizard.
LAMB and SHEEP (cabretta, capeskin, mocha, shearling)	Africa Asia Europe North America South America	Lighter than other leathers. Tends to stretch easily. May be sueded to imitate doeskin. Shearling leather is sheepskin tanned with a short length of wool left on. Chamois is oil-tanned leather made from undersplits; mocha, the skin of hair sheep buffed on the grain side; cabretta, a durable leather from South African or South American hair sheep with a glazed finish.	Chamois, garment linings, jackets, gloves, handbags, other personal leather goods, sweatbands for hats, parchment, shoe and slipper uppers and linings.

store the soft, supple feel, are recommended for washable leather. To press suede, use a dry iron at a low setting and brown wrapping paper as a press cloth. If leather articles are not marked washable, the should be dry-cleaned by cleaners who specialize in handling leather.

In contrast to smooth-surface leathers, suede articles should be brushed with a special brush in a circular motion unless the suede has a dustproof finish. If suede becomes shiny, a very fine sandpaper or emery board may be used gently to brush up the nap. The original color may be restored to suedes that have become grayed by the use of prepared colored dressings. Suede shoes, bags, and other accessories may be resueded commercially.

WOMEN'S SHOES

It is estimated that a person walks approximately 65,000 miles during a lifetime. It is also estimated that 95 per cent of all babies born in America are born with perfect feet, yet 80 per cent of the adult population have foot defects. The medical profession indicates that much of this trouble stems from improper footwear.

As a child, you probably had no control over the type, size, and fit of the footwear you wore. Now that you make your own selections, it is advisable to keep in mind several factors when you choose shoes. To make wise choices from the great variety of footwear available can be difficult. There are variations in design, material, and construction; in sizes, in brands, and in cost. Added to these are other considerations, including fit, comfort, health, serviceability, color, style, and care. If appearance is your first interest, the shoes' fashion rightness and their suitability to you, to a particular costume, and to the time of year are all significant.

The types of shoes from which to choose are many. Throughout history, shoe styles have varied widely: from the high top to the very low cut with scarcely any top beyond a single strap; from extremely thick to extremely thin soles; and from pencil-thin, stilt-like high heels and slim spikes down to thick, square heels or no heels at all. The toes have been long and narrow as in the needle toe, broad, turned up, and cut out to reveal the toe. At times, shoes have been extremely plain; at others, highly ornamented with embroidery, jewelry, and other decoration. With many women leading active lives, working and participating in community affairs and other activities, a comfortable yet smart style has developed—the casual shoes made of soft leather, with medium or low heels and unstiffened toes.

Types of shoes

Shoes have been classified into a few basic types with several subdivisions each, greatly simplifying communication between the salesman and the customer.

The *sandal* is one of the oldest types of shoes; in earliest times it consisted of a slab of leather held to the foot by means of straps. Over the years, some types have covered the foot, others revealed it; all made use of straps to hold the shoe on the foot. Common examples are the Mary Jane, open quarter, open shank, open toe, ankle strap, and T-strap. Some T-strap shoes have straps of different colors that can be changed to go with different outfits.

With few exceptions, the *high-top* shoe has become obsolete in women's wear. This style is confined now to shoes for specialized activities like skating, basketball, and horseback riding. Jodhpurs and monk shoes for riding are specific examples.

The *oxford* had an early predecessor in the animal skins that were laced on the foot with thongs. It is used for comfort-type footwear. The shoe is cut below the ankle and held on the foot by laces in the center of the instep or at the side of the shoe. The heel may be any height. The *saddle oxford* has a low heel and the section of the shoe across the instep is in a contrasting color. The *balmoral* is laced with a closed throat, while the *blucher* is laced with an open throat. The *ghillie* is a laced shoe with a slotted front; the laces tie around the ankle. The *shawl tongue*, in which style a folded, slashed tongue covers the lacing, is another variation of the oxford. A *sneaker* is a laced canvas shoe with rubber or plastic sole.

The *pump* has been one of the most popular styles for several years. It is low cut but not held to the foot by straps. The *opera pump* is a classic plain pump. Pattern pumps have fancy cut-out sections,

Sandal

Moccasin

Sling back

Boot

Pump

Oxford

T-strap

Ballerina

Ghillie

D'Orsay

Mule

bows, buckles, or other trim. The *step-in* is a type of pump that comes up across the instep; it is either made entirely of elasticized material or has elastic inserts in the sides. This latter variation is sometimes called a *gore shoe*. The *D'Orsay pump* has a V-cut top side line. The *sling-back pump* is an open-back shoe with a curved halter strap to keep the sling back from slipping off. The *spectator pump* is usually white with contrasting leather toe, heel, or trim. A pump with one or more straps across the instep is called a *strap pump* as distinguished from the real sandal.

The *moccasin* is a molded one-piece bottom that cradles the foot with a vamp plug

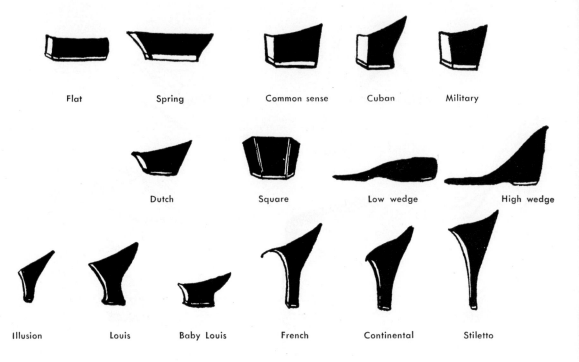

Flat	Spring	Common sense	Cuban	Military

Dutch	Square	Low wedge	High wedge

Illusion	Louis	Baby Louis	French	Continental	Stiletto

stitched to shape the shoe. The Indian moccasin does not have a heel lift, but a heel can be added to a plain moccasin. The flat shoe ranges from the ballet to the sneaker with little or no heel and a low-cut upper.

Heels fall into the general classifications of flat, medium, high, and novelty. Further breakdowns include spring, common-sense, military, Cuban, high Cuban, illusion, high, Louis, Baby Louis, French, Continental, Dutch Boys, wedge, Spanish, spike, and whatever other terms fashion may develop. Heel heights are measured in eighths of inches; a heel one and three-fourths inches high, for example, is referred to as a four-teen-eighths heel. The range is from two eighths to twenty-eight eighths.

Besides shoes there are boots and slippers. *Boots* may be any heavy high-top shoes used for sports, like ski boots and riding boots. Campus boots, like chukka boots

in either smooth or brushed leather, are popular all-weather footwear among students. Stadium boots with fleece or fur linings are popular cold-weather footwear. The *slipper,* a lightweight shoe worn chiefly indoors, can be either low cut or high cut. The *mule slipper* is a high-heeled slipper without counter or quarter.

All of these styles of footwear are made from a variety of materials. Although leather is considered best for comfort, durability, and serviceability, many other materials are used for shoe uppers and soles. Fabric, fur, mesh, straw, and vinyl plastics are used for uppers; cork, plastic, rope, rubber, and wood are used for soles.

Shoe leathers
Leather used in shoe uppers for women's shoes is made from the hides or skins of cattle, hogs and pigs, kangaroos, reptiles, sheep, and goats.

Calfskin is firm and porous, with a distinctive grain pattern that takes a high luster on polishing. It is pliable enough to shape itself to the foot. The thinner calf leathers used in women's shoes can be given a smooth, boarded, printed, embossed, patent, or sueded finish. Cowhide, less expensive than calfskin, is durable, attractive, and excellent for sport shoes, waterproof footwear, and patent leather. It resembles calfskin but is coarser grained and not so pliable.

Pigskin is one of the most porous leathers because of its tiny bristle holes. Shoe uppers made from pigskin are cool and comfortable. It is highly resistant to deterioration by mold and relatively immune to damage from moisture and humidity. Genuine domestic pigskin has gained in importance in the shoe industry. In women's shoes pigskin is often imitated.

Kangaroo leather, in appearance resembling kid leather, has a fine grain and is strong for its weight and thickness, attractive in appearance, durable, and comfortable. Sueded kangaroo leather is popular because of its distinctive napped surface and the close resemblance to true buckskin, which is scarce. Kangaroo leather is usually used only in comfort shoes, primarily in men's shoes.

Kidskin, made from the skins of both young and mature goats, is lighter than calf and one of the strongest leathers for its weight. It is flexible, fine-grained, and porous; it does not crack but will scuff more easily than calf. It is one of the coolest leathers, and its pliability and softness make it popular in women's shoes. It is finished in many colors, including gold and silver, and in smooth, glazed, embossed, patent, and suede finishes.

Ostrich skin is sometimes used for women's shoes, but the skin is rare and the leather consequently expensive. This unusual leather has its own natural textured look. It is extremely strong and durable.

Reptile skins used in footwear include those of alligators, lizards, and snakes. Alligator leather, like most other reptile skins, is tough, durable, and resistant to scuffing. It can be dyed in many colors. Genuine alligator leather is used in luxury footwear. It is often imitated by embossing smooth leather. Lizard skin is naturally tough but must be carefully cut to give adequate thickness for good wear. It dyes well and is available in many colors. Snake skin is not as durable as other reptile leathers. It dyes well and comes in many colors. The patterns vary from large to pinpoint markings.

Sheepskin is used as an imitation for several other skins and is embossed, printed, buffed, napped, and sueded to resemble buckskin, doeskin, pigskin, and others.

Shoe fabrics

Fabrics of many kinds are used in making shoe uppers. Usually, shoe fabrics are stronger and more durable than those made for clothing use. The exception is when a fabric is used for shoes to match a garment worn with them. Some fabrics may have elastic threads woven in to provide extra comfort. Fabric uppers can provide durability, flexibility, good appearance, and porosity. Serviceability depends on the material and how it is used. Fabric uppers may not wear so long as good leather, but when properly woven and cut they are comfortable. Fabrics in light colors can be dyed after the shoes are purchased, if desired.

Brocades are fabrics woven with an all-over design, generally floral and slightly raised. To accent the pattern, contrasting surfaces or colors or gold and silver threads are woven into the design. Silk or one of the synthetic fibers may be used.

Canvas is used for casual shoes and sneakers. It is comfortable, durable, and available in many colors.

Crepe for shoe fabrics has a rough, pebbly surface and may be made of any one of the natural or synthetic fibers or a blend of these fibers.

Faille, poplin, and similar ribbed fabrics are made of silk or one of the synthetics. These fabrics are soft and lustrous and have either a fine or coarse horizontal rib, depending upon the weave variation and the size of the yarn.

Gabardine and other twills are closely woven twill-weave fabrics with a pronounced diagonal rib and may be made of cotton, wool, or rayon or other synthetics, or a blend of these.

Linen fabrics are usually plain weave. The irregularity of the fiber gives linen texture and luster.

Mesh fabrics provide a cool, open weave that is strong, durable, and comfortable. Cotton, metallic threads, and nylon are used. *Antron* nylon straw is long-wearing.

Satin is used for dress and evening shoes, and for slippers. It may be of silk, acetate, rayon, or nylon. Its luster is appealing, but it is less durable than other fabrics.

Sisal and other straws are used for casual and resort-type shoes. They are strong, comfortable, and may be dyed.

Plastics and other materials

Plastics may be in the form of plastic sheeting, transparent or opaque; coatings of plastic on fabrics; or plastic yarns that are braided, crocheted, or woven into novelty shoe fabrics in several colors. The finish may be plain or embossed with a variety of imitation grains. Since solid plastics are nonporous, the use of an absorbent fabric lining will make the shoe more comfortable. A cut-out design provides ventilation. Since plastics do not stretch, the shoes

remain comfortable and retain their shape, provided they fit correctly when purchased.

Corfam, a poromeric man-made material offers breathability, comfort, and easy care; *pattina* is an olefinic shoe material with high gloss for shoe uppers.

Sole leather

Leather is used more than any other material for the soles of shoes. Sole leather, usually made from thick cattle hide, varies in quality according to the section of the hide from which it was taken and the method of tanning. The best sole leather is bend leather, which comes from the section of the hide from the shoulder to the tail and from the backbone to the upper edge of the belly. Bend-leather soles wear longer than those cut from the belly and shoulders.

Vegetable-tanned soles are firm, solid, and water resistant and do not slip. Chrome-tanned sole leather is very durable, but becomes slippery when wet, absorbs moisture, and is best suited for wear in dry climates.

Additional sole materials

Rubber is widely used for soles of casual and sport shoes; crepe rubber is especially desirable for sports footwear. Synthetic rubber withstands cold, heat, oil and grease, and abrasion. Rubber and rubber composition soles do not permit the passage of air through the material and may therefore not be as healthful as soles that are permeable to air. Chemically blown sponge is more porous. Rubber or composition soles will, however, give longer wear than will inexpensive leather soles. Variations in the bottom surface of the outer sole include the "saw tooth" and rib effects.

Cork, rope, and wood are used for soles on casual or novelty footwear. Cork is porous, absorbent, and comfortable but not very durable. Rope or hemp soles are flexible but have limited serviceability.

Additional materials used in other parts of the shoe—insole, lining, counter, toe, box, heel, and trim—include split leathers, pyroxylin-impregnated fabric, foam-back tricot linings, buckram, latex-impregnated felt, metals, and thread for stitching.

Shoe construction

Learning something about the construction of shoes may be of interest and value to the consumer concerned with making the best selection possible. A great amount of work is done by shoe designers and manufacturers before the actual construction is begun.

After the shoe is designed, patterns for each part are cut to scale and prepared for use. Each variation in the shape or the size of the last means that a new pattern must be cut for that particular shoe. These parts are cut by hand or machine from the patterns and are stitched together on sewing machines. The designing of the last is a very important part of shoe manufacture. The last is a wooden form or mold over which most shoes are made. The shape of the shoe is determined by the shape of the last on which it is made. The last is carefully made according to exact measurements. Since, however, feet of the same length and width may vary considerably in shape, lasts of many different shapes are used for the same shoe size. The length of the last from the toe joint to the end of the toes varies. The shape and contour of the bottom of the last determine how well the weight of the person will be distributed and where the main points of weight will be located in the shoe. The heel seat is a very important part of the last, and should be shaped so that the shoe grasps the heel firmly without binding yet controls it so the shoe fits the heel comfortably. Factors affecting the shape of the last are the size and shape of the foot, the type of shoe to be constructed, and the height of the heel to be placed on the shoe. Standard lasts are for the normal foot, combined lasts are for the slender heel, and orthopedic lasts are for the structurally weak foot and for specific foot troubles.

The parts of the shoe that are put together and shaped over the last are divided into two groups, the upper—including all the parts of the shoe above the sole and heel—and the sole. The outside sections of the upper include the *tip*, a separate piece of material covering the toe section of the vamp; the *vamp*, the front part of the shoe from the toe to the instep; the *quarter*, the section of the shoe from the instep to the center back of the heel; the *saddle*, a separate piece of material covering the instep section of a saddle shoe; and the *tongue*, the reinforcement behind the lacing, which may be a part of the vamp or stitched on separately.

The inside sections of the upper shoe include the *toe box*, a stiff or mellow reinforcement under the tip, arched to help the shoe retain its shape; the *counter*, generally a stiff reinforcement at the heel under the quarter of the shoe to preserve the shape of the shoe and make it fit snugly at the heel; the *linings*, reinforcements that make the inside of the shoe more comfortable by covering joinings and seams and by absorbing perspiration; the *doubler*, a cotton flannel interlining under the outer material of the shoe, adding to comfort by acting as an insulating material; and the *sock lining*, lining in the shape of the sole to provide a smooth inside surface for the sole of the foot.

The sole of the shoe, made of one or more layers of leather or other substance, depending on the type of shoe and its con-

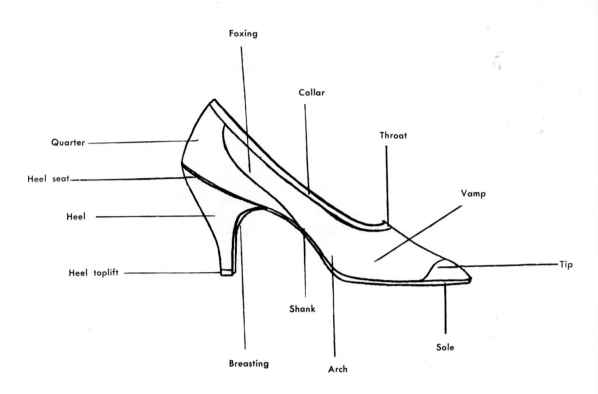

Foxing

Collar

Throat

Quarter

Heel seat

Vamp

Heel

Heel toplift

Tip

Shank

Sole

Breasting

Arch

The parts of a shoe.

struction, includes the *outsole*, the *insole*, the *filler*, the *shank*, and the *welt*.

The outsole is the outside sole on the bottom of the shoe. The thickness of the sole is measured by *irons*. An iron is equal to one forty-eighth of an inch; women's shoes are usually four to six irons thick. The insole is an innersole directly under the sock lining; it acts as a foundation for the shoe and adds to comfort and durability. The filler takes up the space between the insole and the outsole, adding to comfort, making the sole more water resistant, and eliminating squeaks; it usually is either cork, felt, leather, or rubber. The shank is a bridge—generally steel—between the heel and the ball of the shoe. It gives added support to the arch of the foot and aids in keeping the shoe in shape. Wood and fiberboard are also used. The welt is a narrow strip of leather that helps to hold the sole to the upper part of the shoe.

Heels are made of a variety of materials, including composition, leather, metal, plastic, wood covered with fabric or plastic, with leather, plastic, or rubber lifts. The lifts can be replaced when worn down. Built-up heels are made of layers of leather or leather board. High heels are made of a combination of wood and metal for strength; they may be copper-plated or coated with resin; some are thermoplastic with a steel dowel driven through the axis.

When the shoe uppers are completely sewed together, they go to the operation known as lasting. The insole is tacked to the wooden last, and the completed top is pulled over the last and attached to the insole. Counters and toe boxes are inserted, filler is pasted on the bottom of the insole, and the outsole is then attached to the insole.

Joining upper and sole

There are three basic methods of construction for joining upper and sole—cementing, nailing, and sewing. Within each of these are several types of shoes, some made by a combination of methods.

The principle of the cemented shoe construction is the use of an adhesive to fasten the upper to the sole. Waterproof plastic and rubber cements are used instead of stitching, staples, or tacks. In some types, lasting tacks or welt construction are combined with cementing processes. This process is practical and produces flexible and comfortable footwear.

The nailing method is seldom used for women's shoes, with the exception, perhaps, of very heavy shoes or ski boots. The upper is attached to the insole by tacks or wire. Occasionally these shoes are stitched on the outside to simulate welt construction. Although this construction is not too flexible, it is very durable.

There are several methods of sewing or stitching uppers to soles. Cotton, linen, Dacron, and nylon thread is used. The *Goodyear Welt* method is considered one of the best constructions for the oxford-type shoe. The welt is attached to the insole by a thread stitched with a curved needle. A channel or groove cut into the side of the insole is used to hold the welt. The space between the insole and the outsole is filled with cork and the outsole is stitched to the welt around the outside of the shoe. This shoe is comfortable, flexible, durable, strong, and easily repaired.

In the *Littleway* construction, staples are used but do not come through to the surface next to the foot and are invisible in the finished shoe. Cement is used to hold the lining and the toe position of the upper in place and a lockstitch joins outsole and insole to the upper. The identifying marks of the Littleway process are the presence

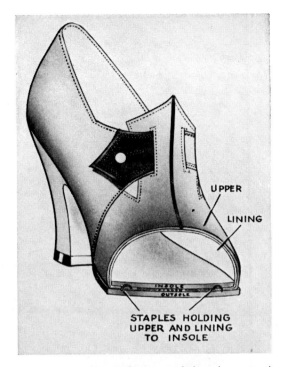

Cross section of a Littleway staple-lasted cemented shoe. (Courtesy United Shoe Machinery Corporation.)

of a lockstitch under the sock lining and the absence of visible tacks.

In the *McKay sewed* process, used for inexpensive shoes, the insole and the upper are fastened together with tacks that may be seen under the sock lining. The outsole is then stitched to the insole with a one-thread chainstitch; the stitches are left exposed on the outsole.

The *stitchdown* method, often used on children's shoes and inexpensive sandals, consists of stitching the upper, which is turned out, to the outsole so that the inside of the shoe presents a smooth surface and the finished shoe resembles Goodyear Welt.

In the *turned shoe* method, the shoe is turned inside out before the sole is sewed to the upper. Only the sock lining covers the seam where the upper and the sole were joined. Since only one sole is used,

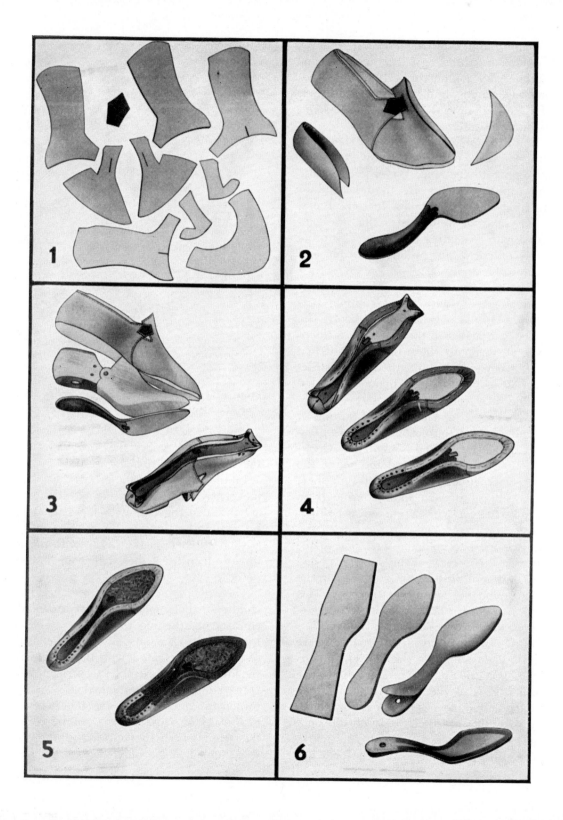

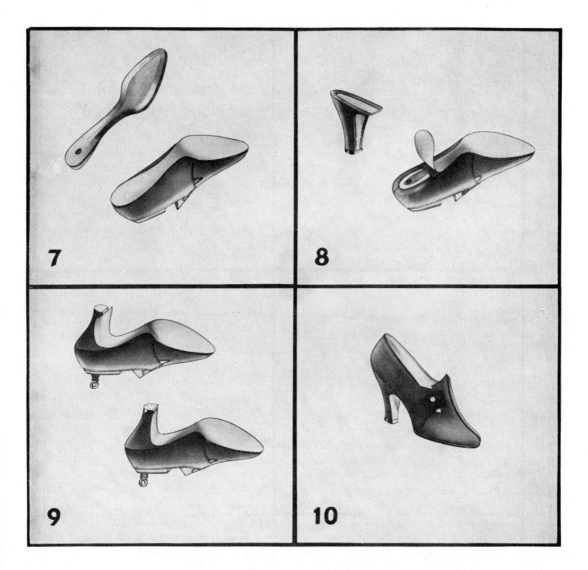

7

8

9

10

the shoe is very flexible and light in weight. With the shortage of skilled hand workers, it has gone almost completely out of use. It was one of the most expensive methods of construction, and as other constructions became more flexible, it was used less and less.

(Opposite and above) The construction of a cemented shoe. (Courtesy United Shoe Machinery Corporation.)

The *vulcanized* sole shoe has a complete rubber out-sole and heel unit vulcanized to an assembled upper in one operation. The *injection-moulded* sole shoe has a specially compounded polyvinyl chloride out-sole and heel unit moulded and attached to the assembled upper in an injection-type machine.

Some sport shoes and house slippers are made by the moccasin method, in which the upper begins on the side of the foot

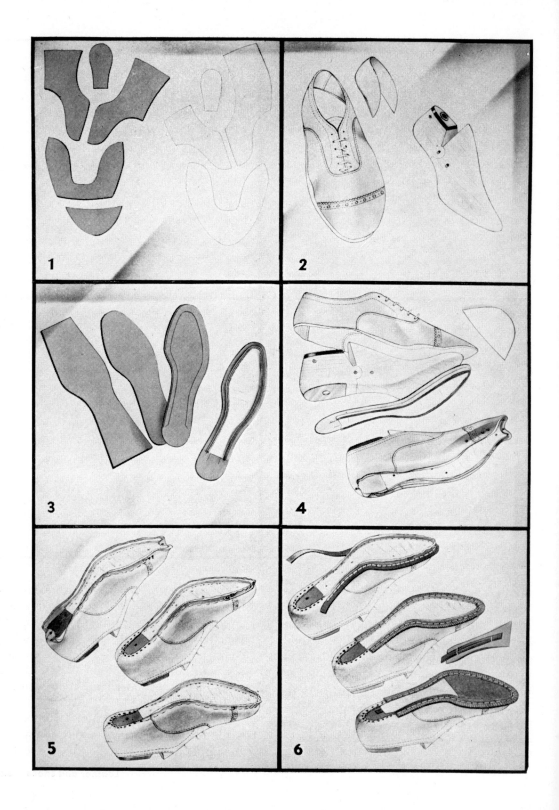

1

2

3

4

5

6

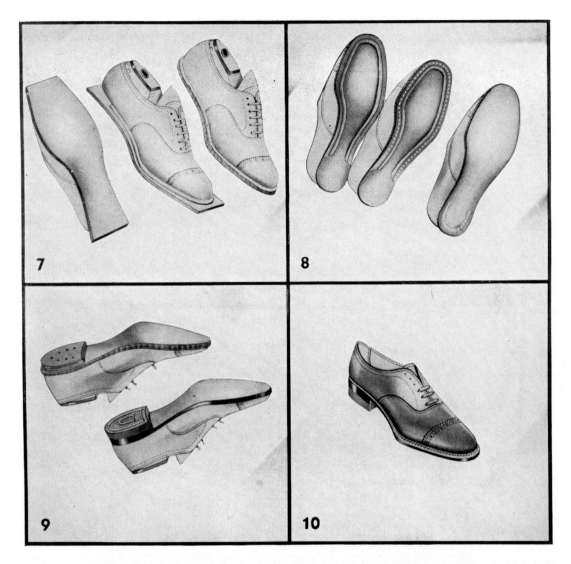

7

8

9

10

and goes under the foot in place of the insole. The outsole is then stitched to the upper. Hand stitching is used to attach the parts of the uppers together on the top of the shoe in the form of a U.

Slip lasting is not really a lasting process but one in which all parts are accurately

(Opposite and above) Progressive steps in the construction of a Goodyear welt shoe. (Courtesy United Shoe Machinery Corporation.)

cut and stitched to insure good fit in the finished shoe. After the uppers have been completely assembled, the shoe is slipped over a platform filler. The platform sole is then pressed into place, the platform cover is lasted, and the sole and heel are fastened. Since there is no opportunity to take up stretch or surplus material in the lasting operation, this method depends for results on accuracy in pattern making, cutting, and stitching. It is used for casual shoes only.

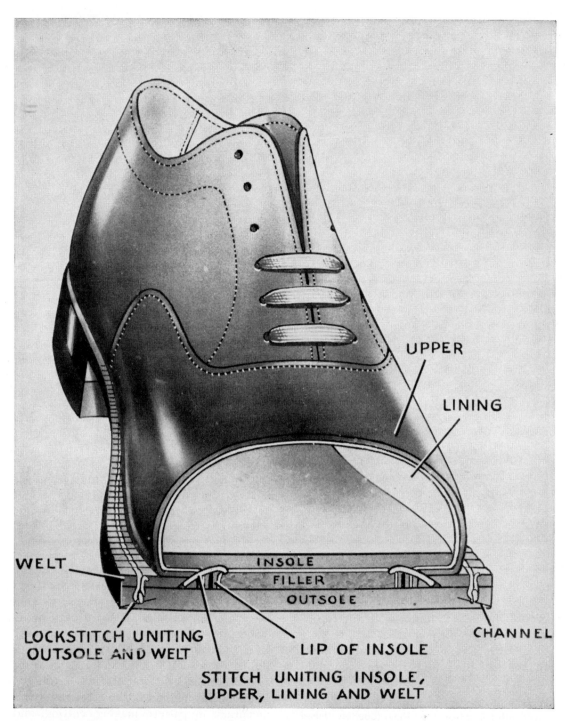

UPPER

LINING

WELT

INSOLE
FILLER
OUTSOLE

CHANNEL

LOCKSTITCH UNITING
OUTSOLE AND WELT

LIP OF INSOLE

STITCH UNITING INSOLE,
UPPER, LINING AND WELT

Cross section of a Goodyear welt shoe. (Courtesy
United Shoe Machinery Corporation.)

Heels are joined to the back part of the shoe by glue, nails, pegs, or screws. Top lifts are nailed to the heels. From two hundred to three hundred steps go into the finished shoe; it takes from a week to ten days for one pair of shoes to go through all the steps.

After the shoes have been completely assembled, they are removed from the lasts, sock linings are put in, and all edges are trimmed. Then the shoes are cleaned, polished or sprayed, inspected, wrapped in tissue paper, and placed in labeled shoe boxes, ready for delivery to the retailer.

It should be remembered that many brands and types of shoes will in construction vary from these steps. The construction of a cool, lightweight fabric shoe that can be washed in an automatic washer will differ from that of an opera pump. Constant innovations in shoe machinery help produce better shoes for less money.

Judging quality

It is difficult to judge the quality of shoes even with some knowledge of design, materials, and construction. Shoes may look alike yet be entirely different in wearing qualities. Factors affecting quality include design, quality of materials, method of cutting, lining, type of thread, fineness of stitching, details of workmanship, and standards of inspection. In order to produce inexpensive shoes, the manufacturer has to economize in the cost of labor, materials, and equipment. Instead of a separate pattern's being cut for each width, several widths may be cut by the same pattern and later shaped to the desired size on the lasts. Some shoes may be made of good materials but with poor workmanship and consequently give poorer service than shoes made of poorer materials but with better workmanship. With so many possible variations affecting quality, the consumer must consider details of shape, fit, material, and construction and try to get information as accurate as possible at the point of sale.

In the discussion of leather, it was pointed out that grade depends upon the age, diet, and condition of the animal from which the hide was taken, the section of the hide, the climate in which the animal was raised, and the method of tanning. Usually, good leather has fine grain and is flexible and firm, while poorer grades have coarse grain, are less elastic, stretch easily, and tend to be stiff. Full-grain leathers, usually superior to split leathers, are used in the better grades of shoes. If the hair holes can be clearly seen in full-grain leather, it is probably of good quality. If the leather is blemished, the mark may be buffed to make the leather look uniform. Split leather, being more porous than grain leather, does not take a shine or hold its shape as well as grain leather and is used in less expensive footwear.

Vegetable tanning produces a firm, solid, water-resistant leather used chiefly for sole leather, although some upper leathers are vegetable tanned. Chrome tanning produces a soft, pliable leather used mainly for shoe uppers, although it is also used for some sole leather. If the two processes are combined in tanning, the resulting leather is comfortable, durable, flexible, soft, and water-resistant.

The finishes applied to shoe leathers include boarding or crushing to simulate irregular grain on an uneven surface; embossing to imitate a grain or to create a special effect directly on the skin or on a coating that has been applied to the leather; glazing, produced by polishing the leather with rollers under heavy pressure or by coating it with varnish or shellac; dyeing smooth or grained leather; sueding, buffing the leather on the flesh side and occasionally the grain side; and patent finish, obtained by stretching the leather very tightly and coating it with a varnish-like substance. There is also a pebbled-surface patent. Patent leather is not guaranteed against cracking; new developments make it crack resistant. The aniline finish, which brings out all the depth and luster of fine smooth leathers, improves with every polish. Knowing what the terms mean and recognizing the purpose of each process should be of value to the consumer who is fortunate enough to find a well-informed salesman.

Considering the other materials used in shoes, it is advisable to ask questions and look for descriptive labels concerning color fastness, water resistance, crocking, abrasion resistance, cracking and splitting, tarnishing, and other characteristics peculiar to fabrics, metallics, plastics, rope, straws, and wood.

The quality of the insole is important to the durability of a shoe since it is the part of the shoe to which both the upper and the sole are attached. Therefore, the inner sole influences the length of wear and how a shoe keeps its shape. Insoles of buffed top-grain leather are more durable than those made of thin split leather reinforced with fabric. Impregnated paperboard, leatherboard, combined foam rubber, cork, felt, and plastic are also used. In cement-lasted shoes, inner soles are often made of more than one component—the toe piece for rigidity, the ball section flexible, the shank piece molded, and the heel piece cushioned to hold the heel nails. The insole can be examined by lifting the sock lining on top of the insole.

In the better grades of shoes, the sock lining is made of leather, while very thin split leather pasted over heavy paper or a leather substitute is used in less expensive shoes.

The lining varies with the quality and the price of the shoe. Some shoes are leather lined throughout, others are leather lined in the back part and fabric lined in the front part. The leather lining is either calf, kid, or sheepskin in better shoes and split cowhide in medium-priced shoes. Fabric linings are either closely woven drill or twill treated to resist perspiration, or loosely woven, heavily sized fabric. Vinyl-coated cotton fabrics impregnated with rubber offer great resistance to cracking from wear. Whatever the lining, to be comfortable, it must be smooth, without pleats or wrinkles.

Although it is impossible to examine the counter and toe box of the shoe, it may be of interest to know that materials used vary in quality. Counters are made of many grades of leather, hemp, flax, or fiberboard. Cellulose and leather fibers combined with latex or other plastics have gradually been replaced by polyethylene, which has even greater resistance to wear. The toe box may be made of leather, pyroxylin-impregnated fabric, buckram, flexible cork, or latex-impregnated felt. Polystyrene, a colorless chemical, is used to make the rigid dome of the hard toe box. Thermoplastics conforming exactly to the last are used for women's open-toed shoes and pointed shoes. The important point is whether the toe box and counter will hold their shape permanently.

Foot structure

Some knowledge of foot structure and of the correct size and fit of shoes for the individual is very important in judging the value of shoes. Many of the complaints about shoes are caused by incorrectly fitted shoes. Not only does incorrect fit cause discomfort, but it may be the cause of uneven wearing and breakdown of the shoe. Often when the feet are uncomfort-

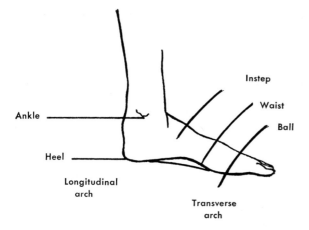

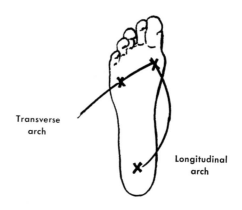

able because of incorrectly fitted shoes, the victim changes his posture to minimize the pain. If the new posture becomes habitual, damage to other parts of the body may result, with headaches and backaches as consequences.

Most people's feet are normal at birth. The normal foot has twenty-six small bones, held together by ligaments and muscles that permit flexibility in the use of the feet, hold body weight, and absorb shock when the feet propel the body. In walking or standing, the toes point straight ahead and the large toe acts as a lever. If the toes are crowded in the shoe, muscles and ligaments are strained and bones pulled out of place. Normal movement is restricted, the feet will tire and ache, and the discomfort causes pain in other parts of the body. The bones of the foot are arranged to form arches that give elasticity and spring, provided the fit of the shoe does not interfere. Length, width, and circumference are important in considering the size and fit of shoes. The length includes not only the total length but the distance from the end of the large toe to the joint and the distance from the joint to the heel. In width, there is a difference at the ball and at the heel. Another variation is in the circumference and the height and shape of the instep. The various proportions of all of these measurements make each individual's feet different, and therefore require special attention in fitting. Feet differ not only in size but in shape, amount of flesh, and height of arch.

Fit

One of the first steps in obtaining a good fit in shoes is to have the feet measured. It is impossible to select shoes accurately by the size of the shoe a person is wearing. A low-heel walking shoe may be comfortable, but a high-heel dress-up shoe in the same size may not fit. Feet should be measured each time shoes are bought. The measuring devices used include size sticks that give not only the total length but the correct ball-to-heel and toe-to-heel length and the width of the foot. Measurement should be taken of both feet, in a relaxed sitting position as well as in a standing position, since some feet become longer when supporting the full weight of the body. Often one foot is larger than the other; it should be fitted unless a different shoe size can be ordered for each foot. Measuring devices are used as guides; they cannot give the exact stated size because of the differences in lasts. After the salesman has selected a pair of shoes according to this measurement guide, the customer has to decide upon the fit and comfort. A shoe that fits properly should be neither too tight nor too loose on the foot. One should never buy shoes that are too tight with the mistaken idea that they will stretch and be more comfortable after the breaking-in period. A shoe that fits properly should not stretch that much, and a breaking-in period should not be necessary.

Guides in judging fit include the following: The widest part of the large toe joint should be directly over the widest part of the sole of the shoe. The shape of the toe of the shoe should conform to the shape of the individual's toes with sufficient room so that in walking the toe does not touch the lining of the toe box; in open-toed shoes, the tip of the toe should extend to the end of the insole but not over it when the person is standing. The heel of the shoe should be wide enough at the base to support the heel and at the same time so snug that the heel of the foot does not slip in walking or rub up and down inside the shoe. The foot should tread evenly, with most of the wear on the sole under the ball of the foot. The shoe should conform to the arch of the foot without exerting pressure against it. The fit of the shoe over the instep and from the ball to heel is very important; if it cuts into a fleshy foot or presses against the bones of a thin foot, discomfort follows.

Abnormal feet or those deformed by incorrect footwear require special shoes, and it is advisable to consult a specialist who will prescribe corrective, orthopedic shoes or custom-made shoes designed and lasted exactly to the requirements of the individual.

The height of the heel on the shoe is important to comfort and health. Very high heels throw the body off balance, and the extra weight resting on the ball of the foot may cause callouses. Constant wearing of high heels causes back leg muscles to shorten so that when a person changes to low heels or flat shoes she often feels pain in the back of her leg. On the other hand, the person who wears flat shoes constantly often finds great discomfort when wearing heels that shift the weight to the ball of the foot. It is advisable to change heel heights occasionally. A heel not over one and three-fourths inches high is adequate for women's general wear. With the illusion heel, which gives the appearance of greater height without exceeding the above-mentioned height, many women can enjoy comfort and smart appearance at the same time.

Size

Women's shoe sizes range from 1 to 13, with a half size for each regular size. The normal range is from 5 to 10, with 60 per cent of all shoes sold in sizes 6½ to 8½. Each half size is approximately one sixteenth of an inch longer than the preceding size. In width, sizes range from AA to D, with each width size approximately one sixteenth to one twelfth of an inch wider across the bottom of the sole; size AA, for example, is about one sixteenth of an inch narrower than size A. Extremely narrow, AAAAA and AAAA, and the wide E widths are usually found in corrective footwear. The combination last provides a heel section narrower in proportion to the rest of the shoe for people whose feet are so shaped.

Another point to recognize when selecting shoes is that there are differences in fit and comfort in shoes of the same size but in different types and brands. Many consumers make a comparative study of various brands of shoes, and, when they find a particular last that proves comfortable and satisfactory, purchase the same last each time. Sometimes the number or the name of the last is found printed on the inside of the shoe. Even though these markings may not be in all shoes, a good salesman should be able to identify the last, so that the customer can buy the same brand of shoe in a variety of styles, all made on the last best for her.

Buying

The cost of footwear seems to be more important to some consumers than to others. The amount spent for shoes varies with the individual, according to her life, the condition of her feet, the skill with which she buys, and the care given the shoes. People who plan their shoe wardrobes as carefully as they do the rest of their apparel decide on their need and the amount of money they can afford to spend and then look for the shoes in that price range to fit their purpose, their feet, and their pocketbook. People who wait until the day they want to wear the shoes with a particular outfit or for a special occasion often buy hastily, pay more than they can afford, and ignore some of the other factors of selection that are important to long-term satisfaction. Some people are fascinated by sale prices and buy for price, ignoring quality, size, and fit. It is quite possible to buy on sale shoes that are entirely satisfactory, but customers should follow the same practices in selecting these shoes they follow otherwise. Some people buy all of their shoes from the same retailer, who stocks shoes that suit their requirements. The salesman who is well informed on feet and shoes learns the special needs of his customers and can so give them the service they desire. From the standpoints of appearance, economy, and health this practice is often the wisest.

The relationship of shoes to the individual and to the rest of her wardrobe is a consideration which puzzles some women.

A few points to keep in mind before going shopping for shoes include knowing what one wants: the type of shoes, the purpose they will serve, and how they will fit into the present wardrobe.

Just as there are women who have a mania for hats and buy a hat every time they go shopping, there are women who have a similar mania for shoes. In contrast, there are women who maintain that one type of shoe serves all purposes. The ideal shoe collection takes care of all of the activities in a woman's life, does not include shoes that fail to serve the purpose of the individual, and includes some shoes that can be worn with more than one outfit. If her budget is limited, a woman chooses one type of shoe to serve many purposes. Shoes are designed for casual wear, dress wear, and for leisure, sports, walking, and other activities. While comfort, durability, and good fit are especially desirable for walking shoes, appearance often takes precedence over comfort and durability in shoes for dancing; if these shoes fit properly and are well made they will not cause serious discomfort during the short periods they are worn for evening wear or dress purposes. Casual and general sports shoes may serve a dual purpose for walking and general utility wear. The sneaker and loafer so popular with teen-age and college women serves many purposes in their schedule of activities.

Shoes and the individual

Not only are there shoes for different purposes, but there are different types of shoes, as indicated earlier—from the balmoral to the strap. The lines of the shoe design, the material, and the color can enhance the assets and camouflage the liabilities of an individual's feet and legs. With due consideration to the proportions of the figure, leg, ankle, and foot, one can through clever choice of shoes create optical illusions: adding or subtracting height, decreasing the apparent width of the ankle, and giving the whole figure an appearance of slenderness. The shoe should also be in keeping with the individual's age and personality. The ankle-strap sandal may not be the smartest selection for the middle-aged woman who usually wears a dark classic suit minus all frills.

The same principles you learned in previous chapters on color, line, proportion, and texture apply to the selection of shoes. For example, the heavy person wishing to emphasize length and slenderness of line chooses shoes of simple design and line, with trim heels that will provide a firm foundation and at the same time create a graceful line; the shoes should match rather than contrast with the color of her outfit. The woman with a thick calf and ankle can minimize this effect by choosing shoes free from fancy stitching and detailed ornamentation, with V-throated cut and of a single color and texture.

To summarize, the shoes should harmonize in color and style with the costume, with the activity for which worn, and with the wearer; they should fit the budget and the feet and be durable, wearable, and of the best quality for the price.

Care

Now that the customer has finally made the best selection possible, her next responsibility is the proper care of the shoes. As already mentioned, if the shoe fits well, it will retain its original lines, the soles will wear evenly, and the heels will retain their strength and position, provided the shoe is worn for the appropriate purpose; for instance, evening shoes used for casual wear will not last as long as they would if used properly, and lightweight street shoes are a poor selection for active sports. Shoes

should be allowed to rest and dry out thoroughly between wearings in order to regain their original shape and give longer service. This may mean that a person should have two pairs of shoes, to be worn on alternate days. Some women whose jobs require that they stand nearly all day often have an extra pair of shoes on the job so that they can change during the day, allowing their feet and the shoes to profit by the change. Unless shoes are specially lined to be worn without foot coverings, they should be worn over footlets, socks, or stockings to protect the shoes from the effect of perspiration, to keep them sanitary, and to increase foot comfort. Shoes should be stored with shoe trees or similar support inside or placed on shoe racks with shoe-shaped supports to restore the original shape and prevent wrinkled linings. Shoe trees should fit the shoes. Newspaper or tissue paper stuffed into the toes is a good substitute. Careful storage away from dust saves unnecessary cleaning and keeps the appearance of shoes. Shoes should be kept in good repair by having heels straightened and the lifts on heels replaced, rips mended, and soles replaced or half-soled as needed. Worn-down heels and threadbare soles throw shoes out of line and put undue strain on the uppers. Be familiar with the best care for the various materials from which the uppers are made. The consumer should consult the shoe salesman about the specific care of each pair of leather shoes. There may be other suggestions besides the usual wiping with a damp cloth, polishing with waterproof paste polish, and brushing suedes with a rubber sponge or brush. Polishing keeps the leather pliable and more resistant to water as well as improves the appearance. On most fabric shoes that are not washable like the washable casuals, spots can be removed with cleaning fluids or mild soap and water.

However, here again, follow the suggestions of the salesman. Wiping with a damp cloth is usually sufficient for cleaning plastics and other materials. Since plastics are thermoplastic, they should be kept away from heat to prevent softening. Most cleaning fluids should not be used on plastics. In addition to being cleaned, shoes should be protected from moisture, rain, and snow by rubbers or boots, which are available in fabric, plastics, and rubber. Boots are made in ankle length and above; rubbers either cover the whole shoe or cover only the toe and vamp, in which case they are known as toe rubbers. To protect shoes from friction, many people put heelless socks over the shoes before putting on the protective footwear. If shoes do get wet, they should be stuffed carefully with paper and allowed to dry away from heat. Although leathers are treated and finished to resist moisture, they tend to dry out and become brittle, hard, and uncomfortable if exposed to moisture and heat frequently. Water tends to rot both leather and thread. Wet leather stretches out of shape and the stitches cut through easily; quick drying does not give the leather a chance to contract properly.

In putting on shoes, a shoe horn should be used to prevent breaking the backs of the shoes and wearing out the uppers at the back.

When leather shoes are not to be worn for a long time, such as seasonal shoes stored during seasons when not worn, they should be cleaned thoroughly and polished, stuffed well with paper, covered to protect them from dust and dirt, and stored in a cool, dry place. When the shoes are taken out of storage, they should be given a dressing of oil or a polish containing oil before being worn again.

In some sections of the country where mildew and mold collect on shoes, dampening the shoes with a weak solution of carbolic acid in water after cleaning is effective. After drying, they should be polished and stored. On removal from storage, shoes that have been so treated should be given a thorough airing before being worn.

MEN'S SHOES

While women may choose their shoes more as items of decoration, men tend to choose shoes more from the standpoint of comfort. That may be the reason why there are more women than men with foot trouble. In prehistoric times, women's and men's feet were similarly wrapped in pieces of animal hide. Since for centuries the only way of traveling was on foot, protection and comfort in footwear were essential. As women's feet came to be considered attractive, their footwear became more decorative. There have been periods in history when men's feet were cramped by fashion—even as late as the Victorian era. Since that time, comfort, utility, value, and appearance seem to have been the influential factors in the selection of men's shoes.

However, men have come to realize that good-looking shoes are important parts of a well-dressed man's wardrobe. The man who once bought one pair of shoes for all seasons, all occasions, and all outfits has at least six pairs—two business; one dressy; two casual; one in-between times. Men seem to be aware of the relationship of shoes to their appearance and realize that a change of dress frequently calls for a change of shoes.

One of the reasons for this change of attitude may be that there is an increasing array of men's shoes from which to choose. Designs, materials, colors, constructions, brands, and costs are nearly as numerous as in women's shoes. There are shoes for formal and semi-formal evening wear, weddings and formal daylight affairs, cold weather, hot weather, business, school and college, casual wear, and active sports.

Shoe types

The typical designs in men's shoes include the *balmoral, blucher, boot, brogue, chukka boot, gore shoe, jodhpur, loafer, moccasin, monk, oxford, pump,* and *sandal.*

The *balmoral* is a laced shoe with closed throat. The *blucher* is also a laced shoe, with the vamp continued up beneath the top, which laps over the vamp from the sides; there are the two-eyelet Continental with contrasting trim, the Italian blucher,

Balmoral

Blucher

Brogue

Buckle-and-strap

Boots

Oxfords

Sandal

Pump

Loafer

Slip-on

the two-eyelet blucher with moccasin toe, the plain toe, and the straight tip. The *boot* is any shoe with the top reaching above the ankle. The *brogue* is a heavy waterproof shoe or a strong low shoe with large ornamental perforations. The *chukka boot* is slightly above ankle length, laced or with a buckle, and made of suede with a crepe sole.

The *gore shoe* has an elasticized side or front. The jodhpur is a high ankle boot with a two-eyelet closing. In the *loafer,* the U-shaped vamp is topped with a wide strap. The *moccasin* has a one-piece vamp with attached circular tongue; there is also a slip-on type with a tassel. The *monk* shoe features a three-piece upper with side buckle. The *oxford* is a balmoral or blucher type with three or more eyelets; there are the wing tip, with the toe tip cut in wing shape; the plain tip without perforations; and the spectator sport, in which the toe and the heel are of perforated contrasting leather. The *pump* is a low-cut slipper. The *sandal* is an open shoe with interfaced straps.

Heels

The heels of men's shoes are similar in all types of shoes. Although men do not wear heels of varying heights, they may use a construction known as an elevator to gain additional height. By means of a specially constructed raised platform on the inside of the shoe, elevators actually increase a man's height to over one and a half inches more than it would be if he wore regular shoes. These shoes are available in all styles and in a wide range of sizes. Outwardly, the heels of "elevators" are no higher than those of regular shoes. The only visible difference is that the shoe's back upper half rises a little more than usual to accommodate the built-up inner

ramp, but this is under the trouser cuff and is seldom seen.

Additional footwear

Men also wear weather-boots, galoshes, rubbers, and slippers. Rubber boots may be calf, knee, or hip length for protection from rain and snow; leather boots are for skiing, riding, and other sports. Galoshes are usually above ankle length and made of either rubber or fabric. Rubbers that are ankle length completely cover the shoe; the shell type covers the sole and about a third of the depth of the upper. Slippers are a lightweight kind of footwear worn chiefly indoors; they may be low cut or high cut and are made of leather or fabric.

Materials

All of these designs are made from a variety of materials, but leather seems to be the most popular in men's footwear. Fabrics, meshes, and straw are used for uppers, while cork, plastic, rope, rubber, and composition are used for soles.

Many of the leathers used in women's shoes are used also in men's shoes. Split leather is often used in men's work shoes. Cowhide and the heavier grades of calfskin are much used for men's shoes. Men's shoes of kid are usually made from the skins of mature goats. Pigskin is used in limited quantities; buffalo leather, from the hides of domesticated land and water buffalo, is used as a substitute. Cordovan leather, from the rump of horsehide, is used for riding and military boots and for men's daytime shoes. It is a tough, stiff, scuff-resisting, long-wearing leather with very fine pores, so fine that it is almost airtight. Genuine cordovan is expensive; it is frequently imitated in less durable leathers. Suede kangaroo leather, called kangaroo buck, is used for men's shoes because of its strength and durability. Patent leather is sometimes used for pumps for formal wear.

Fabrics used in men's shoes include canvas, gabardine, linen, mesh, and plastic-coated fabrics. The other materials used are similar to those used in women's shoes.

Construction

One of the most popular constructions in men's shoes is the welt construction used in the better grade of shoes. The nailed construction is used extensively in making men's work shoes. The stitchdown process is used for some shoes. The parts of men's shoes are similar in name to those of women's shoes, and many of the steps in construction resemble the steps in the construction of women's shoes. The tip, a separate piece of material covering the toe section of the vamp, is common in the oxford type of shoe for men. Many advertisements of men's shoes emphasize important construction features, such as oak bend leather soles, welts as in hand-sewn shoes, hand lasting over combination lasts, leather insoles, top-grain leather uppers, full linings of natural calf, and rubber heels. The soles of men's shoes are usually from nine to twelve irons in thickness.

Sizes

In length, sizes for men's shoes range from 5 or 6 to 12 or 13, with half sizes. The average size is from 8 to 13. In width, men's sizes usually range from AAA to EE, where AAA is the narrowest. The average range is from B to E. Sometimes numbers as well as letters are used to indicate size, 8½ C, for example, 8½ length and C width. In another notation, a zero following the key figure indicates a full size and the numeral 5 a half size; 70 here would mean size 7 and 75, size 7½. Width may also be indicated by numbers: thus, 00 is AAA; 0, AA; 1, A; 2, B; 3, C; 4, D; 5, E; and 6, EE.

Under this system 070 means 7AA, and 375 would stand for 7½C. In some shoes, widths are also indicated by narrow (N), medium (M), and wide (W). Proper fit is just as important in men's shoes as in women's, and the same care should be taken in measuring and fitting.

Shoes for the occasion

In addition to the different types of shoes, there are shoes for different occasions in men's wear. Opera pumps of patent leather are worn with formal evening wear and also with semi-formal evening costume in town or in the country. For weddings and other formal daylight affairs where a cutaway is worn, plain-tip calf or patent leather shoes are appropriate. For travel in cold weather and at a resort, stout brogues are comfortable; moccasins or sandals are ideal for warm climates. Moccasins or loafers are good for the country or a cruise. Buckskin oxfords, loafers, and chukka boots are popular for casual and campus wear. Plain-tip or wing-tip bluchers or bals serve for business and informal social affairs. The tassel slip-on shoes with diamond-panel hose are for casual clothes. Plain-toe bluchers with argyle socks go with tweeds. Wing-tip shoes with dark-ribbed hose are for dressier occasions. Straight-tip shoes and hose with diamond patterns brighten casual outfits. There should be as much co-ordination of the shoes with the style and the fabric of the rest of the outfit in men's clothing as there is in women's clothing.

Care

The care of men's shoes is similar to that of women's shoes. Emphasis should be placed on frequent care and on the need for extra pairs to provide a rest period for shoes that tend to be worn daily. The hurried use of the old shoe brush once a week is inadequate.

Shoe Terms

Ankle. The joint between the foot and the leg bones.

Bal. (Balmoral.) A tie shoe with the tongue of the shoe stitched to the vamp.

Ball. The widest and fleshiest part of the foot, at the base of the toes.

Blucher. A tie shoe in which the tongue is a part of the vamp.

Clogs. Thick, heavy-looking soles (often wood) used in shoes for beach wear and play use.

Counter. A stiffening of leather or other material inserted at the back of the shoe above the heel.

Crepe sole. A thick, spongy-looking rubber sole used on heavy oxfords and play shoes.

D'Orsay. A pump with a V-cut top side line.

Espadrilles. Play shoes with thick rope soles and fabric uppers.

Everett slipper. A shoe shaped like a pump, with a protruding tongue covering the instep.

Galoshes. Also called *arctics,* a kind of protective footwear usually worn over the shoes; made of rubber, plastic, or fabric and closed with snap or slide fasteners; may have genuine or imitation fur trim.

Ghillies. Low-cut shoes fastened by means of long laces that tie around the ankle.

Heel. The part of the foot directly behind the arch and below the ankle; the corresponding part of the shoe.

Heels. *See illustration.*

Huaraches. Uppers of strips of leather braided or woven together and stitched or laced to the sole.

Insole. The piece of leather on the bottom of the inside of the shoe.

Instep. The top of the arched part of the foot directly in front of the ankle.

Jodhpur. A low-cut riding boot.

Last. The wooden form over which the shoe is formed.

Loafer. A low-cut, heavy-soled shoe with a U-shaped vamp topped with a wide strap.

Longitudinal arch. The bridge-like elevation of the foot from the base of the heel to the base of the large toe (inner) or from the base of the heel to the base of the small toe (outer).

Mary Jane or **party shoe.** A flat-heeled, broad-toed plain sandal with a single strap across the instep.

Metatarsal arch. The so-called arch across the bottom of the ball of the foot.

Moccasin. A shoe with a one-piece vamp with attached circular tongue.

Mules. Backless slippers that cover just the top of the toes, usually with high heels; some dress shoes are very similar in design.

Open-shank sandal. A sandal with the sides cut out to the sole.

Opera pump. A classic plain pump, with no cut-outs, bows, or other fancy trim.

Opera slipper. A shoe shaped like a pump but cut low on the side.

Outsole. The heavy bottom part of the sole.

Platform sole. A built-up sole of cork or wood with an attached leather outsole.

Quarter. The part of the shoe's uppers that covers the counter.

Rubbers. A *toe rubber* covers only the toe part of the shoe; there is a back strap to hold the rubber on the heel. *Storm rubbers* have a tongue that covers the instep.

Shank. The part of the shoe sole under the arch of the foot from the heel to the ball.

Slippers. Shoes for indoor wear. (See *Everett, Mules,* and *Opera slipper.*)

Sneakers. Laced canvas shoes with rubber soles.

Toe box. A piece of stiff or soft leather or other material inserted between the toe cap and the lining of the shoe.

Toe cap or **tip.** That piece of the uppers covering the toe of the shoe.

Transverse arch. The highest arch of the foot, under the instep, measured across the width of the foot.

T-strap sandal. A sandal in which a strap comes up the instep to meet a regular strap coming up from the sides, the two straps together somewhat resembling the shape of the letter T.

Vamp. The forepart of the shoe uppers.

Waist. The portion of the foot about halfway between the instep and the ball.

CHILDREN'S SHOES

It has been pointed out that no item of apparel should be more carefully selected than a pair of shoes. This is especially true of children's shoes, since a tight, short shoe can warp a tiny foot beyond repair.

Until the child is about nine months old, a very soft shoe that offers some warmth and is amply large is all that should be used. As soon as the infant can stand, he should have a pair of shoes with semi-hard soles. A good choice is a supple leather shoe that provides flexibility and free movement, yet has a firm heel counter to hold the heel bone straight. The instep should be loose enough to permit free blood circulation. As soon as the child starts running about, he should have shoes with thin lifts or spring heels of about one fourth to three eighths of an inch. Up to the age of six, the heel should not exceed a half inch in height; after that it can be increased gradually to an inch. There is little difference between the shoes of boys and girls from two to five years of age. The soles should be stiffer than those of the first shoes but still flexible, the uppers pliable, the inside line straight, and the heels low or built in under the sole.

The advantages of the high-top shoe over that with low-cut uppers are that it helps prevent slipping on the heel, which is not fully formed, and that it offers more support and some protection from the weather. Plain oxfords or other lace shoes are usually used for boys and girls. Sometimes a single- or double-strap shoe is used for girls.

Since children's feet grow very rapidly from one to fifteen years of age, constant checks should be made on whether a child has outgrown his shoes, at least every four to eight weeks for children up to five years and every two to four months for children over five. Improperly fitted and poorly made shoes prevent the normal development of the bones; toes become bent and twisted; and the child's participation in activities is hindered. If a child's shoes hurt him, he will usually take them off whenever possible. Checking to see if the toe is against the end of the shoes is one method of checking the fit of shoes. With a stiff toe cap this is difficult, but the toe prints inside the shoe show how close the toes are to the end of the shoe. Shoes that are outgrown but not worn out are often handed from one child to another in a family. This is an unwise practice, because the hand-downs may force a child's soft, delicate bones into the foot shape of the first wearer, and usually the shoe does not properly fit the second wearer for length and width and causes strain and discomfort, and sometimes even permanent damage.

Walkers

Oxfords

Snap-
locks

Loafers

Sneakers

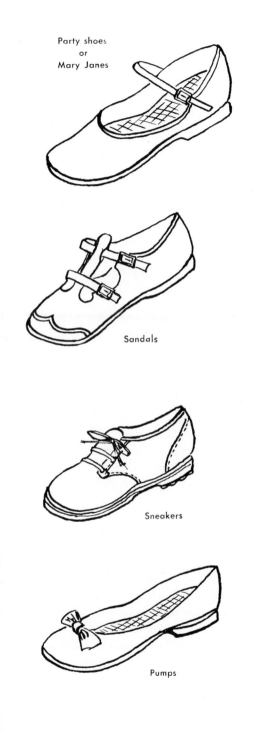

Party shoes
or
Mary Janes

Sandals

Sneakers

Pumps

Types of shoes

Choosing the best type of shoes for their children is a major concern for many parents. Typical children's shoes include *oxfords* (plain, wing tip, and moccasin tip), *Mary Janes, loafers,* and *sneakers.* For everyday wear, shoes made with flexible leather soles, supple leather uppers, a firm counter, and a rigid shank are recommended by specialists. This type of shoe provides for foot motion, freedom for the toes, and support for the heel bone and the longitudinal arch. There is a wide and attractive variety of children's shoes for everyday wear, shoes that wear well and are comfortable. Children as well as adults like a shoe wardrobe, so that other types of shoes for special occasions are often requested. Little girls like dress-up or ballet shoes, which may not be as practical in wear as their everyday shoes. The high-heel shoe for girls is frequently desired early. While no harm will result from wearing high heels for a few hours at a time on dress occasions, it is not advisable for a girl to wear heels all day until her feet are fully developed, and even then a frequent change is recommended. Sneakers for both boys and girls are very good for active sports, but they are objectionable for constant wear, especially during hot weather when feet perspire more freely. Any child who wears sneakers all day and on hard surfaces may be in for trouble. Sneakers should be fitted as carefully as other shoes. Loafers and high-heeled cowboy boots are all right for short periods of time but not for all-day-long wear. Some people buy shoes of medium quality for children, thinking they get full value for their money since the child is likely to wear out one pair of shoes by the time he is ready for a larger size. This is a poor practice, because shoes of lesser quality do not hold their shape and give as good support as those of better quality.

At some time during the life of almost every child there is a period of going barefoot. Walking or running barefoot on a sandy beach or a well-kept lawn, where the whole foot is subjected to different stress is not harmful; hardwood floors, cement sidewalks, and asphalt playgrounds, however, provide such a uniformly flat surface that the step becomes strained by the full weight of the body falling on the same areas of the foot, unless the foot is supported by a properly fitted and constructed shoe.

Fitting

The actual fitting should be done by an expert shoe fitter in a store, one who understands foot structure and the growth of children's feet. The shoe should be fitted for length, width, and foot action to the arch and over the instep. As with adults, both feet should be measured and then the longer foot fitted. One should never buy shoes by the size of the previous pair. The shoe should be one half to three fourths of an inch longer than the end of the longest toe. The toe box should be rounded in width and height to give room for toe movement. The heel should fit snugly and offer firm support. The child should not decide upon the size. A good shoe fitter can usually be relied upon to determine the correct size and type of shoe for a child. If properly fitted, shoes should not require a breaking-in period; however, the first wearings should be limited to allow the new shoe to become fully flexible and supple. The usual size ranges are infants 0–6; babies 6½–8, children 8½–13½, youths 12½–3, boys 3–6, and growing girls 3½–10.

Even with carefully selected shoes, some children develop foot problems. It is wise to let a doctor determine the seriousness and recommend treatment. If corrective shoes or shoes with special features are needed, it is better to follow the advice of a doctor than to make a selection from the great numbers available.

Construction

Methods of construction of children's shoes include some of those used for adults'. Both girls' and boys' shoes are made with the welt construction, especially the oxford type. The single-sole stitchdown shoes are designed for infants, with the two- and three-sole stitchdowns being made extensively in children's sizes. In low-priced shoes for boys and girls, composition or rubber soles give longer service than will cheap leather soles. Metal plates for heels and tips of shoes help prevent those parts from wearing down.

Children's shoes are made of calf, kip, or elk-tanned cowhide leather. Calf is most expensive and most desirable, but kip and elk are very satisfactory. Patent leather is usually used for girls' Mary Jane shoes.

Care

The care of children's shoes is similar to that of adults'. The directions for care given by the shoe salesman should be followed. Keeping shoes in good repair is especially important with children's shoes so that the original shape is maintained and the shoes continue to give adequate support.

REFERENCE READINGS

Books
Bacharach, Bert, *Right Dress,* A. S. Barnes, New York, 1955.

Evans, Mary, *Better Clothes for Your Money.* J. B. Lippincott Co., Philadelphia, 1952.

Pareti, John J., Jr. *How to Sell Footwear Profitably.* Fairchild Publications, Inc., New York, 1967.

Wilcox, Ruth Turner, *The Mode in Footwear,* Charles Scribner's Sons, New York, 1948.

Wingate, Isabel B., Gillespie, Karen R., and Addison, Betty, *Know Your Merchandise,* 3rd Ed., McGraw-Hill, New York, 1964.

Bulletins
Better Buymanship #5, *Shoes,* Household Finance Corporation, Chicago, 1948.

Dollnig, Berneice, *How to Buy Shoes—Hidden Values,* Consumer Education Division, Sears, Roebuck & Co., Chicago.

Herbst Shoe Manufacturing Co., *Shoe Facts and Foot Care for Children's Feet,* Herbst Shoe, New York.

Leather Industries of America, *Leather in Our Lives,* New York, 1959.

National Shoe Manufacturers Association, *Facts and Figures on Footwear,* New York, 1958.

Research Bureau for Retail Training, *Merchandise Facts to Help You Sell Shoes,* University of Pittsburgh.

United Shoe Machinery Corporation, *How American Shoes Are Made,* Boston, 1961.

Chapter 20

Gloves, other accessories, and luggage

Gloves have been an important accessory of dress since early times. Like the early foot coverings, the first hand coverings were crude, probably animal skins covering the hands to keep them warm and to protect them from scratches, bruises, and cuts. The word glove is thought to be derived from the old Saxon word *glof*, meaning to hide or to cover. Through the years, gloves became symbols of love, loyalty, friendship, security, high honor and integrity, hatred, defiance, and challenge.

WOMEN'S GLOVES

Gloves are now considered the finishing touch of the costume. In some sections of the country, custom rules on the propriety of wearing gloves, especially for formal wear, other social occasions, and religious activities. Gloves matching, contrasting, or harmonizing in color and material with suit, bag, or shoes lend beauty to an outfit.

Gloves also provide protection and warmth; they seem to be popular with all age groups. Fashion affects color, design, and material in gloves just as it does in other items of apparel. Bright colors may be popular one season, only to be succeeded by neutral tones the next. In choosing colors, one should consider the effect they may give to the costume, to the apparent size of the hands, and the relationship to the size of the individual. Bright or light colors can lend a spotty effect, make hands seem larger, and draw attention to the hipline when the arms are held at the sides. Gloves of low or medium color value and closely harmonizing colors are usually in good taste.

Since the climate is different in various sections of the country, comfort should be considered. Many fabric gloves are cooler than leather gloves in warm weather; knitted woolen gloves or mittens and fully- or skeleton-lined leather gloves are ideal for cold weather.

Glove styles

Glove styles seem to be endless in number, but they are all designed from a few basic types based on "button length." Regardless of the presence or absence of buttons, the term is used in the trade to indicate length. Each "button" is a French inch, about one twelfth of an inch larger than the standard inch. Length is measured from the base of the thumb to the top of the glove; a one-button glove is approximately one inch in length from the thumb. A twelve-button glove, about thirteen inches in length, is approximately elbow length.

The *button* or *clasp glove* is of short or medium length with a button or other fastener at the wrist, either on the palm side or on the back of the glove. The *cadet*

(Opposite) Styles in women's gloves.

344

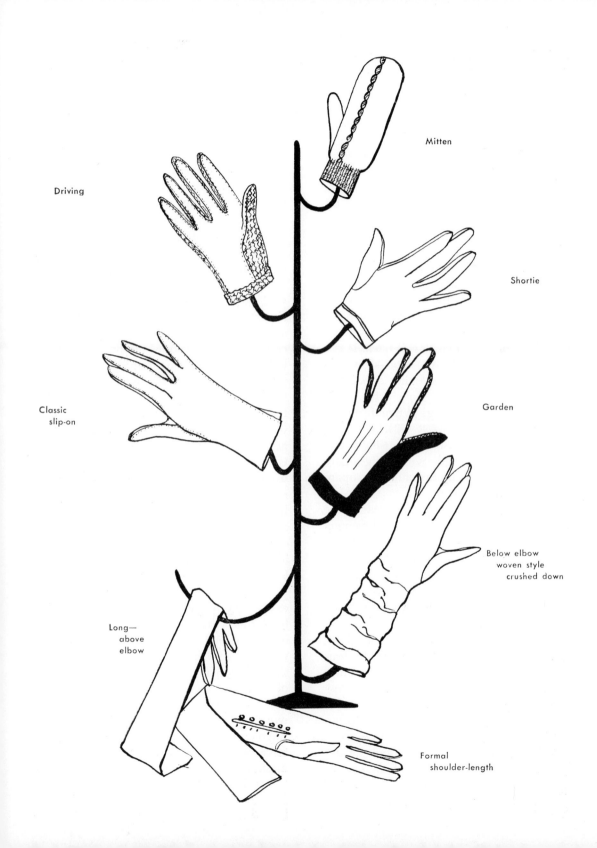

Mitten

Driving

Shortie

Garden

Classic
slip-on

Below elbow
woven style
crushed down

Long—
above
elbow

Formal
shoulder-length

glove is made to fit the hand of regular width but with shorter than average fingers. The *finger-free glove* has a strip of leather or fabric extending around both sides and around the end of each finger; there is no seam at the tip. The *gauntlet* is a four- or six-button slip-on glove with a flared top obtained by the insertion of a separate triangle-shaped gore above the wrist. The *mitten*, which presumably preceded the fingered glove, has one section for the thumb and another larger one for the fingers and hand. The mitten is used mainly for warmth in casual dress or sportswear. The *mousquetaire* (a term seldom used now) is a long glove—eight to twenty buttons—with an opening at the wrist. This allows the hand to be put out through the placket and the fingers of the glove to roll back. It is a dressy glove worn with short-sleeve or sleeveless afternoon or evening dress. The *shorty* is a wrist-length glove with either a side or center opening. When fastened, it is fastened at the wrist with a button, clasp, or strap. The *slip-on* is usually two to four buttons in length, with a slight flare above the wrist but no fastenings or openings; it is just slipped on.

One novel style for evening wear is the two-piece glove, where the short glove may be removed and the arm section left on the arm. Novelty gloves are made with unusual combinations of material, trimmings, or cuffs; they are often made of the same fabric as the dress with which they are to be worn.

Fasteners used on gloves include buckles, buttons, clasps, and slide fasteners. Buttonholes are costly to make and sometimes stretch and tear. Clasps may pull out unless the fabric or the leather is well reinforced with stays. Slide fasteners are very satisfactory in some types of gloves or mittens.

In choosing gloves, one may look for design, color, material, comfortable fit, ease of care, price, and suitability to oneself, one's wardrobe, and the occasion for which the gloves will be worn. The emphasis placed on any one of these factors will vary with individual tastes and needs.

Materials

Some consumers stress materials, many preferring leather to fabric for all gloves; others, again, buy more fabric gloves. For warm weather, gloves of woven or knitted fabric are popular; they are also less expensive than leather gloves. Woven materials like gingham, organdy, and piqué must be well constructed and closely woven to prevent pulled seams. Moderately priced fabric gloves for nearly all occasions are available. Fabrics commonly used include cotton, crochet, piqué, meshes, and string knit; there are also double-woven gloves with a soft, suedelike finish, resembling fine doeskin in appearance. Although the term double-woven is used, the fabric is not woven but knitted so that the fabric looks alike on both sides. Double-woven material is considered the best-wearing of all fabrics used in gloves; it is long lasting and sturdy, retains its shape, and usually shrinks very little in washing. It may be made of cotton, rayon or nylon and the surface may be flat or sueded. Single-woven fabric is similar in appearance but less firm and will not last as long as double-woven fabric.

String gloves in nylon or Orlon launder easily, dry quickly, shrink very little, and hold their shape. Nylon and Dacron are used in stretch gloves, which have the advantage of fitting several different hand sizes. Nylon is popular in gloves because of its appearance and easy care; it is available in tricot, meshes, velvets, double-woven fabrics, and simulations of leather. Rayon gloves, which are comfortable, easy-to-clean, and colorful, are available in knits, meshes, nets, suede-finish fabrics, and velvet. Wool gloves range from sheer wool gloves to heavy woolen knits for cold weather and sportswear. Combinations of fabrics offer interesting variety. Knit and tricot palms have been combined with backs of woven fabric like shantung, broadcloth, or piqué. Knitted palms provide better fit and help eliminate splitting of seams, which may occur in woven-fabric gloves.

There are two types of finish used on knitted fabrics: the calendar finish, in which the material is rolled and pressed to a softness resembling the doeskin finish used on leather; and the suede finish, where the surface of the material is lightly brushed to resemble sueded leather. Angora mittens or gloves are included in the knitwear group; they are often worn by college students for dressy winter wear. Leather trim is sometimes used on fabric gloves and mittens. Leather-faced fabric gloves are warm and comfortable gloves for driving. Fur and fur-lined gloves are popular in cold weather for driving, sports, and outdoor work.

Some of the leathers discussed earlier are used in glove manufacturing. Glove leathers must be comfortable and durable, yet soft, supple, and easy to care for. Fine leather has body even if it is thin and feels soft, supple, and lively. Less desirable leather may be paper-thin or stiff and boardlike, and it feels dead. Thickness is not necessarily an indication of strength. Leathers usually used include cabretta, calfskin, capeskin, chamois, doeskin-finished lambskin, goatskin, kidskin, lambskin, mocha, and pigskin. The more sturdy leathers are calfskin, capeskin, goatskin, and pigskin.

Here, as with leather for shoes and other accessories, type and quality are determined by the type of animal skin used, the tanning and dyeing processes, and the type of finish. Generally, the coarser the hair, the finer the skin, and the finer the hair, the

coarser the skin. Consequently the skins of hair sheep often make better glove leather than those of the fine domestic wool sheep. Chrome- and oil-tanned leather is made into soft, durable, washable gloves. Chrome tanning is applied to calfskin, kidskin, and sheepskin. Oil tanning is used for light, natural-color leathers like buckskin and chamois. White washable glove leathers are tanned with formaldehyde. Doeskin is tanned by this method or the chrome process. Alum-tanned leathers are sometimes given another tanning by the chrome process to improve washability. Glove leathers are either brush dyed or dip dyed. In brush dyeing, the surface of the leather is dyed; the inside of the glove remains white or cream colored; and the color of the gloves does not rub off on the hands. Heavier leathers are usually dip dyed, so that the dye penetrates the entire skin. Crocking, the transfer of color to the hand when the hand perspires, may occur with dip-dyed gloves. In dark gloves that have been brush-dyed, parts of the glove that receive considerable abrasion, such as the fingertips, may show a slight grayness. High-quality black gloves seldom lose their color. In gloves made with outseams, the white edges of brush-dyed leather will show. Sometimes these are colored after the glove is made. In some dip-dyed leathers it is possible to shave off a thin layer to leave the white surface on the inside. Dark colors and bright colors are not always guaranteed to be colorfast to light, washing, or dry cleaning.

Leather finishing and staking. Two types of finishes are used for glove leathers, called smooth, glacé, or grain finish, and nap, degrained, sueded, or velvet finish. The smooth finish is obtained by polishing the grain or outside of skins like cabretta, capeskin, and pigskin. Blemishes or defects are easily noticed on this shiny surface, so only the nearly perfect skins are finished

Glove Leathers

Cabretta. From the hair sheep of Brazil, thought to be a cross between a goat and a sheep. The leather has a glacé finish, is very durable, and is tanned for washability; it resembles kid and is often sold as capeskin.

Calfskin. From young calves from Poland, Russia, and the United States; it has tight, even grain and is smooth, glossy, and supple. It is little used except for imitation pigskin; may be given a velvet finish. It is made into a durable, washable glove.

Capeskin. Originally, from the hair sheep of South Africa, shipped from Cape Town. Now loosely used to mean any dip-dyed sheepskin with a grain finish. Genuine capeskin is light, flexible, and very durable; it has firm, fine grain, is tough and resistant to wear, and feels glossy and slippery when rubbed with the fingers. It dyes well in many colors by dip or brush method and can be tanned washable. The skins of South African, French, Spanish, and Oriental wool sheep closely resemble those of the hair sheep.

Chamois. Originally, from the chamois, a species of antelope; the term now applies also to a split sheepskin leather dyed yellow.

Doeskin. Originally, the skin of a young antelope or female deer; now loosely applied to sheepskin or lambskin finished to look like it, which should be labeled as doeskin-finished lambskin. There is American, English, and French doeskin, depending upon the country of origin and the method of tanning. The grain leather is shaved off the body of the hide and applied to a fine emery wheel to produce a soft, pliable, velvety nap finish, making a porous, absorbent, serviceable leather.

Goatskin. A soft, supple, and durable leather from India, Europe, Africa, and South America; usually washable, it is used for sportswear gloves. The grain is fine and tight, with a pebble pattern giving the effect of circles. It has high gloss.

Kidskin. Obtained from very young milk-fed goats from Belgium, France, and Italy. The baby goats are carefully raised and guarded against bruises and scratches to produce smooth, perfect skins for making fine-grain, glacé-finished gloves. When the leather is brush dyed, the insides of the gloves remain white. Some kidskin gloves are tanned for washability. The term is often erroneously applied to glacé-finished lambskin or sheepskin. Kidskin gloves are lightweight, thin, and flexible, with fine, tight grain.

Lambskin. From young sheep—not baby lambs—from the Balkans, France, Germany, and Italy. The leather is fine, lightweight, and pliable, with smooth, thin grain; it resembles kidskin but is not as fine, resilient, or durable. The same method of tanning is used as with kidskin. Domestic lambskin has also been used for gloves and may be sueded as well as glacé finished.

Mocha. From the hairy blackhead sheep of Arabia and northeastern Africa, named after the town in Arabia from which the first skins were brought; a nap finish is given to the grain side of the skin. Mocha is generally used in full thickness and finished with the grain side out, called frizzed. After the thin grain is soaked and scraped off, the grain side is buffed. The result is a strong, close-grained, velvet finish, usually heavier than suede and with finer, closer nap. Goatskins can be tanned to resemble mocha but lack the velvety feel of real mocha. Mocha is often used for lined gloves. The leather can be dip dyed or brush dyed and can be tanned for washability.

Pigskin. Obtained from wild hogs from Mexico and Central and South America, including the carpincho and the peccary. The leather is soft, strong, and rugged and carries the markings of bristle holes, scars, and scratches. Imitation pigskin is made from other leathers by embossing bristle holes by machine. Genuine pigskin is usually so labeled. The Mexican peccary seems to furnish the finest leather for gloves. Genuine pigskin is washable. Pigskin gloves are used for casual wear, driving, and sportswear.

Suede. A nap finish given to the flesh side of any leather. The finish is named after Sweden, where it originated. For gloves, kidskin, lambskin, and sheepskin are usually used. Suedes are used for formal daytime and evening wear. They are often brush dyed and are seldom washable.

this way. The term glacé is applied to the bright, shiny finish of kid and lambskin. The nap finish is obtained by buffing the leather against an emery wheel to give a soft finish. Degrained leather has the top grain, the hair side of the leather, shaved or skinned off, leaving plump, fleshy, porous leather. Mocha leather and imported doeskin are nap-finished on the grain side. Suede is a nap finish given to the flesh side of the skin, as in doeskin-finished lambskin. Gloves with this velvet-like finish are luxurious in appearance and texture but tend to wear shiny and collect soil easily. Since skins vary in thickness from the heavier parts on the back of the animal to the thinner parts at the sides and belly, all tanned skins have to be leveled off on the flesh side to an even thickness. Some skins are still too thick for glove leather after leveling. They are then split. A very thin layer of the grain, a *skiver*, results from the first split. The undersplit, from which chamois leather is produced, is called a flesher. Some splits and fleshers make tough, sturdy glove leather. When the grain side of the leather is to be worn next to the hand, the grain usually is removed by splitting or buffing so the glove will feel soft but not slippery.

After tanning, dyeing, and finishing, the leathers used for gloves go through yet other operations. Staking is done by machine or by hand; in this operation, the leather is stretched to exactly the point at which it will retain the proper amount of pliability and resiliency. Machine staking is used on heavy grain leathers. Hand staking, which is done on lightweight leathers, involves a slow, careful drawing of the leather back and forth across a large, convex, dulled blade until every inch of the leather has been stretched. *Doling* means shaving the leather to a uniform thickness over rollers equipped with fine blades. If this process is done over emery wheels instead of fine knives, it is called wheeling.

Construction

Workmanship and method of construction affect the appearance, fit, and wear of the gloves. Some gloves are completely handmade while others are hand guided on machines for some operations. Deciding how many pairs of gloves can be cut from one skin, called *taxing*, is the first operation before cutting. Among the fifty or more operations involved in making a pair of gloves, cutting is one of those requiring the greatest amount of skill. The three methods of cutting gloves are known as table, pattern, and block cutting.

The finest gloves are *table cut,* which means that each piece of leather for each glove is dampened slightly and then pulled and stretched by hand to insure just the proper amount of stretch. Each piece is cut with shears according to accurate measurements made with a French rule, and each pair of gloves is cut from the same piece of leather. Table-cut gloves are usually marked by the glovers guild symbol or by the words Table Cut stamped on the inside.

In the *pattern-cut* or *pull-down-cut* method, the whole leather is stretched in the opposite direction from which the glove is to be taken. Pattern impressions for glove pieces are made by tracing cards, and the body of the glove is cut roughly around them. Then these pieces are pulled down or stretched to fit the glove pattern and are put into piles and cut by a machine operated with a weighted, sharp steel die. This method is less expensive than table cutting and is used by many volume manufacturers.

Block or *die cutting* is used on heavy leathers that cannot be cut by hand. Singly or in piles, the leathers are placed under a machine-driven sharp die that stamps out the pattern from the whole piece of leather, a process somewhat like cutting cookies with a cookie cutter. Scars or cuts on the leather can seldom be avoided with this method as they can in table cutting.

The parts of the glove

The parts of the glove cut by these methods include the trank, thumb, fourchettes or forks, and quirks or gussets. The *trank* is the general outline that forms the palm, back, and fingers of the glove. Before the fingers are slit, it resembles an oblong. The next step is finger slitting, in which the trank is cut for the fingers and the hole for the

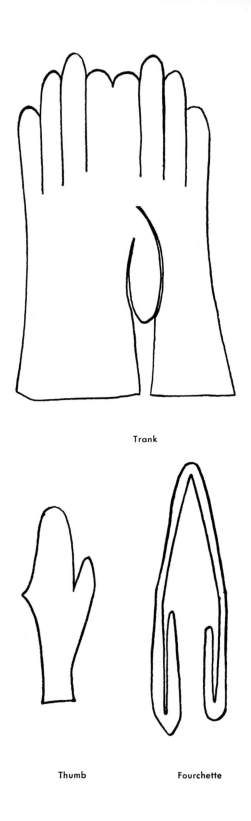

Trank

Thumb   Fourchette

thumb; the tiny triangles called *quirks* are also cut from the trank in this step. The *thumb* is made from a separate piece of material and is later stitched into the hole cut for it in the trank. *Fourchettes* are small oblong pieces used as side pieces between the front and back finger sections of the trank, providing ample space for finger width. *Gussets* or quirks are used at the base of some fourchettes and thumbs.

After the parts of the glove are cut, decorative stitching, called *pointing*, is done on the back of the tranks of some gloves. The traditional three rows of stitching have given way to many designs of stitching and tucks. Points tend to make the hand appear long and slender. Decorative stitching dates back to the leather gloves made in several sections, with seams or lacings on the back. Beads, braid, contrasting color thread and other materials are either hand or machine stitched. Gloves are trimmed in various ways; they may be made of combinations of leathers with different finishes and with two-toned contrasts; buttons, slide fasteners, and buckles; appliqués and bows; scalloped edges and hand-rolled hems; lacings, cordings, and pipings; and perforations and embroidery.

Seams

The various methods of closing the glove are determining factors in quality. Most of the sewing is done by machine. Gloves requiring hand sewing are usually sent to Puerto Rico after cutting, where they are expertly sewed; when finished, they are shipped back to this country.

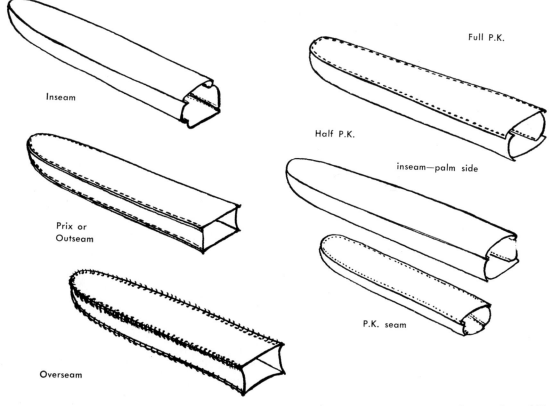

Inseam

Prix or Outseam

Overseam

Full P.K.

Half P.K.

inseam—palm side

P.K. seam

The size of the thread should correspond to the weight of the material. The stitches should be small, regularly spaced, and at the same distance from the edge through-

English or Bolton thumb.

out. Lockstitching is done with two separate threads looped into a single stitch, with one thread showing on top and one underneath. In chainstitching, which makes a more elastic seam than lockstitching, each stitch consists of a loop on the underside and a single thread on top.

The *inseam* is made by stitching the seam on the wrong side of the glove and then turning the glove inside out so that no stitching is visible. This seam is the least expensive and the easiest to make. It is used on some inexpensive leather gloves and on some fabric gloves.

The *outseam*, also called Prixseam or P.X.M. seam, is made with cut edges on the outside, the threads going through them as in a flat seam. Sometimes these seams are handsewn to resemble saddle stitching. Since the fingers are bulkier in appearance with this seam, it is usually used only on men's gloves or on sportswear gloves for women.

The *overseam*, or round seam, is one in which two raw edges are placed together on the outside of the glove and are either sewed over and over by hand or whipstitched by machine. A very fine seam results that is attractive and desirable for dressy gloves. However, the seam is not as durable as other seams since a very narrow strip of leather is caught in the seam. The *osann* stitch is a coarse machine-made overseam stitch used decoratively in medium-priced heavy sport gloves.

The *Piqué*, or P.K. or lap seam, is flat and is made by lapping one edge over the other, the sewing being done so that one raw edge shows. This is considered the most durable seam for street and dress gloves. This is the most difficult seam to make in glove closing and is usually used on expensive gloves of good quality. With the half P.K. or half-inseam seam, the fingers are piqué-sewn on

French thumb.

the backs and inseam-finished on the palm side. It is used on medium-priced gloves. The *tyseam* or tystitch is a machine stitch that simulates a hand-sewn stitch.

There are various methods of cutting and inserting the thumb, including the English, French, set-in, insert, and reverse thumb.

In the *English* or *Bolton thumb,* the thumb and its quirk are cut in one piece; it is one of the strongest and best-fitting constructions.

The *French thumb* is made with a thumb quirk, a small triangular piece inserted at the base or arch of the thumb.

The *set-in thumb* is made of one piece without a quirk and set in a round hole cut in the trank of the glove.

The *insert thumb,* cut in one piece without a quirk, differs from the set-in thumb in that it has no seam at its base but extends all the way to the cuff of the glove.

The *reverse thumb* is flat and does not turn into the palm, making it possible for the glove to be reversed and worn on either the right or the left hand.

After the gloves are stitched, they require shaping, known as laying off. The gloves are dampened and then slipped on metal hands the exact size and cut of the glove. These metal forms are heated by steam or electricity and the glove is perfectly shaped on them. At this stage, some manufacturers give the gloves another napping or polishing. Grooves along the sides of the fingers permit the fourchettes to be folded in like bellows. After a final inspection, the gloves are wrapped in tissue ready for shipment.

Fabric and lined gloves

Some of the construction methods used on leather gloves are used also in making fabric gloves. Tranks of fabric are cut and placed in exact piles, and the glove is pattern die cut by a knife-edge glove die forced through the entire pile of tranks. The

Set-in thumb.

Kip seam often used on fabric gloves is similar to the half-piqué seam for leather gloves, where the lap or piqué seam is used on the top of the glove and the inseam on the palm side. A full inseam is used on inexpensive fabric gloves. The full piqué seam is used on fabrics not subject to excessive fraying. The laying-off or shaping process for fabric gloves is the same as that for leather gloves.

When gloves are lined for extra durability, warmth, and protection, the linings are made of knitted wool, cotton, rayon, silk, and sueded fabrics and leather, fur, and shearling. Wool linings are of two types. The seamless is knit as a separate glove and inserted into a finished outer glove and attached or left free so that it may be worn separately. The second type is made from a knit wool tubing, die cut and sewed to the size of the glove and inserted and attached.

Other fabric linings are often pasted onto the leather trank and dried before the die is cut; then the lining and glove are sewed in one operation. Leather-lined gloves are lined with a very lightweight, nap-finished leather applied with an adhesive to the outer leather glove, and the two layers are cut and sewed as one. Furs used for linings include mole, rabbit, and squirrel. Knitted fourchettes are used with the fur to reduce the bulk. Fur-lined gloves are seldom warmer than others, because the fluffy fur, which usually holds a layer of air, is matted flat as the glove is worn. The shearling linings, made of lambskin with the short wool left on, are often tanned and dyed to simulate furs. In skeleton linings, the sides of the fingers are open, with no fourchettes being used.

Insert thumb.

Knitted gloves and mittens continue to be popular in cold weather. They are made of Angora, cashmere, mohair, camel hair, wool, cotton, Dacron, nylon, and Orlon. They stretch and give with the movement of the hand and generally fit better than gloves of woven fabric. Knitted fabrics used for gloves are usually warp knit, made on either the tricot or the milanese knitting machines. Duplex gloves are made from two thicknesses of knitted material that are pasted together and then made up as a single fabric. Some of the gloves are knitted with a cotton or rayon outside while the inside is made of lamb's wool. Designs are drawn and transferred to knitting machines, which, properly set up, automatically knit plain or patterned gloves and mittens. After knitting, the mitten or glove is washed and then dried on a wooden frame the exact size and shape of the original pattern. A final brushing raises the soft nap to produce a fluffy, warm-looking glove or mitten.

Sizes

Size is determined when the trank is cut. Sizes in women's leather gloves range by quarter inches, while in fabric gloves the sizes range by half inches. Glove sizes range from 5½ to 8, with the average for women 6½. Lined gloves and mittens are small (5 or 6), medium (6½ or 7) and large (7½ or 8). For children sizes are generally marked as one half the child's age:

Age	1	2	4	6	8	10	12	14
Size	0	1	2	3	4	5	6	7

All glove manufacturers make the same range of sizes, but the cut of one make may vary from the cut of another. Although the wrong size in a glove is not harmful to health, it may cause annoyance, discomfort, and rapid wearing out. A glove that is too small is likely to wear at the seams and fingertips. When purchasing gloves, it is wise to have the right hand, which is usually larger, measured. This may not be true for a left-handed person. The measurement is taken around the knuckles, at the widest part of the hand, with a tape measure. If the measurement were 7 inches, the person would usually take a size smaller, or 6¾, in a leather glove, since the leather has enough give to provide adequate room for the hand. However, in washable doeskin gloves the customer would be wise to buy a size larger than usual to allow for shrinkage. Lined gloves should be bought a size larger than the hand measurement.

Before the glove is tried on for size, a good salesperson will ask the customer to double her hand and then stretch the back of the glove across the customer's knuckles to see if it will fit. The correct width will reach from the inside knuckle to the outside one. The length of the fingers of the glove is also important. A customer who has very long fingers or long, pointed fingernails may find it necessary to buy a larger size or to find a brand that has extra long fingers. The correct finger length may be checked by placing the tip of the middle finger of the glove at the base of the middle finger of the hand. The two measurements should be the same. If gloves are too short, they will rip easily between the fingers.

With a new glove being tried on for the first time, it may be necessary to put talcum powder on the glove. A new leather glove also has to be eased on, each finger being pushed on separately until the whole glove covers the hand and is smooth in appearance. Then the customer and the salesperson decide whether the fit of the glove is correct. An easy-fitting glove looks better than one that is too small, because a tight glove makes the hand appear larger. A glove that is too snug does not give maximum wear, because the strain may cause the stitches to break or to cut the leather. A glove with a loose fit has warmth in cold weather, with the layer of air between the glove and hand acting as insulation.

Care

Care is as important for gloves as it is for any other item of apparel, yet many people are very careless with their gloves. The care should begin with the proper method of putting on and removing gloves. One should follow the same method in putting on gloves that one used when trying them on before purchasing. In removing gloves, one should first loosen the fingertips by pulling them slightly, then turn the glove inside out and ease it off the hand. Then the glove is turned right side out, the fingers are straightened, and the glove is smoothed into its original shape and appearance. Proper fit is another feature that helps to keep the glove in good condition and prevents unnecessary strain on the glove.

Ring settings should be turned toward the palm to prevent strain on the top of the glove. When not being worn, the gloves should be placed in a glove guard attached to the lady's handbag or inside the bag. Gloves should be aired before being stored in a glove box or drawer, to allow the perspiration from the hands to evaporate.

Even if gloves are labeled washable, extreme care should be taken when washing and drying them. Gloves should not be allowed to become too soiled before washing, because the extra rubbing to remove the dirt may tear the gloves and rub off the color. Ripped seams should be repaired before the gloves are washed or dry-cleaned. If no directions for washing are given with the new gloves, it is best to use lukewarm, mild soap suds and wash the gloves either on the hands or on perforated glove forms. Chamois and doeskin gloves should not be washed on the hands. The suds should be squeezed and pressed through the leather with no rubbing. A soft brush may be used to remove spots. While the gloves are on the hands and under water, they should be rolled back from the wrist and slipped over the fingers so that the inside can be washed. After careful rinsing, excess moisture should be pressed out of the gloves by rolling them in a towel, starting at the fingertips. Blowing air into the gloves will help shape the fingers and prevent the leather from sticking together. Finally the gloves should be smoothed out, placed on glove forms or on a towel, and allowed to dry in a cool, shady place, never near heat or in the sun. When nearly dry, they should be finger-pressed to prevent the leather from becoming harsh and brittle. Gentle massaging with the fingers also causes the leather to absorb some of the natural oil from your fingers.

Nonwashable gloves should be dry-cleaned by a reliable dry cleaner. Leather gloves that have been dry-cleaned should not be washed. Some lined gloves and dark-colored ones should be dry-cleaned.

Wool gloves and mittens should be washed carefully before they are stored and then dried on frames or blocked. These as well as fur-lined gloves should be protected from moths with spray, crystals, or other effective repellent and then stored in airtight containers.

Fabric gloves are usually washed—off the hands—in lukewarm water and mild soap suds, avoiding friction and wringing. Water may be removed by rolling the gloves in a towel after rinsing. The gloves should be dried away from sunlight and extreme temperatures.

MEN'S GLOVES

Gloves are as indispensable for the well-dressed man as for a woman, yet many men fail to recognize the importance of gloves in their wardrobes. Warriors in the thirteenth century wore gloves of chain mail or scale or plate armor for protection during combat. Gloves were adopted by men of all classes in the fourteenth century. Following fashion and custom, delicate white or gray leather gloves are considered appropriate for formal day or semi-formal evening functions. For business and sportswear, sturdy leathers in darker colors are used. Men's gloves continue to be simple in style for all occasions.

Leathers

Many of the same leathers used for women's gloves are also used for men's gloves. Mocha was originally tanned for men's gloves because of its thickness and weight. Then the leathers were shaved to a fine thinness, finished in a nap or velvet finish, and used for women's gloves as well as for men's. Pigskin is a popular leather for men's gloves for casual wear and driving. Cabretta is used for men's dress gloves. Heavy capeskin is also used for men's gloves. Goatskin gloves are popular with men because they are of strong, sturdy, washable leather. Servicemen's gloves are made of goatskin, cabretta, or horsehide.

Buckskin, calfskin, deerskin, doeskin, and reindeer, imported in limited quantities from various countries, are also used. Men's gloves made from these leathers are coarse-grained, durable, heavy, pliable, warm, and washable.

Other materials

For work gloves, heavy canton flannel with the nap on the inside and the twill weave outside, double-thickness quilted canton flannel, leather-covered or leather-reinforced gloves, asbestos gloves, and waterproof rubber gloves are all common; the materials used depend on the specific end uses of the gloves. Linings include chamois, fur, and wool.

Construction

Of the constructions discussed in women's gloves, the outseam is very often used for men's gloves, especially on pigskin gloves. The *gauge-sewn* seam corresponds to the plain outseam in women's gloves. The triple stitch—two stitches forward and one back over—is a machine lockstitch, or ripproof stitch, that seldom ravels and is often used in men's gloves. The *osann* seam is also used frequently in men's gloves, as is the swagger stitch, which is similar to diagonal overcasting. Some gloves have a double side wall, which means that the fourchettes on the outer fingers extend to the wrist of the glove. The pointing or decorative stitching on the back is called *silking* in men's gloves.

While many gloves are table or pattern cut, the inexpensive lined glove for men is usually block cut.

Types of gloves

Men sometimes wear mittens for warmth in sportswear and for some outdoor work. The gauntlet glove seen in western films is used mostly by cowboys, who often use elaborate beading and fringes as decoration. This type of glove is worn also by some men in other sections of the country.

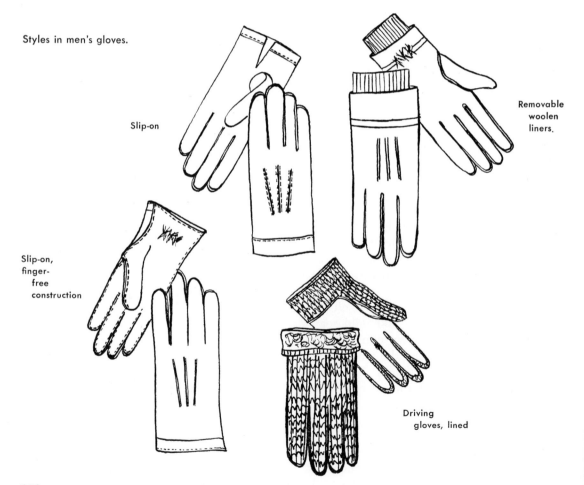

Styles in men's gloves.

Slip-on

Removable woolen liners.

Slip-on, finger-free construction

Driving gloves, lined

The cadet glove was originally made only for men and was eventually adapted for women.

The shorty glove, popular in men's wear, is usually called a clasp or pull-on glove. Like the women's shorty, it is wrist length and fastens with buttons, clasps, or straps at the side or center.

The slip-on glove with a flare opening or front vent is also common in men's gloves.

The work glove, or general utility glove, for men is a basic style made in various materials. It is usually made with a snug-fitting knitted cuff at the wrist. It is designed to keep the hands warm, clean, and protected. It is used by farmers, factory workers, mechanics, and men in similar occupations.

Size and color

Sizes in men's leather gloves range by quarter inches, and by half inches in fabric gloves, from 7 to 10, with 8½ as the average. Knitted gloves with leather palms are sized as small, medium, and large.

Colors in men's gloves are more limited than in women's gloves. They include natural, tan, brown, gray, cork, oatmeal, saddle, putty, red tan, black, buff, and white.

In selecting gloves, men tend to choose for comfort, fit, durability, price, material, style, and color. Although ease of care is important, few men are concerned with this. A few have definite preferences as to leather and style. More men need to recognize that gloves complete the outfit and that color and texture should match, contrast, or harmonize for the best in appearance.

Care

The care of men's gloves is similar to that of women's gloves, and so easy that men can take care of their own gloves. To wash washable gloves, rub damp white soap into the soiled parts and roll the gloves to allow the soap to soak in for a while; then turn the

Men's specialty gloves. From left to right: gauntlets, ski mittens, and work gloves.

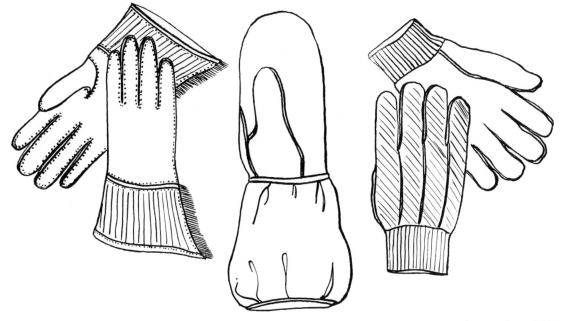

gloves inside out and rub them with soap, put the gloves on the hands, and wash them well in warm water; rinse them and roll them in a terry towel to remove excess moisture; reshape them; blow into each glove finger; and then allow them to dry away from direct heat. If a washable glove has been dry-cleaned it cannot be successfully washed again.

Gloves can be stretched if put on and taken off incorrectly. The fingers should be worked on one at a time and eased over the hand, especially with new gloves. The cuffs should be rolled over the palm and the fingers pulled gently when removing gloves. Gloves should not be stuffed in a topcoat pocket but folded neatly and placed in the inside breast pocket.

HANDBAGS

To men, a woman's handbag and its endless contents can be an amusing topic of conversation; but to the woman, it is one of the most essential accessories in her wardrobe. It is much more convenient, handy, comfortable, and attractive than it would be to have numerous pockets bulging with billfolds, cigarettes, combs, compacts, keys, letters, lipstick and numerous miscellaneous items. In addition to being a convenient container, a well-chosen handbag is a smart addition to a well-dressed woman's outfit. A good bag is a good investment.

Many women are very particular about their handbags in regard to color, texture, design, size and space, materials, construction and workmanship, convenience, ease of carrying, appropriateness to the individual and the occasion, and price. Bags are available for every costume, individual, occasion, and wardrobe. The silhouettes of the garments worn should help determine the size and the type of bag used.

A bag for everyday use should be large enough to hold the many items a woman carries without being out of proportion to the woman's size. The opening should be large enough to allow for the rummaging around women seem to do. The bag for less utilitarian use, designed for afternoon and evening, is more formal in appearance, due to the design, material, trimming, and, often, its smaller size.

Leather and other materials

Several of the leathers and other materials used for women's shoes are used also for handbags because shoes and handbag often form a matching set. Whenever handbag and shoe manufacturers co-operate in selecting colors and materials, customers can find matching bags and shoes to wear with some costumes.

Woven fabrics used for bags designed for afternoon and evening occasions often are less durable and less expensive than leather. Fabric bags are difficult to keep clean and require frequent cleaning, and those that cannot be cleaned easily entail rather expensive upkeep. Fabrics used for afternoon bags include bengaline, bouclé, broadcloth and cordé, crepe, faille, felt, gabardine, gingham, linen crash, metallic, moiré, petit point, piqué, taffeta, tapestry, and velvet. Evening bags are made of brocade, lamé, satin, or leather and decorated with beads, embroidery, marcasites, rhinestones, and sequins.

Various kinds of straws, natural and synthetic, are also used for bags; they are durable but often difficult to clean. Fur is sometimes used to match a hat or fur trim on clothes.

Plastic bags are popular in warm weather, being cool to carry, less expensive than leather, durable, easy to care for, and washable. The smooth plastics can be embossed to resemble leather. Some plastics are also used successfully for all-season bags.

Handbags for general wear are made of

alligator, buffalo, calfskin, capeskin, cow-hide, kipskin, crocodile, kid, morocco, ostrich, lizard, patent leather, pigskin, pin seal, sealskin, sharkskin, sheepskin, snakeskin, and sueded kid and lambskin. Alligator, calf, kipskin, cowhide, lizard, and sealskin are the most prevalent. Suede sometimes flattens and becomes shiny and tends to crock, soiling hands and gloves, although many of today's suedes are crock-proof. Patent leather formerly had a tendency to crack, but new developments in tanning have produced a crack-resistant patent leather.

Linings vary according to the type of bag and the material on the outside. Dressy fabric bags are usually lined with faille, moiré, taffeta, and satin. The linings of leather handbags include cotton or rayon fabrics, plastic, and leather, usually skeepskin skivers. Felt fillers line the cardboard and buckram to soften fabric bags.

The kind of frame used depends upon the design and the cost of the bag. In inexpensive handbags, the bag and the frame are attached to each other by pushing the edges of the bag and its lining into the frame. A more durable and expensive method involves pushing the lining into the frame first, then bringing the leather over the frame and inserting it from the inside of the bag, covering the frame, and distributing the weight.

Frames are made of brass, plastic, steel, tortoise shell, and wood and may be plated with chromium, gold, or silver or covered with fabric or leather. Other materials, for mountings and clasps, include lucite and marcasite. The material covering the parts of the frame exposed to wear should be resistant to abrasion, or the frame covering will wear out before the rest of the handbag.

The handles and fastenings on handbags should be made of sturdy materials and securely attached. There are shoulder straps for sports and streetwear, top handles hung across the arm, and small side handles for dress bags to be held in the hand. Fastenings should close the bag securely and at the same time be easy to manipulate in closing and opening. Slide fasteners should operate easily.

The hidden parts of the bag which lend body, shape, and support include cardboard, celluloid, cotton felt, heavy duck fabric, muslin, and paper. The better the material, the longer the bag holds its original shape and rich appearance.

Gussets or side gores on bags to give ample space for the contents whether the bag is open or closed should be deep, strong, and securely fastened.

Coin purses inside handbags may be loose or attached or may swing from the frame on an elastic cord or a chain. They should be of the same quality material and workmanship as the handbag. Some bags are fitted with other items such as mirrors, combs, and compacts, which may be desirable but add to the cost of the bag.

Types of bags

The general types of handbags for women include the box, envelope or underarm, pouch or vagabond, novelty, satchel, swagger, and vanity.

The *box bag* is shaped like a square or rectangular box and may have one or two strap handles or a shoulder strap.

The *envelope bag*, resembling an envelope with a top flap, is made with or without handles and may be carried under the arm. This type of bag is usually large and convenient. It may have a flat handle along the top or the back.

The *pouch bag* is any type of handbag with a slide fastener, frame closing, drawstring top, or a top handle. It is usually soft, and pleated or gathered to a top opening.

Satchel

Swagger

Pouch

Tote bag

Shoulder bag

Clutch

Box

Envelope

The *vagabond* is a pouch-shaped bag with a smooth envelope closing.

Novelty bags include beach bags, belt bags, carpetbags, gypsy bags, knitting bags, muff bags, saddlebags, tote bags, and other unusual types.

The *satchel* is a roomy bag with top handles and a flat bottom and is good for shopping and traveling.

The *swagger,* which is similar to the satchel, is a roomy bag with a two-strap handle and an 8-, 10-, or 12-inch frame; it usually has a slide fastener opening.

The *vanity bag* is a box-like bag with built-in sections for cosmetics, comb, file, and mirror. The box may be square or round and sometimes even takes on novel shapes, resembling binocular cases, lunch baskets, fish baskets, and picnic boxes.

Construction

The first step in manufacture is the designing of the bag. The designer's drawing is made up in muslin for approval and then the muslin is used as the master pattern from which cardboard or metal patterns for the different parts of the bag are cut. The material from which the bag is to be made is cut out by hand or with metal dies. The parts are assembled and sewed by hand or machine. Linings, filler, interlinings, and stay materials are glued or cemented into the bag, the edges of the fabric or other material are turned in by hand, and then the bag goes to the frame worker, who inserts the bag into the appropriate frame and applies the fasteners. The handbags are inspected, cleaned or polished, stuffed with tissue, and shipped to retailers.

When purchasing a bag, the shopper should make sure that the material is suitable for the use she expects to give the bag and that the bag is large enough to hold all of the possessions she carries. The opening should be wide enough and the depth convenient, not so deep that it is difficult to find articles. She should also check the gussets, lining, and compartments for material and construction. She should carefully check the size of the bag, considering her height, her figure, and the occasion for which the bag will be used. A bag that is in proportion to the individual's size indicates good taste in selection.

To summarize, quality in handbags includes comfort in carrying and holding, convenience of compartments and other details, the finish of the materials, firm mountings, good interiors and fittings, the quality of the leather or other materials, and workmanship. The trade name of a reliable and well-known manufacturer is often an indication of quality.

Care

Handbags require care for maximum wear, but many women do not realize this. The worst offenders are the women who carry too many articles in a handbag, thus stretching it out of shape and causing the material to pull away from the frame. Whenever bags are stored for a season they should be thoroughly cleaned inside and outside and stuffed with tissue paper to retain their shape.

Fabric bags should be cleaned frequently by brushing, spot cleaning, or dry cleaning. Some fabric bags have a removable cover that is washable. The lining should be kept clean by brushing or vacuuming. Polishing leather helps preserve the life of the bag and maintain its original appearance. A cream polish on smooth leathers helps protect the bag from mars and scratches. Suede bags require brushing with a rubber or fine bristle brush. Flattened, shiny nap may be improved by the careful use of fine emery paper. However, resueding by a reliable repair shop is usually more satisfactory than any home method.

Evening bags made of beads or sequins should be repaired immediately when a thread breaks, because many beads are attached to one thread and a whole row will fall off.

Wiping bags of plastic and washable leather with a damp cloth is usually sufficient care for this kind of bag. Wiping and brushing is recommended for straw bags.

Fur bags require the same care in cleaning, storing, and wearing as other fur items in the wardrobe.

BELTS

Women's belts

Separate belts for women are usually articles of decoration which lend accents of color and texture to several outfits and also define the waistline when fashion is emphasizing the natural line. Belts are made of braid, elastic fabric, leather, metal, plastic, straw, and combinations of these materials. Widths vary from half an inch to four and five inches, and the belt may be straight or curved in the contour or cummerbund style. Length is marked according to waist measurement in inches or labeled small, medium, and large. A variety of fastenings are used, including lacings, buckles, hooks and eyes, snaps, buttons, and gripper fasteners. Belts made of metal or metallic yarns, heavy leathers, and straw are often unlined in order to reduce their bulk. Many fabric belts, like those of felt, grosgrain ribbon, satin, and velvet, have a backing of real leather, simulated leather, plastic, or plastic-coated fabric to lend body and substance to the belt and prevent wrinkling and crushing.

In purchasing a belt, one should consider whether an accent at the waistline will be flattering and whether the belt will be used with one outfit or several. The width, length, color, and material should be appropriate for the individual, the quality of the material, and the cost. Belts should be colorfast and should not crock. Metal and simulated metal fastenings and trim should not tarnish, wear off, or otherwise lose the original finish before the leather or other material wears out. Buckles or other fastenings covered with the same material as the belt often wear out before the belt, and the belt has to be discarded for that reason. The eyelets, edges, and stitching on belts should be examined for durability. If no instructions are given for cleaning the belt, the customer should ask for information or try to decide how the belt should be cleaned. A soiled belt that has to be discarded because it cannot be cleaned is an expensive purchase. Some belts are washable; others can be wiped off with a damp cloth or cleaning fluid. Leather belts can often be cleaned with a neutral cream wax or with saddle soap and then polished, but one must make sure that all excess polish is removed before the next wearing. When belts are not in use, they should be hung on a belt rack so that perspiration and dampness will evaporate. The application of colorless nail polish to metals helps prevent tarnish and discoloration.

Men's belts

The belt, a gadget that ties a man in the middle and keeps his shirt in and his trousers up, is an important accessory in most men's wardrobes. Many men rely upon belts instead of suspenders to hold up their trousers; a few men wear both. Some men wear belts not only for the obvious practi-

Styles in women's belts.

Styles in men's belts.

cal purpose, but to add a note of contrast, especially with slacks. Leather is preferred by many men who realize that a well-made genuine leather belt is more durable than one of any other material. The leathers used are alligator, calfskin, cowhide, ostrich, pigskin, pin seal, snakeskin, shark, and walrus. A tooled leather belt can be a prized possession. The one-piece leather belt is preferable to one of two or more leather pieces stitched together. If the belt is lined, leather is often used; the lining is either held by an adhesive or stitched to the piece of leather used for the outside of the belt. Widths vary from half an inch to an inch, with in-between sizes popular. Belts are also available in a wide range of colors and patterns —such as tartans, bold striped cotton, and checked cotton. Some are elastic, both braided and cord. Others have plaid and rep nylon coverings that match ties. Rep belts can be found in many different patterns with pigskin or cowhide leather fronts. Comfortable braided nylon has been fashioned in bright colors for leisure wear as well as in solid shades for dress wear. Another sport-time favorite has a double loop of elastic cord hooked to a cowhide front. For warm weather and in some areas of the country these belts are cooler and more comfortable than leather ones. Transparent vinyl resin seems to be less popular than other materials for men's belts. Buckles are made of brass, gold, nickel, silver, and white metal. Many are decorated with chasing, carving, or engraving or are monogrammed. The buckles are either the regulation type, with one ring and a spine that fits in punched holes, or the two-ring cinch buckle.

In selecting a belt, a man needs to keep in mind his wardrobe—the kind of suits and slacks—the color, fabric, texture, width, length, material, design, and buckle of the belt, how securely it is attached, and whether it works easily. Men's belts should be cleaned frequently; wiping the inside with a damp soapy cloth will prevent discoloration and permanent soiling. Belts should be hung on a rack when not being worn. Leaving the belt on the trousers is not good for the belt or the trousers.

SUSPENDERS

The popularity of suspenders, or braces, as they are called in England, has been on the wane for some time. However, there are some men who prefer them to a belt or even wear them with a belt to insure greater security and comfort. Many of the men who do not wear suspenders might improve their appearance by wearing them.

Suspenders are made of fabric, elasticized belting, leather, rayon webbing, transparent plastic, and combinations of these materials. Some are neutral in color; others come in bright solid colors, plaids, checks, and figured patterns to match other furnishings. The heavy work suspenders have buttonholes in the ends and fasten to buttons on the trousers. Other suspenders have clips that clamp to the top of the trousers. Suspenders are usually adjustable in length and are available in various widths.

The important points to keep in mind when choosing suspenders are the quality of the material, the device for attaching to the trousers, the width, the provision for adjusting length, the color, and whether the material will discolor the shirt.

SMALL LEATHER GOODS

Small or fancy leather goods, being common gift items, are often selected by price only, with a minimum of attention given to color, construction, material, or size. Sometimes they are made of simulated leather, plastics, and fabric, and there is quite a difference in durability and service.

Included in this group are billfolds and

wallets, cigarette cases, coin or change purses, key cases, luggage tags, passport folders, and other similar items. The billfold, which is a small, flat, convenient folder to hold identification cards and bills, is popular with both men and women. In ladies' billfolds there is also a compartment for coins. There are so-called secret compartments for extra bills and checks in billfolds for men and for women. There is some variation in design, fastenings, size, and shape. In place of or in addition to this regulation billfold, some men use the flat folder that is carried in the inside breast pocket of the coat instead of the back hip pocket of the trousers. This type of folder has more compartments, is larger than the billfold, makes less of a bulge, and is seldom lost or stolen from the inside pocket.

Cigarette cases, used by both men and women, vary in size, material, and method of opening. Some are the shape of a package of cigarettes with a variety of openings such as the slide, zipper, and flap, while others are flat to accommodate cigarettes that have been removed from the original package. Many users have very definite preferences on the design and size of these cases.

The coin or change purse, which is a small holder for coins and bills, sometimes having two or more compartments, fits inside the handbag or in a pocket. Coin purses equipped with compartments or slots for coins of different denominations prove convenient when one has to cope with parking meters, toll gates, buses, and subways.

Key cases are small holders with attached rings for keys and sometimes with space for driver's license and auto registration. These cases are available in various sizes, and some also have a coin compartment.

Luggage tags can be bought separately if they are not a part of the luggage. They are markers that have celluloid or other transparent spaces for the name and address of the owner and are attached to the handles of luggage.

Nearly all of the above items are available in a wide variety of leathers, including alligator, calfskin, cattle hide, ostrich, pigskin, sealskin, goatskin, sheepskin, and reptile leather. Some are made of split leather and others of top-grain leather. Simulated leather and plastic are also used. Cigarette cases are also made of metal and may be gold and silver plated. Women's coin purses may be made of fabrics similar to those used in handbags.

When choosing these small items, one should keep in mind the size that will be most convenient; the various compartments; fastenings, closings, and ease of operation; and the material and color that will be the most serviceable and will harmonize with the other accessories and the apparel with which they will be used.

LUGGAGE

Americans, who have always been on the go, keep going places faster, farther, and more frequently, have broken all records for European and domestic travel and, consequently, all records for buying luggage. To select luggage adequate and appropriate for an individual's needs requires careful consideration of the numerous types of luggage available. At one time, a heavy leather suitcase or a heavy wood-frame trunk was considered adequate for any trip.

Luggage is needed for travel by auto, boat, bus, plane, and train, and weight and space limitations are important items to consider. Travelers like to have luggage wardrobes with different bags for different journeys. They like luggage that is fashionable and at the same time provides economy of space, is easy to pack and unpack, and is designed to eliminate extra folds in

Men's luggage. From left to right: three-suiter, courier case, two-suiter, and one-suiter. (Courtesy American Luggage Works, Inc.)

clothing. Since luggage is handled by many people other than the owner, durability is very important. Good-quality, well-built luggage can take rough handling much better than inexpensive luggage, yet many people hesitate to pay the price of good luggage.

It is possible to buy luggage with the right amount of space and accessories to fit every specific need. The types of luggage include hand luggage such as the brief case, bellows case, Boston bag, fitted case, Gladstone bag, hat case, kit bag, Oxford bag, shoe case, suitcase, and wardrobe case. Trunks—either box or wardrobe—are classified as large luggage.

Types of luggage

The *brief case* used by business men is not only used for important papers and documents, but will carry shirts, socks, toilet kit, handkerchiefs, pajamas, and underwear for the person who has a long, busy schedule requiring a change of clothes for an evening appointment. It is small and flat, with two or more compartments, and may have a flap or a slide fastener closing reinforced with straps.

The *bellows case*, with a top which expands to provide extra space, is used by some men who travel a great deal and need several changes of clothes.

The *Boston bag*, a small luggage case, has flexible rather than rigid sides and is packed in the upright way in which it is carried.

The *fitted case* or dressing case usually

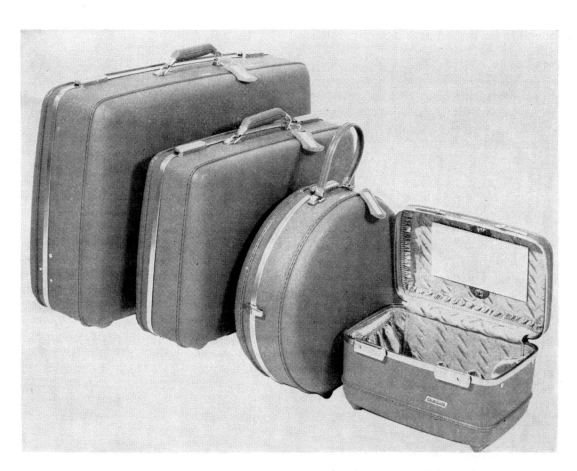

used by women varies in size from the 14-inch cosmetic case or 16-inch train case to the 21-inch weekend bag. The small size provides space and containers in the lid or on a tray for cosmetics and toiletries, as well as room in the lower half of the case for the clothing essential for an overnight trip. A fitted or dressing case for men is a small, compact leather container holding brushes, comb, shaving equipment, file, and other toilet items.

The *fortniter* is a suitcase larger than a wardrobe case, with hangers for dresses and suits in the lid and compartments in the bottom for hose, shoes, and accessories.

The *Gladstone bag* is a sturdy suitcase with straps, generally used by men on an extended trip requiring several changes of clothing. The case is not rigid and is built to allow for some expansion in packing. It opens flat and often has a center partition to keep clothes in each section separate. It is similar to the two-suiter.

The *hat case* is designed primarily for carrying hats, but is often used for other apparel and accessories. It is deep and square or round in shape in 15–20-inch size.

The *jewelry case* is a boxlike case small

enough to be carried as a handbag, fitted with a tray and velvet lined.

The *kit bag* is a heavy type of bag with a square top and straps in addition to the fasteners to keep it closed. The contents of the bag are carried in the position in which they are packed. Extra material in the top folds over to allow ample room for extra items. It is often used for men's shoes.

The *overnight case* is a small suitcase that holds enough clothing for a short trip or an overnight visit.

The *oxford bag* is a type of box bag that resembles the Boston bag, but is larger.

The 54-inch *service-pak*, designed for service men, is a combination portable bag for three uniforms or suits with places for shirts, socks, toilet goods. It extends full length so that garments may be hung as in a closet and folds over into a sectioned case for carrying.

The *shoe case* is similar to the hat case. In fact, either of these bags can be used for carrying shoes or hats or both.

Suitcases vary in size and shape, ranging from the weekend case to the wardrobe case. The original suitcase was a rigid, flat, rectangular case to hold suits. Other sizes are also called Pullman cases in 24–27-inch size and 30-inch overseas cases. In men's luggage, suitcases are often called two-suiters or three-suiters. The two-suiter is a suitcase with a tray to hold two suits. Ties may hang in the lid section. Under the suits are compartments for accessories.

The *wardrobe case,* equipped with hangers, keeps the folding of clothing to a minimum and is desirable for extended travel. It is smaller than a fortniter.

The *box trunk* is convenient for storage or long trips. The *wardrobe trunk,* which has hangers, drawers, and compartments for accessories, may serve as a closet as well as a means of carrying clothes.

The matched travel sets modeled on the service-pak, made of fabric with reinforced corners and edges, include several sizes, which fit one inside the other when not in use, and a hang-up bag. These are popular with both men and women for auto and plane travel. The hang-up bag eliminates all folding, and little pressing is required at the end of the trip.

Materials

Luggage is made from a variety of materials, from leather to cardboard. The leathers used for the outer covering of luggage include alligator, calfskin, cattle hide, ostrich, pigskin, rawhide, sealskin, and sharkskin. Some inexpensive pieces of luggage are made of split leathers, which do not have the quality or the appearance of top grain.

Luggage today reflects the great revolution brought about by air travel. Air travel made luggage lighter, and this led to experiments with new shapes, frames, and materials. Leather, of course, is still widely used in luggage, but plastics and synthetics have become important rivals. Some of these do not crock, chip, or peel, are waterproof, and usually cost less than leather. Pyroxylin-coated linen and canvas are quite satisfactory. Aluminum and fiberglass make very satisfactory lightweight luggage. Fiberglass will not scuff, warp, dent, or puncture. It is water-repellent and washable and has dustproof aluminum tongue and grove closures and hard polished hardware. Paper-covered cardboard is used in some inexpensive luggage. Leather and metal are used for the reinforcement of corners and edges of luggage made of other materials.

The materials used underneath the outside coverings are fiberboard and basswood. Fiberboard varies in quality, from cardboard to specially treated fiberboard. Three-ply basswood is close-grained, lightweight, soft, and strong and does not warp or crack under ordinary care and use. The layers of wood are sandwiched together by heat, pressure, and waterproof adhesives, making it light as a feather yet extremely strong. Linings are made of cotton, linen, paper, rayon, and sheepskin or other thin leather. Plastic linings are used in cosmetic cases so that stains may be easily wiped off.

The hardware on luggage—clasps, hinges, locks, and rings for handles—is made of solid brass, stainless steel, nickel, or brass-plated steel. Some of the plated ware may rust if scratched. Metal studs on the bottom of luggage protect it from abrasion when it is set upright or when pushed across a floor. The addition of casters on one end makes it easy to roll rather than carry heavy luggage. Locks with finger-tip action and concealed rivets and mechanism are desirable. Try the lock to make sure it closes with a secure-sounding snap. The dial lock with a "safe-like" combination eliminates the need for a key. Solid-brass handle loops, hand-riveted handles, and handles designed with room for the palm and fitted to the contour of the hand are other important construction details.

Adequate hinges are important to prevent gaposis in luggage, with three on small cases and four on large ones. A good case should also have a center clip or catch as well as a lock on each end.

Construction

Although no two types of luggage are made by the same method of construction, there are some details and features to be examined in all luggage. In the chapter on leather, the differences between top-grain leather and split leather as well as the differences in the thickness of leather were discussed, and these apply to luggage also. Run a hand over the cover to make sure that it is firmly glued to the box and has no bumps or creases. Well-made luggage has rounded, leather-reinforced edges that resist handling and wear. The quality of the hardware, the number of catches and locks, and the ease with which they work are important in luggage. The salesman should be able to tell the customer whether the base of the luggage is cardboard or wooden. If the sides of luggage are molded into shape from one continuous piece of plywood, there are no corner joints to come apart or split. The quality of the lining, hangers, dust-resistant curtains, pockets, and other accessories should be noted. The weight of the luggage should also be checked, especially if the luggage is to be used for plane travel. Swing the luggage around to see if it is light enough. Tapered luggage is designed to fit body contours for carrying ease. If it is tapered high, it holds more clothes with fewer folds. Some luggage is treated for scuff- and scratch-resistance, water-repellency, and soil-resistance. Most luggage is washable.

After checking specific points of construction, the customer should decide upon the color, design, and number of pieces to fit his needs. In choosing luggage from open stock, it is possible to buy one piece at a time and to acquire gradually a luggage wardrobe to accommodate any kind of clothing and meet the requirements of any trip. Some customers purchase a complete set of matched luggage at one time. Identification tags or monograms are often applied at the time of purchase.

Care

Luggage requires care as does any article of fabric, leather, metal, or plastic. Leather should be polished, and fabric, metal, and plastic should be wiped with a damp cloth. Luggage should not be overloaded so that hinges and clasps are subjected to excessive strain. Since luggage is treated roughly by porters, bellhops, and others, some travelers cover their luggage with a protective jacket or sack to prevent scratching and marring. The inside should be brushed, aired, and wiped out occasionally. Luggage should be repaired immediately if stitches, handles, hinges, or other parts are broken.

REFERENCE READINGS

Books

Bacharach, Bert, *Right Dress*, A. S. Barnes, New York, 1955.

Chambers, Bernice G., *Fashion Fundamentals*. Prentice-Hall, Inc., New York, 1947.

Collins, C. Cody, *Love of a Glove*, Fairchild Publications, New York, 1947.

Evans, Mary, *Better Clothes for Your Money*. J. B. Lippincott Co., Philadelphia, 1952.

Gillespie, Karen R., *A Work Manual for the Study of Non-Textile Apparel Accessories*, Prentice-Hall, Inc., New York, 1947.

Wilcox, Ruth Turner, *The Mode in Footwear*, Charles Scribner's Sons, New York, 1948.

Wingate, Isabel B., Gillespie, Karen R., and Addison, Betty, *Know Your Merchandise*, 3rd Ed., McGraw-Hill, New York, 1964.

Bulletins

Better Buymanship, *Gloves*, Household Finance Corporation, Chicago, 1937.

Heal, Edith and Walker, Robert, *Gloves-Fashion and Etiquette,* Hansen Glove Corporation, 1961.

Tanner's Council of America, Inc., *Dictionary of Leather Terminology*, New York, 1955.

Tanner's Council of America, Inc., *Leather*, U. S. Naval Supply Corps Reserve, J. Sterling Livingston, 1949.

Tanner's Council of America, *The Romance of Leather*, New York, 1937.

Chapter 21

Furs

Interest in furs may start at an early age, when a child enjoys the sensation of feeling the fur of his favorite pet. Little girls playing at being grown up like to borrow a fur piece to make the play acting more realistic. Manufacturers, recognizing this, have provided imitation fur neckwear along with hats and high-heeled shoes for children's fun and play. Nearly every young woman hopes to own furs sometime, whether a coat, jacket, cape, stole, or a fur-trimmed or fur-lined coat. Furs seem to appeal to nearly all women, regardless of interests, occupation, personality, size, and age. A student may not have furs while in college, but will probably plan to own a fur piece later. A fur piece is one of the most important investments in a woman's wardrobe.

Although furs are not as popular in men's wear as in women's apparel, most men are interested in furs—having to pay, they want to know something about this major expenditure. Many men are proud to have their wives dressed in furs. A few do their own gift shopping for furs; others go along while the women shop. Some men allow the women to make the selection and content themselves with signing the check. The majority of Christmas fur purchases are made by men.

FUR KNOW-HOW

Although it takes years to learn all about furs, with a little study of types of furs, processes, and criteria for judging, it is possible for a woman to learn enough to enable her to make an intelligent selection for herself. There is a great variety—of more than forty types—from which to choose, which is often confusing for the uninformed. A woman may have a particular type of fur in mind—perhaps because a friend has one or because she thinks a certain color is becoming to her. Or her budget may restrict her to a specific price range. With such ideas in mind, the consumer needs some accurate information. If she listens to a reliable furrier, she will have no difficulty in making a wise decision.

CHOOSING FURS

It should be kept in mind that there are beautiful, well-styled, and serviceable furs in all price ranges. Furs are classified as to color, durability, length of hair, type of fur, and price. Then there is the classification of the pieces and garments in which furs are used—from scarves, stoles, capes, jackets, three-quarter- and full-length coats, and fur-lined and fur-trimmed coats and jackets to boas, coatdresses, skirts, suits, over-blouses, pants, slacks, separates, hats, shifts, and gowns. There are also the ready-made and the made-to-order classifications. If a customer is willing to pay the price of a made-to-order garment, she can select the skins and the style of the garment. From a variety of samples, she may choose the body of one garment, the sleeve of another, and the collar of another. A good custom furrier then creates a coat according to the customer's selection and measurements. However, in buying a ready-made coat, she also has a variety of furs and styles from which to choose. Usually, she will pay less for a ready-made coat than for a custom-made one. Of course, it is also possible to choose the color, fur, and style in a ready-made coat and then have one similar to it made to order, with a better fit and any special details desired.

FASHION IN FURS

There are fashions in furs as well as in other types of apparel, and the silhouette in furs tends to change with that of fabric coats, jackets, and other outerwear. A few high-fashion furs appear nearly every year and then go out of fashion in a short time. Examples are the empire line's high-waisted shape, full back panels, pleats, partial belts placed anywhere from the shoulders on down, and low bloused effects. However, the trend in styles of fur coats does not change radically. There are classics in fur fashions, and one can usually find a coat with a loosely fitted, soft, casual, slightly flared back and sides and regulation set-in sleeves with deep cuffs and of varying lengths from wrist to elbow.

The popularity of different kinds of furs seems to follow fashion, too. At one time, fox, sheared beaver, seal, and raccoon may dominate, only to be succeeded by mink, Persian lamb, and muskrat. Brown furs may be in fashion one year, and black furs the next.

In keeping with fashion, color in furs is no longer limited to black, brown, and gray. Pastel pinks, blues, blonde tones, suntans, grays, and white are often seen. In mink, colors range from muted tones such as autumn haze, cerulean, and desert gold to rich-toned dark ranch mink and beautiful natural wild mink. White, a one-time formal-wear color in furs, is now also styled for daytime wear. Both long-hair and sheared muskrat are dyed in a variety of colors. The sides or flanks have shorter hair and are often dyed in soft, light colors. Muskrat backs can be dyed to resemble mink. Per-

sian lamb is dyed black or brown. Beaver is sometimes dyed red, white, or blue. Alaska fur seal is often dyed black or golden brown.

Fur trim on coats, jackets, suits, dresses, hats, gloves, and shoes is often fashionable. Fur belts, bags, hats, muffs, and other accessories may be promoted one season and then sink into oblivion the next. Mink earrings, cuff links, and Peter Pan collars had a short period of popularity at one time. During the course of a fashion cycle, many of these items may be revived with but a few changes, and new emphasis placed on the use and ways of wearing.

FURS AND THE INDIVIDUAL

One of the important considerations in choosing furs is the relationship of the type of fur and the design of the garment to the wearer, her needs, and her wardrobe. The person who does not wish to add bulk to her appearance or to detract from her height will avoid the very long-haired, very thick furs, which are more becoming to a person with a tall, slender figure. Women of average build are not greatly limited as to the kinds of fur they can wear. In general, the flat, short-haired furs in dark colors are becoming to chubby women and the long-haired furs in lighter colors to tall, slim women. The short-haired furs with pelts or stripes running vertically are the most flattering to short women.

Without very careful selection, the short person with a full figure may not look as well in a fur coat as in a cloth coat that has slimming lines and is trimmed with a touch of fur. A small fur piece, preferably in a flat or short-haired fur, may be flattering. On the other hand, a poorly selected cloth coat may not do as much for this woman as a fur coat that has been especially designed for her figure. A woman with a short neck can wear a fur coat if she sticks to a flat fur, a natural shoulder line, and a small collar such as a mandarin, a tiny shawl, a rollback, or a cardigan neckline.

A woman over five feet, five inches in height who has a full figure can wear any moderately full coat if it is long enough to slenderize her figure; the fur should be flat, or short-haired, such as fur seal, Persian lamb, or sheared muskrat.

The slender, petite woman looks well in a full-length coat if the fur is not too bulky. The slightly fitted, the semi-loose, or the straight wrap coat, when scaled to the petite size in all details, are very flattering.

In fact, styling and smarter-looking silhouettes designed for the petite woman have come to the rescue of the "little person lost in the big fur coat." There is quite a wide choice of furs to fit small women, and their budgets. The petite fur coat, scaled to fit and flatter the figure 5′5″ and under, is available in many places. It is designed with the shorter woman in mind, for smaller shoulders, shorter arms, and fuller hips. Furs for the smaller woman need not be custom made; they can be furnished from stock. Every intricate detail and fashionable fur silhouette may be scaled proportionately to fit her. Nearly every kind of fur is now fashioned for the petite woman to make her look taller by creating a long, slender line and eliminating the "dumpy" look.

FUR ACCESSORIES

If a person prefers a fur-trimmed coat, a fur scarf, a stole, or other fur accessories to be worn with coats, suits, or dresses, she should keep in mind the effect these create on her appearance. Since a fur hat, collar, scarf, or stole accents the face and upper portions of the figure, it should flatter the individual's coloring as well as her height and proportions. Fur muffs and cuffs, fur-trimmed gloves, and fur bands and flounces on coats, all draw attention to other areas of the figure, and here again the over-all effect should be considered. The size of the pieces and the length and bulk of the fur are significant for women of all sizes and heights. The selection of any fur that will flatter the wearer takes a great deal of trying on and careful consideration. The importance of line, design, color, texture, proportion, and optical illusion is as great in furs as in other apparel.

FULL-LENGTH COATS

Full-length coats are preferred by many women, but there are many three-quarter-length coats sold, too. Although a woman is warm in any fur coat that falls below the hips, she is not so well protected from rain and snow in a three-quarter-length coat as in a full-length one. Also, the shorter coat allows a woman less leeway in the choice of colors and styles of dresses and skirts over which it can be worn for the most pleasing appearance. Many women like capes, stoles, scarves, and short jackets—but here again warmth and practicality are often sacrificed for style. However, these garments can be worn over nearly everything, from early fall into winter, from spring into summer, and sometimes even all summer long, especially in places such as air-conditioned restaurants and theaters. In some states, such as California, they are preferred to full-length coats.

STOLES AND JACKETS

Stoles are made in many shapes—the straight dramatic one that can be shaped to specific tastes and occasions, the contour stole with collar or sleeve or cuff treatments, and the conventional cape-stole.

Jackets generally follow the fashionable silhouette. The "box" jacket may have a flat center back and fullness on the sides. Details include smart pocket treatments, contrasting trims, buttons, tabs, and half-belts. The tapered jacket is a variation of the slim line and often features tapered push-up sleeves.

ONE COAT ONLY

The woman who can afford only one fur coat often chooses a conservative type of fur in a classic style. She wants a durable fur and one she will enjoy wearing for a long time. Although nearly all furs are appropriate for many occasions, some women tire of conspicuously marked furs. However, leopard is one of the most desirable furs and can be as expensive as mink. Natural raccoon is used mostly in sportswear; sheared raccoon is an all-occasion fur. Extreme styles go out of fashion more quickly than classic designs. The cost of restyling a fur coat depends upon the craftsmanship of the furrier and the condition of the fur. A color that is becoming to the wearer and goes well with the rest of her wardrobe is a wise choice.

Warmth and longevity used to be the consumer's chief requirements for furs, but nowadays the majority of furs are purchased for fashion and lightness of weight. There is a handsome fur coat to fit nearly every budget due to improvements in the techniques of fur breeding, manufacture, and design. There are few "neglected" furs. New processes have put many luxury furs within the reach of more people, and less expensive furs are made to look like luxury furs. Muskrat that has been dyed and sheared looks like Alaska seal. American broadtail looks as soft and silky as the expensive Russian variety. Persian lamb has been improved in new lightweight, lustrous varieties. Sheared raccoon and sheared fox have a luxury look. Rabbit is dyed to look like anything from chinchilla to ermine.

For the college girl, there are gaily dyed furs in all the colors of the rainbow, employing such various skins as mole, muskrat, broadtail, mouton, and rabbit. Improved processes make them soft, light in weight, long-wearing, and handsome. Simple lines, such as back-belted polo coats and chesterfields, as well as many varieties of jacket styles, from bolero to cardigan, are available.

If a person lives in a very cold climate, she buys a fur that will give the greatest warmth, while a fur with moderate warmth is preferable in less frigid areas. A stole or cape for dress and evening wear in air-conditioned buildings is the only type of fur needed in many sections of the country.

The most popular all-occasion furs for daytime, dress, and evening wear are Alaska fur seal, sheared muskrat, mink, nutria, otter, Persian lamb, and squirrel. Unless the protection of a full-length coat is needed, a simply styled jacket, short coat, or stole gives the wearer a feeling of luxury and is adaptable for multiple-purpose wear. Jackets or coats with small collars, straight or adjustable-length sleeves, a minimum of trim, and straight or moderately full body lines, go with a variety of clothes. The straight stole can be worn in many different ways. It goes with more clothes, any place, any time, than a more formal contoured style.

DURABILITY

The degree of durability desired in a fur often depends on the uses to which the wearer puts the garment. If she expects to wear the fur daily—riding in or driving a car, traveling crowded subways and elevators, or sitting in it often and long—then the greater the durability of the fur and the more practical the design of the coat, the better the selection. However, if she wants a fur only for dress and evening wear, more fragile, less durable skins and a less practical design may serve her needs.

For example, the coat that would give the most wear and comfort to a career woman in a very cold climate would be any one of the durable furs in a full length with modified fullness for easy movement and comfortably cut armholes to go over suits. This style can be worn over any silhouette, from the slender to the full-skirted. Mouton-processed lamb, for example, good looking and low priced, would fill these needs.

Still another example is the person who travels a great deal—commutes to work, rides buses when shopping, or drives a car. She might be wise to buy a durable fur in an in-between length rather than a full-cut, full-length coat. The shortness would eliminate much of the wear caused by sitting, and, being less bulky, a short coat would be easier to handle in traveling. Since lengths range from bolero to three-fourths, there is a wide selection from which to make the choice most becoming to the individual's figure.

FUR AND YOUR WARDROBE

Which fur design will best fit into the rest of a person's wardrobe? What color, what fur, what type of garment—all fur, fur-lined, or fur-trimmed—will go best with what she already owns? For instance, she might wonder whether a short coat can be worn with a full skirt. If it is a waist-length coat, a waist-fitting jacket, a very short cardigan, or a barrel jacket that wraps snugly just below the waist, it can.

A short coat can also be worn with a suit, provided it is long enough to cover the suit jacket and it goes with the suit silhouette. The armholes of the fur coat should be deep enough to accommodate the sleeves of the suit jacket.

A stole should be selected in relation to the wearer's proportions and height. It should not be so deep as to be overpowering. One that extends to the waistline may not be as flattering to a woman as a narrower one.

The cape-stole, a popular combination garment, is a fairly good-sized fur piece made in a large variety of furs. It is considered dressy, but it may be worn in daytime over simply-styled clothes.

For the woman who can afford a fur wardrobe, there are fur slacks, suits, and gowns designed in furs appropriate to the garment and the occasion.

Is it possible to substitute a fur coat for a heavy cloth coat? Will a woman who buys a fur coat still need a cloth coat to make the transition from winter to spring, and from fall to winter, in climates where differences in temperature are quite extreme? To justify the purchase of a fur coat, a person may say that the coat will provide unique protection against cold and icy winds, and that its long service—as compared with a cloth coat's—justifies the greater cost. This may be quite true if a wise selection is made. However, a great many furs are purchased in order to provide glamour, luxury, and prestige rather than warmth and serviceability.

A fur-lined cloth coat or jacket is often preferred to a fur garment. Being on the inside, the fur is protected from bad weather, but it still lends warmth to the coat. Short straight-hair or curly furs are generally used. The cut of a fur-lined, all-purpose coat is ordinarily a box or a semi-fitted flare, to allow for the extra bulk. A good multiple-purpose garment is the cloth coat with a removable fur lining, which can be put in and removed by the use of a slide fastener around the complete length of the front and neck facings. The fur used in linings should be of good quality to withstand the friction of wear and should be easy to clean.

FUR TERMINOLOGY

In order to be able to interpret labels and advertisements, to understand the sales talk of furriers or retail personnel, and to select furs intelligently, a customer needs to understand some of the terms used.

Furs, as defined by the fur trade, are articles of wearing apparel or trimmings made from the skin of an animal, with all or part of the hair intact, used as attire for warmth or adornment, and accepted by the fur industry as a fur product.

Nearly all fur-bearing animals have two kinds of hair covering—the soft, thick, short hair next to the skin, known as *fur fibers* or *underfur,* and the long, glistening, and somewhat stiffer hairs, known as *guard hairs,* which act as a protection for the soft fur fibers by shedding rain and moisture. A full-furred animal has both thick underfur and long guard hair. Sometimes the guard hairs are sheared to a predetermined length to beautify the fur by giving it a rich, velvety texture, as in sheared muskrat, fox, and raccoon. A process that gives a similar effect is plucking; here the guard hairs are completely plucked out, leaving only the soft underfur. This is often done to beaver, nutria, and otter. Some long-haired furs, such as fox, depend upon the length and beauty of the guard hairs for attractiveness.

The *pelt* is the entire skin, including both fur and leather; *peltry* refers to fur skins collectively. A *prime* fur is a first-quality fur, usually taken when the winter is at its coldest and the animal has a thin supple skin, dense underfur, and silky guard hair. When warmer weather comes, the animal begins to shed the underfur and the hair becomes irregular and dull in appearance.

Seconds, thirds, and *fourths* are terms applied to furs taken either in the fall, before the development of the best quality of fur fiber and guard hair, or after they have passed their prime. These "late-caught" skins are often off in color; the fur is thin and shedding and the skins are tough. The term *springs* refers to spring-caught muskrat, beaver, nutria, and others that have their best fur in the springtime when the icy mountain streams thaw down.

Other factors that affect the condition of skin and fur are altitude, amount of moisture, sunlight, and food available to the animal. Animals living in very cold climates usually have full fur fibers with erect guard hairs. Animals that live in water or in rainy climates develop very strong guard hairs.

WILD AND RANCH FURS

Furs are taken from two general categories of animals—wild ones, which are trapped, and those raised in captivity. Although we import many furs, we have a large number of fur-bearing animals in North America. Furs are often classified according to family groups—such as cat, canine, hoofed, rodent, and weasel. There is also a miscellaneous group, composed of animals that are not members of any of these families.

Wild animals sometimes fight each other, with the result that their pelts are marred and damaged. It is often difficult to catch wild animals in the prime season, especially with traps, since other animals often devour the trapped animals. Clubbing animals and shooting them are other methods, but these are not very practical because of the possible damage to the skins.

Chinchilla, mink, muskrat, fox, nutria, and Persian lamb can be raised successfully on ranches. Ideal conditions can be provided, including adequate diet, careful breeding of fine strains, protection against disease, climate and altitude best suited to the animals' needs, and a quick and painless death when the pelts are in their prime. Skins from mink raised in captivity tend to be more uniform in color, texture, and weight than the skins of wild mink. Because of great advances in the field of applied heredity, ranch *mutation* mink are available in almost any shade of color, ranging from brown-black to pure white, including light and dark grays, pale blue, and pale pink.

PROCESSING

After the skins are removed and processed, they are sold at auctions to manufacturers who treat them for use in apparel. *Dressing* is one of the first processes and corresponds to tanning in the leather industry. The pelts are treated to protect the leather from bacterial decay and insect damage, to enhance the beauty of the fur, and to remove any unnecessary guard hairs. They are washed to remove dirt, scraped to removed excess flesh and fat, and sheared or plucked to remove guard hairs. The skins are then placed in machines called "kickers," where large wooden or rubber blocks or rubber tires kick the furs against one another, breaking up the fibers in the skins until the skins are soft and pliable.

The next step is *drumming*, in which skins and sawdust are revolved together for a specified time; the sawdust takes out dirt, grease, and grime and leaves the furs shiny and clean. After the removal of the sawdust, chemicals are applied to the skin side of the pelts, to preserve them and change the raw skin to soft, pliable leather. After application of a lubricant and further drumming, the skins are stretched and the fur is "fluffed" by compressed air to add softness and beauty. If this dressing is not thoroughly done, peeling occurs in lamb and kid skins, because they dry out and the top layer of skin separates from the lower layer.

Many furs are used in their natural color. If furs are to be dyed, this is usually done after they are dressed. At one time, *dyeing* was used to make less expensive furs look like better furs; now it is done to enhance the beauty of a number of furs. Natural color varies with the type of fur and is affected by season, climate, and habitat. Some animals have a natural camouflage; some are white in color like the surrounding country during cold weather, while others that live in swamps and forests are darker than those living in open country. Colors range from white, yellow-brown, blue-brown, yellow, and red to black. If the fur has been immersed in a dye bath, it is specified as being *dyed* or *dipped;* the skin side as well as the fur will be changed in color. If color is applied by brush, feather, spray, or otherwise only on the fur side in order to darken the natural color of the fur without affecting the skin, the furs are known as *tip-dyed.* *Bleaching* is a process of removing a yellow tinge to make a fur pure white, used with, for example, ermine or white fox. It is also used to lighten the color of dark furs in order to make it possible to dye these furs in light colors or to improve their color. Bleaching and redyeing must be done very carefully, so as not to impair the wearing quality of the furs. *Plasticizing* is a process used on mouton-processed lamb to make the fur rain resistant. Plasticizing agents can also be used on other furs for water repellency.

The construction of fur garments is unique, and certain terms are peculiar to the fur industry. Before a fur garment is begun, a muslin pattern is usually made up and checked for fit, design, and details. When the muslin is approved, it is taken apart and a paper copy of it is made. This is used as the pattern for designing and shaping the various pieces of the garment.

The fur cutter takes over from here. His chief tools are a ruler and a very sharp knife resembling a razor blade with a handle. He arranges the skins that have been selected for the garment to fit the various parts of the pattern. He then cuts the skins, being careful that each part will match the color and markings of that next to it and that the desired length will be attained. As he cuts and fits the pieces of fur together, he also removes any small holes or imperfections by cutting them out. Later these edges will be sewed together inconspicuously, with a

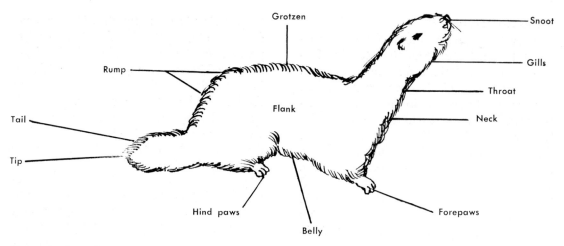

The parts of a pelt.

minimum loss of fur. This process, known as *damaging out,* is done more frequently on inferior furs than on the better furs. In joining skins, the head-to-rump connection in the length is either a long triangular zig-zag seam or a circular wave. These joinings conceal the connections better than a straight seam.

Dropping, or *letting out,* is a process used especially on beaver, mink, muskrat, raccoon, skunk, and fox. It consists of cutting a skin into long, narrow diagonal strips and resetting them in stagger formation so as to extend the length of the skin and make the center back very distinct. In this way, one skin can be extended to the entire length of the coat, giving a narrow line to the skin and bringing out the characteristic marking. Since the cuts are often as little as one-eighth of an inch apart, the resulting strip is very narrow. *Semi-let out* construction increases each skin's length only slightly, instead of to the full length of the garment.

In *skin-on-skin* method, the peltries are sewed together without any change in the original length and width. When zigzag or circular seams are used, the joining of the skins by this method is not obvious.

After the cutter finishes his work, the pieces are sewed together, a process that requires a great deal of skill. The operator uses a machine that stitches a seam similar to the overseam on leather gloves. He holds the two edges of the leather side of the fur together and stitches row after row, with great speed and accuracy, forming the various sections of the garment. Next, the closer puts the parts together—sleeves, collars, backs, fronts, and whatever other pieces the original pattern included. He uses different kinds of seams, depending upon type of fur, location of seam, and design.

Leathering means inserting alternate narrow strips of leather or tape into thick, bulky, long-haired furs like fox. Leathering adds to the skin area, minimizes bulk, reduces the amount of fur needed, and gives the garment a more slenderizing effect. This process can be detected by blowing the fur aside or by looking at the skin side of the peltry. Furs for trimming are usually handled this way.

Staying is a process used to reinforce some thin-skinned furs such as ermine, mole, and Russian broadtail. A thin piece

A first step in "letting out" is the delicate job of cutting the pelt into thin strips about a quarter of an inch wide. Great skill is required, and the cutters usually are true craftsmen. (Courtesy Fur Information and Fashion Council.)

The operator sews the strips together, changing the skin from its original dimensions into a long, narrow section. The garment made from these sections will be more flexible and better looking. (Courtesy Fur Information and Fashion Council.)

of strong fabric is stitched to the backs of the skins to prevent their ripping. It should not be done to hold skins of poor quality together.

The fur operator also stitches together sections of the peltry, such as the neck, the paws, and parts of the belly. He joins these pieces, either by hand or machine, into large rectangular pieces. These sections, or *plates*, are the "yard goods" from which the pattern of a garment is cut. When these pieces are carefully made

into plates, they can be excellent, although quite different from the way the fur of the same animal usually looks.

Following the sewing, it is necessary to flatten the seams by drawing them over a stake and to shape the various pieces to conform exactly to the original pattern. As they come from the operators, the various pieces are dampened and stretched to fit the pattern pieces, which have been traced in chalk on a large wooden board. The back, front, sleeves, and collar are nailed to the board, leather side up, and left to dry to the shape set by the pattern. Thousands of nails are used; all edges and seams are nailed to

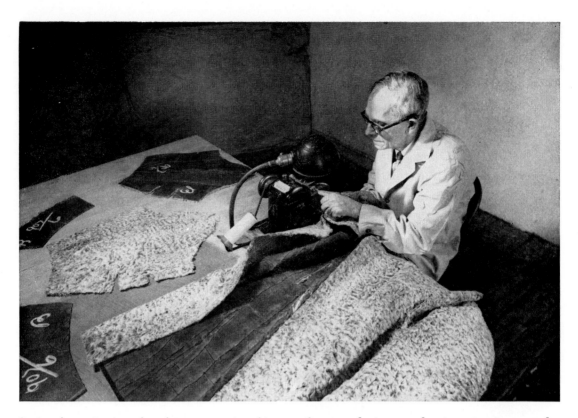

Sewing the sections together, the operator gives this Persian lamb coat its initial form. The parts have been cut from plates over a pattern as for a cloth coat, but furs demand more skillful handling than fabrics. Taping, lining, putting on buttons, and other operations will follow. (Courtesy Fur Information and Fashion Council.)

hold the pieces firmly in place, to eliminate stretching out of shape, and to assure a graceful hang and drape to the garment. Stapling is sometimes used instead of nailing, to speed up the operation.

After adequate drying, the pieces are removed from the board. Then all edges are closed and taped, the lining is sewed in, and all necessary fastenings are attached.

WHERE TO SHOP

In addition to the foregoing information, what should the woman who is selecting furs or the man who is going to pay for them keep in mind? Where to shop is a very important consideration. Shopping in a department store or at a furrier's with a reputation for reliability is wise. A reliable dealer tells the truth and stands behind his statements. The retailer with experience in the fur business buys ready-made fur garments that he sells as he would any merchandise. The retail-custom furrier usually has had years of experience in appraising furs, cutting and sewing them, and dealing with customers. He handles made-up models as well as custom-made garments. Long

(Opposite) Thousands of nails are required for this step in making a fur garment. The fur, moistened on the skin side, will dry in a day and will take its shape from the pattern. (Courtesy Fur Information and Fashion Council.)

establishment and a reputation for fair dealing are good indications of reliability. Even when dealing with a reliable furrier, it is wise to take a few precautions. If a person plans to have the garment delivered instead of taking it upon purchase, she should write her name in indelible ink on the leather side of the fur as a means of identification. If the dealer provides repairs for one year, allows furs out on approval, provides for deposits with the privilege of refunding, or adds a carrying charge to his budget plan, a written statement explaining those conditions should be provided—for the protection of both the customer and the dealer.

WHEN TO SHOP

When to shop is also a very important consideration. In some post-Christmas inventory sales, stores may cut prices, so that some furs may be less costly at that time than in the fall. August fur sales, which are promotion sales, do not necessarily offer lower prices. Two advantages of the August sales are that there is the largest stock from which to choose and the provisions of the lay-away plan are tempting. One should not be misled by offers of "bargains," which, in furs, may turn out to be garments of inferior quality, either in the skins or in the workmanship used in construction. Exaggerated claims, amazing bargain prices, extra-liberal trade-in allowances, and enormous savings in clearance sales often are high-pressure selling techniques that can be misleading. Because many people purchase furs more for appearance and becomingness than for warmth and durability, it is difficult to judge fur prices. Popularity as well as serviceability influences price; a certain type of fur currently in fashion may cost more than one that will give more warmth and better service.

WHAT TO BUY

It is usually better to buy the best grade of a moderately priced fur rather than a lower grade of a costly, rare fur. Looking at the fur of her choice in several price ranges may help the customer. Price is usually determined by the grade of the fur, its rarity, and the quality of workmanship in the construction of the garment.

The quality of the fur depends upon the primeness of the fur, its luster, density, and color, the softness and pliability of the skin, and freedom from damage.

Some animals such as the lamb, the kid, and the pony do not have double hair growth (that is, both underfur and guard hair), by which many furs are judged. They have either wool or one type of hair only. The value of such a skin is established by its characteristic curl or moiré pattern. Persian lamb, which has tightly knuckled curls lying flat in an unbroken pattern, is considered the best type. The coarse-textured Persian lambs from Russia have thicker skins, which means that a coat made from their fur will be heavier than one made of South African Persian lamb.

Some of the less expensive furs include kid, marmot, mouton-processed lamb, rabbit, and skunk. Among the moderately priced furs are processed-broadtail lamb, beaver, Japanese mink, pieced mink, raccoon, and squirrel. Nutria, ocelot, opossum, and otter are expensive furs. Very expensive are broadtail, chinchilla, ermine, mink, and sable.

It is a good idea to select a fur that is becoming to you and is within your price range. Sometimes, buying quality in furs pays for itself in the end. With the repeal of the federal excise tax, your fur dollar goes further.

QUALITY

The best sections of the skin are used for

the better-quality garments. There is little waste in furs, and the other parts of the skin are not discarded. They are sewed together to make less expensive fur garments. Although the fur is not comparable to that of the best sections of the peltry in color, density, pliability, and texture, garments made from these pieces give satisfactory service if the workmanship is good. They cost less, but may also be less durable.

The durability of furs also depends upon the amount of wear they get and the kind of care they receive. When the humidity is very high, furs have a tendency to mat or felt; if, on the other hand, the atmosphere is very dry, the guard hairs may become brittle and break off. Average humidity in the air keeps furs soft and flexible. Among the most durable furs are beaver, lamb, mouton, Persian, marten, mink, muskrat, otter, raccoon, and seal. Moderately durable furs are fitch, krimmer, Chinese and Japanese mink, and opossum. The less durable furs include fox, kidskin, leopard, marmot, nutria, ocelot, sable, and squirrel. The least durable of all furs are chinchilla, ermine, mole, and Russian broadtail.

In addition to durability, there are other features, which the purchaser can examine—the uniformity of the fur and the thickness of the skins, the color, the tendency to shed, the staying and taping, the interlining, front facings, and lining fastenings. Working the garment between the fingers is one way of feeling the thickness of the skins. Determine the shedding by shaking the fur briskly. Shedding is the coming out of fur at the roots; it is not the same thing as the breaking of the hairs that happens with dirty furs.

INNER CONSTRUCTION

A look at the skin side of a fur garment reveals the seam construction. The "French bottom" allows the lining to be folded back for examination of the skin side. Except with let-out skins, there should not be a great many small seams or odd pieces. There are a few exceptions, like Persian or broadtail, where many seams are a part of the normal construction. The seams should be flat and inconspicuous. In a better coat, thin, delicate skins will be stayed with cloth sewed on by hand. All seams are rubberized, and seams at the shoulders, neckline, armholes, and underarms are reinforced with tape at points of strain. An innerlining of cotton, flannel, quilted cotton, wool, chamois, or lamb's wool is used in garments made of furs that do not give much warmth. Innerlinings also protect the seams on the leather side of the furs—as well as the lining—from abrasion.

LININGS

The lining may be even more important in a fur garment than in a cloth one. Where once most linings were neutral in color and plain in fabric, they have changed just as furs have. Nowadays they may be gay, shining, bold and brilliant, enhancing the appearance of the wearer as well as of the fur. Taffeta designed in stripes, florals, or small prints, and satins, crepes, and failles are colorful in dark coats, while honey beiges blend with the light coats. There are prints on crepes for casual coats and plaid linings for the sports-minded. Many black fur coats with dressmaker details have brocaded silks and ottomans on the inside, either in the darker colorings or in muted reds on black or blues on black; silvery tones on black are also smart. Many luxury coats are lined with silks of different shades with variations in design—such as a metallic thread shot through—to create interest.

Fur coat linings should be smooth, closely woven, abrasion resistant, heavy enough to support the coat, and colorfast to cleaning, perspiration, atmospheric fading, and crocking. The lining should fit without sagging, and should have extra folds at the neck and shoulders. The use of shields of the same fabric under the arms gives some protection to the lining. Storm cuffs in flared sleeves add to the comfort of the wearer. Waist ties help keep the coat closed when the wearer is walking. All such items, as well as the lining itself, should be securely fastened with fine, even, invisible stitches.

FIT

The serviceability of a fur garment is affected by the fit. A coat or jacket should never fit so tightly at the shoulders, underarms, armholes, or hips that there is strain on the seams or the skins. A coat that fits well should never feel cumbersome. In very cold temperatures, many people wear a fur coat or jacket over a suit; there should be adequate room for the suit under the coat.

CARE OF FURS

Good furs deserve tender, loving care. Improper care can easily ruin even a very durable fur, while a less serviceable one may be kept in good condition a long time with proper care.

Friction should be avoided whenever possible. Books, packages, and handbags carried under the arm when a fur coat or a cloth coat with fur cuffs is worn tend to wear the fur. Accessories, such as some necklaces and heavy costume pins, with sharp edges that catch the fur will twist and break guard hairs.

Don't apply perfume directly to fur. Don't pin flowers or jewelry through it. A handbag with shoulder straps will rub the shoulder and the side areas of the coat, producing worn spots.

One should never sit on a fur coat when it is possible to push it aside or hang it up. Buttons should be unfastened before sitting

down to avoid strain both on the skins and on the fastenings.

Wearing a neck scarf will help to protect a fur collar from abrasion and from oils from the wearer's hair and neck.

After wearing, a fur coat should not be tossed in a heap, which will cause rips, tears, and loss of shape. It should be shaken by the hem to fluff and straighten the hairs, flex the skins, and stimulate the flow of oil; placed on a padded hanger designed for fur coats; and hung in a dry, cool, roomy closet. Hangers that conform to the shape of the neck and shoulders of the coat will not cut the fur or form sharp creases. Too much heat in storage dries out some of the oils in the furs. Fur coats should not be crushed against other garments in a closet; such treatment causes the fur to flatten and become matted.

A fur coat is not a raincoat and should not be used as one. Wet furs bulge and stretch wherever there is pressure or pull. If furs have been dampened by rain, they should be removed as soon as possible, carefully wiped in the direction of the flow of hair, then gently shaken and allowed to dry naturally. Hanging a fur coat over heat will dry the skins, and a draft will cause the exposed side to shrink. The best way to dry a wet fur is to hang it in a draftless, airy room for from 12 to 24 hours. Unless this is done, furs tend to lose their softness and flexibility. Never, never leave your fur coat carelessly thrown over a chair if it is damp from rain or snow. Do not brush or comb furs that are wet. In fact, whether the fur is wet or dry, harsh brushing causes friction that splits the hairs.

Furs should be kept away from strong sunlight and heat. Sunlight may fade the colors. Never place furs near a radiator, an open fire, or any other source of intense heat.

Rips and tears should be repaired immediately, preferably by a reliable furrier. Although there are publications available giving specific directions for home care, cleaning, repairing, and remodeling of furs, it is wiser to leave such care to a furrier. Even with a good reference at his elbow, an amateur cannot give furs the kind of care they deserve.

Even in top-quality garments, seams sometimes open and small leather tears appear; this should not alarm you unless it occurs so frequently as to indicate defective skins. Furs should be cleaned once a year to keep them in good condition; cleaning prevents matting and breaking of the guard hairs. Most furs should also be glazed.

Remodeling

The workmanship in remodeling must be as skilled as that in the original garment. A good furrier who can tell whether or not the furs are worth remaking is the person to whom your worn furs should be entrusted. When the estimate for restyling a fur coat exceeds twenty-five per cent of the original price of the garment, it is wise to consider converting it into a cape, jacket, or stole; using it as a lining for a cloth garment; or exchanging it. The allowance on the old garment is included in figuring the price of a new coat.

Remodeling or restyling furs is a difficult, time-consuming job. In most instances, the furrier must take an old coat apart pelt by pelt before he can reassemble it in a new style. He must then reassemble the furs so that the markings are properly matched. He often has to add new skins to the usable ones from the old coat, all of which adds to the cost. In addition, it is almost always necessary to reline the coat. Even with an expert job, what you get back is not a new garment. Many furs fade somewhat with wear; the life expectancy of a remodeled fur coat is not the same as that of a new one.

Although the style is changed, the fur is still the same texture and color—unless dyed or redyed—that you have worn for years.

There are some cases in which remodeling would be wise. For instance, if a person has worn a fur coat very little because its style was unbecoming or went out of fashion, it might be worth the cost to have the little-used skins converted into a smarter or more becoming style.

When not wearing furs for an extended period of time, should you store them at home or put them in commercial storage? Summer storage in a closet at home—even long exposure to room temperature during the winter—will dry skins. Dried-out, brittle furs are difficult to revive. Plastic bags should never be used to cover fur; a linen or cotton sheet is a good cover. There should be adequate space around the coat. Unless you can provide conditions comparable to those provided by the facilities of reliable commercial storage, it is usually wise to pay the price and feel secure about your furs in storage during hot weather. Often the firm where you bought your furs provides safe storage. If not, be sure to find a reputable merchant. Inquire about the method of storing; the use of moth-repellent chemicals; whether the cost of storage includes insurance against burglary, fire, moths and theft; and where your coat would be stored—at the furrier's, in some central storage, or in a warehouse. You should get a receipt giving a description of your furs and stating their value, the type of storage, the protection included, and whether the garments are fully insured for the value indicated.

The various balls, bombs, flakes, vapors, and sprays to prevent moth damage are effective only in airtight storage, with the air inside completely saturated and free of moisture and heat. Since these conditions

Fur Terms

Bleaching. A process for producing a lighter shade of a certain fur or removing off-color spots and stains.

Broadtail lamb. The skin of a prematurely born, stillborn, or very young lamb of the Karakul breed of sheep, having flat, light-weight fur with a moiré pattern.

Broadtail-processed lamb. Lambskin that has been sheared, leaving a moiré pattern on the pelt, to have the appearance of true broadtail.

Damaging out. Removing damaged sections of pelts by cutting and resewing so that the damage does not show from the fur side.

Dipping. See *Dyeing*.

Dressing. A process that protects pelts from bacterial decay and insect damage.

Dropping or **letting out.** Cutting skins in diagonal lines and then resewing the cut sections to make the skin long and narrow, making the center back of the skin very distinct. Mink, muskrat, skunk, and fox are often cut this way.

Drumming. Revolving and tumbling the skins in drums containing sawdust, the purpose being to clean the fur and pelt without losing suppleness or luster.

Dyeing. The process of applying dyestuffs to the hair or fur by immersion in a dye bath or by application of the dye by brush, feather, spray, or otherwise for the purpose of changing the color of the fur or hair, or to accentuate its natural color.

—Dipping. Applying the dyestuff to the entire pelt, by dipping or by brushing on the dye in layers.

—Tip dyeing. Applying the dyestuff only to the ends of the hair or fur by feather or brush.

Electrifying. A process (beating, brushing, dampening, or ironing) for generating static electricity in fur to restore brilliance, character, and life.

Full-furred. Having both an abundance of underfur and well-developed guard hairs, characteristic of prime furs.

Fur families. Family grouping is one way of classifying commercial furs with related characteristics. The common groups are the *aquatic*, including the fin-footed animals like the fur seal and the hair seal; the *canine*, including the foxes and wolves; the *cat* family, including the leopard, lynx, and ocelot; the *hoofed*, including the calf, guanaco, lamb—broadtail, Karacul, krimmer, Persian—and pony; the *rodent* family, both the water rodents like beaver, muskrat, and nutria and the land rodents like the burunduki, chinchilla, hamster, marmot, rabbit, and squirrel; the *weasel* family, including the badger, ermine, fisher, fitch, kolinsky, marten, mink, otter, sable, skunk, weasel, and wolverine; and a *miscellaneous* group that includes the opossum, raccoon, mole, and monkey.

Fur fiber or **underfur.** The soft, thick hairs, shorter than the guard hairs, next to the skin of the pelt.

Glazing. A process for giving luster to dull-looking fur.

Guard hair. The long outer hair of double-furred peltries protecting the underfur.

Lapin. Rabbit.

Late-caught skins. Skins taken after they have passed their prime season, usually inferior in quality.

Leathering. Inserting alternate narrow strips of leather into thickly-furred peltries such as fox to increase the skin area and reduce bulkiness.

Let-out. See *Dropping*.

Matching. Sorting and matching skins of similar quality and appearance.

Moiré. Wavy, rippled pattern or design on some natural and processed furs like broadtail and pony.

Mouton-processed lamb. Lambskin that has been sheared and the hair straightened, chemically treated, and thermally set to produce a moisture-repellent finish.

Mutation fur. Term applied to furs of various shades and colors produced in captivity. An unusual or rare variation in color in a litter is reproduced through selective breeding, and the strain is continued.

Nailing. Damp skins are nailed to a board in the shape set in the pattern; when dry, the skins continue to hold the shape in which they were nailed. (See illustration on p. 383.)

Pelt. The entire skin, including fur and leather.

Peltry. Pelts, collectively; fur skins in general.

Persian broadtail lamb. The skin of the very young lamb of the Karakul breed of sheep; the hair is formed in flattened knuckled curls with a moiré pattern.

Persian lamb. The skin of the young lamb of the Karakul breed. The hair is formed in the characteristic knuckled curls.

Plates. Large sections of fur made by sewing whole skins or pieces together; the yard goods of the fur trade.

Plucking. Removing guard hairs by pulling them out by hand or machine.

Prime. The season—midwinter for nearly all fur-bearing animals—when both skin and fur are best developed; also, the quality of pelts taken at that time.

Scarf. Fur in its original shape, with the head mounted and attached and the paws and tail left attached. Scarves are worn over suits and cloth coats.

Seconds. Furs of the next quality after prime; second-grade pelts are more thin-furred and have tougher skin than prime.

Shearing. Cutting the guard hairs and the underfur to a predetermined, uniform length.

Shearling. The skin of a lamb, sheared and combed.

Skin on skin. The method of sewing together skins without changing the original length or width, in contrast to the let-out process.

Skirts. Two or more plates that have been sewed together.

Slunk. The pelt of an unborn animal. The term applies especially to calfskin with the hair left intact, which is used in sportswear.

Springs. Spring-caught animals of those species that develop their best quality of fur in the spring—particularly beaver, muskrat, and nutria.

Staying. The application of thin, strong cloth to the skin side of pelts for reinforcement.

Taping. (1) Sewing strips of leather into a skin; similar to leathering. (2) Sewing cloth tape along the edges of pelts to be attached to cloth garments. (3) Sewing cloth tape on seams for reinforcement.

Thirds. Peltry lower in quality than seconds; generally, low-grade, inferior skins.

Tip dyed. See *Dyeing.*

Underfur. Fur fibers.

Zigzag. Triangular ridges of seams joining skins; usually invisible at a distance.

are difficult to maintain, cold storage or gas treatment, or a combination of both, are used commercially. The color, flexibility, softness, and natural oils of the skins are preserved, and the furs are protected from moths.

In the cold-storage method, cold air is blown into the storage vaults; the temperature is maintained at 40° Fahrenheit; and the humidity is controlled to prevent drying out of the skins, or—at the other extreme—matting and mildewing because of too much dampness.

In the gas treatment, the furs are placed in airtight vaults where the temperature and humidity are controlled, and fumigating gases are used regularly. Properly controlled, this method is scientifically safe and is not injurious to the dye and the oils of the furs.

Before furs are stored, they should be thoroughly cleaned commercially. Furs should never be home cleaned. Cleaning furs with any available household cleaning fluid will dry the skin, and strenuous rubbing action will split and wear off the hairs. Professional cleaning by a reliable furrier once a year will rejuvenate the pelts; remove dirt, dust, grease, insect eggs, and other soil; and prolong the life and serviceability of the garment. An accumulation of soil may cause unpleasant odors, decrease the luster of the fur, and cause the fur to rot and decay. Different kinds of fur require specific care, which the furrier, not the wearer, is capable of giving.

Commercial cleaning of furs is done by custom furriers, fur cleaners, and fur retailers, who often use the services of specialists such as fur dressers and dyers. These specialists are familiar with the characteristics of different furs and provide special handling for each kind. One of the largest fur dyers in the country has a process that includes inspection, cleaning, repairing, revitalizing, and storing, with a registered guarantee tag affixed to every garment. Attention is first given to the lining of a garment. It is dampened to soften the soil and dirt; if extremely soiled, it is spot-cleaned or may even be removed and cleaned separately. The fur then is tumbled in a drum containing very fine sawdust—much as it was when it was first processed—for a carefully controlled period of time. Then the furs are revolved in a screen-covered drum in which air, tumbling, and suction remove the sawdust from the furs. The next step is to restore each kind of fur to its natural luster, softness, and character.

Glazing is a process used to restore luster to dull-looking furs. It not only improves the appearance, but also helps keep fur from becoming brittle. One method of glazing involves wetting the fur with a solution and passing a warm iron over it; this attracts oils and waxes to the surface of the hair and improves the luster. Ironing with wax paper over the furs is another way to improve the luster.

If a garment has fur trimming, usually the trimming is separated from the garment and each cleaned separately, since the dry cleaning solutions used on fabrics tend to dry out the natural oils of the fur, leaving the leather side either very tender or stiff and hard and subject to cracking.

LABELING

One of the greatest aids to the consumer who is in the market for a fur garment is the Fur Products Labeling Act, discussed in Chapter 10. It imposes a severe penalty on any retailer who sells a fur without labeling it with its true name. Former terms such as beaverette, coney, Hudson seal, lapin, mermink, mink-dyed muskrat, mountain sable, sealine, and many others were merely misleading names for marmot, muskrat, opossum, or rabbit.

Federal law requires the retailer to attach a tag at least 2 x 3 inches in size to every fur and fur-trimmed garment. On this tag must appear:

1 The true name of the animal from which the skins were taken, in large type.
2 If the skins were imported, the country of origin.
3 If the fur is dyed, bleached, or otherwise changed from its natural state, a statement of such alteration.
4 If the fur contains pieces or less valuable parts of the animal, a statement of that fact in plain language. This provision also applies to used and second-hand furs.
5 The name of the store selling the fur or the full name and address of the manufacturer or his identifying number.

The law also provides that the store must give you a sales check with your purchase, on which are stated the same facts that appear on the tag. The law is applicable equally to cash sales and to instalment buying.

None except the true name of the animal from which the skins in the garment were taken is permitted to appear on tags, sales checks, or advertisements. The term "Hudson seal" has been replaced with *black-dyed muskrat* or *sheared black-dyed muskrat.* "Mink-dyed muskrat" must now be called only *dyed muskrat* or *brown-dyed muskrat.* The term *dyed rabbit* is used in place of "sable-dyed coney." "Mermink" is properly called *marmot.* "Mountain sable" is *dyed bassarisk;* "lapin" is *sheared dyed rabbit* or *dyed rabbit.*

Rabbit was at one time turned out under thirty or more different names. Although the labels identify the rabbit, it can still masquerade as any one of several other furs. It used to be bought mainly by college students, but it can, in sheared form, be made to look like mink or ermine and is bought by many women at a cost much lower than that of luxury furs.

"Mink-dyed squirrel" must be described as *dyed squirrel,* and the description of color may be added: color—brown. The term slunk, which means the pelt of an unborn animal, is applied to calf. This is not an imitative fur, even though it is sometimes printed to look like leopard or dyed in bright colors. It must be identified as to origin of animal. Since Bombay lamb comes from various parts of India, this fur is now labeled *dyed lamb,* with India the country of origin.

The term "Persian lamb" posed a problem since there is no longer a country called Persia. However, the chief value of the skin is in its curly-patterned appearance, and so the law permits the continued use of the name, with the provision that the country of origin of the skin appear on the tag.

The law provides that all the required information must appear on one side of the tag. The store may, if it wishes, use the reverse side of the tag for directions concerning care, storage, and repair; but no wording may be used that could in any way be misleading.

When a coat is restyled or repaired and new material is added, the furrier must state on the sales check the true name of the added fur as well as its country of origin.

As indicated in the chapter on textiles, the Wool Products Labeling Act and the Textile Products Identification Act require that all fibers used in apparel be identified and percentages given, so that interlinings in fur coats and the fabric of a fur-trimmed cloth coat must be labeled as well as the furs.

| FUR | ORIGIN | | CHARACTERISTICS | | | USES | WARMTH | DURA-BILITY | COST * |
	COUN-TRY	FAMILY	COLOR	HAIR LENGTH	APPEAR-ANCE				
Badger	Canada United States	Weasel	Cream with brown and silver tip	Long guard hair	Fluffy under-fur, silky guard hairs	Trimmings on cloth and fur coats Guard hairs used in pointing fox furs	Good	Good	Moder-ate
Beaver	Alaska Canada United States	Rodent	Pale brown to bluish brown, dark brown, black or brown guard hairs	Long	When proc-essed (plucked or sheared) is soft, dense, light-weight.	Coats, jackets, trimmings for sports and general wear	Very good to ex-cellent	Good	Moder-ate to expen-sive
Burunduki	China Russia	Rodent	Dark stripes on light yellow or brown background	Short	Short, flat, coarse fur; thin leather	Trimmings on sports out-fits; lining for jackets, coats	Little	Low	Low
Chinchilla	South America United States (fur farms)	Rodent	Bluish gray with black-tipped white guard hairs to ash-gray tinged with yellow	Short ¾ to 1 inch	Smooth, silky, lightweight, delicate, luxurious	Capes, coats for dress wear	Little	Low	Expen-sive
Ermine (American weasel)	Canada Russia United States	Weasel	White with black tip tail; brown	Short	Dense, deli-cate silky, soft lus-trous; lux-urious	Evening capes, wraps, jack-ets, trimmings for dress and evening wear; popu-lar in warm climates	Fair	Fair	Expen-sive
Fisher	Canada	Weasel	Medium-dark brown with black tipped guard hairs	Long	Soft, full underfur	Scarves, capes, jackets, coats	Good	Good	Expen-sive
Fitch	Central Europe	Weasel	Yellow with black guard hairs	Medium	Lustrous, soft; pliable leather	Scarves, jack-ets, trimmings	Good	Fair to good	Moder-ate
	Russia		White with black tipped guard hairs	Medium	Soft	Coats	Fair	Good	Expen-sive
Fox— Blue	Alaska Greenland Iceland Scandi-navia	Canine	Smoky bluish-brown	Very long	Thick, bushy fur	Scarves, stoles, short capes, jackets; trimmings; rarely in coats	Moderate	Fair to low	Moder-ate to expen-sive

* "Costs are based on Summer 1965 prices; this can definitely vary over the years." Jess Chernak, Fur Information and Fashion Council.

FUR	ORIGIN		CHARACTERISTICS			USES	WARMTH	DURA-BILITY	COST *
	COUN-TRY	FAMILY	COLOR	HAIR LENGTH	APPEAR-ANCE				
Fox—Cross	Europe North America	Canine	Red-silver with black cross at back of neck	Long	Bushy	Jackets; scarves, trim-mings; occa-sionally capes and coats	Moderate	Fair to low	Moder-ate
Fox—Kit	North America Russia	Canine	Off-white	Long	Soft fur, dense, silky	Coats, trimmings	Very good	Good	Moder-ate
Fox—Platina or Platinum	Scandi-navia United States	Canine	Platinum-shaded cream to light blue with silvery cast; light blue-gray underfur; white, pale gray top fur	Very long	Full, dense, lustrous fur; white marking on head, neck	Dressy capes, stoles for dress wear; trimmings	Moderate	Fair to low	Moder-ate
Fox—Red	Alaska Canada Siberia United States	Canine	Orange-yellow, orange-red, brown-red	Long	Same as Cross	Casual jackets, coats, trim-mings for general wear	Moderate	Fair to low	Low to mod-erate
Fox—Silver	North American and Scan-dinavia fur farms	Canine	Blue-black with silvery banded guard hairs	Very long	Dense, glossy, lustrous, smooth silver; ranges from $3/4$, $1/2$, $1/4$ to all black	Stoles, capes, scarves, jack-ets for dress, casual, evening wear; trim-mings	Moderate	Fair to low	Moder-ate
Fox—White	Alaska Canada Greenland Siberia	Canine	White with yellow streaks	Very long	Thick, silky, lustrous, bushy fur	Capes, stoles, evening wraps; trim-mings; dyed for day-time wear	Moderate	Fair	Moder-ate to expen-sive
Guanaco or Guanaquito	South America	Hoofed	Yellow-red, red-brown (copper color)	Medium to long	Soft, full un-derfur, silky guard hair	Jackets, coats for general wear; trim-mings	Moderate	Fair to low	Inexpen-sive
Jaguar	South America	Cat	Brownish-yellow, large rosettes	Short	Flat hair	Jackets, coats	Fair	Fair to low	Moder-ate to ex-pen-sive
Kolinsky	Siberia	Weasel	Yellow-brown	Medium	Straight, fine	Jackets, capes, trimmings	Moderate	Fair	Moder-ate
Lamb—Broadtail	Afghan-istan Russia South Africa	Hoofed	Black, brown, Gray	Very short	Flat with moiré pat-tern; high luster; fragile skin; pliable	Dress coats, capes, jack-ets, trim-mings, linings	Poor	Poor to fair	Expen-sive

* "Costs are based on Summer 1965 prices; this can definitely vary over the years." Jess Chernak, Fur Information and Fashion Council.

FUR	ORIGIN		CHARACTERISTICS			USES	WARMTH	DURA-BILITY	COST *
	COUN-TRY	FAMILY	COLOR	HAIR LENGTH	APPEAR-ANCE				
Lamb—Broadtail processed	South America	Hoofed	Off-white	Short-sheared	Similar to real broad-tail but duller, less silky; an even moiré pattern	Coats, capes, jackets for general wear; lin-ings; trim-mings	Little	Low to fair	Low to mod-erate
Lamb—Kidskin	Africa China India South America	Hoofed	Black, gray white	Short to me-dium	Sleek moiré look, high luster	Coats, jackets for general wear	Little	Low to fair	Low to mod-erate
Lamb—Mongo-lian	Outer Mongolia	Hoofed	Off-white	Long	Silky, shaggy	Coats, jackets, stoles, pants	Good	Good	Moder-ate
Lamb—Mouton process	Australia North America South America South Africa	Hoofed	Off-white black brown	Short	Sheared, straight-ened, smooth lustrous pile	Coats, jackets for general wear; trim-mings; lin-ings	Very good	Fair to good	Low
Lamb—Persian	Afghanistan Russia South Africa	Hoofed	Black, brown, gray	Short	Lustrous, tightly rolled curls running in continuous ridges; coarse texture	Coats, jackets, trimmings; general and dress wear	Moderate	Fair to good	Moder-ate to ex-pen-sive
Leopard	Ethiopia India Somaliland	Cat	Black rosettes on cream or yellow background	Short	Flat, sleek, colorful; supple skin	Coats, jackets for general wear trim-mings; lin-ings	Fair	Low to fair (sheds)	Expen-sive to very ex-pen-sive
Lynx	America Canada Russia	Cat	Brown-gray with blue-white or gray guard hairs	Long	Fluffy, light color with attractive shadings	Scarves, short jackets for sports, day-time, even-ing wear; trimming	Moderate very good	Fair (sheds)	Moder-ate
Lynx cat	America Europe	Cat	Light color, small rosettes	Medium long	Semi-fluffy	Coats, trimming	Good	Good	Moder-ate to ex-pen-sive
Marmot	Asia Europe Russia	Rodent	Blue-gray to yellow-brown; upper ⅓ of fur brown; mid-dle ⅓ yel-low	Short	Coarse, harsh hair with high glassy gloss	Coats for gen-eral wear	Fair	Poor to fair	Low

* "Costs are based on Summer 1965 prices; this can definitely vary over the years." Jess Chernak, Fur Information and Fashion Council.

| FUR | ORIGIN | | CHARACTERISTICS | | | USES | WARMTH | DURA-BILITY | COST * |
	COUN-TRY	FAMILY	COLOR	HAIR LENGTH	APPEAR-ANCE				
Marten—American	United States Canada	Weasel	Tan to yellow to dark brown	Medium	Straight silky hair; dense fur; smooth texture	Scarves, jackets for general wear	Moderate	Fair	Moderate
Baum	Asia; Europe	Weasel	Tan to dark brown; white-gray	Medium	Silky	Coats	Good	Good	Expensive
Marten—Stone	Asia Europe	Weasel	White-gray underfur with brown guard hair	Medium	Slightly coarser than other martens	Scarves, jackets trimmings for dress wear	Moderate	Good	Moderate
Mink—Wild	China Europe Japan North America	Weasel	Yellow to pale brown; to very dark brown; narrow, dark stripe on center back	Short	Dense fur with lustrous glossy silky, guard hairs; flexible light-weight skins	Scarves, coats jackets, wraps stoles, for all occasions	Very good	Fair to good	Moderate to expensive
Mink—Ranch	Europe North America	Weasel	White to blue-brown; mutation in many colors	Short	Uniform color density and textures; gills, pieces, paws give patterned effect	Scarves, coats jackets, wraps stoles for evening wear	Very good	Good	Moderate to very expensive
Mole	Belgium Great Britain Holland	Rodent	Deep blue gray	Very short	Straight, sleek fur; delicate skin	Jackets, coats capes, trimmings	Little	Low	Moderate
Muskrat	Canada Russia United States	Rodent	Dark brown backs; golden brown sides; silver bellies	Short	Dense even fur with long guard hair	Coats, jackets; for general wear	Moderate to very good	Fair to good	Moderate
Nutria	South America United States	Rodent	Blue-brown to yellow-ish-red	Short	Soft; resembles beaver but shorter fur	Coats for general wear; trimmings; linings	Moderate to very good	Fair	Moderate to expensive
Ocelot	South America Mexico	Cat	Tawny colored with black, brown, white oblong dash and ring shapes	Short	Straight, deep flat fur, clear markings	Coats, jackets, capes; trimmings; for sportswear	Fair	Good	Expensive

*"Costs are based on Summer 1965 prices; this can definitely vary over the years." Jess Chernak, Fur Information and Fashion Council.

FUR	ORIGIN		CHARACTERISTICS			USES	WARMTH	DURA-BILITY	COST *
	COUN-TRY	FAMILY	COLOR	HAIR LENGTH	APPEAR-ANCE				
Opossum—American	America	Miscella-neous	Cream white with silvery tip guard hairs; gray white with black-tip guard hairs	Medium	Bulky, coarse; dull	Coats, jackets; trimming for sports, casual wear	Moderate to very good	Poor to fair	Low to moderate
Opossum—Australian	Australia	Miscel-lane-ous	Blue-gray; yellowish-reddish	Medium	Soft, smooth, dense fur	Coats, jackets, trimmings	Moderate to very good	Fair	Moderate to expensive
Otter	North America South America	Weasel	Light to dark brown	Short	Thick, soft, with lustrous sheen; resembles beaver when plucked	Coats for general wear, trimming	Moderate to very warm	Good to very good	Expensive
Pony	Poland Russia South America	Hoofed	Medium Gray, tan, brown, black	Short	Resembles kidskin but heavier skins; flat moiré pattern; lustrous	Sport coats, jackets; trimmings	Little	Low to fair	Low to moderate
Rabbit	Australia Europe France Belgium	Rodent	White, gray, brown	Short	Thick, fine, soft, straight glossy hair; sheared resembles many other furs	Coats, jackets, capes, stoles for all occasions trimmings, linings	Good	Good	Low
	Japan	Rodent	Beige to white	Short	Soft	Trimmings	Fair	Low	Low
Raccoon	North America	Miscel-lane-ous	Gray-brown with silvery cast; dark silvery brown	Medium to long	Dense with high sheen; guard hairs plucked; fur sheared	Coats, jackets for general wear	Good to very good	Good to excellent	Moderate
Sable	Japan Manchuria Siberia	Weasel	Dark brown or black with bluish cast; yellow to yellow-brown	Medium	Thick, soft fur; lustrous sheen; fluffy guard hairs	Scarves, stoles, capes, jackets, coats; for dress, evening wear; trimmings	Good	Fair	Expensive

* "Costs are based on Summer 1965 prices; this can definitely vary over the years." Jess Chernak, Fur Information and Fashion Council.

FUR	ORIGIN		CHARACTERISTICS			USES	WARMTH	DURA-BILITY	COST *
	COUN-TRY	FAMILY	COLOR	HAIR LENGTH	APPEAR-ANCE				
Seal— Fur	Alaska Asia South Africa South America	Aquatic	Brown	Short	Lustrous, soft, fine after guard hair plucked. Alaskan most dense	Coats, jackets, capes, stoles, scarves, trimmings	Very good	Good to ex-cel-lent	Moder-ate to ex-pen-sive
Seal— Hair	Canada Scandi-navia	Aquatic	Gray or spotted	Short	Bristly hair; compact leather; no underfur; flat, sleek, slight pat-tern	Coats for sportswear	Moderate to good	Fair to good	Low to mod-erate
Skunk	North America South America	Weasel	Dark brown and black with white stripes along back	Long	Straight, thick fur; long, lus-trous guard hair	Jackets, stoles, capes, trim-mings, sports and general wear	Very good	Good	Moder-ate
Spotted cat	South America	Cat	Cream color small rosettes	Short	Soft, silky, sleek	Trim, neck-wear	Moderate to good	Fair	Moder-ate
Squirrel	Canada China Siberia	Rodent	Gray, steel blue, black	Short	Full furred and fine textured	Coats, jackets, trimming	Moderate	Poor to fair	Moder-ate
Tiger	India	Cat	Tawny orange & black stripe	Short	Deep, flat hairs	Coats, jackets	Fair	Fair to low	Expen-sive
Wolf	North America	Canine	Pale blue; gray under-fur; black guard hairs	Medium	Soft, dense underfur; long-flow-ing guard hairs	Trimmings, jackets, scarves; sports, cas-ual wear	Very good	Fair to good	Low to mod-erate
Wolverine	North America	Weasel	Wide dark brown center stripe on back; light brown streaks on sides	Long	Coarse tex-ture	Trimmings; bulky jack-ets, and coats; sports-wear	Very good	Good	Moder-ate
Zebra	Africa	Horse	Creamy-white, brown, black stripes	Short	Deep, straight, flat	Coats	Fair	Low	Moder-ate

* "Costs are based on Summer 1965 prices; this can definitely vary over the years." Jess Chernak, Fur Information and Fashion Council.

The Fur Label Authority label on a garment indicates that that garment was produced under fair labor standards. This is a result of a co-operative effort between management and labor for the consumer's protection.

The Mutation Mink Breeders' Association, acknowledged producer of the world's finest mutation mink, uses protective trademarks; the carefully graded and sorted varieties of natural-color mink are labeled, stamped, and sold only under the association's trademark. Each one of the trademark colors has descriptive terms identifying the exact natural color of the skins and indicating that they are not blended or retouched in any way. The trademark is in a woven label sewed to the lining of the garment; it is also stamped on the skins and included on the bill of sale.

The Fur Information and Fashion Council conducts a public relations program for the fur industry and launches industry-wide campaigns to promote furs.

IMITATION FURS

The synthetic fibers made to imitate furs should not be confused with real furs. Various combinations of fibers—Orlon and Dynel, for example—in a pile fabric offer silky thickness, lightweight warmth, beautiful styling, long wear, and mothproofness. Colors range from pale grays, beiges, and browns to charcoal tones. In general, coats of imitation fur are inexpensive; those with real fur trim cost proportionately more.

After four years in the laboratory, fabric duplicates of several costly furs were put on the market. The process of making imitation furs—which were first produced in 1953 by "mating" Orlon and Dynel—culminated in a fabric whose painted-on stripes come remarkably close in appearance to genuine mink and have been called "mock-mink."

Laboratory mink is one of the fanciest entries. The original fabric, which resembled beaver, was rain- moth- and mildewproof; it shed a little, but it was warm and inexpensive. Soon other companies began turning out imitation furs under intriguing trademarks and names. Better dyes and finishes made imitation fur look like sheared beaver, raccoon, sealskin, fox, otter, lamb, monkey, jaguar, leopard, zebra, giraffe, and Russian broadtail.

A cleaner for the home care of these pile fabrics was developed. Dry cleaners are cautioned to use fur-cleaning methods instead of the usual dry-cleaning process on these imitation furs.

FUR FOR MEN

Throughout history, men have worn furs from time to time. During the twentieth century, fur apparel for men has been pretty much limited to the raccoon coat of the 1920's, which enjoyed a revival with the brief raccoon-coat fad among college students and sport-coat enthusiasts during the 1950's.

Fur-trimmed and fur-lined coats and jackets have been more popular than fur coats. The alpaca-lined coats and jackets and the lambskin shearlings used during World War II and the Korean War for warmth and durability seemed to create a desire for similar serviceability in civilian clothing. Although alpaca and lambskin shearlings are not furs in the true sense of the word, they seem to be the closest approximation of furs for men. The hair-like wool is made into a pile fabric used in jackets, car coats, and full-length coats. "Lambskin shearling" is a skin tanned with a uniformly-clipped short length of wool on it.

If an alpaca fabric is made from a specialty hair fiber, it is labeled according to the provisions of the Wool Products Labeling Act. The person who contemplates buying an alpaca-trimmed or alpaca-lined garment should check the label to make sure he is paying for wool and not for one of the synthetic fibers.

If a man does buy a real fur coat, jacket, vest, hat, or other fur accessories, he should keep in mind the same suggestions made for the wise purchase of furs for women.

REFERENCE READINGS

Books

Ashbrook, Frank G., *Furs, Glamourous and Practical,* D. Van Nostrand Co., Inc., New York, 1954.

Bachrach, Max, *Fur, a Practical Treatise,* Prentice-Hall, Inc., New York, 1953.

Evans, Mary, *Better Clothes for Your Money,* J. B. Lippincott Co., Philadelphia, 1952.

Fuchs, Victor Robert, *The Economics of the Fur Industry,* Columbia University Press, New York, 1957.

LaBarthe, Jules, *Textiles, Origins to Usage,* The Macmillan Co., New York, 1964.

Lester, Katherine and Oerke, Viola Bess, *Accessories of Dress,* Manuel Arts, Peoria, Illinois, 1940.

Samet, Arthur, *Pictorial Encyclopedia of Furs,* Arthur Samet, New York, 1950.

Tate, Mildred Thurow and Glisson, Oris, *Family Clothing,* John Wiley & Sons, New York, 1961.

Wilcox, Ruth Turner, *The Mode in Furs,* Charles Scribner's Sons, New York, 1952.

Wingate, Isabel B., Gillespie, Karen B., Addison, Betty, *Know Your Merchandise,* 3rd Ed., McGraw-Hill, New York, 1964.

Bulletins

Better Buymanship No. 8, *Furs,* Household Finance Corporation, Chicago, Illinois, 1951.

Born, W., "Alaska Sealskins," *Ciba Review,* Basle, Switzerland, 1952.

Butt, Gladys, L., *Make Your Furs Wear Longer,* Cornell Extension Bulletin 838, New York State College of Home Economics, Ithaca, New York, June, 1955.

Federal Trade Commission, *Rules and Regulations Under the Fur Products Labeling Act,* 1952.

The Fur Information and Fashion Council, Inc., "The Softest Touch," New York, 1964.

Great Lakes Mink Association, *Some Questions and Answers About Your New Mink Coat,* Kenosha, Wisconsin.

Magazines

Changing Times, "Fur Coat Guide for Husbands Only," The Kiplinger Magazine, Washington, D. C., November, 1953.

Consumer Reports, "Furs," Mount Vernon, New York, November, 1955.

Greene, Nona Lou and Taylor, Jan Martineau, "The Fashionable Life Is Wrapped in Fur," The Fur Information and Fashion Council, Inc., New York, 1965.

Chapter 22

Hosiery

O ver 2,000 years ago Eskimos wrapped their legs in grass. The Vikings devised crisscross leather straps that partially covered the legs and at the same time kept their shoes from falling off. Hand-knitted hose, which came into existence in the fifteenth century, were about the only kind available until the 1900's. With the invention of the knitting machine, mass production of hosiery, now a multi-million-dollar industry, developed. The primary function of modern hosiery seems to be to make legs look shapely and slender and to complement the entire costume of the wearer.

TYPES OF HOSIERY

Today there are socks and stockings for every occasion, in a great variety of colors, materials, sizes, and textures. Women's hosiery is available in body length, ankle length, and any length in between. Anklets are made in elastic, flat, and ribbed knit tops. Knee-length and above-knee-length hose are knit with either an elastic top or a double hem. Body hose, leotards, and tights reach to the waist. Footlets worn inside shoes when regular socks or stockings are not worn are also classed as hosiery.

Hosiery is usually full fashioned or circular knit. *Full fashioned* means that the stocking is knitted to conform to the shape of the leg and foot. *Circularknit* or seamless stockings are knit in tube form and heat-set to conform to leg and foot shapes. Seams may be closed with yarn of either matching or contrasting color. *Tubular* hosiery, another form of circular knit, stretches to the desired shape. *Support* hosiery provides extra support for the leg through the use of all-stretch nylon or a combination of nylon and spandex. Seamless stockings without toe and heel reinforcements are designed to be worn with sandals or toeless or sling-back shoes to give a bare-legged effect. Fads in decorative hosiery include clocks of sequins, jewels, and other filigree on the sides of the ankles and tops decorated with appliqué of lace, flowers, and similar motifs. Patterned hose in a variety of designs and sheerness are fashionably acceptable.

FASHION IN HOSIERY

The length of the skirt influences the emphasis placed on hosiery—in design, sheerness, and color. In the 1920's when skirts started climbing, women wanted their legs to look glamorous—and legs have been in the spotlight nearly every season since then. Fashion news has been made by stretch hose, metallic-thread seams, sparkling nylon, and sequin clocks. Tights, leotards, colored hose, body hose, stretch hose, textured hose, and printed hose are fashionable.

It has been estimated that the average American woman buys a pair of stockings every three weeks. Mass-production methods have made hosiery available to her at a minimal cost. The extreme sheerness of hosiery does not afford much warmth, but most women do not feel completely dressed unless wearing hose.

For many activities and in some climates, hosiery is not worn at all. In contrast, many women have large hosiery wardrobes, with different types for different occasions, activities, and costumes. The varying degrees of sheerness include ultra or evening sheer, dress or daytime sheer, walking sheer, and sport or service sheer.

With the introduction of colored and textured hose, fashion stressed co-ordinating hosiery with shoes, skirts, tops, jumpers, sweaters, and hats with a resulting "total" look. Hosiery colors to complement basic skin tones have also been promoted. Shaded hose, to create the optical illusion of straighter and more slender legs, were developed at one time. Some of the patterns of textured hose have a tendency to make the leg look larger.

HOSIERY FIBERS

The quality of the fiber, the size of the ply, the twist of the yarn, and the finish are important factors in the appearance, strength, and durability of hose. Cotton, nylon, rayon, silk, wool, acrylics, olefins, spandex, linen, and combinations of these fibers are used in hosiery yarns.

Cotton fibers are carded before being spun into yarns. *Combed* cotton yarns are firmer, smoother, and stronger than carded yarns of the same size. Cotton hose are made of single- or multiple-ply yarns. Cotton is spun into yarns of different degrees of fineness, from the extremely fine, tightly spun to the coarse, loosely spun. Size is indicated by numbers—the higher the number, the finer the yarn. *Mercerized* cotton

yarns are lustrous, strong, and take dye readily. *Lisle,* a smooth, two-ply combed-cotton yarn, tightly twisted and singed to remove fuzz, makes fine, smooth, strong cotton hosiery. There is no great general demand for cotton hose; however, cotton socks and stockings are worn by some consumers. They absorb perspiration and are easy to launder. Cotton lisle soles replacing the usual nylon are preferred by some women.

Nylon is one of the most popular fibers for hosiery. Nylon is used in monofilament and multifilament form. Spun nylon is used in socks and sometimes in full-length stockings; it is often mixed with other fibers and used for reinforcement in hosiery.

The qualities that make nylon popular for hosiery are its abrasion resistance, elasticity, and strength. Nylon-covered elastic yarns may be used in the flexible tops of hose requiring no garters for support. The fine monofilaments go into the making of the gossamer-like hose many women seem to prefer for appearance if not durability. Nylon can be heat-set, so that the process of shaping, or preboarding, can give permanent shape to nylon hosiery.

Nylon is also used in stretch hose, both full-fashioned and seamless, which fit a range of sizes. They cling to the leg and give without binding under the strain of knee bending. Stretch is built into nylon by a permanent twist similar to that of coil-spring knitting yarn. Many types of stretch yarn have been developed, under a variety of brand names. Stretch hose are comfortable, fit well, and wear well. Cantrece nylon, a self-crimping monofilament, has a resiliency that improves the fit of hose.

Sparkling nylon hosiery, popular at one time, was made from a monofilament yarn in which a change in the amount of exposed surface area produces a multitude of

Textured stockings. (Courtesy Berkshire Knitting Mills.)

highlights. This hosiery, intended for evening wear, was available in a wide range of colors—including gold and silver—and a choice of textures.

Both *viscose* and *cuprammonium* rayon are used primarily in men's hose. During World War II, rayon was the chief fiber used in all hosiery. Rayon may be made with any degree of luster and in either fine or coarse filaments. Rayon's chief advantages are its affinity for dyes and its low cost. The high-twist rayon yarn used in hosiery increases sheerness, strength, and elasticity. Spun rayon is used to make wool-like yarns generally used in socks. The denier range of rayon yarn is 40, 50, 75, 100, and 150.

Acetate is a thermoplastic fiber, and hosiery made from it can be pre-boarded to make the shape permanent.

Silk produces clear-textured, elastic, smooth, strong yarn for hosiery. The sheerness is stated by threads, the number of strands of silk twisted together for stocking

yarn. Two thread are very sheer; three threads are sheer; four and five are service sheer; six to twelve threads are service weight. Highly twisted silk yarns improve the appearance and service of silk hose. Silk hosiery is less and less available, except by special order for women's hose.

Wool yarns are used mainly for ankle- and knee-length socks for women. Worsted yarns make the finest and most desirable wool hosiery. Wool retains heat, absorbs moisture, and, when treated, is shrinkage resistant.

The *synthetic* fibers—Dacron-polyester, Dynel-modacrylic, Orlon-acrylic, Vectra-olefin, Lycra-spandex, and combinations—are used in hosiery. Orlon, Dacron, and Dynel are quick drying, and durable.

Blends and combinations of fibers in hosiery are made in various ways—by mixing fibers together before yarns are spun; by making a core of a yarn of one fiber and twisting another fiber about this core; by making two-ply yarns, one of the strands of one kind of fiber and the other of another kind; by plaiting—by having one side of the

The parts of a stocking.

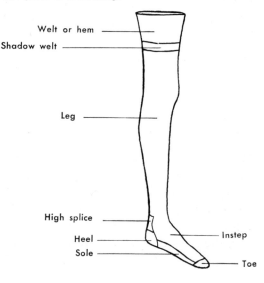

402

fabric of one kind of fiber and the other side of another kind; and by using one textile fiber, such as nylon, for the main part of the base and another, like cotton or silk, for the reinforcements at the heel, sole, splicing, and garter welt. For people who find that nylon stockings are not absorbent enough, hose with a nylon leg and a cotton or silk sole may be comfortable.

CONSTRUCTION

The construction of hosiery is also very important. The yarn is usually made by one firm and then sold to other manufacturers, who make the hose by various methods and techniques. Most hosiery is weft knit.

Full-fashioned

Full-fashioned stockings are knit flat in a shape that conforms to the shape of the leg

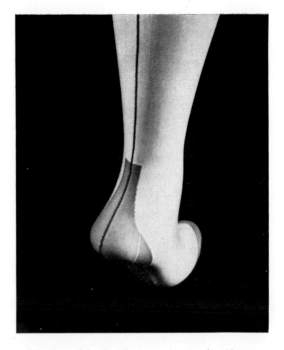

Full-fashioned heel with narrowing marks. (Courtesy Berkshire Knitting Mills.)

Full-fashioned heel and toe construction. (Courtesy Berkshire Knitting Mills.)

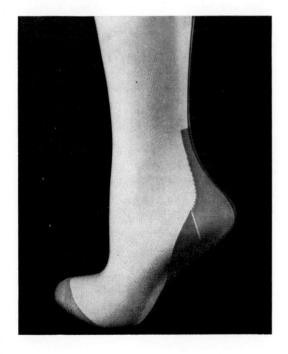

and foot, and then are closed along the bottom of the foot and up the back of the leg. The open area inside the welt at the top is due to the fact that the seaming machine cannot allow the operator to proceed any further; this opening is not an imperfection in construction. Full-fashioned hose are usually made in full-length stockings and sometimes in socks.

Beginning with the welt or hem, the stocking is knitted with a full count of stitches or loops to provide maximum circumference at the top. As the knitting progresses in a downward direction the number of stitches is lessened. Each "dot," or *fashion mark,* near the seam of the stocking and in the foot indicates that stitches or loops have been knit together at that point. This narrowing process provides the desired shape to fit the knee, calf, ankle, and foot.

To recognize full-fashioned hose, look for fashion marks on each side of the back seam below the welt, at the calf, and near the heel and for lengthwise rows of stitches that run parallel to the seam. Fashioning at the calf may also be observed by the shape of the stocking and its elasticity. The number of stitches dropped in shaping the stocking from calf to ankle depends on the gauge. The coarser the gauge, the fewer the narrowings. Fashion marks that are very close together in the leg of the stocking may indicate skimping.

Seamless and tubular

Circular-knit, or seamless, hose are knit in round tubular form with the same number of stitches throughout the leg and foot. Sometimes the stitches are tighter around the ankle and looser at the top to give the stocking shape. Body length hose, over-the-knee hose, knee socks, and anklets are made by this method. Circular-knit hose can be distinguished by the fact that all lengthwise rows of stitches run parallel the full length of the stocking. Seamlesss stockings made of nylon and other thermoplastic

Seamless foot. (Courtesy Berkshire Knitting Mills.)

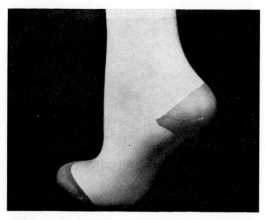

404

fibers are shaped on heated drying forms. Because this shaping is permanent, it is important to buy the correct size and proportions in seamless hose.

Tubular hosiery, knitted in a circular fashion in a uniform size throughout the length, stretches to fit the foot and leg. Although the low price appeals to some consumers, the fit and comfort do not.

Semi-fashioned and cut-and-sewn

Another method of making stockings is to start at the toe and finish at the hem, adding stitches as the stocking is knit. The stitches meet in the form of a V at the back of the leg without a seam. This semi-fashioned method is usually confined to cotton, heavy rayon, wool, and surgical hosiery. Some cut-and-sewn hose and tights are cut from knitted fabric according to a pattern and then sewn together.

Knitting stitches

The knitting stitches used in making hosiery are plain, mesh, and ribbed knit.

Plain knit is smooth and even textured, with lengthwise rows of loops or ridges showing on the right side, and crosswise rows of loops visible on the wrong side.

Mesh knit is a type of yarn interlooping forming an open, lacy pattern. Of the many variations of mesh knit used in hosiery, the run-resistant mesh seems to be the most popular. The stitches of run-resistant hose are locked together in such a way that a snagged stocking will not develop a run, although a hole may result.

Ribbed knit, with its vertical ridges, is more elastic, more durable, and heavier than plain knitting. It is used in socks and anklets, but is too coarse for full-length hosiery. There are true ribs and imitation ribs in hosiery; the true rib has ridges alternating on either side of the fabric. The imitation rib may be made by dropping

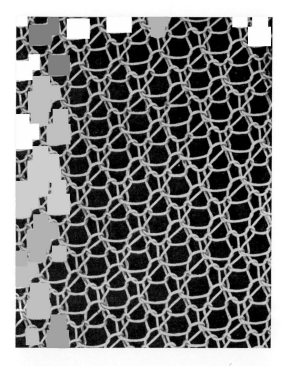
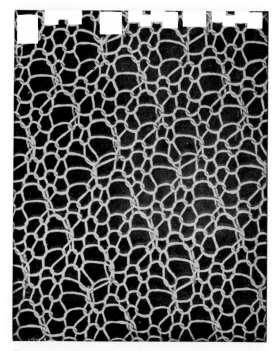

Two types of nonrun mesh, 7 × actual size. (Courtesy Textile Machine Works, Reading, Pa.)

stitches at regular intervals to give a ribbed appearance or by a special stitch that looks like a rib on one side of the fabric but is merely caught together on the back. A distinguishing feature of imitation ribs is the presence of eyelets wherever the ribbing is changed, usually at the foot, heel, or hem. Sheer textured hose in a variety of designs have patterns produced by a combination of stitches.

Denier and gauge

Fineness of knitting is determined by denier and gauge. *Denier* is the term used to designate the fineness of nylon, rayon, or silk yarn; the lower the denier, the finer the yarn. One-thread silk is approximately 14 denier; two-thread is 28; and three-thread, 42. The great strength and transparency of nylon make possible a wide range, from 7 or 10 through 15, 20, and 30 up to 70 denier.

Gauge is the number of needles per 1½ inches on the needle bar of the machine used in knitting full-fashioned hosiery. The higher the gauge, the more closely knit is the fabric; the usual range is from 39 to 72.

In order to produce varying degrees of sheerness in hosiery, different combinations of denier and gauge must be used. As the denier, or size of the yarn gets finer, which is indicated by a lower number, the gauge usually increases, as the higher number indicates. High-gauge hose are smoother and tend to resist snagging; since a high gauge requires finer yarn, the stitches are closer together. Thus, 60-gauge, 15-denier nylon hose tend to wear better than 15-denier hose of lower gauge. Since the numbers proved confusing to many consumers, "walking sheer" or "business sheer," "dress sheer," "evening sheer," and similar terms have gradually replaced the original terminology. To designate the closeness of the loops in

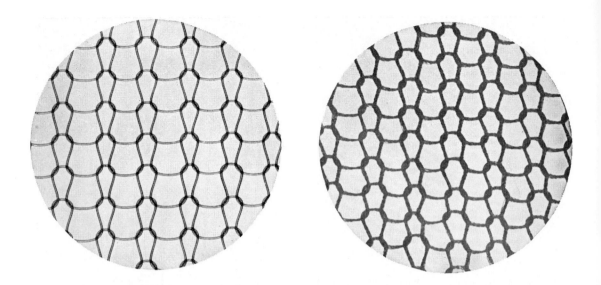

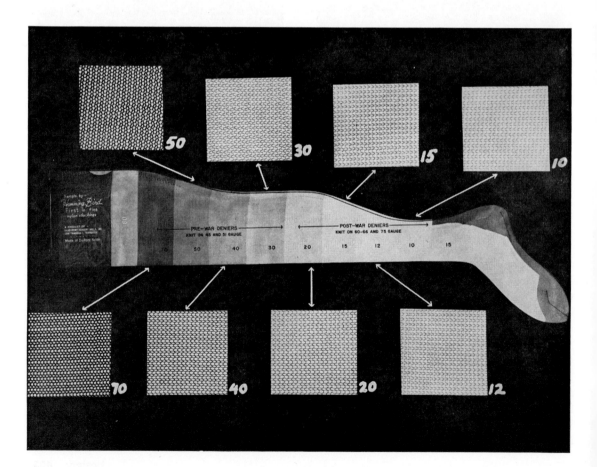

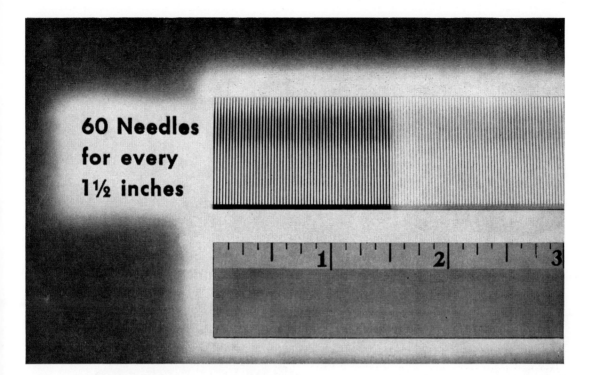

**60 Needles
for every
1½ inches**

circular-knit hosiery, the number of needles used in knitting the tube is indicated; the common range is from 260 to 432 needles. Variations between coarse and fine circular knits are similar to those between low- and high-gauge full-fashioned knits. Although hosiery is made in ultra sheer, sheer, medium sheer, and service weights, American women tend to choose very sheer hose for all occasions.

Cotton and wool yarns are numbered, and the higher numbers are used in the finer socks and stockings. The slight vertical ridges of loops, or "wales," on the right side of a stocking indicate the gauge; as the

(Opposite) Top: left: Fifteen-denier nylon hose magnified 10 times; right: Thirty-denier nylon hose magnified 15 times. (Courtesy E. I. du Pont de Nemours & Co.) Bottom: Range in deniers. (Courtesy Davenport Hosiery Mills.)

Gauge: the number of needles or loops in each inch and a half across the top of the stocking. (Courtesy Berkshire Knitting Mills.)

gauge number increases, the wales appear finer and closer together.

Finishing and dyeing

The amount of twist in the yarn influences the luster of the stocking. A high twist stretches the surface of the yarn and makes the yarn more elastic and run-resistant. Stockings are *ingrain* dyed before knitting or *dip dyed* after knitting, or a combination of the two methods may be used. Dyeing may also be done before the yarn is spun; this method is called *stock dyeing*. Improved dyes and methods of dyeing make it possible for the consumer to purchase hosiery that is colorfast to laundering, which means that the colors do not fade or stain. Dark-colored socks and an-

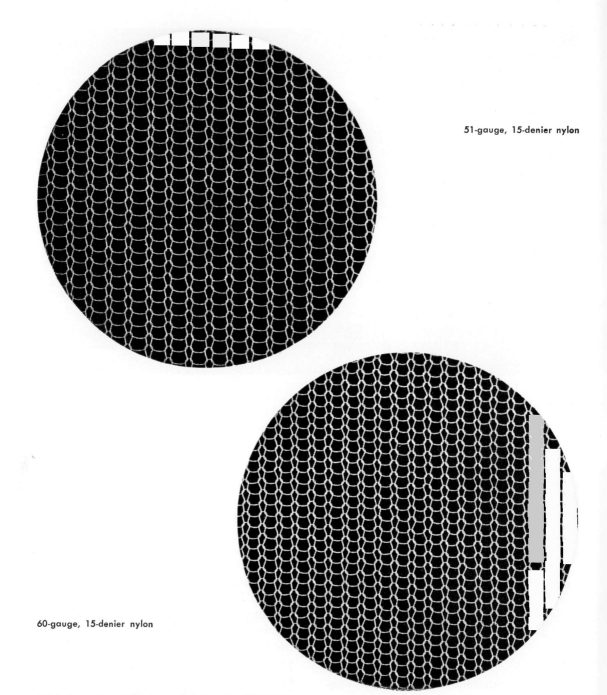

51-gauge, 15-denier nylon

60-gauge, 15-denier nylon

Stitch formation of fabric produced on the READING
Full-Fashioned Knitting Machine. Fabric enlarged to
seven diameters. (Courtesy Textile Machine Works,
Reading, Pa.)

klets should be washed separately until it is evident that the color will not run.

Various finishes have been developed for hosiery, including those that make hosiery resistant to water spotting, snagging, and shrinkage. Some nylon stockings have a finish that makes them more absorbent; these are more comfortable for persons who tend to perspire. Other finishes, like those that retard the development of odors and resist bacteria and germs, are used on some hosiery. Finishes to reduce the sheen were developed when low-sheen stockings seemed to be preferred.

Sizes

To insure proper fit and, consequently, adequate service, hosiery is made in a wide range of sizes. The foot size is the length of the foot in inches. The leg length is the distance from the bottom of the heel to the top of the stocking. Because of the variations in shape and size of women's legs regardless of foot size, proportioned hosiery has been developed for average, full, short-slender, slender, and tall styles. Outsize hose, which are designed for the large thigh and calf, are knit on wider needle bars than regular size and are usually longer. The increased elasticity due to the greater amount of fabric causes less strain and gives comfort to the wearer.

The foot of the stocking should be half an inch longer than the foot of the wearer. A foot that is unusually fleshy may require a longer stocking to allow for extra take-up in the width and depth of the foot. In contrast, a very thin foot and leg may require a shorter stocking. The length of the regular stocking from the welt to the edge of the sole should be long enough for the garter to be attached to the welt, not below it. The stocking should be comfortable when the wearer is seated and without wrinkles when she is standing. Short

lengths are 28 to 29 inches; medium, 30 to 32 inches; long, 33 to 34 inches, opera, 40 to 44 inches. However, there is some variation in these figures among different brands of hosiery. Body hose are proportioned to foot, leg, and body size.

The relationship of the shoe size to the corresponding hosiery size should be noted:

Shoe Size	Stocking Size
1, 2N, 2½N	8
2W, 2½W, 3, 3½, 4N, 4½N	8½
4W, 4½W, 5	9
5½, 6, 6½N	9½
6½W, 7, 7½N	10
7½W, 8, 8½N	10½
8½W, 9, 9½	11
10, 10½, 11	11½

When buying two or more pairs of hose of the same color and foot size, the customer should be sure that the leg length of all pairs is the same.

The sizes recommended in stretch stockings are as follows:

Small—If regular sizes are 8, 8½, or 9 short, slender, or medium, or 9½ short or slender.

Medium—If regular size is 9 long or ample; 9½ medium, long, or ample; size 10 short, slender, or medium; or size 10½ short or slender.

Long—If regular size is 10 long or ample, 10½ medium, long, or ample, or 11 and 11½, all lengths.

POINTS IN BUYING

Brands

When buying hosiery, many women buy by brand name, having found a size and construction that gives them greater satisfaction than any other kind. Brand name is usually a manufacturer's guarantee of quality and value in each price range. Other women do comparative shopping and buy what seems to be the best quality at a particular price. For many women hosiery is an expensive item in their wardrobe—because of poor selection, improper care, or rough wear. Care should be taken in choosing the style of stocking—full-fashioned or seamless; the type—conventional or stretch; the knit—plain or mesh; the weight or denier—sheerness; the gauge or needle count—closeness of stitches.

Full knit

Hose that are full knit, that have adequate size and length for the wearer, careful workmanship, and clear texture, usually give good service. Hose knit to full size, and not skimped, give good elasticity and good wear. The hem or welt of an over-the-knee stocking should stretch to about 12 inches, an outsize stocking should stretch to 14 or 15 inches at the top. Adequate stretch in the thigh area is necessary to prevent discomfort from poor circulation. In socks and anklets, the ribbed top should be firmly knit to insure permanent elasticity. An average size sock will stretch to 7¼ inches through the instep to the heel.

Seams

Seams in full-fashioned stockings should be flat, narrow, neat, firmly sewed with good quality thread, and have 14 stitches to the inch, on the average.

The inside of hosiery should be smooth, with thread ends securely fastened and carefully clipped to prevent raveling and to increase comfort.

Reinforcements

In hosiery designed for durability rather than for the bare look required by fashion and some shoe designs, the reinforcements are important. However, the stocking that has little or no reinforcement looks prettier with a sandal. Reinforced areas are at the

points of wear and strain. The double section under the foot, the sole, is usually wide for general wear, but narrow and less durable for hose to be worn with sandals. The toe reinforcement of regular hose should be heavy enough to prevent its being cut by toenails. The "splice," or reinforcement of the heel above the top of the shoe, varies in size and shape, but usually ends far enough above the heel to withstand the rubbing from the edge of the shoe. A narrow, tapering heel reinforcement has a slenderizing effect on the ankle. The hem, or welt, at the top of the stocking should be well reinforced in order to withstand the strain put upon it by garters. The double thickness should be 3½ to 4 inches wide. Just below

Seamless toe with a patented band that stops runs starting in the toes from moving up into the body of the stocking. (Courtesy Berkshire Knitting Mills.)

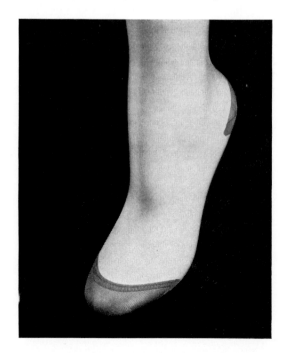

this welt is a narrow strip about 1½ inches in width; this "shadow welt" forms a transition between the welt proper and the leg of the stocking. A row of lock stitches, called a run-stop, between the shadow welt and the leg prevents a run that starts in the welt from continuing down the leg.

Color

When choosing colors in sheer hosiery, the customer should examine a stocking over the salesperson's hand, because the color looks much lighter over skin than in the box or package. Colored, patterned, and bulky hose should also be checked this way for appearance.

Irregulars

Occasionally hose marked "seconds," "thirds," or "irregulars" are put on sale or reduced in price. These are stockings that do not meet the specifications of a manufacturer's first quality. Seconds and thirds are those in which there are mends, runs, or other obvious imperfections in construction or finish. Irregulars are imperfect in dimension, size, color, or knit. The defects are often so slight that these hose are sometimes a bargain for some consumer uses. It is a government requirement and accepted procedure among hosiery manufacturers to mark hosiery of other than first quality by these terms.

Price

Price is not necessarily an indication of quality in hosiery. Some low- and medium-priced stockings wear as well as, if not better than, some higher-priced hose. Novelty or super-sheerness features may add to the cost of expensive hose.

Labels

Informative labeling is available on most hosiery. The information may be either stamped on the hose, printed on the package, or given on a paper insert in the folds of the packaged hose. This information is limited to denier, gauge, and fiber content on some hose; other brands include size charts, information on special construction features, and directions for care.

The Federal Trade Commission's *Trade Practice Rules for the Hosiery Industry* are beneficial to the consumer in providing her with information about the hosiery at the point of sale. The fibers used are named together with the part of the stocking in which they are used, e.g., "nylon with silk sole." Many technical terms, as defined in the rules, are included in labeling, such as "irregulars," "cotton lisle," and others.

It should be remembered that hosiery yarns are made by textile producers and then sold to hosiery manufacturers, who knit the yarn on standard hosiery machines; yet hosiery varies in construction and workmanship with different manufacturers. Consequently, the purchaser should examine hosiery carefully before buying, unless a particular brand with which she is familiar meets all of her needs.

Socks

When choosing knee socks or anklets, it is important to check the way the top is joined to the leg to see whether all loops are caught. A true ribbed-top sock is elastic enough to stay up in place without binding. The machine-sewed rib often leaves a rough edge and is not as neat, flat, elastic, and well made as the real rib, but it wears well and is less expensive. Socks should be well reinforced in heel, sole, and toe.

Care

The care of hosiery begins with the buying—choosing the correct size and weight is very important. Evening sheers are a poor choice for casual wear if durability is desired. Many women buy sheers almost automatically and wear them for all occasions. Stockings of a more durable gauge and denier will last longer. Buying the sheer-as-cobweb hose for street wear means getting runs almost as a person walks. Denier for denier, nylons wear as well today as they did when they first appeared on the market, but the first ones made were no sheerer than 40 denier. 8-, 10-, and 12-denier hose should not be expected to wear as long as the heavier ones.

If the foot of a stocking is too short, the toes and heels wear out rapidly; if the leg is too short, the stocking wears out or develops runs at the knee; if the leg is too long, runs may develop quickly because the wearer usually has to fasten her garters in the shadow welt rather than in the double welt. Since stockings are about the only item of clothing that cannot be tried on when it is bought, it is important to know the exact size needed.

Buying two or more pairs of the same color at one time allows rotating of hosiery and matching remaining hose when one of a pair has to be discarded.

Sheer hosiery should be handled with care when being put on and taken off. Hands and nails should be smooth, and so should the feet and the legs. The stockings should be inspected after each wearing so that any catches or runs may be repaired immediately.

Socks and stockings should be washed after each wearing to remove soil and perspiration that might weaken the fibers. Rubbing, twisting, and wringing is hard on fine hosiery. They should be cared for by gently squeezing mild, lukewarm suds through them, rinsing them carefully, wrapping them in a towel to remove excess moisture, and hanging them to dry on a smooth line away from direct sunlight or heat. All hosiery that is not colorfast to washing should be washed separately. It is possible to launder some socks in automatic washers —but make sure the label indicates this method. Usually several pairs are placed in a nylon bag, which is then placed in the washer and washed in the shortest cycle possible. All hosiery should be thoroughly dry before storing or wearing. This is especially true of rayon, which weakens when it is wet but regains its strength when thoroughly dry. Wool hosiery can be dried on forms that are made especially for the purpose of stretching the hose back into shape.

MEN'S HOSIERY

Men can and should have plenty of variety in the socks they wear. It is estimated that men over fifteen average 10.8 pairs per person; and that solid-color, ribbed, elastic-top slack socks account for nearly 80% of the market. Some men own many more socks than they habitually wear, either because they do not like certain gift socks or because they wear the socks that are on top of the collection over and over. In general, if the basic color of the socks complements a man's suit and shoes rather than being keyed to his tie or shirt, the wearer shows good taste.

Types

There seem to be three types of socks— plain, patterned, and casual—with each type having its own special place in the wardrobe. Plain-colored socks in a smooth, flat knit and in dark colors are appropriate for evening wear. For daytime wear, most men prefer ribbed knits or nubby textures, wearing black and navy with black shoes and brown with brown shoes or gray, maroon, tan, blue, or green to complement or match the suit. The regular or elastic-top half-hose length socks are usually worn for general and dress wear.

Patterns are a variation for daytime and look best when worn with plain suits. The patterns include inconspicuous clocks, overall small figures, or stripes. They are lightweight and are held up by elastic tops. The fashion acceptance of more conspicuous patterns such as Argyles fluctuates over the years.

Casual socks are heavier in feel and knit and often have bold colorful designs. They are worn with tweeds and sport clothes. For general wear and sportswear, elastic-top, knees-length, short-length socks, or anklets are the lengths usually worn. For active sports, the "sweat," or boot sock, and knee sock are worn.

Men's socks may be either circular knit or full fashioned, in a Jacquard, a plain, or a ribbed stitch. The rib stitch may be used throughout the sock or confined to the top. Usually the ribbed sock clings to the leg, fits well around the ankle, and requires no garters. Elastic thread knitted in several rows in the top keeps socks in place on the leg. The imitation ribbed sock, often found in inexpensive hose is not as strong or elastic as the true ribbed knitting. It can be distinguished by tiny holes at the hem, in the foot, or at the heel of the sock. Many men prefer circular-knit hose, maintaining that a seamless foot is more comfortable than that of the full fashioned foot. The number of needles for men's socks varies with the type of sock, 56 being an average for heavy work socks. Knee length support hose provide comfort for "standees."

The clock, which is a decorative feature on the side of some hose, is either knitted in as a part of the hose and called "true wrap" or several strands of yarn are held loosely during the knitting operation, leaving long loose ends of thread on the inside of the sock. Socks made by the latter method, called "mock wrap," tend to wear out more quickly, because the loose threads pull out as the sock is worn and laundered.

Men's socks should be colorfast or vat dyed. If not, colored socks—especially the dark ones—should be washed separately until they no longer bleed in the water.

Size

Men's socks are made in several lengths: athletic socks, 7 to 8 inches; slack socks and anklets, 8 to 9½ inches; half socks, 14 to 14½ inches (with ½-inch tolerance, either longer or shorter); work socks, 14 to 15½ inches; and knee socks, 17½ to 20 inches. Corresponding shoe and sock sizes are:

Shoe	Hose
7–7½	10½
8–8½	11
9–9½	11½
10–10½	12
11–12	13

Measuring the foot of a well-fitting sock from the point of the toe to the end of the heel is another way of checking the size in nonstretching socks. Men with large feet and legs can buy stout sizes to insure comfort and wear. Socks should fit neatly and well. Socks that droop over shoe tops or bare the legs do not fit properly. Short socks with elasticized tops give most men the maximum in comfort and neatness. Men with heavy or very thin legs usually look better in longer socks worn with garters.

Fibers

Men's socks are made in a variety of fibers. *Spun nylon* is used a great deal, because hose made from it are comfortable, durable, non-stretching, non-shrinking, and soft. The filament nylon that is used in men's socks is of heavier weight than that used for women's hosiery, so that men's lightweight dress socks are never as sheer as women's hose. Nylon reinforcements in heels and toes are common in socks made of other fibers.

Stretch hose are available to men as well as to women. Stretch socks have a soft, crinkly surface texture. They look like any other socks, except that they are much smaller. They are made of nylon filament yarn that is specially twisted to give extraordinary elasticity. This nylon is combined with spun nylon and other fibers. The socks will stretch easily and comfortably to fit any man's feet. As they stretch, they fit snugly and trimly over the ankle and leg, which makes them the neatest-looking socks a man can wear. They do not shrink or stretch out of size in laundering. However, the continuous-filament nylon does not absorb perspiration readily. Combining stretch nylon yarn with cotton increases the absorbency if the cotton yarn is on the inside of the sock, where it comes in contact with the skin. Sometimes the stretch nylon and cotton are twisted together before knitting to form a single yarn. Some nylon socks are lined with cotton.

Spun rayon—made of rayon fibers cut to special lengths and spun into soft, fluffy yarns—is also used in men's hosiery. Spun rayon is widely used in pattern hosiery. The pattern may be produced by cross dyeing—in which rayon yarn is twisted or knitted with acetate or some other yarn that will take a different color in the same dye bath, thus producing a design. Patterns are also "knitted in" by the Jacquard knitting method.

Silk is sometimes used in men's hose, either alone or in combination with other fibers. In contrast to the two and three threads used in women's hose, 8 to 20 strands are used, since the heavier yarns give better wear than lightweight ones.

Cotton has been a popular fiber for men's lightweight socks and for work socks in warm weather. Mercerized cotton yarns and cotton lisle are lightweight, comfortable, and desirable for dress wear. With the development of the nylon stretch hose, a one-size cotton sock was developed. It looks hand knit, is shaped for comfort, and is neat in appearance. Its two-way ribbing,

which prevents wrinkling, keeps the sock neat on the foot and leg. It is made of fine mercerized long-staple cotton reinforced with nylon for extra strength.

Wool is used in nearly all types of men's socks—from sheer, lightweight cashmere to heavy work or active-sport socks. Many men whose feet perspire excessively prefer wool socks to any other, because wool can absorb moisture without feeling clammy. Wool socks are very warm, excellent in cold climates for outdoor work and sports. The blending of wool with other fibers—to reduce shrinkage—is common. Blends are popular in men's socks. *Cashmere* for softness, lamb's wool for body and warmth, and nylon for washability and drying ease are combined in sretch hose. *Dacron*-polyester, *Orlon*-acrylic, and *vectra*-olefin are used either alone or in blends.

One of the finishes developed for men's hose is designed to make them hygienically clean. This finish retards the development of odors. It is nontoxic and nonirritating, bacteria- and germ-resistant, and effective against athlete's foot.

Care

The care of men's hosiery is easy, and more and more men seem to take care of their own socks—especially men who travel and college students. Socks should be washed after each wearing in lukewarm water and neutral soap suds. The washing should be followed by thorough rinsing and pressing out of excess moisture. Then the socks should be hung to dry, away from direct heat or sunlight, or placed on sock drying forms—especially wool socks. Colored socks should be washed separately until all bleeding of color has disappeared.

Many socks are so well made and thoroughly reinforced against strain and abrasion that they rarely wear out. Socks that have had too much wear and too many washings will lose their color and their fit long before they develop holes or tears. That is the time to replace them.

If a sock does develop holes, the holes should be darned before the sock is beyond repair. A sock should not be pulled on the foot all at once, causing holes and runs. The foot of the sock should be eased on first, and then the rest of the sock pulled up the leg.

Wool socks should be bought a size larger than is usually worn to allow for shrinkage. Wool socks should be washed in not-too-hot water to prevent excess shrinkage. Placing wool socks on metal or plastic sock dryers helps maintain their original shape and size.

If garters are worn they should not pull too tightly on the socks. The strain may cause holes and runs.

CHILDREN'S HOSIERY

Buying

Important points to consider when buying socks for children are color, fabric, size, heel, sole, toe, and top. Socks labeled colorfast or vat dyed may cost a little more than an unlabeled pair, but they will look better longer, with no excessive fading or bleeding. The sock should be closely knitted. It may be made of combed mercerized cotton, spun nylon, Orlon-acrylic, rayon, wool, or combinations of these fibers. Choice would depend upon the climate and the needs of the child. A fancy, plain, or ribbed stitch may be used.

The heel, sole, and toe should be of a heavier knit than the rest of the sock. Reinforcement should extend above the back of a low shoe. There should be no loose ends of yarn to catch on the foot. Four- or six-ply yarn or nylon reinforcements give added wear.

Whether the top of the sock is finished with elastic or lastex or has a ribbed or flat-knit top, it should have plenty of give. A skimpy top will be uncomfortable and will wear out sooner. Circular ribbed knits are common, although some short socks are full-fashioned. Tights and leotards are usually circular knit, but some are cut-and-sewn.

Size

Remembering that a child's foot grows quickly, one should not buy the same size bought last time, because a sock, like a shoe, affects the healthy growth of a young foot.

Children's socks are classified in length as ankle-length; half-length; five-eighths- or mid-length, seven-eighths- or knee-length, and full-length. Shoe sizes and corresponding sock sizes are:

Shoe	Socks
0–1	4
1½–2	4½
2½–3	5
3½–5	5½
5½–6½	6
7–8	6½
8½–9	7
9½–10	7½
11–12	8
13	8½

REFERENCE READINGS

Books
Bacharach, Bert, *Book for Men*, A. S. Barnes & Co., New York, 1953.
Bacharach, Bert, *Right Dress*, A. S. Barnes & Co., New York, 1955.
Evans, Mary, *Better Clothes for Your Money*, J. B. Lippincott Co., Philadelphia, 1952.
Wingate, Isabel B., Gillespie, Karen R., and Addison, Betty C., *Know Your Merchandise*, 3rd Ed., McGraw-Hill, New York, 1964.

Bulletins
Better Buymanship, Use and Care, *Hosiery*, Household Finance Corporation, Chicago, 1948.

Magazines
Consumer Reports, "Men's Socks," Mount Vernon, New York, January, 1957.

Chapter 23

Lingerie

In his choice of lingerie and underwear, the individual has an opportunity to add variety to his wardrobe and do exactly as he pleases without concern for offending others. Although women's outerwear may demand a certain kind of foundation, the robe and nightgown or pajamas of the individual often express the whims and preferences convention does not always allow in outerwear. Even the most conservative man might wear gay patterned shorts or brightly colored pajamas.

ROBES

Robes have come to refer to many kinds of clothing. For the women, there are negligees and housecoats. For the men, there are lounging robes and bathrobes. Individual preferences in lounging wear are just as varied as the kinds available. Individuals vary a great deal in the amount and the kind of wear they give to robes. College girls may study in a robe. In many households a robe is acceptable at breakfast. Other families are very strict in not allowing informal wear at the table. There are those who for TV and reading like the easy comfort of a robe or housecoat. Some people have a number of robes; others find one robe adequate for their needs. Design in robes varies from the classic line in flannel or other woolen fabrics to housecoats in intricate and elaborate damasks. A woman's robe may follow the fashion silhouette of the day. However, there is generally a wider variation in styles than will be found in dress wear. For example, the oriental influence is often found; mandarin collars, kimono sleeves, or decorative frog fasteners are usually seen in some styles every season.

A woman can really express her personal preferences in choosing her lounging wear. She may have very frilly, fancy negligees or the classic flannel robe. Many women have a variety of kinds. The classic robe is not always severe but may be made in lovely fabrics with added decoration in the seams or on the lapel. It may give a very elegant appearance and still be easy to put on and pack well for travel. A negligee has come to mean a robe designed for the bedroom, dainty, sheer, and usually with added decoration such as lace or cording. Negligees are frequently found in nylon tricot, a soft crepe, or satin in rayon or silk. The material is generally a soft one with a decorative, elegant feeling. A hostess gown is designed more as a dress would be. It is often full length and usually of a luxurious, lovely fabric such as satin, lamé, damask, or taffeta. Velvet has always been a favorite. This type is usually designed to fasten securely either with a zipper or fly front. It is necessary that the hostess coat be fashioned to stay shut. The peignoir is a loose-fitting negligee that generally hangs free from a yoke or from the shoulders. It has come to mean a dressy kind of robe. The duster, originally worn to protect clothing from dust, is imitated in the style of many robes. It falls free from the shoulder and is loose in fit, generally a little less decorative in design, and may be made of plain fabric. Hostess gowns and lounging pajamas, which are popular from time to time, are made to look appealing and

Robe styles. Left: negligee or peignoir; right: kimono.

suitable to be worn to receive people. They are often fitted to the figure. The design is enhanced by the way the outfit fits the individual.

The choice of fabric for a robe is determined to a great extent by the use one ex-pects to give the robe. We have already indicated that negligees and some dusters are made in very delicate fabrics. Despite its filminess and lightness, a negligee made

Robe styles. Left: quilted. Center: Empire, back zipper. Far right: negligee.

of nylon tricot is exceedingly strong, durable, and easily laundered. Nylon tricot has also been used a great deal in quilted dusters and robes, which launder very successfully. Nylon tricot robes or negligees should not be pressed, and one must take care when wearing them not to get near a hot iron, open fireplace, or the stove, which might melt the fabric. Nylon tricots, if trimmed, regardless of weight or style, should have nylon trimmings that have the same properties in washability and wear. Cotton trim will not dry as quickly nor launder under the same conditions as nylon tricot. Quilted robes are also made in cotton, most of which

"At home" lounge wear for the hostess.

now can be laundered. Rayons, silks, and acetates are also often quilted, but should be dry-cleaned unless the label definitely states washability. Among the napped fabrics we find brushed fleecy finishes, doeskin, velveteen, and velvets. These fabrics may be silk, triacetate, nylon, acrylic, or rayon, or a blend of fibers. Velveteen is a cotton fabric. The classic tailored robe is made in numerous fabrics, although a woolen flannel is usually the most popular.

At various times other fabrics, such as chenille, become popular. A blend of cotton and wool such as Viyella makes a lovely soft washable robe. Many of the wool flannels are now made to be fully washable. Terry cloth is a favorite for a robe to slip into after the bath. It is absorbent, easily laundered, and practical. Men frequently use terry robes as beach coats. Terry is nice for children since it is usually

The oriental influence in lounge wear for men and women.

machine washable and can be bleached. Many companies make terry robes in a greatcoat style that will fit both men and women. Summer robes come in wide varieties of fabrics and, except for the negligee, will usually be opaque. Seersucker, piqué, gingham, chintz, and cotton satin are all satisfactory. These come in a wide variation of designs and with many different kinds of trim. Trim and buttons are particularly important on robes. Very often buttons cut thread because of the sharpness of the shank, and the individual can spend a great deal of time sewing on buttons. It may be simpler to replace those buttons that are always in need of attention. Robes that have buttons of self fabric should indicate that

the buttons are washable and will not rust. Better robes come with extra buttons.

The individual woman will choose her robe for becomingness to her figure. In selection, one should remember that most robes are not worn with foundation garments. If warmth is desired, a long robe might be the natural selection. If lightness in weight for travel is needed, one that does not crease readily and packs into a small space will be desirable. In your choice of style, an easy fit and becoming color will be important. Robes are sold in misses', junior, and in larger sizes corresponding to dress sizes such as 38 and 40. Occasionally, robes are marked small, medium, and large.

Most bedjackets are chosen for warmth, but, for summer, lightweight bedjackets are also available. The bedjacket is a short version of the robe, made of the same fabrics and with the same care features. Since housecoats, negligees, and bathrobes are very personal items and are worn in your own home, you can have what you would like with no consideration for anyone but your family. This may be where a woman who normally does not need decorative clothes can express her love of luxury. It may be that if you do not wear plaids and gaily patterned fabrics in your everyday clothes, you would enjoy the change to a patterned fabric.

Men's robes are generally made in a classic style, frequently with a shawl collar. If warmth is desired, the robe will probably be in a good wool flannel or Viyella. In a lighter weight fabric, a foulard or tie silk in small geometric patterns is a favorite. Summer robes are of cotton piqués, plissés, or other washable fabrics. Some men find that a lightweight lounging robe that slips on over the shirt for chilly evenings is an attractive and comfortable addition to the wardrobe. This might be in a fine wool or a

Men's robes. From left to right: classic robe, shawl collar, and kimono.

lovely damask. Style may vary from the kimono in a hip length, to a plaid in the lapel coat style. Men's robes are sold in small, medium, large, and, occasionally, in extra-large sizes. Small usually corresponds to 35, 36, and 37 in suit sizes; medium is for sizes 38 and 40, and large for 42 and 44. Extra-large sizes are for those whose suit sizes would be 46 or over.

WOMEN'S LINGERIE

All of the various kinds of lingerie and underwear have some factors of selection in common but beyond these factors the articles have different requirements. High on the list of requirements for all underwear is the ease of launderability and care. Lingerie will need good construction for durability and should have desirable performance features like colorfastness, sanforization, and durable-press in fabric and trim. Fashion will have an influence on all underwear, particularly on women's lingerie. The silhouette of women's fashion will govern the design and fitting of the foundation garment. Petticoats will be popular when the bouffant silhouette is in fashion and disappear when the silhouette is slim. A properly fitted garment is essential to comfort and appearance.

Foundation garments

Foundation garments are a typically American garment. Until recently, European and South American women rarely wore girdles and brassières. Foundation garments are selected to enhance the proportions of the body, to give support to the body where needed, and to improve the appearance of outer clothing. They should be comfortable to wear and should not bind at any point on the body. These garments are for control of the figure and should not distort it in any way. A girdle that is too tight will create rolls that will make a person look larger.

Brassières. For health, as well as appearance, a brassière should not bind at any point. A brassière that binds may impair

circulation. Support is essential to protect delicate body tissues. Size and style are important considerations for a comfortable and becoming bustline. Styles are available in different designs and fabrics. Brassières are also now molded to shape. It is especially important that the young girl's figure be properly controlled from the time she begins to develop. The control throughout the garment is achieved by intricate and varied designs and by a fabric that is suitable for the purpose. Heavy broadcloth, lace, and net are used frequently in combination with elastic for movement without binding. The well-designed style will give complete coverage for the soft flesh. Support in the garment will come from the straps and from the band base of the brassière. If the straps are too narrow or too long there will be no support. A band that is loose rides up in back and control is lost. Support is gained through design, boning, wiring, or stitching. Design varies from the narrow bandeau to the long-line brassière. Stitched-in polyurethane foam, acetate or polyester fill or cotton batting material is used to give additional fullness to the bust

Find a becoming proportion for your figure. From left to right: midway between shoulder and waist, low line, and high line.

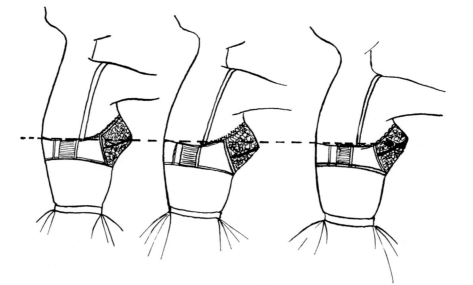

contours. It is important when padded brassières are chosen that they appear entirely natural. The long-line brassière is used where a smooth, continuous line is needed.

Size is the most important factor in selecting a good brassière. Unfortunately, there is little size standardization, and sizing varies from one manufacturer to another. Most good stores have well-trained personnel to assist in proper fitting. Brassières are bought by bust and cup size. Measuring the chest above the bust may be a better indication of bra size. Because of the variation in sizing and styles, it will be necessary for you to try different makes in order to find the correct type for you. In selecting size, there are several methods various manufacturers suggest. One is to measure the bustline directly at the fullest part and to take a high chest measurement, above the bust. From the difference in these measurements you can determine cup size. The bust that measures one inch more than the chest usually requires an A cup, two inches more requires a B cup, three inches more requires a C cup, etc. Other manufacturers suggest the measurement be taken directly below the bustline around the diaphragm. If the measurement under the bust is an odd number, add five inches to determine size. If the result of the measurement under the bust is an even number, add six inches to find the proper size. Neither of these methods is infallible. Since fabric construction and the tone of the flesh may affect the fit, it is best to try foundation garments carefully. Once you have determined the style best for you, you will be able to recognize features of design and fabric good for your figure.

Girdles. Your choice of girdles or corselets will be dependent on many different things. In your analysis of your figure, you discovered which physical characteristics you

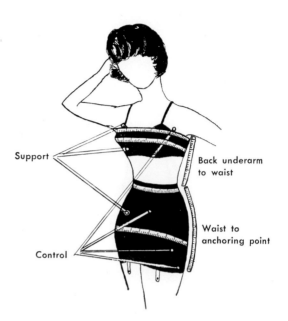

Support

Back underarm to waist

Control

Waist to anchoring point

wanted to camouflage or to emphasize. You also noted the lengths of various areas of the body. Your activities will determine to a great extent the kind of girdle that will be satisfactory to you. The person who is on her feet a great deal may need support for her back muscles. The very active person will not want anything that restricts or interferes with movement.

Girdles should give a smooth line to your figure. This is done through giving firm contours and control. A girdle must not be so tight as to create added rolls or bulges. When you analyzed your figure, you noted your bone structure, which you know you cannot change. If you are wide in the hips because of bone structure, you cannot decrease width, but you can obtain a smooth line. However, if you are fleshy, a girdle may control the fat and make you appear somewhat slimmer. Padded girdles add curves. A girdle should not ride or move on the body. It should move with the body.

The control or support in a girdle is obtained by use of different kinds of fabrics and of design. Girdles will vary from the

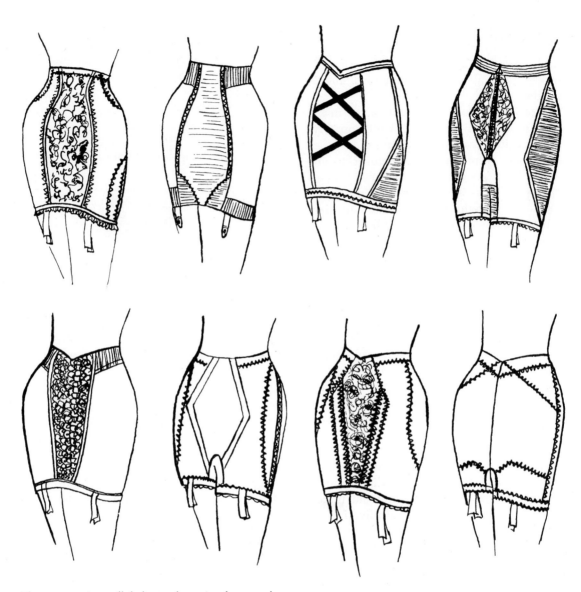

The construction will help to determine how much support and control the girdle will give. All paneling aids in control. Fabric panels give support; elastic panels help in control yet allow movement.

lightweight nylon net or two-way stretch, which gives a minimum of support, to a garment of heavy, nonelastic quality that is boned, paneled, and often laced for the very heavy figure that needs support. A firm,

closely woven, heavy fabric is used when support is needed. A fabric that does not stretch is combined in design with elastic that permits the movement of the body. Elastic may be made to stretch in either direction or, as in the case of a one-piece girdle, give a two-way stretch. The two-way stretch girdle is used for the figure that needs a smooth line and a little control but does not need support. Most girdles that

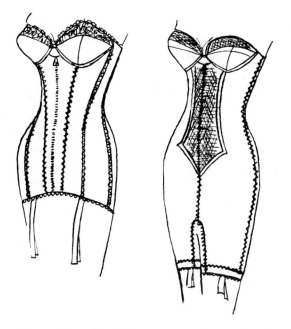

The one-piece foundation garment gives a smooth line through the midriff, supports the bustline, and aids in hip control. The long leg panty controls the thigh.

have control are made with paneling. The center panels, front and back, may be of a rigid material for support and control and the side panels elastic to allow movement of the body. Sometimes the side panels are made in a firmer fabric which does not give and which controls side flesh. New fabrics, such as those made of spandex fibers, are replacing the heavy fabrics of the past. These fabrics serve the same purpose as rubber but have more restraining power. The lightness in weight gives comfort without loss of control and support. Gussets or criss-cross panels are used to give extra freedom for leg movement. Boning is needed for large figures. In some cases, boning has been replaced by stays of fabric or by Mylar plastic stays, which are lighter and softer than steel but which do give control. Boning is used to keep a girdle from rolling at

the top and to control and flatten excess flesh. Boning may interfere with comfort, and in trying on the girdle, one should make sure it is not going to press or bind and that when one sits it will bend with the figure. The garment should be long enough to cover the fleshy part of the hips but not so long as to interfere with walking. Panty girdles control flesh over the upper leg. If the panty leg is too tight, it may affect circulation. A leg edge with lacy stretch prevents interference with circulation and eliminates a bulge where the girdle ends. The panty girdle gives a smooth appearance under close-fitting clothing. Proper length of girdle and of stockings helps to keep them correctly in place.

The garter belt is chosen for the sole purpose of holding up stockings. It has no value as a fat support and for control of body. It is important when a garter belt is worn that skirts do not cling. The slim skirt is best worn with a girdle for a smooth line. If a garter belt is substituted, a fuller skirt might be more attractive. Garter belts need to be fitted to stay put. They should not slip or twist on the figure, or create ridges or bulges under outer clothes. It is important that the length of the stockings and the length of the garter hold the stockings in place without twisting and/or sagging.

Girdle sizes are designated as junior, teen, average, full hip, and straight hip. Neither age nor measurement can give you your figure type. You have analyzed your body; with experimentation you can determine the most flattering fit and style.

Slips and panties

Slips are available in numerous colors; there even are two-toned slips made to be worn with a white blouse and a dark skirt. Evening slips are available which are designed to go with the silhouettes worn in a particular season. The slip may have a low decolletage to correspond to that of the dress, or the half-slip may be adequate with a dress made with a lining.

Slips and panties are made in similar fabrics. Designs follow the fashion silhouette of the day and should not interfere with the appearance of the outside garments. Choice of fabric and style will affect the appearance and comfort of slips or panties. Crepe and satin made from nylon, polyester, rayon, or cotton are the woven fabrics used most frequently. Most knitted slips are of nylon or rayon and are seldom seen in silk. Stretch satin and stretch taffeta made of nylon or polyester and spandex allow excellent fit and a smoother line under knits because they stretch horizontally only. Some nylon tricots are finished to prevent stretching or sagging. Many slips, called dress shapers, use a combination of seaming and fabric to fit the body closely. The man-made fibers and finishes on cotton have revolutionized the care of lingerie. They allow for dainty, delicate lingerie that is easily laundered and requires little or no ironing.

The design and the fit of slips is important to appearance. Slips and half-slips should fit closely to the body when worn under a fitted garment. Knitted fabrics and the use of bias in design allow movement without creating great bulk. Knits need little ironing and are easily cared for. Woven fabrics that do not give as readily may be desirable for use under woven and knitted fabrics that tend to give and stretch. Taffeta, for example, helps prevent sagging and stretching by relieving the strain on the outer garment. Stretch lace of spandex and nylon is used in bodices for a close fit that allows movement of the body. Nylon is very strong and durable; however, unless treated for static electricity, it tends to cling in dry weather. There are those who find pilling in nylon lingerie a problem. Rayon makes an inexpensive, durable slip

but it is weaker when wet. Cotton is enjoyed in summer because it is cool, absorbs moisture, and does not cling to the figure. Blends of polyester and cotton do not need more than "touch up" ironing.

Trim is an important factor in the durability of the article. Very sheer, delicate fabrics combined with heavy fabrics have an uneven pull and tend to split. However, many of the nylon nets have great strength and are used for trim. The best-wearing slips and panties have lace and trim of nearly the same weight as the body of the garment or are made without excessive trim. In panties, not only trim but the quality of the elastic is important. Many panties are discarded long before the fabric has worn out because the elastic has. Woven rayon or silk fabrics may slip and pull when the seam is stronger than the fabric. This is referred to as "slippage." The yarns of the fabric separate from each other and from the seam. Most fibers used in lingerie that is washed a great deal will become yellowed, grayed, or dingy unless properly laundered.

Slips that have strong, well-sewn, adjustable straps have eliminated much tedious mending. Where the ribbon straps are of a quality inferior to that of the fabric, considerable time will be spent in replacing them.

An important design feature in slips is the molding of the fabric to fit the human form. The design should eliminate any excess material but provide freedom of movement for the body. This molding is done in various ways. Inset bias bands for the rib and waist area are excellent for the small waist. A perfectly straight slip will be bulky under outer garments. The advent of the tricot knit has helped considerably to make a closer fit possible. Even tricot knits are shaped by seams or separate bands in a well-fitting slip. If

Inset   Darted   Gored   Bias center panel

Slip styles.

the skirt of a woven slip is cut on the bias, it will mold more readily to the figure but tends to twist on the figure and hang unevenly. The skirt may be cut in gores, with the side gores on the bias and straight grain in the front. The gores help to give a smooth contour and fit to a stocky figure. Combinations of bias tops, straight grain in skirts, all-bias slips, or straight top, straight skirt, and a bias fit inset in the midriff allow for figure variations. Trying on slips of various designs will help you determine the kind for you. The gored or bias slips allow for greater differences between bust and hip measure.

Skirts come proportioned in lengths—short, medium, and long. Generally, the short are for 5'4" and under, medium for

5'4" to 5'6", and long for over 5'6". In considering length, remember that a heavy figure will fill out the slip and make it shorter, and the tall, slender girl who does not fill out the slip will not necessarily need the added length of a long slip. When trying to find a nicely designed slip, it is wise to try on new makes. When you find a slip you like, take down the style, size, and proportion. The length of the slip should not be adjusted by the straps. Adjustable straps should alter the length from the bustline fullness to the shoulder.

Petticoats are designed to give added shape to the skirt silhouette. If the skirt is gored or flared, the petticoat should be

Left: Half-slip; right: Petticoat.

Half-slips are made in the same fabrics as full-length slips, such as tricot, crepe, satin, and taffeta.

The construction of the slip is an important item in durability. Many slips of good fabric have split seams and broken shoulder straps long before the fabric has worn out. Straps of the self material are best; when ribbon is used, it should be of a fine weave. Self fabric straps should be double stitched and securely fastened to the slip. The fastening to the strap is often a point reinforced with double stitching, V-stitching, or an added piece of fabric. Straps on slips which have lace should either be reinforced or attached to the body of the slip. Seams should have close, even stitches. The best-constructed slips are those that are double stitched. A plain seam with top stitching will be flat and neat. Flat-felled seams will be bulkier than top-stitched plain seams but will not have edges that may fray. A zigzag stitch is frequently used for top stitching and is an excellent stitch to use in mending knit fabrics. Zigzag stitches do not break as readily as straight stitches. Most knitted fabrics are made with an overcast edge. This overcasting is a little bulkier, but, if carefully done, it does not show on the right side. Lace that is hand sewn is seamed with a close satin stitch. With machine-made slips, lace is attached with the zigzag stitch. Appliqué and embroidery, frequently applied on lingerie as decoration, may be very fine hand work or may be done by machine. It is important that the embroidery is not too heavy for the fabric or the fabric may wear readily.

Panties and pettipants are very similar to slips in fabric construction, with the exception that we find a wider variety of fibers used. Wool and part-wool fabrics are used for warmth. Knee-length styles are often used for outdoor activities. Nylon stretch materials are being used both in above-the-knee-length and in full-length panties.

gored or flared. Some skirts have four gores and some, two. Many petticoat silhouettes have a fitted hipline and flare at the bottom of the skirt. The fitted hipline in the petticoat is generally more becoming with full skirts because it adds less bulk at the hipline and waist. With stiff petticoats, it is essential to find out whether the stiffness is permanent. Many crinolines are given a very stiff finish that later washes out. Some stiff petticoats have rough seams that snag or cause runs in hose. Cotton petticoats can be starched for stiffness. Too many petticoats can create more fullness than the outer skirt and so make the skirt look skimpy.

The number of dresses that are completely lined have made the half-slip popular. The half-slip that fits closely at the waistline generally has a zipper closing. Others, in knits, have elastic waist control. The elastic should provide enough control so that the slip does not pull down in sitting.

Full-length tights or panty hose are often worn and are not covered.

Sizing in lingerie varies with the manufacturer, but the knitwear industry has more than others adopted the sizing suggested by the Department of Commerce. Women's slips are generally sold by bust measure and length proportion. Women's panties run from 4 to 10.

Sleeping wear

Nightgowns and pajamas are the most personal items of clothing. Preferences in nightwear are as varied as the personalities of people. To some, nightwear is only a covering, and the only considerations are comfort and ease of care. Others indulge whims for luxury, color, and decoration. Whatever the choice, most people desire that night-gowns or pajamas require little time in upkeep and be comfortable and reasonably durable.

Nightgowns and pajamas differ little from slips and panties in fabric, construction, and trim. The range of designs in nightwear offers greater variety in choice. There are long-sleeved nightgowns, shorty night-gowns, and long and short pajamas. The only limitations of design are considerations for comfort, durability, and designing for the human figure. Designs are chosen which look well on the figure without foundation garments. Nightgowns have many of the design features found in robes—puffed sleeves, small collars, and full skirts. In a

Nightgown styles. Left: Full-length; right: waltz-length.

Nightgown styles. Left: Old-fashioned long-sleeve style; right: coat-style shortie.

Pajama styles. Left: shortie pajamas or Baby Dolls; right: three-piece travel set.

jamas can be found in hand as well as in machine construction. Pajamas require a well-reinforced crotch with adequate length to allow freedom of movement.

Size in nightgowns and pajamas is usually stated by bust measure, although many manufacturers are beginning to use dress sizes, such as 10, 12, etc. Junior sizes are also available.

Small accessories such as nightcaps are fashionable from time to time. The need for a head covering results from pinning up the hair for bed. Nightcaps in frilly and delicate fabrics are supposed to prevent the "spook look" and hold the hair in place. There are those that may create an odd look instead of preventing it.

MEN'S UNDERWEAR

Men choose underwear primarily for comfort and protection. Fashion in these items is primarily in the fabric and does not affect the appearance of outer garments.

Shorts

The most frequently worn shorts include knit briefs, French-back shorts, boxer shorts, or designs combining design features of the other styles. French-back shorts have a tab like that in some trousers which adjusts the waistband. Boxer shorts have a full elastic waistband. Other shorts have elastic either

French-back shorts.

long or knee-length nightgown, fullness adequate for comfort of the legs is needed. Button-down-the-front varieties, especially, will need this fullness to prevent pulling at the buttonholes. Many people find that with those that button all the way down the front, the buttons may tend to slip out of the buttonholes with the strain of movement.

Fashion plays a big part in nightwear for women. It influences the kind of article and fabric, color, and design. The long-sleeved nightgown has been in and out of fashion many times. Design is frequently influenced by current fashion in outerwear.

The fabrics that are found in slips are also the most popular in nightwear, but one will also find flannels, brushed nylons, and challis for warmth in cooler weather.

The construction of nightgowns is similar to that of slips. Lovely nightgowns and pa-

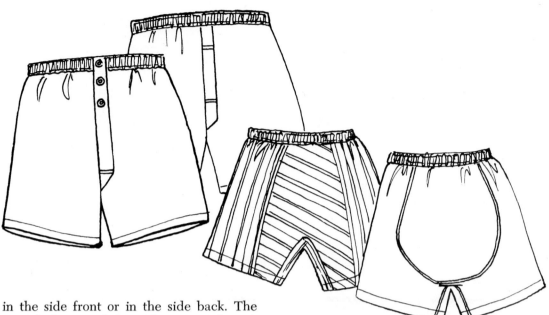

Men's boxer shorts with bias center panel or contour seat.

in the side front or in the side back. The French shorts and those that are made partially of elastic are generally made with grippers or buttons in a fly front. The fit will to a large extent determine comfort. Style will be the individual's decision after he has experimented with the various designs for comfort and appearance. It is important that men's trunks do not bind, pull, or creep. Shorts will generally be more comfortable when designed with a center panel cut on the bias which gives fullness without a center seam.

The choice of fabric will be an important factor in comfort. Smoothness and softness of material should be given first consideration. Polyester, nylon, cotton, silk, rayon, and blends of these fibers are used in shorts. Most cottons are given a durable-press finish. Broadcloth and batiste are favorite woven fabrics in French and boxer shorts. Knits that allow plenty of stretch are particularly suited to briefs. In all shorts the quality of the elastic should be equal to the quality of fabric used. It is annoying to have trim or elastic wear out when the item is otherwise in excellent condition. You will also want to check la-

bels for complete shrinkage and colorfastness. New laundry equipment such as dryers has created problems of shrinkage with knitted fabrics. Some fabric finishes may rule out the use of bleaches in laundry.

Well-constructed shorts will have strong, flat seams free of rough edges that may irritate. Points of strain should be reinforced with fabric or double stitching. The zigzag stitch does not break readily in knit fabric or in bias seams of woven fabric.

Sizing in shorts varies from manufacturer to manufacturer. Men's shorts are sold by waist measurement; sizes range from 28 to 44. Height may make quite a difference, and a person who is very tall may need a larger size to obtain the proper fit.

Undershirts

T-shirts and undershirts are designed primarily for comfort and protection. T-

Elasticized men's shorts for abdomen control.

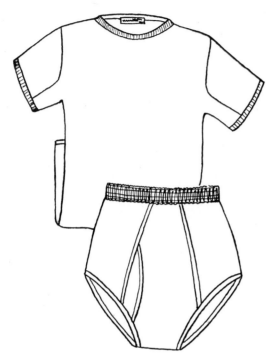

T-shirt and knit briefs.

shirts have short sleeves, while undershirts have narrow shoulder straps that leave the neck and arms free. A good fit is essential for wear and comfort. Important features of the T-shirt include adequate width across the shoulders for movement and sufficient length to allow tucking it into the trousers. Strain on the armscye is a frequent cause of wear. Some T-shirts have a separate panel in the undersleeve which gives added room. For the person who perspires a lot, the sleeves of the T-shirt give protection to the shirt and comfort to the wearer. Undershirts are made primarily in knit construction. Since the T-shirt has no openings, it is necessary for the neck edge to stretch. The binding of the neck edge, usually of rib knit construction, should return to its original shape and fit closely to the neck or body. Nylon 420, a fiber developed specifically to reinforce cotton, has been used for added

strength at the neck and in other areas that receive strain. Cotton and cotton-and-polyester blends are the fibers most frequently used in undershirts. They launder easily and require a minimum of care. The polyester-cotton blend dries quickly and is light in weight. In the selection of the undershirt, ease of care, shrinkage, fit, and durability will be important factors.

Pajamas

Men's pajamas come in numerous styles and fabrics. There are three major types: the middy styles, which slip over the head, the coat type, which button down the front, and the knitted type, which slip over the head. Sleeves in the various styles may be raglan style or the two-piece set-in. A gusset that extends into the sleeve may be incorporated for extra movement. The two-piece sleeve might have the underarm panel cut on the bias to allow for ease in movement. Well-cut tops will have a pleat under the arm for extra fullness and to prevent binding about the body.

Trousers, which may be long or short, are made with adjustable waist bands like those found in shorts. Designs that have a bias-cut

Men's pajama styles.

center panel eliminate the center seam and increase comfort. Trousers of knit fabric usually have ribbed cuffs that allow a close fit but stretch for putting on.

Fabrics used in men's pajamas are varied. Broadcloth, percale, and batiste of cotton or cotton-and-polyester blends are often favored because they are easy to launder, but there are men who prefer the luxurious feel of, say, a silk crepe. Knitted types are made of cottons, nylons, and blends of triacetate, acrylic, cotton, polyester, etc. Fleecy fabrics or flannels are available for cold climates. In selecting fabric, consideration should be given to factors of shrinkage, colorfastness, smoothness, weight, and climate.

Pajamas should be made with durable, smooth seams. Flat-felled or double-stitched seams will be needed for durability. Points of strain should be reinforced with fabric or stitching.

Since there are men who wear only the tops or trousers of pajamas, many stores sell these items separately. Nightshirts are available for those who prefer them. Nightshirts will have the same design and style features found in pajama tops.

Men's pajamas are sold in sizes A, B, C, D, and E. Generally, size A fits the man of 100 to 135 lbs., B the one of 135 to 165 lbs., C the one of 165–185 lbs., D fits those who weigh 185–215, and E fits those whose weight exceeds 215 lbs.

Chapter 24

Jewelry

Jewelry is purely decorative. Its prestige or status value has changed little throughout the ages. It has a place in folklore and romance, and it has become a symbol of sentimental value. Of all decorative additions, jewelry is perhaps the most expressive of personality. Since it is a nonfunctional item used purely for pleasure and adornment, individuals should definitely have a philosophy about jewelry and its use. People often form a real attachment for beautiful jewels, and everyone is familiar with the sentiment of the wedding or engagement ring. Jewelry, whether custom, symbol, or investment, is purely for adornment and enjoyment. There has always been the financial aspect; many people have felt that an investment in fine jewels is the one secure investment. For whatever purpose one buys jewelry, it is wise to know something about jewelry before making a large purchase.

Jewelry has always been one of the most personal of art forms. There is a fascination about jewelry few can resist. To the designer it is an art form. The individual may buy it because of a love of beauty or the desire to impress others with a show of wealth. Jewelry is a definite reflection of personality and of the taste of the person who chooses it, although the person may herself often be unaware of her reasons for choosing it.

At one time, it was considered in extremely poor taste to wear anything but real jewelry; pearls and precious stones were thought the only suitable kinds of jewelry. It was the incomparable Madame Coco Chanel whose influence caused the fashion world to change to the wearing of more jewelry and to accept costume jewelry. At the height of her popularity in the 1920's, Chanel introduced costume jewelry and made imitation pearls and jewels the last word. Bulky papier-maché jewelry in gay, strong colors reflected the mood found in the Mondrian dress of Saint-Laurent. It is the same break from traditional design that is found in the colorful jewelry of Kenneth Lane. Obviously fake, frequently large, the jewelry is purchased not as an investment but to give variety. Fashion plays a part in determining what kind of jewelry and how much is worn, in what way, when, and for what occasions.

JEWELRY AND THE INDIVIDUAL

Jewelry must enhance the beauty of the outfit yet be subordinate to the wearer to be truly decorative. Personal preferences for gold or silver or certain precious stones help create individuality. Some people really dislike diamonds; others may not like silver. Each individual has some reaction to different materials and designs. Choice of jewelry is usually dictated by personal taste and by one's pocketbook. Jewelry is never a necessity, and it should be decorative and express one's personality. How much jewelry to wear is also a matter of good taste. A set number of pieces cannot be stated since the importance of a piece of jewelry will make a great deal of difference. Occasion and place will be governing factors. Marianne Ostier, for example, says that gold is a daytime metal because it softens,

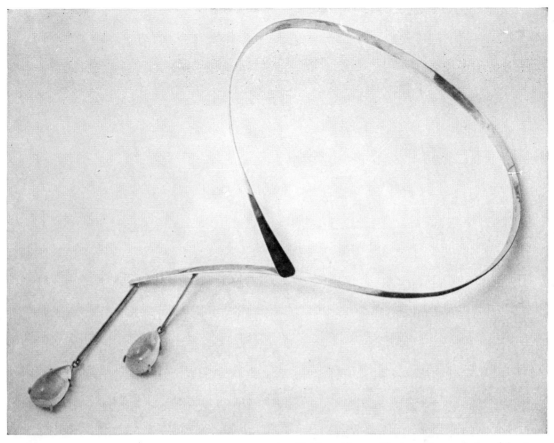

Gold necklace with moon-stones designed by Irena Brynner. (Courtesy Irena Brynner.)

flatters, and is very elegant with daytime clothes. She believes that jewelry for a dressy evening must glitter.[1] Irena Brynner feels that jewelry must not only be wearable and function with the body but that it reflects the life we lead.[2] For the individual, the importance of the other articles of dress is a consideration in addition to occasion and place. Too many decorative additions, whether flowers, trim, or jewelry, will result in an overdone look. A dress that is simple in line and worn with simple accessories

might allow more jewelry than one that has other decorative additions. In considering decorative additions, one should remember that fabric in itself or a hairdo may be elaborate; the individual must consider the whole picture before deciding how much jewelry can be worn.

Pearls are the one item of jewelry considered good with all kinds of clothes and at any time. As with many other items of clothing, one finds that matched pieces of jewelry frequently detract from each other. A truly fine piece of jewelry, whether a contemporary piece or a conventional design,

---

[1] Laura Riley, "America's Most Fabulous Jewels," *Ladies' Home Journal*, July, 1958.

[2] *Craft Horizons*, Vol. XVI, No. 5 (September–October, 1956), 27; Vol. XIX, No. 2 (March–April, 1959), 33.

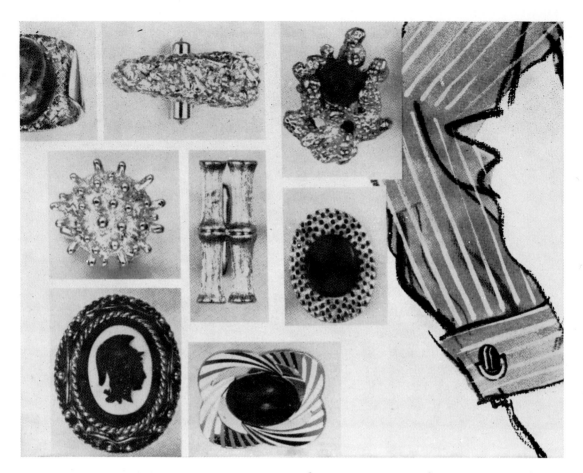

A man has a wide variety of patterns, textures, finishes, stones, and metals from which to choose cuff links that express his preferences. (Courtesy American Institute of Men's and Boys' Wear, Inc.)

is in itself important and loses importance when matched with similar jewels.

JEWELRY OF THE PAST AND PRESENT

The person interested in jewelry can study design and basic materials by observing the beautiful historic pieces of jewelry on display in museums. Many of the better-known contemporary craftsmen have exhibits in museums as well as shows held in large cities or at craft centers. Not only are some of the most precious stones in the world in museums, but the whole legacy of the past is there at the disposal of the average person as well as the designer. There are historic designs that are a study in themselves. It is not difficult to see the influence of some of the periods of the past in contemporary design. Etruscan jewelry, for example, has inspired several of our better-known contemporary craftsmen. Many of the techniques of the past are used and have been improved upon today.

Many costume pieces are copied from rare and valuable jewelry of the past or from the work of well-known jewelry artists. Contemporary craftsmen in the field are numerous. The truly outstanding contemporary craftsmen reflect the technological developments of the times. Most are contributing to the development of techniques and of new ways of using metal and stones. An excellent example is that of John Paul Miller, who in recent years rediscovered the lost art of granulation. To name but a few others, there are Robert Ingstrom, Margaret DePatta, Irena Brynner, and Ed Weiner. Each has his own view on designing and making jewelry and his individual approach. Alma Davies creates jewelry in papier-maché with a primitive design quality. Many contemporary designers do pieces that are within the means of many people yet might well become the heirlooms of the future.

In the field of design of precious and valuable jewelry there are Harry Winston, Jean Schulumberger of Tiffany's, Duc de Verdura, Mr. Felix, and Marianne Ostier; they are just a few of the well-known people who exert a strong influence in fashion jewelry.

TYPES OF JEWELRY

Jewelry is usually spoken of as "real" or "costume" jewelry. Real jewelry is made from natural or genuine stones mounted in fine metal. Both precious and semi-precious stones are genuine gems from natural sources. The precious gems—including diamonds, pearls, sapphires, and emeralds—are both more expensive and more difficult to work. The semi-precious stones include agates, lapis lazuli, malachite, and amethyst. Gold, silver, and platinum are precious metals. There are also man-made stones closely resembling natural stones like sapphires, rubies, and emeralds. Cultured pearls are not really man-made; they are the result of man's lending nature a helping hand. Stones are purchased and sold by the carat, which is a unit of weight rather than size, equal to one-fifth of one gram. The carat is composed of 100 points. A diamond with 25 points would be one-fourth carat. The carat is also used to measure gold; in this sense of the word we will write karat. The karat measures the proportion of gold in an alloy, not the weight; it is one twenty-fourth part. Pure gold is 24 karats; 14-karat gold is 14 parts gold and 10 parts alloy. Since pure gold is too soft to be used by itself, it is generally alloyed with nickel or copper. Sterling silver is 925 parts of silver and 75 parts of alloy, or 925/1000 silver, per ounce. In coin silver, the ratio of pure silver to pure alloy is 900 to 100. Mexican silver cannot be stamped since its pure silver content is not reliably consistent.

Pure gold is too soft to withstand much wear. A *gold-plated* article must have a gold covering that is 1/100,000th of an inch thick. In a *gold-filled* article, 1/20th of the weight is 10-karat gold. *Rolled gold* must be 10-karat gold but the gold may be less than 1/20th of the weight and gives a lighter gold finish. If a piece is gold flashed or gold finished, the layer of gold is thinner than that of gold plate. When an article is gold or silver plated, a base metal is covered with a thin coating of gold or silver by an electroplating process. The thickness of the coating and its precious-metal content will determine the value of the finished piece. An article that is silver flashed or silver finished has a thinner coating than silver plate.

Alloys of nickel, copper, and zinc are frequently referred to as German silver, liberty silver, or nickel silver. The names are misleading; the alloys contain no silver at all. Lacquer is often applied to plated articles, particularly to those gold flashed, for more lasting finish.

Costume or fashion jewelry is jewelry that follows the mode of the day; it may be made of various kinds of materials, such as

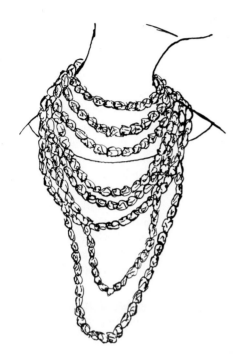

Chanel rope beads.

cult to distinguish from the genuine; the untrained eye may think an imitation or a synthetic jewel finer than precious stones or real pearls.

Pearls are genuine, cultured, or simulated. Genuine pearls are formed around an accidental irritant within the shell of certain mollusks, mainly the pearl oyster. Cultured pearls are deliberately "encouraged" by providing carefully bred oysters with the necessary irritant. There are two kinds of simulated pearls—indestructible and destructible. Indestructible pearls are made by covering a glass bead with one of various kinds of mixtures, one being a lustrous material made of fish scales. Destructible pearls are made by filling hollow, pearl-like beads with wax. These pearls generally discolor in contact with perfume and other cosmetics. Pearls, both genuine and cultured, are not always white but may be cream, silver rosea, cream rosea, pink rosea, and black. Pearls are graded according to size, the thickness of the shell, shape, freedom from imperfection, and depth of color. It is difficult to distinguish the finest cultured pearls from the natural; the identification is usually made by means of X-ray. The shell of natural pearls is much thicker than that of cultured pearls.

Numerous attempts have been made to simulate rubies, sapphires, and diamonds. The man-made product frequently is a very good imitation, and of course is considerably less expensive. Rutile and fabulite, beautiful stones in their own right, resemble diamonds, but they are very carefully marked to prevent their being called imitations.

A synthetic gem is one produced by man to have the same properties as a genuine stone. Imitation jewels are those that resemble one or another of the precious stones in color or appearance but not in other properties; they are frequently made of glass. Most synthetic gems can be recognized by

synthetic stones, wood, enamel, or inexpensive or nonprecious stones. Fashion jewelry is generally sold in stores other than jewelry stores. It is not to be inferred that costume jewelry is always inexpensive imitation jewelry; it may be very fine and often is also expensive. The quality of a piece of fashion jewelry depends upon the material of which it is made and the craftsmanship with which it was executed.

Many plastics are being developed that are excellent for costume jewelry. They have made possible more variety in color and are lightweight in addition to being inexpensive. Good imitations are often diffi-

(Opposite) Top left: Bracelet styles; top right: Earring styles; center: Pins; bottom: Necklace styles. From left to right: Choker, matinee length, and opera length.

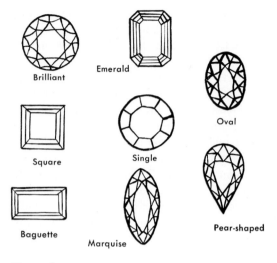

Diamond cuts.

the perfection with which they are made; genuine stones generally exhibit some imperfections and lack uniformity. There are about thirty of the precious stones that are really outstanding in importance.

The diamond, of course, is the best known, and because of its association with engagements it is perhaps bought more than any other. Diamonds are usually colorless; red, blue, green, or black diamonds are exceedingly rare, those with a yellow tinge being far more common. Diamonds are the hardest substance known. They are formed of nearly pure carbon in isometric crystals. The cost of a diamond depends on the *carat, color, clarity,* and the *cut* of the stone. A small diamond with fewer flaws, clearer color, and more beautiful cut may cost more than a larger stone.

In the past, the brilliant or the round cut has been the most popular for diamond rings. In the last few years, the oval has become increasingly popular. It is the newest of diamond cuts. It gives the illusion of the stone's being much larger than it actually is. Most engagement rings are mounted in narrow bands to make them seem larger.

The cut of the diamond is chosen to enhance the natural brilliance and beauty of the stone. The facets, minute surfaces on the stone, pick up and reflect light rays. A stone that is cut and polished but not faceted is known as a *cabochon*. Certain cuts require larger rough diamonds than others.

The techniques of making jewelry are as numerous and varied as the materials used. Stones, whether precious, semi-precious, or synthetic, are cut to reflect light rays and increase their brilliance and are then polished by the method best suited to the material. Stones are polished by hand, fire, or acid. Hand-polished stones are polished on a revolving wheel, each facet separately. Fire polishing is used on inexpensive articles; in this process, the stone is exposed to intense heat. In acid polishing, the stone is immersed in an acid bath. After being polished, the stone is set. A hand-set stone may be held in place by metal prongs or a *bezel*, a thin band of metal that fits around the stone. In machine sets, the stone is glued into the setting. The workmanship of a piece of jewelry is judged by the secure setting of the stone, the smoothness of the edges, the cut and polish of the stone, and the beauty of the design.

Gold, silver, and copper are the most popular metals used in making jewelry; they are particularly suitable for handmade jewelry. All three of these metals can be alloyed with other metals to create different effects. White gold is produced by combining alloys of silver, zinc, and either copper or nickel. These metals are easily shaped and easily joined by solder or by fusion. They are the best for use with the enameling process. Copper has been gaining in popularity and is frequently used as a contrasting element in combination with other materials. Copper tarnishes readily, and a finished piece of copper jewelry is usually given a lacquer coating to prevent oxidation. The warmth and richness of copper appeals to many people. Contemporary craftsmen combine it with precious and semi-precious stones for new and beautiful effects.

Designs are produced on metal jewelry by numerous techniques such as piercing, granulation, hammering, twisting, etching, and enameling. An important part of a hand-wrought piece is the finishing process. Metals may have a dull or a bright finish. They may be textured or smooth or may be made in a combination of several finishes such as satin and mat or partly oxidized. Oxidation changes the color of the metal in recessed or carved areas; it is also used in areas around stones or pearls for accent. It is sometimes referred to as antique finish, but it is done deliberately by the artist.

CARE

Fine jewelry deserves good care. Good care will extend the life of inexpensive jewelry. Precious stones if securely set can be washed in warm water with a small amount of detergent and a drop of ammonia. A soft brush or cotton will clean both the metal and the stones. Inexpensive jewelry that has been glued or cemented should not be washed. Wiping the surface of the stone and the metal with a cloth dampened in a little ammonia will increase luster. Imitation pearls should never be washed but can be wiped carefully with a soft cloth. If immersed in any cleaning fluids, imitation pearls will generally discolor and the finish chip. Watches and cultured pearls should always be cleaned professionally. Settings of valuable jewelry should be checked often by a jeweler. Metals can be polished with a good metal polish or pumice rubbed. Oxidation that is part of the design of a silver piece should not be removed.

If liquid jewelry cleaners are used, special attention should be given to instruc-

tions. Many of these liquids will remove oxidation and may harm the metal if left on too long. Some metals—copper, for example—react with perspiration to form a green stain on the skin. There are some people for whom this is a greater problem than for others. Colorless nail polish can be used to protect against this staining, but the treatment is likely to detract from the appearance of the jewelry. Precious stones, pearls, and metals should be stored where they will not come in contact with other stones and metals. Most stones—with the exception of diamonds—are easily scratched; they should be stored in a soft jeweler's cloth or in cotton to prevent contact with other jewels.

BUYING JEWELRY

When investing in jewelry, regardless of what kind, you can find assistance in making your selection. The Federal Trade Commission requires that metals and precious and semi-precious stones used in jewelry be accurately described in order to prevent misrepresentation. The buyer of fine jewelry is dependent upon the integrity of the jeweler with whom he is dealing. Jewel identification is a science, and in buying fine jewelry, one must rely upon the opinion of a trained person. There are many jewels in the country that are practically worthless and as investments are poor. Jewelry of poor quality, whether precious, semi-precious, or costume, is never a good investment. In all kinds of jewelry, the value of the piece is dependent upon the quality of the basic materials and of the workmanship. Size is never an indication of quality. It is better to have a semi-precious stone well executed than to have a diamond of poor cut and poor quality. The person who chooses jewelry for the occasion, for adornment, and to express his personality will find pleasure regardless of cost.

REFERENCE READINGS

Books

Harth, A. C., *Beaten Metal Work*, Sir Isaac Putnam & Son, Ltd., London, 1947.

Ostier, Marianne, *Jewels and the Woman*, Horizon Press, New York, 1958.

Stoutenburgh, John L., Jr. (ed.), *Dictionary of Arts and Crafts*, Philosophical Library, Inc., New York, 1956.

Weinstein, Michael, *The World of Jewel Stones*, Sheridan House Inc., New York, 1958.

Winebrenner, D. Kenneth, *Jewelry Making*, Laurel Publishers, Scranton, Pa., 1953.

Wingate, Isabel B. Gillespie, Karen R. Addison, Betty J., *Know Your Merchandise*, 3rd Ed., McGraw-Hill Co., New York, 1964.

Wooster, N., *Semi-Precious Stones*, Penguin Books, Harmondsworth, Middlesex, 1952.

Booklets

Research Bureau for Retail Training, *Merchandise Facts to Help You Sell Fashion Jewelry*, Research Bureau for Retail Training, University of Pittsburgh.

Conference Reports

Asilomar, First Annual Conference of American Craftsmen, The American Craftsmen's Council, 1957.

Periodicals

Craft Horizons, New York: Vol. XVI, No. 5 (September–October, 1956), 27; Vol. XIX, No. 2 (March–April, 1959), 33.

Design Quarterly, Minneapolis, Minnesota.

Riley, Laura, "America's Most Fabulous Jewels," *Ladies' Home Journal*, July, 1958.

The Washington Post, "Jewelry Section," May 18, 1952, Washington, D. C.

Chapter 25

Children's clothing

Although many of the factors that affect clothing selection apply to all age groups, the young child does have specific requirements quite different from those of adults. The role of clothing in the child's life assumes added importance because of its relation to his growth and development. As a child grows, he wants to do things for himself. He tries to put on his socks or pull on his T-shirt or comb his hair. His clothes, then, are one means of helping him to increase his physical dexterity and to become self-reliant. Clothing can also affect his emotional adjustment. From infancy, the child is learning to adjust and conform to the society in which he is going to live. The way he is dressed can aid in this adjustment. He should feel happy about his clothes and enjoy wearing them. He will gain greater confidence in himself when he feels he is making a good impression on his group.

Awareness of clothing comes at different ages, but even the small child may have definite ideas as to what he wants in clothes and how he wants to look.

Clothing should help the child express himself. Too often a parent gives so little thought to the clothing of children that the parent is expressing his own personality and not the child's. Clothes should help develop creativity and individuality.

The small child may have a great deal of common sense about his clothing needs. He deserves to be heard and have his ideas considered. He should be given an opportunity to help select clothing suitable to himself and his age. The mother might select several articles of different colors and designs that she finds acceptable and let the child choose from them. Mothers should remember that there are times when children learn by making mistakes. In the adult world being well dressed depends upon whom one is with. Children also sense this and want to appear well dressed in the eyes of their companions. Many parents object to their children's strong desire to conform to the group and at the same time oppose experimentation, which is the first step toward individuality.

In the teen years, conflict between mother and daughter about the kind of clothes the daughter will wear is common. Mothers may try to keep their daughters little girls while the daughters are trying to find their style. Another point for parents to keep in mind is that quantity in clothes may be more important to teenagers than quality.

COMFORT

Comfort is essential for all ages but doubly so for the growing, active toddler and preschooler. Comfort in clothes results from the consideration of different factors such as fabric, cut, and fit. Fabrics should not irritate or scratch the child's skin and should give the desired amount of warmth or coolness. The cut of the garment should not interfere with body movement and should al-

443

low for safety in play. A child should not be bothered by overalls that bind in the crotch, sleeves that cut across the arm when he reaches for his favorite toy, or dangling ribbons that get caught in tricycle wheels. The garment may be designed for comfort, but unless it fits the child, may be very uncomfortable. Clothing that is too large overpowers the child, hinders movement, and is not safe. The child not only feels uncomfortable but looks it. Clothing that is too small cramps the child's movements and may cause him to pull and tug at his clothes to try to reduce the strain on his body. Clothes that grow with the child can help to answer some of these problems of fitting the child during the period of rapid growth.

EASY CARE

Recent developments in textiles and household equipment have eliminated many tedious hours in laundering and ironing. Durable-press and man-made fibers have released many hours for other activities. However, care in selection is necessary since the mother wants her family clean and neat. The child doesn't want to have to worry about his clothes getting dirty when he plays or when he falls down on his way to school. The child of school age wants clothes with "low nuisance value." They should be durable, of strong construction, and easy to wash and iron.

ATTRACTIVE CLOTHES

In selecting attractive clothes for the child, parents should consider many of the same factors that affect the attractiveness of clothes for the adult. Colors should be becoming. The young child generally has a petal-smooth skin and may be able to wear many colors better than adults. Lines will be chosen to emphasize good features and play down less attractive features like large stomachs or a pudgy appearance. When

the child is born, the head is about one fourth of the body length, and the proportions of children's clothing should be adjusted until the body has grown to correspond to the adult proportions. The figure and shape of the child will play a large part in the selection of styles. The little girl's figure is straight, and will generally look most attractive in dresses and clothes that fall from the shoulder or from a yoke. The very young child has a large abdomen, and will look better in a design without a definite waistline.

As with adults, a definite mood is created in children's clothes through the use of design in fabric, trim, texture, and color. Delicate colors, bows, lace, and frills have long been associated with small children. A feeling of daintiness can come from a delicately printed fabric as much as from additional trim. Emphasis is on interesting fabric combinations and bolder color schemes, with trims that do not require extra care. Although some design features, such as smocking, are usually associated with children's clothes, the design is usually kept simple and carefree.

FASHION

Fashion in children's clothing frequently follows that of adults'. Fashion is not always functional and can make a child appear foolish. At times, when the style does not interfere with the action and comfort of the child and if the proportions of the design are suited to the figure of the child, it can be an effective tool. For example, the shift and tent styles for little girls are excellent for the body proportions and movement. Stretch tights when properly sized allow movement without bulk. The bright gay colors of the "young" fashion delight children. The new era of fashion for children stresses interest in fabrics, clean lines, and simplicity rather than the fussy elaborate designs. The late Claire McCardell designed children's clothes that stressed the importance of movement and of using decorative fabrics in simple, easily cared for styles. She made a point of eliminating tight little necklines, sleeves, and frills. There are also designers who specialize just in children's clothing.

THE INFANT

The infant's clothing needs are limited to a few items essential to his protection and comfort during the early months of his life. His activities are primarily concerned with eating and sleeping.

Diapers are first on any layette list. Diapers must be soft, lightweight, absorbent, easily washed, and quick drying. Fabrics most commonly used in diapers are birdseye, gauze, knits, and flannelette. Cotton is the most satisfactory fiber for diapers; it is easy to wash and can be boiled if necessary.

Diapers come in rectangle, square, and contour styles, or may be cut to avoid folding. Regular diapers of gauze or birdseye are oblong in shape, about 20 × 40 inches, and are folded to give the infant proper protection. This type of diaper allows for changes in size as the baby grows. Special scoop-type pins make pinning easier and safer because of the shape and the safety lock of the plastic head. Gauze diapers are available with snap or Velcro fasteners that adjust as the baby grows. This diaper opens flat and eliminates pinning. Stretch-weave diapers fit well without binding. The center of a self-shaping diaper draws in when washed, becomes more absorbent and shapes itself to fit the waist line. Pre-shaped diapers are available with extra layers at the center where absorbency is most needed. Diapers also come pre-folded with construction of the center panel thicker, which allows less bulk on side panels. Diaper services are a time-saving way of providing clean diapers but may be a little more expensive. Many of these services carry prefolded and shaped diapers as well

The essentials in the new baby's wardrobe.

as the regular style. Many of the companies return the same diapers each time to the same customer.

Disposable diapers and liners reduce staining and laundry and are available with medicated finishes which prevent rashes. The disposable diaper with the water-repellent backing eliminates the need for plastic panties. Disposable diapers can serve as a crib pad to protect bedding and are a great aid to the traveling mother. Disposable diapers pin on like regular diapers. They have a soft cotton surface to protect the baby's skin. If a disposable diaper is to be used, it is wise to try a brand for satisfactory performance before buying a large number. Different kinds will meet the needs of babies at different ages. Disposable diapers are more expensive to use than regular diapers. The parent will decide when cost becomes more important than time, or vice versa.

It is wise never to allow the diapers to become too soiled. Some mothers immediately put the soiled diapers into a covered pail containing detergent or soap. Whenever possible, laundry should be done daily to prevent stains on diapers from becoming set. Fabrics should be washable in hot water with a mild soap or detergent. Where hard water is a problem, a water softener should be used. At certain times it may be necessary to boil the diapers. Whenever laundered, they should be rinsed thoroughly to remove all soap. Knitted fabrics, although sanforized, may shrink in automatic dryers.

Protective panties are used as diaper covers to aid in keeping clothing and bedding dry. There are two kinds of protective panties, those that are waterproof and those knitted of wool and called soakers. With protective panties, it is important that the parent change the baby often and keep a careful watch on the condition of the baby's skin. Babies may be susceptible to diaper rash, and it may be necessary to allow more evaporation than protective panties permit. The knitted soaker absorbs moisture and allows more circulation of air than rubber or plastic. It is important that soakers be washed thoroughly. There are different styles and a wide variety of fabrics available in waterproof panties. Styles include bloomers, which have to be pulled on, the snap-on style, and fancy pants in both styles. Fancy pants may have gathered nylon net or trim, which makes them easy to care for. Waterproof panties are generally made of acetate tricot, coated inside with plastic but some are available with polyurethane foam interlining for extra protection. A cotton terry cloth lining next to the baby's body gives more comfort and protection. All styles should include features for the baby's comfort and health: looseness around the legs to allow for proper ventilation and to help prevent diaper rash, no tight elastic or other bands around the waist, and soft fabrics that are light and cool. Styles that allow for easier dressing and quicker changes are those that open flat and are snapped. All protective panties should be machine washable and soft to the touch. Soakers are limited to the first few months of a baby's life. Protective panties are used especially for going visiting or traveling and as a protection both for furniture and for floor coverings when the child begins to crawl.

Shirts give the baby added protection from sudden changes in temperature. The double-breasted shirt makes life easier for the mother because it opens flat and is put on the baby without undue pulling and twisting of arms. Double-breasted shirts are fastened with tie tapes or grippers. The shirt should have smooth seams and sleeves that give with body movements and should be made of a soft, fine, cotton knit. The double-breasted shirt should have diaper tabs, which increase the wearing qualities of the shirt. The double-breasted shirt will expand and grow with the child more readily than the over-the-head styles. Many babies do not wear shirts in summer, although there is a diaper shirt made of a lightweight batiste that protects the child when little warmth is needed. This shirt should have ample armholes, pin tabs, and front openings; the neck should not bind.

Although the baby sleeps most of the time, he is very active in his sleep and will need room for stretching. Many mothers use a kimono as a wrapper after the bath and for daytime wear. Some mothers use the wrapper instead of nightgowns. Kimonos with raglan or kimono sleeves and tie tapes or gripper openings are very satisfactory. Ribbon ties become twisted and difficult to untie when wet. The kimono may be put on with the opening in the front or in the back. In this way, the kimono can remain dry while the child is sleeping and does not have to be changed every time the diaper is changed.

The nightgown or the kimona is chosen by some mothers for both day and night wear. It should be long enough to allow ample room for the baby to kick. Generally, nightgowns are at least 27 inches long and wide enough around to allow for movement and comfort. The nightgown is either of the envelope fold-over kind or of the kind with a draw string at the bottom. The advantage of the gown is that if the baby kicks off the covers he is still protected. Nightgowns with full-length front openings are the easiest to put on. Those with partial openings down the center front are put on from the feet up over the body and involve more handling of the baby. The one-piece stretch garment with feet and a long center opening which extends into the entire crotch area is the most practical and popular of all infants wear. It serves the purpose of many garments.

Sacques and sweaters are used for addi-

tional warmth and as a decorative item in the baby's wardrobe. The sacque is a loosely fitted garment made in numerous fabrics such as cotton knit, brushed rayon, terry cloth, quilted cotton, and silk. Wool challis is often used and should generally be lined with a very soft, washable silk or rayon. Gripper-type fasteners are preferable for easier fastening. The sweater should also open down the front and should preferably have kimono sleeves. When wool is used it should be very soft or lined.

Sleeping bags are designed to keep the baby warm and covered through chilly evenings. Sleeping bags are easy to use; they have long zipper openings that make it easy to put the child in. They will grow with the child in width as well as in length. They are safe because the child cannot become uncovered, and are useful in travel or in the carriage. Fabrics for sleeping bags are made in different weights of acrylic, wool, acetate, and cotton and frequently interlined with polyurethane foam.

Buntings are considered a luxury because they are used for only a very short time. Buntings give the baby protection from changing outdoor temperature. The garment should be large enough to give the baby room to move in but not so large that he will be lost in it. The front opening should be long enough to put the baby in with ease. The two-piece buntings with separate sleeper jackets that convert to pram suits and then to snowsuits will give longer wear. They are designed for convenient dressing, with two zippered sides that allow the suits to open flat. They should have a gripper crotch. The pram suit is a one-piece zipper suit that can be converted to a snowsuit by unsnapping and unbuttoning the boots and mittens. It is generally used for children about six months old. Pram suits come in washable, water-repellent cottons, nylon, and acetate.

Bibs are a functional part of the baby's

wardrobe and should be chosen to be practical and easily cared for. An absorbent fabric like terry cloth will be satisfactory. The older child will need larger coverings to protect his other clothing. The gripper-style bib adjusts to the baby's size and eliminates the annoying problem of strings that must be tied. Some of the terry cloth bibs are plasticized for greater protection.

Bonnets or hoods are made for the protection of the baby's head in warm weather and for warmth, if a bunting is not used, in winter. Those made of woolen fabric may have to be lined to protect the child's head from irritation. Bonnets should be washable and easy to put on.

It is doubtful that many mothers will have to include dresses when buying clothes for the baby since dresses are frequently given as gifts and the baby is not put in dresses very often. Panty dresses and topper sets for boys and girls are very useful. These are available in charming printed and colored cotton knits that are absorbent, easy to launder, and do not require ironing. The design of baby dresses should include full-length openings, front

Toppers for the diaper set—comfortable for Baby and easy for Mother.

or back; smooth seams finished to prevent scratching of the child's skin; and fullness from the shoulder that allows for adequate body movement. Tight bands or elastic should not be used. Fabrics should be soft, light in weight, and easily laundered. Trim should be soft and easily cared for. Most buttons on dresses are much too small, and should be increased in size. Newer fabric blends like polyester and cotton have made possible many dresses that keep to a minimum the care needed for the new baby's clothes.

THE TODDLER

The baby develops quickly. Before he is a year old, there will be many changes in his size and in his needs. When he begins to crawl, he will need clothes that are very durable and protect him while he is crawling and learning to stand and walk. The mother should check frequently to see that clothes are large enough. Creepers and sun suits are ideal for summer wear. Baby's clothes should not catch on furniture as he crawls around. Slip-over T-shirts and sweaters are suitable if they have large openings at the shoulder or down the front so that they may be easily slipped over the child's head. Knit trousers and shirts are ideal. At this age he will need crawler sets, sun suits, and overalls that open with snap openings at the legs and crotch to allow easy diaper changes. The toddler will be very active and the mother will want to change him as quickly as possible. Some of the topper sets and overalls have waterproof plastic lining to protect furnishings and floors. The clothes should still have the necessary softness, absorbency, and stretch for easy movement. Overalls, which are excellent for both boys and girls, protect the young child while he is crawling and learning to walk. They should be of a sturdy, soft fabric and have straps that not only cross in back but are shaped or guarded at the

Clothes for the toddler to crawl and grow in.

shoulder to prevent their slipping off during play. Denim, seersucker, and corduroy are durable and need little care. Even in warm weather, if the child crawls a great deal, lightweight cotton overalls or stretch jumpsuits are needed. No-iron machine washables are a must for tiny tots who are exploring the new world around them.

Knit or stretch training pants with a section through the crotch to allow for stretch and better fit may be used when the child is ready for toilet training. They are cut with the ribbing going across the crotch and up and down the side panels. Polyurethane foam between two layers of cotton knit increases absorbency.

In many areas, children will need snowsuits that allow for activity without bulk and for warmth and durability; they should be easy to put on and, preferably, should not need to be dry-cleaned. Children, regardless of age, are very active; they are hard on their clothes and are easily annoyed when clothing interferes with play. Design features that provide for comfort and allow for growth include those like the raglan sleeve, seen in the smaller child's clothing. The one-piece snowsuit generally used for the smaller child should have front openings that extend into the leg and make it easier to put the suit on. Some one-piece suits having two zippers are easier to put on. The older child will generally use the two-piece snowsuit with adjustable straps or the stretch-type snow pants. The most important factor, other than design, in choosing a snowsuit is the fabric. Man-made fabrics have made lighter and more comfortable snowsuits. A child should not be burdened with cumbersome clothing. The weave of the fabric will be important to the wearing qualities of the suit. Closely woven poplins and gabardines would be excellent since they take water-repellent finishes well. This finish is essential in a snowsuit. All the materials in the suit—interlinings, interfacing, and rib knit cuffs—must be washable.

For milder weather, a nylon jacket lined with cotton flannel or acrylic fleece is ideal for outdoor play. Stretch slacks permit activity without bulk.

THE PRESCHOOLER'S GROWING-UP CLOTHES

The young child is anxious to learn to dress himself, and the patient mother will find that in the end this will not only be a great time-saver but will give the child a sense of accomplishment. Design features that help the child to dress himself are openings that make it easy to put the garment on and openings located where the child can reach them, sleeves that are easy to get into, and fasteners—such as buttons —large enough for the child to handle.

Wide hems on a little girl's dress and

Clothes that fasten easily—with large buttons and zippers in front—and clothes that grow—no definite waistlines and raglan or kimono sleeves—are best for the preschooler.

sleeves that may be let out grow with the child. Kimono or raglan sleeves eliminate a definite shoulder line, which must, for comfort and for appearance, be properly placed. Adjustable shoulder straps and waist bands allow for additional growth in skirts and trousers. Dresses that hang from a yoke or from the shoulder line and have no definite waistline seam allow for longer wear.

Longer life for the garment will result from sturdy, durable fabrics, strong construction, secure, well-made trimmings and fasteners, and properly sized articles. Many of the features that make clothing easy for the child to cope with also contribute to easy care. Designs that open down the

front, with kimono or no sleeves and simple styling, and dual-purpose garments such as the blouse-slip or coverall simplify laundering. For dress-up clothes, fabrics should be chosen that need little or no ironing; trim and lace should not have to be ironed.

SCHOOL TIME

As the child reaches school age, there will be an increase in his group activities. He will participate in more social activities and will need a wider variety of clothing. Besides attending school, children are exposed to varying kinds of weather, they play hard, and attend more occasions for which they have to dress up. They will need to add to their wardrobes things such as raincoats, cold-weather jackets, and trousers. As in the wardrobes of their high school or college brothers, there will be an emphasis on separates that are versatile. The child will need more variety in every-

The child from six to twelve will need clothes for many occasions.

day clothing since the clothes he wears to school will be changed to play clothes after school hours. At this age, boys wear things out quickly. Knees are forever coming through pants, and parents should consider buying reinforced trousers for greater durability. Shoes scuff quickly and wear out fast. The family will have to consider these factors in the over-all clothing plan. Children dress up for Sunday School or church and parties and will need more dressy clothing than the less social younger child.

It is very important that the clothes fit at the time the child is wearing them. Many mothers feel that if they buy clothing a little larger, it can be worn for a longer period of time. In this scheme of buying, chances are the clothes will never quite fit the child. He grows so rapidly that by the following year he will have outgrown the article that did not fit him when it was purchased the year before. He might wear the article of clothing out before it does fit him, and therefore he never has clothing that fits

Boys' clothes must be serviceable, sturdy, and comfortable.

him correctly. It is better to have fewer clothes that fit the child than to have a lot of clothes that do not. An article that is too large will catch and slip on the body and will not be comfortable. It will not look attractive if it does not fit. An article that fits correctly feels right, looks right, and is comfortable to wear.

Durable-press has been an outstanding development for the clothing of school age children. It has meant many less hours in laundering and makes possible the use of many designs which were not practical before. It has the drawback of holding stains, particularly grease. Stains should be pretreated with concentrated detergent or solvent before washing. Durable-press does not allow alteration and remodeling since creases are permanent. A real effort is being made to solve the staining and the alteration problem. However, because it

does not need ironing, fewer clothes will be needed and clothes can be purchased to fit the child.

Fabric-to-fabric bonding will also increase the design and wear qualities in children's wear—particularly outerwear. Fabrics which formerly were not practical will become more useful with bonding techniques.

The child is at the mercy of his parents' tastes and standards. The child who is dressed "different" at school is immediately on the defensive. He may try to prove and establish himself by behavior that is unbecoming and undesirable. Thought should be given to his real needs. It will be less expensive to dress him appropriately with a few clothes than to have many clothes that do not look or feel right for him. It is important to listen to the child's opinions on clothes and to observe the customs of his school group.

SIZING

Sizing has in the past been a real dilemma for the consumer. Today it is possible, as a result of the sizing studies done by the Department of Commerce, to buy children's clothes that fit. Children's clothes should be sold by height and weight. Most conscientious buyers of children's clothing are now stocking only clothes that are sized in this way. Infants' clothing is also sized by weight and height. The sooner mothers demand more uniform sizing, the sooner manufacturers will comply. Sizes from 7 to 14 have been developed for girls and sizes from 2 to 20 for boys. Classifications such as sub-teen and teens give no reliable way of determining size. The size charts given below are being used by many manufacturers in this country. For boys' trousers, waist and inseam measurements should be considered as well as height and weight. The wise mother will look for a chart for sizing and for laundry instructions on all children's clothing.

INFANTS', TODDLERS', AND CHILDREN'S SIZING

Size	Weight	Height
0	up to 13 lbs.	24″
½	14–18 lbs.	26½″
1	19–22 lbs.	29″
1½	23–26 lbs.	31½″
2	27–29 lbs.	34″
3	30–34 lbs.	36½″
4	35–38 lbs.	40″
5	39–44 lbs.	43″
6	45–49 lbs.	46″
6X	50–59 lbs.	48″

BOYS' SIZES
(by body measurements and weight)

Size	Neck	Chest	Height	Weight
2	10″	21″	34″	29 lbs.
4	10½″	23″	40″	38 lbs.
6	11″	25″	46″	49 lbs.
8	11½″	26½″	50″	59 lbs.
10	12″	28″	54″	73 lbs.
12	12½″	29½″	58″	87 lbs.
14	13″	31½″	61″	100 lbs.
16	13½″	33″	64″	115 lbs.
18	14″	34½″	66″	126 lbs.

GIRLS' SIZES
(by body measurements and weight

Size	Height	Weight	Chest	Waist
7	50″	60 lbs.	26″	23″
8	52″	67 lbs.	27″	23½″
10	56″	83 lbs.	29″	24½″
12	58½″	95 lbs.	30½″	25½″
14	61″	107 lbs.	32″	26½″

REFERENCE READINGS

Books
Thompson, Henrietta M. and Rea, Lucille, *Clothing for Children*, John Wiley and Sons, Inc., New York, 1949.

Booklets
Boettke, Eleanor M., *Suggestions for Physically Handicapped Mothers on Clothing for Preschool Children*, School of Home Economics, The University of Connecticut, Storrs, Conn.

Consumer Education Division, *Infants' and Children's Clothing, Equipment, and Toys*, Consumer Education Division, Sears, Roebuck, and Co., Chicago, Ill., 1957.

Unpublished studies
Boettke, Eleanor M., *The Development of Dress Designs Suitable for Preschool Children*, Master's Thesis, Pennsylvania State College, 1953.

Travel clothes

America has become a mobile nation. There are men who fly to work daily; some travel across the country for a business appointment and return the same day. Whole families travel long distances by plane—families of servicemen or families on vacation.

Much has been written on what to take on a trip and how to pack. So much emphasis has been placed upon "traveling light" that specific requirements are often neglected.

PLANNING

Part of the excitement of travel is planning the wardrobe you will take with you. Whether you are planning a short trip over the weekend or a summer tour of Europe, you will find that the time and care put in on choosing and packing your wardrobe will pay off in good grooming and extra hours for relaxation and enjoyment. You can, if you are not careful, spend all of your energy on nonessentials. If you have to spend your time dressing, changing, packing, and repacking, you will miss a lot of fun, people, and places.

As in the planning of your wardrobe in general, there are certain things you should consider when planning for travel—where you are going, the activities in which you will participate, how you will travel, how long you will be away, and what seasonal weather you can expect. A trip by car involves clothes different from those worn for traveling by public conveyance. Whether on vacation or business, when you travel you are in the public eye. A person is more likely to be on display when traveling away from home or when visiting than he would be at home. When traveling by car, some people tend to take too much luggage because "there is plenty of room." This may cause problems on arrival; extra bags mean more worry, tips, and inconvenience.

In addition to clothes for unexpected activities, you should provide extra clothing and clothes that are easy to care for in emergencies; spilled liquids, ripped or torn fabric, or a sudden shower can force you to spend your vacation laundering, pressing, or shopping. While you would not want too many clothes to take care of, be sure to pack the extras that will take care of all occasions. It is annoying to be invited to go swimming and not have a swimsuit.

En route

Air or train travel is much like being in a public place. You will want to appear neat, clean, and attractive but not ostentatious or overdressed. Slacks and scoop-neck blouses or T-shirts and dungarees are appropriate at-home clothes but most inappropriate on a public conveyance. Those who travel by car may wear more casual attire; they should keep in mind, however, that they may have to stop at a hotel or a restaurant. Tourists in Washington have been criticized for their "too-casual" appearance.

Changes of weather

Seasonal changes in the weather usually require that, regardless of how you travel, you have a coat or a sweater available. Or one might start in fairly cool weather and arrive at one's destination to find it very warm. A dress or suit, fairly lightweight, that will be comfortable in warm weather but has a jacket or coat for cool weather should be worn. The weather may well be different at each stop along the way as well as at your destination.

Care and comfort

Most travel involves more soiling of clothes than ordinary wearing, and dark clothing and accessories generally prove more satisfactory for travel. Color contrast could be obtained through jewelry, scarves, or other bright color accents. In any mode of travel you will be seated for most of the time, and wrinkle-resistant fabrics or knits are desirable. Tight skirts tend to work up and can be very uncomfortable. A slightly full skirt lends itself well for comfort in sitting for long periods of time; a skirt that is too full, however, will tend to drag on the floor. Skirts with durable-press pleats are preferred by many travelers.

In the air

Most airlines place limitations on either the weight of baggage or the number of bags per person. Even if you are not going by air, there may be times when you have to carry your own bags—and the lighter and fewer the better. If you will be traveling for any length of time, you will find a large tote bag an excellent way of carrying things you will need en route; it might include things like an extra pair of stockings and, in case you will need to look a little dressier, a small dress purse. Some people will carry, besides cosmetics, a change of shoes and a fresh blouse. Pressurized containers are not advisable for air travel. Plastics and small tubes that can be disposed of when finished are best for cosmetics. Some people also carry a large and a small towel and a bar of soap in the tote bag. Many men who leave by plane in the morning and return at night carry a clean shirt in a brief case or attaché case. Many men's suits are now made in lightweight wash-and-wear fabrics; they are excellent for trips on which the individual does not want a great amount of luggage.

Time and place

How long one will be away will make a considerable difference in how much one takes. It is not always possible to obtain shoe repairs or cleaning services in out-of-the-way places, particularly on short notice. Spares carefully planned to go with the outfits worn should be taken. Women might carry a little laundry soap in their cosmetic bags for washing out slips, hose, or a blouse.

A little thought about where one is going and what services will be available there, the activities in which one will participate, how one will travel, for how long one will be away, and what clothes will best meet one's needs in all these situations will prove of great value.

Clothes for the occasion

Some wash-and-wear clothes will need a little touch-up ironing. Travel irons—regular and steam—are available for the tourist. Unless you buy European makes, it is not advisable to take an electric travel iron, razor, or alarm clock to Europe. The plugs of the cords will not fit European fixtures, and there are three different standard voltages in Europe, two alternating cycles, and DC as well as AC. Not all of the portable converters will turn DC into AC.

Places

There is a great deal one can work out as to what will be suitable in a place to which one has never been. Resort areas in rather rough, rustic settings call for sturdy trousers, shoes, and shirts, weatherproofed jackets and hats, and swimsuits and bathing shoes.

At the seaside, if you are going to spend a great deal of time at the beach, you may require more than one bathing suit. Since it is generally fairly humid there, clothes will not dry readily and a spare bathing suit can add to comfort and appearance.

Winter resorts vary from place to place, but clothes and equipment for skiing, ice skating, and other sports are pretty much the same. Winter resorts generally do not require formal attire, so that simple wools or quilted skirts with jersey tops are acceptable dinner dress.

When visiting in the home of a friend, try to remember the activities she has mentioned and go prepared. It is annoying for the hostess to have to supply clothes for her guests, and of course no one else's clothes can do justice to the individual. In some areas of the country, as at some resorts in rustic surroundings, cleaning services are not available and it is rather difficult to get laundry and pressing done, so that the few items like sweaters and jerseys that do not need pressing are always a real boon to the traveler. If you will be doing something entirely different for part of the trip, pack the clothes for this part separately. You should be orderly in planning and packing, and make sure that you pack a complete outfit—including accessories.

Basics and variations

Basic wardrobes for travel are recommended but are not equally acceptable to everyone. You do not have to take certain items just because a list suggests you do so. The list is only a guide; use your individuality in planning your clothes for your trip.

A trip may be a week end away from college—at home, at the home of a friend, at another college, in the country, or in the city. It may be a sight-seeing trip abroad

or a stay-put, rest-and-relaxation vacation in the United States. It is wise to check the locale for types of clothing that will be adequate, comfortable, and acceptable.

There is less variation in clothing needs in European countries. Slacks and shorts are acceptable aboard ship but not everywhere else in Europe; they should not be worn on city streets. Americans are often resented for their inappropriate attire in Europe. You should be appropriately dressed for sightseeing; if you plan to visit cathedrals, take a head covering—chapel caps are adequate—in your purse, and wear a dress with sleeves.

A clean traveler

There are innumerable aids to keeping clean while traveling. Small items that are easy to pack include small face cloths with plastic bag, soap pellets and wafers, purse-size towelettes moistened with cleansing lotion, hand lotion packaged in foil envelopes, the folding toothbrush in a case that also holds a small tube of toothpaste, small sponges of rubber or plastic in place of the clothes brush, spot-cleaning packets, and laundry kits—plastic bags, clothespins with hooks, inflatable rubber hangers, cold-water soaps or capsules, indoor clotheslines, and detergents in packets. Toilet tissue should be included for European travel if one desires the customary American quality.

WOMEN'S PACKING

It is not necessary to invent a new system for each trip, or to arrive with wrinkled clothes and without proper accessories.

Pullman case

The right clothes must be properly packed in a minimum of space. There is a technique to packing a travel wardrobe so as to keep it from wrinkling and to have all items conveniently accessible. In your Pullman case, pack shoes, encased in fabric or plastic bags, toe to heel, at the bottom in one end of the bag; tuck hosiery and other small items in the shoes; at the opposite end, place your waterproof cosmetic bag, unless you are carrying it in a tote bag; put your jewelry case and lingerie in the same end. Fill the center space in the bottom with your flat handbag, gloves, blouses, packable hat, scarves, handkerchiefs, belts, sewing kit, bathing suit, and other items not used regularly. This first layer should be level before you begin a second layer.

The next layer includes skirts, jackets, and dresses, placed with as few folds as possible. To pack a skirt, fold it so that it fills the suitcase on all sides, with a fold at the hip.

To pack a dress, fold back the sleeves and the sides in a straight line from shoulder to hem and fold the dress at the waistline to fit in the case lengthwise. Leave belts fastened loosely; fasten alternate buttons; and be sure that lapels and collars are smooth.

To pack a jacket, fasten alternate buttons. Lay the jacket face down across the width of the suitcase. Lay the sleeves across the bottom of the jacket. Flip the tail of the jacket over into the case, with the fold at the waistline.

An alternate packing method for jackets is to turn the jacket inside out except for the sleeves, fold it in half, tuck one shoulder inside the other.

The top layer is reserved for items you will need to get at readily: night gown or pajamas, robe, slippers, sweater, and rainwear.

If you pack your case in layers, it is possible to take out or replace items in the ends of the first layer by picking up any bottom corner of the second layer. The whole second layer can be lifted out without repacking if you need something from the center of the bottom layer.

Small cases

You may carry a train case, carryall, tote bag, or airline bag for small articles to provide more space in your Pullman case. Roll your robe, nightgown, or pajamas and place them on the bottom; tuck travel slippers in one corner and fill the remaining space with your waterproof cosemetic bag, other kits, and miscellaneous travel necessities.

Wardrobe case

If you use a wardrobe case, place dresses and suit coats on hangers; either cross the sleeves over the front or let them hang down along the side seams of the garment. Pin skirts to the hangers or snap them on with hanger clips and fold side panels towards the center. Snap the holding bar into position. The remaining items are packed in the bottom.

Hang-up wardrobe

This travel bag is used for auto, train, and air travel. Skirts are hung on regular skirt hangers or on combination jacket-and-skirt hangers. Dresses folded at the waistline over the crossbar of a sturdy metal hanger will travel well if clipped to the hanger with clothespins. If the clothes do not extend to the bottom of the bag, shoes will ride well in this space. It is necessary to have adequate space for the car sack so the hems of the clothes do not become wrinkled. Unless the sack is carefully packed, hung, and carried, the clothes will wrinkle more than if packed in a suitcase.

MEN'S PACKING

Men should plan ahead when packing in order to have everything they will need at their destination while keeping their baggage to a minimum. If a man's clothing is made of synthetic fibers, he can reduce the number of items to take along; pajamas, robes, underwear, socks, shirts, and suits in several of the synthetics can be washed easily and dried quickly, and can be worn after little or no ironing.

Any traveling man can have that band-box look if his clothes have been packed properly. No matter what kind of bag is used, the principles of packing are the same.

When packing for a trip, begin with the heavy items. Fill shoes with extra socks, cover them with an old pair of socks and fit them in the bottom or back of your luggage. Add the shaving kit, brushes, and toiletries and other heavy items. Pack so that nothing can move around, but do not pack too tightly.

To pack jackets, let the front sections overlap and curve the sleeves over the side seams. Place trousers in alternate directions with the front creases facing the hinges of the bag. Accordion-pleated tissue placed in the folds of the suit is a good precaution against creasing. Shirts are placed front to front with the collars at opposite ends. You can protect the collars by filling the necks with handkerchiefs. An alternative method is to unfold the shirt to its full length and refold it with the shirttail up over the front and tucked under the back of the collar.

Ties can be carried in a tie case or rolled over tissue from the top of the fold to six inches from the end. Ties can also be folded over the center pages of a magazine.

Two-suiter

To pack a two-suiter, remove the hangers and place trousers lengthwise in the hanger section in alternate directions, with the front creases toward the bag's hinges. Let the trouser legs hang over the edges of the case. Lay in jackets on hangers, smooth them out carefully, and put in divider board or drop metal divider. Fold the trouser legs over the divider and the jackets over the trousers. Place heavy articles in the bottom of the other half of the two-suiter or in pockets if provided. Place shirts on top of this layer of bulky items.

Pullman case

To pack a Pullman case, pack shirts, shoes, belts, socks, toilet kit, and slippers in the bottom layer. For trousers and jackets, follow the same procedure as with the two-suiter. Put pajamas, handkerchiefs, ties, and underwear flat in the pocket of the lid of the case.

Brief case

An expandable brief case is adequate for overnight trips for businessmen or college students on an interview. Slip a sheet of cardboard inside shirts and put the shirts in the bag with the collars downward. Besides shirts and business papers, there is room for socks, toilet kit, and handkerchiefs. If pajamas and underwear are rolled, there is room for them, too.

Hang-up bag

The car sack is often used for auto, air, or train trips. Put trousers in first, on hangers. Curve jacket sleeves over the side seams. Use crushed tissue to stuff the shoulders. Fold clothing flat for packing the pockets of the bag. Place shirts as indicated previously. Put rolled ties and socks in collar openings of pajamas. Place shoes so they will ride at the bottom when the bag is folded for carrying.

GENERAL TIPS FOR EVERYONE

Lingerie or underwear will come out fresh and smooth if you use four-compartment plastic "books." These cases also are great time-savers; no need to unpack them, just slip the case into a dresser drawer. Keep one section free for soiled clothes. The compartments have zippers, so that you can even pack a bathing suit still damp from your last dip.

An alternative method for packing lingerie or underwear is to place each item on several full-length sheets of tissue paper and roll it, with the tissue on the outside.

Never stuff bags to the point of overflowing; a few clothes ready to wear on arrival are better than an extensive wardrobe that is forever in need of pressing.

On arrival, hang up your clothes. Most creases will hang out of fabrics made with wrinkle-resistant finishes or fibers. Stubborn creases in wool will disappear when clothes are hung over a steaming tub or brushed with a dampened brush before hanging.

When traveling over long distances, you can arrive looking fresh and crisp if you will carry your basic cosmetic needs, a fresh blouse or shirt in a plastic case, and a pair of soft-soled slippers to wear on the train or plane in your tote bag, train case, or brief case.

You can save time by keeping your traveling cosmetic case fully equipped at all times. There is no reason why you should have to pack these items every time you go away for a week end.

If you are flying, fill plastic bottles only three-quarters full and wrap perfume bottles in foil or seal them with paraffin to prevent leaks.

If you like to pack with tissue paper, place an accordion-pleated sheet against the side of the case where the fold-back of a dress or suit falls. The garment is then folded back over the tissue. Do not place sheets of tissue paper indiscriminately between clothes. A flat sheet has no function and merely adds weight.

A sheet of heavy plastic cut to fit each suitcase as an inside cover tucked down around the edges prevents clothes from wrinkling when straps are tied over them.

A suggestion for students who travel every week end is to pack bulky items like sneakers, wool socks, books, and shoes in a separate bag rather than in the suitcase. Put these items in plastic bags, using a separate one for each pair of shoes.

If you are traveling abroad, be sure to take toilet soap and laundry soap that will suds well in hard water.

Tight girdles and tight shoes should be avoided when traveling.

A loosely packed suitcase is as bad as one packed too tight.

For persons traveling abroad, the inevitable collection of purchases often poses a problem. The best solution is to buy an inexpensive, lightweight suitcase locally. If you are returning by air, it is advisable to repack personal items not needed on the return trip in the inexpensive suitcase and ship it home by air express. This will cost less than excess baggage charges. The purchases should be packed in the suitcase you keep with you for customs inspection.

Luggage allowances
Plane. For domestic flights most airlines accept two big bags and a cabin bag; the largest bag cannot exceed 62 inches in total length, height, and width; the second piece is limited to 45 to 55 inches, and the carry-on bag must fit under the seat. 44 pounds on international tourist flights, and 66 pounds on international first-class flights are allowed.

Bus and train. You may take two cases that you can, if necessary, carry yourself. There is a weight limit of 150 pounds on some trains and buses. No single piece of luggage exceeding 300 pounds in weight, seventy-two inches in the greatest dimension, or $2,500 in value will be checked on a railroad ticket. A case 27 x 17 x 9 inches will fit under your Pullman seat.

Steamships. On an ocean voyage 350 pounds of luggage per person is allowed; 150 on a coastal cruise.

For easy travel ashore, two cases are suggested. A minimum of luggage, which you can handle yourself in emergencies and keep track of easily, adds to carefree traveling.

Planning. If in your planning you must take weight allowances into consideration, the following approximate weights of some common items in travel wardrobes may be helpful. The exact weight, of course, will vary with the material.

Approximate weights in pounds of items of women's clothing: coat—3, suit—2½, dress—1, skirt—¾, slacks—1½, sweater—½, blouse—¼, lingerie—1¼, robe—1, bathing suit—½, hose—⅛, shoes—1, hat—¼, purse—1, and scarf—¼.

Approximate weights in pounds of items of men's clothing: topcoat—3, tweed suit—4½, worsted suit—2½, flannel slacks—1¾, shirt—½, wool sweater—1, socks—¾, shoes—4, necktie—½, and handkerchief—⅛.

REFERENCE READINGS

Dodge, David, *The Poor Man's Guide to Europe*, Rev. Ed., Random House, New York, 1959.

Newman, Harold, "Newman's European Travel Guide," A. S. Barnes & Co., New York, 1963–64.

Joseph, Richard, *Worldwide Travel Guide*, Doubleday & Co., Inc., New York, 1953.

"How to Pack," Good Housekeeping Bulletin, New York, 1965.

Jones, Candy, *Look Your Best*, Harper & Row, New York, 1964.

Olson's Complete Motoring Guides to Europe, J. B. Lippincott Company, 1967 & 1968.

Pan American, *New Horizons World Guide*, Simon and Schuster, New York, 1958.

Scudder, Muriel Wilson, *Europe in a Suitcase*, Muriel Wilson Scudder, Manhasset, New York.

Strong, William M. and Runyon, A. Milton, *How to Travel Without Being Rich*, 3rd Ed., Doubleday & Co., Inc., New York, 1959.

"Travel in Style," Union Label Department, I.L.G.W.U., New York, 1964.

Index